I0885490

AI-Driven Decision-Making for Diversity, Equity, and Inclusion in Marketing

Theodore Tarnanidis
https://orcid.org/0000-0002-4836-3906
International Hellenic University, Greece

IGI Global Scientific Publishing
Publishing Tomorrow's Research Today

Vice President of Editorial	Melissa Wagner
Director of Acquisitions	Mikaela Felty
Director of Book Development	Jocelynn Hessler
Production Manager	Mike Brehm
Cover Design	Jose Rosado

Published in the United States of America by
IGI Global Scientific Publishing
701 East Chocolate Avenue
Hershey, PA, 17033, USA
Tel: 717-533-8845 | Fax: 717-533-7115
Website: https://www.igi-global.com E-mail: cust@igi-global.com

Library of Congress Cataloging-in-Publication Data

Names: Tarnanidis, Theodore, 1977- editor
Title: AI-driven decision-making for diversity, equity, and inclusion in marketing / edited by Theodore Tarnanidis.
Description: Hershey, PA : IGI Global Scientific Publishing, [2026] | Includes bibliographical references and index. | Summary: "This book examines how Generative AI intersects with Diversity, Equity, and Inclusion in marketing. It offers frameworks, case studies, and strategies to embed fairness, cultural competence, and transparency into AI-assisted decision-making, ensuring ethical and effective engagement with diverse global audiences"-- Provided by publisher.
Identifiers: LCCN 2025041867 (print) | LCCN 2025041868 (ebook) | ISBN 9798337367316 hardcover | ISBN 9798337367323 paperback | ISBN 9798337367330 ebook
Subjects: LCSH: Artificial intelligence--Marketing applications | Marketing--Social aspects
Classification: LCC HF5415.125 .A425 2026 (print) | LCC HF5415.125 (ebook)
LC record available at https://lccn.loc.gov/2025041867
LC ebook record available at https://lccn.loc.gov/2025041868

British Cataloguing in Publication Data
A Cataloguing in Publication record for this book is available from the British Library.

Editorial Advisory Board

Table of Contents

Detailed Table of Contents

ignore marginalized groups. This creates ethical and commercial risks related to DEI. Biased systems can damage consumer trust, harm brand reputation, and clash with new regulatory standards. This chapter looks at how bias shows up in marketing systems, why it matters, and what technical, organizational, and regulatory methods can promote more inclusive AI practices. It draws from literature, industry cases, and fairness frameworks. It outlines strategies like auditing datasets, designing inclusively, ensuring human oversight, and improving governance. Ultimately, it views DEI as the ethical basis for responsible AI marketing that can handle future challenges.

Artificial Intelligence (AI) is transforming contemporary marketing by enabling brands to create inclusive, equitable, and culturally resonant communication at scale. This chapter explores how AI-driven systems—through advanced segmentation, generative content, fairness-aware algorithms, and accessibility technologies—can enhance diversity, equity, and inclusion (DEI) across global markets. Drawing from theoretical foundations, empirical studies (2018–2024), and methodological frameworks, the chapter demonstrates both the transformative potential and the risks of algorithmic bias, representational inaccuracies, and ethical dilemmas. It proposes human-centered, culturally grounded, and policy-aligned approaches to mitigate discrimination and strengthen trust. Ultimately, the chapter positions inclusive AI-driven marketing as a pathway to ethical innovation, equitable digital participation, and socially responsible brand engagement.

The digital age has fundamentally reshaped the dialectical relationship between sports organizations and their fan bases, transforming a traditionally passive consumer into an active and influential stakeholder. This paper explores the shifting priorities of these digitally-empowered customers, who now operate as 'prosumers'—simultaneously consuming and co-creating the sporting experience. Focusing on the burgeoning professional sports landscape in India, this study utilizes a qualitative, comparative case study methodology to analyze the blurring boundaries and emergent benefits of digital fan engagement within the Indian Premier League (IPL) and the Indian Super League (ISL). It examines three key pillars of this new dynamic: fan-led digital protests, multifaceted expressions of online support, and the evolving landscape of participatory merchandising. The chosen case studies—Chennai Super Kings (CSK) from the IPL and Kerala Blasters FC from the ISL—provide a rich context for this analysis.

Generative Artificial Intelligence (GenAI) is redefining branding by enabling large-scale, personalized, and creative content generation. However, in a global marketplace, cultural sensitivity is essential to ensure that AI-generated messages resonate authentically with diverse audiences. Culturally aware GenAI systems recognize and respect local customs, language nuances, and societal values, avoiding stereotypes and misrepresentation. By integrating diverse datasets, cultural expertise, and ethical oversight, brands can create inclusive narratives that strengthen trust, loyalty, and emotional engagement. This chapter explores the intersection of cultural intelligence and GenAI in branding, examining its role as both a strategic tool and an ethical responsibility. It also addresses challenges, risks, case studies, and future directions for building meaningful, culturally attuned brand identities.

Artificial intelligence has been quickly shifting into the pioneer of contemporary marketing. AI powered systems influence how brands communicate with culturally diverse audiences through automated content creation and hyper personalized targeting. These systems, while highly efficient, are proving to have major cultural blind points in which algorithmic decision making fails to detect or interpret cultural, social, and representational subtleties. Such lapses appear as biased outputs, homogenization of identity, and reinforcement of stereotypes, growing into public controversies and reputational crises. This chapter explores cultural blindness in marketing-focused AI systems through four case studies: Amazon's recruitment tool, H&M's culturally insensitive campaign, Dove's beauty representation controversy, and Levi's AI generated diversity models.

AI-based customization technology enables business operations to develop unique market positions which results in new marketplace offerings. Artificial intelligence technologies on platforms let businesses deliver customized sessions to their individual customers through advanced data processing and machine learning systems. Real-time data processing enables individual users to get precise solutions through service-based goods that integrate advanced user segmentation methods. The ongoing commercial success of businesses depends on successful customer demand forecasting through personalized solutions that result in heightened performance and better customer retention. The delivery of tailored customer interactions through AI technology provides businesses with two essential benefits which support their development of unique market leadership above competitive offerings. The ability of online businesses to identify current customer behavior patterns becomes essential for sustained success as an e-commerce service because it creates enduring market benefits in the industry.

Modern structure of financial system relies strongly on live trend of stock-market price and the real-time deviations of values that enriches a healthy competition and instant decision-making capability in a fast-moving market environment. Due to the inherent dynamic properties of big data, it becomes challenging for typical data-mining tools, technologies, methods and techniques to be applied on big-data streaming task. The significant resistance faced by real time streaming of big data involves lack of adaptability, controllability and programmability. Apache kafka is one of the best frameworks to work with for resolving real time data streaming tasks for its unique characteristics of being reliable, distributed and having high throughput and low latency. The essential features of kafka are thoroughly summarized in this abstract which empowers market regulators to manage and analyze stock value movement in a real-time manner to cop up with momentary changes.

In a time when artificial intelligence redefines marketing practice pillars, the concern is not innovation but conscience-driven innovation. While AI tools promise unmatched precision in reaching customers, segmenting, and budgeting, they carry a silent danger of deepening existing disparities, if they were to be unleashed without caution. This article advocates for the practice of Equity by Design, and it insists that Diversity, Equity, and Inclusion (DEI) must be made a part of the actual design of AI-driven marketing systems. By borrowing cross-disciplinary insights from finance, organizational ethics, and digital strategy, the case is argued through illustrations of how equitable design cuts down on algorithmic bias, expands financial service access to marginalized communities, and enhances consumer trust in a more data-driven market. Beyond compliance or corporate social responsibility, embedding DEI in AI is a competitive strategy, attaching ethical obligation to long-term brand worth, sustainable growth, and global competitiveness in the digital economy.

This chapter explains how artificial intelligence has evolved customer segmentation from a marketing tool into a socio-technical decision mechanism with implications for fairness, inclusion, and cultural representation. In the chapter, algorithmic segmentation is analyzed using clustering methods, explainable frameworks such as LIME and SHAP, and fairness metrics to identify or alleviate structural bias in multicultural markets. It discusses accuracy fairness trade-offs, transparency, emotional trust, and organizational capability gaps, especially when segmentation outputs flow into generative AI driven personalization. Through case studies on multicultural targeting, AI sales agents, misinformation flows, and exclusion in finance, employment, and welfare, the authors show how segmentation systems affect society. The chapter concludes with strategic, ethical, and policy recommendations for responsible, inclusive AI marketing grounded in fairness aware segmentation.

Generative Artificial Intelligence (GenAI) has come in a wave as earth-shattering innovation in world marketing offering capabilities in real-time content generation, hyper-personalization, predictive analytics, and dynamic audience engagement in a global marketing world that is culturally diverse. While these abilities promise increased efficiency and further connection of consumers, they also have some important issues surrounding fairness, representational accuracy and culture. In multicultural environments, AI-driven marketing systems which fail to include the principles of Diversity, Equity and Inclusion (DEI) could play a role in the reinforcement of harmful stereotypes, the marginalization of minority communities and the loss of public trust. Biases inherent in training data, model architectures and even automated decision pipelines can be used to create arbitrary audience segmentation and culturally inappropriate messaging - creating reputational, ethical and regulatory problems for organizations.

F1 or Formula 1 used to be an underdeveloped sport, but now, it has grown to be a globally appreciated brand with more than 200 countries encompassing an audience. Despite its sponsorships, technological innovations, and elite status, the sport has faced critiques and controversies pertaining to its lack of diversity, equity, and inclusion. F1 has been and continues to be, marketing a brand image that exudes exclusivity, and having an audience that is mostly dominated by white male drivers and male heads that run the socioeconomically European framework, has been easily alienating to more marginalized parts of the world. Campaigns like "We Race as One" have been seen as an attempt of inclusivity, but the intention behind them seems more like an attempt to placate the opposition by most critics. On the other hand, artificial intelligence has ushered in a new era of automated self-engaging marketing where exclusion is tailored for exclusivity.

Preface

The focus of this book is on the connection between Generative Artificial Intelligence (GenAI) and Diversity, Equity, and Inclusion (DEI) when it comes to AI-assisted marketing decision-making in multicultural domains. AI systems are now essential for marketing automation, personalization, and audience targeting, but if they are not designed with diversity in mind, biased decisions, cultural missteps, and inequitable reach can occur. An examination is conducted in this book on the integration of DEI principles into GenAI models to guarantee ethical, inclusive, and efficient marketing strategies across global cultures. In this book, the focus is on global marketing management practices in the digital age, which necessitate effective communication strategies across borders. We believe that the book will bring together researchers from diverse research backgrounds with that in mind. The objectives of the edited book are to explore: How Diversity, Equity and Inclusion (DEI) principles can be operationalized in AI-assisted marketing tools; The ethical challenges and risks of bias in AI systems targeting multicultural consumers; Strategies to embed fairness, transparency, and cultural competence into GenAI marketing workflows; Frameworks and tools to audit and mitigate algorithmic bias Real-world marketing applications where inclusive GenAI has created or destroyed brand value. This publication is an important reference source for academics and researchers, undergraduate students, postgraduate students, consultants, technology developers and policymakers interested in exploring the challenges of AI-Driven Decision-Making for Diversity, Equity, and Inclusion in Marketing for Multicultural Marketplaces.

The book is made up of 15 chapters that aim to showcase the main research areas on the subject and thus provide valuable findings to practitioners and readers.

Chapter 1 examines how marketing strategies targeting global Gen Z segments conceptualize, implement, and evaluate diversity and inclusion (D&I) across different regions. The chapter gathers relevant theoretical frameworks, methodological approaches, and empirical findings about inclusive marketing through the synthesis of contemporary academic literature and practitioner insights. Special attention is paid to the differences between developed and emerging markets when it comes to

Gen Z expectations, illuminating both shared generational values and culturally specific interpretations of inclusion. In addition, the analysis examines Gen Z's disapproval of performative activism, stressing the significance of genuineness, transparency, and consistency in brand messaging and organizational practice. The incorporation of cross-cultural viewpoints helps this chapter identify essential challenges and opportunities for marketers who are trying to engage Gen Z through credible D&I initiatives.

Chapter 2 gives a brief overview of AI Bias in Marketing. Specifically, it looks at how bias shows up in marketing systems, why it matters, and what technical, organizational, and regulatory methods can promote more inclusive AI practices. It draws from literature, industry cases, and fairness frameworks. It outlines strategies like auditing datasets, designing inclusively, ensuring human oversight, and improving governance. Ultimately, it views DEI as the ethical basis for responsible AI marketing that can handle future challenges.

Chapter 3 explores the role of AI-Driven Campaigns Inclusive Targeting and Messaging for Diversity, Equity, and Inclusion in Marketing. Artificial Intelligence (AI) is transforming contemporary marketing by enabling brands to create inclusive, equitable, and culturally resonant communication at scale. This chapter explores how AI-driven systems—through advanced segmentation, generative content, fairness-aware algorithms, and accessibility technologies—can enhance diversity, equity, and inclusion (DEI) across global markets. Drawing from theoretical foundations, empirical studies (2018–2024), and methodological frameworks, the chapter demonstrates both the transformative potential and the risks of algorithmic bias, representational inaccuracies, and ethical dilemmas. It proposes human-centered, culturally grounded, and policy-aligned approaches to mitigate discrimination and strengthen trust. Ultimately, the chapter positions inclusive AI-driven marketing as a pathway to ethical innovation, equitable digital participation, and socially responsible brand engagement.

Chapter 4 focuses on the AI-Driven Decision-Making for Advancing Diversity, Equity, and Inclusion Insights from Indian Brands. The digital age has fundamentally reshaped the dialectical relationship between sports organizations and their fan bases, transforming a traditionally passive consumer into an active and influential stakeholder. This paper explores the shifting priorities of these digitally-empowered customers, who now operate as 'prosumers'—simultaneously consuming and co-creating the sporting experience. Focusing on the burgeoning professional sports landscape in India, this study utilizes a qualitative, comparative case study methodology to analyze the blurring boundaries and emergent benefits of digital fan engagement within the Indian Premier League (IPL) and the Indian Super League (ISL). It examines three key pillars of this new dynamic: fan-led digital protests, multifaceted expressions of online support, and the evolving landscape of participatory merchandising. The chosen case studies—Chennai Super Kings (CSK) from the IPL and Kerala Blasters FC from the ISL—provide a rich context for this analysis.

Chapter 5 investigates the Branding and Identity through Culturally Sensitive GenAI. Generative Artificial Intelligence (GenAI) is redefining branding by enabling large-scale, personalized, and creative content generation. However, in a global marketplace, cultural sensitivity is essential to ensure that AI-generated messages resonate authentically with diverse audiences. Culturally aware GenAI systems recognize and respect local customs, language nuances, and societal values, avoiding stereotypes and misrepresentation. By integrating diverse datasets, cultural expertise, and ethical oversight, brands can create inclusive narratives that strengthen trust, loyalty, and emotional engagement. This chapter explores the intersection of cultural intelligence and GenAI in branding, examining its role as both a strategic tool and an ethical responsibility. It also addresses challenges, risks, case studies, and future directions for building meaningful, culturally attuned brand identities.

Chapter 6 explores cultural blindness in marketing-focused AI systems through four case studies: Amazon's recruitment tool, H&M's culturally insensitive campaign, Dove's beauty representation controversy, and Levi's AI generated diversity models.

Chapter 7 tries to elucidate Customer Targeting in Digital Marketing through AI-Powered Personalization for Market Differentiation AI-based customization technology enables business operations to develop unique market positions which results in new marketplace offerings. Artificial intelligence technologies on platforms let businesses deliver customized sessions to their individual customers through advanced data processing and machine learning systems. Real-time data processing enables individual users to get precise solutions through service-based goods that integrate advanced user segmentation methods. The ongoing commercial success of businesses depends on successful customer demand forecasting through personalized solutions that result in heightened performance and better customer retention. The delivery of tailored customer interactions through AI technology provides businesses with two essential benefits which support their development of unique market leadership above competitive offerings. The ability of online businesses to identify current customer behavior patterns becomes essential for sustained success as an e-commerce service because it creates enduring market benefits in the industry.

Chapter 8 refers to stock market analytics. Modern structure of financial system relies strongly on live trend of stock-market price and the real-time deviations of values that enriches a healthy competition and instant decision-making capability in a fast-moving market environment. Due to the inherent dynamic properties of big data, it becomes challenging for typical data-mining tools, technologies, methods and techniques to be applied on big-data streaming task. The significant resistance faced by real time streaming of big data involves lack of adaptability, controllability and programmability. Apache kafka is one of the best frameworks to work with for resolving real time data streaming tasks for its unique characteristics of being reliable, distributed and having high throughput and low latency. The essential features of kafka are thoroughly summarized in this abstract which empowers market regulators to manage and analyze stock value movement in a real-time manner to cop up with momentary changes.

Chapter 9 explores the role of equity by design and it insists that Diversity, Equity, and Inclusion (DEI) must be made a part of the actual design of AI-driven marketing systems. By borrowing cross-disciplinary insights from finance, organizational ethics, and digital strategy, the case is argued through illustrations of how equitable design cuts down on algorithmic bias, expands financial service access to marginalized communities, and enhances consumer trust in a more data-driven market. Beyond compliance or corporate social responsibility, embedding DEI in AI is a competitive strategy, attaching ethical obligation to long-term brand worth, sustainable growth, and global competitiveness in the digital economy.

Chapter 10 explains how artificial intelligence has evolved customer segmentation from a marketing tool into a socio-technical decision mechanism with implications for fairness, inclusion, and cultural representation. In the chapter, algorithmic segmentation is analyzed using clustering methods, explainable frameworks such as LIME and SHAP, and fairness metrics to identify or alleviate structural bias in multicultural markets. It discusses accuracy fairness trade-offs, transparency, emotional trust, and organizational capability gaps, especially when segmentation outputs flow into generative AI driven personalization. Through case studies on multicultural targeting, AI sales agents, misinformation flows, and exclusion in finance, employment, and welfare, the authors show how segmentation systems affect society. The chapter concludes with strategic, ethical, and policy recommendations for responsible, inclusive AI marketing grounded in fairness aware segmentation.

Chapter 11 investigates the paradox of performative ethics and authentic sustainability marketing that emerges when looking at the trajectory of marketing ethics from its origins to current overall coherence or divergence between theory and practice in our global world. The conversation is informed by recent examples from a range of industries, from Volkswagen's "Dieselgate" and H&M's "Conscious Collection" to Patagonia's radical transparency, Dove's inclusivity campaigns, and Nike's social justice activism that illustrate how greenwashing erodes consumer trust while genuine sustainability becomes a source for loyalty, resilience, and cultural relevance.

Chapter 12 analyses the capabilities and challenges of generative AI in marketing. Marketing has always been influenced by technological innovation, ranging from the development of the printing press and mass media promotion to the advent of digital platforms and algorithmic targeting. In the digital economy of the day, perhaps the most revolutionary development is the rise of generative artificial intelligence (GenAI). GenAI has not only opened up new avenues for automating and scaling personalization but also added the capacity to produce compelling, adaptive, and context-aware communication at a scope not before possible.

Chapter 13 presents a comprehensive examination of the paradigm shift in sports fandom,driven by Artificial Intelligence from physical stadiums to personalized digital ecosystems. It posits that AI,when designed with foundational principles of Diversity, Equity, and Inclusion and Algorithmic Justice,can transcend being a mere technological tool to become a catalyst for equitable access and profound engagement. The analysis introduces an original four-layer framework for deconstructing and designing inclusive fan supported by global case studies and adaptive solutions for underserved regions.Moving beyond accessibility, the chapter establishes a robust economic rationale by integrating the Fan Lifetime Value model, demonstrating how inclusive AI investments drive long-term loyalty, unlock new revenue streams, and enhance brand equity. It confronts critical ethical challenges data privacy, algorithmic bias, digital divides and provides actionable guidance through a step-by-step implementation roadmap for sports organizations.

Chapter 14 concerns with the competence in AI-Driven Decision Systems. Generative Artificial Intelligence (GenAI) has come in a wave as earth-shattering innovation in world marketing offering capabilities in real-time content generation, hyper-personalization, predictive analytics, and dynamic audience engagement in a global marketing world that is culturally diverse. While these abilities promise increased efficiency and further connection of consumers, they also have some important issues surrounding fairness, representational accuracy and culture. In multicultural environments, AI-driven marketing systems which fail to include the principles of Diversity, Equity and Inclusion (DEI) could play a role in the reinforcement of harmful stereotypes, the marginalization of minority communities and the loss of public trust. Biases inherent in training data, model architectures and even automated decision pipelines can be used to create arbitrary audience segmentation and culturally inappropriate messaging - creating reputational, ethical and regulatory problems for organizations.

Chapter 15 analyses the role of racing toward inclusion in Formula 1 marketing. F1 or Formula 1 used to be an underdeveloped sport, but now, it has grown to be a globally appreciated brand with more than 200 countries encompassing an audience. Despite its sponsorships, technological innovations, and elite status, the sport has faced critiques and controversies pertaining to its lack of diversity, equity, and inclusion. F1 has been and continues to be, marketing a brand image that exudes exclusivity, and having an audience that is mostly dominated by white male drivers and male heads that run the socioeconomically European framework, has been easily alienating to more marginalized parts of the world. Campaigns like "We Race as One" have been seen as an attempt of inclusivity, but the intention behind them seems more like an attempt to placate the opposition by most critics. On the other hand, artificial intelligence has ushered in a new era of automated self-engaging marketing where exclusion is tailored for exclusivity.

This publication is an important reference source for academics and researchers in marketing and management, undergraduate students, postgraduate students, consultants, technology developers and policymakers interested in exploring how the DEI principles can be integrated into GenAI models to guarantee ethical, inclusive, and efficient marketing strategies across global cultures

Acknowledgment

This publication is an important reference source for academics and researchers, undergraduate students, postgraduate students, consultants, technology developers and policymakers interested in exploring the challenges of AI-Driven Decision-Making for Diversity, Equity, and Inclusion in Marketing for Multicultural Marketplaces. .We are confident that this book will be essential for readers to upgrade their current work and education.

We would like to express our gratitude to all those who contributed to this project, particularly the authors and reviewers who took part in the evaluation process. Their help was instrumental in the success of this book. We express our sincere appreciation to the chapter writers who contributed their time and knowledge to this book from all over the world. Thank you to all the peer reviewers for their valuable ideas that have improved the quality, coherence, and substance of the chapters. We are thankful to the writers who gave up their time to act as reviewers. This book would not have been possible without the production staff at IGI Global. Throughout this process, they were extremely helpful and encouraging and provided the highest level of service. The work of many individuals goes into publishing a successful book, not just those who are acknowledged as authors or editors.

Book edited by:

Theodore Tarnanidis, International Hellenic University, Greece

Chapter 1

A Cross-Regional Analysis of Diversity and Inclusion in Marketing for Global Generation Z

Theodore Tarnanidis
https://orcid.org/0000-0002-4836-3906
International Hellenic University, Greece

Vijaya Kittu Manda
https://orcid.org/0000-0002-1680-8210
PBMEIT, India

Bruno Barbosa Sousa
https://orcid.org/0000-0002-8588-2422
Polytechnic University of Cávado and Ave, Portugal & UNIAG, Portugal

ABSTRACT

This chapter examines how marketing strategies targeting global Gen Z segments conceptualize, implement, and evaluate diversity and inclusion (D&I) across different regions. The chapter gathers relevant theoretical frameworks, methodological approaches, and empirical findings about inclusive marketing through the synthesis of contemporary academic literature and practitioner insights. Special attention is paid to the differences between developed and emerging markets when it comes to Gen Z expectations, illuminating both shared generational values and culturally specific interpretations of inclusion. In addition, the analysis examines Gen Z's disapproval of performative activism, stressing the significance of genuineness, transparency, and consistency in brand messaging and organizational practice.

DOI: 10.4018/979-8-3373-6731-6.ch001

The incorporation of cross-cultural viewpoints helps this chapter identify essential challenges and opportunities for marketers who are trying to engage Gen Z through credible D&I initiatives.

1. INTRODUCTION

The global marketplace has seen the rise of Generation Z (Gen Z), which is commonly described by those born between the mid-1990s and early 2010s, as an influential and values-driven consumer group (Tarnanidis et al., 2026c; Velinov, 2025). Gen Z demonstrates heightened awareness of social justice, equity, and inclusion, as demonstrated by their unparalleled racially and ethnically diverse nature, increased openness to gender identity and sexual orientation, and deep immersion in digital technologies (Konishi et al., 2025; Mandania et al., 2025; Sardashti & Calantone, 2022). Marketing is no longer a peripheral or symbolic branding practice, as these attributes have elevated Diversity and Inclusion (D&I) to a central strategic concern. The constant exposing has enhanced their understanding of social inequality, cultural diversity, and systemic injustices in various societies. Gen Z customers place a high value on representation, equity, and inclusion, deeming these values as essential in establishing relationships with brands (Choi et al., 2025). Gen Z is a diverse global market, not a single uniform market. It is instead formed by regional, cultural, economic, and social contexts (Whitwam, 2025).

Racial justice, gender equality, disability inclusion, and LGBTQ (diverse community of people whose sexual orientations and/or gender identities differ from traditional heterosexual) representation are often prioritized by Gen Z consumers in Western markets like North America and Europe. In contrast, parts of Gen Z in places like Asia, Africa, and Latin America may place emphasis on economic inclusion, affordability, cultural authenticity, digital access, and possibilities for social mobility (Marti, 2025). In spite of regional variations, global Gen Z groups have a similar expectation of transparency, ethical behavior, and meaningful social engagement from brands operating in an interconnected market (Shepperson et al., 2025). Gen Z uses a critical lens to evaluate brand authenticity, unlike previous generations. This generation expects brands not only to showcase diversity in marketing communications but also to embed inclusion into their organizational practices, product development, employment policies, and corporate governance (Estanyol et al., 2025). Social media platforms, where Gen Z actively voices approval or criticism, quickly expose and reject superficial or performative approaches to D&I. Gen Z requires sustained action for inclusion instead of symbolic gestures (Ochis, 2024).There are three objectives in this chapter.

The first objective is to examine the concept of diversity and inclusion in modern marketing and how it is becoming more relevant for Gen Z consumers worldwide. The second objective is to examine the perception and response of different global Gen Z segments to D&I initiatives, with a focus on both shared values and regional variations. Finally, this chapter is about evaluating the effects of digital and human-centered marketing strategies on brand trust, loyalty, and long-term competitiveness in a globalized economy. The chapters objectives allow for a thorough understanding of the importance of diversity and inclusion in engaging the global Gen Z market.

2. DETERMINING GENERATION Z AND ITS SIGNIFICANCE TO D&I

Individuals born between 1995 and 2010 are commonly known as Generation Z (Gen Z), but some scholars vary the upper bound slightly depending on national context and data availability. Gen Z is rapidly becoming a significant part of consumers, employees, and cultural influencers across the globe as of the mid-2020s. Gen Z is regarded as the most racially and ethnically diverse generation in history, specifically in significant consumer markets including the United States, the United Kingdom, and parts of Western Europe (Zimand-Sheiner & Lissitsa, 2024). In marketing contexts, the understanding and evaluation of diversity and inclusion (D&I) are fundamentally reshaped by this demographic reality. Gen Z stands out due to its apparent identity fluidity beyond demographic diversity. The rejection of rigid identity categories related to gender, sexuality, nationality, and culture is more prevalent among Generation Z than previous generations. The research conducted by Cantó & Rodó-Zárate (2024) shows that people have a higher likelihood of identifying with nonbinary gender identities, multicultural backgrounds, and intersectional social positions. The complexity of this fluidity impedes traditional segmentation strategies that depend on static demographic labels and elevates the significance of inclusive marketing approaches that acknowledge multiplicity, hybridity, and self-expression instead of fixed categories.

Gen Z has another distinctive feature, which is cultural hybridity. The continuous exposure to global cultural symbols, narratives, and communities is what Gen Z consumers experience when growing up in digitally networked environments. The integration of local and global identities is made possible through social media platforms like TikTok, Instagram, and YouTube, enabling Gen Z individuals to construct self-concepts that draw from multiple cultural repertoires simultaneously. From a marketing perspective, this means that inclusive representation must move beyond nationally bounded or monocultural frames and instead reflect transnational, hybrid, and intersectional identities (Eisend, 2025; Eisend et al., 2023; Rößner & Eisend,

2023). Understanding Gen Z requires a deeper understanding of its heightened social awareness and moral sensitivity. In this generation, social justice movements that have become highly visible include Black Lives Matter, MeToo, LGBTQ rights advocacy, disability inclusion campaigns, and global conversations about mental health and climate justice. Gen Z has a different expectation of institutions, such as corporations and brands, because of these movements. Gen Z consumers are more inclined to base their attitudes, trust, and purchase intentions on a brand's approach to diversity, equity, and inclusion than older generations, empirical studies consistently demonstrate (Branca et al., 2024; Rohmanue & Jacobi, 2024).

Criticism has been leveled against Gen Z's engagement with discrimination and harassment. Research suggests that Gen Z is both values-driven and skeptical, particularly when it comes to what they perceive as 'performative' or symbolic inclusion. If superficial diversity cues like tokenistic representation in advertising are not backed up by credible organizational practices, they may result in backlash and are often insufficient. As a result, inclusion for Gen Z is evaluated holistically, encompassing not only marketing communications but also corporate policies, leadership diversity, supply chain ethics, and consistency over time (Park et al., 2023). Gen Z's marketplace perceptions and behaviors are particularly relevant to D&I due to these generational characteristics. Authenticity, transparency, and participation are key elements in inclusive marketing efforts that resonate with Gen Z, encouraging consumers to co-create brand meanings instead of passively consume them. Gen Z's reliance on peer networks and social media for information sharing and accountability can result in brand legitimacy being quickly damaged by lack of inclusion, whether through exclusionary messaging (Hortillo et al., 2025). In short, the diversity and inclusion of Generation Z is now a primary organizing principle in marketing research and practice due to their demographic diversity, identity fluidity, cultural hybridity, and heightened social consciousness. Understanding Gen Z requires reversing traditional demographic segmentation towards a more nuanced, intersectional, and ethically informed approach to analyzing consumer behavior in inclusive marketplaces.

3. KEY ASPECTS OF THE THEORETICAL CONTEXT

The research into Generation Z and Diversity and Inclusion in marketing is based on several complementary theoretical traditions that aid in explaining why inclusion is significant to this generation and how inclusive marketing efforts influence consumers' perceptions and behaviors (Licsandru & Cui, 2022; Licsandru & Cui, 2018). Social identity theory, self-congruity theory, and consumer culture theory are some of the most influential frameworks (Kolańska-Stronka & Singh,

2024; Rabbanee et al., 2020). The cultural negotiation of inclusion and exclusion in contemporary marketplaces is highlighted by these perspectives when they are combined. Understanding Gen Z's distinctive responses to inclusive marketing initiatives is made easier when these theories are integrated.

3.1 Group-Based Representation and Social Identity Theory

According to social identity theory, individuals rely heavily on their social group membership to shape their self-concept (Turner et al., 1979). In contexts where identity cues are salient, these group affiliations have an impact on attitudes, preferences, and behaviors. Social identity theory suggests that marketing can have a positive impact on consumer responses to brands and messages that affirm valued group memberships and show respect for their identities (Yang et al., 2025). Social identity processes are especially important due to the high diversity and attention to representation and equity among Gen Z. Research suggests that Gen Z consumers are more capable of noticing who is included or excluded in advertising campaigns than older cohorts (Branca et al., 2024; Munsch, 2021). Inclusive representation is a method of symbolizing recognition that can verify consumers' identities and generate positive brand associations (Cheah & Phua, 2025).

Gen Z individuals often identify with multiple social groups at the same time, which is often the case with their identities. The complexity of social identity theory that is focused on single-category representations challenges its simplicity. Recent marketing research emphasizes that inclusive messaging overlaps with identities and stereotyping (i.e. it is important to consider race, gender, disability, and sexuality (Eisend et al., 2023; Tuli et al., 2025). This suggests that social identity theory needs to be extended to include layered and fluid group affiliations, especially when studying Gen Z consumers, from a theoretical standpoint.

3.2 Identity Alignment and Self-Congruency Theory

Social identity theory is used to support self-congruity theory, which focuses on coordinating a consumer's self-concept with the brand's symbolic image (Sirgy, 1982; Jamal & Al-Marri, 2007). This framework suggests that consumers are more likely to develop positive attitudes, trust, and loyalty towards brands that reflect their own or aspiring personalities. By acknowledging, respecting, and aligning with consumers' identities and values, inclusive marketing can enhance self-congruency. Gen Z views self-congruency as more than just surface-level identity markers and includes moral and value-based alignment. Gen Z consumers tend to evaluate brands not just on their looks, but also on their commitment to fairness, social justice, and inclusion (Tsougkou et al., 2024; Zimand-Sheiner & Lissitsa, 2024 . Symbolic representation and ethical perception of values are the two ways in which inclusive marketing influences self-congruity.

Gen Z's trust in a brand, emotional attachment, and advocacy are significantly enhanced when they perceive high self-congruence with an inclusive brand, as shown by recent studies (Mishra & Gupta, 2025; Srivastava et al., 2023). If perceived misalignment, such as exclusionary corporate practices contradicting inclusive advertising, is perceived, it can reduce self-congruity and result in negative reactions. The reason Gen Z is particularly sensitive to accusations of 'woke-washing' or performanceative inclusion is largely due to this dynamic (Opoku-Dakwa & Rice, 2024).

3.3 Inclusion negotiation and Consumer Culture Theory

Consumer culture theory argues that inclusive marketing is more contextual in broader cultural, social, and ideological contexts than social identity and self-congruity theories, which are focused only on individual-level psychological processes. This theory holds that Gen Z consumers are active participants in shaping the meaning of inclusive marketing messages, not just passive recipients. Brand narratives related to diversity and inclusion are publicly evaluated, interpreted, and sometimes rejected by Gen Z consumers through social media (Arsel et al., 2021; Coman et al., 2022).

In D&I marketing, power and ideology play a role, as highlighted by the theory. Inclusive campaigns are not isolated from culture; they connect with more extensive discourses on race, gender, capitalism, and inequality (Pop et al., 2024). Marketing messages are often perceived as ideological statements by Gen Z, who have been politically influenced by visible social justice movements. Brands are assessed not just as players in the market but also as agents of social change with ethical obligationsn (Kipnis et al., 2021).

3.4 Authenticity and Inclusion

Authenticity is a central construct that connects identity, culture, and inclusion across these theoretical traditions (Lehman et al., 2019). The definition of authenticity is a perception that a brand's inclusive actions are genuine, consistent, and based on real commitments instead of opportunistic trends. It has been suggested by theoretical work that authenticity has a negative impact on the effectiveness of inclusive marketing by influencing whether identity alignment and cultural resonance result in positive outcomes (Schwarz & Williams, 2020).

Gen Z places a high value on authenticity in a holistic and dynamic manner. In order to ensure inclusive representation in advertising, internal diversity practices, credible partnerships, and sustained engagement need to be in place (Aday & Schmader, 2019. This expectation is in line with the importance of cultural coherence and the focus of self-congruity theory on aligning values. The comprehensive framework for understanding D&I research on Gen Z in marketing can be derived from social identity theory, self-congruity theory, and consumer culture theory when combined (Brekhus, 2020).The psychological mechanisms and cultural dynamics that underlie Gen Z's response to inclusive marketing can be captured by researchers by integrating these perspectives.

4. METHODOLOGICAL PERSPECTIVES

The diversity and inclusion (D&I) aspects of Generation Z marketing research are examined by scholars using a diverse range of methodological approaches, which reflects both the complexity of D&I constructs and the unique characteristics of Gen Z consumers. Surveys, experiments, field data analyses, and qualitative approaches are commonly used methods that have been highlighted in recent work, especially when it comes to causal inference, mixed-method designs, and behavioral outcomes.

In Gen Z and D&I marketing studies, survey research remains a crucial method, especially for assessing attitudes, values, and perceptions related to inclusion, authenticity, and brand trust. For Gen Z's consumer decision-making, the normative beliefs they hold regarding diversity, equity, and social justice matter (Francis & Hoefel, 2024). In recent studies, a multi-item scale has been developed to determine the perceived inclusivity, representational fairness, and moral alignment between consumers and brands using a combination of different factors (Djafarova & Foots, 2022; Tuli et al., 2025). However, we can say that the use of survey-based methods in D&I research is limited by social desirability bias, among other important limitations. Gen Z respondents, who are typically knowledgeable about socially accepted inclusion rules, may exaggerate their positive attitudes towards inclusive marketing or neglect to report their negative reactions. As a result, scholars increasingly caution against relying solely on self-reported intentions or attitudes when studying Gen Z and D&I. Recently designed surveys have incorporated indirect questioning, anonymity assurances, and implicit measures to mitigate these concerns, as well as triangulating survey responses with behavioral data.

In addition, establishing causal relationships between inclusive marketing stimuli and Gen Z consumer responses is dependent upon the use of experimental methods. In laboratory and online experiments, researchers are able to manipulate specific marketing communications elements, such as the presence of diverse spokespersons, inclusive language, or explicit social justice messaging, while still keeping other variables unchanged. Using these designs allows for a clear assessment of observed effects on outcomes, such as perceived authenticity and willingness to buy (Narayanan & Singh, 2025). For example, Gen Z is not a homogenous group, as evidenced by recent experimental research that emphasizes heterogeneous treatment effects. More and more studies are investigating whether people respond to inclusive marketing differently depending on factors like political ideology, cultural background, identity salience, or previous experiences with discrimination (Van den Bergh, et al., 2023). The goal is to achieve a more nuanced analysis in D&I marketing research, which aligns with the demands for more nuanced and intersectional analyses (Eisend et al., 2023). Furthermore, scholars are utilizing more advanced experimental strategies, including pre-registration, manipulation checks aimed at perceived authenticity, and mediation analyses to discover the underlying causes. In recent studies, it has been demonstrated that inclusive advertising has an indirect effect on Gen Z's purchasing intentions through perceived moral legitimacy and value congruence, not just representation (Chhabra et al., 2025; Tuli et al., 2025). Overall, the shift in methodological approaches to studying Gen Z and inclusive marketing is reflected in a shift towards research designs that are rooted in behavioral science, causality, and ethics. More and more scholars are realizing that capturing Gen Z's social awareness and skepticism requires methods that can capture both expressed values and actual behaviors. Researchers can create more comprehensive and actionable knowledge about how D&I impacts Gen Z's marketplace experiences by combining surveys, experiments, field data, and qualitative insights.

5. AN OVERVIEW OF MAJOR TRENDS AND THEIR IMPLICATIONS.

The most significant empirical findings that have emerged from recent research are summarized in this section. The value placed on inclusive practices, representations, and brand values by this cohort is consistently demonstrated by empirical research on Generation Z (Gen Z) and diversity and inclusion (D&I) in marketing. Findings from quantitative, experimental, and qualitative studies indicate that representation alone is not enough. Authenticity, consistency, and alignment between marketing communications and corporate actions strongly influence Gen Z's reactions to inclusive marketing.

The general attitude of Gen Z consumers towards diversity and inclusion in marketing is generally positive, according to a robust body of empirical evidence. In multi-market surveys, Gen Z is more likely to give favorable brand evaluations than older cohorts when advertising uses racially diverse models (Eisend et al., 2023). On average, inclusive representation has positive effects on brand attitudes and ad liking, as suggested by meta-analytic evidence, especially among younger consumers (Barari et al., 2025).

The perception of brand warmth, moral legitimacy, and social relevance among Gen Z audiences is enhanced by inclusive cues, as demonstrated by experimental studies. Controlled experiments that have manipulated the diversity of advertising spokespersons have found that engaging and communicating messages are more credible when representation aligns with Gen Z's lived realities and social norms. The findings point to the fact that inclusive representation is a baseline expectation rather than a distinguishing feature for many Gen Z consumers (Cheah & Phua, 2025; Nazir & Wani, 2025).

Studies show that when diversity cues are perceived as tokenistic, such as the inclusion of a single marginalized individual (Eisend et al., 2023). In qualitative interviews, it is revealed that Gen Z consumers are especially sensitive to stereotyped portrayals and symbolic inclusion that lack substance or continuity. The use of social media data in field studies indicates that tokenistic campaigns are more likely to spark public criticism, particularly when brand histories reveal minimal prior involvement with D&I initiatives Gen Z's positive marketplace outcomes can only be achieved by incorporating inclusive representation into broader, credible strategies, as demonstrated by these findings (Hietanen et al., 2022). Authenticity is consistently identified as a moderator in empirical studies of Gen Z and inclusive marketing (Campagna et al., 2023). The concept of authenticity is typically defined as perceived sincerity, consistency over time, and consistency between a brand's stated values and observable actions. In surveys and experiments, it has been found that authenticity has a significant effect on the relationship between inclusive messaging and positive outcomes like brand trust, emotional attachment, and advocacy intentions (Tuli et al., 2025). The importance of consistency is another important empirical finding, particularly across marketing touchpoints and over time. Longitudinal and panel studies indicate that Gen Z consumers evaluate inclusivity holistically. Initiated or episodic inclusive campaigns have a weaker effect than ones that are part of a sustained, organizational-wide effort (Branca et al., 2024). Gen Z customers actively track brands' consistency through the use of digital trace data, which involves cross-referencing marketing claims with publicly available information, including reviews, social media discourse, and activist reporting (Hietanen et al., 2022). The importance of aligning marketing communications with corporate actions is being highlighted more and more by empirical research. Gen Z consumers are more likely to give praise to brands that demonstrate support for inclusive messages through tangible actions, such as equitable hiring practices, supplier diversity programs, or political advocacy aligned with stated values, according to studies (Goedertier et al., 2024; Zimand-Sheiner & Lissitsa, 2024). Perceived moral legitimacy is enhanced and self-congruence is strengthened, which in turn predict loyalty and word-of-mouth intentions. Although aggregate findings demonstrate strong support for D&I, empirical studies also show that there is heterogeneity within Gen Z. Political ideology, cultural background, identity salience, and prior experiences with marginalization all play a role in the responses to inclusive marketing. Gen Z consumers who are marginalized across multiple dimensions tend to have more positive reactions to genuine inclusion, but they are also more susceptible to misrepresentation (Boyd et al., 2020; Eisend et al., 2023). Considering Gen Z as a homogeneous segment is not recommended due to this heterogeneity, which also supports the need for more nuanced, intersectional analyses in future research.

Digital platforms and algorithmic systems have a fundamental impact on how Gen Z interacts with brands, determining what content is visible, amplified, or marginalized. Because Gen Z is the first generation to grow up within algorithmically media environments, they mostly experience marketing through social media platforms, such as TikTok, Instagram, YouTube, and emerging creator economies. Not only do these platforms send marketing messages, but they also actively shape marketplace inclusion by determining who gets heard, what identities get represented, and how narratives about diversity and inclusion (D&I) circulate. Thus, research is becoming more focused on how algorithmic inclusion and exclusion affect Gen Z's perceptions of brands and their inclusive legitimacy. Digital platforms use algorithms to select content according to engagement metrics, personalization models, and commercial incentives. While these systems are often described as neutral or meritocratic, empirical research suggests that algorithms can re-establish and even worsen existing social inequalities. Inclusion for Gen Z, who rely heavily on algorithmic feeds to mediate brand encounters, is felt not only through brand-controlled advertising but also by the different visibility of creators, influencers, and user-generated content (Noble, 2018). At the intersection of digital platforms, algorithms, and inclusion, influencer marketing is crucial. Brand values are often translated into relatable narratives for Gen Z consumers by influencers who act as cultural intermediaries. Platform algorithms have an impact on influencer visibility, with some creators being favored and others being marginalized. Gen Z consumers are becoming more attentive to these dynamics and may criticize brands that claim inclusion while working with influencers who adhere to narrow standards of attractiveness, ability, or cultural expression (Eisend et al., 2023).

In a nutshell, based on empirical research, Gen Z considers diversity and inclusion in marketing to be important, but they consider inclusive representation to be necessary but not enough for positive brand evaluations. Gen Z's responses are shaped by authenticity, consistency, and alignment between messaging and corporate action. The findings suggest that inclusive marketing for Gen Z requires strategic integration, ethical grounding, and sustained over time to make a meaningful impact. Inclusion in Gen Z marketing cannot be understood entirely through content analysis or brand-controlled messaging, as research on digital platforms and algorithmic inclusion highlights. In digital marketplaces, algorithms act as powerful intermediaries that determine who is seen, heard, and valued. The broader sociotechnical systems that regulate visibility and voice govern inclusive marketing for Gen Z, as their consumer identities are deeply intertwined with platform participation.

The table below summarizes the key implications for practice and research regarding generation Z in global markets.

Table 1. Key Insights for Generation Z Global Market Segments

Trends	Primary conclusions	Implications for practice	Implications for research	Sources
Diversity and inclusion are interconnected	Gen Z is dedicated to representation that includes race, gender, LGBTQ, and culture, and tokenism is detrimental to their effectiveness.	Incorporate inclusion authentically in campaigns; avoid gestures that are motivated by performance.	In the future, it is important to examine how different dimensions of intersectionality are interconnected. (e.g. product and brand evaluations among Gen Z are influenced by race, gender, and sexuality in cultural contexts. It is necessary to conduct longitudinal studies to determine the long-term effects of authentic versus performative inclusion on brand trust and loyalty.	Branca et al. (2024) da Fonseca et al. (2025) Eisend et al. (2023) Goedertier et al. (2024) Tarnanidis et al. (2026a) Tarnanidis et al. 2026b) Tarmanidis (2025) Whitwam (2025)
Authenticity and consistency are important	The alignment of messaging and corporate actions is crucial, as inconsistent campaigns can lead to backlash.	The organization's practices and long-term commitment must be reflected in communication messaging and campaigns.	Gen Z's ability to detect inauthenticity can be explored through research into the mechanisms involved, such as social media scrutiny and peer discourse. Testing how perceived hypocrisy influences boycott intentions and online activism among Gen Z consumers can be done through experimental research.	Tuli et al. (2025) Hortillo et al. (2025) Boyd et al. (2020) Velinov (2025)
Algorithmic platforms and digital platforms.	Algorithmic bias affects visibility; influencer partnerships amplify reach.	Collaborate with a variety of influencers; keep track of the outcomes of algorithms.	Additional investigation is required to examine the way platform algorithms influence Gen Z's exposure to brands, identities, and social causes. Investigating the relationship between algorithmic bias, influencer diversity, and consumer perceptions of fairness and inclusion should be a priority for scholars.	Noble (2018) Eisend (2025) Hortillo et al. (2025) Pop et al. (2024)

continued on following page

Table 1. Continued

Trends	Primary conclusions	Implications for practice	Implications for research	Sources
Co-creation and participation are intertwined.	Gen Z is engaged in participatory marketing, UGC, and influencer content.	Promote the participation of consumers through co-created campaigns.	Examining the power dynamics of co-creation should be a focus of future studies, especially as it pertains to Gen Z's perception of participation as either empowerment or exploitation. The ability to analyze cultural differences in brand co-creation could be explored through cross-market research.	Eisend et al. (2023) Ochis (2024) Park et al. (2023)
Ethical Considerations	Privacy, identity representation, and algorithmic fairness are essential considerations.	Assure that data is being used ethically, represented fairly, and is transparent.	The focus of research should be on Gen Z's ethical guidelines for data usage, personalized AI, and surveillance marketing. By conducting comparative studies across regions, it is possible to clarify the influence of regulatory environments and cultural norms on ethical expectations.	Tuli et al. (2025) Licsandru & Cui (2022) Zuboff (2024)

Source: The authors

The table shows that Generation Z is a market segment that is value-driven, participative, and highly critical, with expectations that go beyond traditional marketing approaches. The main point is that authenticity and interconnectedness are necessary for diversity and inclusion. Gen Z's approach to representation involves evaluating whether inclusion is meaningful and embedded in brand values, not just responding to it. Credibility can be undermined by tokenistic gestures, which can be perceived negatively, leaving authenticity as a prerequisite instead of a differentiator. Authenticity and consistency between messaging and action are closely connected. Gen Z is observant of the alignment between organizational communication and operational behavior, as demonstrated by the table. Backlash can be triggered by campaigns that are inconsistent or exploitative, especially in digital spaces where information is spread quickly. The findings indicate that Gen Z's trust is fragile and built over time through sustained, coherent practices rather than isolated campaigns.

Digital and algorithmic platforms have a significant role to play, which is another key insight. Algorithms have the power to shape visibility, strengthen power structures, and amplify whose voices are heard. The role of influencers in mediating is crucial, but algorithmic bias can limit representation. This highlights the need for both platform presence and an understanding of how algorithmic systems shape reach, fairness, and cultural narratives to effectively engage with Gen Z. Gen Z engagement is defined by co-creation and participation, as highlighted in the table. Gen Z favored interactive relationships with brands by creating user-generated content, participating in campaigns, and collaborating with influencers over passive consumption. Consumer expectations to shape brand meaning and identity are reflected in this shift in power. In the end, ethical considerations become a universal theme. Fundamental expectations include privacy, fair representation, and transparency in data use. Gen Z's demand for ethical accountability, meaningful inclusion, and active participation is reflected in these findings, which fundamentally transform the way organizations design, communicate, and sustain their market strategies.

6. DISCUSSION AND CONCLUSIONS

Gen Z (Gen Z) is a distinct consumer group that has high expectations for diversity, inclusion, and authenticity in the brands they support. To adapt to the unique characteristics of this generation, managerial strategies need to incorporate D&I considerations across the marketing mix while also using digital channels, participatory marketing, and socially conscious narratives. Marketing scholarship is focusing on the critical frontier of diversity and inclusion research targeting Generation Z. Due to the demographic diversity, digital naivity, social consciousness, and value-driven decision-making of this cohort, it is necessary to conduct research that is rigorous, ethically informed, and methodologically sophisticated. It is clear from key findings that inclusion cannot be merely represented; authenticity, consistency, and alignment between corporate actions and messaging are crucial to shaping positive consumer responses.

It is important for managers to incorporate D&I into all marketing activities, utilize participatory co-creation, and ensure transparency and ethical responsibility in all brand interactions. Gen Z's heterogeneity and evolving values must be reflected in robust theoretical frameworks, intersectional analyses, and longitudinal studies by researchers. Achieving inclusive marketing for Gen Z can be achieved by incorporating insights from social identity theory, self-congruity theory, and consumer culture theory, while taking account of algorithmic mediation in digital spaces. Ultimately, Gen Z's interaction with brands has both advantages and disadvantages. inclusive strategies can promote loyalty, advocacy, and social legitimacy, but missteps can lead to backlash and reputational harm. Gen Z is both a driver of marketing innovation and a benchmark for authentic and ethical inclusion, which is why scholars and practitioners need to take this issue seriously.

REFERENCES

Aday, A., & Schmader, T. (2019). Seeking authenticity in diverse contexts: How identities and environments constrain "free" choice. *Social and Personality Psychology Compass, 13*(6), e12450. https://doi.org/https://doi.org/10.1111/spc3.12450

Arsel, Z., Crockett, D., & Scott, M. L. (2021). Diversity, Equity, and Inclusion (DEI) in the Journal of Consumer Research: A Curation and Research Agenda. *The Journal of Consumer Research, 48*(5), 920–933. DOI: 10.1093/jcr/ucab057

Barari, M. M., Eisend, M., & Jain, S. P. (2025). A meta-analysis of the effectiveness of social media influencers: Mechanisms and moderation. *Journal of the Academy of Marketing Science*. Advance online publication. DOI: 10.1007/s11747-025-01107-3

Boyd, C. S., Ritch, E. L., Dodd, C. A., & McColl, J. (2020). Inclusive identities: Re-imaging the future of the retail brand? *International Journal of Retail & Distribution Management, 48*(12), 1315–1335. DOI: 10.1108/ijrdm-12-2019-0392

Branca, G., Grosso, M., & Castaldo, S. (2024). Value through diversity: A systematic literature review to understand diversity and inclusion in consumer research. *Psychology and Marketing, 41*(11), 2854–2873. https://doi.org/https://doi.org/10.1002/mar.22088

Brekhus, W. H. (2020). *The sociology of identity: authenticity, multidimensionality, and mobility*. John Wiley & Sons.

Campagna, C. L., Donthu, N., & Yoo, B. (2023). Brand authenticity: Literature review, comprehensive definition, and an amalgamated scale. *Journal of Marketing Theory and Practice, 31*(2), 129–145. DOI: 10.1080/10696679.2021.2018937

Cantó, J., & Rodó-Zárate, M. (2024). Gender-Ideology Trouble? Ideology, Gender, and Generation as Factors in LGB+ Self-identification among Gen Z and Millennials in Catalonia. *Sexuality & Culture, 28*(6), 2745–2769. DOI: 10.1007/s12119-024-10252-w

Cheah, I., & Phua, P. (2025). Generational advertising: Literature review and practitioner insights on key pitfalls and implications. *International Journal of Advertising, 44*(2), 286–312. DOI: 10.1080/02650487.2024.2429904

Chhabra, S., Singh, A., & Maddela, D. (2025). Brand, causes, and the credibility gap: Gen Z purchase intentions in emerging markets. *Journal of Asia Business Studies*, •••, 1–21. DOI: 10.1108/jabs-05-2025-0302

Choi, L. S. L., Chan, K. W., & Fock, H. (2025). Deepening exploration of socially responsible consumption in generation z: The impacts of environmental knowledge and perceived consumer effectiveness. *Journal of Consumer Marketing*, *42*(7), 877–892. DOI: 10.1108/jcm-05-2024-6857

Coman, I. A., Yuan, S., & Tsai, J.-Y. (2022). Toward an Audience-Centric Framework of Corporate Social Advocacy Strategy: An Exploratory Study of Young Consumers from Generation Z. *Sustainability*, *14*(7), 4099. DOI: 10.3390/su14074099

da Fonseca, M. J. S., Aleixo, A. S. M., Teixeira, A. S., & Sousa, B. B. (2025). Drive the Purchase Intentions of Generation X and Z Tourists through Marketing Activities. In *Customer Insight in Tourism* (pp. 151–161). Routledge.

Djafarova, E., & Foots, S. (2022). Exploring ethical consumption of generation Z: Theory of planned behaviour. *Young Consumers: Insight and Ideas for Responsible Marketers*, *23*(3), 413–431. DOI: 10.1108/yc-10-2021-1405

Eisend, M. (2025). Diversity in Interactive Advertising. *Journal of Interactive Advertising*, •••, 1–13. DOI: 10.1080/15252019.2025.2513236

Eisend, M., Muldrow, A. F., & Rosengren, S. (2023). Diversity and inclusion in advertising research. *International Journal of Advertising*, *42*(1), 52–59. DOI: 10.1080/02650487.2022.2122252

Estanyol, E., Mas-Manchón, L., Fernández-Cavia, J., & Van-Bergen, P. (2025). Raising the bar? How Generation Z perceives corporate reputation and environmental commitment. *Young Consumers: Insight and Ideas for Responsible Marketers*, 1-20. https://doi.org/DOI: 10.1108/yc-06-2025-2596

Goedertier, F., Weijters, B., & Van den Bergh, J. (2024). Are Consumers Equally Willing to Pay More for Brands That Aim for Sustainability, Positive Societal Contribution, and Inclusivity as for Brands That Are Perceived as Exclusive? Generational, Gender, and Country Differences. *Sustainability*, *16*(9), 3879. DOI: 10.3390/su16093879

Hortillo, J. N., Moore, K., & Covington, S. M. (2025). AI and DEI: Do inclusive ads speak to the culture? An examination of marketing advertisement's efficacy to Gen Z consumers. *Journal of Cultural Marketing Strategy*, *10*(1), 81–93. DOI: 10.69554/CYUE5388

Jamal, A., & Al-Marri, M. (2007). Exploring the effect of self-image congruence and brand preference on satisfaction: The role of expertise. *Journal of Marketing Management*, *23*(7–8), 613–629. DOI: 10.1362/026725707X2266

Kipnis, E., Demangeot, C., Pullig, C., Cross, S. N. N., Cui, C. C., Galalae, C., & Williams, J. D. (2021). Institutionalizing Diversity-and-Inclusion-Engaged Marketing for Multicultural Marketplace Well-Being. *Journal of Public Policy & Marketing*, *40*(2), 143–164. DOI: 10.1177/0743915620975415

Kolańska-Stronka, M., & Singh, B. (2024). Five decades of self-congruity in consumer behaviour research: A systematic review and future research agenda. *International Journal of Consumer Studies*, *48*(1), e12983. https://doi.org/https://doi.org/10.1111/ijcs.12983

Konishi, C., Vargas-Madriz, L. F., & Tesolin, J. (2025). Fostering equity, diversity, and inclusion through social-emotional learning: The role of digital technologies. *Journal of Research on Technology in Education*, •••, 1–13. DOI: 10.1080/15391523.2025.2455054

Lehman, D. W., O'Connor, K., Kovács, B., & Newman, G. E. (2019). Authenticity. *The Academy of Management Annals*, *13*(1), 1–42. DOI: 10.5465/annals.2017.0047

Licsandru, T. C., & Cui, C. C. (2018). Subjective social inclusion: A conceptual critique for socially inclusive marketing. *Journal of Business Research*, *82*, 330–339. https://doi.org/https://doi.org/10.1016/j.jbusres.2017.08.036

Licsandru, T. C., & Cui, C. C. (2022). Ethnic marketing: the good, the bad and the unknown. In *Handbook of Research on Ethnic and Intra-cultural Marketing* (pp. 29–40). Edward Elgar Publishing.

Mandania, R., Cadogan, J., Liu, J., & Kazmi, N. (2025). Optimizing Promotional Campaigns to Maximize Customer Lifetime Value: A Dynamic Learning Approach. *Journal of Service Research*, *0*(0). Advance online publication. DOI: 10.1177/10946705251365524

Martí, G. (2025). Antiracism as Inclusivity: The Racial Justice Paradigm of White Progressive Churches. *Journal for the Scientific Study of Religion*, *64*(2), 173–186. https://doi.org/https://doi.org/10.1111/jssr.12949

Mishra, V., & Gupta, P. (2025). Drivers of consumer brand advocacy in the metaverse. *Journal of Fashion Marketing and Management*, •••, 1–19. DOI: 10.1108/jfmm-04-2024-0145

Munsch, A. (2021). Millennial and generation Z digital marketing communication and advertising effectiveness: A qualitative exploration. *Journal of Global Scholars of Marketing Science*, *31*(1), 10–29. DOI: 10.1080/21639159.2020.1808812

Narayanan, S., & Singh, G. A. (2025). From Stimulus to Response: Understanding the Causes and Outcomes of Consumer Activism. *Journal of Consumer Behaviour*, *24*(2), 820–845. https://doi.org/https://doi.org/10.1002/cb.2438

Nazir, M., & Wani, T. A. (2025). Human vs virtual influencers and message framing: Enhancing environmental awareness, activism and sustainable purchase intentions through effective messaging. *Management Research Review*, *48*(5), 685–708. DOI: 10.1108/mrr-08-2024-0630

Noble, S. U. (2018). Algorithms of oppression: How search engines reinforce racism. In *Algorithms of oppression*. New York university press.

Ochis, K. (2024). *Gen Z in work: A practical guide to engaging employees across the generations*. Routledge.

Opoku-Dakwa, A., & Rice, D. B. (2024). A Place for Critical Race Theory and Wokeness in Diversity Strategies. *The Academy of Management Perspectives*, *38*(2), 214–224. DOI: 10.5465/amp.2023.0015

Park, Y. W., Voss, G. B., & Voss, Z. G. (2023). Advancing customer diversity, equity, and inclusion: Measurement, stakeholder influence, and the role of marketing. *Journal of the Academy of Marketing Science*, *51*(1), 174–197. DOI: 10.1007/s11747-022-00883-6

Pop, L., Morales, L., Peev, I., Soulé, M. V., Coetzer, J. H., & Gilani, H. (2024). Inclusivity and Diversity: Marketing Exercise or a Real Commitment? In *Decolonizing Marketing Theory and Practice* (pp. 114-136). Routledge.

Rabbanee, F. K., Roy, R., & Spence, M. T. (2020). Factors affecting consumer engagement on online social networks: Self-congruity, brand attachment, and self-extension tendency. *European Journal of Marketing*, *54*(6), 1407–1431. DOI: 10.1108/ejm-03-2018-0221

Rohmanue, A., & Jacobi, E. S. (2024). The influence of marketing communications agencies on activist brands' moral competency development and ability to engage in authentic brand activism: Wieden+Kennedy 'Just Does It'. *Journal of Brand Management*, *31*(2), 126–139. DOI: 10.1057/s41262-023-00340-x

Rößner, A., & Eisend, M. (2023). Ethnic Minorities in Advertising. *Journal of Advertising*, *52*(5), 774–784. DOI: 10.1080/00913367.2023.2255247

Sardashti, H., & Calantone, R. J. (2022). Does equity-based compensation motivate executives to build strong brands? *Journal of Marketing Management*, *38*(13–14), 1433–1460. DOI: 10.1080/0267257X.2022.2041068

Schwarz, K. C., & Williams, J. P. (2020). Introduction to the social construction of identity and authenticity. In *Studies on the social construction of identity and authenticity* (pp. 1–24). Routledge.

Shepperson, L., von Rosing, M., & Czichos, H. (2025). Diversity of perspectives. In *The Sustainability Handbook* (Vol. 1, pp. 359–373). Elsevier.

Sirgy, M. J. (1982). Self-Concept in Consumer Behavior: A Critical Review. *The Journal of Consumer Research*, *9*(3), 287–300. DOI: 10.1086/208924

Srivastava, R., Gupta, P., Kumar, H., & Tuli, N. (2023). Digital customer engagement: A systematic literature review and research agenda. *Australian Journal of Management, 50*(1), 220-245. https://doi.org/ (Original work published 2025)DOI: 10.1177/03128962231177096

Tarnanidis, T., Manda, V. K., Sousa, B. B., Vlachopoulou, M., & Papachristou, E. (2026c). Marketing Complexity of Smart Consumer Products to Global Millennial Segments. In Tarnanidis, T., Sousa, B., Vlachopoulou, M., Papachristou, E., & Kittu Manda, V. (Eds.), *Diversity and Inclusion-Driven Marketing for Multicultural Marketplaces* (pp. 1–16). IGI Global Scientific Publishing., DOI: 10.4018/979-8-3373-2111-0.ch001

Tarnanidis, T., Papachristou, E., Andreou, V., Stergiou, A., & Manda, V. K. (2026b). Inclusive Marketing Strategies for Adaptive Fashion. In Tarnanidis, T., Sousa, B., Vlachopoulou, M., Papachristou, E., & Kittu Manda, V. (Eds.), *Diversity and Inclusion-Driven Marketing for Multicultural Marketplaces* (pp. 17–30). IGI Global Scientific Publishing., DOI: 10.4018/979-8-3373-2111-0.ch002

Tarnanidis, T., Sousa, B., Vlachopoulou, M., Papachristou, E., & Kittu Manda, V. (Eds.). (2026a). *Diversity and Inclusion-Driven Marketing for Multicultural Marketplaces*. IGI Global Scientific Publishing., DOI: 10.4018/979-8-3373-2111-0

Tarnanidis, T. (2025). Digital marketing and AI integration with robotics for the fight against racism in football: A cross-cultural investigation. International Journal of Business and Applied Social Science, 11(3), 28-34. http://dx.doi.org/10.33642/ijbass.v11n3p4

Tsougkou, E., Karampela, M., & Balabanis, G. (2024). Drivers and mechanisms of consumer attitudes toward global brand activists: A mediated approach. *International Marketing Review*, *41*(6), 1330–1357. DOI: 10.1108/imr-09-2023-0237

Tuli, N., Kumar, H., Upadhyay, S., & Ciszek, E. (2025). Distance between 'them' and 'us': Identity stigmatization in the age of consumer inclusion. *International Journal of Advertising*, •••, 1–30. DOI: 10.1080/02650487.2025.2592469

Turner, J. C., Brown, R. J., & Tajfel, H. (1979). Social comparison and group interest in ingroup favouritism. *European Journal of Social Psychology*, *9*(2), 187–204. https://doi.org/https://doi.org/10.1002/ejsp.2420090207

Van den Bergh, J., De Pelsmacker, P., & Worsley, B. (2023). Beyond labels: Segmenting the Gen Z market for more effective marketing. *Young Consumers: Insight and Ideas for Responsible Marketers*, *25*(2), 188–210. DOI: 10.1108/yc-03-2023-1707

Velinov, E. (2025). Generation Z in Focus: Behavioral Insights from Emerging and Advanced Markets. In *Gen Z at Work in Central and Eastern Europe* (pp. 26-41). Routledge.

Whitwam, B. (2025). Global Cultural Convergence in Social Commerce: How Platforms Transform Trust-Building among Gen Z Consumers. *Journal of Internet Commerce*, *24*(4), 325–347. DOI: 10.1080/15332861.2025.2547067

Yang, S., Goh, E., & Fan, Y. (2025). Advancing self-congruity theory in senior tourism: A perspective on theoretical, methodological and contextual progress. *Asia Pacific Journal of Marketing and Logistics*. Advance online publication. DOI: 10.1108/apjml-08-2024-1152

Zimand-Sheiner, D., & Lissitsa, S. (2024). Generation Z - factors predicting decline in purchase intentions after receiving negative environmental information: Fast fashion brand SHEIN as a case study. *Journal of Retailing and Consumer Services*, *81*, 103999. DOI: 10.1016/j.jretconser.2024.103999

ADDITIONAL READING

Bakare, L. (2024). *Responsible Marketing: How to Create an Authentic and Inclusive Marketing Strategy*. Kogan Page Publishers.

Cross, S. N. N., Galalae, C., Licsandru, T. C., Martín Ruiz, V., Cui, C. C., Mari, C., & Kearney, S. (2025). Co-creating sustained impact for diversity and inclusion engaged marketing. *European Journal of Marketing*, *59*(6), 1458–1468. DOI: 10.1108/ejm-04-2024-0326

Ferraro, C., Hemsley, A., & Sands, S. (2023). Embracing diversity, equity, and inclusion (DEI): Considerations and opportunities for brand managers. *Business Horizons*, *66*(4), 463–479. https://doi.org/https://doi.org/10.1016/j.bushor.2022.09.005

Francis, T., & Hoefel, F. (2018). True Gen': Generation Z and its implications for companies. *McKinsey & Company, 12*(2), 1-10.

Galalae, C., Kipnis, E., Cui, C. C., Johnson, E., Licsandru, T., Vorster, L., & Lindsey-Warren, T. M. (2023). A Multicontextual Lens on Racism and Discrimination in the Multicultural Marketplace. *Journal of the Association for Consumer Research, 8*(1), 95–106. DOI: 10.1086/722704

Licsandru, T. C., & Cui, C. C. (2019). Ethnic marketing to the global millennial consumers: Challenges and opportunities. *Journal of Business Research, 103*, 261–274. https://doi.org/https://doi.org/10.1016/j.jbusres.2019.01.052

Śliwa, M., Anderson, L., Black, K., Chaffer, C., & Webb, J. (2025). Introduction to the Handbook of Inclusive Learning and Teaching in Business and Management. In *Handbook of Inclusive Learning and Teaching in Business and Management* (pp. 1–12). Edward Elgar Publishing.

Van den Bergh, J., & Behrer, M. (2016). *How cool brands stay hot: Branding to Generations Y and Z*. Kogan Page Publishers.

KEY TERMS AND DEFINITIONS

Diversity and Inclusion (D&I): is a key term that describes the deliberate practice of acknowledging, appreciating, and cherishing differences among individuals, while ensuring that everyone feels welcome, respected, and able to participate fully.

Gen Z: is the demographic cohort that was born between 1997 and 2012

Tokenism: is the act of doing things (such as employing someone from a minority group) solely to avoid criticism and create the impression that people are being treated fairly.

Chapter 2
AI Bias in Marketing:
Challenges, DEI Concerns, and Mechanisms for Ethical Innovation

Anu C. Haridasan
https://orcid.org/0000-0002-2985-7919
VIT Business School, Vellore Institute of Technology, Chennai, India

Naveenraj Xavier
https://orcid.org/0000-0003-2681-5964
SRM Institute of Science and Technology, India

ABSTRACT

Artificial Intelligence is changing modern marketing through personalized engagement, trend prediction, and large-scale content generation. As generative models spread across advertising, consumer analytics, and creative work, worries about bias, fairness, and representation are increasing. When AI is trained on unbalanced data, it can reinforce stereotypes, misrepresent cultural identities, or ignore marginalized groups. This creates ethical and commercial risks related to DEI. Biased systems can damage consumer trust, harm brand reputation, and clash with new regulatory standards. This chapter looks at how bias shows up in marketing systems, why it matters, and what technical, organizational, and regulatory methods can promote more inclusive AI practices. It draws from literature, industry cases, and fairness frameworks. It outlines strategies like auditing datasets, designing inclusively, ensuring human oversight, and improving governance. Ultimately, it views DEI as the ethical basis for responsible AI marketing that can handle future challenges.

DOI: 10.4018/979-8-3373-6731-6.ch002

1. INTRODUCTION

Artificial Intelligence (AI) is rapidly changing marketing. It allows for precise targeting, automated decision-making, and scalable creative production. As algorithms manage more brand-consumer interactions, marketing relies more on data insights and predictive modeling instead of human judgment (Kietzmann et al., 2018; Rust, 2020). Generative AI speeds up this change by creating text, images, and design assets on a massive scale. This offers greater efficiency but also raises ongoing concerns about fairness, representation, and cultural sensitivity.

This technological progress presents a key paradox. The same systems that enable better personalization and creative flexibility may also reinforce inequalities found in historical and digital data (Bender et al., 2021; Crawford, 2021). Without careful oversight, AI models trained on non-diverse datasets can misrepresent identities, marginalize vulnerable groups, or produce outputs that continue harmful stereotypes. These issues are particularly important in marketing, where visibility and cultural impact are significant (Sheng et al., 2021; Suresh & Guttag, 2021).

1.1. AI's Transformative Role in Marketing

AI has become essential to marketing strategy. It influences segmentation, pricing, promotional optimization, and customer relationship management ((Haridasan et al., 2025). Predictive analytics improves marketers' ability to identify customer needs, optimize user journeys, and deliver relevant content in real time (Kietzmann et al., 2018; Wedel & Kannan, 2016). Machine learning models track patterns across millions of data points. This enables detailed personalization that far exceeds traditional marketing analytics (Odlin & Benson-Rea, 2021; Rust, 2020).

Generative AI deepens this change. It helps with scalable idea generation, copywriting, product visualization, and testing creative variations. This allows marketers to quickly experiment with different stories and visual concepts (Dwivedi et al., 2023; Huang & Rust, 2022). However, this power comes with risks. Generative systems can unintentionally reinforce biases found in their training data. This can lead to content that reflects oversimplified or distorted cultural views (Bender et al., 2021; Luccioni et al., 2023).

In marketing, where imagery, language, and symbolism matter greatly, these issues can cause representational harm, misinterpretation, or cultural exclusion.

1.2. The Rise of Generative AI and Its Dual Promise

Generative AI offers new creative possibilities. It makes content production easier and speeds up campaign development. Its advantages include low production costs, quick iterations, and the ability to create personalized media at scale (Dwivedi et al., 2023; Kaplan & Haenlein, 2019).

Generative AI is like a partner in creativity in marketing. It doesn't take away from human ingenuity; instead, it helps to optimize workflows and enhance efficiency across marketing departments.

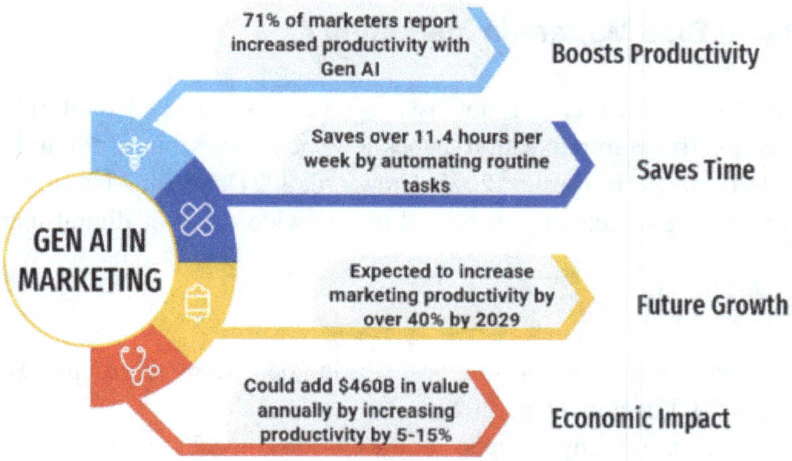

Source: www.adonis.media/insights/understanding-generative-ai-for-marketing-success

However, several studies point out that generative models often reflect stereotypes or demographic gaps, especially regarding race, gender, and socioeconomic status (Birhane & Prabhu, 2021; Luccioni et al., 2023). Language models replicate patterns of occupational, gender, and ethnic bias found in training data (Sheng et al., 2021; Bender et al., 2021). Similarly, diffusion models may produce idealized, Western-centered, or sexualized images unless guided carefully (Luccioni et al., 2023; Perera & Patel, 2023).

This creates a dual promise:

(i) Promise of value:

- faster creative production
- lower cost
- scalable personalization

(ii) Promise of harm:

- stereotype reinforcement
- exclusion of minority identities
- biased depictions in marketing campaigns
- culturally insensitive or inaccurate content

Thus, generative AI needs proper governance to ensure its benefits do not overshadow ethical responsibilities.

1.3. Why AI Bias Matters in Marketing?

Bias in AI-driven marketing is not just a technical issue; it is also cultural, social, and legal. Marketing communication shapes how society sees things, cultural stories, and shared meanings (Borgesius, 2025; Crawford, 2021). When AI systems create biased outputs, the effects are magnified by the wide reach of digital marketing channels.

Key harms include:

- Representational harm (erasing or distorting depictions of groups) (Blodgett et al., 2020; Luccioni et al., 2023)
- Allocative harm (denying opportunities in jobs, housing, or credit) (Cowgill & Tucker, 2019; Lambrecht & Tucker, 2019; 2024)
- Cultural harm (appropriating or misusing cultural symbols) (Birhane & Prabhu, 2021; Crawford, 2021)
- Trust erosion, as consumers lose confidence when they see AI-driven interactions as unfair or exclusionary (Kaplan & Haenlein, 2019; Rust, 2020)

Regulatory pressures are increasing. Frameworks like the EU AI Act require companies to ensure fairness, transparency, and risk management. Firms that do not deal with AI bias may face compliance penalties, damage to their reputation, and a long-term loss of customer loyalty.

1.4. Positioning DEI as the Ethical Core of Marketing Innovation

Diversity, equity, and inclusion (DEI) must serve as the ethical foundation for AI-driven marketing because this technology shapes representation, influences cultural narratives, and determines access to information and opportunities. Integrating DEI into AI systems requires us to recognize that data is not neutral. Datasets reflect historical inequities, power structures, and cultural biases (Crawford, 2021; Suresh & Guttag, 2021).

DEI-centered AI development requires:

- Inclusive data collection to ensure demographic representation (Castro et al., 2020; Gebru et al., 2021)
- Bias auditing and fairness evaluation during model development (Mehrabi et al., 2021; Mitchell et al., 2019)
- Transparent and accountable governance mechanisms (Floridi & Cowls, 2022; Jobin et al., 2019)
- Collaboration between marketers, data scientists, ethicists, and DEI teams (Dwivedi et al., 2023; Huang & Rust, 2022)

Marketing sits at the intersection of technology, culture, and society. Therefore, embedding DEI principles into AI workflows is not just an ethical necessity; it is also a strategic choice. Inclusive AI strengthens brand reputation, improves market reach, and helps organizations meet changing consumer expectations for ethical behavior and cultural sensitivity (Kaplan & Haenlein, 2019; Rust, 2020).

2. OBJECTIVES AND RESEARCH QUESTIONS

Artificial Intelligence (AI) continues to change modern marketing by impacting decision-making, content creation, and consumer engagement. However, as algorithmic systems become more common in marketing processes, concerns about fairness, bias, and representation increase. Scholars highlight that AI systems can unintentionally mirror historical and social inequalities, especially when they are trained on unbalanced datasets or used without proper oversight (Mehrabi et al., 2021; Suresh & Guttag, 2021). In marketing, where cultural representation, inclusivity, and social views are important, these risks have greater ethical and reputational consequences.

Therefore, this chapter aims to examine how algorithmic bias appears in AI-driven marketing practices and how diversity, equity, and inclusion (DEI) principles can be included in responsible AI development.

2.1. Chapter Objectives

The first objective of this chapter is to explain how algorithmic bias works and how it impacts AI outputs in marketing. Algorithmic bias can come from biased training data, model designs, feedback loops, or social patterns that influence decisions in advertising, personalization, segmentation, and content generation (Blodgett et al., 2020; Suresh & Guttag, 2021).

The second objective is to explore the effects of AI bias on DEI, especially in areas like representational accuracy, cultural sensitivity, and fair access to opportunities. Marketing systems that depend on biased AI can uphold exclusionary norms, underrepresent minority groups, or unevenly distribute benefits, which can harm consumer trust and brand reputation (Crawford, 2021; Lambrecht & Tucker, 2019).

The third objective is to identify ways to reduce bias, such as auditing datasets, using inclusive design, implementing fairness-aware algorithms, integrating human oversight, and setting up strong governance structures. Scholars highlight the importance of systemic approaches—not just technical solutions—to ensure that AI systems follow ethical guidelines (Floridi & Cowls, 2022; Jobin et al., 2019).

Finally, the chapter aims to provide recommendations that align with policy, drawing from global regulations like the EU AI Act and ethical AI guidelines in industry and academia.

2.2. Central Research Questions

Based on the above objectives, this chapter looks into the following research questions:

- How do algorithmic biases emerge within AI systems used in marketing?

This question examines data-driven, systemic, and socio-technical sources of bias (Suresh & Guttag, 2021; Mehrabi et al., 2021).

- What cultural, ethical, and representational risks do biased AI models pose for marketing practice?

Previous research indicates that misrepresentation and exclusion can significantly affect brand equity and social norms (Blodgett et al., 2020; Crawford, 2021).

- How can marketers integrate DEI principles into AI development and deployment?

This includes designing inclusive datasets, conducting fairness evaluations, using participatory approaches, and ensuring interdisciplinary governance (Floridi & Cowls, 2022; Jobin et al., 2019).

- What mechanisms, including technical, organizational, and regulatory aspects, are most effective for reducing AI bias in marketing environments?

These research questions guide a combined analysis of theory, practice, and policy to support ethical, inclusive AI marketing.

2.3. Scope and Limitations of the Study

This chapter looks at the connection between AI bias, marketing practices, and DEI frameworks, focusing on generative AI, algorithmic targeting, content personalization, and automated decision systems. It covers both technical aspects, such as training data imbalance and model fairness metrics, and social dimensions, like representation, inclusivity, and consumer trust.

Several limitations need to be noted. First, this chapter does not include empirical experimentation; instead, it combines existing academic and industry research. Second, AI technologies develop quickly, so some insights may change as models become more advanced or as new regulations come into play (Dwivedi et al., 2023). Third, cultural views on bias differ across regions. While the chapter uses global case studies, it mainly reflects the leading regulatory frameworks and research from North America and Europe.

Despite these limitations, the chapter provides a solid conceptual basis for understanding AI bias in marketing and promoting inclusive, equity-focused innovation.

3. THEORETICAL BACKGROUND AND LITERATURE REVIEW

Artificial Intelligence (AI) systems are increasingly involved in brand–consumer interactions, bringing up new concerns about fairness, representation, and ethical responsibility. This section combines theoretical ideas related to algorithmic bias, diversity, equity, and inclusion (DEI) in marketing, fairness metrics in machine learning (ML), and governance frameworks. The review shows how these areas connect to influence responsible AI marketing practices, forming a basis for the chapter's later analyses.

3.1. Algorithmic Bias: Definition and Mechanisms

Algorithmic bias means systematic and unfair discrimination caused by computational systems. This often leads to unequal results across demographic groups (Mehrabi et al., 2021; Suresh & Guttag, 2021). Bias can arise from various sources throughout the ML process, such as data collection, labeling, model design, optimization goals, and deployment settings.

3.1.1 Data-driven learning and representational imbalance

Machine learning models find statistical patterns from training datasets. If these datasets underrepresent certain groups or mainly reflect dominant cultures, the model learns biased associations (Barocas et al., 2020; Buolamwini & Gebru, 2018). Representational imbalance happens when demographic groups are either missing or inadequately represented, leading to decreased performance and stereotypical outputs for those populations.

In marketing, this imbalance can result in skewed audience segmentation, exclusionary ad targeting, or content personalization that favors majority identities (Lambrecht & Tucker, 2019). For example, consumer data may include historical spending trends and socio-demographic connections that inadvertently lead to discriminatory targeting results.

3.1.2 Bias amplification in generative models

Generative AI presents unique bias risks because models do not just classify or predict; they actively create new images, text, and media. Research shows that diffusion and transformer-based models often amplify societal stereotypes found in their training data (Luccioni et al., 2023; Bender et al., 2021). Factors that worsen bias amplification include:

- Skewed training data (e.g., overrepresentation of Western beauty standards in image datasets).
- Semantic associations learned by large language models (e.g., connecting leadership terms with male-dominated contexts).
- Prompt sensitivity, where neutral prompts lead to biased outputs.

In marketing, this can lead to generative content that routinely shows lighter-skinned individuals, gender stereotypes, or culturally inaccurate imagery. This can harm brand equity and reinforce negative social patterns (Sheng et al., 2021).

3.2. Diversity, Equity, and Inclusion (DEI) in Marketing

DEI principles have long influenced marketing conversations, especially in areas like multicultural marketing, cultural branding, and inclusive advertising. Traditionally, multicultural marketing focused on customizing campaigns for specific demographic groups (Cui, 2001). Over time, this evolved into inclusive marketing, which stresses authentic representation, cultural sensitivity, and fair treatment of consumers at all touchpoints (Rosengren et al., 2020).

Recent research on diversity and inclusion in marketing highlights that modern marketing strategies need to incorporate DEI principles into technology-based and data-driven decision-making processes. This is especially important when reaching out to multicultural and global consumer groups (Tarnanidis et al., 2026).

3.2.1 From multicultural marketing to inclusive AI strategies

The shift from multicultural marketing to AI-driven inclusivity reflects changing consumer expectations and technological capabilities. Consumers now demand accurate, respectful, and diverse representation in advertising. Brands that do not meet these expectations risk losing trust or facing public backlash (Dwivedi et al., 2023; Crawford, 2021).

AI offers new opportunities—and risks—for DEI

Opportunity: AI can personalize campaigns for diverse audiences at scale, enhancing cultural relevance and identity representation.

Risk: AI-generated content may unknowingly stereotype or exclude groups if not managed carefully.

For example, research shows that targeted advertising algorithms may send job ads mainly to men or housing ads to specific racial groups. This reinforces structural inequalities (Lambrecht & Tucker, 2019; Ali et al., 2019). Thus, DEI-aware AI practices need systematic bias checks, diverse training data, and human oversight.

3.3. Fairness in Machine Learning: Technical Perspectives

Fairness in ML aims to ensure that algorithmic decisions do not disproportionately harm or disadvantage certain groups. Several established fairness concepts have emerged in the literature.

3.3.1 Demographic parity

Demographic parity requires that outcomes do not depend on protected attributes (e.g., gender, race). Formally, an algorithm meets demographic parity when all groups have an equal chance of receiving a positive outcome (Dwork et al., 2012). While useful for finding high-level disparities, demographic parity may ignore subtle contextual differences important in marketing (e.g., consumers' genuine preferences).

3.3.2 Equalized odds

Equalized odds requires equal true positive and false positive rates across demographic groups (Hardt et al., 2016). It accounts for performance differences and is commonly used for classification tasks. In marketing, ensuring predictive models perform equitably across consumer groups supports fair personalization, segmentation, and recommendation systems.

3.3.3 Counterfactual fairness

Counterfactual fairness considers whether a system's decision would remain the same if the individual belonged to a different demographic group in a hypothetical scenario, while keeping everything else the same (Kusner et al., 2017). This concept aligns closely with ethical marketing principles by isolating the influence of sensitive attributes from model decisions.

Given the complexity of marketing situations, where preferences, identities, and cultural factors interact, no single fairness definition applies universally. Scholars argue that fairness must be sensitive to context and linked to societal and organizational values (Mitchell et al., 2019; Floridi & Cowls, 2022).

3.4. Ethical AI and Governance Frameworks

Ethical AI frameworks stress accountability, transparency, fairness, and responsibility throughout the AI lifecycle. These frameworks come from interdisciplinary research that includes ethics, law, computer science, and policy studies.

3.4.1 Accountability

Accountability in AI requires organizations to establish clear responsibilities for decisions made by automated systems (Jobin et al., 2019). In marketing, accountability means that human decision-makers need to oversee algorithmic results, especially in areas affecting vulnerable populations (Cowgill & Tucker, 2019).

3.4.2 Transparency

Transparency involves explaining how AI systems work, what data they use, and how they make decisions. Transparency tools, such as model cards and data documentation, help stakeholders understand and reduce information gaps (Mitchell et al., 2019; Gebru et al., 2021).

3.4.3 Responsibility

Responsibility includes taking proactive steps to prevent or lessen harm. This involves thorough evaluation, documentation, stakeholder review, and following ethical and regulatory standards (Floridi & Cowls, 2022). The EU AI Act and similar initiatives promote responsibility by categorizing AI risks, requiring impact assessments, and demanding risk mitigation plans.

Together, these governance principles help ensure that AI systems align with organizational values, regulatory requirements, and ethical norms.

3.5. The Intersections of DEI, Fairness, and Marketing Ethics

DEI, fairness, and marketing ethics intersect in their shared goal of promoting respect, equity, and accountability. Algorithmic bias challenges basic marketing ethics principles related to fairness, non-discrimination, and truthfulness (Murphy et al., 2017; Palmer & Hedberg, 2013). Integrating DEI into AI practices boosts fairness efforts by ensuring cultural context, inclusive representation, and consideration of social justice issues.

Marketing ethics focuses on consumer well-being, dignity, and the need to avoid harm—values that closely connect with fairness metrics and DEI practices. For example:

- Fairness metrics help measure disparities.
- DEI frameworks provide context for disparities and reveal their social and cultural implications.
- Ethical governance guarantees accountability and transparency.

This intersection highlights that creating fair and inclusive AI is both a technical challenge and a social-ethical responsibility. As marketing increasingly relies on AI for creative and strategic decisions, connecting DEI with fairness frameworks is crucial for building trust, promoting respectful representation, and ensuring fair access to opportunities.

4. CHALLENGES IN PRACTICE: HOW AI BIAS MANIFESTS IN MARKETING

As AI-driven systems increasingly influence how brands connect with consumers, worries about fairness, representation, and ethical choices are rising across industries. While AI offers substantial benefits in efficiency, personalization, and creative tasks, using it in marketing reveals serious weaknesses. Biased algorithms can skew audience targeting, misrepresent cultural identities, erode consumer trust, and create legal issues. These challenges stem not just from technical problems but also from oversights in governance, accountability, and ethical guidelines (Suresh

& Guttag, 2021; Crawford, 2021). This section explores how AI bias appears in marketing practices and the resulting consequences.

4.1. Algorithmic Bias in Ad Targeting and Personalization

Algorithmic advertising systems use machine learning models to decide which content appears for which consumers. These systems analyze large datasets of behavior and demographics to predict user preferences, bidding strategies, and ad placements. However, optimizing based on data can unintentionally lead to discrimination—both in representation and allocation—when the training data includes historical biases (Lambrecht & Tucker, 2019; Ali et al., 2019).

4.1.1 Discriminatory Ad Delivery

Research shows that advertising platforms can disproportionately deliver high-paying job ads for technical roles to men, even without specific gender targeting (Lambrecht & Tucker, 2019). Similarly, housing and credit ads may be distributed along racial lines based on predicted click-through rates rather than explicit targeting criteria (Ali et al., 2019). Because marketing algorithms aim for engagement, they may unintentionally mirror demographic patterns from historical data. Recent research on dynamic learning in promotional optimization shows that while these systems can significantly improve customer lifetime value, they may also reinforce existing behavioral patterns if fairness and governance constraints are not included (Mandania et al., 2025).

4.1.2 Feedback Loops

Feedback loops happen when algorithmic decisions reinforce the very patterns they are based on. For instance, if ads for STEM jobs are primarily shown to men, then click-through rates from women may stay low, further solidifying biased expectations (Cowgill & Tucker, 2019). Over time, personalization systems may create self-reinforcing pathways that exclude some groups.

4.1.3 Impact on Consumer Segmentation

Traditional segmentation methods relied on human judgment and oversight. However, AI-based segmentation identifies hidden demographic groups that may closely relate to sensitive traits (like race or income) without clear labeling. This unclear grouping can lead to unintentional discrimination or unfair targeting, raising ethical questions about transparency and consent (Baracas et al., 2020).

4.2. Cultural Blind Spots and Representation Failures

Marketing communication shapes cultural stories and identity representations. Yet, AI systems often show biases in representation due to limited training sets, incomplete cultural contexts, or an overabundance of dominant identity groups (Blodgett et al., 2020; Buolamwini & Gebru, 2018).

4.2.1 Bias in Generative Content

Generative AI models, including large language models and image generators, typically reproduce majority norms. Studies reveal that neutral prompts, such as "a professional person," often lead to images of lighter-skinned men, highlighting biases in training datasets (Luccioni et al., 2023). Language models may create stereotypical links, associating nurturing roles with women and leadership roles with men (Sheng et al., 2021). For marketers using automated creative tools, such outputs risk reinforcing harmful stereotypes in ads, reducing the cultural inclusivity of campaigns.

4.2.2 Underrepresentation and Erasure

When AI systems fail to represent minority identities adequately, marketing content can exclude or misrepresent marginalized groups. For example, this may involve mislabeling cultural attire, creating inaccurate depictions of non-Western environments, or not representing diverse body types, ages, and abilities (Crawford, 2021). Such misrepresentation can alienate audiences and hurt brand authenticity.

4.2.3 Cultural Appropriation Risks

AI systems trained on collected internet data may reproduce cultural symbols without proper context, which can lead to cultural appropriation. For instance, generative models may mix sacred or traditional artifacts into commercial images, raising ethical concerns about cultural misappropriation—a growing issue in marketing ethics (Murphy et al., 2017).

4.3. Ethical and Legal Risks of AI in Marketing

AI-driven marketing is facing increasing scrutiny from regulators, as governments and civil society groups express concerns about discrimination, privacy issues, and a lack of transparency (Jobin et al., 2019; Floridi & Cowls, 2022).

4.3.1 Regulatory Compliance Challenges

New laws like the EU AI Act require organizations to assess risks, ensure transparency, and reduce harm. AI systems used for profiling and targeted advertising may be labeled "high risk" if they significantly impact economic opportunities. Companies must show fairness, maintain documentation, and ensure human oversight to remain compliant.

4.3.2 Algorithmic Discrimination Liability

Brands may be legally responsible when their algorithmic marketing systems lead to discriminatory outcomes—even if there was no intent to discriminate. U.S. anti-discrimination laws that govern employment, housing, and credit have already applied to online advertising (Cowgill & Tucker, 2019). If an AI system unfairly excludes protected groups, companies may be held accountable for the consequences.

4.3.3 Privacy and Data Protection Risks

AI-driven personalization depends on gathering extensive consumer data, which raises concerns under global privacy regulations like GDPR and CCPA. Issues include insufficient informed consent, unclear data-sharing processes, and the potential for reidentifying sensitive traits through inference (Crawford, 2021).

4.4. Erosion of Consumer Trust and Brand Reputation

Consumer trust is essential in marketing, and AI bias threatens reputational integrity. Studies indicate that consumers respond negatively if they perceive algorithms as unfair or exclusionary (Kaplan & Haenlein, 2019).

4.4.1 Loss of Perceived Fairness

When consumers see biased recommendations or discriminatory ad patterns, their trust in AI systems diminishes. For instance, women or minority consumers may feel left out when product suggestions consistently favor other demographics. This can reduce engagement, loyalty, and brand connection (Rust, 2020).

4.4.2 Public Backlash and Social Media Amplification

Failures in representation or culturally insensitive AI-generated content can quickly go viral on social media, escalating into public relations crises. Cultural missteps that might have once been contained can now blow up into global controversies due to rapid online sharing.

4.4.3 Impact on Brand Equity

Biased marketing practices may cause lasting damage to a brand, lowering its perceived authenticity and inclusivity—qualities increasingly important to younger consumers (Dwivedi et al., 2023). Brands seen as insensitive or discriminatory risk losing diverse audiences and face difficulties in rebuilding trust. Research on brand-building and executive incentives indicates that long-term brand strength is connected to governance structures and leadership accountability. This reinforces the case for ethical and responsible AI-driven marketing practices (Sardashti & Calantone, 2022).

4.5. Governance and Accountability Gaps in Industry Practice

Despite a growing awareness of AI risks, many organizations lack proper governance to ensure ongoing fairness and compliance.

4.5.1 Lack of Internal Oversight

Many companies adopt AI solutions without formal review processes, ethical oversight boards, or collaborative risk assessments (Jobin et al., 2019). AI decisions often reside within technical teams, restricting marketers' ability to spot cultural or ethical issues.

4.5.2 Insufficient Bias Auditing

Although tools exist for measuring fairness and documenting datasets, they are not commonly used in marketing. Bias audits remain uncommon due to perceived costs, expertise shortages, or fear of uncovering compliance liabilities (Mitchell et al., 2019; Gebru et al., 2021).

4.5.3 Opaque Vendor Models

Many marketing teams depend on third-party platforms (like ad networks and recommendation engines) whose algorithms are proprietary and unclear. This lack of transparency limits organizational control and accountability, even when downstream impacts arise (Cowgill & Tucker, 2019).

4.5.4 Misalignment Between DEI and AI Teams

DEI teams often concentrate on human-centered initiatives—like hiring, culture, and branding—while AI teams prioritize optimization and performance. Without coordination, AI development may miss DEI considerations, resulting in harmful outcomes despite a company's stated commitment to inclusivity (Floridi & Cowls, 2022).

5. CASE STUDIES AND INDUSTRY SNAPSHOTS

Case studies provide important examples of how AI bias shows up in real marketing scenarios and how organizations have responded, whether successfully or not. Looking at both failures and successes reveals the underlying causes of bias, gaps in governance, cultural impacts, and chances for ethical improvements. This section examines two examples of failure and two examples of success, followed by combined lessons that promote responsible AI marketing.

5.1. Case of Failure: Facebook Ads and Algorithmic Discrimination

Facebook, now known as Meta, has experienced ongoing criticism for algorithmic discrimination in its advertising systems. Even when advertisers set neutral audience targets, Facebook's machine learning algorithms adjusted ad delivery based on predicted engagement. This led to discriminatory trends linked to race, gender, and income level (Ali et al., 2019).

5.1.1 Biased Delivery of Housing, Employment, and Credit Ads

In a significant study, Ali et al. (2019) showed that Facebook's algorithms favored white users for housing ads, targeted younger men with ads for delivery jobs, and sent credit card offers mainly to higher-income groups—even without specific targeting limits. These practices violated U.S. civil rights laws related to housing and employment.

Lambrecht and Tucker (2019) also highlighted gender discrimination in ad delivery for STEM job opportunities. Even without gender targeting, job postings for technical roles mostly appeared to men due to algorithmic optimization that favored historically higher male engagement.

5.1.2 Legal and Ethical Consequences

These discriminatory results led to several legal actions, including a 2019 settlement where Facebook agreed to improve its ad-targeting tools for sensitive categories. The U.S. Department of Housing and Urban Development (HUD) also filed charges claiming violations of the Fair Housing Act.

From an ethical standpoint, these failures show how algorithmic personalization can unintentionally replicate systemic inequalities, especially when models optimize for engagement without fairness checks (Cowgill & Tucker, 2019; Barocas et al., 2020).

5.1.3 Marketing Implications

For marketers, the Facebook case demonstrates that:

- Optimization goals, such as click-through rates and conversions, may conflict with fairness.
- Lack of transparency from vendors poses serious reputational and legal risks.
- Even "neutral" models can lead to discriminatory effects in real-life situations.

5.2. Case of Failure: Bias in Generative AI Imagery

The rise of generative AI models, such as DALL·E, Stable Diffusion, and Midjourney, has allowed marketers to automate creative production. However, these models show strong biases due to their training data and reinforcement learning processes.

5.2.1 Stereotypical and Exclusionary Outputs

Research by Luccioni et al. (2023) finds that diffusion models often reinforce gender and racial stereotypes. Neutral prompts like "CEO" or "engineer" usually produce images of white men. Prompts for "nurse" or "teacher" tend to generate images dominated by women. These patterns reflect societal stereotypes embedded in training datasets.

Sheng et al. (2021) similarly discovered that language models create stereotypical associations, such as linking Muslims with violence or African Americans with crime, when developing narratives or marketing texts.

5.2.2 Commercial Harms in Marketing Contexts

Several brands using generative tools have faced backlash:

- A major clothing retailer created promotional images that visibly lacked representation of people of color.
- A travel company's AI-generated ads featured culturally inaccurate depictions of Asian and African regions, drawing online criticism.
- Social media outcry raised concerns about AI-generated "Eurocentric beauty standards."

These incidents harmed brand trust and highlighted the risks of unreviewed AI-generated marketing content (Crawford, 2021).

5.2.3 Underlying Causes

Bias in generative imagery arises from:

- Skewed datasets scraped from the internet (Bender et al., 2021).
- Reinforcement of dominant cultural aesthetics.
- Absence of fairness measures in model designs.

Generative systems risk erasing or misrepresenting diverse cultural identities unless actively managed.

5.3. Case of Success: Olay's "DecodeTheBias" Campaign

In contrast to failure cases, some companies have effectively applied AI and DEI principles to address systemic bias in beauty and advertising. One notable example is Olay's "Decode The Bias" initiative, which aims to confront gender and racial underrepresentation in STEM fields.

5.3.1 Addressing Representation through Data and Storytelling

Olay recognized that women, particularly Black and Latina women, are significantly underrepresented in STEM careers (Dwivedi et al., 2023). The company used data-driven storytelling, expert partnerships, and inclusive imagery to promote awareness and encourage more women to pursue scientific careers.

While not focused specifically on AI models, the campaign showed how brands can shift from biased or exclusionary narratives to inclusive, data-supported representation. It established industry standards for:

- Inclusive creative guidelines.
- Accurate depiction of women in STEM roles.

- Partnerships with diverse creators and institutions.
- DEI-Driven Marketing Effectiveness

Research in inclusive advertising indicates that diverse representation can boost brand perception, strengthen cultural connections, and build consumer trust (Cui, 2001; Rosengren et al., 2020).

Olay's success highlights the benefits of:

- Inclusive visual design practices.
- Avoiding stereotypical portrayals.
- Integrating DEI considerations into branding strategies.

Though not specific to AI, it offers a model for applying DEI principles to AI-generated marketing content.

5.4. Case of Success: Human-in-the-Loop AI Governance

Human-in-the-loop (HITL) systems have emerged as a best practice for preventing harmful AI outputs in marketing. Several companies now weave human oversight into their creative processes, algorithmic choices, and dataset evaluations.

5.4.1 Brand Example: Adobe's Responsible AI Program

Adobe, a leader in creative AI tools, serves as a strong example of HITL governance:

- Adobe Firefly integrates safeguards and human-corrective workflows to limit biased or harmful outputs.
- Datasets undergo human review to avoid inappropriate or stereotypical imagery (Gebru et al., 2021).
- Transparency features, like "Content Credentials," help marketers identify AI-generated assets.

5.4.2 Retail Example: Human Oversight in Recommendation Systems

A major U.S. retail chain reportedly adopted a HITL framework in its product recommendation systems. Human reviewers monitored algorithmic performance for signs of demographic exclusion (Rust, 2020). This resulted in:

- Reduced leakage of stereotypes in recommendations.
- Fairer distribution of promotional offers.
- Increased engagement from underrepresented consumer groups.

Why Human Oversight Works
HITL systems support:

- Context and cultural understanding that AI lacks.
- Ethical review aligned with marketing principles.
- Prevention of biased outputs before they reach the public.

By combining machine learning automation with human judgment, companies enhance both fairness and creative quality.

5.5. Lessons Learned: Comparing Failures and Best Practices

The cases shown reveal that the risks of biased AI in marketing are not just theories—they are well-documented and have serious consequences. Several key lessons emerge.

1. Optimization without fairness leads to discrimination.

Failures like Facebook Ads show that engagement-based optimization often results in biased outcomes if left unchecked (Ali et al., 2019). In contrast, HITL models manage performance alongside equity.

2. Representation matters in both data and creative output.

Generative failures highlight how inadequate representation in datasets leads to stereotypical or culturally insensitive imagery (Luccioni et al., 2023). Olay's success emphasizes the commercial advantages of inclusive representation.

3. Transparency and documentation improve accountability.

Using model cards, dataset documentation, and human audits enhances oversight and diminishes algorithmic opacity (Mitchell et al., 2019; Gebru et al., 2021).

4. DEI must be embedded, not added, to AI pipelines.

Organizations that weave DEI into algorithmic development fight bias more effectively than those that make after-the-fact corrections (Floridi & Cowls, 2022).

5. Human oversight remains essential.

In all successful cases, human review processes played a significant role in preventing harmful outcomes. Automation without oversight is inadequate for culturally sensitive marketing situations.

6. MECHANISMS FOR ETHICAL AND INCLUSIVE INNOVATION

As AI becomes a key part of marketing decision-making and creative work, ensuring ethical and inclusive innovation requires more than just technical skills. It needs a socio-technical approach based on fairness, accountability, diversity, and transparency. This section highlights six important mechanisms for building responsible AI systems in marketing: bias detection and dataset auditing, inclusive design, fairness-aware algorithms, human oversight, corporate governance, and the involvement of DEI and regulatory actors. Together, these mechanisms help avoid harmful outcomes, improve consumer trust, and enhance organization integrity.

6.1. Bias Detection and Dataset Auditing

Bias detection and dataset auditing are crucial for making sure that AI systems work fairly. Machine learning models learn patterns from their training data, so any imbalance or stereotype in that data affects the model's results (Barocas et al., 2020; Mehrabi et al., 2021).

6.1.1 Dataset Documentation and Transparency

Datasheets for datasets (Gebru et al., 2021) and Data Statements for Natural Language Processing (Bender & Friedman, 2018) offer structured ways to document:

- Data sources
- Collection methods
- Demographic distributions
- Potential risks or representational gaps
- Intended uses and limitations

These documentation practices help marketing teams see if their data underrepresents certain demographic groups or overrepresents dominant cultural patterns.

6.1.2 Auditing for Representational Bias

Representational bias happens when specific groups are not included enough or are misrepresented in the dataset. For example:

- Beauty and fashion datasets might feature mainly lighter-skinned individuals.
- Consumer sentiment datasets may lean toward Western dialects of English.
- Behavioral targeting datasets can reflect past inequalities in purchasing power or digital access (Crawford, 2021).

Audits can include statistical tests, demographic distribution analysis, or comparative sampling to spot imbalances.

6.1.3 Auditing for Allocative Bias

Allocative bias deals with the unequal distribution of resources or opportunities, such as credit offers, job ads, or targeted promotions. Studies show that ad delivery algorithms can distribute opportunities unevenly across gender or racial groups (Ali et al., 2019; Lambrecht & Tucker, 2019). The auditing process might involve:

- Counterfactual testing
- Sensitivity analysis by demographic attribute
- Fairness metrics like demographic parity or disparate impact ratios

These insights help marketers fix models that focus on predicting engagement over ensuring fairness.

6.2. Inclusive Design in AI Systems

Inclusive design aims to integrate DEI principles right into AI system development. Instead of dealing with bias after the fact, this approach considers the diverse needs, identities, and cultural contexts of users from the start (Norman & Nielsen, 2019).

6.2.1 Co-design with Diverse Stakeholders

Inclusive AI design benefits from having diverse teams—designers, customers, experts, and marginalized communities—who can highlight cultural nuances that algorithms might miss. Diverse teams have been shown to better frame problems, reduce exclusionary assumptions, and increase cultural relevance (Cui, 2001; Rosengren et al., 2020).

6.2.2 Persona Diversity in Marketing Applications

Marketers often use personas to model customer segments. Inclusive AI improves this practice by creating personas that:

- Represent a wider range of racial, gender, age, and ability identities
- Include intersectional experiences
- Consider different levels of digital literacy

This ensures that AI-generated recommendations, creative work, and customer journeys do not default to majority norms (Dwivedi et al., 2023).

6.2.3 Inclusive Evaluation Frameworks

Evaluation processes should include:

- Cultural quality checks
- Bias stress tests
- Sensitivity reviews for harmful outputs

These checks ensure that technical performance metrics align with ethical marketing goals.

6.3. Fairness-Aware Algorithms and Testing Tools

Fairness-aware algorithms aim to reduce biased results by adding fairness constraints during model training and evaluation.

6.3.1 Pre-processing Methods

Pre-processing techniques lower bias before training in the following ways:

- Rebalancing datasets
- Removing sensitive attribute correlations
- Using synthetic augmentation for underrepresented groups

These methods help close representational gaps (Kamiran & Calders, 2012).

6.3.2 In-processing Algorithms

In-processing directly integrates fairness into model optimization. Examples include:

- Adversarial debiasing
- Fairness-constrained loss functions
- Counterfactual fairness estimators (Kusner et al., 2017)

These algorithms penalize discriminatory patterns during training, leading to more balanced decision-making.

6.3.3 Post-processing Tools

When retraining or changing datasets is not feasible, post-processing tools adjust model outputs to meet fairness metrics. These include:

- Threshold adjustments across demographic groups
- Re-ranking algorithms to lessen disparate impacts
- Output filtering in generative AI models (Luccioni et al., 2023)

6.3.4 Testing and Benchmarking

Tools like AI Fairness 360 (IBM) and Fairlearn (Microsoft) support systematic testing of fairness metrics. Model cards document:

- Performance disparities
- Known biases
- Appropriate versus inappropriate use cases (Mitchell et al., 2019)

For marketing teams, these tools can reveal whether personalization or targeting systems treat different demographic groups fairly.

6.4. Human Oversight and Hybrid Decision-Making

While automation speeds up marketing processes, human oversight is crucial for ensuring ethical outcomes. Human-in-the-loop (HITL) decision-making combines algorithmic efficiency with human judgment, allowing for oversight during training, testing, and deployment (Rust, 2020).

6.4.1 Why Human Oversight Matters

AI lacks understanding of context and cultural sensitivity. Humans can:

- Recognize cultural nuances (e.g., religious symbols, body norms)
- Spot harmful or offensive outputs
- Consider ethical issues beyond statistical patterns

This is especially vital for generative AI used in creative marketing, where nuance matters greatly.

6.4.2 Forms of Hybrid Oversight

Effective HITL mechanisms include:

- Pre-deployment review panels with legal, DEI, and marketing experts
- Real-time monitoring of algorithmic outputs
- Escalation processes for concerning results
- Manual review of high-risk outputs (e.g., images involving sensitive identities)

6.4.3 Reducing Automation Bias

Automation bias occurs when users place too much trust in AI outputs, assuming they are objective. Training and governance must ensure that employees critically assess model recommendations.

6.5. Corporate Governance, Accountability, and Transparency

Strong governance enables organizations to systematically monitor AI systems, maintain ethical standards, and ensure regulatory compliance.

6.5.1 AI Ethics Boards and Governance Structures

More organizations are creating AI ethics committees made up of technical experts, ethicists, legal advisors, and DEI specialists (Jobin et al., 2019). These boards focus on:

- Model approval processes
- Risk assessments
- Ethical guidelines for data use
- Compliance with privacy and anti-discrimination laws

6.5.2 Transparency Mechanisms

Transparency tools include:

- Model cards (Mitchell et al., 2019)
- Datasheets for datasets (Gebru et al., 2021)
- Algorithmic impact assessments
- Interpretability tools, such as LIME and SHAP

These tools help marketers understand how AI systems work and allow consumers to make informed choices.

6.5.3 Accountability Frameworks

Accountability makes sure that companies take responsibility for AI-driven decisions. This involves:

- Documenting model behavior and decision pathways
- Assigning clear responsibility for failures
- Maintaining audit trails for algorithmic decisions

As regulations like the EU AI Act grow, accountability becomes both a moral and legal obligation (Floridi & Cowls, 2022).

6.6. Role of DEI Teams, Ethicists, and Regulators in AI Marketing

Ensuring ethical AI marketing needs interdisciplinary governance that brings together expertise from DEI professionals, ethicists, and regulators.

6.6.1 Role of DEI Teams

DEI teams offer cultural insight and help prevent representational harms by:

- Developing inclusive creative guidelines

- Reviewing marketing imagery and narratives
- Collaborating with data science teams on dataset audits
- Identifying potential cultural sensitivities

Their input ensures that AI marketing aligns with organizational values and respects cultural diversity. Empathy-based frameworks in management education stress the importance of understanding different viewpoints and being aware of moral issues. This is crucial when incorporating DEI principles into decisions related to organizations and technology (Licsandru et al., 2025).

6.6.2 Role of Ethicists

Ethicists assist with:

- Evaluating the impact of bias
- Aligning values between AI systems and organizational goals
- Creating strategies to prevent potential harm

They bring philosophical and contextual insight that quantitative fairness metrics cannot fully capture.

6.6.3 Role of Regulators

Regulators set boundaries that guide responsible AI development. Their role includes:

- Enforcing anti-discrimination measures
- Protecting privacy (GDPR, CCPA)
- Setting auditing requirements (EU AI Act)
- Mandating transparency

Regulatory frameworks encourage companies to adopt ethical AI practices and create accountability mechanisms (Jobin et al., 2019).

7. POLICY, REGULATION, AND GLOBAL FRAMEWORKS

As AI technologies become essential to marketing practices, governments and organizations worldwide are creating regulations to reduce bias, ensure transparency, and protect consumers from unfair or manipulative effects. Marketing applications, like personalized advertising, profiling, content generation, and automated decision-making, intersect with data protection, anti-discrimination laws, and consumer rights (Crawford, 2021). This section looks at new policies, self-regulation by companies, ethical certification frameworks, and practical policy suggestions for fair and responsible AI marketing.

7.1. The EU AI Act and Emerging Global Policies

The EU Artificial Intelligence Act (EU AI Act) is the most extensive global framework aimed at regulating AI based on risk categories. It directly affects marketing systems involving profiling, content personalization, or automated decision-making.

7.1.1 Risk-Based Categorization and Marketing Implications

The Act classifies AI systems into:

- Unacceptable risk (e.g., manipulative systems exploiting vulnerabilities)
- High risk (e.g., AI used for credit evaluations, hiring, or essential services)
- Limited risk (e.g., chatbots needing disclosure)
- Minimal risk (e.g., basic AI tools)

While marketing systems aren't always labeled as high risk, those that heavily influence consumer access to credit, housing, or jobs may qualify for regulation (Floridi & Cowls, 2022). Targeted advertising that abuses sensitive data or vulnerable groups may also face regulatory scrutiny.

7.1.2 Global Policy Trends

Other nations are adopting complementary policies:

- United States: The White House blueprint for an AI Bill of Rights focuses on fairness, explainability, and privacy protections.
- Canada: The Artificial Intelligence and Data Act (AIDA) mandates responsible development and documentation for AI used in commercial settings.
- United Kingdom: The UK takes a sector-specific regulatory approach that highlights transparency and accountability.
- Asia-Pacific: Singapore's Model AI Governance Framework provides practical guidelines that align with accountability and human oversight principles.

These global frameworks together emphasize the importance of fairness, transparency, and consumer protection for marketing organizations (Jobin et al., 2019).

7.2. Corporate Compliance and Self-Regulation Mechanisms

Beyond government regulation, organizations are increasingly adopting internal management systems and self-regulatory practices to promote responsible AI use.

7.2.1 Internal AI Ethics Policies

Many large companies have created AI ethics guidelines that focus on:

- Non-discrimination
- Transparency
- Accountability
- Safety
- Human oversight

Firms like Google, Microsoft, and Salesforce share their principles for responsible AI and have internal review processes for sensitive systems (PwC, 2022).

7.2.2 Self-Regulation Through Impact Assessments

Algorithmic Impact Assessments (AIAs), popularized first by Canadian and European regulators, are now commonly used by companies to assess risks related to:

- Discrimination
- Privacy violations
- Cultural insensitivity
- Consumer manipulation (Véliz, 2021)

In marketing, AIAs help to identify harmful trends in ad targeting, personalization algorithms, and content generation workflows.

7.2.3 Transparency Practices

Organizations implement transparency tools such as:

- Model cards (Mitchell et al., 2019)
- Datasheets for datasets (Gebru et al., 2021)

- Explainability dashboards for internal stakeholders

These resources assist marketing teams in understanding model behavior and explaining AI usage to consumers and regulators.

7.3. Ethical Certification and Audit Standards

Third-party certifications and audit frameworks provide outside validation of ethical AI practices, which is crucial for consumer-facing roles like marketing.

7.3.1 ISO Standards for Ethical AI

The ISO/IEC 42001 AI Management System Standard (AIMS), introduced in 2023, offers a structured guide for:

- AI governance
- Risk and quality management
- Transparency requirements
- Data lifecycle management

Organizations that adopt ISO AIMS improve their compliance and show commitment to responsible AI.

7.3.2 Algorithmic Fairness and Audit Tools

Independent audit agencies use fairness metrics to assess algorithmic systems for bias and discrimination. Common evaluation tools include:

- AI Fairness 360 (IBM)
- Fairlearn (Microsoft)
- Google's Model Cards framework
- Responsible AI dashboards

These tools aid marketing firms in detecting imbalances in ad delivery, customer segmentation, and recommendation outputs (Dwivedi et al., 2023).

7.3.3 Ethical Certification Initiatives

Certification frameworks such as:

- IEEE 7000 Series Standards for ethically aligned design
- B Corp certification that integrates social impact into governance
- Digital Trust Labels developed in Switzerland and Singapore offer credibility and demonstrate a commitment to ethics for consumers.

In marketing, ethical certification can enhance brand reputation and trustworthiness.

7.4. Policy Recommendations for Fair and Responsible AI Marketing

To promote ethical and inclusive AI in marketing, a collaborative approach involving policymakers, businesses, and industry players is vital. The following recommendations build on insights from global frameworks and academic studies.

1. Mandate Fairness Audits for High-Impact Marketing Systems

Fairness audits should be required for:

- Ad targeting systems
- Generative AI used for extensive campaign creation
- Segmentation and recommendation algorithms

Audits must assess both representational harms (like stereotypes and exclusion) and allocative harms (such as unequal opportunity distribution).

2. Strengthen Transparency Requirements in Advertising Platforms

Platforms like Meta, Google, and TikTok should be required to:

- Disclose targeting parameters
- Provide tools for understanding to advertisers
- Publish reports on fairness and demographic impacts

Transparency supports accountability and enables informed consumer choices (Cowgill & Tucker, 2019).

3. Prohibit the Use of Sensitive Attributes for Harmful Profiling

Policies should limit the use of attributes like race, ethnicity, religion, and sexual orientation for discriminatory profiling, in line with GDPR and the EU AI Act.

4. Incentivize DEI Integration in AI Development

Governments can encourage inclusive AI design by offering:

- Tax benefits
- Grants for innovation focused on diversity, equity, and inclusion
- Public-private partnerships for creating inclusive datasets

This promotes cultural change across the industry (Rosengren et al., 2020).

5. Support Independent AI Oversight Bodies

Regulators should set up independent AI oversight boards or ombudsman roles to:

- Review high-risk AI implementations
- Investigate consumer complaints
- Enforce fairness and transparency standards

6. Promote Human-in-the-Loop Mandatory Review for Generative AI Marketing

Given the risks of bias and cultural insensitivity, human review should be mandatory for AI-generated advertising in sensitive areas (Rust, 2020).

8. FUTURE DIRECTIONS AND OPPORTUNITIES

As AI technologies develop, marketing faces unique opportunities to create more inclusive, transparent, and culturally aware practices. While previous sections covered challenges and governance strategies, it is also important to explore new opportunities that could reshape the future of ethical AI in marketing. Key directions include integrating fairness-by-default principles into generative AI systems, responding to changing consumer expectations, encouraging innovation across disciplines, and building trust through clear communication.

8.1. Fairness by Default in Generative AI Systems

Generative AI models, such as large language models (LLMs) and diffusion models, are becoming common in creating marketing content, branding, and advertising. However, research shows that these models tend to amplify biases found in training datasets, leading to representational gaps (Bender et al., 2021; Luccioni et al., 2023).

To tackle this issue, future AI systems should incorporate fairness-by-default mechanisms into their design. These mechanisms include:

i. Bias-Resistant Training Pipelines

Models should use well-curated datasets that represent demographic diversity and cultural nuances. Tools like Datasheets for Datasets (Gebru et al., 2021) and Model Cards (Mitchell et al., 2019) help developers document potential risks, maintain transparency, and identify representational gaps before deployment.

ii. Integrated Fairness Constraints

Fairness-aware training methods, such as adversarial debiasing, demographic parity constraints, and counterfactual fairness estimators, can help reduce output discrepancies (Kusner et al., 2017). Applying these constraints during training ensures that fairness is part of the system from the start, rather than added later.

iii. Real-Time Output Monitoring

As generative models create dynamic content, real-time monitoring systems should identify and flag potentially discriminatory or culturally insensitive outputs. This has become more achievable with automated safety classifiers and human-in-the-loop review systems (Rust, 2020).

Future marketing environments will rely on generative AI that is not only creative but also fair, culturally sensitive, and consistent with diversity, equity, and inclusion (DEI) principles.

8.2. Evolving Consumer Expectations and Ethical Branding

Consumer expectations are changing quickly. There is a rising awareness of digital rights, privacy, and the ethical risks associated with AI. Studies show that younger consumers, especially global millennials, prefer brands that show cultural sensitivity, inclusivity, and ethical innovation in technology-driven marketing environments (Dwivedi et al., 2023; Rosengren et al., 2020; Tarnanidis et al., 2026).

i. Ethical Branding as Competitive Advantage

Brands that openly share their ethical AI practices are more likely to gain trust and stand out in the market. Ethical branding includes:

- Clear disclosure of AI use in marketing interactions
- Fair treatment across different consumer demographics
- Responsiveness to concerns about representation and cultural accuracy

Marketing research indicates that ethical branding positively impacts brand perception, loyalty, and purchase intent (Cui, 2001; Kaplan & Haenlein, 2019).

ii. Demand for Inclusive Representation

Consumers increasingly expect marketing content to showcase global diversity in body types, cultures, genders, abilities, and age groups. AI-generated content that does not meet these expectations could face backlash or lose trust. Therefore, representation must be intentional and not accidental.

iii. Data Privacy as an Ethical Imperative

Consumer concern about surveillance, targeting, and data misuse is on the rise. Fair, privacy-respecting AI systems comply with evolving norms under GDPR, CCPA, and upcoming global regulations (Floridi & Cowls, 2022).

8.3. Cross-disciplinary Collaboration for Inclusive Innovation

The future of inclusive AI marketing depends on collaboration across technical, ethical, social, and creative fields.

i. Integrating DEI, Marketing, and Technical Teams

Research shows that diverse teams produce more innovative and culturally sensitive solutions (Crawford, 2021). Cooperation between:

- Data scientists
- DEI professionals
- Marketing strategists
- Behavioral scientists
- Ethicists

ensures that AI systems are built with both technical skill and cultural insight.

ii. Academic-Industry Partnerships

Universities and research institutions are essential for developing fairness metrics, auditing techniques, and ethical guidelines. Industry partnerships can speed up:

- Bias detection innovations
- Creating inclusive datasets
- Context-sensitive AI evaluation frameworks (Jobin et al., 2019)

iii. Global and Cross-cultural Perspectives

Marketing increasingly operates in global markets with diverse cultural norms. Future AI systems should include multidisciplinary cultural knowledge to avoid misrepresentation, stereotyping, or appropriation, especially in cross-border contexts (Cui, 2001).

8.4. Building Trust Through Ethical AI Communication

As AI becomes common in consumer interactions, transparency and communication will be crucial for maintaining trust.

i. Communicating AI Use Clearly

Transparency practices suggest informing consumers when they are interacting with AI-generated content or personalized algorithms. Clear disclosure aligns with global standards for trustworthy AI (Floridi & Cowls, 2022).

ii. Explaining Decision-Making

Consumer trust grows when brands clarify how AI systems:

- Personalize content
- Use consumer data
- Protect privacy
- Ensure fairness (Kaplan & Haenlein, 2019)

Explainability dashboards and user-facing summaries can help clarify automated decisions.

iii. Responding to Mistakes Transparently

AI systems may occasionally fail, leading to biased or inappropriate results. Brands that address mistakes quickly and honestly can avoid long-term reputational harm. Strategies for crisis communication based on accountability and authenticity can strengthen consumer loyalty (Rust, 2020).

iv. Public Education and Awareness

Organizations can also promote a better public understanding of AI by:

- Publishing clear guides
- Hosting community workshops
- Supporting digital literacy programs

This encourages informed consumer engagement and empowers individuals to navigate AI-driven marketing environments responsibly.

9. CONCLUSION

Artificial Intelligence is changing marketing by enabling better personalization, predictive insights, and scalable creative production. However, as shown in this chapter, these benefits come with important ethical challenges, especially around fairness, representation, and discrimination. Responsible AI marketing needs a balanced mix of technical solutions, organizational accountability, and strong rules.

9.1. Key Insights and Reflections

Algorithmic bias does not happen by chance; it is a predictable result of data-driven systems that rely on flawed datasets, gaps in representation, and unclear optimization methods (Mehrabi et al., 2021; Barocas et al., 2020). In marketing, these biases can result in unfair ad delivery, stereotypical outputs, and unequal access to opportunities (Ali et al., 2019; Luccioni et al., 2023). These problems cause cultural and commercial damage: misrepresentation erodes consumer trust, harms marginalized communities, and puts firms at risk of regulatory issues (Crawford, 2021; Lambrecht & Tucker, 2019).

To tackle these challenges, we need solutions that combine social and technical approaches. Algorithms that promote fairness, audits of datasets, model documentation, and human oversight work best when combined with principles of Diversity,

Equity, and Inclusion (DEI), ethical governance, and teamwork across fields (Floridi & Cowls, 2022; Gebru et al., 2021).

9.2. The Business and Moral Imperative of DEI in AI Marketing

Integrating Diversity, Equity, and Inclusion (DEI) into AI systems is both an ethical duty and a business advantage. Marketing plays a key role in shaping cultural stories; biased AI systems risk reinforcing negative stereotypes (Blodgett et al., 2020; Crawford, 2021).

From a business standpoint, DEI enhances:

- Brand trust and loyalty, as consumers favor transparent and inclusive brands (Kaplan & Haenlein, 2019; Rosengren et al., 2020).
- Market relevance, with inclusive campaigns achieving better engagement (Cui, 2001).
- Compliance with regulations, as fair AI practices lower the legal risks linked to emerging laws like the EU AI Act (Floridi & Cowls, 2022).

DEI is not optional; it is crucial for responsible AI-driven marketing.

9.3. Towards a Future of Ethical and Inclusive AI

The way forward requires rethinking how we design, govern, and communicate about AI. Fairness must be built into the design, supported by inclusive datasets, fairness guidelines, and culturally aware evaluation methods (Luccioni et al., 2023). Working together across disciplines—bringing together data scientists, DEI experts, marketers, ethicists, and regulators—is vital to ensure both technical reliability and cultural understanding (Jobin et al., 2019).

Transparency will be increasingly important. Organisations should make it clear how AI affects personalisation, how data is used, and how fairness is maintained. They must also address mistakes with accountability and openness (Rust, 2020). Lastly, rules and internal governance must grow together to ensure innovation meets societal values and consumer rights.

The future of AI in marketing depends on the industry's commitment to fairness, transparency, and inclusive design. Ethical AI is not just a regulatory necessity; it is also a competitive edge that allows marketers to foster growth while promoting equity and social well-being.

REFERENCES

Ali, M., Sapiezynski, P., Bogen, M., Korolova, A., Mislove, A., & Rieke, A. (2019). Discrimination through optimization: How Facebook's Ad delivery can lead to biased outcomes. Proceedings of the *ACM on human-computer interaction*, 3(CSCW), 1-30.

Barocas, S., Hardt, M., & Narayanan, A. (2020). Fairness and machine learning. *Recommender Systems Handbook*, *1*, 453–459.

Bender, E. M., & Friedman, B. (2018). Data statements for natural language processing: Toward mitigating system bias and enabling better science. *Transactions of the Association for Computational Linguistics*, *6*, 587–604.

Bender, E. M., Gebru, T., McMillan-Major, A., & Shmitchell, S. (2021, March). On the dangers of stochastic parrots: Can language models be too big? In Proceedings of the 2021 *ACM conference on fairness, accountability, and transparency* (pp. 610-623).

Birhane, A., & Prabhu, V. U. (2021, January). Large image datasets: A pyrrhic win for computer vision? In 2021 *IEEE Winter Conference on Applications of Computer Vision (WACV)* (pp. 1536-1546). IEEE.

Blodgett, S. L., Barocas, S., Daumé Iii, H., & Wallach, H. (2020). Language (technology) is power: A critical survey of" bias" in nlp. *arXiv preprint arXiv:2005*.14050.

Borgesius, F. Z. (2025). Discrimination, artificial intelligence, and algorithmic decision-making. *arXiv preprint arXiv:2510*.13465.

Buolamwini, J., & Gebru, T. (2018, January). Gender shades: Intersectional accuracy disparities in commercial gender classification. In Conference on *fairness, accountability and transparency* (pp. 77-91). PMLR.

Castro, D. C., Walker, I., & Glocker, B. (2020). Causality matters in medical imaging. *Nature Communications*, *11*(1), 3673.

Cowgill, B., & Tucker, C. E. (2019). Economics, fairness and algorithmic bias. *The Journal of Economic Perspectives*, *34*(4), 54–77.

Crawford, K. (2021). *The atlas of AI: Power, politics, and the planetary costs of artificial intelligence*. Yale University Press.

Cui, G. (2001). Marketing to ethnic minority consumers: A historical journey (1932-1997). *Journal of Macromarketing*, *21*(1), 23–31.

Dwivedi, Y. K., Hughes, L., Wang, Y., Alalwan, A. A., Ahn, S. J., Balakrishnan, J., & Wirtz, J. (2023). Metaverse marketing: How the metaverse will shape the future of consumer research and practice. *Psychology and Marketing*, *40*(4), 750–776.

Dwork, C., Hardt, M., Pitassi, T., Reingold, O., & Zemel, R. (2012, January). Fairness through awareness. In Proceedings of the *3rd innovations in theoretical computer science conference* (pp. 214-226).

Floridi, L., & Cowls, J. (2022). A unified framework of five principles for AI in society. *Machine learning and the city: Applications in architecture and urban design*, 535-545.

Gebru, T., Morgenstern, J., Vecchione, B., Vaughan, J. W., Wallach, H., Iii, H. D., & Crawford, K. (2021). Datasheets for datasets. *Communications of the ACM*, *64*(12), 86–92.

Hardt, M., Price, E., & Srebro, N. (2016). Equality of opportunity in supervised learning. *Advances in Neural Information Processing Systems*, •••, 29.

Haridasan, A. C., Xavier, N., Krishnan, M. A. N., & Glorindal, G. (2025). AI Washing in Marketing: Feasibility, Viability, and Ethical Constraints. In *Strategic Blueprints for AI-Driven Marketing in the Digital Era* (pp. 495–528). IGI Global Scientific Publishing.

Huang, M. H., & Rust, R. T. (2022). A framework for collaborative artificial intelligence in marketing. *Journal of Retailing*, *98*(2), 209–223.

Jobin, A., Ienca, M., & Vayena, E. (2019). The global landscape of AI ethics guidelines. *Nature Machine Intelligence*, *1*(9), 389–399.

Kamiran, F., & Calders, T. (2012). Data preprocessing techniques for classification without discrimination. *Knowledge and Information Systems*, *33*(1), 1–33.

Kaplan, A., & Haenlein, M. (2019). Siri, Siri, in my hand: Who's the fairest in the land? On the interpretations, illustrations, and implications of artificial intelligence. *Business Horizons*, *62*(1), 15–25.

Kietzmann, J., Paschen, J., & Treen, E. (2018). Artificial intelligence in advertising: How marketers can leverage artificial intelligence along the consumer journey. *Journal of Advertising Research*, *58*(3), 263–267.

Kusner, M. J., Loftus, J., Russell, C., & Silva, R. (2017). Counterfactual fairness. *Advances in Neural Information Processing Systems*, •••, 30.

Lambrecht, A., & Tucker, C. (2019). Algorithmic Bias? *Management Science*, *65*(7), 2966–2981.

Lambrecht, A., & Tucker, C. (2024). Apparent algorithmic discrimination and real-time algorithmic learning in digital search advertising. *Quantitative Marketing and Economics*, *22*(4), 357–387.

Licsandru, T. C., Mari, C., Kipnis, E., Galalae, C., Johnson, E., Cross, S. N., & Yoruk, I. (2025). Integrating diversity, equity and inclusion in management education: An empathy framework. *British Journal of Management*. Advance online publication. DOI: 10.1111/1467-8551.70008

Luccioni, S., Akiki, C., Mitchell, M., & Jernite, Y. (2023). Stable bias: Evaluating societal representations in diffusion models. *Advances in Neural Information Processing Systems*, *36*, 56338–56351.

Mandania, R., Cadogan, J., Liu, J., & Kazmi, N. (2025). Optimizing Promotional Campaigns to Maximize Customer Lifetime Value: A Dynamic Learning Approach. *Journal of Service Research*. Advance online publication. DOI: 10.1177/10946705251365524

Mehrabi, N., Morstatter, F., Saxena, N., Lerman, K., & Galstyan, A. (2021). A Survey on Bias and Fairness in Machine Learning. *ACM Computing Surveys*, *54*(6), 1–35.

Mitchell, M., Wu, S., Zaldivar, A., Barnes, P., Vasserman, L., Hutchinson, B., . . . Gebru, T. (2019, January). Model cards for model reporting. In Proceedings of the conference on *fairness, accountability, and transparency* (pp. 220-229).

Murphy, P. E., Laczniak, G. R., & Harris, F. (2017). Ethics in marketing. *International cases and perspectives*.

Norman, D., & Nielsen, J. (2019). The definition of user experience (UX). Nielsen Norman Group. https://www.nngroup.com/articles/definition-user-experience/

Odlin, D., & Benson-Rea, M. (2021). Market niches as dynamic, co-created resource domains. *Industrial Marketing Management*, *95*, 29–40.

Palmer, D., & Hedberg, T. (2013). The ethics of marketing to vulnerable populations. *Journal of Business Ethics*, *116*(2), 403–413.

Perera, M. V., & Patel, V. M. (2023, September). Analyzing bias in diffusion-based face generation models. In 2023 *IEEE International Joint Conference on Biometrics (IJCB)* (pp. 1-10). IEEE.

PwC. (2022). AI Ethics and Governance Report. PwC Global. https://www.pwc.com/gx/en/issues/data-and-analytics/artificial-intelligence/what-is-responsible-ai/pwc-responsible-ai.pdf

Rosengren, S., Eisend, M., Koslow, S., & Dahlen, M. (2020). A meta-analysis of when and how advertising creativity works. *Journal of Marketing*, *84*(6), 39–56.

Rust, R. T. (2020). The future of marketing. *International Journal of Research in Marketing*, *37*(1), 15–26.

Sardashti, H., & Calantone, R. J. (2022). Does equity-based compensation motivate executives to build strong brands? *Journal of Marketing Management*, *38*(13-14), 1433–1460. DOI: 10.1080/0267257X.2022.2041068

Sheng, E., Chang, K. W., Natarajan, P., & Peng, N. (2021, August). Societal biases in language generation: Progress and challenges. In Proceedings of the 59th annual meeting of the *association for computational linguistics and the 11th international joint conference on natural language processing* (volume 1: long papers) (pp. 4275-4293).

Suresh, H., & Guttag, J. (2021, October). A framework for understanding sources of harm throughout the machine learning life cycle. In Proceedings of the 1st *ACM Conference* on *Equity and Access in Algorithms, Mechanisms, and Optimization* (pp. 1-9).

Tarnanidis, T., Manda, V. K., Sousa, B. B., Vlachopoulou, M., & Papachristou, E. (2026). Marketing Complexity of Smart Consumer Products to Global Millennial Segments. In *Diversity and Inclusion-Driven Marketing for Multicultural Marketplaces* (pp. 1–16). IGI Global Scientific Publishing., DOI: 10.4018/979-8-3373-2111-0.ch001

Véliz, C. (2021). *Privacy is power*. Melville House.

Wedel, M., & Kannan, P. K. (2016). Marketing analytics for data-rich environments. *Journal of Marketing*, *80*(6), 97–121.

KEY TERMS AND DEFINITIONS

Algorithmic Bias: Systematic and repeatable errors in AI systems that lead to unfair or unequal outcomes for certain groups. These often stem from biased data, model design choices, or optimization objectives.

Allocative Harm: This type of harm occurs when AI-driven marketing systems unfairly distribute opportunities or resources, such as job ads, credit offers, or promotions, among different demographic groups.

Representational Harm: Representational harm happens when AI-generated or AI-mediated marketing content misrepresents, stereotypes, marginalises, or excludes specific social or cultural groups.

Generative AI: These are artificial intelligence systems that create new content, such as text, images, or videos, by learning patterns from large datasets rather than relying solely on predefined rules.

Diversity, Equity, and Inclusion (DEI): This guiding framework focuses on ensuring fair representation, equal access to opportunities, and meaningful inclusion of diverse identities, perspectives, and experiences in marketing and technology practices.

Fairness-Aware Algorithms: These machine learning models explicitly include fairness objectives or constraints to reduce biased outcomes during training, evaluation, or deployment.

Human-in-the-Loop (HITL): This approach to AI governance combines automated decision-making with human oversight. It allows people to review, intervene in, or correct AI outputs when necessary.

Dataset Auditing: Dataset Auditing involves the systematic review and analysis of training data to identify demographic imbalances, representational gaps, or embedded biases that may affect AI system performance.

Transparency: This practice includes clearly documenting and communicating how AI systems use data, make decisions, and generate outputs. It enables accountability and informed oversight.

Ethical AI Governance: Ethical AI Governance are the organizational policies, structures, and accountability mechanisms that guide the responsible design, deployment, and monitoring of AI systems according to ethical principles and regulatory requirements.

Bias Amplification: Bias Amplification is the process by which AI systems intensify existing social or cultural biases found in training data. As a result, they produce outputs that exaggerate stereotypes or inequalities.

Feedback Loops: These are self-reinforcing cycles in AI systems where earlier algorithmic decisions influence future data inputs, often strengthening biased patterns over time.

Inclusive Design: This design approach proactively considers the needs, identities, and experiences of diverse users to prevent exclusion and bias in AI-driven marketing systems.

Algorithmic Transparency: Algorithmic Transparency refers to how well stakeholders can understand, inspect, and question how an AI system operates, including its data sources, logic, and decision-making processes.

Automation Bias: This is the tendency for humans to rely too heavily on AI-generated recommendations or decisions. People often assume they are objective or correct, even when errors or biases are present.

Fairness Metrics: Fairness Metrics are quantitative measures used to evaluate whether AI systems produce equitable outcomes across different demographic groups, such as demographic parity or equalized odds.

Cultural Sensitivity: Cultural Sensitivity is the ability of marketing systems and content to respect, accurately represent, and appropriately engage with diverse cultural values, symbols, and social contexts.

Chapter 3
AI-Driven Campaigns:
Inclusive Targeting and Messaging for Diversity, Equity, and Inclusion in Marketing

Priyanka Srivastava
https://orcid.org/0009-0002-6831-9977
Indira Institute of Management, Pune, India

ABSTRACT

Artificial Intelligence (AI) is transforming contemporary marketing by enabling brands to create inclusive, equitable, and culturally resonant communication at scale. This chapter explores how AI-driven systems—through advanced segmentation, generative content, fairness-aware algorithms, and accessibility technologies—can enhance diversity, equity, and inclusion (DEI) across global markets. Drawing from theoretical foundations, empirical studies (2018–2024), and methodological frameworks, the chapter demonstrates both the transformative potential and the risks of algorithmic bias, representational inaccuracies, and ethical dilemmas. It proposes human-centered, culturally grounded, and policy-aligned approaches to mitigate discrimination and strengthen trust. Ultimately, the chapter positions inclusive AI-driven marketing as a pathway to ethical innovation, equitable digital participation, and socially responsible brand engagement.

DOI: 10.4018/979-8-3373-6731-6.ch003

1. INTRODUCTION

1.1 The Rise of AI in Contemporary Marketing

Artificial Intelligence has become central to the evolution of modern marketing, reshaping how brands understand audiences, automate decisions, personalise experiences, and design campaigns that resonate with diverse populations. In an era where consumer expectations revolve around hyper-personalisation and representation, AI is not merely a technology but a transformational force that redefines inclusivity and engagement. From audience segmentation to real-time content optimisation, AI tools—such as natural language processing (NLP), machine learning (ML), deep learning (DL), sentiment analysis, and predictive analytics—empower marketers to build data-driven communication strategies that reach consumers meaningfully. The growing reliance on AI across industries demonstrates a paradigm shift where computational intelligence is becoming integral to identity formation, self-expression, and brand perception. Marketing teams are now adopting AI to interpret complex behavioral patterns, decode cultural signals, and craft messages that align with values of diversity, equity and inclusion (DEI). This confluence of AI and DEI serves as a landmark moment where technology and ethics intersect to influence societal narratives.

In the last decade, AI applications in marketing have evolved from mere automation support tools to sophisticated engines that drive decision-making at scale. The digital advertising ecosystem—Google Ads, Meta Platforms, TikTok, LinkedIn, Amazon, and programmatic ad exchanges—now relies heavily on machine learning algorithms for real-time bidding (RTB), recommendation systems, and targeted ad delivery. These systems analyze millions of user interactions, demographic details, search patterns, and social signals to determine the most suitable audience for content. As a result, AI delivers unprecedented precision in targeting customers who are more likely to engage, convert, or show brand loyalty. However, this precision also comes with ethical concerns, especially related to fairness, transparency, representation, and algorithmic bias. As organizations increasingly use AI to influence public opinion, buying behavior, and cultural habits, the responsibility to ensure fairness becomes non-negotiable. Thus, DEI-driven marketing emerges as one of the most critical domains where AI's potential must be guided by clear ethical principles and socially sensitive frameworks.

1.2 Understanding Diversity, Equity, and Inclusion (DEI) in the Marketing Context

Diversity, Equity, and Inclusion—collectively known as DEI—have become strategic imperatives for contemporary brands. In the marketing ecosystem, DEI represents much more than demographic or cultural representation: it reflects an organization's commitment to acknowledging and celebrating differences, ensuring fair access to messaging and resources, and creating a sense of belonging among all consumer segments. Diversity represents the mosaic of identities—race, ethnicity, gender identity, age, socio-economic status, disability, neurodiversity, sexual orientation, geographic location, religion, and linguistic backgrounds—that shape consumer perceptions. Equity focuses on eliminating systemic barriers to ensure that individuals receive fair treatment and equal opportunities. Inclusion emphasizes the creation of marketing content, messages, and experiences where every individual feels valued, visible, respected, and acknowledged.

In marketing, DEI is more than a moral obligation; it is a business necessity. Several studies from McKinsey & Company and Deloitte indicate that brands with strong DEI values outperform those without inclusive strategies, both in customer loyalty and financial returns. A diverse customer base expects accurate representation, culturally sensitive messaging, and ethical personalization. When consumers feel misrepresented, stereotyped, or ignored, brand reputation suffers. The failure of several global advertising campaigns—such as insensitive portrayals of ethnic minorities or tokenistic inclusion—illustrates why DEI must be rooted deeply within strategy, not treated as a symbolic gesture.

AI enters this environment as a double-edged sword: it holds tremendous power to advance DEI but can also reinforce bias if deployed carelessly. If training datasets reflect unequal social structures, AI models may reproduce stereotypes and discriminatory outcomes. This is visible in gender-biased search suggestions, racially skewed facial recognition systems, and unequal advertisement exposure detected in social media algorithms. However, when developed responsibly, AI can play a significant role in identifying representation gaps, monitoring bias, expanding audience reach, and creating messages inclusive of marginalized communities. The central challenge is to align AI capabilities with DEI values and ensure ethical governance across the marketing lifecycle.

1.3 Why Inclusive AI-Driven Marketing Matters Today

The global digital consumer landscape is more diverse than ever. As people from various backgrounds access social media, e-commerce platforms, and digital content, brands face cultural expectations and ethical responsibilities that were previously unknown. Inclusivity is now central to brand identity, customer retention, and social reputation. Consumers want to see themselves reflected authentically, not symbolically. They want brands to understand their values, respect their identities, and support their journeys. AI has the potential to amplify inclusion by reducing human bias, scaling representation efforts, and creating customised experiences that cater to varied cultural and demographic groups.

Several global trends highlight why inclusive AI-driven campaigns are now unavoidable:

A. Increasing Social Awareness and Digital Activism

Movements such as #BlackLivesMatter, #MeToo, LGBTQIA+ rights campaigns, disability rights advocacy, and anti-racism activism have elevated global consciousness. Consumers today instantly spot stereotypical, insensitive, or tokenistic messaging. AI-driven systems must therefore be trained to detect harmful language patterns, microaggressions, or misrepresentations within advertising content. The integration of AI with social sentiment analysis gives brands real-time insights into how audiences react to campaigns, enabling adjustments that align with public expectations of fairness.

B. Rapid Growth of Multicultural Markets

Countries such as India, Brazil, the United States, Indonesia, and the UAE are experiencing rapid demographic diversification. Global migration, mixed identities, multilingual populations, and multicultural youth demand inclusive marketing narratives. AI enables marketers to analyze cultural nuances, language preferences, and localized behaviors at scale, ensuring campaigns resonate authentically across geographies.

C. Personalisation as a Consumer Expectation

Consumers expect tailored recommendations, curated feed content, and personalised communication. AI excels at building personalised journeys but must avoid discriminatory targeting. For example, AI-based systems must not exclude individuals from job ads, credit offers, healthcare promotions, or educational content based on sensitive attributes. Ethical AI ensures that personalization does not compromise fairness.

D. Regulatory and Ethical Pressures

International regulatory bodies, including the EU (through GDPR and the upcoming AI Act), the US FTC, and privacy commissions across Asia, enforce guidelines on fairness, transparency, and responsible data usage. Brands are now required to evaluate biases, disclose automated decision-making processes, and protect users from algorithmic harm. DEI-focused AI governance is not optional—it is a compliance necessity.

1.4 How AI Enhances Inclusive Targeting and Messaging

AI empowers marketers to transform inclusive intent into measurable, scalable, and sustainable strategies. Key AI capabilities that advance DEI in marketing include:

1. AI-Assisted Audience Segmentation Without Stereotyping

Traditional segmentation often relied on rigid demographic categories (age, gender, income), which may perpetuate stereotypes. AI shifts segmentation toward behavioral, psychographic, and contextual analysis—focusing on what people value rather than who they are. This reduces discriminatory assumptions and delivers campaigns that resonate with personal meaning instead of demographic generalizations.

2. Real-Time Bias Detection in Content Creation

NLP-based bias-detection tools can scan copy, visuals, hashtags, and scripts to identify potentially insensitive language or exclusionary phrasing. These tools help brands avoid reinforcing stereotypes in representation.

3. Sentiment & Emotion Analysis Across Cultures

AI models analyze emotions expressed in multiple languages and dialects across regions, helping brands measure how different groups perceive their messaging. This supports culturally sensitive campaign optimization.

4. Inclusive Visual Recognition Systems

Computer vision algorithms can now evaluate the diversity of people shown in ads—counting representation across skin tones, ages, genders, and disabilities. This ensures equitable representation in promotional materials.

5. Voice and Language Inclusion

AI facilitates multilingual campaign creation via translation systems, sentiment evaluation, and speech recognition tuned for regional accents. This provides accessible experiences for non-native speakers, rural populations, and marginalized communities.

6. Accessibility Enhancements

AI generates subtitles, sign-language avatars, image alt-text, screen-reader optimised content, and voice-assistive navigation—making campaigns inclusive for persons with disabilities.

1.5 Challenges in AI-Driven Inclusive Marketing

Despite its potential, AI introduces serious risks that marketers must acknowledge and mitigate:

Algorithmic Bias

AI models often reflect the biases present in training data, leading to racial, gender, and cultural discrimination.

Stereotyping Through Automated Targeting

Hyper-personalized ads may reinforce sensitive labels—such as assuming interests based on ethnicity or gender.

Underrepresentation in Datasets

Marginalized groups may not appear sufficiently in datasets, leading to inaccurate algorithms.

Lack of Transparency

Opaque AI systems make it difficult to understand how targeting decisions are made, preventing accountability.

Privacy Concerns

Using personal and behavioral data for targeting raises issues of consent, especially when involving vulnerable groups.

1.6 The Road Ahead: Towards Ethical, Inclusive AI-Driven Marketing

Responsible AI frameworks—such as Explainable AI (XAI), Fairness Metrics, Algorithmic Audits, and DEI-aligned data governance—ensure that AI-powered campaigns follow transparent, ethical, and inclusive standards. Organizations must focus on:

- Inclusive dataset design

- Bias testing before campaign launch
- DEI-trained marketing teams
- Human-in-the-loop oversight
- Continuous auditing of AI systems
- Cultural co-creation with diverse communities

AI-driven DEI marketing is ultimately about creating meaningful, accurate, and empowering representation across cultures. Brands that adopt inclusive AI approaches not only build trust but also shape a more equitable digital society.

2. LITERATURE REVIEW

A. Theoretical Foundations of AI-Driven Inclusive Marketing

The intersection of artificial intelligence and diversity-oriented marketing draws from several foundational theories within communication, behavioural science, and ethical technology design. The concept of inclusivity in marketing is grounded in Multicultural Marketing Theory, which emphasizes authentic representation, cultural sensitivity, and equitable engagement across diverse consumer groups. Early scholars such as Hall (1997) argued that representation is not merely a reflection of culture but a process that shapes cultural meaning itself. This theory provides a crucial basis for understanding how AI-generated content—text, images, or recommendations—now plays a semiotic role in constructing identity narratives in digital environments. Similarly, the principles of Consumer Culture Theory (CCT) highlight how individuals use marketplace resources to construct identities, reinforcing the need for a marketing ecosystem that recognizes multiple realities and lived experiences. AI, with its predictive and generative capabilities, has the power to accelerate or distort these constructions depending on how inclusive its algorithms are.

Another relevant theoretical lens comes from Algorithmic Fairness Theory, which examines the presence of bias, discrimination, and unequal outcomes in automated systems. Authors such as Barocas and Selbst (2016) explain that algorithms can unintentionally replicate social inequities when trained on skewed or incomplete datasets. The concept of *disparate impact*—where groups experience unequal consequences despite neutral intentions—is central to understanding why AI-driven marketing sometimes fails diverse consumers. Similarly, *disparate treatment* explains how explicit use of sensitive attributes (race, gender, caste, religion) in decision-making leads to harmful exclusions. These theoretical frameworks stress the importance of fairness-aware machine learning, bias audits, and ethical data governance, which form the backbone of inclusive AI marketing strategies.

The Theory of Personalisation and Relevance further shapes the foundation of AI-driven campaigns. According to this theory, individuals respond positively to content that reflects their needs, values, and identities. AI elevates personalisation from a demographic approach to a behavioural and psychographic orientation, using pattern recognition to interpret multi-layered consumer behaviours. However, theoretical critiques from scholars such as Noble (2018) warn that overly personalised systems may reinforce echo chambers, stereotyping, and exclusion, restricting exposure to broader perspectives. Thus, while personalisation increases campaign relevance, it requires careful ethical boundaries to avoid discriminatory targeting.

Finally, Inclusive Design Theory provides another theoretical basis for AI-driven DEI marketing. Proponents such as Waller, Clarkson, and Cardoso argue that inclusivity must be built into systems from the beginning—not added as an afterthought. Inclusive design seeks to create solutions that accommodate the widest spectrum of human diversity, including abilities, languages, socio-economic backgrounds, and cultural affiliations. As AI becomes embedded in creative generation and targeting decisions, this theory becomes essential for ensuring accessible content (alt text, subtitles, sign-language avatars) and balanced representation. Together, these theoretical frameworks provide the intellectual scaffolding for understanding how AI may promote or undermine diversity, equity, and inclusion in marketing ecosystems.

B. Global Developments in AI, Bias, and Inclusive Communication

The global adoption of AI in marketing has accelerated rapidly over the past decade, but this rise has been accompanied by intense discussions on fairness, accountability, and transparency. Global research reveals that AI systems often replicate racial, gender, and cultural biases embedded in society. One of the earliest and most influential studies is Buolamwini and Gebru's (2018) foundational work, which found that commercial facial recognition systems exhibited error rates as high as 34% for darker-skinned women compared to less than 1% for lighter-skinned men. Although not strictly within marketing, this study demonstrated the consequences of biased datasets and led to global conversations about inclusive algorithm development, prompting marketing platforms to reassess their own visual recognition and ad targeting systems.

In the marketing domain, research by Ali et al. (2019) demonstrated that Facebook's ad delivery algorithm could skew job advertisements along gender lines even when advertisers selected neutral targeting criteria. Similarly, Lambrecht and Tucker (2019) found that ads for STEM jobs disproportionately reached men because of algorithmic optimisation strategies that reinforced existing behavioral patterns. These studies highlight how algorithmic personalisation—while beneficial for efficiency and engagement—can unintentionally perpetuate discrimination. Therefore, they reveal the critical need for fairness-aware systems that ensure equal exposure across diverse consumer groups.

International regulatory developments further shape inclusive AI practices. The EU General Data Protection Regulation (GDPR) and the upcoming AI Act impose strict requirements for fairness, explainability, and human oversight. Companies must demonstrate that their algorithmic decisions do not harm protected groups. Research by Wachter, Mittelstadt, and Floridi (2017) introduced the concept of a "right to explanation," influencing how marketers globally approach transparency in automated targeting. This has inspired brands to develop explainable AI dashboards that reveal why particular consumers receive certain ads, mitigating mistrust among diverse communities.

Emerging economies also contribute important insights. Studies from India, Brazil, and South Africa highlight the importance of linguistic and cultural inclusion in AI tools. A 2021 report by NITI Aayog noted that AI systems often perform poorly in regional languages and dialects, excluding millions from equitable access to digital services. In Brazil, research by Vieira et al. (2020) found that social media algorithms sometimes amplify content stereotypes related to race and socio-economic status. Such findings underscore the necessity for localized, culturally aware dataset development, which is essential for inclusive marketing in multilingual and multicultural contexts.

C. Empirical Studies on AI-Driven Marketing, Representation, and DEI (2018–2024)

Empirical research from the last six years reveals a mix of positive advancements and critical challenges in AI-driven inclusive marketing. One significant line of research examines representation in advertising content generated or curated by AI systems. A 2019 analysis by the Geena Davis Institute, conducted in partnership with Google, showed that machine learning tools used to assess diversity in media found severe underrepresentation of women, people with disabilities, and ethnic minorities in global advertising. This study led several brands—such as Dove, P&G, and Unilever—to adopt AI-based bias detection tools to ensure accurate representation in their visual campaigns.

Another important empirical contribution is the work of Sloane et al. (2021), who examined how AI-driven recommendation systems shape cultural consumption patterns across streaming platforms. Their study found that algorithms often narrow exposure to culturally diverse content, especially for minority groups, thereby reducing opportunities for inclusive storytelling in digital marketing contexts. Similarly, Koenecke et al. (2020) documented racial disparities in automated speech recognition systems from major tech companies, with accuracy rates significantly lower for African American Vernacular English (AAVE). Such findings directly influence voice-based marketing strategies, impacting how brands interact with diverse linguistic groups.

In the domain of consumer responses to AI-driven inclusive campaigns, a 2022 study by Bhandari and Rodgers found that consumers from underrepresented groups respond more positively to ads that use representation aligned with their identity. However, audiences were quick to detect tokenism or superficial inclusion, leading to backlash. The study further showed that AI-enhanced sentiment analysis can be used to detect negative reactions early, assisting brands in adjusting messaging strategies in real time.

Research on ethical personalization also reveals important insights. A 2023 report by Accenture found that 62% of consumers prefer brands that personalise communication while maintaining fairness and transparency. However, 41% expressed concern that algorithmic targeting sometimes makes them feel stereotyped or pigeonholed. This dual sentiment illustrates the delicate balance marketers must achieve: leveraging AI for relevance without crossing ethical boundaries.

Large-scale empirical audits of social media platforms have also shed light on algorithmic inequity. A study by Ali and Sapiezynski (2021) found that political ad delivery on Facebook displayed racial and ideological biases even when identical ads were submitted. Similarly, a 2024 study by MIT revealed that TikTok's content recommendation system can unintentionally suppress content by creators belonging to minority groups. These findings prompted global tech companies to adopt fairness checks and open-source bias mitigation tools to improve representational equity.

D. Integrative Insights: What the Literature Suggests for Inclusive AI Marketing

The combined body of theoretical and empirical research reveals several interconnected insights critical for designing inclusive AI-driven marketing strategies. First, algorithms do not exist in isolation—they are shaped by sociocultural realities, and without deliberate intervention, they tend to replicate existing inequalities. Theories of algorithmic bias and inclusive design highlight that fairness must be intentional, measurable, and embedded across all levels of development. Second, representation matters not only in content but also in data. Empirical evidence repeatedly shows that underrepresentation in datasets leads to exclusion in outcomes. Whether in visual recognition, voice systems, or ad delivery mechanisms, inclusive datasets form the backbone of ethical AI systems.

Third, personalisation and inclusion must coexist, but this coexistence requires human oversight, fairness auditing, and DEI-driven governance models. Consumers want tailored experiences, yet they reject discriminatory or stereotypical assumptions. This underscores the need for transparent, explainable AI tools that allow marketers to understand and justify algorithmic decisions. Fourth, global studies make it clear that inclusivity is context-specific. Linguistic diversity, cultural nuance, regional socio-political dynamics, and local consumer identities must shape the training and deployment of AI systems in marketing.

Finally, the literature suggests that inclusive AI marketing is most successful when it integrates human creativity, technological intelligence, and ethical responsibility. The human-in-the-loop approach emerges as a recurring recommendation, ensuring that automated processes do not override cultural sensitivity or ethical judgment. Overall, the literature confirms that AI has the transformative potential to make marketing more inclusive, empathetic, and socially accountable—but only when guided by intentional, equity-focused frameworks.

3. CONCEPTUAL FRAMEWORK OF AI-DRIVEN INCLUSIVE MARKETING

A. Foundations of Inclusive AI in Marketing Ecosystems

The conceptual foundation of AI-driven inclusive marketing is built upon the integration of three critical pillars: technological intelligence, ethical governance, and socio-cultural representation. These pillars form a dynamic ecosystem in which AI tools interact with human values, shaping how marketing messages are produced, targeted, and distributed. At the core of this framework is the recognition that marketing is both a communicative and cultural practice. It not only reflects societal norms but actively constructs meaning, influencing how individuals see themselves in relation to brands, communities, and the larger social world. AI intensifies this cultural power by processing large datasets and generating personalised content at unprecedented scale. However, for this power to advance diversity, equity, and inclusion (DEI), marketing systems must be designed with a deep awareness of how technology can reproduce or disrupt social inequities.

This foundation begins with data, the principal resource that fuels machine learning models. Inclusive datasets must capture the diversity of global populations across languages, identities, geographies, and socio-economic contexts. Without equitable representation at the data level, AI systems risk perpetuating stereotypes or misrecognising marginalized groups. Thus, the first component of the conceptual framework highlights the need for inclusive data governance practices, such as balanced sampling, demographic weighting, contextual annotation, and bias audits. Yet data alone is insufficient; the second pillar is algorithmic design, which determines how AI interprets patterns, makes decisions, and prioritises certain outputs. Fairness-aware machine learning frameworks—such as adversarial debiasing, equalized odds, demographic parity, and calibration strategies—ensure that the algorithm's internal logic aligns with principles of equity and ethical decision-making.

The third foundational pillar involves representation theory, which emphasizes how marketing messages construct identity and belonging. AI-generated text, visuals, and recommendations must be evaluated through lenses of cultural sensitivity, narrative accuracy, and contextual relevance. This aligns with the broader theoretical tradition that sees representation as a social practice with political implications. When AI is used to create or amplify messages, the responsibility to maintain representational justice becomes central to the framework. Together, these pillars establish the conceptual grounding through which inclusive AI-driven marketing can be understood, analyzed, and operationalized.

B. Structural Components of the Inclusive AI Marketing Model

The conceptual model is further organized into a set of structural components that reveal how inclusive AI-driven marketing functions in practice. The first structural element is Audience Intelligence, which focuses on how AI identifies, segments, and understands consumer groups. Unlike traditional demographic segmentation, AI allows for dynamic, behavior-based, psychographic, and contextual segmentation that respects individual diversity without relying on stereotypes. For instance, rather than assuming preferences based on gender or ethnicity, AI learns from user behavior, content interaction, and sentiment patterns—thereby focusing on personal motivations rather than demographic assumptions. Audience Intelligence repositions consumers not as static categories but as fluid, multi-dimensional individuals whose diversity can be understood through data-driven empathy.

The second structural element is Inclusive Creative Generation, which involves using AI tools such as natural language models, computer vision, and generative AI systems to create content that reflects diverse realities. This includes inclusive text (bias-free language), inclusive imagery (representational balance), and inclusive narratives (culturally grounded messaging). AI-based content evaluation tools—such as text toxicity classifiers, gender-balance detectors, and diversity visual analyzers—support marketers in identifying how inclusive or exclusive a campaign may appear to different audiences. These tools do not replace human judgment, but they empower creative teams with evidence-based insights that enhance representational fairness.

A third structural component is Ethical Personalisation, which ensures that AI-driven targeting and recommendation systems do not reinforce discrimination. Ethical personalisation involves transparency (users understanding why they see certain messages), fairness (avoiding exclusion based on sensitive attributes), and value alignment (ensuring that recommendations serve user interests rather than exploiting vulnerabilities). In this component, marketers design personalisation rules that prevent harmful profiling, restrict the use of protected attributes, and prioritize consumer well-being. Ethical personalisation transforms AI from a tool of efficiency into a mechanism of empowerment, ensuring that diverse consumers experience marketing as relevant, respectful, and non-discriminatory.

The fourth structural component is Accessibility Integration, which ensures that AI-generated content is accessible across diverse physical, sensory, cognitive, and linguistic abilities. This includes AI-driven subtitles, sign-language avatars, screen-reader compatible formats, multilingual voice interfaces, and contextual translation systems. Accessibility is often overlooked in marketing frameworks, yet it is a cornerstone of inclusivity. Through AI-enabled accessibility integration, brands can reach individuals who were previously marginalized in digital ecosystems, expanding the reach and social impact of marketing communication.

C. The Inclusive AI-Marketing Cycle: Inputs, Processes, and Outputs

The conceptual framework conceptualizes inclusive AI marketing as a continuous cycle with interconnected stages: inclusive inputs, fairness-centered processes, and equitable outputs. This cycle helps marketers understand how inclusivity must be integrated across the entire AI lifecycle rather than added at the end of campaign development.

The cycle begins with Inclusive Data Inputs. This stage includes data collection, dataset annotation, and representational mapping. Inclusive data inputs ensure that the dataset used to train AI models contains adequate representation of different identities, backgrounds, socioeconomic groups, languages, and lived experiences. Inclusive annotation practices—such as diverse annotator teams, cultural-context labels, and community validation—ensure that data interpretation aligns with real-world diversity. Without this foundation, every subsequent step in the cycle risks reproducing systemic biases.

The second stage is Fairness-Centered Algorithms. Here, AI models undergo bias detection, bias mitigation, fairness calibration, and explainability processes. Fairness metrics are applied to detect whether the system favors or disadvantages particular groups. If biases are detected, mitigation strategies such as reweighting, algorithmic adjustments, or data augmentation are applied. Explainable AI (XAI) mechanisms allow marketers to understand how decisions were made, fostering trust and accountability. This stage ensures that algorithmic intelligence aligns with DEI objectives rather than contradicting them.

The third stage consists of Ethical Marketing Outputs. These outputs include equitable targeting decisions, bias-free advertising content, culturally relevant messaging, accurate representation, and accessible formats. Ethical outputs prioritize transparency, dignity, and positive identity reinforcement. For instance, rather than showing financial product ads only to specific racial or socio-economic groups, an inclusive AI system ensures equitable exposure while tailoring content to individual behaviors. Similarly, inclusive content generation avoids harmful stereotypes, misrepresentation, or cultural insensitivity. Accessibility outputs—such as alt-text, audio descriptions, and multilingual content—ensure that campaigns reach audiences with diverse needs.

The cycle concludes with Evaluation, Feedback, and Continuous Learning, where performance metrics are analyzed not only for conversion or engagement but also for fairness and inclusivity. AI systems learn from real-world reactions, sentiment analysis, and user feedback. This iterative learning process refines the system, ensuring that inclusivity grows stronger over time. Marketers, technologists, and DEI specialists collaborate to update datasets, refine models, and enhance representational accountability. This cyclical process emphasizes that inclusive AI-driven marketing is not a static achievement but an evolving practice that deepens with each iteration.

D. Stakeholder Roles in Operationalizing the Inclusive AI Framework

The conceptual framework identifies multiple stakeholders whose collaboration is essential for building inclusive AI marketing ecosystems. The first critical stakeholder group is Marketing Teams, who must adopt inclusive creativity practices, challenge stereotypes, and ensure that content resonates authentically with diverse audiences. Marketers are responsible for ensuring that AI-generated recommendations, visuals, and narratives align with DEI principles and do not harm or misrepresent any group.

The second stakeholder group includes Data Scientists and AI Engineers, who design, test, and deploy machine learning systems. These professionals carry the responsibility of ensuring fairness at the algorithmic level through inclusive dataset creation, bias mitigation techniques, XAI integration, and ethical model governance. Their technical decisions shape how equitable or discriminatory AI systems may become, highlighting the importance of DEI training for technical teams.

A third group of stakeholders consists of DEI Specialists, cultural researchers, and community organizations. These stakeholders serve as ethical guardians and cultural validators, offering insights into lived experiences, intersectional identities, and social sensitivities. Their involvement is crucial in developing inclusive datasets, validating marketing messages, and auditing representational balance.

The fourth stakeholder group is Regulators and Policymakers, who set legal and ethical frameworks governing AI use in marketing. Their role includes establishing fairness standards, requiring transparency in algorithmic decisions, protecting consumer rights, and ensuring accountability for discriminatory outcomes. Laws such as GDPR, the EU AI Act, and various national data-protection frameworks influence how companies operationalize inclusive AI marketing.

The final stakeholder group includes Consumers, who are no longer passive recipients of marketing messages but active participants in shaping brand narratives. Their feedback, digital activism, and social expectations guide brands toward equity-centered practices. Consumers increasingly demand transparency, fairness, and representation, pushing companies to adopt inclusive AI systems not as a trend but as a social responsibility.

Together, these stakeholders create a collaborative ecosystem that supports the conceptual framework of inclusive AI-driven marketing. Their roles intersect and reinforce each other, demonstrating that inclusivity is not a technological achievement alone but a collective, value-driven endeavor.

4. METHODOLOGICAL PERSPECTIVES AND RESEARCH DESIGN FOR STUDYING AI-DRIVEN INCLUSIVE MARKETING

A. Philosophical and Epistemological Underpinnings of the Research

Understanding AI-driven inclusive marketing requires a methodological orientation that recognizes the complexity of both technology and human diversity. The field is inherently interdisciplinary, drawing from marketing science, computer science, sociology, cultural studies, and ethics. At the philosophical level, research on inclusive AI is rooted in critical realism, an epistemological stance that acknowledges both the observable phenomena (e.g., ad targeting outcomes) and the underlying, unobservable mechanisms (e.g., algorithmic rules, systemic biases) that shape those outcomes. Critical realism is particularly suitable because AI systems operate within layers of abstraction, where biases may be embedded in data structures, coding practices, or cultural assumptions. Researchers must therefore examine not just what AI does, but why it behaves in specific ways.

Another relevant philosophical grounding is found in interpretivism, which highlights the need to understand how consumers interpret, experience, and respond to AI-driven marketing messages. Inclusive marketing is as much a cultural phenomenon as a technological one. It involves human perception, emotional resonance, identity negotiation, and social meaning-making. Thus, interpretivist methods—interviews, ethnographic observation, discourse analysis—enable researchers to understand the lived experiences of diverse consumers interacting with AI-generated content.

At the same time, AI-related studies require positivist methods because algorithmic performance must be measured objectively using quantitative metrics such as accuracy, fairness scores, false positives, demographic parity, and exposure rates. This dual epistemological framework—interpretivist and positivist—forms a mixed-method foundation that allows researchers to capture both the technical realities of algorithms and the human realities of consumer experience. Inclusive AI must therefore be studied through a lens that combines mathematical precision with cultural empathy.

B. Research Designs Suitable for AI-Driven Inclusive Marketing

Given the multi-layered nature of AI and DEI, no single research design is sufficient. Instead, scholars typically rely on multi-method and multi-source designs that allow them to triangulate findings and validate insights across contexts.

A dominant approach is the experimental design, commonly used to test how AI algorithms behave under controlled conditions. For example, researchers may simulate ad delivery using different algorithms and evaluate whether certain groups receive disproportionate exposure. Experiments also help test interventions such as data reweighting, algorithmic corrections, or fairness constraints. Laboratory-style simulations allow researchers to manipulate variables (e.g., input datasets, demographic attributes, interest signals) to observe causal relationships between algorithm design and marketing outcomes.

Another important design is the algorithmic audit, now widely used in AI ethics research. Algorithmic audits involve systematically testing real-world AI systems—like Facebook Ads Manager, Google AdWords, TikTok algorithm, Amazon recommendation engine—to detect biases or discriminatory patterns. These audits may be internal (conducted by companies) or external (conducted by independent researchers). The methodological rigor comes from creating synthetic user profiles, tracking algorithmic responses, and comparing exposure patterns across demographic groups. Audit-based research is particularly crucial for uncovering hidden biases in opaque, proprietary systems.

Survey-based research designs are equally vital for understanding consumer perceptions of AI-driven inclusive marketing. Surveys help capture public attitudes toward algorithmic fairness, trust in AI, perceived inclusivity in brand communication, and emotional reactions to AI-generated content. For example, surveys can measure whether consumers feel stereotyped, respected, or accurately represented in targeted ads. These insights allow researchers to connect algorithmic behavior with human experience.

Qualitative case studies also play a major role, especially for understanding organizational adoption of inclusive AI. Case studies of brands like Nike, Dove, Google, P&G, or Tata can reveal how companies embed DEI into their AI workflows—data collection, creative generation, targeting rules, accessibility practices, and internal governance. These case studies also provide insight into challenges such as limited datasets, cultural misinterpretations, and cross-border ethical dilemmas.

Finally, mixed-method longitudinal designs allow researchers to track how AI-driven inclusive marketing evolves over time. These studies examine long-term changes in algorithm performance, representation patterns, brand perception, and consumer engagement. Longitudinal designs are essential because AI systems continuously update, learn, and adapt—meaning fairness must be assessed repeatedly, not once.

C. Data Sources, Tools, and Analytical Techniques Used in Inclusive AI Research

Research on AI-driven inclusive marketing requires access to diverse data sources and advanced analytical tools capable of capturing both algorithmic behavior and human reactions. At the algorithmic level, the most critical data sources include training datasets, which may consist of images, text, audio, and behavioral patterns. Inclusive research requires that datasets be annotated for demographic attributes (race, gender, disability, language, geography), while maintaining privacy and ethical safeguards. Researchers often use open-source datasets such as COCO, ImageNet, OpenFace, and Google's Inclusive Images Dataset to analyze representation gaps.

For evaluating marketing outcomes, researchers rely on social media platform data, including ad impression logs, engagement metrics, ranking information, sentiment scores, and user-level demographic indicators (when ethically accessible). API tools from Twitter (now X), Reddit, YouTube, and Facebook can provide valuable insights into how different groups interact with AI-driven content.

Analytical techniques include machine learning classification, sentiment analysis, topic modeling, and computer vision analysis. Sentiment analysis tools (BERT, RoBERTa, GPT-based models) help researchers gauge cultural or emotional responses to AI-generated messages. Meanwhile, computer vision tools examine representational diversity within ad imagery, detecting patterns of overrepresentation (e.g., young, light-skinned models) or exclusion of marginalized identities.

Fairness metrics are central to analytical work in inclusive AI research. Common measures include:

- Demographic parity
- Equalized odds

- Predictive parity
- False positive rate balance
- Exposure fairness metrics
- Toxicity and bias scoring in NLP outputs

These metrics quantify the inclusiveness or discriminatory tendencies of AI systems.

On the qualitative side, researchers use thematic analysis, critical discourse analysis (CDA), and semiotic analysis to interpret how AI-generated messages represent identities, cultures, and communities. These approaches help decode hidden stereotypes, narrative patterns, or cultural assumptions that algorithms may unintentionally reinforce.

Emerging tools such as Explainable AI (XAI) frameworks—SHAP, LIME, Grad-CAM—allow researchers to understand algorithmic decision-making processes. For example, XAI can show which features caused an AI model to classify an image or decide to target a certain user segment. This transparency is essential for diagnosing bias and guiding remediation.

D. Ethical Procedures, Bias Mitigation, and Research Integrity

Because AI-driven inclusive marketing involves sensitive demographic and behavioral data, ethical considerations are central to the methodological framework. Ethical research begins with informed consent, ensuring that participants understand how their data will be used, stored, and analyzed. Privacy regulations, including GDPR, CCPA, and India's Digital Personal Data Protection Act (DPDP Act), require researchers to anonymize data, limit attribute usage, and protect personally identifiable information (PII).

Researchers must pay particular attention to algorithmic bias mitigation. Ethical procedures include testing models across demographic subgroups, using fairness-aware ML algorithms, and evaluating the impact of data augmentation techniques (e.g., balancing underrepresented groups). Researchers must also consider the social implications of biased systems, especially when dealing with communities historically marginalized or misrepresented in media.

Transparency is an essential ethical requirement. Researchers should document how datasets were selected, how models were trained, and what fairness constraints were applied. Methodological transparency allows other scholars to replicate findings, improving the reliability and integrity of inclusive AI research.

Another ethical priority is avoiding stereotyping and harm. When studying minority groups, researchers must avoid labeling, essentialism, or reinforcing negative associations. This requires cultural sensitivity training, diverse research teams, and community involvement in the interpretation of findings.

Finally, inclusive AI research must uphold research integrity by avoiding conflicts of interest, disclosing industry funding, and ensuring that AI systems deployed in studies do not harm or misinform participants. Ethical AI research is not only about complying with regulations—it is about aligning technological inquiry with human dignity, justice, and respect for diversity.

5. APPLICATIONS OF INCLUSIVE AI IN CONTEMPORARY MARKETING PRACTICE

A. Inclusive Audience Segmentation and Market Understanding

One of the most transformative applications of AI in contemporary marketing lies in audience segmentation—an area that has historically suffered from oversimplification, stereotyping, and reductionist assumptions about consumer behavior. Traditional segmentation relied heavily on demographic indicators such as age, gender, race, income, location, or marital status. While these categories provide useful high-level insights, they often fail to capture the complexity of modern identities, especially as individuals increasingly reject rigid categories and embrace diverse self-expressions. AI changes this paradigm by making segmentation more dynamic, fluid, and behavior-driven. Inclusive AI-based segmentation examines how consumers think, what they value, how they interact with content, and what cultural or socio-linguistic contexts shape their decisions. This allows marketers to move beyond "one-size-fits-all" and avoid stereotypical assumptions tied to demography.

Through machine learning techniques such as clustering, unsupervised pattern recognition, and deep learning–based embeddings, AI can recognize nuanced user behaviors without forcibly assigning individuals into biased or predefined groups. For example, instead of assuming women prefer soft colors or men prefer technology, AI can identify clusters based on real behavioral patterns—such as sustainability-minded users, value-driven consumers, or people drawn to empowerment narratives. This reduces the risk of demographic determinism, a phenomenon where brands assume people behave in certain ways simply because of their identity markers. Also, inclusive segmentation allows marketers to detect underrepresented or overlooked segments, such as rural digital-first consumers, bilingual audiences, or individuals with disabilities who interact differently with digital platforms.

Importantly, inclusive segmentation also integrates contextual signals. AI systems analyze language preferences, cultural markers, browsing habits, and emotional responses, allowing brands to design culturally resonant campaigns. Linguistic AI enables marketers to target multilingual users without assuming a primary language based on geography or ethnicity, thus respecting linguistic diversity. For example, in India's diverse linguistic landscape, AI-driven tools can recognize consumer behavior across Hindi, Tamil, Bengali, Marathi, Urdu, and more — framing segmentation not as a demographic category but as a dynamic communication preference. This approach enhances both precision and inclusivity, ensuring that diverse communities are not only targeted but respected.

B. AI-Enhanced Inclusive Content Creation and Representational Fairness

The rise of generative AI has significantly reshaped creative content generation in marketing, offering unprecedented opportunities to enhance representation and cultural inclusivity. Generative models—such as GPT for text, diffusion models for images, and voice synthesis systems—enable marketers to produce diverse narratives, multilingual content, and culturally grounded imagery at scale. Unlike traditional creative workflows that rely on limited human perspectives, AI tools allow for a wider exploration of identity expressions, enabling brands to produce content that reflects different skin tones, body types, age groups, gender identities, religious symbols, and cultural artifacts.

AI-based content analysis tools play a critical role in achieving representational fairness. For example, machine learning models trained on diversity evaluation tasks can scan campaign visuals to detect imbalances, such as overrepresentation of a particular race, absence of older adults, or stereotypical portrayals of gender roles. These tools highlight problematic areas before campaigns go live, acting as an automated DEI lens. They can even detect subtle forms of exclusion, such as tokenism, lack of intersectional representation, or imagery that reinforces dominant cultural narratives. For marketers striving for authenticity, these tools provide invaluable support—ensuring that campaigns do not inadvertently perpetuate biases.

Natural Language Processing (NLP) tools also enhance inclusivity by detecting bias or harmful language patterns in textual content. AI can identify gendered wording, culturally insensitive metaphors, microaggressions, or phrases that might alienate certain communities. This is particularly important in global marketing, where cultural interpretation varies across contexts. For example, a slogan that feels empowering in one cultural region may appear offensive or dismissive in another. AI-powered linguistic sensitivity checkers help marketers tailor messages across geographies, ensuring respect, accuracy, and cultural resonance.

Beyond detection, AI actively supports the creation of inclusive content. Generative models can produce multilingual versions of ads, write disability-inclusive messaging, and generate alternative text for visually impaired users. They can also help brands write narratives that celebrate diversity — such as stories of empowerment, resilience, community strength, and cultural pride. However, it is essential that human oversight remains central; AI can enhance diversity but cannot fully interpret cultural meaning. Therefore, best practices require a synergy between human creativity, DEI expertise, and AI capabilities to achieve authentic representation.

C. Ethical Personalisation, Fair Targeting, and Consumer-Centric Campaign Delivery

In modern digital marketing, personalisation is the primary driver of engagement, but it also carries significant ethical concerns. AI-driven personalisation must ensure that targeting decisions do not reinforce discriminatory patterns or expose consumers to harmful content. Inclusive personalisation models prioritize fairness, transparency, and respect for user autonomy.

AI systems can analyze user interactions to personalize content that reflects individual preferences without relying on sensitive attributes such as race, caste, religion, sexual orientation, or disability unless explicitly stated by the user. This approach prevents discriminatory ad delivery—such as excluding certain groups from job or financial product ads, which has been documented in multiple empirical studies. Ethical personalisation sets boundaries on what data can be used, how it can be interpreted, and how it impacts consumer experiences.

One powerful application is fairness-constrained ad delivery. Modern advertising platforms now use fairness constraints that ensure proportional ad exposure across demographic groups. For example, if a job advertisement is meant for all genders, fairness algorithms ensure that algorithmic optimization does not disproportionately deliver the ad to only one gender. Similarly, ads for credit card offers, educational programs, or health services must be accessible to diverse consumers, preventing discriminatory exclusion.

AI also enhances inclusivity through context-aware targeting. Instead of using sensitive demographic labels, AI uses contextual cues such as browsing behavior, content engagement patterns, sentiment indicators, and cultural preferences. This leads to more respectful personalization that avoids stereotyping. For instance, an algorithm may target users based on an interest in entrepreneurship rather than assuming entrepreneurial interest based on gender or race.

Transparency is another critical component. Inclusive marketing requires brands to communicate how personalization works, allowing users to understand why they see specific ads. Some platforms now offer "Why Am I Seeing This?" features that provide explanations driven by Explainable AI (XAI). This transparency builds trust, especially among diverse consumers who may fear being surveilled or targeted unfairly.

Finally, inclusive personalisation includes well-being oriented content delivery, where algorithms avoid exploiting psychological vulnerabilities. Instead, they prioritize messages that support empowerment, agency, and positive identity formation. For example, a plus-size consumer should not be targeted with weight-loss ads unless they explicitly seek such content. Inclusive AI thus shifts personalization from profit-maximising tactics to human-centered design principles.

D. AI for Accessibility, Linguistic Inclusivity, and Participation of Marginalized Communities

A crucial but often overlooked application of AI in inclusive marketing is its ability to enhance digital accessibility and provide equitable experiences for users with disabilities, linguistic challenges, or limited digital literacy. AI-driven accessibility tools transform how consumers interact with digital content, allowing brands to reach audiences long excluded by traditional marketing channels.

AI-powered captioning systems generate accurate subtitles for audio and video content, ensuring that users with hearing impairments can engage meaningfully with advertisements, product launches, and brand stories. Advanced models trained on diverse accents, dialects, and speech patterns improve accuracy for global audiences. Similarly, AI-based speech recognition enables voice-search accessibility, empowering visually impaired consumers to navigate digital products using natural language.

Another major advancement is the rise of AI-generated alt text, which describes images for users relying on screen readers. Previously, alt text required manual entry and was often neglected in marketing workflows. AI automates this process, ensuring visually impaired users have equitable access to visual brand messages. Additionally, innovations in sign language avatars—powered by deep learning—now allow brands to communicate with deaf communities using real-time, AI-rendered gesture translations.

Linguistic inclusivity is another transformational area. AI-based translation systems—backed by transformer models, neural machine translation (NMT), and multilingual embeddings—enable brands to communicate in over 100 languages with improved accuracy and cultural sensitivity. This is particularly important in linguistically diverse nations like India, Nigeria, South Africa, Canada, and Indonesia. AI does not merely translate words but attempts to contextualize cultural expressions, idioms, and localized sentiment patterns. This ensures that marketing messages maintain meaning and emotional resonance across linguistic boundaries.

AI enhances inclusion for rural, low-literacy, or digitally inexperienced communities through voice-based interfaces, visual search tools, and conversational AI in local languages. These innovations reduce barriers to participation, enabling consumers from marginalized backgrounds to interact with brands confidently and independently. By integrating accessibility and linguistic inclusivity, AI transforms marketing from a privilege-limited domain into a space where all individuals—regardless of ability or background—can participate meaningfully.

6. BENEFITS, LIMITATIONS, AND CHALLENGES OF AI-DRIVEN INCLUSIVE MARKETING

A. Strategic and Societal Benefits of AI-Driven Inclusive Marketing

AI-driven inclusive marketing offers transformative benefits that extend far beyond improved business performance. At a strategic level, AI empowers brands to analyze vast data ecosystems, revealing hidden consumer needs and behavioral patterns that traditional methods cannot identify. This allows organizations to design marketing strategies that reflect the lived experiences of diverse audiences, thereby strengthening brand loyalty, trust, and emotional connection. Consumers today seek representation and authenticity; they gravitate toward brands that see them, hear them, and validate their identities. AI enables brands to scale this recognition across millions of individuals simultaneously. For instance, machine learning algorithms can identify emerging subcultures, multilingual micro-communities, and marginalized consumer groups, enabling brands to tailor campaigns with precision and cultural sensitivity. As a result, companies that embrace inclusive AI significantly expand their market reach, generating higher engagement and customer retention.

On a societal level, inclusive AI-driven marketing acts as a catalyst for positive cultural change. Marketing has historically shaped public perceptions of gender, race, disability, beauty standards, and social norms. When AI enhances representation, identifies stereotypes, and designs diverse narratives, it challenges dominant societal ideologies and promotes more equitable cultural contexts. AI-enabled content evaluation tools can correct harmful portrayals before they reach the public, thereby reducing the risk of reinforcing discrimination. Also, inclusive AI supports greater participation from consumers who were traditionally excluded due to disabilities, linguistic limitations, or geographic marginalization. Tools such as automated captioning, AI-generated sign-language avatars, speech-to-text interfaces, and contextual translation systems democratize access to brand content, ensuring equitable participation in digital economies. Ultimately, inclusive AI-driven marketing contributes to a more just society by promoting representation, accessibility, and cultural inclusiveness at scale.

B. Technological and Ethical Challenges in Implementing Inclusive AI

Despite its potential, the implementation of inclusive AI-driven marketing presents significant technological and ethical challenges. One major challenge lies in the quality and diversity of datasets used to train AI models. Many datasets exhibit historical biases, cultural imbalances, or underrepresentation of marginalized identities. When such datasets feed into marketing algorithms—whether for image generation, ad targeting, or sentiment analysis—the system may produce discriminatory or stereotypical outcomes. For example, facial recognition systems have been shown to misclassify individuals with darker skin tones; similarly, NLP models may misinterpret dialects like African American Vernacular English or regional Indian languages, leading to flawed personalization or exclusion. Overcoming dataset bias requires extensive investment in culturally diverse data collection, annotation, and auditing, but many organizations either lack the resources or underestimate the importance of truly inclusive datasets.

Another challenge is the opacity of AI systems, often referred to as the "black box" problem. Many machine learning algorithms—particularly deep learning models—produce outputs without offering clear explanations of how decisions were made. This is problematic for inclusive marketing because marketers cannot correct unfair or discriminatory patterns if they cannot trace the root cause. Explainable AI (XAI) tools are emerging, but they are not yet universally integrated across marketing platforms. Additionally, brands must navigate ethical dilemmas related to privacy, consent, and surveillance. Personalization based on implicit behavioral data can feel intrusive, especially among minority communities who may already feel targeted or monitored. Ethical marketing requires balancing personalization with respect for consumer autonomy, but platforms often prioritize engagement and conversion metrics over user well-being.

AI-driven inclusion also faces the challenge of global diversity, where cultural norms, linguistic structures, gender identities, and social expectations vary widely. What is inclusive in one cultural context may be inappropriate or insensitive in another. AI models trained primarily on Western datasets may fail to understand cultural nuances in Asia, Africa, Latin America, or Indigenous communities. This creates a mismatch between algorithmic behavior and local cultural expectations, leading to misrepresentation or stereotyping. Ensuring global inclusivity requires region-specific datasets, local consultations, and ongoing model adaptation—which many multinational brands struggle to operationalize. Finally, ethical challenges arise when AI systems unintentionally reinforce echo chambers by narrowing user exposure to diverse content, thus undermining inclusivity efforts.

C. Organizational and Operational Limitations Affecting Implementation

AI-driven inclusive marketing also faces significant internal, organizational challenges. One major limitation is the lack of DEI literacy among marketing teams, AI developers, and leadership executives. While technical teams may understand algorithms, they may lack awareness of cultural representation, intersectionality, or identity politics. Conversely, DEI professionals may not understand algorithmic structures or AI design principles. This creates a knowledge gap that hinders effective collaboration. To implement inclusive AI successfully, organizations must build cross-functional teams that combine technical expertise, cultural competency, and marketing strategy. Without such integrative capacity, AI-driven inclusivity remains superficial and reactive rather than transformative.

Operational limitations also arise from the resource-intensive nature of inclusive AI. Ensuring fairness requires continuous dataset updates, bias audits, model retraining, stakeholder consultations, and ethical evaluations—all of which demand financial investment, time, and human expertise. Many small and medium enterprises lack the infrastructure to implement these processes rigorously. Even large corporations may prioritize short-term ROI over long-term inclusivity goals, leading to fragmented or inconsistent implementation. Furthermore, organizations may struggle with legacy systems and outdated workflows, making it difficult to integrate new AI technologies into existing processes. This includes challenges in aligning diverse data sources, ensuring privacy compliance, and redesigning marketing workflows to include fairness checks at every stage.

Another limitation concerns institutional resistance to change. Many organizations operate under performance-driven cultures where marketers focus heavily on speed, conversion, and revenue. Inclusive AI requires slowing down processes to evaluate fairness, representational accuracy, and community impact—steps that some leaders may consider "non-essential." This mindset prevents companies from embedding inclusivity as a core operational value. Additionally, internal biases among decision-makers can influence how AI tools are implemented. If leadership fails to see inclusivity as a strategic priority, AI systems may be deployed without sufficient ethical oversight, creating potential reputational and legal risks.

D. Consumer-Related Challenges and Public Trust Concerns

Consumers' concerns and perceptions also play a critical role in shaping the success of inclusive AI-driven marketing. One major challenge is the trust deficit that many consumers feel toward AI systems. High-profile incidents of algorithmic discrimination—whether in job ads, facial recognition, or social media content moderation—have raised public skepticism. Marginalized communities, in particular, may be wary of AI-driven marketing due to historical exclusion or misrepresentation in media. This distrust can undermine the effectiveness of campaigns, even when they are designed with inclusivity in mind.

Another challenge lies in the consumer's ability to interpret personalization ethically. While many users appreciate personalized content, some interpret targeted ads as intrusive or manipulative, especially when based on sensitive attributes or behavioral surveillance. Inclusive AI must therefore prioritize transparency—explaining how personalization works and giving consumers control over what data they share. Without transparency, brands risk appearing exploitative rather than inclusive.

Consumers also expect authentic representation, not tokenism. AI-generated inclusive content that feels superficial, automated, or disconnected from lived experience may trigger backlash. Communities can quickly recognize when brands use diversity as a marketing tactic rather than a genuine value. This risk becomes greater with AI-generated visuals or text that may unintentionally perpetuate stereotypes or misrepresent cultural elements. For example, generative image models may inaccurately portray cultural dress, religious symbols, skin tones, or disabilities, leading consumers to question authenticity.

A final consumer challenge relates to digital inequality. While AI-driven inclusivity increases accessibility for many, there remains a digital divide—particularly in rural regions, low-income communities, or places with limited internet access. AI-driven personalization depends on user data; however, not all consumers produce sufficient digital footprints. This leads to data poverty, where individuals with limited internet usage receive less personalized or less inclusive marketing experiences. This challenge underscores the importance of designing inclusive systems that serve both high-data and low-data users equitably.

7. FUTURE DIRECTIONS, INNOVATIONS, AND EMERGING TRENDS IN INCLUSIVE AI-DRIVEN MARKETING

A. The Rise of Ethical and Human-Centered AI as the Foundation for Inclusive Marketing

The future of inclusive marketing will be shaped by a broad movement toward ethical and human-centered AI systems, where technology is designed not merely for efficiency but for social responsibility and consumer empowerment. As global regulatory frameworks become stricter—through the EU AI Act, Canada's AIDA, and India's DPDP Act—brands will increasingly be required to justify algorithmic decisions, mitigate bias proactively, and demonstrate equitable marketing practices.

This shift will force organizations to adopt ethical-by-design principles, where fairness, transparency, and inclusivity are embedded at every stage of the AI lifecycle. Human-centered AI emphasizes contextual sensitivity, participatory design, and user autonomy, ensuring that algorithms respect individual dignity and cultural diversity.

Future marketing ecosystems will rely on interdisciplinary DEI councils, consisting of sociologists, ethicists, technologists, and community representatives who oversee AI tools, review datasets, and evaluate representational fairness. Additionally, the growth of "Responsibility-as-a-Service" platforms—software that evaluates fairness, explains predictions, and implements algorithmic corrections—will become a standard component of marketing workflows. In this emerging context, AI becomes a partner that supports human values rather than an autonomous system that shapes culture unchecked. Brands that adopt human-centered AI early will build a long-term competitive advantage rooted in trust, loyalty, and ethical leadership.

B. Advances in Multicultural AI, Linguistic Intelligence, and Context-Aware Systems

A major future trend in inclusive marketing will be the development of multicultural AI systems capable of understanding cultural nuances, multilingual cues, sociolinguistic variations, and region-specific symbolism. Current AI models, despite their sophistication, are still disproportionately trained on Western-centric datasets and often misunderstand cultural expressions from Africa, Asia, Latin America, and Indigenous communities. The next generation of AI systems will use cultural ontologies—structured knowledge frameworks representing local customs, histories, identities, and traditions. These ontologies will guide AI models to produce content that is accurate, culturally respectful, and emotionally resonant.

The rise of advanced multilingual AI will revolutionize how brands communicate with global and local audiences. Innovations such as massively multilingual language models (MMLMs), improved neural machine translation, and real-time speech synthesis will enable marketing messages to shift seamlessly across 100+ languages while preserving cultural intent. AI will also learn multilingual sentiment patterns, enabling more accurate emotional analysis across diverse languages. This development is particularly transformative for countries like India, where linguistic inclusivity determines market participation. AI-driven hyperlocal personalization will allow brands to tailor content based on dialect, cultural festivals, subcultural identities, and regional idioms.

Another future trend is context-aware AI, where algorithms use social, cultural, emotional, and environmental context before making decisions. Rather than reacting to surface-level patterns, AI will interpret deeper meanings—distinguishing humor from sarcasm, activism from aggression, celebration from appropriation. This contextual intelligence will minimize misinterpretation and harmful outputs, making personalization more respectful and accurate. Context-aware AI will also support inclusive accessibility features, dynamically adjusting content for neurodivergent users, elderly consumers, or individuals with sensory processing differences.

C. Integration of Generative AI, Synthetic Media, and Responsible Creative Automation

The rapid evolution of generative AI will redefine the future of inclusive content creation, introducing new opportunities and risks. Generative AI tools—capable of producing realistic images, videos, narratives, voices, and virtual environments—will enable brands to create vast libraries of diverse content at unprecedented scale. This will make it possible to represent a broad spectrum of identities, including individuals of different ages, skin tones, body types, abilities, and cultural backgrounds. Synthetic media can be used to populate advertisements with inclusive characters, avoiding tokenistic representation or reliance on stereotypical imagery.

However, this future also demands responsible creative automation, where generative systems are constrained by fairness rules, cultural expertise, and ethical guidelines. To prevent the reinforcement of stereotypes, next-generation generative AI will include embedded diversity constraints that regulate skin tone variation, gender representation, disability portrayal, and cultural symbols. AI will also support brands in designing adaptive visual campaigns, where parameters shift depending on the cultural context of the viewer. For example, a beauty ad viewed in Japan versus Nigeria versus Brazil may automatically adjust visual styles to reflect local beauty norms and cultural values—without losing the core brand message.

Another emerging trend is the use of synthetic datasets generated through AI to train inclusive models without compromising privacy or relying heavily on sensitive demographic data. These synthetic datasets can be engineered to represent diverse identities intentionally, helping mitigate the underrepresentation problem that limits current machine learning. Moreover, AI-driven creative studios will integrate human feedback loops, involving communities in evaluating generated content for authenticity and cultural accuracy.

The commercialization of immersive technologies such as AR/VR marketing, virtual storefronts, and metaverse environments will further elevate the role of inclusive AI. Brands will need to ensure that virtual avatars, metaverse representations, and digital experiences accommodate users with disabilities, cultural preferences, and varying digital identities. Generative AI will help build these inclusive virtual ecosystems, ensuring equitable representation in emerging digital spaces.

D. Emergence of Participatory AI, Community Co-Creation, and Inclusive Governance Models

Future inclusive marketing will move beyond top-down brand communication and embrace participatory AI, where consumers—especially those from marginalized communities—actively contribute to the design, evaluation, and governance of AI models. This shift recognizes that communities have the experiential knowledge necessary to guide representation, correct stereotypes, and validate cultural narratives. Participatory AI frameworks allow users to edit AI-generated content, vote on representational accuracy, flag problematic outputs, and co-create marketing assets. This democratization of AI-driven creativity ensures that campaigns reflect lived experiences rather than corporate assumptions.

Community co-creation will expand through AI-powered creative platforms, where users generate content representing their stories, identities, and culture. Brand campaigns may be built collaboratively with consumers, activists, artists, and cultural scholars. For example, a global empowerment campaign may invite users to generate AI-based visuals celebrating cultural heritage, which are then curated into a unified brand message. This participatory approach deepens engagement, fosters belonging, and strengthens the social legitimacy of AI-generated narratives.

Future inclusive marketing will also rely on multi-stakeholder governance models, where brands, regulators, NGOs, and civil society organizations work together to establish fairness standards, evaluate AI tools, and ensure accountability. New institutions, such as Ethical AI Boards or Marketing Transparency Councils, will monitor representational fairness, dataset equity, and cross-cultural accuracy. As AI-generated content becomes ubiquitous, society will expect brands to prove that their algorithms do not perpetuate discrimination. Auditable AI pipelines, inclusive dataset registries, and algorithmic accountability reports will become standard elements of marketing governance.

Finally, we will witness the growth of AI literacy and consumer education, empowering users to understand how AI-driven marketing works and how they can control their own personalization ecosystems. As consumers become more informed and assertive, brands will be compelled to adopt radical transparency and ethical design. The future of inclusive AI-driven marketing is therefore not only technological—it is fundamentally social, participatory, and justice-oriented, driven by collective responsibility and shared cultural stewardship.

8. IMPLICATIONS FOR POLICY, PRACTICE, AND FUTURE RESEARCH

A. Policy Implications: Creating Ethical, Transparent, and Fair AI Marketing Ecosystems

AI-driven inclusive marketing compels policymakers across the world to rethink the regulatory concern governing digital communication, data use, and algorithmic accountability. Governments must recognize that AI systems are not simply neutral technologies but powerful actors shaping representation, cultural narratives, and social access. As a result, policy frameworks must enforce algorithmic fairness, mandating that marketing platforms evaluate and mitigate bias in datasets, content, and audience targeting. Emerging laws such as the EU AI Act set a global benchmark by classifying certain AI applications as high-risk and requiring extensive transparency, risk assessments, and human oversight. Other nations—including India, Canada, Brazil, Australia, and South Africa—are moving toward similar regulations. These frameworks should include explicit requirements for inclusive design, equitable representation, and non-discriminatory ad delivery.

Another policy implication concerns data governance. Legislations such as GDPR, CCPA, and India's DPDP Act emphasize user consent, data minimization, and privacy protection. However, inclusive AI requires policymakers to also consider dataset diversity as a regulatory standard. Just as financial audits ensure fiscal transparency, "data diversity audits" can ensure that training datasets reflect the demographic and cultural realities of society. Policymakers should also enforce transparency by requiring platforms to disclose how personalization works, what attributes are used in targeting decisions, and how fairness is monitored. Additionally, the creation of public-interest algorithm registries, where companies submit descriptions of AI systems used for large-scale marketing, can advance accountability and promote public trust.

Policymakers must also protect vulnerable groups who may be disproportionately impacted by discriminatory AI systems—such as persons with disabilities, ethnic minorities, rural populations, and LGBTQIA+ communities. Regulations should enforce accessibility requirements and promote language inclusivity, ensuring that marketing does not exclude individuals based on linguistic or physical limitations. Ultimately, policy must evolve toward a rights-based governance model, where fairness, representational justice, and cultural dignity are treated as fundamental digital rights.

B. Practical Implications for Marketers and Industry Stakeholders

For practitioners, inclusive AI-driven marketing demands a profound shift in how campaigns are conceptualized, designed, deployed, and evaluated. Marketers must embrace a fairness-first mindset, ensuring that inclusivity is not added superficially but embedded throughout the marketing lifecycle. This begins with the adoption of inclusive data strategies, where teams deliberately curate datasets that reflect demographic, cultural, linguistic, and ability-based diversity. Marketers should partner with diverse communities to validate representational accuracy, ensuring that AI-generated content is culturally respectful and contextually appropriate.

Another practical implication is the need for cross-functional collaboration. Inclusive AI requires marketing teams to work closely with AI engineers, DEI specialists, accessibility experts, and cultural researchers. Such collaboration ensures that technological efficiency is balanced with ethical and cultural sensitivity. Organizations must also invest in AI literacy training, equipping marketers with the ability to interpret fairness metrics, analyze AI-generated outputs, and spot representational biases. Inclusive marketing is no longer limited to creative intuition; it requires scientific evaluation of algorithmic behavior.

Practitioners must also integrate transparency and user empowerment into their strategies. This includes providing clear explanations of personalization, offering opt-out options, and enabling users to customize their targeting preferences. Brands that demonstrate transparency will gain trust, especially among marginalized groups historically excluded or stereotyped in marketing. Additionally, practitioners should adopt inclusive accessibility standards, ensuring campaigns are equally consumable by individuals with disabilities, language barriers, or limited digital literacy. Tools such as alt-text, multilingual captions, voice navigation, tactile-friendly design, and AI-generated accessible formats must become standard practice rather than optional add-ons.

Finally, practitioners must rethink evaluation metrics. Traditional metrics such as conversion rates or click-through rates are inadequate for assessing inclusivity. Brands must adopt representational metrics, fair exposure metrics, and accessibility performance indicators that measure how well campaigns engage diverse populations. This shift from performance-only to fairness-inclusive evaluation marks a new era in marketing analytics.

C. Scholarly Implications: Directions for Advancing Research on Inclusive AI Marketing

The academic community plays a vital role in advancing the theory and practice of AI-driven inclusive marketing. Scholars must continue to investigate algorithmic bias, including how biases emerge, how they propagate across systems, and how they can be systematically mitigated. Future research should focus on developing new fairness frameworks tailored specifically to marketing, since current fairness metrics were largely developed for sectors like finance, healthcare, or criminal justice. Marketing has unique variables—representation, emotional resonance, cultural meaning—which require new methodologies for fairness evaluation.

Additionally, scholars must explore cross-cultural AI performance, examining how algorithms behave differently across geographies, languages, and cultural contexts. This requires global datasets, comparative studies, and participatory research methods involving diverse communities. Another promising area is research on AI accessibility, including how AI systems can better serve persons with disabilities and neurodiverse individuals. Studies are needed to evaluate how adaptive AI tools—such as context-aware interfaces, real-time assistive technologies, and multimodal content—can enhance participation in digital marketplaces.

Future research should also explore consumer psychology in AI-driven contexts, investigating how identity, trust, autonomy, and perceived fairness influence user responses to AI-generated content. The rise of generative AI introduces new psychological questions: How do consumers interpret synthetic characters? Are AI-generated cultural symbols considered authentic? How do consumers judge the ethicality of AI-driven inclusivity? These questions open new interdisciplinary pathways bridging marketing, psychology, computer science, and cultural studies.

Finally, scholars should develop longitudinal research designs to track how AI-driven inclusivity evolves over time. AI systems learn continuously; therefore, inclusivity must be measured periodically, not merely during initial deployment. This longitudinal inquiry will generate valuable insights into the durability of fairness interventions and the evolving nature of AI-society interaction.

D. Implications for Future Innovation, Global Equity, and Digital Society

Looking forward, inclusive AI-driven marketing has the potential to play a transformative role in advancing global equity and creating a more just digital society. As AI becomes deeply embedded in marketing, communication, and everyday digital life, its influence on cultural representation and access will only grow. This underscores the need for innovations that prioritize equitable digital futures. Future AI systems must be designed to bridge—not widen—gaps between communities. This includes prioritizing digital access for rural populations, low-income communities, Indigenous groups, and other historically marginalized segments.

Technological innovations should support the creation of AI systems that adapt to cultural evolution, allowing models to update their understanding of identity as society changes. For example, evolving gender identities, emerging cultural symbols, and shifting linguistic patterns must be recognized by AI systems to maintain inclusivity. Similarly, innovations in synthetic data, cultural embeddings, and fairness-aware generative models will enable more equitable representation in digital media.

Future global equity also depends on international collaboration. Nations must work together to build inclusive datasets representing the full spectrum of human diversity—across continents, languages, and cultures. Collaborative AI initiatives can ensure that low-resource languages, Indigenous knowledge systems, and minority communities are appropriately represented in global AI ecosystems. Additionally, innovations in open-source AI can democratize access, enabling smaller organizations and developing economies to implement inclusive marketing practices without prohibitive costs.

Ultimately, inclusive AI-driven marketing must contribute to a digital society founded on justice, accessibility, and representation. As digital identities become intertwined with economic, cultural, and social opportunities, inclusive AI will determine who gets seen, who gets heard, and who participates in the digital world. Therefore, the ultimate implication is profoundly societal: inclusive AI-driven marketing has the potential to build cultures that celebrate diversity, uplift marginalized voices, and foster global solidarity.

9. CONCLUSION

In the rapidly evolving scenario of digital communication, AI-driven inclusive marketing stands at the intersection of technology, ethics, culture, and human identity, offering a transformative opportunity to reshape how brands engage with diverse audiences. This chapter has demonstrated that artificial intelligence—when guided by principles of fairness, transparency, equity, and cultural sensitivity—can become a powerful force for advancing representation, accessibility, and social belonging. Through an exploration of theoretical foundations, empirical findings, methodological approaches, practical applications, benefits, and challenges, it becomes clear that inclusive AI is not merely a technological enhancement but a profound cultural responsibility. AI's ability to analyze complex behavioral data, generate multilingual and culturally relevant content, and support accessibility for marginalized communities provides unprecedented opportunities to create marketing ecosystems that honor the plurality of human experience. Yet, the risks are equally significant. Biased datasets, opaque algorithms, stereotypical generative outputs, and exclusionary personalization practices can reinforce discrimination, perpetuate harmful narratives, and undermine public trust. Therefore, the future of inclusive AI-driven marketing depends on sustained commitment from policymakers, industry leaders, researchers, and communities to build ethical governance frameworks, invest in culturally diverse datasets, promote participatory co-creation, and integrate fairness checks throughout the AI lifecycle. Ultimately, the purpose of inclusive AI marketing extends beyond brand performance—it aims to cultivate a digital world where every individual, regardless of identity, ability, language, or background, is recognized, valued, and represented with dignity. In this vision, AI becomes not only a tool for innovation but a catalyst for social progress, cultural equity, and collective empowerment in the global digital era.

REFERENCES

Aayog, N. I. T. I. (2021). *Responsible AI for all: Operationalizing principles for responsible AI.* https://www.niti.gov.in/sites/default/files/2021-02/Responsible-AI-21022021.pdf

Accenture. (2023). *Personalization and trust in the age of AI: Global consumer study.* https://www.accenture.com/us-en/insights

Ali, M., Sapiezynski, P., Bogen, M., Korolova, A., Mislove, A., & Rieke, A. (2019). Discrimination through optimization: How Facebook's ad delivery can lead to skewed outcomes [Preprint]. arXiv. https://arxiv.org/abs/1904.02095

Barocas, S., & Selbst, A. D. (2016). Big data's disparate impact. *California Law Review, 104*(3), 671–732. https://papers.ssrn.com/sol3/papers.cfm?abstract_id=2477899

Bhandari, A., & Rodgers, S. (2022). How identity representation in ads influences consumer trust and engagement. *Journal of Advertising Research.* https://www.journalofadvertisingresearch.com

Buolamwini, J., & Gebru, T. (2018). Gender shades: Intersectional accuracy disparities in commercial gender classification. *Proceedings of Machine Learning Research, 81*, 77–91. http://proceedings.mlr.press/v81/buolamwini18a.html

Deloitte. (2020). *The diversity and inclusion revolution: Eight powerful truths.* Deloitte Insights. https://www2.deloitte.com/us/en/insights/deloitte-review/issue-22/diversity-and-inclusion-at-the-workplace.html

Geena Davis Institute on Gender in Media. (2019). *See it, be it: Analyzing representation in advertising using machine learning.* https://seejane.org

Hall, S. (1997). *Representation: Cultural representations and signifying practices.* Sage Publications. https://uk.sagepub.com/en-gb/eur/representation/book227613

Koenecke, A., Nam, A., Lake, E., Nudell, J., Quartey, M., Mengesha, Z., Toups, C., Rickford, J. R., Jurafsky, D., & Goel, S. (2020). Racial disparities in automated speech recognition. *Proceedings of the National Academy of Sciences of the United States of America, 117*(14), 7684–7689. https://www.pnas.org/doi/10.1073/pnas.1915768117 PMID: 32205437

Lambrecht, A., & Tucker, C. (2019). Algorithmic bias? An empirical study of apparent gender-based discrimination in the display of STEM career ads. *Management Science*, *65*(7), 2966–2981. https://pubsonline.informs.org/doi/abs/10.1287/mnsc.2019.3098

McKinsey & Company. (2021). *Diversity wins: How inclusion matters*. https://www.mckinsey.com/featured-insights/diversity-and-inclusion/diversity-wins-how-inclusion-matters

Noble, S. U. (2018). *Algorithms of oppression: How search engines reinforce racism*. New York University Press., https://nyupress.org/9781479833641/

Sloane, M., Moss, E., & Chowdhury, R. (2021). A silicon valley love triangle: Hiring algorithms, pseudo-science, and the quest for diversity. *AI & Society*. https://link.springer.com/article/10.1007/s00146-021-01314-4

Vieira, R., Paiva, D., & Ochoa, C. (2020). Algorithmic stereotypes in Brazilian social media ecosystems. *Brazilian Journal of Communication*. https://bjc.emnuvens.com.br

Wachter, S., Mittelstadt, B., & Floridi, L. (2017). Why a right to explanation of automated decision-making does not exist in the General Data Protection Regulation. *International Data Privacy Law, 7*(2), 76–99. https://academic.oup.com/idpl/article/7/2/76/3860944

Waller, S., & Clarkson, J. (2021). *Designing for inclusion: A practical guide*. University of Cambridge Inclusive Design Toolkit. https://www.inclusivedesigntoolkit.com

World Economic Forum. (2022). *The future of jobs and AI's ethical integration*. https://www.weforum.org/reports

Chapter 4
AI-Driven Decision-Making for Advancing Diversity, Equity, and Inclusion:
Insights From Indian Brands

Mitrajit Biswas
https://orcid.org/0000-0002-0409-867X
O.P. Jindal Global University, India

ABSTRACT

The digital age has fundamentally reshaped the dialectical relationship between sports organizations and their fan bases, transforming a traditionally passive consumer into an active and influential stakeholder. This paper explores the shifting priorities of these digitally-empowered customers, who now operate as 'prosumers'—simultaneously consuming and co-creating the sporting experience. Focusing on the burgeoning professional sports landscape in India, this study utilizes a qualitative, comparative case study methodology to analyze the blurring boundaries and emergent benefits of digital fan engagement within the Indian Premier League (IPL) and the Indian Super League (ISL). It examines three key pillars of this new dynamic: fan-led digital protests, multifaceted expressions of online support, and the evolving landscape of participatory merchandising. The chosen case studies—Chennai Super Kings (CSK) from the IPL and Kerala Blasters FC from the ISL—provide a rich context for this analysis.

DOI: 10.4018/979-8-3373-6731-6.ch004

1. INTRODUCTION

The growing complexity of global markets has intensified the need for branding and communication strategies that are both culturally sensitive and institutionally credible. As consumers and citizens increasingly evaluate organizations through the lenses of sustainability, equity, and inclusion, branding has evolved from a purely promotional function into a mechanism of governance and legitimacy. Recent research emphasizes that diversity- and inclusion-driven marketing is no longer peripheral but central to how global brands and institutions navigate fragmented and multicultural marketplaces (Tarnanidis et al., 2026a; Tarnanidis et al., 2026b). Moreover, these dynamics are amplified by the rise of digitally mediated engagement, where feedback loops, algorithmic learning, and real-time data optimization shape strategic decision-making. Mandania et al. (2025) demonstrate how dynamic learning approaches enable organizations to adapt campaigns over time, prioritizing long-term value creation over short-term visibility. Such insights are particularly relevant in contexts where branding intersects with ethical responsibility and social outcomes.

Because of all this, what fans want has totally changed. It's not just about buying tickets or snagging a signed cap. Now, people want to feel like they matter. They want team bosses to be upfront, players to actually respond to DMs (even if it's just a fire emoji), and maybe even a say in how the club runs things. There's a word for this: 'prosumer.' Not just a consumer, not just a producer, but both—someone out there making memes, posting hot takes, and basically shaping the vibe of the whole league. Sometimes the energy in the comments section is as important as what happens on the pitch.And hey, if you want to see this whole transformation play out in real-time, just look at India's sports scene. The IPL and ISL? Total game-changers. These leagues were born in the age of smartphones and WiFi, so their fans are, like, digital natives to the core. Young, tech-savvy, obsessed—sometimes a little too obsessed. The way these folks support their teams? It's next level.

So here's the main question: How has going digital rewritten the rulebook for sports fans in India, and what's the fallout (good and bad) for both the fans and the teams in these mega-leagues?

To tackle this, the plan is to dive deep into a few things:

1. Break down how fans turned into these digital 'prosumers'—think mashup of culture, online crowds, and everyone pitching in.
2. Check out how fans use the web to get organized, protest, or even pressure team management to do things differently.
3. Map out all the different ways people show support online—building clubs, showing loyalty, making friends across the planet.

4. Take a hard look at merch: how digital engagement is changing what gets sold, how it's marketed, and who gets a say in the designs.

We'll zoom in on two teams that basically live and breathe this digital fandom: Chennai Super Kings (IPL) and Kerala Blasters FC (ISL). Their fans? Relentless. By digging into their stories, maybe we'll get a real sense of what's working, what's a mess, and where it's all headed. At the end of the day, it's about figuring out how teams can keep up, how fans can actually shape what happens, and what it all means for the business of sports in the digital age. Buckle up, because it's a wild ride.

2. LITERATURE REVIEW

2.1 The Theoretical Underpinnings of Fandom: From Identity to Community

Honestly, before everything went digital, being a fan was a totally different beast. You had to actually show up—think stadiums packed with sweaty bodies, or your local bar with the regulars screaming at the TV. That whole vibe? It set the stage for what fandom would become once the internet crashed the party. Suddenly, you didn't have to be anywhere near your team to be part of the action. Message boards, weird old blogs, chat forums—eventually Twitter, Insta, TikTok—these became the new bleachers. Now, some dude in Seoul or Lagos could lose his mind at the same time as a lifelong Liverpool fan, all thanks to a dodgy stream and a hashtag.

But here's the twist: as sports went global, things got messy. Teams started racking up fans from every corner of the planet. Sure, anyone could jump into the chaos, but that also meant all these debates popped up—like, are you a "real" fan if you've never been to a match? Or are you just one of those bandwagon folks who only pop up when the team's winning? Suddenly, sharing a meme or spamming the comments became just as important (or maybe more) than actually being there in person.

Scholars increasingly argue that effective branding in global and institutional contexts must be grounded in diversity, equity, and inclusion (DEI). Tarnanidis et al. (2026a) conceptualize marketing complexity as a function of cultural heterogeneity, symbolic interpretation, and ethical sensitivity, highlighting the risks of standardized narratives in multicultural environments. Their edited volume (Tarnanidis et al., 2026b) further situates inclusion-driven marketing as a strategic necessity rather than a normative add-on. Complementing this perspective, Licsandru et al. (2025) introduce an empathy-based framework for management and education, emphasizing perspective-taking as a mechanism for institutional trust and legitimacy. This framework is particularly relevant for branding and policy narratives that seek to resonate across socio-cultural divides without reproducing exclusionary or extractive logics.

And you can't ignore the algorithm. Social media doesn't just let you shout into the void; it pushes certain stuff to the top—big emotions, hot takes, crazy reactions—because clicks are currency. It's wild. Back in the day, being a fan was about shared memory and inside jokes. Now, it's about getting seen. If your tweet doesn't pop off, did you even really support your team? Still, at the core, not much has changed. People want to belong, they want to pick sides, they want to show who they are. Tech just cranked the volume and threw us all into the world's biggest, weirdest stadium, where everyone's talking at once and algorithms are referee and DJ. So yeah, digital fandom didn't kill the old ways—it just remixed them, made them louder, and gave everyone a front row seat (even if you're watching in your pajamas at 3am).

2.2 The Digital Turn: The Rise of the 'Prosumer' Fan

Web 2.0 totally flipped the script in the early 2000s—suddenly, it wasn't just TV and radio blasting stuff at us anymore. The internet turned media into this wild, messy many-to-many playground. People could actually talk back, make their own stuff, and pass it around. Henry Jenkins called it "convergence culture"—basically, old and new media smashing together, and suddenly you can't tell the difference between who's making stuff and who's just watching. This wasn't just about tech upgrades; it actually changed the way we see ourselves and each other. Suddenly, anyone could be a creator, not just some suit in a media office. Fans, especially, got loud. People started remixing, editing, and bouncing stuff off each other like never before. Axel Bruns even coined "produsage" for this—users producing and using content at the same time. Fans didn't just take what they were given—they twisted it, added to it, kept it alive way past its "official" shelf life. Nowhere is this more obvious than in sports. Sports fans are wild, no joke: they're making memes, live-tweeting games, editing TikToks, and dropping hour-long podcasts about what the coach should've done. All this isn't just a hobby. It's work—actual digital labor. Every highlight reel or meme boosts a team's brand, whether the fans mean to or not. And the reason all this fan-made content hits different? It's real. It's raw. Official team posts look like they've been through five rounds of legal approval, but fans? They'll roast the team, make inside jokes, and spill their guts in ways the PR department could never dream of. That's why this stuff spreads so fast—it just feels more honest. But here's where it gets sticky. While fans are out there hustling, posting, and sharing, the big companies and platforms are scooping up all that energy and turning it into cash. Every post, every click, it's all data and ad money for someone else. Yeah, fans get clout—likes, followers, a bit of bragging rights—but the real money? It's not landing in their pockets. Unpaid labor, basically. All for the love of the game. And let's talk about how time works now. Fandom used to be about ninety minutes on a Sunday, maybe a pint at the pub. Now? It never stops. There's always a new take, a new meme, a new highlight reel. You can be a die-hard fan from halfway across the world, hanging out in Discord servers or Reddit threads at 3 AM, arguing about the same match. The community isn't just local anymore; it's global, it's chaotic, and honestly, sometimes it gets toxic. Who's a "real" fan? Who's just riding the bandwagon? Online drama's a whole thing. So, in the end, the modern fan is stuck in this weird spot. Super empowered, making cool stuff, but also kinda being used by the system. Free, but not really. Creative, but also just another cog in the big digital machine. Fandom's never been weirder—or more fun.

The increasing use of artificial intelligence and adaptive analytics in branding and governance raises important ethical and strategic questions. While data-driven optimization offers efficiency and personalization, it also risks reinforcing bias or reducing inclusion to a technical variable. Mandania et al. (2025) caution that learning systems must be designed with long-term relational value in mind, rather than purely transactional outcomes. This insight aligns with broader concerns regarding responsible innovation and the avoidance of performative inclusion.

2.3 Platforms of Power: Social Media as a Double-Edged Sword

Let's be real: digital platforms aren't just passive venues where fans show up and do their thing—they're more like weird, unpredictable playgrounds that totally shape how fandom works. Each one's got its own vibe, its own set of rules, and the tech itself nudges people to act a certain way. So, sports fandom online? It's a patchwork of wild, overlapping scenes, not some boring, one-size-fits-all deal. Every platform brings its own flavor of drama, connection, and sometimes, way too much chaos.

Take X—yep, Twitter, but X now, I guess. It's basically the digital cousin of screaming at your TV in a bar. Everything's fast, loud, and hashtag-powered. Stuff like #INDvPAK or #YNWA? Those aren't just hashtags, they're rallying cries, pulling in fans from all over the world like moths to a stadium-shaped flame. Blink and you'll miss something outrageous, hilarious, or downright stupid. The whole system rewards whoever's quickest with the snark or the meme. And sometimes, yeah, a single tweet blows up and actually changes the conversation—hell, every now and then it even nudges what you see on ESPN. But, man, this speed comes at a price: people jump to outrage or sarcasm way faster than they stop and think. Today's viral joke? Tomorrow's online brawl.

Now, Instagram's playing a different game. It's all about the visuals, the vibes, the pretty filter on top of the chaos. Athletes and influencers flex their lifestyles, fans post their merch and stadium selfies, and suddenly, rooting for a team looks a lot like personal branding. Everyone's curating, everyone's "authentic"—at least, as long as the algorithm thinks so. The more you look like you're living and breathing your fandom, the more likes and attention you rake in. It's fandom as a fashion statement, and honestly, who knew supporting a team could be so… glossy?

Leadership incentives play a critical role in determining whether branding strategies prioritize long-term credibility or short-term gains. Sardashti and Calantone (2022) demonstrate that equity-based compensation structures can motivate executives to invest in enduring brand strength rather than symbolic compliance. This finding reinforces the argument that inclusive and sustainable branding must be institutionally embedded through governance mechanisms, rather than delegated solely to communication functions.

Swing over to Reddit and you'll find the opposite energy: slower, nerdier, and super community-driven. Subreddits like r/Cricket or r/Soccer are these sprawling, self-policed forums where people can argue about stats, relive old games, or write the internet's longest think-pieces. Instead of chasing virality, fans build up mountains of knowledge and inside jokes. The upvote system means the crowd decides what matters, not some faceless algorithm. But the flip side? These spaces can get a little echo-chambery, with everyone agreeing just a bit too much and getting weirdly defensive about their little corner of the internet. So, what's the big picture? There's this wild tension running through all of it. On good days, these platforms feel like democracy in action—fans calling out clubs, pushing for justice, or actually making real-world change. Remember when the European Super League idea got nuked, partly because fans online lost their collective minds? That stuff matters. But, let's not kid ourselves: most of the time, it's a lot of surface-level posturing. Hashtag activism, profile pic changes, retweets that don't mean much. The algorithms? They're not helping. They push the loudest, angriest voices to the top, so you end up with tribal echo chambers, way too much grandstanding, and—if we're being honest—plenty of straight-up abuse. It's messy, it's noisy, and it's definitely not as simple as just "fans connecting online."

2.4 The Indian Context: A 'Mobile-First' Fandom

If you wanna get what's really going on with digital fandom in India, you kinda have to throw out the Western playbook. The Indian internet scene is a totally different beast—think wild growth, everyone skipping the desktop era and just going straight to smartphones. It all basically exploded after Reliance Jio crashed the party in 2016 with dirt-cheap data and towers popping up everywhere. Suddenly, folks from tiny villages and big cities alike got online, and boom—half a billion new users in no time. That's not just a blip; it flipped the whole script for sports fans, how people watch stuff, and how online communities even form.

Now, here's where things get spicy. India isn't just one language, one vibe. It's a swirling mess of languages, cultures, and inside jokes. So, unlike the West where most of the fan chatter online is in English, Indian fans are out here on Facebook, WhatsApp, and ShareChat dropping memes and hot takes in Hindi, Tamil, Bengali, Malayalam, you name it. The result? You've got hyper-local fan groups riffing in their own slang, cracking jokes only they'd get, and reacting to sports in ways that would just confuse a Manchester United fan on Twitter. It's like everyone's watching the same game, but telling their own story in their own flavor. Kinda beautiful, honestly.

And let's not forget—video rules everything. With all that cheap data and everyone glued to their phones, short videos are the new normal. YouTube, Insta Reels, Moj, Josh—they're all crammed with fans making highlight edits, adding their own commentary, remixing clips, and turning every wicket or goal into a meme-able moment. It's not just watching anymore; it's this whole feedback loop where fans set the tone and even the "official" sports accounts jump in, borrowing memes and jokes from the crowd. The IPL, Pro Kabaddi, ISL—they've all jumped on this train, and it's only getting noisier.

Then there's the sheer numbers game. India's online crowd is massive—like, mind-boggling. So when fans get hyped (or mad), stuff goes viral in hours, sometimes minutes. Hashtag campaigns, meme floods, boycotts, whatever—if it catches on, it's everywhere, across languages and platforms. Sports teams and leagues basically live on a tightrope now, because anything they do can blow up in their face, or turn them into overnight legends. And sometimes, this fan energy spills out of sports and into politics or social issues—because in India, sport isn't just sport; it's identity, pride, rebellion, you name it.

So, you end up with this wild hybrid fan: rooting for Liverpool at 1am, but also losing their mind over Chennai Super Kings or their local kabaddi team. They might tweet in English about the World Cup, but switch to Hindi for the WhatsApp group or Bengali on Facebook for some spicy banter about the neighborhood team. This mashup—what the academics call "glocal fandom"—is peak India: global and local, digital and totally real-life, all at once.And don't even get me started on the platforms themselves. Twitter and Instagram? Sure, they're big, but mostly for the city crowd flexing their English. If you zoom out to smaller cities and towns, it's all about ShareChat, Moj, YouTube Shorts—apps that actually get the local languages, let you send voice notes, and serve up memes tailored for your state. Suddenly, anyone can jump in and be heard, not just the English-speaking elite. It's democratization on steroids, honestly.

3. METHODOLOGY

This study employs a qualitative, comparative case study approach, a methodology well-suited for conducting an in-depth, holistic investigation of a contemporary phenomenon within its real-life context (Yin, 2014). This approach was chosen to move beyond broad generalizations about digital fandom and to explore the specific, nuanced ways in which shifting fan priorities are manifesting within the Indian professional sports ecosystem.

3.1 Case Selection

The selection of Chennai Super Kings (IPL) and Kerala Blasters FC (ISL) was purposive. These two cases provide a compelling comparative framework:

- Chennai Super Kings (CSK): Representing the globally recognized, commercially dominant IPL, CSK provides the case of an established and highly successful team. Its fanbase is not only large but is renowned for its intense loyalty and digital savvy, particularly demonstrated during periods of organizational crisis. The team's association with a superstar captain, M.S. Dhoni, adds a layer of analysis regarding parasocial relationships.
- Kerala Blasters FC (KBFC): Representing the younger, growing ISL, KBFC provides the case of a team whose identity is deeply intertwined with its regional culture and passionate, community-driven fanbase. Their fan group, 'Manjappada', is a benchmark for organized fan support in Indian football, adept at translating digital coordination into tangible, real-world spectacle.

Comparing these two allows for an analysis of the similarities and differences in digital fan engagement across two different sports, league structures, and stages of market maturity.

3.2 Data Collection

So, over two years—yeah, a full-on marathon, not a sprint—this researcher dove headfirst into the wild world of Indian digital sports fandom. We're talking all the leagues, all the drama, the highs, the "why is this happening?" lows. No one just dipped a toe in; this was more like cannonballing into every platform you can name. The whole idea? Get the inside scoop on how fans actually behave as the seasons shift, when off-season boredom turns into tournament fever, and when the internet loses its mind over a player snub or a viral meme war. Plus, tech stuff changes every five minutes, so keeping up with that was a whole job in itself. The researcher mixed things up: hung out in fan spaces, stalked memes, watched comment sections explode, and even did some digital archaeology in old forums. It was like being part anthropologist, part digital detective—just minus the fedora and magnifying glass. Let's break it down: 1. Digital Ethnography (Netnography) First up, the big one: digital ethnography—yeah, netnography if you're feeling fancy. Think of it as people-watching, but online. The researcher basically became a digital ghost, haunting everything from official team Twitter/X and IG accounts, to those chaotic fan-run pages and meme factories, to the deep recesses of Reddit (shoutout to r/CSK and the football heads). It wasn't just about watching the big stuff, either—it was about soaking up the everyday noise, the random banter, and those never-ending debates about who should've been picked or why the ref is allegedly blind. Everything got archived: screenshots, threads, memes—you name it, it went into the vault. And it wasn't all words, either. Visuals were huge: memes, GIFs, emojis, even the way people timed their posts. The researcher nerded out over how humor, sarcasm, and pure emotion get wrapped up in digital stuff. The end result? A sort of "fan culture zoo," showing how people flex their loyalty, fight for status, and cook up meaning together, all through pixels and punchlines. 2. Content Analysis But wait, there's more. On top of lurking, the researcher actually analyzed what fans were saying and doing. This wasn't just "vibe-checking"—it was a deep dive into the receipts. They split the data into two big buckets: angry protest energy (like when fans go all #StandWithCSK) and the business side (jersey drops, merch hype, influencer shilling). For the protest side, they grabbed the 500 spiciest posts under each big hashtag—stuff that was getting all the likes and retweets during peak rage. Every post got dissected for mood (is this person hyped, mad, just being salty?), emotional flavor (pride, nostalgia, "I'm gonna lose it"), and how fans spun their hot takes (are they invoking tradition, calling out the suits, or just memeing?). Basically, trying to figure out how online mobs rally and make themselves heard. Then there's the merch side. Here, the action was in the comments under jersey launches and ads. Fans weren't shy—dropping feedback, roasting the designs, demanding "local flavor" or just affordable prices for once. These threads turned into a weird mashup of shopping, identity, and grassroots activism. Buying a shirt became a mini-political act. Go figure. To keep things from getting messy, the researcher coded everything—first just spotting the random trends, then grouping stuff into themes like "real fans vs. bandwagoners," "fans fighting the man," and so on. Since the data came from everywhere—Twitter, Insta, YouTube, Facebook—it was wild to see how the same campaign could blow up in totally different ways, depending on where it landed. And that's the gist. Not just a bunch of numbers, but a deep, sometimes messy, very human look at how digital sports fans in India do their thing.

3.3 Data Analysis

Alright, so here's how it actually went down:

The whole process was built around Braun and Clarke's six-step thematic analysis thing (yeah, that one from 2006—kind of the gold standard, honestly). It's solid because it lets you chase patterns in just about any type of qualitative mess—tweets, memes, sketchy screenshots, you name it. And because the data was all over the place (different platforms, formats, vibes), this method was the only way to keep things from spinning out of control. Plus, I didn't just do analysis after collecting data—I was already poking at ideas and making mental notes while still deep in the trenches, which, honestly, made the whole thing way more interesting.

Step 1: Getting Cozy with the Data

This part? It was basically me marathoning fan videos, doomscrolling old tweets, and flipping through fieldnotes like a detective who's had too much coffee. Not just reading, but really soaking in the tone—laughing at inside jokes, cringing at old memes, getting weirdly nostalgic or angry along with everyone else. I scribbled a lot of half-baked thoughts and gut reactions in memos, which later turned out to be gold for finding themes. Connecting what people said online to what was happening in real life (big matches, scandals, weird corporate moves)—that kept things honest and grounded, not just floating in internet-land.

Step 2: The Code Scramble

Next up: coding. Not the Matrix kind, sadly. I went through everything and slapped on labels to parts that felt juicy or important—sometimes because they surprised me ("humor as resistance" popped up and I loved it), sometimes because they matched stuff I'd read in fandom studies ("fan labor" is classic). It was this mashup of going with my gut and also keeping an eye on what the experts say. Every meme, Reddit rant, or snarky comment got treated like its own tiny story. Sometimes a dumb meme would say more about collective frustration than a thousand-word essay. I kept a codebook (nothing fancy, just a Google Doc with lots of highlights and crossed-out ideas) and kept tweaking it as new stuff came up.

Step 3: Chasing Down Themes

After a while, it was like, okay, I've got all these codes, now what? So I started lumping them together—some codes naturally grouped up, like all the stuff about "digital activism" or "community building" through memes and homemade content. I drew a bunch of mind maps (not pretty, but whatever), just to see how stuff connected across platforms. Sometimes a joke would start on X, then morph on Reddit, and end up in a YouTube compilation, all carrying the same underlying message. That's when I started seeing patterns that weren't obvious at first—like, people whining about overpriced merch wasn't just about being broke, it was about who gets to "own" the club's identity. That's real power struggle stuff, hiding under memes.

Step 4: Theme Reality Check

This is where I got picky. Had to make sure the themes actually made sense—not just to me, but to anyone else who might read this. I went back over every quote and meme I'd thrown into a theme, double-checking: Is this really all about "authenticity"? Or am I just seeing what I want to see? I kept asking, does this theme actually answer the big research questions, or am I forcing things to fit? Some themes got the boot; some merged together. The whole thing was a constant back-and-forth, a little bit like herding cats, but with more memes and fewer scratches.And that's how it went—messy, sometimes chaotic, but honestly, that's how good qualitative research always feels. If it was neat and tidy, I'd be worried I missed something.

3.4 Ethical Considerations

This study adhered to strict ethical guidelines for conducting research in online spaces. All data collected was publicly available. To protect user privacy, all usernames were anonymized, and no direct quotes were used in a way that would make the individual user identifiable. The research treated the online communities with respect, approaching the analysis from the perspective of an observer rather than a participant to avoid influencing the discourse.

4. CASE STUDY ANALYSIS

The Chennai Super Kings franchise is a titan of the IPL, not just for its on-field success but for its cultivation of an intensely loyal global fanbase. This loyalty was tested and ultimately fortified through digital engagement during the team's most significant crises and triumphs.

4.1 Protest: The Fan as Watchdog and Brand Defender

Alright, buckle up, 'cause this ain't your average cricket fandom story. CSK's online crew? They're not just fans—they're like a digital cult forged in fire, or well, in suspension. Seriously, those two years (2016–2017) when the team got the boot? Most groups would've just fizzled out, but nope, not these folks. The absence became their rallying cry. The #StandWithCSK hashtag wasn't just some random trend—it was a lifeline and a battle flag rolled into one. You'd see people pouring their hearts out online, grieving, raging, and hyping the team, all at once. It was wild.

You know what really stuck out? The way they basically turned M.S. Dhoni into some kind of digital Gandalf. The guy didn't say much—classic Dhoni—but fans spun his silence into this whole "strong but silent" martyr vibe. Old match clips, Dhoni quotes, memes—you couldn't scroll for five minutes without bumping into another tribute. It was all so extra, but also kind of moving, honestly.

But it wasn't just heart emojis and nostalgia dumps. The #StandWithCSK wave went full rebel mode. Fans started calling out the IPL bigwigs and the media, saying the whole suspension was way over the top. Satirical videos, spicy memes, open letters—you name it. It was like, "Hey, you can ban the team, but you can't kill the family vibe." And "Lion sleeps, not dies"—that one was everywhere. The whole punishment turned into this badge of honor, not a death sentence.

And get this: while the official CSK socials basically went into hibernation, the fans hustled hard. Posters, countdowns, fantasy lineups—they did it all themselves. It's what smart academics call "relational labor," but honestly, it just looked like love and a bit of obsession. They kept the brand alive, not just as consumers, but as caretakers. Archivists, activists, whatever you wanna call it—CSK's heartbeat never flatlined.When the squad finally came roaring back in 2018, it wasn't like the brand had vanished and returned. It felt more like the fans had been holding the torch the whole time, and the team just picked it up again. "Whistle Podu is back" wasn't just about cricket. It was a tip of the hat to everyone who kept the spirit burning. Basically, digital fandom turned out to be the team's secret insurance policy.

Fast forward to the 2022 IPL Mega Auction—now, this is where things got messy. CSK didn't take back Suresh Raina ("Chinna Thala" for the diehards), and fans straight-up lost it. Within hours, #BringBackRaina and #NoRainaNoCSK were blowing up everywhere—X (Twitter), Insta, YouTube, you name it. Emotional edits, open letters to management, some folks were probably lighting virtual candles.

And the vibe? It wasn't just "bad strategy, bro." People were genuinely mad, tossing around words like "betrayal" and "disloyal." You could feel the sting through your screen. For these fans, this wasn't just about cricket—it was about breaking a promise, a betrayal of trust. Suddenly, team management wasn't just making business moves; they were answering to a digital jury, and the court of public opinion was in session.Did the protest bring Raina back? Nah, but it sure showed just how deep this fandom runs. This isn't just about supporting a team—it's about owning a piece of its soul. And honestly? That's kinda rare.

Look, the protest didn't exactly bring Raina back, but it did get the CEO to break the silence and put out a public explanation. That's something. Basically, it forced the higher-ups to admit that all those people shouting online actually matter, not just as background noise but as a real crowd demanding answers. Wild how fans went from just watching games to, well, sticking their noses right into management's business. Now, thanks to Twitter (or X, whatever we're calling it) and Insta, fans have actual power. They're not just spectators anymore—they're watchdogs, poking and prodding, making sure teams don't just sweep stuff under the rug.

Honestly, this isn't just a CSK thing. Everywhere you look in sports, fans are using social media to call out teams, demand explanations, keep receipts, all that jazz. If a franchise tries to pull a fast one, someone's gonna tweet about it, and it snowballs. Fans have become this collective memory bank and, sometimes, a bit of an ethics committee—ready to throw shade or rally support, depending on the day.So, what happened with CSK's digital fanbase is basically a snapshot of how sports fandom has totally flipped in the social media age. Fans used to just buy tickets and cheer; now they're shaping the story, building the brand, and making sure the team sticks to its roots. When the team got suspended, the fans stepped up to keep the spirit alive online, and that movement has only gotten stronger. Now, it's not just about celebrating wins. Fans are calling out the club if it slips up, making sure loyalty and identity actually mean something. The digital world's become both therapy and a battleground—a place where fans hash out what their team stands for and aren't afraid to drag management into the conversation.

4.2 Support: Co-Creating the 'Yellove' Narrative

CSK fans—aka the Whistle Podu Army or Yellove Family—aren't just your average sports crowd screaming at the TV. Nah, this is a full-blown digital movement. It's wild how a cricket team turned a bunch of WhatsApp forwards and memes into something that honestly feels more like a family reunion than a marketing campaign. You don't even have to be from Chennai to get swept up. If you vibe with the yellow, you're in. It's like a giant digital festival that mashes up nostalgia, new tech, and a weirdly touching sense of belonging. Let's break it down. Three big things make CSK's online world tick: memes and storytelling, that fake-but-still-real intimacy with the players, and a global network that feels like your cousin's group chat exploded across continents. And they all kinda feed off each other, turning random internet posts into emotional fuel. So, memes. This is where the magic happens. CSK memes aren't just jokes—they're survival tools. Seriously. Twitter, Insta, wherever—fans are out there firing off memes, GIFs, jokes, and videos, remixing the team's ups and downs into legends. Dhoni as "Thala" (the boss, basically) is meme royalty. Dude's practically a South Indian Yoda at this point—always calm, always plotting three steps ahead, even when the team's tanking. Memes like "Thala knows" or "Trust the process – Dhoni never panics" pop up every. single. time. The team loses? Doesn't matter. Out come the memes about destiny, fate, and tactical pauses. Losing just becomes part of some epic CSK soap opera. It's like therapy, but with GIFs. And these memes aren't generic either. They're packed with Tamil slang, inside jokes, movie references—stuff you'd only get if you grew up on Kollywood films and filter coffee. It's local pride, but with a global twist. You've got fans in the US or Dubai dropping "Whistle Podu" in the comments like they've lived in T.Nagar their whole lives. That's what makes it so cool—it's not just about cricket, it's about culture, identity, and repping where you're from (even if you're technically not from there). Now, let's talk about this whole "I feel like I know the players" thing. CSK fandom isn't just cheering from the stands; it's peeking behind the curtain. Insta stories of Dhoni chilling with his dog, goofy locker-room reels from Gaikwad or Chahar, random training videos—fans eat this stuff up. Dhoni, especially, is a legend. He barely posts, but when he does, the internet basically stops breathing. One blurry video of him on a bike? Instant classic. The less he talks, the more fans obsess. It's like he's cricket's Bigfoot—mythical, mysterious, and oddly comforting. The younger guys get in on the act, too. More selfies, more banter, more chit-chat with fans. The more "normal" they seem, the harder fans ride for them online. Someone trolls a player? Oh boy. The Yellove crew will defend that dude like he's their actual brother. Supporting CSK isn't just "I like this team"—it's "I'd fight for these guys." So yeah, CSK's digital world is less about stats and more about stories, jokes, inside references, and feeling like you're part of something bigger than just cricket. It's messy, loud, kinda chaotic—and honestly, that's the best part.

Global Community Hub and Transnational Belonging

Alright, here's the thing—CSK fans don't just watch cricket anymore; they basically live it together online, no matter where they are. The digital world's given them this wild, global hangout. So instead of just screaming themselves hoarse in Chepauk, now you've got people blowing up Twitter Spaces, spamming emojis in YouTube chats, or going off in Reddit threads. And honestly, sometimes those "virtual stadiums" get even wilder than the real thing. You see #WhistlePodu, #Yellove, #ThalaForAReason flying around like digital flags—doesn't matter if you're in Chennai or chilling in Chicago, everyone's plugged into the same hive mind.

What's really cool? This whole thing's become a lifeline for Tamils and Indians scattered everywhere. It's not just about cricket—jumping into meme wars or watch parties online is a way to tap back into home vibes, even if you're half a planet away. All those inside jokes, the Tamil catchphrases and slogans, they keep that thread to "home" alive. CSK fandom's basically this double shot: you get to lose your mind about cricket, and you get to feel like you still belong to something bigger, even when you're eating instant noodles in Toronto.But hey, it's not just blind cheering and posting memes. These fan spaces are full of heated debates, player analysis, and the occasional full-on rant about management choices. There's proper nerding-out too—some of those Reddit debates and fan podcasts go way deep, like borderline cricket PhDs. It's not just noise; it's a messy, passionate collective trying to make sense of the chaos that is T20 cricket. Everyone's got a theory, everyone's got receipts.

Now, CSK's not just sitting back and watching this happen. The franchise is pretty savvy—they keep boosting fan memes, fan art, whacky tribute videos, you name it. It's not just corporate PR; it actually feels like they're in on the joke with everyone else. Campaigns like #WhistlePoduDiaries and #SuperFansOfCSK? That's them tossing the ball right back to the fans, letting them shape the whole story. Suddenly, you're not just following the brand—you're sorta writing it.

And check this even CSK's official posts have picked up the fan lingo. The admin's dropping Tamil-English slang, making pop culture references, all that. It's not cringe, either—it's got some real flavor. That's the trick: the brand keeps it real without totally hijacking the vibe. It's this weird, awesome mix of chaos and marketing, but it works.So what's the takeaway? CSK fandom online isn't just a crowd—it's like a living, breathing organism. There's meme battles, there's random banter, there's intense tactical breakdowns, and this sense that you're part of something way bigger than just a game. Memes are the language, parasocial bonding is the glue, and the internet's the stadium that never closes. CSK's whole digital thing is a masterclass in mixing deep-rooted culture with slick online game. It's not just about cricket—it's about finding your people, telling your own story, and turning a sports team into a global community where everyone gets a say. Pretty wild, honestly.

4.3 Merchandising: From Fan Gear to Lifestyle Brand

CSK's merchandising strategy exemplifies how a sports franchise can translate digital fandom into economic participation, transforming affective loyalty into tangible consumer behavior. Rather than treating merchandise as a static revenue stream, CSK approaches it as an extension of fan identity and digital engagement, allowing the community to participate in the brand's aesthetic and symbolic universe. The team's merchandising success lies in its ability to blend data analytics, cultural intuition, and fan intimacy, creating a model of participatory commerce that aligns with the ethos of the *"Yellove"* community.

Data-Driven Design and Responsive Innovation

At the core of CSK's merchandising ecosystem is a feedback-oriented, data-driven approach that draws directly from the digital vernacular of its fan base. Social media platforms—especially Instagram, X (formerly Twitter), and YouTube—serve as real-time focus groups, where fans express opinions about product quality, design aesthetics, and pricing. The franchise actively monitors these digital conversations, using social listening tools to track recurring complaints, preferences, and visual trends. For example, when fans criticized the 2020 jersey for being "too cluttered" and lacking the signature bright *Yellove* tone, the management acknowledged the feedback publicly. The following season's redesign featured a sleeker, minimalist aesthetic with enhanced fabric quality and symbolic motifs—such as the roaring lion emblem subtly embossed on the torso—responding directly to fan sentiment.

Such responsiveness transforms the merchandise design process into a dialogic loop between brand and audience. The digital fan thus becomes a co-designer, whose collective voice shapes aesthetic outcomes. This participatory model not only enhances product relevance but also strengthens fans' sense of ownership. Each jersey or accessory becomes more than a commodity—it becomes a socially co-produced artifact, imbued with the emotional labor of the community that inspired it. This also reflects a deeper data-literacy within the franchise, where analytics are used not merely for marketing but for cultural calibration, ensuring that merchandise embodies the evolving values and tastes of its audience.

Limited-Edition "Drops" and the Gamification of Consumption

Drawing inspiration from streetwear and sneakerhead culture, CSK has reimagined merchandising as a cultural event rather than a transactional activity. The franchise frequently releases limited-edition "drops", often timed with significant milestones—such as Dhoni's birthday, playoff qualifications, or season launches. These are announced exclusively on digital platforms, with cryptic teaser videos, countdowns, and influencer collaborations building anticipation. The ephemeral nature of these releases taps into the psychology of scarcity and exclusivity, encouraging immediate purchase and social signaling.

In this model, buying a limited-edition CSK hoodie or cap is not simply about acquiring a product—it becomes a ritual of belonging and status within the digital fan hierarchy. Fans proudly post their purchases online using hashtags like #YelloveDrop or #WhistlePoduStyle, transforming consumption into a performative act of fandom. The digital sphere amplifies this effect: every photo, unboxing video, or meme contributes to a feedback loop of visibility and desire, fueling further engagement.

The strategy effectively gamifies the consumption experience—where timing, participation, and display are as important as ownership. In doing so, CSK has aligned its merchandising ecosystem with the logics of digital culture itself: immediacy, virality, and co-performance. The fandom's participation in these "drops" mirrors their participation in online rituals like live tweeting or meme-making, thereby blurring the line between consumption and community performance.

Player-Driven Marketing and Parasocial Commerce

CSK's player-driven marketing marks a decisive shift from traditional celebrity endorsement to authentic digital influence. The team leverages the parasocial intimacy cultivated between fans and players to drive organic marketing outcomes. Unlike conventional advertising campaigns, where players appear in stylized shoots or scripted promotions, CSK's digital merchandising relies on micro-moments of authenticity: a casual Instagram story of Ruturaj Gaikwad wearing new training shorts, a YouTube clip of Dhoni unboxing a new jersey, or Deepak Chahar joking about team kits on his vlog. These unscripted moments feel spontaneous and personal, making fans perceive the products as part of players' lived experience rather than marketing props.

This approach exemplifies parasocial commerce, where emotional proximity translates directly into purchasing behavior. Fans interpret such gestures as acts of shared participation rather than persuasion—buying the same merchandise becomes a way of *mirroring the emotional intimacy* they feel with players. This relational dynamic amplifies the symbolic value of every product: owning a jersey worn or mentioned by Dhoni, for instance, becomes akin to possessing a fragment of his aura.

Moreover, by diversifying its range beyond standard sportswear to include everyday lifestyle items—such as phone covers, tote bags, caps, and even face masks—CSK has successfully extended its brand into fans' daily routines. Each product functions as a subtle performative marker of identity, allowing fans to inhabit the team's ethos in both public and private spaces. This "lifestyle turn" reflects a broader strategy of cultural embedding, transforming the franchise from a seasonal sporting entity into a 24/7 lifestyle brand sustained by digital visibility.

Digital-First Ecosystem and the Reinvention of Sports Commerce

Alright, here's the thing about CSK's merch game: they're not just slapping a lion on a t-shirt and calling it a day. They've actually figured out how to turn all that wild online hype—the constant memes, the "Yellove" chants, the endless Dhoni worship—into real cash. It's not just about selling you a jersey; it's more like they're letting fans wear their obsession on their sleeves (literally). The merch isn't some boring afterthought, it's a badge of honor that says, "Yeah, I'm part of this madness." And the way they do it? Total masterclass in blending data-nerd stuff, gut feeling, and just… knowing the fans inside out. The whole thing feels like an inside joke only the CSK fam gets.

Now, let's talk about how they actually cook up these products. CSK's always lurking on Insta, X, and YouTube, checking what the fans are vibing with (or absolutely roasting). It's like they've got a 24/7 focus group happening right in their DMs and comment sections. Remember that 2020 jersey disaster? Fans hated it—said it looked like a banana explosion, too much happening, and not enough of that classic Yellove pop. CSK didn't just brush it off. They went, "Alright, we hear you," and the next season, boom: sleeker design, better fabric, subtle lion flex on the torso. Fans noticed, and honestly? Respect. It's not just about selling a shirt—it's about this back-and-forth, fans shaping what gets made. Suddenly, that jersey isn't just merch, it's a piece of the whole CSK story, co-created by the people who care most.

And then there's the "drop" culture. Straight up, these folks took notes from sneakerheads and hypebeasts. Limited edition hoodies, caps, or whatever—dropped outta nowhere when something big happens (Dhoni's birthday? You know there's a special edition coming). They tease it online with cryptic posts, influencer hype, countdowns, all that jazz. You blink, you miss it. And of course, everyone who scores a piece is flexing it all over socials—#YelloveDrop, #WhistlePoduStyle, the works. It's not just buying a hoodie, it's a whole event. If you get one, you're in the club. Miss out? Better luck next time.

This whole setup turns shopping into a game. You've gotta be quick, you've gotta be in the loop, and yeah, you better show off when you win. It's like merch drops are just another way for fans to play the CSK fandom game—live-tweeting, meme-making, and now, racing to snag the latest drop. The line between being a fan and being a collector? Pretty much gone. Everything just feeds back into the hype machine, and CSK's sitting there, loving every minute of it. And honestly? Can you blame them?You know what's wild about CSK's merch game? They've gone all-in on digital—like, every step, from coming up with ideas to getting feedback, launching stuff, and getting it out there, it's all online. We're talking Insta stories, collabs with influencers, stores on e-comm sites like FanCode and ShopTheArena… they're everywhere fans already hang out. Physical shops? Yeah, those exist, but honestly, they're just there as backup, not the main deal.

Makes sense, right? India's glued to their phones, so CSK basically meets fans where they live—scrolling, liking, voting on their favourite jersey designs, dropping comments in Hinglish or Tamil or whatever. They're not just selling tees; they're spinning stories. Every drop is tied to some memory or player moment, like that one Dhoni quote you keep seeing on Twitter. Buy a cap, and suddenly you're in on the story, part of the legend. It's kind of genius. Fans hype things up, CSK reposts or riffs on those reactions, and the whole thing snowballs. It's not just about selling stuff anymore—it's like this cycle where fandom and business keep feeding off each other. Feels more like a culture than a shop.To wrap it up (because I could ramble forever), CSK's basically turned merch into a whole vibe. It's not just about slapping a logo on a shirt and calling it a day; they're mixing in storytelling, digital culture, and a heavy dose of "we see you." Fans aren't just buying stuff, they're helping build the brand's story, flexing their loyalty for all to see. Limited drops, player shoutouts, designs that actually listen to what people want—CSK gets it. That's the magic: merch that means something, not just something you wear once and forget about. Fandom here is loud, proud, and totally alive. Whistle Podu, indeed.

4.4 Kerala Blasters FC (ISL): How a Region Became a Football Frenzy

Let's be honest, Kerala Blasters haven't exactly been racking up trophies like CSK in cricket, but man, the energy their fans bring? Off the charts. There's something about Kerala's football DNA—decades of street football, local legends, and a touch of stubborn pride. All this gets whipped into a frenzy by Manjappada, the fan group that basically lives online and then storms stadiums in real life.

4.4.1 Protest: When Fans Get Loud (and Organized)

Manjappada isn't just about yelling from the stands—they're a straight-up movement. Their online hustle? Yeah, it's not just about hyping up the team on match day. It's more like a megaphone for fan power, turning every phone into a protest sign. On X (still feels weird calling it that), Facebook, Telegram—they're everywhere. The Yellow Army runs like a decentralized squad, flipping between wild celebrations and, when things go south, pure chaos.

Digital Accountability and Tactical Outrage

Let's be real. When Kerala Blasters start blowing games, the mood online sours fast. Fans go from posting love letters to the team to full-blown roast sessions. Hashtags like #OutWithTheCoach, #RebuildKBFC, and #BlastersDeserveBetter pop up outta nowhere and suddenly, it's all anyone can talk about. It's not just one dude having a meltdown—this is organized rage. Mods and admins shoot out ready-made posts, graphics, and hashtag plans via WhatsApp and Telegram. Everyone's on the same page, pushing the message hard.The club has to listen—no hiding from that kind of coordinated noise. You see coaches getting the boot, new players signed, management forced to say sorry. What looks like angry fans venting is actually a proper negotiation—fans flexing their digital muscles and making stuff happen.

From Local Grievance to League-Level Advocacy

But it doesn't stop with just KBFC drama. Manjappada's got bigger game. When there's dodgy refereeing or stadiums charging a kidney for tickets, they team up with other supporter groups and blast the league with hashtags like #SaveISL or #FansFirstFootball. Suddenly, it's not just about one club—it's about the whole Indian Super League. Fans aren't just buying tickets anymore. They're demanding a seat at the table.Bottom line? For Manjappada, protest isn't just about crying when the team loses. It's about making sure fans actually matter in Indian football. It's messy, hilarious, sometimes a little unhinged, but always about taking charge and making noise where it counts.

4.2.2 Support: From Screens to Stadiums

Online, Manjappada's fierce. But offline? It's a full-on family reunion with a thousand cousins you actually want to hang out with. WhatsApp, Facebook, Telegram—all those chats are like secret planning rooms for the madness you see on match days.

Tifo Culture and Collective Production

Those giant yellow banners in Kochi's Jawaharlal Nehru Stadium? Not magic. They're the result of months of nerdy group chats. Designs get tossed around in WhatsApp groups, everyone votes on which legend to feature or what meme to slap on, and then someone drops a crowdfunding link. By the time match day comes, fans know the songs, the moves, the spot they're supposed to stand—no one's winging it.These tifo projects are wild. It's like a multiplayer art project: some people design, others paint, someone's organizing snacks. Everyone's pitching in. It's messy, emotional, and somehow it all clicks. Fans aren't just shouting from the stands—they're literally building the club's vibe piece by piece.

Linguistic and Cultural Authenticity

Manjappada keeps it real—everything's in Malayalam, packed with inside jokes, movie quotes, and memes only someone from Kerala would get. Forget the corporate, vanilla branding you see in IPL. Here, it's all about coconut emojis, Mohanlal punchlines, and local slang. The digital feed is just dripping with Kerala's flavor. Makes you homesick even if you're already home.And for fans chilling in Dubai or Toronto or wherever, being part of Manjappada is like carrying a piece of Kerala in your pocket. It's fandom with roots—glocal, if you wanna get fancy.

Logistics of Passion: The "Away Day" Machine

When KBFC's on the road, Manjappada turns into a well-oiled chaos machine. Volunteers are out here organizing train rides, booking buses, sorting out hotel rooms—Google Sheets flying everywhere. Telegram threads blow up with ticket updates and food plans. Suddenly, you've got a swarm of yellow shirts taking over rival stadiums in Bengaluru or Goa. It's a whole vibe—Kerala follows you, whether you want it to or not.All this? It flips the script on what it means to be a fan. No more just sitting and watching. This is active, sweaty, emotional, and a little bit nuts. But man, it's community at its best—the kind you wish every club had.

4.3 From Fandom to Networked Publics: Theorizing Manjappada's Digital Power

Manjappada's whole online thing? It's not just about football and memes for the LOLs. This is 21st-century Indian fandom turned up to eleven, where being a fan is basically a kind of digital citizenship. They're not just scrolling and liking stuff—they're organizing protests, flooding timelines with memes, co-designing merch, and generally acting like they own the place (because, honestly, they kinda do). danah boyd calls this "networked publics"—fancy term, but it fits. Basically, you've got regular people, digitally connected, constantly visible, and able to scale up their voice at the tap of a screen. They're not just soaking up whatever the club feeds them; they're out here setting the agenda, fighting about what the club stands for, and how it should be run.

For Manjappada, X (ugh, still calling it Twitter in my head), Instagram, WhatsApp—these aren't just apps. They're more like digital playgrounds where anyone can jump in to argue, plan, vent, or just vibe with fellow fans. Every hashtag protest, meme war, or viral video—those are tiny political acts. They turn feelings into noise the club can't ignore. The authorities end up reacting, not because some official letter landed on their desk, but because the fans' collective outrage, joy, or sarcasm just can't be swept under the rug. Papacharissi labeled this "affective publics"—when digital crowds use emotion as a kind of power. Nailed it.

Affective Publics and Emotional Infrastructure

Papacharissi's theory totally explains what's powering Manjappada's activism. Online, emotions don't just stay personal. Anger, pride, nostalgia, whatever—they get meme-ified, hashtagged, and passed around until everyone's riding the same emotional wave. Every campaign (#SaveISL, #OutWithTheCoach—you know the drill) is less about cold logic and more about collective feels. That's the real infrastructure: not wires and servers, but networks of shared emotion. Fans aren't just rational actors, they're emotional engines—fueling both unity and rebellion.And this changes the whole hierarchy. The old-school power gap between club bosses and fans? Way less rigid now. Someone in a tiny Kerala town can drop a meme that blows up nationally in hours. That's not just engagement. That's fans grabbing the mic and rewriting the script. Suddenly, everyone's got a say in what the club means and where it's headed.

Participatory Culture and the Co-Creation of Meaning

Bring in Henry Jenkins (yeah, the fandom guy). He talks about "participatory culture," where the line between consumer and creator is basically erased. That's Manjappada in a nutshell. Fans aren't just buying jerseys—they're making memes, writing chants, designing merch, shooting fan films, and just generally remixing the club's identity 24/7. The club drops something, the fans spin it into a thousand new forms, and the cycle keeps rolling. Jenkins' "convergence culture" is alive and well here—grassroots creativity feeding back into the official brand.

And it's not just Manjappada. Look at Whistle Podu Army (CSK fans)—same deal, different city. Both groups are like unofficial creative agencies for their teams. But Manjappada's got that regional flavor—Malayalam memes, local slang, the whole cultural package. It's not just about supporting a team; it's about repping Kerala on a global digital stage. That's next-level participatory culture—borderline rebellious, honestly.

From Audience to Assembly

Thing is, Manjappada isn't content to just talk online. They've moved from group chats to real-life protests, from tweetstorms to stadium banners. Media nerds call this "networked assembly" (shoutoutGerbaudo): when digital buzz translates into boots on the ground. These fans have gone from "armchair experts" to actual movers and shakers—organizing away-day travel, demanding accountability, defending their turf. They're proof that "affective publics" can morph into "deliberative publics"—fans who don't just emote, but negotiate, organize, and push for real change.

So yeah, Manjappada totally messes with the boundaries between fandom and activism, culture and politics, "just football" and "something bigger." Their digital world is part soapbox, part archive, part battleground. Football, for them, isn't only a game—it's a way to flex regional pride, push back, and build something that's both local and global.

5. DISCUSSION: WHERE'S THE LINE? DIGITAL FANDOM GETS MESSY (AND KIND OF AWESOME)

Honestly, just look at the madness around the Chennai Super Kings (CSK) and Kerala Blasters FC (KBFC). Fandom's not just about screaming at a TV anymore—now it's almost like fans are part of the club itself. Social media's basically ripped the fence out from between "the team" and "the people who care way too much about the team." X, Insta, Reddit, WhatsApp… all these platforms have turned fans into co-authors of the story, not just people on the sidelines. Teams get a whole vibe shift because of online fans—sometimes for better, sometimes for chaos.

5.1 Power Swap: From Teams Yelling at Fans to Actual Conversations (or Fights)

Back in the day, teams would just blast PR at the masses and hope we'd clap along. No backtalk, no feedback loop—fans were basically just living room cheerleaders. Now? Total 180. Teams and fans bicker in public, they meme each other, they call each other out. It's wild.

Look at Manjappada or the Whistle Podu Army. These aren't just fan clubs; they're digital mobs with hashtags that can make or break a manager's day. #OutWithTheCoach, #SaveISL—those aren't just whiny hashtags. They're pressure campaigns. Clubs and league bosses have to respond or risk looking clueless. Remember when CSK dropped Suresh Raina in the 2022 IPL auction? Fans went ballistic, CEO had to come out with an official "Hey, calm down, here's why…" That would've never happened in the old days.Basically, fans have hacked the system. The comment section is the new boardroom. Social media's turned into this weird, unofficial parliament for sports, where a meme can actually nudge the club's decisions. It's messy and loud and sometimes petty, but it's real power.

5.2 Fan Creativity: Free Labor or Just a Labor of Love?

Here's where it gets a bit sketchy. All this digital energy? It's basically work. Fans spend hours making memes, cutting slick highlight reels, running forums, building up the club's legend. You can't put a price tag on it, but clubs are cashing in. Every meme, every viral tweet feeds the algorithm monster, making teams more popular and—let's be honest—more profitable.Take CSK: they'll retweet a fan's graphic, slap a meme into an official post, and boom—that's free marketing. KBFC crowdsources T-shirt designs, and fans love it… but it's also free R&D. There's a fine line between "we're all in this together!" and "thanks for the free ideas, now go buy this jersey."

So yeah, is it co-creation, or just clubs milking free labor? Kind of both. Fans get a rush from seeing their stuff go viral, maybe even a sense of belonging. But at some point, someone's gotta ask: shouldn't there be more than just likes and retweets as payback? Still, for most diehards, the buzz of being noticed by their club, the community feels, and the sheer fun of it all—that's the real payoff. Fandom's always been a labor of love, just now it's a bit more public, and a lot more complicated.

So, here's the kicker—digital fandom is basically obsessed with "keeping it real," while everything's being filtered, staged, or edited behind the scenes. Folks want to see clubs and players drop the act, spill some tea, show us life beyond the PR machine. Locker-room jokes, random life updates, that sort of stuff. But, let's be honest, even those "unguarded moments" are getting run through a blender of algorithms and branding teams. There's always a little performance in the "realness," isn't there?That's the weird loop fans get stuck in: you're not just watching, you're performing too—posting, hashtagging, trying to look like the ultimate supporter online. Clubs and players know this game. They've turned authenticity into a whole strategy. Take someone like Dhoni or Adrian Luna—they don't flood social media, but when they do, it feels raw, maybe a little messy, and people eat it up. It's not the loudest or flashiest folks who win online hearts; it's the ones who feel like, yeah, they could just be your neighbor on an off day.Basically, "being authentic" online isn't anti-performance—it's just another flavor of performance. It's the emotional gold fans crave and the marketing trick clubs need to seem less like faceless brands and more like your quirky best friend.

5.3 Boundaries and Benefits: A Comparative Analysis

If you look at CSK and KBFC, you'll see digital fandom isn't some cookie-cutter thing. It's totally shaped by the team's backstory, the place, and the whole vibe of the club.For CSK, their online fanbase is like a fortress. Even when the team was banned, "Yellove" fans kept the spirit alive, turning what could've been just sad nostalgia into some wild myth-making online. For KBFC, it's a different beast. Their digital crew, Manjappada, basically built a movement out of thin air—turning football into a badge of Malayali pride, even when results on the pitch were, let's say, less than inspiring.

But there's drama too. CSK fans are always debating what "legacy" even means—are you loyal to the team, or just the stars? KBFC fans, meanwhile, get fired up about the bigger picture, calling out the mess in Indian football's leadership. Their fandom isn't just about loving a team; it's like a mini social movement.CSK's crowd loves glitz, old-school heroes, and winning—totally Chennai, right? KBFC is about the people, the local culture, that whole "one of us" energy.Put them side by side, you've got two totally different flavors of digital fandom: CSK's slick, global, brand-heavy style versus KBFC's raw, collective, homegrown vibe. Both are proof that digital fandom is no joke—it's a major force for emotion and community in modern sports. And honestly? It's only getting bigger.

Alright, let's just call it like it is: Indian sports fans? They're not just sitting on the sidelines anymore, cheering or groaning at their screens. Nope. They've basically crashed through the velvet rope and started rearranging the furniture. These folks are shaping the whole vibe—from what gets posted online, to what clubs and brands actually do. Fandom right now is this wild mash-up of citizenship, shopping, and pure creativity… and it's all happening at the speed of a retweet.

Look at CSK and KBFC—two totally different flavors of fanatic. CSK's crowd? All about nostalgia, larger-than-life heroes, a bit like Bollywood on a cricket pitch. KBFC, on the other hand, loves inside jokes, local pride, and the kind of memes that don't even make sense outside Kerala. The platforms might be the same (X, Insta, whatever), but the energy? Super local, super personal.So yeah, the old lines—fan, activist, customer, creator—they're not just fuzzy, they're melting. Fans want more than merch drops and hashtags. They want honesty, a say in the big calls, maybe even a slice of the action. For the clubs and leagues, this is both gold and dynamite. You get endless hype and fresh ideas, but also, you're under the microscope 24/7.Bottom line? The winners in the next era of sports aren't going to be the ones "managing" their fan base like a spreadsheet. They'll be the ones who treat fans like a crew—not just a cash register. Think trust, think joint projects, think transparency. The whole "us vs. them" thing? That's just not going to cut it.

So, what should sports orgs do? Four things, honestly:

- Actually talk to people. Not just push PR fluff—get into real convos, hire community folks, run campaigns where fans actually shape the story.
- Let fans make stuff. Jerseys, chants, social causes—give them the keys sometimes, not just a branded megaphone.
- Keep it real. You mess up? Own it. Explain the weird decisions. People respect honesty way more than spin.
- Play fair. If fans are making content or building the buzz, give credit, maybe even cash. It's a two-way street.

Now, if you're the research-y type, there's a ton left to dig into. How does all this online hype actually move the needle—do ticket sales or merch numbers jump? Does this work the same in the US, Europe, or Japan? And what about all these new toys—metaverse stadiums, blockchain fan clubs, AI-driven everything? Plus, who's still getting left out—by language, money, gender? Lots of questions, zero easy answers.

Final thought: This isn't about turning feelings into products. It's about fans using every platform out there to demand better, fairer, more fun sports. They're shaping the stories, calling for accountability, and turning fandom into something that kinda looks like democracy (but with more memes). The next chapter? It's not just about what happens on the pitch—it's the drama, the dreams, and the debates happening everywhere else. Welcome to the real game.

Alright, let's just call it like it is: Indian sports fans? They're not just sitting on the sidelines anymore, cheering or groaning at their screens. Nope. They've basically crashed through the velvet rope and started rearranging the furniture. These folks are shaping the whole vibe—from what gets posted online, to what clubs and brands actually do. Fandom right now is this wild mash-up of citizenship, shopping, and pure creativity… and it's all happening at the speed of a retweet.

Look at CSK and KBFC—two totally different flavors of fanatic. CSK's crowd? All about nostalgia, larger-than-life heroes, a bit like Bollywood on a cricket pitch. KBFC, on the other hand, loves inside jokes, local pride, and the kind of memes that don't even make sense outside Kerala. The platforms might be the same (X, Insta, whatever), but the energy? Super local, super personal.So yeah, the old lines—fan, activist, customer, creator—they're not just fuzzy, they're melting. Fans want more than merch drops and hashtags. They want honesty, a say in the big calls, maybe even a slice of the action. For the clubs and leagues, this is both gold and dynamite. You get endless hype and fresh ideas, but also, you're under the microscope 24/7.

Bottom line? The winners in the next era of sports aren't going to be the ones "managing" their fan base like a spreadsheet. They'll be the ones who treat fans like a crew—not just a cash register. Think trust, think joint projects, think transparency. The whole "us vs. them" thing? That's just not going to cut it.

So, what should sports orgs do? Four things, honestly:

- Actually talk to people. Not just push PR fluff—get into real convos, hire community folks, run campaigns where fans actually shape the story.
- Let fans make stuff. Jerseys, chants, social causes—give them the keys sometimes, not just a branded megaphone.
- Keep it real. You mess up? Own it. Explain the weird decisions. People respect honesty way more than spin.
- Play fair. If fans are making content or building the buzz, give credit, maybe even cash. It's a two-way street.

Now, if you're the research-y type, there's a ton left to dig into. How does all this online hype actually move the needle—do ticket sales or merch numbers jump?

Does this work the same in the US, Europe, or Japan? And what about all these new toys—metaverse stadiums, blockchain fan clubs, AI-driven everything? Plus, who's still getting left out—by language, money, gender? Lots of questions, zero easy answers.This isn't about turning feelings into products. It's about fans using every platform out there to demand better, fairer, more fun sports. They're shaping the stories, calling for accountability, and turning fandom into something that kinda looks like democracy (but with more memes). The next chapter? It's not just about what happens on the pitch—it's the drama, the dreams, and the debates happening everywhere else. Taken together, the literature suggests that contemporary branding operates at the intersection of diversity, empathy, learning systems, and governance. Embedding inclusion and sustainability into institutional strategy—rather than treating them as reputational tools—enhances legitimacy and resilience in complex global environments (Tarnanidis et al., 2026a; Licsandru et al., 2025). However, this shift also demands vigilance against ethical risks, particularly as AI-driven systems increasingly mediate strategic communication (Mandania et al., 2025). Incentive alignment and accountable leadership remain crucial for translating inclusive narratives into durable institutional value (Sardashti & Calantone, 2022).

REFERENCES

Boyd, D. (2010). Social network sites as networked publics: Affordances, dynamics, and implications. In Z. Papacharissi (Ed.), *A networked self: Identity, community, and culture on social network sites* (pp. 39–58). Routledge.

Braun, V., & Clarke, V. (2006). Using thematic analysis in psychology. *Qualitative Research in Psychology*, *3*(2), 77–101. DOI: 10.1191/1478088706qp063oa

Bruns, A. (2008). *Blogs, Wikipedia, Second Life, and beyond: From production to produsage*. Peter Lang.

Gerbaudo, P. (2012). *Tweets and the streets: Social media and contemporary activism*. Pluto Press.

Jenkins, H. (1992). *Textual poachers: Television fans and participatory culture*. Routledge.

Jenkins, H. (2006). *Convergence culture: Where old and new media collide*. New York University Press.

Jenkins, H., Ford, S., & Green, J. (2013). *Spreadable media: Creating value and meaning in a networked culture*. New York University Press.

Jenkins, H., Ito, M., & boyd, d. (2015). *Participatory culture in a networked era: A conversation on youth, learning, commerce, and politics*. Polity Press.

Licsandru, T. C., Mari, C., Kipnis, E., Galalae, C., Johnson, E., Cross, S. N. N., Cui, C. C., Kearney, S., Martín Ruiz, V., Vorster Larsen, L., & Yoruk, I. (2025). Integrating diversity, equity and inclusion in management education: An empathy framework. *British Journal of Management*. Advance online publication. DOI: 10.1111/1467-8551.70008

Mandania, R., Cadogan, J., Liu, J., & Kazmi, N. (2025). Optimizing promotional campaigns to maximize customer lifetime value: A dynamic learning approach. *Journal of Service Research*, *0*(0). Advance online publication. DOI: 10.1177/10946705251365524

Papacharissi, Z. (2015). *Affective publics: Sentiment, technology, and politics*. Oxford University Press.

Sardashti, H., & Calantone, R. J. (2022). Does equity-based compensation motivate executives to build strong brands? *Journal of Marketing Management*, *38*(13–14), 1433–1460. DOI: 10.1080/0267257X.2022.2041068

Tarnanidis, T., Manda, V. K., Sousa, B. B., Vlachopoulou, M., & Papachristou, E. (2026). Marketing complexity of smart consumer products to global millennial segments. In Tarnanidis, T., Sousa, B., Vlachopoulou, M., Papachristou, E., & Manda, V. K. (Eds.), *Diversity and inclusion-driven marketing for multicultural marketplaces* (pp. 1–16). IGI Global Scientific Publishing., DOI: 10.4018/979-8-3373-2111-0.ch001

Tarnanidis, T., Sousa, B., Vlachopoulou, M., Papachristou, E., & Kittu Manda, V. (Eds.). (2026). *Diversity and inclusion-driven marketing for multicultural marketplaces*. IGI Global Scientific Publishing., DOI: 10.4018/979-8-3373-2111-0

Yin, R. K. (2014). *Case study research: Design and methods* (5th ed.). SAGE Publications.

Chapter 5
Branding and Identity Through Culturally Sensitive GenAI

Soumen Ghosh
https://orcid.org/0009-0008-3778-6090
Global Institute of Management and Technology, Krishnanagar, India

Rupam Hazra
https://orcid.org/0009-0003-0332-2128
Global Institute of Management and Technology, Krishnanagar, India

Partha Paul
https://orcid.org/0009-0007-5146-0321
Global Institute of Management and Technology, Krishnanagar, India

Parag Chatterjee
https://orcid.org/0000-0003-1243-9582
Global Institute of Management and Technology, Krishnanagar, India

ABSTRACT

Generative Artificial Intelligence (GenAI) is redefining branding by enabling large-scale, personalized, and creative content generation. However, in a global marketplace, cultural sensitivity is essential to ensure that AI-generated messages resonate authentically with diverse audiences. Culturally aware GenAI systems recognize and respect local customs, language nuances, and societal values, avoiding stereotypes and misrepresentation. By integrating diverse datasets, cultural expertise, and ethical oversight, brands can create inclusive narratives that strengthen trust, loyalty, and emotional engagement. This chapter explores the intersection of

DOI: 10.4018/979-8-3373-6731-6.ch005

cultural intelligence and GenAI in branding, examining its role as both a strategic tool and an ethical responsibility. It also addresses challenges, risks, case studies, and future directions for building meaningful, culturally attuned brand identities.

1. INTRODUCTION

In today's interconnected world, Generative Artificial Intelligence (GenAI) is transforming the way brands craft and communicate their identities, enabling personalized marketing, rapid creative development, and global outreach at an unprecedented scale. Yet, this power comes with the challenge of cultural sensitivity—ensuring that AI-generated content respects local customs, language nuances, and societal values. By integrating diverse datasets, cultural expertise, and ethical oversight, brands can leverage GenAI not only as a creative engine but also as a bridge for meaningful cross-cultural engagement. This chapter examines how culturally sensitive GenAI can shape branding strategies, strengthen emotional connections, and position brands for sustainable relevance in a global marketplace.

2. UNDERSTANDING CULTURAL SENSITIVITY IN THE AGE OF GENAI

Cultural sensitivity in the context of Generative AI (GenAI) refers to the ability of AI systems to recognize, respect, and adapt to the values, traditions, and communication styles of different cultures. As brands increasingly use AI to create marketing content, designs, and narratives, cultural awareness becomes crucial to building trust and avoiding misrepresentation. GenAI can generate powerful, personalized messages, but without cultural context, it risks producing content that feels tone-deaf or offensive. Cultural sensitivity ensures that AI-generated branding aligns with local customs, language nuances, and societal norms. By incorporating diverse and representative datasets, AI can better understand these variations and avoid reinforcing stereotypes. Students provide intentionality, assessment, and contextual awareness, while AI systems provide new combinations and patterns that go beyond traditional human thought (Ramezani & Wagner ,2025). This approach not only prevents harm but also strengthens emotional connections with global audiences. Brands that integrate cultural intelligence into GenAI benefit from higher engagement, loyalty, and authenticity

A. Defining Cultural Sensitivity and Inclusion

Cultural sensitivity and inclusion refer to the awareness, respect, and integration of diverse cultural values, beliefs, and practices in social, organizational, and technological contexts. It emphasizes understanding differences without prejudice and ensuring equitable treatment for individuals from varied backgrounds. In the age of globalization and digital innovation, cultural sensitivity ensures that communication, policies, and technologies do not unintentionally marginalize or offend any group. Inclusion goes beyond tolerance by actively creating opportunities, platforms, and environments where all cultural identities are represented and valued. Together, cultural sensitivity and inclusion foster trust, collaboration, and fairness in multicultural environments. In order to show respect for the potentially shattered company culture, some people wanted management would be more ready and eager to listen, engage in discourse, and be emotionally intelligent and sensitive (Baeten,2025).

a) Respecting Cultural Differences

Respecting cultural differences involves recognizing that people from various backgrounds may have unique traditions, communication styles, and worldviews. By acknowledging these distinctions, organizations and individuals create a foundation for mutual respect and collaboration. This reduces cultural misunderstandings and promotes harmonious interactions.

b) Promoting Equal Opportunities

Inclusion requires not only acknowledging diversity but also ensuring that people from different cultural groups have fair access to opportunities. Equal opportunities in education, employment, and leadership help remove systemic barriers that marginalize underrepresented communities. This strengthens social equity and ensures meaningful participation for all.

c) Creating Inclusive Environments

An inclusive environment is one where individuals feel welcomed, safe, and valued regardless of their cultural identity. This involves designing policies, practices, and communication that encourage participation from everyone. Inclusive environments empower individuals to contribute their perspectives, enriching collective creativity and problem-solving.

B. The Role of Culture in Brand Perception

Culture plays a powerful role in shaping how consumers perceive brands, influencing everything from trust and loyalty to emotional connection. When cultural awareness is lacking, however, even strong global brands may appear insensitive or disconnected, damaging their reputation. Cultural symbols, traditions, and communication styles influence the way consumers interpret brand messages, advertisements, and product design. Therefore, understanding and integrating cultural perspectives is not just about avoiding mistakes—it is a key driver of competitive advantage in global branding. Understanding their attitudes toward use, readiness to embrace, and perceptions of its value is necessary to recognize GenAI's transformative potential and implications for future company operations (Vitellaro et al., 2025).

a) Cultural Values and Consumer Trust

Cultural values guide how individuals evaluate a brand's integrity and authenticity. For example, in collectivist cultures, community-oriented branding often resonates more strongly than individualistic messages. When brands align with local beliefs, traditions, and moral standards, they build a foundation of trust. A lack of cultural sensitivity, however, can make a brand seem foreign, exploitative, or out of touch with its audience. By respecting cultural values, brands can enhance credibility and long-term loyalty.

b) Language, Symbols, and Meaning

Language and cultural symbols carry unique meanings that heavily impact brand perception. A word, gesture, or color may have positive connotations in one culture but offensive ones in another. Similarly, AI-generated slogans without cultural adaptation risk being misunderstood or ridiculed. Brands that carefully adapt language and symbols demonstrate respect for cultural contexts, creating stronger emotional bonds.

c) Cultural Identity and Brand Loyalty

When branding aligns with local traditions, festivals, or shared histories, people feel represented and valued. This sense of belonging fosters brand loyalty that goes beyond product functionality or price. For example, regionalized campaigns during cultural holidays like Diwali or Lunar New Year often deepen consumer attachment. In contrast, overlooking cultural identity can alienate audiences, pushing them toward competitors who show greater cultural awareness.

C. Risks of Cultural Misrepresentation

Cultural misrepresentation occurs when brands misuse, stereotype, or misinterpret cultural elements in their messaging, products, or campaigns. Such missteps can damage brand reputation, offend communities, and create long-lasting distrust among consumers. With GenAI playing a larger role in content creation, the risk increases if datasets are biased or lack cultural nuance. Even small errors—such as an inappropriate slogan, a misplaced symbol, or inaccurate depiction of traditions—can go viral and spark backlash in today's hyperconnected world. Therefore, avoiding cultural misrepresentation is not just about being politically correct—it is essential for brand survival and relevance in diverse markets. An example of this is genocide studies, where content produced by AI might unintentionally downplay or distort facts, which can be deeply damaging and disreputable to both survivors and descendants of those who suffered in genocides (Bjelobaba et al., 2025).

a) Damage to Brand Reputation

When brands misrepresent culture, they risk being perceived as ignorant, insensitive, or exploitative. A single campaign mistake can overshadow years of positive brand-building efforts. For example, several global fashion brands faced criticism for using sacred cultural symbols inappropriately, leading to boycotts. Reputation damage spreads quickly through social media, amplifying consumer outrage. Once trust is broken, it takes significant time and resources to rebuild credibility.

b) Alienation of Target Audiences

Cultural misrepresentation can alienate the very consumers a brand is trying to reach. Instead of feeling valued, audiences may feel mocked or reduced to stereotypes. This alienation not only reduces engagement but may also push consumers toward culturally respectful competitors. For instance, a campaign that overlooks cultural sensitivities during religious festivals may backfire, creating resentment instead of connection. By neglecting cultural respect, brands risk losing long-term loyalty.

c) Ethical and Social Backlash

Beyond reputation and loyalty, cultural misrepresentation often triggers ethical debates and public criticism. Communities may accuse brands of cultural appropriation, exploitation, or disrespecting sacred traditions. In some cases, misrepresentation can even lead to legal or regulatory action. For example, misuse of indigenous art or religious icons without consent has sparked lawsuits and international criticism.

Addressing these risks requires proactive cultural research and ethical collaboration with local communities.

3. GENAI AS A BRANDING TOOL

Generative AI (GenAI) has emerged as a powerful asset for shaping brand identity and delivering personalized marketing at scale. It can produce creative content such as advertisements, social media posts, product designs, and brand stories tailored to specific audience segments. Unlike traditional methods, GenAI can quickly analyze consumer data to understand preferences, behaviours, and emotional triggers, enabling brands to connect more deeply with their audiences. It allows for dynamic storytelling, where narratives can be adapted in real time to suit cultural, seasonal, or situational contexts. GenAI also supports rapid prototyping of visuals and campaigns, reducing creative development time and costs. For global brands, it offers the ability to localize content for multiple regions while maintaining a consistent core identity. Suitable Gen-AI models are selected to classify brand messages according to the desired themes, prompts are created, categories are encoded using AI results, and finally, the consensus among coders is confirmed(Koçak,2025). Moreover, it can help uncover fresh design concepts and marketing angles that human teams might overlook. However, using GenAI as a branding tool requires careful oversight to ensure that generated content remains authentic, ethical, and culturally sensitive.

A. Capabilities of Generative AI in Marketing and Design

Generative AI (GenAI) is revolutionizing marketing and design by enabling brands to produce personalized, scalable, and innovative content with unprecedented speed. It can analyze consumer data, generate creative assets, and adapt messaging to different cultural and linguistic contexts. From ad copy to logos, videos, and even immersive virtual experiences, GenAI reduces time and costs while expanding creative possibilities. More importantly, it allows brands to test multiple variations of campaigns instantly, helping identify what resonates most with target audiences. Numerous major companies are investigating how synthetic data can contribute to the marketing research process, and several industry reports and predictions indicate that this sector is experiencing significant activity and expansion (Hermann & Puntoni, 2025). As a result, GenAI is not only a tool for efficiency but also a catalyst for creativity and innovation in branding.

a) Personalized Marketing at Scale

GenAI enables brands to deliver highly tailored content to individual consumers across multiple platforms. By analyzing browsing behavior, purchase history, and demographics, AI can craft personalized emails, ads, and product recommendations. This level of personalization fosters stronger consumer engagement and increases conversion rates. Unlike traditional methods, GenAI achieves personalization at scale—reaching millions without losing individual relevance. Brands that embrace this capability gain a competitive edge in customer retention and satisfaction.

b) Creative Content Generation

Generative AI can produce a wide variety of creative outputs, including text, images, video scripts, product designs, and even music. This reduces dependence on large creative teams while expanding the scope of experimentation. For instance, AI tools can generate multiple logo variations or campaign visuals in minutes, allowing marketers to quickly test and refine ideas. This balance between automation and creativity transforms the speed and quality of branding efforts.

c) Cross-Cultural and Multilingual Adaptation

One of the strongest capabilities of GenAI is adapting marketing content for different languages and cultural contexts. AI can translate not just words but also tone, idioms, and cultural references, ensuring campaigns resonate globally. For example, an AI-driven campaign can adjust imagery, colors, and symbols to align with regional values and traditions. This reduces the risk of cultural insensitivity while strengthening brand relatability across borders. Brands using this capability can expand globally while maintaining cultural authenticity and local trust.

B. Personalization at Scale

Unlike traditional personalization, which often focuses on broad segments, GenAI can adapt messages to individual preferences, behaviours, and cultural contexts. This creates stronger connections between brands and consumers, as people feel recognized and valued on a personal level. It also drives higher engagement and conversion rates because the content aligns more closely with what customers actually want. Commercial personalization has become the leading approach in this competition, offering the potential to turn standard customer interactions into significant, individualized conversations (Parker et al.,2025), By combining speed, efficiency, and precision, personalization at scale has become a cornerstone of modern marketing strategies.

a) Dynamic Customer Segmentation

Instead of grouping consumers only by age, gender, or income, AI can track browsing habits, purchase patterns, and real-time interactions. This creates more accurate audience clusters that evolve continuously with consumer behavior. For example, an online retailer can instantly adjust recommendations when a customer shifts interest from electronics to fashion. Such dynamic segmentation ensures relevance and improves customer satisfaction.

b) Tailored Content Delivery

With GenAI, brands can customize not only the message but also the format, tone, and timing of content delivery. An AI-powered system can decide whether a consumer prefers a short video, an infographic, or an in-depth article. It can also adapt messaging styles—formal, casual, or humorous—depending on the customer's profile. Tailored delivery ensures that consumers receive content in a way that best suits their preferences and cultural expectations.

c) Real-Time Adaptation

One of the most powerful features of personalization at scale is real-time adaptability. GenAI can analyze live interactions, such as clicks, time spent on a page, or abandoned carts, and instantly adjust responses. This immediacy makes the customer feel understood and valued, while reducing lost sales opportunities. Real-time personalization also builds a sense of ongoing dialogue between the consumer and the brand.

C. Storytelling and Narrative Creation through AI

Storytelling has always been at the heart of branding, as narratives help consumers emotionally connect with products and services. Generative AI enhances this process by crafting stories that are personalized, culturally adaptive, and contextually relevant. Instead of static, one-size-fits-all campaigns, AI enables brands to generate dynamic narratives that evolve with audience behavior and feedback. This makes brand communication more engaging, relatable, and memorable in a fast-paced digital environment. By combining data-driven insights with creative outputs, AI transforms storytelling into a powerful tool for brand differentiation and loyalty-building. They determined that the distorted and eerie viewpoints and stories generated by the AI might serve as either a foundation for innovative, impartial ways for users to contemplate the world or as yet another means for businesses and commercial applications to generate highly personalized content similar to digital advertising (Fabre et al., 2025).

a) Emotionally Resonant Campaigns

GenAI can analyze cultural cues, consumer psychology, and emotional triggers to create stories that resonate deeply with audiences. For example, it can weave narratives around family, tradition, or aspiration depending on the cultural context. This emotional engagement strengthens long-term consumer-brand relationships.

b) Interactive and Immersive Experiences

Beyond traditional storytelling, GenAI enables interactive narratives where consumers actively participate in the brand story. Through AI-powered chatbots, VR/AR, or gamified experiences, users can shape how the narrative unfolds. For instance, a fashion brand could let customers design digital outfits and integrate them into personalized storylines. This immersive approach not only enhances engagement but also creates a sense of ownership and co-creation. By making consumers part of the story, brands build stronger loyalty and advocacy.

4. INTEGRATING CULTURAL AWARENESS INTO GENAI SYSTEMS

Integrating cultural awareness into Generative AI systems involves designing algorithms that can understand and respect cultural differences across languages, symbols, traditions, and values. This starts with training AI models on diverse, representative datasets that reflect global perspectives rather than favouring one dominant culture. Cultural context must be embedded in the AI's content generation process, ensuring that imagery, tone, and messaging align with local customs and sensitivities. For example, marketing visuals might need to adapt clothing styles, colour symbolism, or festive references to resonate with different audiences. Avoiding cultural stereotypes is essential, as AI trained on biased data may unintentionally reinforce harmful narratives. Collaboration between AI engineers, cultural anthropologists, linguists, and brand strategists can help bridge gaps in understanding. Localization should go beyond translation, incorporating idiomatic expressions, humour, and storytelling styles native to each audience. As GenAI rapidly advances and becomes more embedded in educational settings, it is crucial to grasp how it influences the developmental journeys of students during their critical academic years (Siraj et al., 2025).

A. Training AI on Diverse and Inclusive Datasets

The foundation of culturally sensitive GenAI lies in the quality and inclusivity of the datasets it is trained on. By incorporating voices, languages, images, and perspectives from multiple communities, brands can ensure that AI-generated content reflects global diversity. The results indicate that genAI can be beneficial for straightforward quality assessment tasks; however, in intricate situations, the results might lack precision and necessitate innovative evaluation methods (Browning et al., 2025).

a) Reducing Algorithmic Bias

When AI models are trained on biased or incomplete datasets, they can unintentionally produce outputs that misrepresent certain groups. By including balanced representation across gender, ethnicity, religion, and socio-economic backgrounds, biases can be minimized. For example, a beauty brand using AI should include diverse skin tones and facial features in training data. This ensures recommendations and content creation are inclusive rather than exclusionary. Reducing bias not only prevents harm but also enhances brand credibility.

b) Ensuring Global Representation

Brands aiming for international reach need AI systems that recognize cultural differences across regions. Training AI on global datasets helps the system understand variations in language, tradition, humour, and visual aesthetics. By including global perspectives, AI-generated branding becomes more relatable to different audiences. Global representation ensures brands avoid a "one-size-fits-all" approach and build stronger cross-cultural connections.

B. Avoiding Biases and Stereotypes in AI-Generated Content

In the past few years, Generative Artificial Intelligence (GenAI) has transformed the way content is created, resulting in the rise of Artificial Intelligence-Generated Content (AIGC), which includes a diverse range of multi-modal content (Basyoni et al., 2025). One of the biggest challenges in applying GenAI for branding is the risk of reinforcing cultural, gender, or social stereotypes. If left unchecked, AI-generated content can unintentionally marginalize groups, perpetuate harmful assumptions, or misrepresent identities. For brands, such mistakes can lead to public backlash, loss of trust, and reputational harm. Avoiding biases requires careful design of algorithms, regular monitoring, and active inclusion of diverse perspectives. By ensuring fairness and sensitivity, AI becomes a tool for positive representation rather than a source of exclusion.

a) Implementing Bias-Detection Mechanisms

Biases in AI can emerge subtly, making it essential to build systems that can detect and flag problematic outputs. Advanced tools can analyze AI-generated text, visuals, or narratives to identify stereotypical portrayals. For example, if an AI system associates leadership only with men or beauty with light skin, it should be flagged for correction. Proactive bias detection prevents harmful stereotypes from reaching audiences.

b) Human Oversight and Cultural Review

While AI can process vast datasets, human judgment is necessary to ensure cultural appropriateness. Having diverse cultural experts and reviewers validate AI outputs can help identify nuances machines might miss. Human oversight ensures accountability in AI-driven branding processes.

C. Localizing Brand Messages for Regional Audiences

In a globalized marketplace, one-size-fits-all branding often fails because cultural values, languages, and preferences differ across regions. GenAI can help brands modify tone, imagery, and storytelling to align with regional cultural norms and consumer expectations. This approach avoids miscommunication, builds stronger emotional connections, and shows respect for local traditions. Ultimately, localized messaging strengthens both relevance and trust, making brands more relatable and successful in diverse markets. In the field of strategizing and distributing pertinent content through different channels to engage target audiences, GenAI has emerged as an essential element in unifying strategies that foster growth(Adeola,2025).

a) Adapting Language and Tone

By localizing language and adjusting tone, brands can better connect with audiences on a personal level. For example, a friendly, casual tone may work well in Western markets but may require a more formal and respectful style in Asian cultures. Using regional dialects, idioms, and culturally relevant expressions can further enhance relatability. GenAI tools trained on local language data can support this adaptation, ensuring messages resonate authentically.

b) Respecting Cultural Values and Symbols

Symbols, colors, and imagery hold different meanings across cultures, and overlooking these can lead to brand missteps. By tailoring visuals and messages to respect cultural values, brands avoid unintended offense. GenAI can analyze cultural trends and suggest regionally appropriate design elements. This sensitivity helps build positive brand associations across diverse markets.

5. SHAPING BRAND IDENTITY THROUGH CULTURAL INTELLIGENCE

A culturally intelligent brand positions itself as authentic and relatable by aligning its values, tone, and imagery with the expectations of diverse audiences. This means understanding not only surface-level cultural symbols but also deeper aspects such as traditions, beliefs, and emotional drivers. Generative AI can assist in this process by analyzing cultural trends, consumer sentiment, and local narratives to create content that resonates meaningfully. Brands that use cultural intelligence effectively can strengthen trust, loyalty, and emotional engagement with customers. For example, a brand celebrating a festival in one region can tailor its message to honour that tradition while maintaining its global identity. In today's digital era, artificial intelligence (AI) has become an essential resource in numerous fields, including design. The swift advancement of AI technologies has given rise to tools that enable designers to discover creative solutions, examine patterns, and enhance their creative processes(Hassan,2025).

A. Aligning Brand Values with Cultural Contexts

For a brand to truly connect with its audience, its values must resonate with the cultural context of the people it serves. Misalignment, on the other hand, can create dissonance and reduce authenticity in the eyes of consumers. GenAI can help brands analyze cultural sentiment, values, and social issues to align messaging with what matters most to specific communities. This procedure is crucial in collaborative situations like interdisciplinary education, workplace training, and research-practice collaborations, where various areas of expertise need to come together to tackle intricate problems(Ordóñez,2025). Ultimately, cultural alignment transforms brands from being mere businesses into meaningful contributors to society.

a) Reflecting Social and Ethical Priorities

Different societies emphasize different values—such as sustainability, equality, or community service—and brands must reflect these priorities to build trust. For instance, an eco-conscious society may expect brands to highlight their green initiatives, while another region may value social equity and fair trade. GenAI can identify regional ethical priorities and guide brands in tailoring messages to highlight them. By doing so, brands avoid being perceived as tone-deaf.

b) Celebrating Cultural Traditions and Heritage

A brand that acknowledges and celebrates local traditions shows respect for the communities it serves. For example, designing campaigns around festivals like Diwali in India or Lunar New Year in China demonstrates cultural sensitivity. GenAI can generate creative assets that incorporate traditional elements while still reflecting a modern global brand voice. Such alignment makes the brand feel more relatable and emotionally connected to local consumers. Over time, this strengthens cultural loyalty and brand attachment.

B. Building Emotional Resonance with Diverse Audiences

Emotional resonance is the foundation of strong brand-consumer relationships, and it becomes even more critical in diverse cultural settings. When a brand creates messages that reflect the feelings, struggles, and aspirations of different communities, it builds trust and relatability. GenAI can help by analyzing cultural stories, regional communication styles, and consumer sentiment to shape emotionally engaging content. Emotional resonance goes beyond advertising—it creates a sense of belonging and shared identity between the brand and its audience. Ultimately, a brand that connects emotionally across cultures earns loyalty that extends beyond products or services.

a) Telling Culturally Relevant Stories

Stories are universal, but the way they are told differs across cultures. A narrative that resonates in one region may not carry the same weight elsewhere. GenAI can craft localized storytelling that draws on cultural myths, traditions, or real-life experiences familiar to local audiences. This ensures the brand feels authentic rather than generic. By weaving culturally relevant narratives, brands strengthen emotional bonds and deepen customer engagement.

b) Using Symbolism and Imagery that Connect Emotionally

Colors, symbols, and imagery evoke powerful emotions, but their meanings differ across cultures. For example, red may signify luck in China but caution in Western countries. GenAI can recommend visual elements that align with regional emotional triggers, avoiding missteps while maximizing impact. When audiences see symbols that resonate with their cultural identity, they feel acknowledged and respected.

C. Case Examples of Successful Cultural Branding

Case studies of successful cultural branding show how brands can meaningfully integrate cultural values into their identity and campaigns. These examples highlight the importance of respecting local traditions, tailoring messages for specific audiences, and balancing global consistency with local adaptation. They also demonstrate that when cultural sensitivity is authentically applied, it leads to stronger emotional connections and greater customer loyalty. Generative AI can further enhance these strategies by helping brands analyze cultural data and create content that resonates. Studying these cases provides a roadmap for how organizations can build global relevance while staying locally authentic. Although GenAI shows potential in improving communication, speeding up design workflows, and boosting customer interaction and satisfaction, there are several significant challenges, such as the necessity for high-quality datasets, the demand for substantial computational power, and ethical concerns surrounding AI-generated designs (Ngai et al.,2025).

a) Nike's "Just Do It" with Local Adaptations

Nike has successfully adapted its global slogan, "Just Do It," into culturally relevant campaigns worldwide. In China, for instance, campaigns focus on collective progress and community sports rather than only individual achievement. In the Middle East, they have highlighted women athletes to promote empowerment in traditionally restrictive contexts. These adaptations show how a strong global brand identity can flex to align with regional values.

b) Coca-Cola's "Share a Coke" Campaign

Coca-Cola's "Share a Coke" campaign localized branding by printing popular first names on bottles in different countries. In India, they featured names and nicknames common in regional languages, while in Australia they tapped into a culture of casual nicknaming. This small personalization created huge emotional engagement by making customers feel seen and valued. It became not only a branding success but also a cultural phenomenon. The campaign demonstrated how personalization and cultural alignment can fuel emotional resonance at scale.

6. ETHICAL CONSIDERATIONS IN CULTURALLY SENSITIVE GENAI

Ethical considerations are central to ensuring that culturally sensitive Generative AI (GenAI) supports inclusion, fairness, and respect in branding. AI systems must be designed to avoid reinforcing harmful stereotypes or misrepresenting cultural traditions. This begins with building transparency into how AI-generated content is created, so stakeholders can understand the sources and processes behind it. Cultural appropriation is a major risk, where brands might unintentionally exploit cultural elements without proper understanding or acknowledgment. Ethical GenAI development also requires protecting intellectual property, especially when drawing from indigenous or community-owned cultural expressions. The rise of GenAI as an innovative technology and its potential use in promoting learning in an ethical manner deserves our attention (Shen et al.,2025).

A. AI Transparency and Accountability

Transparency and accountability in AI are essential for building trust in culturally sensitive branding. Consumers want to know how AI systems generate content, make recommendations, and adapt cultural elements. When brands openly communicate the role of AI in their campaigns, they prevent misunderstandings and reduce the risk of being perceived as manipulative. Accountability ensures that when mistakes or cultural misrepresentations occur, companies take responsibility and correct them quickly. Together, transparency and accountability establish ethical guardrails, making AI a trusted partner in branding rather than a hidden or questionable tool. The idea that transparency will automatically result from this is misguided. Therefore, accountability encompasses more than just understanding the decision-making process; it also requires insight into the reasons behind it, including the biases and motivations that influenced the final result (Hussain & Hussain, 2025).

a) Clear Disclosure of AI Usage

Brands should inform consumers when AI is involved in creating content, advertisements, or personalization strategies. This fosters honesty and prevents audiences from feeling deceived. For example, a brand could disclose that AI was used to analyze cultural trends but that humans oversaw the creative direction. By being upfront, brands create a transparent relationship with audiences.

b) Mechanisms for Error Correction

Even with the best intentions, AI systems can sometimes produce biased or culturally inappropriate content. Having mechanisms in place to quickly identify, acknowledge, and correct these errors is critical for accountability. This may include consumer feedback loops, cultural advisory panels, or real-time monitoring of campaigns. By responding quickly and responsibly, brands show they value cultural respect and audience trust. This accountability builds resilience and credibility in the long term.

B. Avoiding Cultural Appropriation

Transformative possibilities for preserving and revitalizing cultural heritage are presented by Generative Artificial Intelligence (AI)(Mary,2025). Cultural appropriation occurs when brands adopt elements of a culture without proper understanding, respect, or acknowledgment of its significance. In branding with Generative AI, this risk is heightened, as AI can reproduce cultural patterns, symbols, or traditions without recognizing their deeper meaning. Avoiding appropriation requires brands to engage in genuine cultural research, consult with local communities, and ensure representations are respectful rather than exploitative. By doing so, companies not only protect their brand reputation but also honour the cultural identities they seek to connect with. Respectful use of culture strengthens authenticity and fosters lasting trust with diverse audiences.

a) Engaging with Cultural Experts and Communities

To avoid appropriation, brands should collaborate with cultural experts, historians, or representatives from the communities they aim to portray. This ensures that cultural elements are represented accurately and respectfully. For example, using indigenous designs in fashion should involve consulting indigenous artisans and giving them credit. By including local voices, brands move from exploitation to partnership. This collaboration enhances cultural authenticity and builds mutual respect.

b) Distinguishing Between Appreciation and Exploitation

Brands must differentiate between cultural appreciation—celebrating and honouring traditions—and exploitation, which commodifies them for profit. For instance, incorporating traditional music in a campaign with proper acknowledgment is appreciation, while copying sacred rituals without consent is exploitation. AI-generated branding content should be evaluated through this lens to prevent harmful outcomes. When brands respect the meaning behind cultural elements, they create positive associations instead of backlash. This distinction is key to maintaining integrity.

C. Respecting Intellectual and Indigenous Property

Respecting intellectual and indigenous property is a crucial ethical responsibility for brands using Generative AI in culturally sensitive contexts. Indigenous knowledge, designs, languages, and traditions often carry deep spiritual, historical, and communal significance that cannot be treated as open-source material. By respecting ownership and seeking permissions, brands not only prevent harm but also contribute to cultural preservation. This approach ensures that creativity is inclusive, respectful, and beneficial for both brands and communities.

a) Acknowledging Indigenous Ownership

Brands should recognize this as collective intellectual property and avoid using them without community consent. For example, sacred symbols or traditional medicine practices must not be commercialized as design motifs or marketing slogans without permission. Acknowledgment of ownership helps prevent cultural theft. This practice shows respect and builds equitable partnerships with indigenous groups.

b) Seeking Permission and Fair Collaboration

Before incorporating indigenous or traditional cultural elements, brands should establish formal agreements with community representatives. This ensures that content is used ethically and that communities are fairly compensated. For instance, if AI generates textile patterns inspired by tribal art, royalties or credits should flow back to the community. Such collaboration transforms exploitation into empowerment.

7. CHALLENGES AND RISKS

Implementing culturally sensitive Generative AI (GenAI) in branding comes with several challenges and risks that require careful management. One major challenge is data bias, where training datasets may overrepresent certain cultures while underrepresenting others, leading to skewed outputs. Misinterpretation of cultural nuances is another risk, as AI may generate content that is technically correct but socially or contextually inappropriate. Cultural meanings can shift over time, making it difficult for static AI models to stay relevant without regular updates. Legal and regulatory compliance across multiple regions adds complexity, as cultural representation may intersect with intellectual property laws, advertising standards, and privacy regulations. There's also the risk of cultural appropriation, where brands unintentionally exploit cultural symbols without proper credit or understanding. AI-generated mistakes in sensitive contexts can damage brand reputation quickly in the era of viral social media.

A. Data Bias and Representation Issues

Generative AI systems are only as fair and accurate as the data they are trained on. When datasets lack diversity or overrepresent dominant cultural perspectives, the AI's outputs can perpetuate stereotypes or exclude marginalized voices. This creates challenges for culturally sensitive branding, as biased content may alienate target audiences rather than engage them. Brands that fail to address data bias risk damaging their credibility and trust among diverse communities. Tackling representation issues ensures that AI-generated branding content is inclusive, authentic, and respectful of global cultural diversity.

a) Lack of Diverse Training Data

Many AI systems are trained on datasets dominated by Western, English-language, or majority culture content. This imbalance means that cultural symbols, expressions, or narratives from underrepresented groups are often ignored or misrepresented. For example, an AI image generator may produce stereotypical depictions of African or Asian cultures due to inadequate exposure to authentic cultural data. This creates skewed branding outputs that reinforce inequality. Expanding datasets with diverse cultural input helps ensure inclusivity in AI branding.

b) Perpetuation of Stereotypes

When training data contains biased or stereotypical associations, AI can replicate and amplify them in branding content. For instance, linking certain professions only to specific genders or depicting cultures in outdated ways can harm inclusivity efforts. Brands risk alienating audiences if these stereotypes are reproduced in their campaigns. AI systems must therefore be carefully monitored, audited, and corrected for bias. Preventing stereotype reinforcement creates content that resonates positively with all cultural groups.

B. Misinterpretation of Cultural Nuances

Generative AI often struggles to capture the subtle meanings, traditions, and symbolic elements that exist within different cultures. What may seem like a harmless design, phrase, or gesture in one culture could carry offensive or inappropriate connotations in another. Misinterpretation not only damages a brand's reputation but also risks offending communities and losing consumer trust. Unlike humans, AI lacks lived cultural experiences, which makes it prone to overlooking context or deeper significance. Therefore, careful cultural review and human oversight are necessary to ensure AI-generated branding respects cultural nuances.

a) Symbolic Misuse in Branding

Many cultural symbols carry sacred or historical meanings that AI might misapply when generating logos, visuals, or messages. For example, an AI tool might use religious motifs in casual branding, unintentionally offending followers of that faith. This misrepresentation can make campaigns appear disrespectful or exploitative. Brands need cultural experts to validate the appropriateness of symbols used in AI-driven content. Proper guidance ensures symbols are used with authenticity and respect.

b) Language and Translation Errors

AI translation tools often misinterpret idioms, slang, or culturally rooted expressions, leading to awkward or offensive messaging. A slogan that sounds positive in one language could become confusing or insulting in another if nuance is lost. Such mistakes can make audiences feel misunderstood or undervalued. To avoid this, human linguistic and cultural reviewers should complement AI outputs. Accurate cultural translation builds trust and strengthens brand identity.

C. Legal and Regulatory Compliance Across Regions

When brands use Generative AI for culturally sensitive marketing, they must comply with varying legal and regulatory frameworks across different regions. Intellectual property laws, data protection rules, and cultural preservation policies often differ widely from country to country. A campaign that is acceptable in one jurisdiction might violate copyright, privacy, or cultural heritage rights in another. Failure to adhere to these legal requirements can result in lawsuits, financial penalties, or damage to brand credibility. Therefore, brands must align AI-driven campaigns with local laws to ensure ethical and lawful operations globally.

a) Intellectual Property (IP) Protection

Generative AI can unintentionally create content that replicates or infringes on copyrighted designs, artworks, or traditional knowledge. Different regions have strict IP regulations that must be respected to avoid legal disputes. For example, indigenous art or traditional textile patterns may be protected under local IP frameworks. Brands should establish AI training safeguards and legal audits to prevent misuse. This ensures creative outputs respect ownership rights and support fair cultural representation.

b) Data Privacy and Usage Laws

AI-driven personalization often relies on consumer data, which is heavily regulated under frameworks like GDPR (Europe) or CCPA (California). Mismanagement of sensitive data can lead to privacy violations and hefty penalties. Moreover, some regions impose restrictions on how cultural or demographic data can be used in AI training. Brands must ensure data collection, storage, and use comply with local requirements. Adhering to privacy laws strengthens consumer trust while avoiding legal risks.

8. FUTURE DIRECTIONS FOR CULTURALLY SENSITIVE BRANDING WITH GENAI

The future of culturally sensitive branding with Generative AI (GenAI) lies in creating systems that are both technologically advanced and deeply attuned to human diversity. As AI models evolve, they will increasingly incorporate multimodal cultural understanding, combining text, images, voice, and even gestures to adapt branding for different cultural contexts seamlessly. Brands will be able to engage in real-time cultural co-creation, working alongside consumers to develop campaigns that reflect local traditions and values. Emerging markets will see more personalized and inclusive branding experiences, as GenAI enables content creation in underrepresented languages and dialects. Advances in AI explainability will allow brands to understand how cultural insights are generated, making the process more transparent and trustworthy. Blockchain-based provenance tracking may be used to ensure that cultural elements used in AI-generated branding are properly credited and ethically sourced.

A. AI and Cross-Cultural Co-Creation

AI is becoming a powerful tool for fostering cross-cultural co-creation, where diverse voices, traditions, and perspectives come together to shape brand narratives. Instead of imposing a one-size-fits-all marketing approach, AI can generate content that reflects shared values across multiple cultural groups. This enables brands to create inclusive campaigns that highlight both global unity and regional uniqueness. Co-creation with AI also empowers local communities by giving them a voice in how their culture is represented digitally. Ultimately, this approach builds stronger relationships between brands and audiences, rooted in authenticity and mutual respect.

a) Collaborative Campaign Development

AI can act as a bridge between creative teams from different cultural backgrounds, generating prototypes that incorporate multiple styles, symbols, and expressions. For example, an international campaign could integrate Asian calligraphy with African patterns and Western typography seamlessly. By enabling teams to co-create with AI, brands reduce cultural silos and develop marketing materials that resonate globally. This collaboration not only strengthens inclusivity but also fosters innovation by combining diverse artistic traditions.

b) Empowering Local Voices

Cross-cultural co-creation allows local communities to participate in shaping how their identities are represented. AI can assist by providing tools for local artists, storytellers, and designers to incorporate cultural authenticity into global campaigns. For instance, AI could generate ad visuals using indigenous motifs approved by community representatives. This ensures that branding efforts are not only culturally sensitive but also community-driven. Empowering local voices builds trust and prevents tokenism in marketing.

B. Advancements in Multimodal Cultural Understanding

Modern AI systems are moving beyond text analysis to include images, audio, video, and even gestures in their understanding of culture. This multimodal capability allows AI to grasp cultural symbols, body language, accents, music, and visual aesthetics that define different communities. For branding, this means that campaigns can be adapted more effectively to local contexts, capturing subtleties that go beyond words. For example, an AI can recognize that a color associated with celebration in one culture may signify mourning in another. These advancements ensure that AI-driven marketing strategies are more authentic, inclusive, and emotionally resonant across diverse global audiences.

a) Recognition of Visual and Symbolic Cues

AI can analyze cultural symbols, colors, and traditional motifs to ensure visuals in branding campaigns are respectful and relevant. For instance, while the color white represents purity in Western cultures, it is associated with mourning in parts of Asia. By recognizing such nuances, AI helps prevent cultural misrepresentation. This ability allows brands to design logos, ads, and packaging that are visually aligned with cultural expectations, creating deeper audience connections.

b) Understanding Language, Tone, and Accent

Beyond words, AI can interpret how tone, dialects, and accents influence cultural communication. A slogan delivered in a formal tone might resonate in Japan but may feel too rigid in Brazil, where casual and warm communication is valued. By adapting language delivery, brands can craft messages that feel natural and authentic to regional audiences. This advancement enhances inclusivity by respecting not just what is said, but how it is expressed.

C. Opportunities in Emerging Markets

Emerging markets present significant opportunities for brands leveraging culturally sensitive Generative AI (GenAI). These regions are often characterized by rapid digital adoption, growing middle-class populations, and strong cultural identity, which makes personalization essential. GenAI can help brands craft hyper-localized content, products, and experiences that resonate with diverse traditions and languages. Unlike saturated developed markets, emerging economies offer untapped potential where brands that show cultural respect can quickly build loyalty and trust. By blending

AI innovation with cultural intelligence, businesses can establish themselves as pioneers while contributing to inclusive and sustainable market growth.

a) Localized Branding for Regional Diversity

Emerging markets are not homogenous; they often consist of multiple languages, ethnic groups, and traditions within the same country. GenAI can generate region-specific branding campaigns that respect these distinctions. For example, in India, a food brand could adapt its messaging differently for Tamil Nadu, Punjab, and West Bengal, reflecting language, cuisine, and festive practices. This localization increases relevance and ensures consumers feel authentically represented.

b) Affordable Personalization for Growing Middle Classes

With rising disposable incomes, consumers in emerging markets seek brands that reflect both modern aspirations and cultural roots. GenAI allows brands to deliver personalized marketing at scale without high costs. For instance, AI-powered chatbots in local languages can make luxury services more accessible. This democratization of personalization builds stronger customer loyalty and enables even small businesses to compete effectively.

9. CASE STUDIES

Real-world examples of culturally sensitive Generative AI (GenAI) in branding show how technology can enhance inclusivity and authenticity. A global sports-wear brand used GenAI to create localized ad campaigns for over 50 countries, tailoring visuals, colours, and slogans to match each region's cultural values and fashion trends. In the beauty industry, a skincare company leveraged AI to generate promotional images featuring diverse skin tones, facial features, and cultural dress, ensuring representation across global markets. A food brand used GenAI to adapt recipes and packaging designs for different regions, respecting dietary restrictions, religious customs, and local aesthetics. In entertainment, a streaming platform applied AI to create culturally relevant show recommendations and promotional posters for viewers in different countries. A travel company utilized GenAI to generate personalized itineraries and ads that incorporated local languages, festivals, and traditions, increasing engagement with domestic travellers. In the nonprofit sector, an environmental organization used AI-generated storytelling to connect with indigenous communities, highlighting traditional ecological knowledge respectfully.

A. Global Brand Successes with Culturally Aware GenAI Campaigns

Global brands are increasingly turning to culturally aware Generative AI (GenAI) to ensure their campaigns resonate across diverse markets. By adapting content to local languages, traditions, and values, these companies avoid cultural insensitivity and foster stronger emotional connections. Such campaigns highlight how technology, when paired with cultural intelligence, can elevate brand authenticity and trust. From fashion and entertainment to food and technology, leading global brands have shown that culturally sensitive AI strategies can drive inclusivity, growth, and customer loyalty. These successes set an important precedent for other businesses aspiring to expand responsibly in the global marketplace.

a) Nike's Regionalized AI Campaigns

Nike has used AI-powered tools to generate localized content for different regions, integrating sports traditions, cultural festivals, and languages into their ads. For example, during the Lunar New Year, Nike's GenAI-generated visuals highlighted community celebrations and symbolic colors. This allowed the brand to maintain global consistency while offering region-specific relevance. Such initiatives boosted customer engagement and reinforced Nike's reputation as a culturally adaptive global leader.

b) Coca-Cola's Culturally Adaptive Marketing

Coca-Cola has embraced GenAI to create advertising that reflects local holidays, traditions, and even folklore. In Latin America, AI-generated campaigns incorporated regional music and dance elements, while in Asia, Coke used symbolic motifs like lanterns and cherry blossoms. These campaigns created strong cultural resonance while staying aligned with Coca-Cola's universal message of happiness and sharing. This demonstrated that GenAI can balance global brand identity with local authenticity.

c) Netflix's Personalized and Localized Promotions

Netflix leverages GenAI to produce region-specific promotional posters, trailers, and recommendations tailored to cultural preferences. For example, the same show may have different promotional imagery in Japan, Brazil, and India, reflecting local aesthetics and storytelling traditions. This strategy not only enhances cultural relevance but also increases subscriber engagement. Netflix's approach shows how AI-driven localization strengthens brand loyalty in highly diverse markets.

B. Lessons from Cultural Missteps in AI Branding

While culturally aware GenAI campaigns have brought success, there are also cautionary tales where brands mis stepped due to poor cultural understanding. Misrepresentation, stereotyping, or overlooking cultural sensitivities can harm brand reputation and lead to public backlash. These missteps highlight the importance of cultural intelligence, ethical oversight, and human review in AI-driven branding. When AI lacks diverse training data or brands fail to test campaigns across cultural contexts, mistakes are amplified on global platforms. Learning from these errors is essential to create respectful, inclusive, and authentic AI-powered branding strategies.

a) H&M's Controversial Ad Campaign

H&M once faced criticism for an ad featuring a child in a hoodie with racially insensitive wording. Though not fully AI-driven, it serves as a lesson for GenAI campaigns—automated outputs can unintentionally reinforce stereotypes. A lack of cultural sensitivity checks led to global outrage and damage to the brand's image. Brands must therefore integrate cultural review teams alongside AI systems to avoid similar outcomes.

b) AI-Generated Festival Campaign Misrepresentation

A global beverage company tested AI-generated ads for Diwali in India, but the visuals inaccurately depicted cultural practices, such as placing candles in inauthentic settings. This mistake offended audiences and demonstrated that AI alone cannot capture deep cultural nuance. The incident underscores the importance of consulting cultural experts before deploying AI-generated festival or tradition-related content.

10. CONCLUSION

In the age of Generative AI, cultural sensitivity has emerged as a critical pillar of effective and ethical branding. While GenAI offers unprecedented opportunities for personalization, creativity, and global reach, its true value lies in its ability to adapt content to diverse cultural contexts with authenticity and respect. By embedding cultural intelligence into AI systems, brands can avoid stereotypes, prevent misrepresentation, and foster deeper emotional connections with audiences worldwide. This

REFERENCES

Adeola, F. (2025). *Effects of Generative Artificial Intelligence on Creative Processes Within Local Advertising Agencies* (Master's thesis, Oklahoma State University).

Baeten, T. (2025). *The Influence of Artificial Intelligence Adoption on Educator Perceptions* (Doctoral dissertation, University of Wisconsin--Stout).

Basyoni, L., Qayyum, A., Shaban, K., Elmahjub, E., Al-Ali, A., Halabi, O., & Qadir, J. (2025). Generative AI-Driven Metaverse: The Promises and Challenges of AI-Generated Content. *Authorea Preprints.*

Bjelobaba, S., Waddington, L., Perkins, M., Foltýnek, T., Bhattacharyya, S., & Weber-Wulff, D. (2025). Maintaining research integrity in the age of GenAI: An analysis of ethical challenges and recommendations to researchers. *International Journal for Educational Integrity*, *21*(1), 1–23.

Browning, J. W., McKeever, S., Ferrario, M. A., O'Neill, I., & Stewart, D. (2025, April). Creating sustainable solutions: An inclusive hackathon leveraging genAI in a local context. In *2025 IEEE Global Engineering Education Conference (EDUCON)* (pp. 1-7). IEEE.

Fabre, É., Seaborn, K., Koiwai, S., Watanabe, M., & Riesch, P. (2025, April). More-than-Human Storytelling: Designing Longitudinal Narrative Engagements with Generative AI. In *Proceedings of the Extended Abstracts of the CHI Conference on Human Factors in Computing Systems* (pp. 1-10).

Hassan, M. A. E. (2025). ARTIFICIAL INTELLIGENCE TECHNOLOGIES AND THEIR ROLE IN FOSTERING CREATIVE THINKING IN DESIGN EDUCATION. *Pharos International Journal of Arts and Design*, *2*(01), 287–304.

Hermann, E., & Puntoni, S. (2025). Generative AI in marketing and principles for ethical design and deployment. *Journal of Public Policy & Marketing*, *44*(3), 332–349.

Hussain, A., & Hussain, A. (2025). Transparency and accountability: Unpacking the real problems of explainable AI. *AI & Society*, 1–2.

Koçak, B. B. (2025). HOW TO USE GENAI AS A RATER IN MARKETING: A COMPREHENSIVE GENAI-BASED CONTENT CODING FRAMEWORK. *Yönetim Bilimleri Dergisi*, *23*(57), 1705–1725.

. Mary, B. J. (2025). *Generative AI for Cultural Heritage Preservation.*

Ngai, E. W., Lee, M. C., & Kei, B. C. (2025). A Generative Artificial Intelligence (GenAI) System for Fashion Design: A Case Study. *IEEE Transactions on Engineering Management.*

. Ordóñez, J. M. (2025). Creativity, Ethics, and Regulation in the Age of Generative AI. *AI Impacts on Branded Entertainment and Advertising*, 45-64.

. Parker, L., Hassan, O., & Davis, C. The Role of Generative AI in the Future of Commercial Personalization. *Journal of Electronic Commerce Management, 1*, 1-16.

Ramezani, D., & Wagner, M. (2025). REDEFINING STUDENT AGENCY IN THE AGE OF GENAI. In *EDULEARN25 Proceedings* (pp. 7102-7107). IATED.

Shen, Y., Wang, Z., & Fan, Y. Ethical Issues and Value Tensions in the Context of GenAI-Assisted Learning. In *Learning with Generative Artificial Intelligence* (pp. 222–253). Routledge.

Siraj, M., Duke, J., & Plötz, T. (2025). The GenAI Generation: Student Views of Awareness, Preparedness, and Concern. *arXiv preprint arXiv:2505.02230.*

Vitellaro, F., Schifilliti, V., Buratti, N., & Cesaroni, F. (2025). I won't become obsolete! exploring the acceptance and use of GenAI by marketing professionals. *European Journal of Innovation Management.*

Chapter 6

Cultural Blind Spots in Marketing AI: Case Studies of Failure

Aakriti Jain
https://orcid.org/0009-0008-2179-2955
Christ University, India

Ila Anand
https://orcid.org/0000-0001-8837-4450
Christ University, India

ABSTRACT

Artificial intelligence has been quickly shifting into the pioneer of contemporary marketing. AI powered systems influence how brands communicate with culturally diverse audiences through automated content creation and hyper personalized targeting. These systems, while highly efficient, are proving to have major cultural blind points in which algorithmic decision making fails to detect or interpret cultural, social, and representational subtleties. Such lapses appear as biased outputs, homogenization of identity, and reinforcement of stereotypes, growing into public controversies and reputational crises. This chapter explores cultural blindness in marketing-focused AI systems through four case studies: Amazon's recruitment tool, H&M's culturally insensitive campaign, Dove's beauty representation controversy, and Levi's AI generated diversity models.

DOI: 10.4018/979-8-3373-6731-6.ch006

1. INTRODUCTION

1.1. The Emergence of AI in Marketing Ecosystems

Artificial intelligence has radically changed the marketing field by transforming the field of marketing out of its intuition-based decision making to highly analytical based on data accuracy. AI is used now to guide brand segmentation, content and media placement and comprehend behaviour at huge scale (Kumar et al., 2024). These systems take in huge amounts of consumer data, discern such granular patterns, and facilitate marketing processes that previously were impossible because of human constraints (Mariani et al., 2022). With the growing need to achieve a competitive edge in an environment that is becoming more and more saturated, AI enters, as a strategic resource to help organizations become more efficient, execute timely and correctly, and communicate more accurately.

With the growing aspect of AI-mediated marketing, algorithmic processes are currently defining the transactional and cultural aspects of consumption. Artificial intelligence is also actively used by brands, such as content creation, choosing visuals, analyzing emotions and communication, and the algorithms themselves are directly involved in the process of building representational stories (Burke, 2025). These risks are also multiplied by the fact that AI scalability can be implementable in millions of people in hours, the consequences of mistakes in representation in this example are disproportionately significant (Ali et al., 2019).

Meanwhile, the very fast use of generative AI tools, or programs that can spontaneously generate images, text, and even man-like faces, have dramatically increased the power of algorithms. More brands are resorting to such tools to generate creative output quickly and especially focusing on efficiency rather than engaging in extended cultural screening (Hartmann et al., 2025). Such a turn raises major concerns of authorship, authenticity and accountability. These growing possibilities underscore the priority to oversee culture as AI permeates the value marketing chain.

1.2. Knowing Cultural Blind Spots

Cultural blind spots are when an AI system cannot identify aspects related to culture, interpret meaning symbolically, or reproduce historical-based biases because of shortcomings in training data or model architecture (Akter et al., 2023). The blind spots occur due to the AI models assuming a culturally loaded input as a neutral point of data and depriving it of meaning and context (Chen, 2023).

Cultural blind spots in marketing present in the form of inappropriate imagery, wrong message targeting, uninclusive beauty ideals, representational erasure, and artificial diversity (De Bruyn et al., 2020). Once the exclusionary norms via AI output are reproduced, they strengthen the inequities of society and persist among symbolic harm (Farrington, 2020).

Also contributing to the reasons behind cultural blind spots is that most AI development pipelines have been developed within organizational cultures that apply speed, scale, and efficiency instead of contextual sensitivity (Sebestyen, 2025). Teams also tend to compromise their culture aspects in favor of the technical overall measures of accuracy, precision, or even click-through rates. This logical discrepancy between cognitive computation and cultural significance is the building block of numerous AI-based failures in marketing.

1.3. Significance of Culturally Sensitive AI in Marketing

Cultural sensitivity is no longer a strategic necessity but an ethical add on in the modern world global markets. The current customer is more interested in the aspects of representation, fairness, and identity politics than it has ever been before (Hermann, 2022). Since digital mediums of communication enable faster critique, any cultural faux pas may easily cause reputational disasters with long-term effects (Shakespeare, 2018). When consumers can organize online communities like Black Twitter, feminist networks, or diasporic communities, it increases attention given to the choices made by brands and puts more pressure on cultural competence.

With these expectations, the logic of AI operation is usually inconsistent. Algorithms maximize performance indicators instead of equality or cultural realness (Akter et al., 2021). Unless explicitly designed to protect people, the model can propagate the historic inequalities or reinforce culturally damaging norms by performing their optimization (Akter et al., 2023). This is the reason why human control is essential, especially in such hot areas as beauty marketing, recruitment, identity presentation, and child images (Soleimani et al., 2025).

1.4. Motivation for This Study

Whereas the idea of algorithmic bias is an extensively studied topic in terms of technical research and other ethics literature, the topic of cultural blind spots in marketing AI is under-discussed. This chapter fills this gap by presenting a culturally-inspired discussion of marketing AI failures based on 4 separate industries: recruitment, fashion, beauty, and retail. The case of Amazon, Levi, Dove, and H&M is the result of a premeditated attempt to consider the situations when AI intersected directly with the identity, representation, and culturally sensitive environments (Dastin, 2018).

These cases demonstrate how cultural blind spots are not isolated technical issues. Instead, the problems are systemic and based on wider social structures, organizational culture, and data practices (Georgeson, n.d.). This chapter unites the perspectives of AI ethics, cultural studies, marketing theory and frameworks of DEI to illustrate that representational failures are caused by the intersection of technological design and cultural mismatch (Byrne, n.d.).

1.5. Positioning Within Existing Literature

Existing research on artificial intelligence in marketing has predominantly emphasized algorithmic bias, fairness metrics, personalization efficiency, and predictive accuracy within data-driven decision systems. While this body of work has advanced understanding of technical and statistical inequities, it has largely treated bias as a measurable deviation rather than as a culturally embedded phenomenon. By focusing on cultural blind spots rather than technical bias alone, this chapter extends existing AI and marketing literature through a socio-cultural lens, positioning AI-driven marketing failures as outcomes of sociotechnical design choices rather than isolated algorithmic errors.

2. SCOPE AND OBJECTIVES

2.1. Scope of the Study

This chapter is focused on the investigation of the emergence of the cultural blind spots in the AI-based marketing systems and on how it is reflected in the actual organisational contexts. The paper specifically takes into account such dimensions as culture, representations, and ethics of the AI implementation, instead of addressing only technical performance or accuracy measurements (Arsel et al., 2022).

It does not only place AI as a calculating device, it presents it as a socio-technical system that has a direct impact on mostly shaping public narratives, identity representation, and meaning-making in marketing communication.

The range of the analysis to be provided entails the interaction of AI with culturally sensitive content, how algorithmic-driven systems, particularly in the areas of consumption and branding, influence consumer-facing images and messages, and how automated systems perceive and process markers of identity i.e. gender, race, skin tone and body type. These identity markers are central to contemporary debates on inclusion, representation, and equity in marketing practice (Licsandru et al., 2025).

In order to base this analysis based on lived-in corporate situations, the chapter analyses four significant case studies, including Amazon, Levi, Dove, and H&M,

all instances of varying types of cultural mismatch when supplying AI-mediated situations.

2.2. Research Objectives

The first goal of the chapter aims at such a systematic examination of how AI systems replicate culturally insensitive results based on biased, incomplete, or historical set data. This objective responds to concerns raised in marketing research regarding how data-driven optimization can unintentionally reproduce structural inequalities (Mandania et al., 2025).

The second goal is to consider the implications of such culturally destructive outputs on the image of the brands, customer loyalty, and the discussion in society. Since the current consumers put social-responsible representation on the global brands, any AI-related error in culture may quickly turn into a reputational crisis, causing a backlash among social media, pressure groups, and even mainstream media (Sands and Ferraro, 2025). These reputational dynamics are consistent with research highlighting the strategic importance of managerial decisions in sustaining brand strength and trust (Sardashti & Calantone, 2022).

The third aim is to formulate an interpretive prism of between-industrial comparison of cases. One last goal is to use these findings to provide managerial, academic, and social implications. The chapter is dedicated to identifying ways of developing culturally aware AI, advising forms of governing that should be implemented to ensure no representational failure, and promoting the emergence of multidisciplinary solutions that can be used to introduce cultural intelligence in automated marketing systems (van Esch et al., 2024).

2.3. Rationale for the Focus on Cultural Blind Spots

The reason behind the attention to cultural blind spots is the discrepancy between the technical orientation of mainstream AI studies and the cultural requirements of marketing practice. The accessible research on AI bias is focused on fairness, model explainability, or computational diagnostics, where the interpretation of cultural aspects remains a vast unaddressed area (Mariani et al., 2022).

Marketing, on the other hand, is formed by symbolic space which results as a product of identity, history, and socio-cultural norms. Because of this, algorithmic misunderstandings in this domain disturb uneven cultural influence. This chapter thus places a greater focus on cultural blind spots as a specific category of analysis - it needs the theoretical basis of cultural studies, DEI scholarship, and consumer psychology, rather than merely data science. Such an interdisciplinary orientation aligns with contemporary calls for embedding empathy and cultural awareness into managerial and technological decision-making (Licsandru et al., 2025).

The chosen case studies prove the need for such an approach. This research will be justified by the need to construct structures that incorporate cultural intelligence into the AI development process, establish mechanisms to counteract any harmful effects of automated solutions to ensure that the outputs of the automated systems are consistent with the brand values, and reduce the negative consequences of automated marketing in the future.

3. METHODOLOGY / APPROACH

The qualitative inquiry as the methodology approach chosen in this chapter is based on multi-case analysis and reveals how the cultural blind spots are manifested in separate marketing AI settings. Cultural sensitivity, representational meaning, and algorithmic interpretation are complex and socially conditioned phenomena, which is why with a qualitative design, the evaluation of failures can be richer and situation-conditioned and cannot be quantitatively modelled using quantitative tools only (Arsel et al., 2022).

3.1. Research Design

The chapter follows a qualitative, exploratory research design, which is based on the multi-case research since it aims to comprehend the emergence of cultural blind spots in AI-driven marketing systems. Rather, such phenomena demand interpretive richness, felt context, and proximity to narrative, symbolic and cultural aspects of organizational behaviour.

Considering AI in marketing is a system of the socio-technical networks of datasets, workflow, creative process, and brand strategies, the case study approach enables the analysis of the matter in a holistic manner.

3.2. Nature and Source

The chapter is solely based on the secondary data as all four cases considered, such as Amazon, Levi, Dove, and H&M, occurred in the public sphere and produced a great number of records in news platforms, industry sources, literature, and DEI commentary reports, and company press releases. The use of secondary data is suitable, especially in this study since it is a complex, triangulated insight into the incidences without having to gain direct access to proprietary AI models or confidential organisational data (Byrne, n.d.).

Additionally, the secondary data will allow reflecting on the way the general audiences understood these failures and this is crucial to comprehending the cultural aspects of AI-based marketing scandals.

3.3. Case Selection Criteria

The sampling strategy employed to select the cases was purposive, but it was informed by the factor that different types of cultural blind spots in industries should be represented. The initial criterion was that the case was associated with an AI system that directly affected consumer-facing representation, decision-making, or communication-areas where the sensitivity to the culture is extremely important (Kumar et al., 2024). Second, every incident produced a significant amount of public response, so it became feasible to examine the issue of cultural misalignment not solely through the lens of the organisational lens but also through society interpretation and reaction (Shakespeare, 2018).

Third, varying forms of cultural harm are represented in the cases: the case of Amazon reflects gender discrimination in the hiring process; the case of Levi assumes a synthetic representation and authenticity; the case of Dove, advocates beauty-related representational biasness; the case of H&M, perpetrates the lack of contextual interpretation of racially sensitive imagery (Georgeson, n.d.). Such a set of criteria guarantees the sample is rich in terms of analysis and structurally sound.

3.4. Analytical Framework

A framework of analysis is based on the interpretation supported by AI ethics, cultural studies, marketing theory and representational analysis. This is a framework of interaction considering the data practices, algorithmic decision making, organisational structures, symbolic meaning and consumer reception.

As the analysis is based on cultural theory, the ways in which AI systems encode and recreate historical and social narratives implanted in their training data are explained. The correspondence (or disproportion) of the outputs of algorithms with brand purpose, value commitments, and corporate DEI systems is analyzed through the marketing ethics lens (Hermann, 2022).

3.5. Analytical Procedures

The analysis process served as a planned, three-step process. To determine the conceptual view of each event, all the chosen sources were first summarised as one big data segmented by time and summarised as narrative profiles of the cases (Dastin, 2018). Second, it used an open coding method to determine the main concepts in cases, such as data imbalance, representational errors, contextual misinterpretation, algorithmic opacity, public backlash, and governance lapses (Farrington, 2020). Third, the coded data were synthesized into higher-order thematic categories that made it possible to compare the case meaningfully and even integrate them theoretically (Akter et al., 2023).

3.6. Methodological Rigor

Triangulation, reflexivity, transparency, and contextual grounding have been incorporated into the chapter to achieve the methodological rigour. Triangulation was ensured where the array of secondary sources was broad such as journalistic reports, scholarly critiques, corporate messages, and cultural critiques created a multifaceted conceptualization of each case (H&M apologises..., 2018).

3.7. Ethical Considerations

The study is unlikely to cause serious ethical harm from using publicly available data. The creation of the study was keen on ensuring that no harm or misrepresentation is caused. The problems analyzed are systematic and structural instead of blaming individuals as workers or consumers. Such an ethical position coincides with the overall purpose behind writing this chapter: the development of AI in a responsible, culturally aware way, as opposed to fault-finding.

3.8. Limitations of the Methodology

The methodology has specific limitations even though it has some strengths. Using only secondary data implies that the analysis will not identify internal algorithmic parameters, logs of decision-making, or any other proprietary information that could potentially offer a more detailed view of the failures (Burke, 2025). Moreover, the emphasis on high-profile international brands can not fully generalize the results to smaller companies, still, those cases are crucial to the realization of how the issue of cultural misalignment can be expanded with the help of automated systems (Byrne, n.d.).

3.9. Justification for the Methodological Choice

Finally, a qualitative multi-case design is appropriate due to the essence of cultural blind spots as interpretive, contextual, and socio-technical. Detection of

AI misinterpretation of cultural messages cannot be properly analyzed through technical audits but rather, meaning, power, narrative, and representation. This is the methodology that allows doing just that (Chen, 2023).

4. CASE STUDIES OF AI-DRIVEN CULTURAL MISFIRES

The marketing AI cultural blind spots manifest themselves in their most tangible form, the failure in real life- when automated systems are exposed to culture at its most subtle and misunderstand it, ignore it, or make it flat. The case studies are important as they show both algorithmic flaws and organizational suppositions, data biases, and organizational oversights. The AI systems came into contact with culturally loaded contexts in all the four case studies after Amazon, Levi's, Dove and H&M produced the results that rapidly turned into a controversial topic with the public.

The thing that holds all these together is that none of the organizations wanted to cause harm. The cultural mistakes gained indirectly through the choices that dealt with data curation, automation of workflows, and representational logic. Such failures demonstrate the risks posed by AI when implemented without cultural supervision which could subversively affect brand values, public trust, and diversity promises. This is discussed in later subsections.

4.1. Case Study 1: How Algorithmic Learning Enhanced Gender Bias in Recruitment Tool at Amazon: The use of AI in Recruitment

The recruiting Artificial Intelligence project conducted by Amazon represents one of the latest and most popular examples of emerging cultural blind spots with the help of the technology of algorithmic decision-making. The company invented this system first to automate the process of screening the resumes to enable it to offload the human recruiters and enable more efficiency to the hiring pipeline. The tool, however, had a significant assumption, based on the fact that historical hiring data were based on objective indicators of success and not on the gender imbalance that was common in the technology sector (Dastin, 2018). The model was trained on data consisting mostly of applications that were received within a period of ten years, majority of which were provided by men. Such unrepresentative representation was a reflection of the male-dominated aspect of engineering jobs at Amazon and in the technical sector, in general.

The AI was unable to distinguish between the applicants in terms of their gender. The male applicants were more successful, as the AI was programmed to detect the patterns, which are associated with successful applicants. It started filtering down the resumes with references to indicators that identified women, like women professional organizations, or women colleges (Chen, 2023). Also, the language that was linguistically coded as male was preferred in the model which unwillingly was promoting gendered tropes that prevail within workplace culture and professional writing. This way, the AI emulated the biased nature of past hiring processes by considering such distorted trends as an illustration of a stereotypical recruitment process and carrying the skewed trend at large scale.

The cultural blind spot of this case is due to an organizational assumption of information being objective. The developers perceived historic recruiting performance as an innate result of merit and not a product of gender inequality, learned socially (Akter et al., 2022). The failure of the algorithm was not due to a defect in machine learning but is because it was being asked to learn on a dataset that represented structural discrimination. The cultural aspects of gendered labor patterns were not sufficiently considered within the Amazon organization, which led to the creation of an AI based on the intentionally blind implementation of gender-related bias.

In the event when the problem surfaced, the resentment struck swiftly. The coverage of the incident in the media did not only present the case as a technical gateway but a representative of how discrimination against women could be institutionalized through algorithmic hiring (Soleimani et al., 2025). The reputational cost of such a company as Amazon is great, and more so in the discussion about diversity, equity, and fairness in the tech sector. Even though Amazon stressed that the tool could not be applied in real-time decision-making, the symbolic after effects were still present. The event turned into one of the most important in the world of discussion of the shortcomings of AI-assisted recruitment and the danger of uncontrolled automation.

Implications of the strategy were also important. The Amazon case has shown that AI is incapable of fixing systemic injustice without human supervision and culturally informed system design concepts. It highlighted that dataset composition is not more of a technical problem it is a cultural problem. The experiences of this debacle have had an impact on industry-wide distrust of algorithmic employment and have assisted in the effort to ensure that more broadly people are beginning to appreciate that fairness cannot be reverse-engineered into biased historical data (Hermann, 2022).

4.2. Case Study 2: H&M and The History of the Monkey Hoodie Scandal: Automation of Workflow and Lack of Cultural Control

The controversy of H&M appeared when a picture of a black child wearing a hoodie with the phrase, Coolest Monkey in the Jungle was displayed on the site of the company (H&M apologises..., 2018). Even though the term itself may not be so offensive in other contexts, it has a rich racist historical implication when used in reference to the Black people. The episode elicited a lot of criticism and revealed the effects of the process of automating marketing without cultural scrutiny.

Handover H&M had been deploying automated systems to customize the process of product classification and publishing of its content. The aim of these workflows was to speed up the process of uploading new items in the website, diminish man-power, and have a unified digital catalog. But automation unwillingly emphasized speed over cultural sensitivity. The system was not able to acknowledge the racial connotations of the phrase on the appearance of the child i.e. the image went online without causing internal red flags or human consideration (5 Ways H&M Is Using AI, n.d.).

The cultural blind spot in this case was especially dramatic. The AI could not have comprehended the socio-historical value of racial slurs and stereotypes. It approached the concept of monkey as a neutral word and not a concept that is deeply entrenched in racist stereotypes (Byrne, n.d.). The system was not given the power to contextualise meaning in the absence of humans, and as a result, encountered failure in the representational aspect with universal ramifications.

People's reaction was swift and popular. The image was seen as racially insensitive and received protests in various countries by consumers, activists, and celebrities (Shakespeare, 2018). The overreaction was not only an indication of how problematic the picture was but an assumption that the global brand was rather careless in its functioning.

As a reaction, H&M deleted the photograph, sent official apologies, and hired a Global Diversity Leader, ensuring greater effectiveness of cultural due diligence (Staff, 2018). Such measures emphasized the development of the necessity to implement cultural expertise in technology in the workflow, especially in the case of the brands with a global audience.

The H&M case highlights the risks of the over-automated content pipelines. Once the culturally sensitive decisions are given to an AI system, which does not use the information of contextual intelligence, there is a high probability that the negative cultural harm can be magnified exponentially. The H&M lesson is obvious and can be summarized as the fact that no automation is able to replace human cultural judgment, particularly in a situation of global marketing, where historical context and representational ethics are essential (Soleimani et al., 2025).

4.3. Case Study 3: Dove and the Algorithmic Reinforcement of Beauty Norms: Colorism, Branding, and AI Misalignment

This is because the case of Dove makes it harder to assume that only technologically unsophisticated or unpurposeful brands will be left in the cultural blind spots. With an already evident history of advocating for inclusive beauty standards, Dove, the company of the so-called Real Beauty, has one decade after another to assert itself as such. Although such a powerful brand image, the company received serious reproach when AI-enabled image selection and optimization applications started to create images that solidified Eurocentric beauty standards (Georgeson, n.d.). The incident highlighted how even those brands professing to be inclusive fail, unwillingly, to do cultural harm when they heavily use algorithmic systems.

The automated technology that Dove incorporated into its marketing activities was aimed at maximizing the image performance on the digital platform. Nonetheless, since there were an uneven number of images with a lighter skin color and typical Western facial expressions, AI systems regularly displayed them and ranked them higher (Farrington, 2020). Consequently, the content flow has been distorted in favor of one-sided aesthetic values which negate Dove being diverse as they claimed.

The cultural blindness of the Dove system was the belief that artificial selection of assets would resonate with brand values on its own because of the use of AI. The company viewed AI as a strengthening tool of operations, rather than as a potentially influencing tool of cultural meaning. Such laxity resulted in the historically integrated prejudices of colorists in visual information impacting brand production. It was not, however, only a technical glitch, but a disjuncture between algorithmic logic and brand purpose (Arsel et al., 2022).

The reaction of the people was formed by the self positioning of Dove as a socially minded brand. Customers were dissatisfied to be so cheated by a company that promoted inclusive beauty that its automated processes continued to reinforce negative representational norms (Sands and Ferraro, 2025). The conflict existing between the corporate purpose marketing and the technological action that unintentionally subverts such marketing was brought to light by the critics.

Dove now responded by reassessing their dataset make up, increasing to a bigger visual library-representing a variety of skin tones and body biometries- and reinforcing their human-in-the-loop checks and balances. These positive measures solidified the need to reconcile algorithmic procedures and ethical standards in brands, particularly in culturally consequential industries (Georgeson, n.d.).

The Dove case shows how any well-intentioned brand should be sensitive to the culture implications of AI. Beauty marketing especially has been in the setting of historically charged contexts that are associated with race, colonialism and social hierarchies. AIs are not pre-coded to learn these histories, and left uncontrolled, they have the potential to replicate exclusionary norms that brands have been working to undo (Akter et al., 2023).

4.4. Case Study 4: Levi's Synthetic Diversity: The Problem of Representational Authenticity in AI-Generated Models

The fact that AI-generated models are adopted by Levi is one more but as significant a manifestation of cultural blind spot as traditional one based on representational ethics, as opposed to direct discrimination. In 2023, Levi announced its plans to create AI-generated avatars to better represent its products on its online platforms, believing that artificial models might be able to display its products over a wider spectrum of skin tones, body shapes and demographic characteristics (Burke, 2025). This effort was the work of the company that presented it as a move towards inclusion since it provides a more personalized digital experience to customers during the process of shopping.

However, the rationale of the project indicated a basic misconception of the meaning of authentic representation to the consumer, particularly fashion advertising. Although the AI could be used to generate visually diverse models, they were algorithmic codes generated using image data as composite images and not real persons with lived identity (Hartmann et al., 2025). That is, the diversity was not in-depth. The AI-created models did not feature the cultural discourses, socioeconomic facts, and emotive elements in the real human expression.

The cultural blind spot here was not that Levi intended to omit the real models but it just thought that diversity can be attained simply by having visual differences. Authentic representation does not only have the visual aspects of how a model looks but it is a question of whose voices, bodies and identities are involved in the production process. Representation as a platform of visibility and as an economic opportunity were ignored by the use of synthetic models (Arsel et al., 2022). Through the use of AI, Levi was creating a signal that different communities could be easily replicated in digital form instead of being researched in a significant way.

There was a swift and sharp reaction from people. Critics claimed that the brand practiced performative inclusion as AI-generated diversity did not require hiring actual models who could be benefiting economically and seen (van Esch et al., 2024). This change was seen as the shift in favor of efficiency and cost cutting rather than moral representation. The observers pointed out that the development of synthetic surrogacy to the underrepresented identity may continue the same exclusion that the DEI initiatives seek to address. This standpoint interpreted the effort by Levi as a technology cut-off that was counterproductive to their goals.

Levi replied and explained that the models created by AI systems were intended to complement human models and not to replace them. Regardless of this explanation, the reputational effect remained due to the revelation of a latent disconnection between the DEI communications of the brand and its digital innovation policy. The case brought up more general questions concerning how the representation should be considered by the brands in the age of generative AI. It showed that cultural factors cannot be added as an external factor to technological integration, particularly in areas where AI collides with sensitive issues such as body image, ethnicity, and identity.

In the end, this case can enter into more important debates concerning the morality of synthetic representation. It shows how AI may inadvertently render identities insignificant when organizations consider cultural representation as a visual element instead of an experience. Levi had a point: there is no way the representation can be automated and lose its authenticity and meaning (Hermann & Puntoni, 2025).

5. ANALYSIS AND THEMATIC CONNECTIONS

The cultural blindness aspect of AI-based marketing is systematic and not accidental. The four case studies (Amazon, Levi, dove and H&M) all reveal the intersection of the three aspects (the algorithmic design, organizational behaviour, and representational dynamics) to give culturally-insensitive results. The themes below summarise the patterns prevalent throughout the cases and demonstrate how the structural factors cause AI-based cultural failures.

5.1. Theme 1: Data Bias and Historically Skewed Inputs

In all four cases, the basis of cultural blind spots was data bias, which highlights the inequalities that the AI systems absorb into the data sets that they have been trained on. The Amazon recruitment tool is a clear illustration of how biased datasets may be critical at different times in history and cause discrimination. The model was trained mainly on resumes submitted by men, and this reflected systemic gender imbalances and gave them as the signs of competence (Dastin, 2018). This caused a positive feedback where the algorithm took as a success indicator the patterns that were male coded. The synthetic diversity system developed by Levi also depended on the datasets that represented limited aesthetic standards, which made the AI produce the avatars that do not have the depth, complexity, and the level of authenticity that the real-life human identities possess (Burke, 2025). The dataset used in the visual pipeline at Dove gave results that favored Eurocentric beauty standards, which were implicitly raised (Farrington, 2020). The automated content publishing in H&M also was based on automated procedures in classifications, which could not differentiate between racially charged or neutral words (Byrne, n.d.).

Due to the lack of culturally equalized datasets, there are representational blind spots (especially in areas where identity and symbolism have a social dimension). However, due to the growing attention of scholars to the problem, AI systems mirror the existing social hierarchies when the datasets were built around the majority narrative or do not apply to minority groups (Akter et al., 2022). This interaction is the guarantee that does not make cultural harm accidental but presumes its perspective structure. Such a bias in data also becomes a technical and cultural problem, determining the way AI perceives human identity and the norms it replicates on its huge scale (Chen, 2023).

5.2. Theme 2: Contextual Blindness and the Limits of Algorithmic Meaning-Making

The inability of AI to perceive meaning, history, and cultural nuances is known as lack of understanding of context, and it occurred in each of the four cases. AIs are really good at pattern processing but are unable to gain the socio-historical foundation that helps comprehend why this or that image, word, or association is harmless. The case of H&M shows that it has this limitation: monkey as a racial slur has a long history of being used against Black people, and the algorithm did not see the offensiveness of the text when it was combined with an image of a Black child (H&M apologises..., 2018). It was syntactic, not cultural processing of the phrase. On the same note, the automated image selection option did not acknowledge that the tendency of prioritizing lighter skin tones by Dove strengthened old, colonial, and racial hierarchies, which existed before the emergence of that system (Georgeson, n.d.). The AI used in hiring at Amazon did not contextualize gendered resume indicators, and identified that these were unfavourable correlations only because they were underrepresented in the training data (Soleimani et al., 2025). The model system in which Levi worked synthesized culture identity to mirrors of the skin-color without understanding the socio-political meaning of actual representation (Arsel et al., 2022).

The work of AI systems is based on correlation, but not interpretation. Their lack of knowledge is what makes them fail to comprehend why stereotypes are bad or how imagery can intersect with lived experience. They are deprived of the socio-cultural literacy that human beings attain due to their social experience, education and historical consciousness. Therefore, contextually blind algorithms have escalated harm exactly due to their approach of treating high-stakes aspects of identity such as race, gender, skin tone as a statistical variable without a symbolic meaning (Hermann, 2022). This necessitates highly incorporated human supervision in marketing situations where cultural clues are multifield and extremely decodic.

5.3. Theme 3: Representational Harm, Identity Distortion, and Brand Inconsistency

One of the themes that come out in the cases is representational harm- distortion, omission, or false portrayal of the marginalized identities. The synthetic avatars of Levi show that the idea of representation may become shallow when diversity is created by AI that generates fake bodies and voices without involving actual bodies and voices (Burke, 2025). Synthetic representation can be made visually variant, however, such representation is not authentic and might reduce the identity to algorithmic aesthetics. The case practitioners Dove, a beauty product showing a contrasting aspect of representational harm is the way automated image optimization systems were used to perpetuate the kind of limited beauty ideals that had been against the purpose-driven marketing after which the brand had operated (Farrington, 2020). When representation supports the kind of values that a brand prides itself on then it is the worst kind of representation because it enhances consumer disillusionment as there is no consistency.

The algorithmic hiring processes invented by Amazon caused representational harm by exclusion- the women were being devalued by an algorithm, which was eager to internalize patriarchal hiring patterns and operationalize the identified changes as evidence of merit (Dastin, 2018). The case of H&M depicts representational harm in the form of a contextual mismatch- automated workflows could not identify that the combination of an offensive phrase with the image of a child of the Black racial background reproduced demeaning discourses that were informed by racist conventions (Byrne, n.d.). The notions of power, identity, and cultural legitimacy cannot be considered outside of representation in a marketing context. By botching representation, AI does not only distort the identity but also rewrites the story of the people so as to promote inequality (Akter et al., 2023).

5.4. Theme 4: Organisational Blind Spots and Homogeneous Design Cultures

Outside of technical constraints, the organisational blind spots emerging when these failures happen include cultural assumptions, homogeneity of the teams, and gaps in governance that influence the process of designing and implementing AI systems. As the example of Amazon demonstrates, developers did not consider the problem of gender bias since their team was underinsufficient in terms of gender variety and cultural risk level (Chen, 2023). The failure by Levi to have an accurate understanding of synthetic diversity was an organisational lack of familiarity with the cultural worth of genuine representation and socio-economic reality of marginalized creative labour (van Esch et al., 2024). The issue of misalignment in Dove was in part due to excessive use of automation in a brand that is founded on a purpose-based promise and indicates a lack of communication between technical teams and brand custodians (Georgeson, n.d.). The negligence by H&M was a result of workflow culture that focused on speed and efficiency over cultural scrutiny that illustrates how organisational values inform technical decision-making (Shakespeare, 2018).

These trends echo bigger critiques in that homogeneous AI development teams tend to produce blind spots, or the lack of cultural literacy of the organisational cultures can make them become structural (Arsel et al., 2022). It highlights the fact that the failures of AI cannot be explained only by the ineffective algorithms. They indicate organisational flaws that are so systemic that they enable cultural misinterpretation to pass unnoticed in a design, testing, and deployment (Hermann, 2022).

5.5. Theme 5: Automation Without Oversight and the Escalation of Cultural Risk

Both cases are proof of consequences of deploying automated systems without proper human control. Automation increases efficiency, but it is also increasing the rate and the extent to which mistakes spread. In H&M, insensitive material would be published without a human-crafted control of other sensitive content because of automated publishing (H&M apologises..., 2018). Biased images were exaggerated in automated optimization pipelines of Dove, as algorithms were allowed to make aesthetic choices with no adequate representational criteria (Farrington, 2020). By using AI-developed models, Levi has entirely avoided the process of human decision making in the area of representation, and instead, has been able to create a vulnerability to reputation through a technological compromise (Burke, 2025). The algorithm used by Amazon worked on its own during long durations before internal staff appreciated the discrimination tendencies it generated (Soleimani et al., 2025).

This theme exposes the fact that automation is not a culturally neutral phenomenon-it amplifies organisational values and blind spots. The absence of regulations to check the AI systems results in the system turning into an optimization logic as opposed to being influenced by ethical factors. In many instances, according to the commentary by scholars, efficiency-first designs of AI tend to marginalize concerns of fairness, representation, and inclusion (Hermann and Puntoni, 2025). To forego the risk of culture, organizations need to integrate governance through human-in-the-loop, cultural gateways, and DEI-based review into artificial intelligence processes. Ethical and cultural safety can never be outdone by effectiveness.

5.6. Theme 6: Reputational Risk, Public Outrage, and Cultural Accountability

All four examples show how quickly cultural mistakes can become reputational crises. In a world characterized by constantly networked digital cultures, audiences react to cultural violence quickly and in unison. The algorithm of Amazon was instrumental in turning into a representation of gender discrimination within the tech industry (Dastin, 2018). The initiative of Levi was condemned as play-acted and empty (Burke, 2025). Dove came out to disappointment by the public since the AI outputs went against its claim of being an inclusive brand (Sands and Ferraro, 2025). The incident by H&M sparked worldwide anger and demonstrations, and the brand perception would change permanently (Shakespeare, 2018).

Misalignment in the AI because of cultural differences is not seen as a technical issue but rather as the expression of the values of a brand. This frame of narrative builds the pressure on the cultural responsibility of AI implementation. Beyond the targeted message the brand promises, they are becoming responsible for the hidden results that their algorithmic systems cause. This increases the necessity of cultural cognizant AI governance because reputational harm associated with culturally inappropriate outputs may be lasting longer than technical remedies (Hermann, 2022).

5.7. Theme 7: Need for Cultural Governance and Frameworks for AI Sensitivity

The cross-case thematic analysis highlights the need to have cultural governance, i.e., organizational designs, policies, and processes of review that are needed to promote cultural safety in AI systems. The brands need to embed cultural intelligence at each level of AI development: datasets to work with, model training, performance efficacy, workflow automation, creative self-performing, and post-deployment monitoring (Akter et al., 2021). The oversight of DEI needs to be structured and not reactive and allow the assessment of representational risks as they persist.

Culturally tagged datasets, identity to metadata, ethics boards, localization pipelines, and interdisciplinary evaluation teams are also seen as critical such that cultural risk can be reduced (van Esch et al., 2024). The absence of these structures will keep the AI systems emulating the blind points of the institutions that implement them (Hermann and Puntoni, 2025).

5.8. Synthesis and Implications

Overall, the thematic analysis demonstrates that cultural blind spots in the realm of marketing AI emerge because of the intersection of technical restrictions, organizational frameworks, representational presuppositions, and the disparities of the past. They are not singular incidents but welcome results of rolling out culturally blind AI installations in situations that place great significance on identity and symbolism (Arsel et al., 2022). The examples once again confirm that AI does not process culture on its own- cultural literacy needs to be purposefully implemented into AI governing systems. In the absence of such integration, AI will produce results that promote inequality, damage brand-image, and disrupt cultural legitimacy of corporate communication (Hermann, 2022).

6. EXPECTED CONTRIBUTIONS

This chapter is the synthesis of the analytical insights that were developed in the chapter, and it can be expressed as contributing to the theoretical understanding, practice, society and policy in the broader range. The section starts shifting the gears to conceptualization by determining the implication of these findings to the various stakeholder groups. Viewing such contributions altogether, the chapter proves that the problem of cultural blind spots is much bigger than an individual brand miscalculation and has a considerable applicability to the future of responsible AI design, marketing regulation, and cultural integrity in automated digital spaces.

Beyond its theoretical contributions, this chapter directly addresses managerial, organizational, and policy challenges arising from the deployment of AI in culturally sensitive marketing contexts. By framing cultural blind spots as predictable outcomes of organizational and design choices, the chapter provides actionable insights for marketing managers, AI governance teams, and policymakers seeking to align technological innovation with cultural accountability, ethical branding, and long-term trust in multicultural markets.

6.1. Theoretical Contributions

6.1.1. Expanding the Concept of Cultural Blind Spots in AI

Theoretically, this chapter introduces the concept of cultural blind spots as a specific analytical category in AI and marketing research. Through the examples of Amazon, Levi, Dove, and H&M, this chapter proves that failure of AI can happen even when algorithms do not exhibit a technical error but still encounter a cultural misinterpretation (Hermann, 2022).

6.1.2. Distinguishing Algorithmic Precision from Cultural Precision

The other theoretical input is made by distinguishing between algorithmic precision and cultural precision. Cultural accuracy, in its turn, involves the responsiveness to a socio-historical sense of identity markers (gender, race, skin tone, language, etc.) (Akter et al., 2022). This difference is taking AI theory forward since it demonstrates that the issue of cultural misalignment is neither a performance failure nor a meaning-making failure.

6.1.3. A Multi-Layered Framework for Understanding Cultural Misalignment

The chapter further adds a combined theoretical approach to cultural misalignment that describes the situation using five dimensions, which include data imbalance, contextual blindness, representational harm, organisational blind spots, and governance gaps (Arsel et al., 2022).

6.2. Methodological Contributions

6.2.1. Validating Multi-Case Comparative Analysis for AI Ethics

This chapter provides value to multi-case comparative analysis, which is essential to the study of AI ethics, methodologically. Tthe analysis of four different cases is provided, and a common structural pattern in the industries of HR, fashion, beauty, and retail is identified (Dastin, 2018).

6.2.2. Establishing the Role of Secondary Data in Cultural AI Research

The chapter supports the methodological justification of applying to secondary data, through investigative journalism, corporate statements, academic commentary, and cultural commentary, as a trustworthy evidence base of analyzing AI controversies.

6.3. Managerial and Industry Contributions

6.3.1. Demonstrating the Operational Risks of Culturally Uninformed AI

One of the most significant managerial contributions of this chapter lies in its demonstration of the operational risks associated with culturally uninformed AI systems. Across the four cases examined, it becomes evident that automated marketing and decision-making systems can directly conflict with stated brand values, damage organizational reputation, and erode consumer trust when cultural meaning and symbolic context are not adequately considered (Sands and Ferraro, 2025). For practitioners, this highlights the need to treat AI adoption as a strategic and value-laden process rather than a neutral technological upgrade.

6.3.2. Pathways for Integrating Cultural Oversight in AI Workflows

The chapter also provides managers with clear pathways for integrating cultural oversight into AI-driven workflows. The Amazon case underscores the importance of conducting cultural and historical audits of training datasets prior to model deployment, particularly in sensitive domains such as recruitment. Similarly, the Dove case illustrates the critical importance of aligning AI optimization logic with brand purpose, especially when algorithms are used to shape visual representation and identity-related messaging.

6.3.3. Strengthening Cross-Functional Collaboration in AI Governance

Another key managerial contribution of this chapter is its emphasis on cross-functional collaboration in AI governance. The cases reveal that cultural failures often emerge when AI systems are developed and deployed in isolation, without the involvement of DEI specialists, brand managers, cultural strategists, or creative professionals. By extending AI governance beyond engineering teams to include diverse organizational stakeholders, the chapter advances managerial understanding of how culturally sensitive AI systems can be developed and sustained within complex organizational environments.

6.4. Societal, Ethical, and Policy Contributions

6.4.1. Societal Contributions: Visibility, Representation, and Harm Prevention

On the societal level, the chapter can be valuable in that it presents how the outputs of AI-driven marketing structure affect the discourse among the people of being an individual, being beautiful, being a professional and being a part of the society. The algorithm of Amazon strengthened gender disparity in the workforce; Levi threatened to demote real diversity to algorithm creation; Dove threatened to further propagate colorism; and H&M replicated racist identifications (Arsel et al., 2022).

6.4.2. Ethical Contributions: Embedding Cultural Accountability in AI

The idea of responsible AI is extended in the chapter, turning to cultural accountability on an ethical level. In contrast to the conventional systems of fairness, cultural accountability compels the enterprises to pay attention to how the results of AI use shape the identity narratives and symbolic representation (Hermann, 2022). The subsection is an addition to the ethical marketing AI literature that promotes the establishment of culturally informed oversight boards, various training datasets, and human-in-the-loop review systems (Hermann and Puntoni, 2025).

6.4.3. Policy Contributions: Addressing Regulatory Gaps in Representational Harm

In addition to its theoretical and managerial implications, this chapter contributes to policy discussions surrounding the governance of AI-driven marketing systems. Existing regulatory frameworks addressing artificial intelligence primarily focus on issues of data privacy, transparency, accountability, and discrimination. While these dimensions are essential, they often fail to adequately address cultural misalignment and representational harm arising from AI-generated marketing content.

This need is particularly relevant in multicultural and globalized marketing environments, where automated systems increasingly mediate identity, representation, and symbolic meaning across diverse consumer segments (Tarnanidis et al., 2026). This includes the introduction of representational audits for AI systems used in marketing and advertising, particularly those involved in identity-sensitive domains such as recruitment, beauty representation, fashion imagery, and consumer profiling.

6.5. Overall Significance

Altogether, the works discussed in this chapter promote the significance of the cultural intelligence incorporation to all levels of AI construction, and marketing behavior. The theoretical implications indicate that cultural blind spots are structural and not casual, whereas the methodological considerations encourage methodologies that have the power to test these complexities in all their delicate ways. Working as a manager, the results also show the acuteness of the necessity to develop cross-functional governance models according to which technological innovation is compatible with cultural accountability, authenticity, and representational equity. All these pieces of evidence point to the fact that culturally informed AI is not only an ethical ideal but also a strategic, academic, and societal requirement that will either determine the credibility, inclusivity and legitimacy of future marketing ecosystems.

7. CONCLUSION

The discussion in the chapters has shown that the cultural blind spots in marketing AI are not neither accidental nor random, on the contrary, it is a structural weakness inherent to the sociotechnical systems, within which AI is created, trained, deployed, and regulated. These four case studies; that infused gendered recruitment tool by Amazon, reinforcement of colorist beauty ideals by Dove, and an automated printing event by H&M, show that AI-based cultural failures are created when organisations ignore interpretive, representational and socio-historical aspects of identity.

They are not merely instances of biased output and malfunctioning algorithms, but they portray more profound conflicts between computational rationality and cultural sense. AI systems do not exist in the vacuums. The moment these institutional priorities overshadow cultural awareness, AI is only augmenting the same inequalities and symbolic harms that the brands tend to be opposed to (Hermann, 2022).

One of the key lessons that can be learnt about the chapter is that datasets which are believed to be neutral sources of information are actually historical artefacts that are conditioned by the unequal state of social relations. The system at Amazon internalized decades of the technological industry dominated by men and interpreted this imbalance as a sign of competence instead of trying to consider it as a sign of structural discrimination (Dastin, 2018). The algorithm used by Dove enhanced lighter-skinned visuals given that the base data was skewed or biased to the Euro-centric ideals of beauty in the commercial advertising ecosystem (Farrington, 2020).

The generative models of Levi used simulations of diversity that relied on the incomplete cues of representations and left out the lived, bodily experiences out of which cultural identity is composed of (Burke, 2025).

A different important lesson is associated with the interpretation of incompetency in AI technologies. AI is good in defining statistical tendencies, but cannot perceive historical trauma, marginalization, identity politics or emotional meaning of representation. This tool used by Amazon was not attempting to discriminate on women, it was statistically true in a biased historical trend. The optimization algorithm used by Dove was not trying to encourage lighter skin tones, it was merely making predictions on the most engaged datasets as defined historically.

The system in H&M did not decide to post racially offensive imagery, it was not culturally literate to notice any harmful correlation. It is the interpretative weaknesses of AI that demand organizations to realize that human supervision is not a choice but an essential basis. This distinction underscores why cultural intelligence and empathy-based evaluation cannot be automated and must remain embedded within human oversight mechanisms guiding AI deployment (Licsandru et al., 2025).

In all the four cases, overlooked issues inside the company contributed greatly towards facilitating these failures. Both brands demonstrated some level of overconfidence in automation where they think that the development of technology cannot be a neutral culture. H&M also enabled automated workflows to operate without a cultural inspection and institutions focused on efficiency in operations more than on cultural sensitivity. The use of automated visual optimization by the company Dove demonstrated that there was a discontinuity between the brand purpose and the technology processes in the company, which showed a division among the organizational governance structures.

These deficiencies of the organization help to understand that cultural consciousness of AI is not the process of redressing data, but it is the restructuring of the functioning of institutions, internal competences, and control systems. This finding resonates with managerial research emphasizing that organizational incentives, governance structures, and leadership priorities strongly influence how brand values are operationalized through technology (Sardashti & Calantone, 2022).

Another important aspect of AI-related cultural missteps shown in the chapter is that their consequences have a high reputational cost. The tool created by Amazon developed into a brand symbol of the gender disparity in technology, compromising the public faith in the algorithms in hiring. The move by Levi was criticized as creating a representation as an aesthetic variable, which has led to strengthening arguments that performative diversity is real. The incident experienced by H&M caused protests around the world and the changes in the company became operational and governance-related (Shakespeare, 2018).

There is no such thing as AI-related cultural failure in the age of digital transparency and a globally mobilized social domain, which, despite the operational merits of automation, will cause reputational losses over a long period of time.

On a larger scale, the chapter claims that the idea of culturally aware AI should be perceived as a technical and moral requirement. Companies have to move beyond considering AI governance as a technical compliance matter and start to see it as a cultural duty. To exercise effective AIs governance, the brands should take into consideration the fact that they are not just players in the market but representatives of the culture. This shift aligns with emerging perspectives in diversity- and inclusion-driven marketing, which position brands as cultural actors responsible for shaping inclusive narratives within automated digital ecosystems (Tarnanidis et al., 2026).

The chapter also highlights that future research is required with the aim of increasing the conceptual vocabulary around cultural blind spots in AI. Policy frameworks addressing representational harm as a regulatory issue are also necessary where the organizations have to follow the cultural accountability standards rather than just transparency and privacy standards.

Finally, the conclusion restates that there is nothing like a culturally sensitive AI, but it is the cornerstone of the validity of future marketing ecosystems. Since it is becoming common that brands are delegating creative, operational and representational processes, and representing its brand, to automated means, it needs to develop powerful systems capable of cultural management. The four cases analyzed in this chapter demonstrate that cultural blind spots are predictable and preventable and structural based. It is only under such a circumstance that AI-supported marketing can be carried out in a responsible, inclusive, and ethical manner in an ever more automated world.

REFERENCES

Akter, S., Dwivedi, Y. K., Biswas, K., Michael, K., Bandara, R. J., & Sajib, S. (2021). Addressing algorithmic bias in AI-driven customer management. *Journal of Global Information Management, 29*(6), 27–45. DOI: 10.4018/JGIM.20211101.oa3

Akter, S., Dwivedi, Y. K., Sajib, S., Biswas, K., Bandara, R. J., & Michael, K. (2022). Algorithmic bias in machine-learning-based marketing models. *Journal of Business Research, 144*, 201–216. DOI: 10.1016/j.jbusres.2022.01.083

Akter, S., Sultana, S., Mariani, M., Wamba, S. F., Spanaki, K., & Dwivedi, Y. K. (2023). Advancing algorithmic bias management capabilities in AI-driven marketing analytics research. *Industrial Marketing Management, 114*, 243–261. DOI: 10.1016/j.indmarman.2023.08.013

Ali, M., Sapiezynski, P., Bogen, M., Korolova, A., Mislove, A., & Rieke, A. (2019). Discrimination through optimization: How Facebook's ad delivery can lead to biased outcomes. Proceedings of the ACM on Human-Computer Interaction, 3(CSCW). https://doi.org/DOI: 10.1145/3359301

Arsel, Z., Crockett, D., & Scott, M. L. (2022). Diversity, equity, and inclusion (DEI) in consumer research: A curation and research agenda. *The Journal of Consumer Research, 48*(5), 920–933. DOI: 10.1093/jcr/ucab057

Burke, T. (2025, April 2). What's the biggest AI blind spot in advertising today? AI Digital. https://www.aidigital.com/blog/biggest-ai-blind-spot-in-advertising

Byrne, C. (n.d.). The H&M marketing controversy. Stockton University. https://stockton.edu/diversity-inclusion/h-and-m-marketing-controversy.html

Chen, Z. (2023). Ethics and discrimination in artificial-intelligence-enabled recruitment practices. *Humanities & Social Sciences Communications, 10*(1), 567. DOI: 10.1057/s41599-023-02079-x

Dastin, J. (2018, October 11). Amazon scraps secret AI recruiting tool that showed bias against women. Reuters. https://www.reuters.com/article/world/insight-amazon-scraps-secret-ai-recruiting-tool-that-showed-bias-against-women-idUSKCN1MK0AG/

De Bruyn, A., Viswanathan, V., Beh, Y. S., Brock, J. K.-U., & von Wangenheim, F. (2020). Artificial intelligence and marketing: Pitfalls and opportunities. *International Journal of Research in Marketing, 51*, 91–105. DOI: 10.1016/j.intmar.2020.04.007

Dove apologises for "racist" Facebook advertising campaign. (2017, October 8). BBC News. https://www.bbc.com/news/newsbeat-41542818

Farrington, S. (2020). A case study on Black Twitter's reactions to the framing of Blacks in Dove's 2017 Facebook advertisement (Master's thesis). University of South Florida. https://digitalcommons.usf.edu/etd/8446

Georgeson, T. (n.d.). Dove's "Real Beauty" campaign: A critical analysis. Syracuse University Honors Theses. https://surface.syr.edu/honors_capstone/1271

Hartmann, J., Exner, Y., & Domdey, S. (2025). The power of generative marketing: Can generative AI create superhuman visual content? *International Journal of Research in Marketing*, *42*(1), 13–31. DOI: 10.1016/j.ijresmar.2024.09.002

Hermann, E. (2022). Leveraging artificial intelligence in marketing for social good: An ethical perspective. *Journal of Business Ethics*, *179*(1), 43–61. DOI: 10.1007/s10551-021-04843-y

Hermann, E., & Puntoni, S. (2025). Generative AI in marketing and principles for ethical design. *Journal of Public Policy & Marketing*, *44*(3), 332–349. DOI: 10.1177/07439156241309874

H&M apologises over image of Black child in "monkey" hoodie. (2018, January 8). The Guardian. https://www.theguardian.com/fashion/2018/jan/08/h-and-m-apologises-over-image-of-black-child-in-monkey-hoodie

Kumar, V., Ashraf, A. R., & Nadeem, W. (2024). AI-powered marketing: What, where, and how? *International Journal of Information Management*, *77*, 102783. DOI: 10.1016/j.ijinfomgt.2024.102783

Licsandru, T. C., Mari, C., Kipnis, E., Galalae, C., Johnson, E., Cross, S. N. N., Cui, C. C., Kearney, S., Martín Ruiz, V., Vorster Larsen, L., & Yoruk, I. (2025). Integrating diversity, equity and inclusion in management education: An empathy framework. *British Journal of Management*. Advance online publication. DOI: 10.1111/1467-8551.70008

Mandania, R., Cadogan, J., Liu, J., & Kazmi, N. (2025). Optimizing promotional campaigns to maximize customer lifetime value: A dynamic learning approach. *Journal of Service Research*. Advance online publication. DOI: 10.1177/10946705251365524

Mariani, M. M., Perez-Vega, R., & Wirtz, J. (2022). AI in marketing, consumer research, and psychology: A systematic review. *Psychology and Marketing*, *39*(4), 755–776. DOI: 10.1002/mar.21619

Sands, S., & Ferraro, C. (2025). DEI rollbacks: Consequences and considerations for brand managers. *Business Horizons*. Advance online publication. DOI: 10.1016/j.bushor.2025.02.010

Sardashti, H., & Calantone, R. J. (2022). Does equity-based compensation motivate executives to build strong brands? *Journal of Marketing Management*, *38*(13–14), 1433–1460. DOI: 10.1080/0267257X.2022.2041068

Sebestyén, M. (2025). Focal points and blind spots of human-centered AI. *Humanities & Social Sciences Communications*, *12*(1), 564. DOI: 10.1057/s41599-025-04814-y

Shakespeare, S. (2018, January 17). H&M perception holds up in the UK after controversy—but dips in the US. YouGov. https://yougov.co.uk/politics/articles/20069-hm-perception-holds-uk-after-controversy

Soleimani, M., Intezari, A., Arrowsmith, J., Pauleen, D. J., & Taskin, N. (2025). Reducing AI bias in recruitment and selection: An integrative approach. *International Journal of Human Resource Management*, *36*(14), 2480–2515. DOI: 10.1080/09585192.2025.2480617

Staff, S. (2018, January 18). H&M appoints global diversity leader after "monkey in the jungle" controversy. NDTV. https://www.ndtv.com/lifestyle/h-m-appoints-global-diversity-leader-after-monkey-in-the-jungle-controversy-1801656

Tarnanidis, T., Manda, V. K., Sousa, B. B., Vlachopoulou, M., & Papachristou, E. (2026). Marketing complexity of smart consumer products to global millennial segments. In Tarnanidis, T., Sousa, B., Vlachopoulou, M., Papachristou, E., & Manda, V. K. (Eds.), *Diversity and inclusion-driven marketing for multicultural marketplaces* (pp. 1–16). IGI Global Scientific Publishing., DOI: 10.4018/979-8-3373-2111-0.ch001

Tarnanidis, T., Sousa, B., Vlachopoulou, M., Papachristou, E., & Kittu Manda, V. (Eds.). (2026). *Diversity and inclusion-driven marketing for multicultural marketplaces*. IGI Global Scientific Publishing., DOI: 10.4018/979-8-3373-2111-0

van Esch, P., & Cui, Y. (Gina), & Heilgenberg, K. (2024). Using AI to implement DEI into marketing: The CONSIDER framework. *Australasian Marketing Journal*, *32*(3), 250–262. DOI: 10.1177/14413582241244504

5 ways H&M is using AI. (n.d.). Digital Defynd. https://digitaldefynd.com/IQ/hm-using-ai-case-study/

KEY TERMS AND DEFINITIONS

Algorithmic Bias: Systematic and repeatable distortions in artificial intelligence systems that arise from biased data, model assumptions, or optimization objectives, leading to unfair or exclusionary outcomes.

Cultural Blind Spots: The inability of AI systems to recognize, interpret, or appropriately respond to cultural meaning, symbolic context, and historically rooted identity markers in marketing communication.

Human-in-the-Loop: A governance approach in which human judgment and oversight are integrated into AI decision-making processes, particularly in culturally sensitive or high-impact applications.

Representational Harm: Symbolic or identity-related damage caused when AI systems misrepresent, erase, stereotype, or homogenize individuals or social groups through automated content or decisions.

Sociotechnical Systems: Interconnected systems in which technological components, organizational structures, social norms, and cultural values jointly shape outcomes produced by artificial intelligence.

Synthetic Representation: The use of AI-generated images or models to simulate human diversity, often raising ethical concerns related to authenticity, inclusion, and the displacement of real lived identities.

Chapter 7
Customer Targeting in Digital Marketing Through AI-Powered Personalization for Market Differentiation

Neeraj Kumar Vats
https://orcid.org/0009-0006-4066-2596
Maharishi Markandeshwar University, India

ABSTRACT

AI-based customization technology enables business operations to develop unique market positions which results in new marketplace offerings. Artificial intelligence technologies on platforms let businesses deliver customized sessions to their individual customers through advanced data processing and machine learning systems. Real-time data processing enables individual users to get precise solutions through service-based goods that integrate advanced user segmentation methods. The ongoing commercial success of businesses depends on successful customer demand forecasting through personalized solutions that result in heightened performance and better customer retention. The delivery of tailored customer interactions through AI technology provides businesses with two essential benefits which support their development of unique market leadership above competitive offerings. The ability of online businesses to identify current customer behavior patterns becomes essential for sustained success as an e-commerce service because it creates enduring market benefits in the industry.

DOI: 10.4018/979-8-3373-6731-6.ch007

1. INTRODUCTION

The present business competition drives organizations to build innovative solutions for improving their distinct market position. The pressure of market competition compels businesses to apply AI solutions to capture customer needs which then leads to better market standing along with rising contentment among their clients. Firms intending to expand beyond their country need digital marketing integration with commerce because AI-driven personalization changes customer-business interactions (Luca, 2021). Market uniqueness requires business battles despite multiple available options to customers who need well-designed promotional approaches for differentiation. Organizations needing direction through their orientation challenges can use AI-driven customization as their guiding tool. The implementation of AI-based customer customization uses different methodologies which unite artificial intelligence with data analytics principles (Chaffey, 2020).

Several key aspects of this paradigm shift undergo evaluation by the research including recommender system processes and natural language processing performance of content customization and predictive analytics and machine learning discoveries. This section analyzes the constructive and destructive outcomes of AI technology for e-commerce together with digital marketing operations. Stronger customer commitment forms from AI-generated product sales improvements because the system delivers better conversion rates and reduces cart abandonments.

1.1 Digital Marketing's Evolution

Despite its introduction two decades ago digital marketing has transformed dramatically from basic online advertising into a modern data-based marketing field that employs many technical instruments. When digital marketing first emerged banner advertisements along with emails and web-based advertisements formed its core features. Digital marketing tactics became better targeted and more interactive and personalized when big data analytics alongside mobile technology and social media grew more popular (Kannan, & Li, 2017). This growth occurred alongside developments in automation and artificial intelligence to create powerful platforms like Google, Facebook, and Instagram which enable marketers to generate precise connecting campaigns. This advance now allows businesses to track performance results while optimizing their operational processes in real time and developing their audience outreach strategies (Tuten, & Solomon, 2017). The field grew in reach thanks to the spread of social media platforms along with internet channels and mobile devices. The above study indicates how digital marketing substantially influences product sales through its social media advertisement impact on consumer engagement and brand loyalty formation. Mobile marketing plays a vital role in sustaining client connections for people who are perpetually active (Shankar, & Carpenter, 2020).

The evolution of digital marketing brought forth data-driven marketing as a major advancement. According to the text presentation the authors discussed the power that big data analytics technologies provide to help businesses both take better informed decisions while tailoring exact content for their target audience (Chaffey, 2018). The forward movement of digital marketing demands constant modifications in this constantly evolving field. Since the beginning of internet availability digital market evolve into a complex field which demands in progress innovation coupled with deep perceptive of consumer tastes and conduct (Jarvinen, & Taiminen, 2016).

Figure 1. AI-driven personalization in marketing

1.2 Objectives

The central goal of this chapter consists of three key points:

- Digital marketing and e-commerce benefit from consumer targeting strategies because of its importance in earning success.
- The research will analyze multiple AI-based customization solutions which exist in the market.
- The research will analyze product sales modifications using AI for customization.
- Researchers need to determine the effectiveness of AI-driven customization tools for online promotional advertising.

Targeting Customers in Digital Marketing and E-Commerce

Digital marketing and e-business tactical procedure use customer targeting methods to find groups of consumers most likely to purchase. The marketing practice uses multiple methods that integrate data analytical and machine learning algorithms through tailored content delivery to meet individual customers' needs (Wedel, & Kannan, 2016). The practice enables marketing success by improving customer experiences to boost conversion rates and revenue for online market effectiveness (Chatterjee, & Kumar, 2018).

1.3 The Value of Targeting Customers

The strategic marketing method "customer targeting" provides custom-made offers and goods and services to specific customer groups through classification and targeting procedures. A business achieves greater profitability and gains advantageous results in both customer satisfaction and market positioning through targeting high-value clients along with customized approaches. DM&E has successful targeting of customers as its essential core foundation. (Chatterjee, & Kumar, 2018).

Key Features of Customer Targeting

- **Segmentation**: Divide customers into distinct groups based on demographics, behavior, preferences, or firmographics.
- **Profiling**: Create detailed profiles of target customers, as well as their needs, pain points, and buying habits.
- **Personalization**: Tailor marketing communication, offers, and experience to human being customers or segments.
- **Predictive Analytics**: Use data and statistical models to predict customer behavior, preferences, and responses.
- **Real-time Engagement**: Interact with customers in real-time, using channels like email, social media, or mobile messaging.
- **Omnichannel Experience**: Provide a seamless, consistent experience across multiple touchpoints and channels.

Continuous Optimization: Regularly refine and adjust targeting strategies based on customer feedback, behavior, and performance metrics

Figure 2. Key features of customer targeting

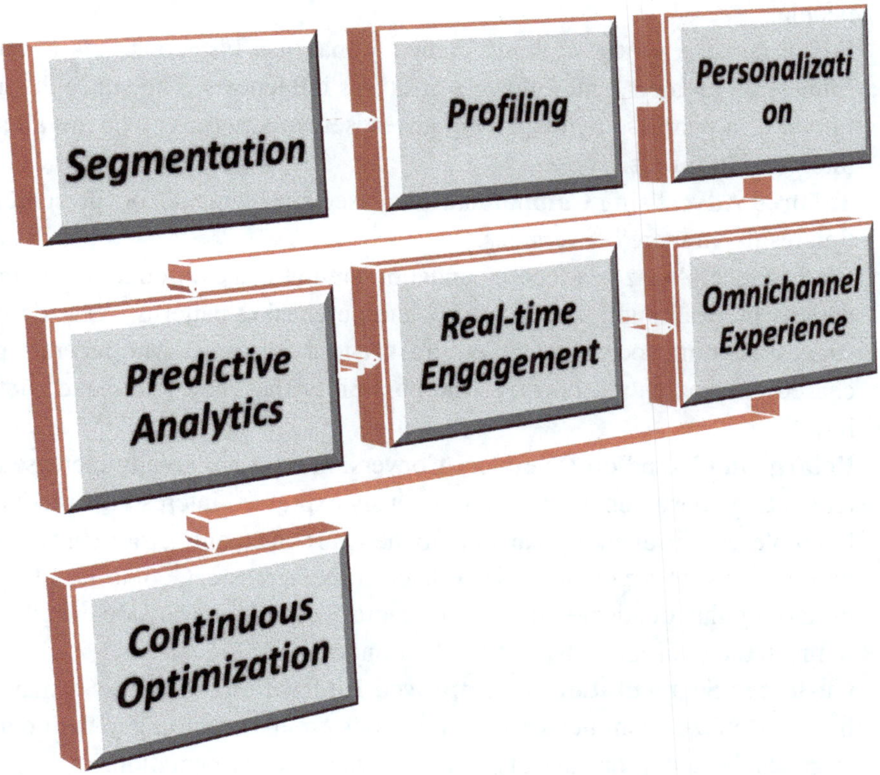

1.4 The Significance Of Targeting Customers In Digital Marketing And E-Business

All firms need successful client targeting to succeed in e-business and electronic marketing operations. This is the reason the e-business sector uses selective consumer targeting as a strategic model to make companies focus their marketing promotions on target audiences who will likely purchase their products. Better targeting strategies enable organizations to elevate their conversion rates substantially which represents the number of users who reach predetermined goals such as purchasing or subscribing or downloading applications (Goes, & Yip, 2020)

1.4.1 How Conversion Rates Are Raised by Targeting?

- **Reaching the Appropriate People at the Appropriate Moment:-**Businesses may lessen the possibility that their marketing efforts will be squandered on individuals who aren't interested in their services by focusing on the correct people.

- For instance, a fitness clothing company may use Facebook Ads to target runners, gym-goers, and followers of fitness influencers. They raise the likelihood of a purchase by displaying advertisements to those who are already interested in fitness.
- **Tailored Advertising Campaigns:-**Increased engagement from personalization results in more conversions.
- For instance, Amazon's recommendation engine makes product recommendations by examining user browsing and purchasing patterns. Amazon may suggest running socks or a fitness tracker to a consumer who recently purchased running shoes, boosting the possibility that they will make another buy.
- **Retargeting Based on Behavior:-**Conversion rates are greatly increased by retargeting consumers who have previously expressed interest in a product.
- Example: A consumer adds an item to their cart on an online store but departs without making a purchase. They later come across a Google Display Ad promoting the identical goods at a temporary discount. They are encouraged to finish the transaction by this kind reminder.
- **Customer Segmentation for Improved Interaction:-** Businesses may deliver customized communications to various groups according to their demographics, behavior, or interests by using customer segmentation.
- For instance, a cosmetics company may divide its clientele into groups like "makeup lovers" and "skincare enthusiasts." Makeup enthusiasts see advertisements for lipsticks and foundations, while skincare enthusiasts see advertisements for moisturizers and serums.
- **Getting Local Targeting Right:-** Businesses may increase relevance by using geo-targeting to reach clients in certain places.
- Example: A restaurant chain restricts consumers within a 5-mile radius from seeing promotions by using Google Ads. Because the audience is local and more likely to come, this method boosts foot traffic.
- **Social Media & Influencer Marketing:-**To reach an interested audience, businesses collaborate with influencers that have a specialized fan base.
- Example: A YouTuber who evaluates electronics teams up with a tech company to introduce a new wristwatch. After reading a favourable review, the influencer's audience—who are already interested in technology—is more likely to convert.
- **Predictive Targeting Driven by AI:-** AI predicts which clients are most likely to make a purchase by analyzing enormous volumes of data.

- In order to increase likelihood that buyer would make a purchase, a fashion e-commerce site employs artificial intelligence (AI) to track which designs the customer browses and sends them an email when those things go on sale.

Businesses may make sure that their efforts reach clients who are already interested or have a high likelihood of making a purchase by utilizing targeted marketing methods. Along with raising conversion rates, this also boosts brand loyalty, improves consumer happiness, and optimizes return on investment (ROI) in e-commerce and digital marketing.

1.5 Optimizes Marketing Spending and Why It's Important?

Mass marketing, in which companies spend money to reach a huge, ill-defined audience, is frequently a component of traditional advertising. This strategy may be expensive and ineffective (Kotler, & Keller, 2016).Businesses may cut down on wasted expenditure by concentrating on particular client groups to make sure their marketing budgets are going to those who are more likely to convert.

- For instance: Inadequate Broad Targeting Campaign: A high-end handbag company targets all women between the ages of 18 and 60 with its Facebook advertising campaign. Many of these ladies might not have the money to purchase expensive handbags or might not be interested in them. Consequently, a significant amount of the cash is squandered on people who are unlikely to become customers (Hughes, 2018).

1.6 Enhances Customer Loyalty and Retention and Why It's Important?

Current consumers is considerably more cost-effective than attracting new client. Businesses may boost client loyalty and promote repeat business by interacting with the appropriate audience through customized suggestions, unique offers, and personalized content.

- For instance, Amazon's Personalized Recommendations leverage a user's browsing and purchase history to recommend items that the user is likely to purchase. This maintains consumer interest and raises the possibility of recurring business.
- Starbucks offers loyalty programs that incentivize consumer to return along with make more purchases by presentation them with points for each transaction.

1.7 Increases Return on Investment (ROI) and Why It Is Important?

Increasing appointment and adaptation rates results in a greater return on investment (ROI) for businesses that target the correct demographic. Targeted campaigns guarantee that every marketing spend produces the most income possible rather than squandering it on people who are unlikely to make a purchase (Chaffey, & Ellis-Chadwick, 2019); Kumar, & Shah, 2017).

For instance, Google Ads Smart Bidding maximizes revenue by automatically adjusting bids to target people who are most likely to convert.

- Nike's Social Media Strategy: To market its products to a specific demographic (athletes and fitness fanatics), Nike collaborates with athletes and sports influencers. Sales and engagement rise as a result, increasing ROI.

2. CHALLENGES IN CUSTOMER TARGETING

2.1 Data-Related Challenges

- Data Quality and Accuracy: Incomplete, outdated, or inaccurate data can lead to ineffective targeting.
- Data assimilation and supervision: gathering records from various sources and managing it effectively can be complex.

2.2 Technical Challenges

- Using cutting-edge targeting tools demands experts who will operate these systems.
- The essential approach contains two parts which demand both unbiased targeting algorithms and full transparency.
- Technical infrastructure experiences difficulties when attempting to handle extensive customer bases during targeting operations..

2.3 Strategic Challenges

- It is challenging to identify the most profitable customer groups among target audiences.
- The ability to discover proper levels of customized marketing that respect customers' privacy remains essential for businesses.

- The procedure to measure and improve targeting strategies shows difficulties because it requires both data analytics and quantitative performance metrics..

2.4 Organizational Challenges

- Targeting operations need inter-team work between marketing and sales and information technology divisions.
- The implementation of new targeting concepts along with technological changes demands extensive organizational transformation to succeed.
- The search for suitable professionals with suitable expertise for customer targeting proves challenging due to what could be termed as a skills and talent gap.

2.5 Regulatory Challenges

The compliance of targeting initiatives with regulations including GDPR and CCPA and other related standards remains essential.

Clear disclosure of targeting activities is necessary because owners need to give permissions before proceeding.

AI Driven Personalised Technique presents businesses with continually developing innovations that and enhance customer satisfaction and engagement. Artificial intelligence (AI) delivers customized experiences to every customer through these modern techniques. This discussion incorporates essential research-based concepts about AI-based personalization from Ricci et al (2015). Recommender systems maintain their status as a vital administrative strategy which researchers find extremely compelling. Analysts at Jannach and Adomavicius provide comprehensive details about these AI-based systems which assess user conduct and tastes using algorithms to create recommendation offer (Jannach, & Adomavicius, 2016). The study investigates numerous methods and algorithms used by recommender systems because they improve customer interaction. The following techniques are among the group of methods

2.6 Predictive Modeling Techniques

- **Collaborative Filtering (CF):** Recommends products base on client behavior with tatse & preferences.
- **Content-Based Filtering (CBF):** Suggested products based on trait and features.
- **Hybrid Recommendation system:** Combines CF and CBF for improved recommendations.

2.7 Machine Learning Techniques

- **Clustering**: Groups users with similar behavior and preferences.
- **Decision Trees**: Creates personalized decision-making models.
- **Random Forest**: Come together multiple decision trees for enhanced forecasting.
- **Neural Networks**: Learns complex patterns in user behavior.

2.8 Natural Language Processing (NLP) Techniques

- **Sentiment Analysis**: Analyzes user sentiment and preferences.
- **Text Classification**: Classifies user-generated content for personalized recommendations.
- **Named Entity Recognition (NER):** Identifies and extracts user-specific information.

2.9 Deep Learning Techniques

- **Convolutional Neural Networks (CNNs):** Analyzes visual data for personalized recommendations.
- **Recurrent Neural Networks (RNNs):** Analyzes sequential data for personalized predictions.
- **Generative Adversarial Networks (GANs):** Generates personalized content and recommendations.

2.10 Real-Time Personalization Techniques

- **Real-Time Analytics:** Analyzes user behavior and preferences in real-time.
- **Real-Time Decisioning**: Makes personalized decisions based on real-time data.
- **Edge Computing**: Enables real-time personalization at the edge of the network.

2.11 Other Techniques

- **A/B Testing:** Tests and optimizes personalized experiences.
- **Personalization Engines**: Uses AI to personalize experiences across channels.
- **Customer Data Platforms (CDPs)**: Unifies customer data for personalized experiences.

2.12 Through user behavior analysis and preference-based AI customization customers experience better performances when enabled with various personalized strategies. Various excellent AI-powered customized approaches include the following:

Recommendation platforms utilize advanced artificial intelligence algorithms to read user behaviors then match appropriate product recommendations. This part of the research depends on authoritative studies from the e-commerce field and the domain of AI-driven customization to enhance our comprehension of recommender systems. A vital data science methodology used in recommender systems exists as collaborative filtering. This research by Koren, Bell and Volinsky (2009) offers detailed revelation about collaborative filtering methods together with their functional mechanisms and possible applications. The technology behind collaborative filtering enhances user satisfaction along with sales conversions by searching through user-tool interactions to make product recommendations that match other users' preferences. Content-based filtering functions as a vital aspect among recommender system tactics. The evaluation of content-based filtering mechanics and its recommendation approach stands out in the research work of Pazzani and Billsus (2007). Scant user-item interaction data makes this method work effectively because it uses personalized recommendations throughout the process.

A more thorough method of providing tailored recommendations is offered by hybrid recommender systems that include collaborative and content-based filtering. The concept of hybrid recommender systems is examined by the researchers in (Burke, 2002), who highlight how they can get over the drawbacks of individual approaches and provide customers with more varied and accurate product options.

3. ANALYTICS FOR PREDICTION AND MACHINE LEARNING

The method of analyzing data using advanced mathematical and statistical techniques for producing predictions falls under Analytics for Prediction and Machine Learning. The development of predictive models through machine learning algorithms allows data learning that produces time-evolving accuracy improvements (Chakraborty, & Dube, 2019). This part explores practical machine learning uses in targeted marketing by drawing evidence from respected research in marketing analytics and machine learning (Hughes, 2018). The modern data-driven organizational decision-making process incorporates machine learning technology which delivers accurate customer prediction abilities for businesses. Through predictions machines enable businesses to create individualized marketing initiatives which target specific customers. Coussement and Van den Poel (2008) explained the machines' capability to forecast user activities. The researchers analyzed how machine learning algorithms perform in customer churn forecasting because these techniques successfully detect business departures among customers.

Key Concepts:

- **Predictive Analytics:** Using data and statistical techniques to forecast future events or behaviors.
- **Machine Learning**: As a branch of artificial intelligence, machine learning entails teaching algorithms to learn from data and generate predictions or judgments.
- **Supervised Learning:** Using labeled data to train computers to anticipate outcomes is known as supervised learning.
- **Unsupervised Learning:**Using unlabeled data to train computers to find trends or connections.

Privacy analytics represents a robust machine learning application according to Davenport, & Harris, (2007). Data predictions through predictive analytics enable companies to forecast customer choices and conduct from past information thus they can predict customer trends. The research group gained knowledge about how predictive analytics enables operational marketing plans and allows better targeting of customers for increased sales performance. The application of machine learning generates customized product recommendations for ecommerce platforms. Deep reinforcement learning analyzes online advertising impressions in recommender systems according to Zhao et al. (2021) who investigated these systems. The research demonstrates the development of machine learning approaches especially deep reinforcement learning together with its potential impact on AI-driven custom strategies in digital marketing.

Figure 3. AI-Driven Personalised Techniques

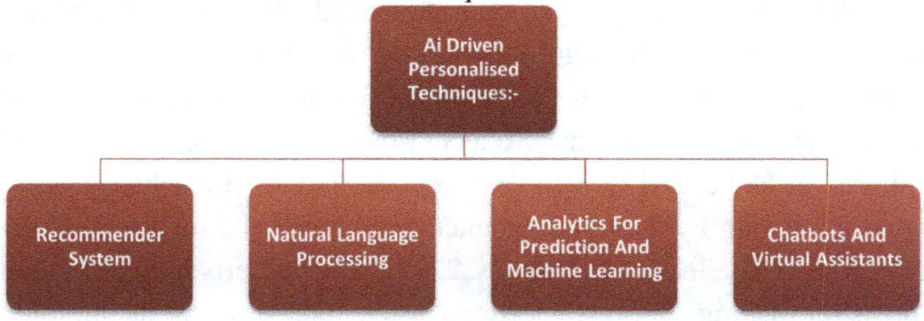

4. OPPORTUNITIES OF AI-DRIVEN PERSONALIZATION IN MARKET DIFFERENTIATION IN DIGITAL MARKETING AND ECOMMERCE

Customization strategies driven by AI have transformed e-commerce and digital marketing by offering fresh methods to consumer interaction (Linden, Smith, & York, 2021) ; Huang, & Rust, 2021). The technique presents several difficulties that must be resolved for proper implementation. The following subsection shows an outline explaining both advantages and potential drawbacks of personalized methods powered by artificial intelligence.

- Businesses implement AI-driven customization to deliver personalized experiences for individual customers thus achieving higher customer satisfaction and loyalty.
- The process of providing suitable recommendations and offers to individual consumers leads to improved conversion rates because tailored content adjusts better to consumer interests.
- The success of AI-driven customization creates market distinctions which allow businesses to differentiate their position from their competitors.
- Organizations gain better customer understanding from AI-powered personalization thus they can develop improved marketing tactics.

The implementation of AI and automation systems simplifies customization projects to decrease the requirement for human resources and generate higher efficiency levels

Figure 4. AI-Driven Opportunities

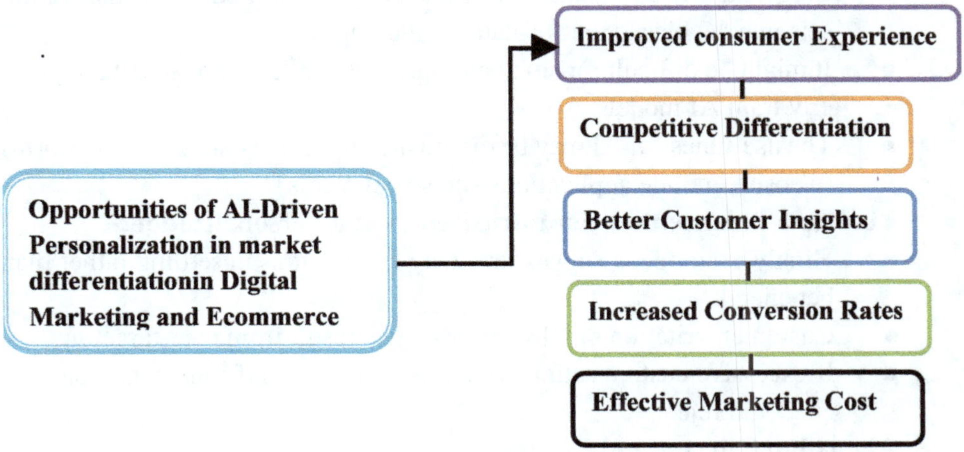

- **Increased Customer Engagement:** AI-powered personalization enables companies to offer highly tailored, pertinent information and recommendations to specific clients, which boosts user engagement and lengthens user sessions (Kireyev, Pauwels & Gupta, 2016).
- **Increased Conversion Rates**: Since customers are given information and products that suit their preferences, personalized experiences usually lead to higher conversion rates, which boost sales (Verhoef, Kannan & Inman, 2015).
- **Increased Customer Loyalty:** Tailored interactions boost customer loyalty, which results in recurring business and enduring alliances (Xiao, & Benbasat, 2007).
- **Effective Marketing Cost**: By accurately identifying the right audience and reducing resource waste, AI can optimize marketing costs (Hogan, 2001).
- **Data-Driven Insights**: Artificial intelligence (AI) provides valuable insights into customer behavior that may inform future product development and marketing plans.

5. CHALLENGES OF AI-DRIVEN PERSONALIZATION IN MARKET DIFFERENTIATION IN DIGITAL MARKETING AND ECOMMERCE

- **Issues with Data Privacy and Compliance:-**
  - Strict guidelines on the collection and use of customer data are enforced by regulations such as the CCPA, GDPR, and other data privacy legislation. Companies must safeguard user data while ensuring openness in AI decision-making. Growing consumer awareness of data tracking has resulted both opposition and opportunities.
- **Availability and Quality of Data:-**
  - Large, high-quality datasets are necessary for AI models, yet these datasets may be biased, out-of-date, or incomplete.
  - It might be difficult for small enterprises to collect enough data to properly train AI models.
  - The usefulness of AI may be diminished by siloed data across platforms (website, mobile applications and social media).
- **Finding a Balance Between Intrusiveness and Personalization:-**
  - Highly customized suggestions may come out as unsettling rather than beneficial.
  - Customer irritation or ad weariness may result from over-targeting.
  - If excessive customisation seems like a privacy infringement, consumers could reject it.
- **Algorithm Fairness and Bias:-**

- If AI is trained on historically biased data, it may propagate prejudices and provide unjust or immoral results (e.g., biased pricing, exclusion of specific groups).
- Constant observation and bias correction are necessary to guarantee fairness in AI models.

- **Infrastructure and Technical Difficulties**
  - Effective infrastructure and a lot of processing capacity are needed for real-time customisation.
  - Large-scale AI implementation can be expensive, particularly for smaller e-Commerce companies.
  - Updating and maintaining AI models requires specialized skills, which is frequently in short supply.
- **Adoption and Consumer Trust**
  - Traditional browsing is preferred by certain clients who do not trust AI-driven recommendations.
  - Brand disengagement and distrust may result from opaque AI decision-making.
  - For AI-driven customization to be credible, it must be consistent with brand identity.
- **Assessing ROI and Efficiency**
  - Clear KPIs are necessary for personalization initiatives, but attribution might be difficult (for example, was a transaction influenced by AI recommendations?).
  - It takes time and money to quantify the true impact of A/B testing AI-driven experiences.
  - Ineffective marketing tactics may result from an excessive dependence on AI without human supervision.

Figure 5. AI-Driven Challenges

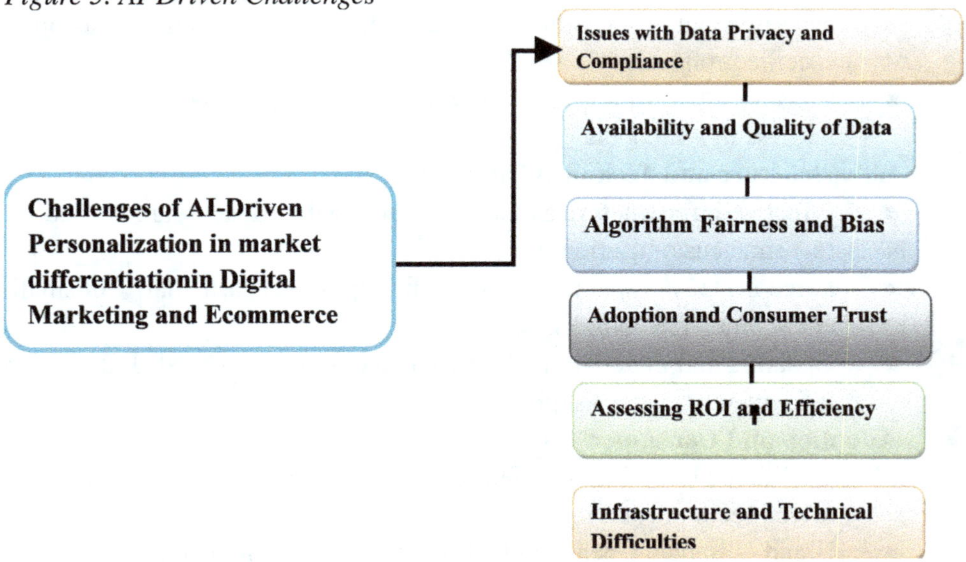

6. IMPACT OF ARTIFICIAL INTELLIGENCE

7 The impact of artificial intelligence (AI) on product sales is one of the most significant facets of digital marketing, and recent studies have highlighted both the opportunities and difficulties in this field. De Bruyn, Viswanathan, Beh, Brock, & Von Wangenheim, (2020) draws attention to the growing significance of AI in marketing and stresses the need to steer clear of potential hazards while utilizing its advantages. Vlacic, Corbo, Silva & Dabic, (2021)contribute to this knowledge by assessing the dynamic environment of AI in marketing and emphasizing how it is always changing. According to Adomavicius, & Tuzhilin,(2005).tailoring recommendations to particular customer preferences improves the significance of customization in the context of product sales

6.1 Positive impacts on product sales are affected by AI-driven customization

- **Higher Rates of Conversion**
- Impulsive purchases are encouraged with tailored suggestions based on browsing interests and history.
- Dynamic pricing powered by AI modifies prices to optimize conversion rates.

- For instance, 35% of overall sales are attributed to Amazon's AI-driven product suggestions.

6.2 Increased Client Loyalty & Retention

- AI-driven loyalty programs increase recurring business by providing personalized rewards.
- Customer engagement and lifetime value (CLV) are enhanced by personalized email marketing.
- For instance, Starbucks has seen a more than 25% boost in sales from loyalty members as a result of using AI to tailor offers.

6.3 A better experience for customers (CX)

- Virtual assistants with AI capabilities and chatbots ease the purchasing process.
- Product discovery is made quicker and simpler with personalized search and navigation.
- For instance, Sephora's virtual try-on capabilities and AI-powered product suggestions increase both in-person and online sales.

6.4 Lower Cart Abandonment Rates

- AI-powered incentives (free delivery, discounts) and reminder lower checkout drop-off rates.
- Real-time AI chatbots help consumers make judgments about what to buy.

Example: Compared to generic emails, which have an average conversion rate of 2–5%, AI-powered abandoned cart emails have an average conversion rate of 10–15%.

6.5 Improved Forecasting of Inventory and Demand

- Best-selling items are constantly accessible because AI anticipates demand trends.
- Revenue and cost effectiveness are increased when stockouts and overstocking are decreased.
- Walmart, for instance, employs AI to estimate inventories, which lowers overstock expenses and boosts sales effectiveness.

6.6 AI-Powered Customization's Detrimental Impacts on Sales

Excessive Personalization May Limit Discovery

- Missed sales chances might result from customers only seeing a small variety of items.
- Cross-selling opportunities and impulsive purchases may be diminished by a lack of diversity.
- For instance, AI may only suggest black shoes to a consumer who consistently purchases them, disregarding other shoe classifications.

7. ETHICAL ASPECTS TO TAKE INTO ACCOUNT

The use of AI in digital marketing raises a number of important ethical issues. Particularly important issues include privacy and data security, transparency in algorithmic decision-making, equity in targeting, and responsibility for AI-driven choices. According to Dignum,, (2019)highlights the ethical concerns that AI in marketing raises, emphasizing the importance of ethical standards and responsible AI governance. Similar to Taddeo & Floridi, (2018) explore the moral ramifications of AI and machine learning across a range of fields, emphasizing the need of foreseeing moral dilemmas.By providing individualized experiences, enhancing consumer engagement, and increasing revenues, AI-powered customization is revolutionizing digital marketing and e-commerce. However, ethical questions about privacy, prejudice, transparency, and fairness surface when companies use AI to stand out in the market. Given that AI depends on enormous volumes of user data, data privacy and consent are crucial ethical issues that frequently raise questions regarding transparency and legal compliance (e.g., GDPR, CCPA). Furthermore, over-personalization may restrict customer choice and liberty, while algorithmic bias may result in discrimination. The ethical environment is further complicated by pricing discrimination, security threats, and the possibility of anti-competitive behavior. Businesses must implement ethical frameworks that put justice, transparency, and customer trust first in order to guarantee responsible AI personalization. Ethical AI improves long-term brand reputation and consumer loyalty in addition to reducing risks.The following section outlines the several ethical issues surrounding the use of AI-based customization techniques in e-commerce and digital marketing.

- **Transparency and Equity**:- AI systems must be impartial and transparent in order to foster trust and ensure moral behavior in the area of AI-driven personalization. Customers that are aware of how their data is being used to personalize their experiences are said to be transparent. Customers can better understand the decision-making processes behind product recommendations and content curation thanks to the openness of AI algorithms' inner workings, which demystifies the customisation process (Eslami, Karahalios, Sandvig, & Fiesler, 2018; Binns, 2018).The "black box" nature of AI judgments makes it difficult for customers to comprehend how customization functions.

- **Ethical Concern**: If customers are unaware of the rationale behind certain recommendations, they may feel duped.
- **Best Practice:** To explain the recommendations for certain items, information, or pricing, use explainable AI (XAI).
- Give customers the ability to modify customization settings through user controls.
- **For instance:** To improve openness, Netflix offers a "Why am I seeing this recommendation?" function.

7.1 Security and Privacy of Data

People are growing more worried about how their data is collected and used in an era of heightened privacy awareness. Therefore, it is imperative that businesses handle this circumstance in a responsible and open manner. Protecting customer information is one of the most significant ethical concerns. This involves guarding against unauthorized access or detrimental use of sensitive data, such as browsing preferences, purchase histories, and personal information. Companies are trusted with this data, and it is their moral obligation to protect it. In addition to being based on moral principles, this duty is reinforced by legal frameworks like the General Data Protection Regulation (GDPR) in Europe (Bhardwaj, Sharma, Goel, Vandana, Sharma, & Verma, 2024). Adherence to such limitations is not only required by law.

Problem: AI-powered customization depends on gathering enormous volumes of personal information, sometimes without the express agreement of the user.

- **Ethical Concern:** Users might not be completely informed about the ways in which their data is gathered, saved, or utilized.
- **Best Practice**:Observe laws such as the CCPA, GDPR, and HIPAA (for the healthcare and finance industries). Provide unambiguous opt-in and opt-out choices, and use straightforward language to describe data usage. Reduce the amount of data you acquire by just gathering what is absolutely essential.
- For instance, Apple's App Tracking Transparency mandates that applications obtain user consent before collecting personal data.

7.2 Well-informed Consent

Obtaining informed consent is a key component of ethical behavior in the era of data-driven personalization. Companies that want to use customer data for personalization must put transparency and respect for individual liberty first. Consumers who give their informed consent are active participants in the data-sharing process rather than merely passive data subjects. Businesses must ensure that their customers fully and clearly understand how their data will be utilized in order to do this. This comprehension covers the extent to which data will be analyzed, disseminated, and maintained in addition to the purposes for which it will be utilized.Another crucial factor is willingness. Consumers must provide their consent voluntarily and voluntarily, free from coercion or pressure (Nissenbaum, 2010). They must be able to choose whether to participate in data collection and customisation activities without worrying about the consequences. To ensure that consent is truly informed and not unfairly persuaded, this component of choice is required. Getting informed consent is a commitment to ethical data processing that goes beyond merely following the law. It promotes a sense of agency and ownership over data by empowering customers to make informed decisions regarding the use of their personal information. Consequently, the customer-business relationship strengthens and trust increases (Martin, 2018).

7.3 Reduction of Bias

Bias prevention inside AI algorithms is a critical requirement in the fields of data-driven personalization and AI-driven decision-making. Whether it comes from algorithmic biases or skewed training data, prejudice may introduce unfairness into AI systems, leading to biased recommendations and even discriminatory outcomes. Therefore, eliminating bias is both a technological challenge and a moral requirement. One of the main causes of bias in AI systems is the training data. The AI system's suggestions could unintentionally reinforce and amplify preconceptions if the training data contains historical biases, injustices, or imbalances. For instance, the AI can unintentionally make offers based on gender stereotypes if past purchase data indicates gender preferences, which would reinforce gender discrimination (Varsha, 2023).

8. EVALUATING AI-POWERED CUSTOMIZATION IN ONLINE ADVERTISING: CASE STUDY & ANALYSIS

By improving ad targeting, raising engagement, and enhancing return on investment (ROI), AI-powered personalization in online advertising is transforming digital marketing. With the support of a case study of Nike's AI-powered advertising campaigns, we will examine in-depth how AI-driven personalization improves online advertising initiatives.

AI-driven personalization in online advertising uses real-time analytics, machine learning (ML), and big data to provide people individualized experiences. AI improves internet advertising in the following ways:

- **Targeting and Audience Segmentation:-**To generate accurate client categories, AI examines user behavior, demographics, interests, and past purchases.
  - For instance, Google Ads use AI to sort users into "affinity groups" (such as tech aficionados and fitness enthusiasts).
- **Real-time bidding and predictive analytics (RTB):-** AI automatically modifies bidding methods in real time and predicts which people are most likely to interact with an advertisement.
  - For instance, Facebook's Lookalike Audiences assist marketers in identifying potential clients who resemble current ones.
- **Customized Messaging & Ad Creatives:-** AI adapts CTAs, images, and ad copy to user preferences.
- For instance, Meta's Dynamic Ads on Facebook and Instagram tailor ad content according to user interactions.
- **Behavioral tracking and retargeting:-** Retargeting driven by AI displays advertisements to consumers who have engaged with a brand but have not made a purchase.
- For instance, consumers are reminded of items they have seen or left in their basket via Amazon's AI-powered remarketing advertisements.
- **A/B testing and performance optimization:-** AI optimizes performance by continually testing various ad versions depending on engagement data. Google's Smart Campaigns, for instance, dynamically modifies ad tactics to increase conversion rates.

8.1 Nike's AI-Powered Advertising Strategy: A Case Study

As a world leader in athletic clothing and footwear, Nike has continuously integrated technology into its marketing plans. The application of artificial intelligence (AI) in digital advertising to produce hyper-personalized campaigns, enhance ad targeting, and improve return on investment (ROI) has been one of its most successful developments.

This case study offers a thorough examination of Nike's use of AI in online advertising, covering its tactics, execution, outcomes, and potential ramifications.

The History and Difficulties of Conventional Advertising:

As a prominent player in the sportswear sector, Nike had a number of difficulties with conventional digital advertising:

- **High Level of Competition**: Fighting for digital advertising space against companies like Adidas, Puma, and Under Armour.
- **Ad Fatigue**: Consumers were growing less receptive to impersonal, generic advertisements.
- **Ineffective Advertising Spend**: Conventional broad-targeting campaigns squandered money on consumers who had no interest in the goods.
- **Abandoned Carts**: A lot of people would peruse Nike's website, put items in their carts, and then walk away without making a purchase.

Nike used AI-driven advertising strategies to boost engagement and maximize marketing efforts in order to overcome these obstacles.

Nike's AI-Driven Marketing Techniques

Nike used AI-powered digital marketing strategies to boost ad performance and consumer engagement. The main tactics Nike employed are listed below:

8.2 Predictive Advertising Driven by AI (Smart Targeting)

Nike used predictive analytics and machine learning (ML) to examine consumer behavior and identify the most effective time, platform, and content for displaying advertisements.

- **How It Operates**: AI examines user data, including search history, social media activity, and purchasing patterns. Forecasts the possibility of a purchase and adjusts ad spots appropriately. Guarantees that consumers see Nike's advertisements at the ideal moment to make a purchase.
- For instance, Nike dynamically displayed tailored advertisements for the newest Nike running shoes to high-intent individuals who had searched for them using Google Ads AI.
- **Outcomes**: A 40% increase in click-through rate (CTR).More users interacted with interest-related advertisements.

- Tailored Advertising Creatives Nike used **Dynamic Creative Optimization (DCO)** technology to employ real-time ad content customization based on user behavior.
- How It Operates:Ad content, pictures, and videos are dynamically altered by AI according to user preferences.Uses location, hobbies, and past purchases to personalize advertisements.
- For instance, Nike's AI system would automatically generate customized Instagram advertising featuring the newest basketball footwear rather than generic Nike ads if a user often viewed the brand's selection.
- **Outcomes**: A 20% rise in conversion rates as a result of consumers seeing advertisements tailored to their interests.
- Increased interaction with digital and social media ads.
- **AI-Powered Abandoned Cart Retargeting**
- Nike employed AI to send tailored offers and reminders to clients who had abandoned their shopping carts.
- **How It Operates:** Users who came to the website but departed without making a purchase were recorded by AI. Google Display Ads, Instagram, and Facebook were used to retarget these people. used push alerts and AI-powered emails to remind people about their abandoned cart.
- **Examples:-** If a buyer put a pair of Nike Air Max shoes in their shopping basket but chose not to check out, they would subsequently see:
- A Google Display Ad urging people to buy the same shoe.
- A social media advertisement promising a 10% reduction if customers made the purchase.
- **Findings**: Cart recovery rates increased by 30%. Personalized retargeting advertising increased the number of consumers who came back to finish their transaction.
- **Chatbots Driven by AI for Interactive Advertising Engagement**

Nike used AI chatbots to their website and Facebook Messenger to improve customer service and product suggestions.

How It Operates: Chatbots with AI capabilities conversed with clients to learn about their preferences.Products are suggested according to their exercise routines, past purchases, and preferred styles.

For instance: Based on their foot shape and running style, a user who messages Nike's chatbot about running gear will receive personalized shoe recommendations.

- Additionally, chatbots offered real-time customer service and responded to questions on product features, shipping, and size.

- **Outcomes:** A Increased direct-to-consumer (DTC) revenues by simplifying product discovery. Higher engagement and lower bounce rates.

Consequences and Impacts of AI-Powered Marketing

Table 1. Nike's success in digital marketing was greatly enhanced by their AI-driven advertising tactics.

Metrics	Nike's AI-Driven Ad Performance
Click- through rate(CTR)	Increased by 40%
Conversion rates	Increased by 20%
Cart recovery rate	Increased by 30%
Return on ad spend(ROAS)	Increased by 25%
Customer engagement	Higher ads interaction and sales

- **Increased ROI**: Nike was able to target just highly intent users and cut down on ad waste thanks to AI.
- **Greater Brand Loyalty**: Customized advertisements maintained consumers' interest in Nike's network.
- **Enhanced Customer Experience**: Smooth interactions were made possible by AI-powered chatbots and predictive advertisements.

9. CONCLUSION

Through AI-powered customization marketing revolution protects organizations in delivering individualized experiences which boost consumer engagement and boost sales potential. Customer trust preservation and regulatory conformity necessitate resolving ethical matters in data privacy combined with algorithm transparency and fair practices to address bias issues. Successful AI-driven customisation in the market depends on an exact alignment between ethical AI practices and personalization combined with substantial competitive advantages. Companies protecting both security and justice standards and customer freedom will build enduring client relationships with their outstanding service model. Using this method businesses accomplish better product sales and simultaneously improve marketing effect efficiency. Moral worries should be the main deciding factor when creating trusting relationships during decision-making processes. Future customer targeting systems heavily depend on the rapid progression of technology that makes AI increasingly essential. Organizations need to handle these matters by conducting truthful business practices. Today's organizations pursue enduring beneficial relationships as a substitute for their previous practice of using deceptive short-term partnerships for customer outreach. Success in business depends on permanent customer contentment over the pursuit of single-time financial gains. Organizations need to develop flexibility as well as creativity alongside maintaining social responsibility to thrive in their consumer targeting process powered by AI.

New AI developments will create meaningful adjustments that will transform e-commerce systems. Current technological innovation together with research that links various fields of technology and sociology allows businesses to thrive in contemporary digital markets. Organizations using an ethical business strategy and forward-thinking approach can resolve future challenges through AI opportunities to generate increased value for their e-commerce customers.

REFERENCES

Adomavicius, G., & Tuzhilin, A. (2005). Toward the next generation of recommender systems: A survey of the state-of-the-art and possible extensions. *IEEE Transactions on Knowledge and Data Engineering*, *17*(6), 734–749. DOI: 10.1109/TKDE.2005.99

Bhardwaj, S., Sharma, N., Goel, M., Vandana, N., Sharma, K., & Verma, V. (2024). Enhancing Customer Targeting in E-Commerce and Digital Marketing through AI-Driven Personalization Strategies. In *CRC Press eBooks* (pp. 41–60). https://doi.org/DOI: 10.1201/9781003450443-4

) Binns, R. (2018).*Fairness in Machine Learning: A Survey. ACM Computing urveys*, 51(6), 1-35.

Burke, R. (2002). Hybrid recommender systems: Survey and experiments. *User Modeling and User-Adapted Interaction*, *12*, 331–370. DOI: 10.1023/A:1021240730564

Chaffey, D. (2018). *Digital Marketing: Strategy, Implementation, and Practice* (7th ed.). Pearson Education.

Chaffey, D. (2020). *Digital Marketing: Strategy, Implementation, and Practice* (8th ed.). Pearson Education.

Chaffey, D. (2020). *Digital marketing: Strategy, implementation, and practice* (8th ed.). Pearson Education.

Chaffey, D., & Ellis-Chadwick, F. (2019). *Digital Marketing: Strategy, Implementation, and Practice* (8th ed.). Pearson Education.

Chakraborty, G., & Dube, J.-P. (2019). Machine Learning in Marketing: Prediction and Targeting. *JMR, Journal of Marketing Research*, *56*(3), 361–374.

Chatterjee, S., & Kumar, A. (2018). Customer Targeting and Personalization in E-commerce: Role of Data Analytics and Machine Learning. *Journal of Retailing and Consumer Services*, *45*, 125–135.

Coussement, K., & Van den Poel, D. (2008). Churn prediction in subscription services: An application of support vector machines while comparing two parameter-selection techniques. *Expert Systems with Applications*, *34*(1), 313–327. DOI: 10.1016/j.eswa.2006.09.038

Davenport, T. H., & Harris, J. G. (2007). Competing on analytics: The new science of Winning. *Harvard business review press. Language*, *15*(217), 24.

De Bruyn, A., Viswanathan, V., Beh, Y. S., Brock, J. K. U., & Von Wangenheim, F. (2020). Artificial intelligence and marketing: Pitfalls and opportunities. *Journal of Interactive Marketing*, *51*(1), 91–105. DOI: 10.1016/j.intmar.2020.04.007

Dignum, V. (2019). *Responsible artificial intelligence: how to develop and use AI in a responsible way* (Vol. 2156). Springer., DOI: 10.1007/978-3-030-30371-6

Eslami, M., Karahalios, K., Sandvig, C., & Fiesler, C. (2018).Faceless Book: 'Like' and the Politics of AI Personalization. *Proceedings of the 2018 CHI Conference on Human Factors in Computing Systems*, 1-13.

Goes, P. B., & Yip, S. (2020). Personalization in E-commerce: Impact on Online Buying Behavior and Conversion Rates. *Journal of Interactive Marketing*, *49*, 15–30.

Hogan, E. A. (2001). "The Attention Economy: Understanding the New Currency of Business by Davenport Thomas H. and Beck John C. Boston: Harvard Business School Press, 15 *(4)*, 145–147, doi: DOI: 10.5465/ame.2001.5898765

Huang, M.-H., & Rust, R. T. (2021). Artificial Intelligence in Service: Applications and Opportunities. *Journal of Service Research*, *24*(1), 3–16.

Hughes, A. M. (2018). Machine Learning and Predictive Analytics in Marketing: A Framework for Application. *Journal of the Academy of Marketing Science*, *46*(4), 494–509.

Hughes, A. M. (2018). The New Marketing Model: How Targeted Marketing Reduces Costs and Increases Conversions. *Journal of Marketing Strategy*, *19*(4), 134–147.

Jannach, D., & Adomavicius, G. (2016). Recommendation Systems: Challenges and Opportunities. *Computer Science Review*, *19*, 1–15.

Järvinen, J., & Taiminen, H. (2016). Research on Digital Marketing: A Review of Literature and Future Research Directions. *International Journal of Advertising*, *35*(3), 340–375.

Kannan, P. K., & Li, H. (2017). Digital marketing: A framework, review and research agenda. *International Journal of Research in Marketing*, *34*(1), 22–45.

Kireyev, P., Pauwels, K., & Gupta, S. (2016, September). Do display ads influence search? Attribution and dynamics in online advertising. *International Journal of Research in Marketing*, *33*(3), 475–490. DOI: 10.1016/j.ijresmar.2015.09.007

Koren, Y., Bell, R., & Volinsky, C. (2009, August). Matrix Factorization Techniques for Recommender Systems. *Computer*, *42*(8), 30–37. DOI: 10.1109/MC.2009.263

Kotler, P., & Keller, K. L. (2016). *Marketing Management* (15th ed.). Pearson Education.

Kumar, V., & Shah, D. (2017). Building and Sustaining Profitable Customer Loyalty for the 21st Century. *JMR, Journal of Marketing Research, 54*(2), 255–270.

Linden, G., Smith, B., & York, J. (2021). The Role of AI in Personalization: Transforming E-Commerce and Digital Marketing. *Journal of Business Research, 124*, 14–23.

Luca, A. (2021). The role of artificial intelligence in customer personalization: Transforming marketing strategies for businesses. *Journal of Business & Technology, 18*(2), 125–139.

Martin, K. (2018). Ethical Issues in the Big Data Industry: Understanding Informed Consent and Privacy. *Journal of Business Ethics, 152*(2), 465–482.

Nissenbaum, H. (2010). *Privacy in Context: Technology, Policy, and the Integrity of Social Life*. Stanford University Press.

Pazzani, M. J., & Billsus, D. (2007). "Content-Based Recommendation Systems," in The Adaptive Web. In Brusilovsky, P., Kobsa, A., & Nejdl, W. (Eds.), *Lecture Notes in Computer Science* (Vol. 4321, pp. 325–341). Springer Berlin Heidelberg., DOI: 10.1007/978-3-540-72079-9_10

Ricci, F., Rokach, L., & Shapira, B. (2015). *Recommender Systems Handbook*. Springer.

Shankar, V., & Carpenter, G. S. (2020). Mobile Marketing: A Strategic Perspective. *Journal of the Academy of Marketing Science, 48*(3), 332–351.

Taddeo, M., & Floridi, L. (2018). How AI can be a force for good. *Science, 361*(6404), 751–752. DOI: 10.1126/science.aat5991

Tuten, T. L., & Solomon, M. R. (2017). *Social Media Marketing* (3rd ed.). Pearson Education.

Varsha, P. S. (2023). How can we manage biases in artificial intelligence systems–A systematic literature review. *International Journal of Information Management Data Insights, 3*(1), 100165. DOI: 10.1016/j.jjimei.2023.100165

Verhoef, P. C., Kannan, P. K., & Inman, J. J. (2015). From multi-channel retailing to omni-channel retailing: Introduction to the special issue on multi-channel retailing. *Journal of Retailing, 91*(2), 174–181. DOI: 10.1016/j.jretai.2015.02.005

Vlacic, B., Corbo, L., Silva, S. C., & Dabic, M. (2021). The evolving role of artificial intelligence in marketing: A review and research agenda. *Journal of Business Research, 128*, 187–203. DOI: 10.1016/j.jbusres.2021.01.055

Wedel, M., & Kannan, P. K. (2016). *Marketing Analytics: A Practical Guide to Real Marketing Science*. Wiley.

Xiao, B., & Benbasat, I. (2007). E-commerce product recommendation agents: Use, characteristics, and impact. *Management Information Systems Quarterly*, •••, 137–209. DOI: 10.2307/25148784

Zhang, J., & Wedel, M. (2019). The Role of Customer Segmentation in E-commerce and Digital Marketing. *JMR, Journal of Marketing Research, 56*(3), 432–451.

Zhao, X., Gu, C., Zhang, H., Yang, X., Liu, X., Tang, J., & Liu, H. (2021, May). Dear: Deep reinforcement learning for online advertising impression in recommender systems. In *Proceedings of the AAAI conference on artificial intelligence* 35(*1*), 750-758). doi: DOI: 10.1609/aaai.v35i1.16156

Chapter 8
Enhancing Stock Market Analytics in Real Time With Apache Kafka

Lavanya Kandasamy
https://orcid.org/0000-0002-2961-321X
Vellore Institute of Technology, India

Swarnava Dey
Vellore Institute of Technology, India

Debdyuti Mitra
Vellore Institute of Technology, India

Dhaivat Jambudia
Vellore Institute of Technology, India

ABSTRACT

Modern structure of financial system relies strongly on live trend of stock-market price and the real-time deviations of values that enriches a healthy competition and instant decision-making capability in a fast-moving market environment. Due to the inherent dynamic properties of big data, it becomes challenging for typical data-mining tools, technologies, methods and techniques to be applied on big-data streaming task. The significant resistance faced by real time streaming of big data involves lack of adaptability, controllability and programmability. Apache kafka is one of the best frameworks to work with for resolving real time data streaming tasks for its unique characteristics of being reliable, distributed and having high through-

DOI: 10.4018/979-8-3373-6731-6.ch008

put and low latency. The essential features of kafka are thoroughly summarized in this abstract which empowers market regulators to manage and analyze stock value movement in a real-time manner to cop up with momentary changes.

1. INTRODUCTION

In this modern era of fast-paced and internally connected global economy system, the stock market serves as a crucial indicator of the health of the economy, a haven for investors, and a field of combat for traders. In 2020, the global stock market capitalization reached an astounding $95.2 trillion, underlining the critical role of real-time data in this vast ecosystem. According to a survey, over 85% of financial institutions and stock market experts believe that real-time data of heavy volume is essential for making wise investment decisions and controlling risk. The global data flood has astronomical hit to every dimension for an estimated production of 2.5 quintillion bytes in each day. Conventional methods are now on the way of getting obsolete and also, not sufficient to address the real-time analytical needs of businesses and industries in this data-driven world. Nearly 76% of firms, according to a recent poll, view real-time data analytics and business insights as essential for their production & operations, highlighting the severe need of developing effective solutions in this area. Real-time data streaming has its own set of difficulties. Tools and procedures that can ingest, process, and analyze data as it flows are required due to the continuous and limitless nature of data arrival. Traditional databases and batch processing methods fail in this modern complex requirement for the financial market analysis, resulting in delays in the availability of data and useful insights. The ability to make informed decisions instantly in the stock market can often make the great difference between financial profit and loss. To gain an edge in this highly competitive arena, market participants need easy access to real-time data that is not only reliable but also efficiently processed and effectively analyzed. This is where Apache Kafka, a powerful and innovative data streaming platform, emerges a new direction to a transformative solution.

This research paper delves deep for the architecture, application cases, and actual implementation of real-time stock market data streaming analysis using Apache Kafka. Through empirical studies, this article aims to shed light on how Kafka has altered the landscape of real-time data analytics, providing organizations and individuals with a potent instrument to navigate the data-driven future business scenarios through a thorough analysis for navigating around the complex and volatile world of financial market. Moreover, Kafka is integrated with Spark in this project for the real-time analytics based on the application of structured streaming API technique. From statistical point of view, stock market data calculation matrix is based on rolling or moving average and volume weighted average. But, Spark itself doesn't prescribe any specific algorithm for real-time streaming whereas it provides the infrastructure and tools to implement analytics-based task as per specific requirement. Stock market price changes occur in a blink of eye because of the vast data pipelines the hold the record of continuous buying and selling of financial assets i.e., stocks, bonds on stock exchanges. These deviations in price in a fraction of second are nothing but the real time streaming events those are provoked by trading activities, market data feeds. To enhance the tracking system of these dynamic data pipeline, this research paper focuses to equip the market players to get an accuracy for forecasting stock prices deviations by drawing appropriate insights and making effective decisions.

2. LITERATURE SURVEY

The paper focused on developing a Lambda Architecture-based, fault-tolerant, scalable model with lower latency. The vast part was covered with the application of support vector regression for predicting the next stock value in a more precise way. On the other hand, it was not enlightened a specific literature review on support vector regression, whether it suggested that this approach had already been studied and can be concluded as a successful approach for stock prediction (Monalisa Jena et al., 2019) . In order to shape the system for real-time data processing and alerting, Kafka's architectural design and process structure were thoroughly examined. It was investigated the usage of Kafka streams in real-time data processing, filtering and aggregation with an objective of generating warnings based on certain circumstances. In a conclusion, the report emphasized Apache Kafka's role as e significant tool business to develop insights from their data streams (Kiran Peddireddy 2023). The growing amount of data and therefore need for event processing, which Kafka can effectively managed is addressed. Also, it described the facts that Kafka can be integrated with standard accounting software/finance analytics tools to grasp business logics. But it didn't give an idea of any probable drawback or limitations possible data loss or the complexity of controlling and observing kafka clusters(Ralph Steurer 2021) . A chance of real-time forecasting of stock market trend based on news, blogs and historical price is primarily based on supervised machine learning algorithms. The model operated in two states: a real-time mode where it is incorporated on live data throughout the stock market timeline and the offline mode where the model worked on past data and as well as current data (after the stock market session). After the addition of sentiment analysis feature from blogs and market news data, the model uplifted the forecast accuracy (Mostafa Mohamed Seif et. al., 2018) . An uncertain autoregressive moving average model provided larger adaptability and general capability for handling situations where past observations & disturbance terms affected current observation (Xin et al., 2022). The impact of the proposed methodology uses matrices such as Symmetric Mean Absolute Percentage Error (SMAPE), Directional Symmetry (DS), and Theil's U Coefficient. The Diebold Mariano (DM) test was used in the paper to evaluate the effectiveness for each pair of models, but it has not mentioned any potential restrictions of this testing strategy (Mohammad Arafat Ali Khan et al., 2022).

An ensemble-based model that combined multi-layer perceptron, long short-term memory, and convolutional neural network models to estimate sentiment in social media posts, achieved a next-hour prediction performance of 74.3% (Hussein Al Osman, 2023) .The use of Apache Kafka in big data stream processing, which involved a major role in real-time streaming data for data analytics. The paper demonstrated that Kafka is a popular architecture known for its scalability, distribution, reliability, and high throughput, providing an API similar to a messaging system (Bhole Rahul Hiraman 2018). The Apache Kafka performance along with experiments based on the producer-consumer API parameters were evaluated. Some significant parameters such as KPI along with CPU utilization and memory usage were determined and tested to evaluate streaming platform performance. In this article, for the data processing technique how validity and dependability are affected by potential biases or limits, was not discussed (Shubham Vyas et al. 2022) . The possibility of dramatic maxima and minima as a process to get an idea about prospective stock pricing behavior in future was examined. In historical data evaluation, the author concluded that LSTM neural network model, powered by the MBGD algorithm & equipped with an attention layer, can forecast stock values. In drawbacks, author also addressed that LSTM neural network has forecast time latency issue (Dou Wei 2019). The Long Short-Term Memory (LSTM) deep learning algorithm forecasted the trend or values of stock indices & volatilities in the stock market. The impact of other financial variables such as open, low, high prices etc., were not considered as well as reasons why market index and volatility projections depend on hybrid momentum for prediction accuracy were not investigated (Kyoung-Sook Moon and Hongjoong 2019). A docker-based Kafka test bed which was applied to gather sufficient training data for the prediction model that estimated the dependability of Kafka under different conFigureurations and network conditions, the article suggested a prediction model involving artificial neural networks (Han Wu et al., 2020). The authors stress that marketplaces are becoming more multicultural as a result of migration and globalization, with customers bringing their own cultural identities, values, and expectations (Tarnanidis et al.,). The authors contend that diversity and inclusion are strategic forces behind innovation, brand distinctiveness, and long-term growth in addition to being moral requirements. Businesses may improve authenticity and build enduring customer trust by including diversity into brand narratives, communication tactics, and product design (Tarnanidis et al.,

2026). Fostering empathy in management courses helps students and future leaders comprehend different viewpoints, confront prejudices, and interact positively across cultural and social divides(Licsandru et a., 2025). The study tackles a significant drawback of conventional advertising campaign planning, which frequently depends on historical data and static segmentation.Their architecture allows marketers to make decisions in real time, customize offers, and more accurately forecast future consumer value by integrating adaptive learning models (Mandania et al., 2025). The study places this analysis in the larger theoretical framework of frameworks for brand value generation and agency theory.The findings show a strong positive correlation: executives who receive greater equity-based incentives are more inclined to devote resources to customer-centric projects, branding, and innovation. This result emphasizes how financial incentives influence organizational culture and marketing strategy (Sardashti & Calantone, 2022).

3. METHODOLOGY

The delays caused by traditional data ingestion techniques frequently result in missed opportunities and elevated risks. Real-time stock market analytics have become essential in a world where the speed and accuracy of financial markets are increasingly defining characteristics. Because the stock market is so dynamic and frequently unpredictable, it is essential to have access to real-time information and be able to analyze and react to it quickly. The demands of today's financial landscape cannot be met by traditional data processing methods. The delays caused by traditional data ingestion techniques frequently result in missed opportunities and elevated risks.

Figure 1. System Architecture for Real-time data streaming and pipelining

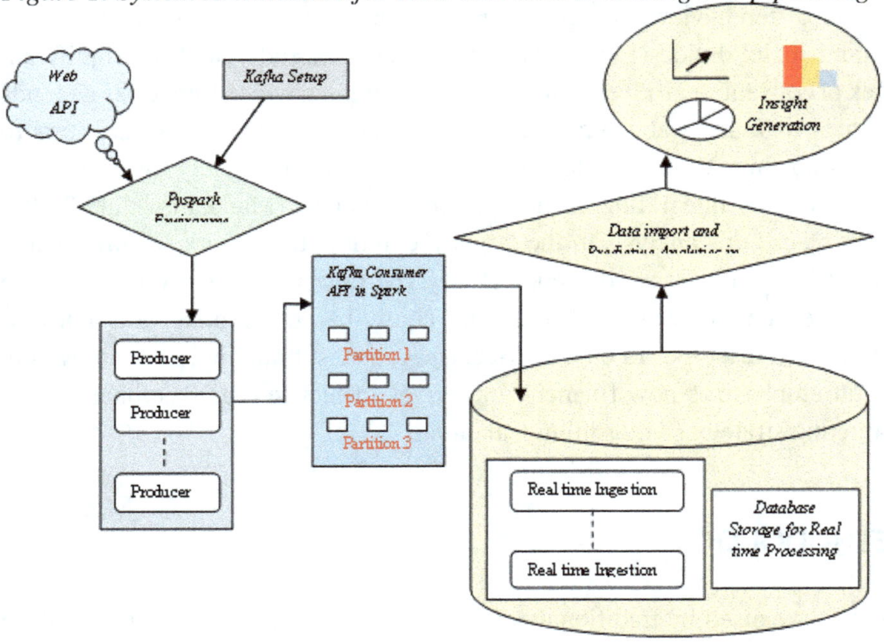

In order to solve this problem, real-time data ingestion, facilitated by technologies like Apache Kafka, is important in addressing this challenge. It guarantees that market data, news updates, and social media sentiment are immediately available for analysis. This timeliness empowers traders and investors to make swift decisions based on the most current information, reducing the risk of missed opportunities or delayed responses. Moreover, real-time data ingestion supports effective risk management by monitoring market anomalies, unusual trading patterns, and news sentiment as they occur. This capability enhances rapid risk assessment and mitigation, contributing to the stability and profitability of market participants. This project is also motivated by the critical need to enhance stock market analytics using Apache Kafka, a technology that offers revolutionary real-time data processing and analytics capabilities, to improve stock market analytics. Kafka's intrinsic features include scalability, fault tolerance, and data integration. Because of its distributed architecture, the system can grow to accommodate ever-growing data volumes while staying operational even in the event of hardware failures. Furthermore, Kafka's seamless integration with various analytics tools and platforms allows us to create a comprehensive view of market conditions, enabling more thorough and accurate analysis.

3.1 Data Collection

The foundation of this research project lies in the acquisition of a comprehensive stock market dataset. The stock market real-time data, sourced from Yahoo finance (https://rapidapi.com/asepscareer/api/yfinance-stock-market-data), comprises essential attributes, including datetime, severity index, current stock value. In this project, the data is directly feed through an API platform for real time streaming.

3.2 Data Preprocessing

This research project addresses the critical task of preprocessing real-time data obtained from an Apache Kafka producer. The process involves a series of meticulously defined steps to refine raw data streams, making them amenable for subsequent analysis or consumption by downstream systems. Initially, a Kafka consumer is set up to subscribe to specific topics where data is being produced, ensuring seamless ingestion of streaming data. Subsequently, the incoming data is deserialized, restoring it to its original format (e.g., Avro, JSON, Protobuf) for further processing and analysis. Rigorous data validation procedures are then applied to ensure conformity with predefined schemas or expected data formats, effectively mitigating potential discrepancies. Following validation, the data undergoes a comprehensive cleaning process to address data quality issues, including missing values and outliers, employing techniques such as imputation and outlier handling. The subsequent step involves the application of requisite transformations, encompassing feature engineering, numerical feature scaling, categorical variable encoding, and natural language data processing. Filter mechanisms are implemented to isolate specific data subsets based on defined criteria or conditions. Additionally, the methodology includes optional steps for data aggregation over designated time windows or based on specific criteria, and data enrichment through the integration of external sources, such as lookup tables or API calls, to provide additional contextual information. Depending on downstream system requirements, optional serialization of the preprocessed data is performed before dissemination to targeted systems, including databases, analytics platforms, or other Kafka topics. The pipeline is designed to incorporate robust error-handling mechanisms, ensuring graceful management of any anomalies or issues encountered during preprocessing. This structured approach aims to enhance the efficacy of data-driven applications by ensuring the integrity and suitability of streaming data for subsequent analysis.

3.3 Experimental Setup

The base of this project is to analyze data which is produce by APIs through the medium of Kafka in real time. Kafka is an open-source distributed event streaming platform originally developed by LinkedIn and later open-sourced as an Apache Software Foundation project. It is designed for efficiently handling real-time data feeds and processing streams of data, making it a popular choice for building event-driven, scalable, and fault-tolerant systems. To install Apache Kafka on Windows, you can follow these steps:

1) Prerequisites:

Java path creation is required as an open-source distribution like Adopt OpenJDK.

2) Kafka Configuration:
   - Download source: https://kafka.apache.org/downloads Choose the binary distribution and download the .tgz file (e.g., kafka_2.13-2.8.1.tgz).
   - Installation of Kafka via downloaded. tgz file into that directory.
   - Inside the Kafka directory, navigate to the "conFigure" folder.
   - Renamed the 'server.properties' file to 'server.properties.old' to keep a backup.
   - Created a new Configuration file named 'server.properties' in the same directory with the following content:
     - Listeners=PLAINTEXT://localhost:9092
     - Log.dirs=/tmp/kakfa-logs
   - Kafka relies on Apache Zookeeper to manage its cluster. Zookeeper was downloaded from the Apache Zookeeper website whether the version included with the Kafka download can also be used.
   - Opened a command prompt and under Kafka directory started Zookeeper by running the following command:

.\bin\windows\zookeeper-server-start.bat .\conFigure\zookeeper.properties

- In the same way in another command prompt, start the Kafka server by running the following command:

.\bin\windows\kafka-server-start.bat .\conFigure\zookeeper.properties

3.4 Building the Topic

- To create a Kafka topic, following command to be executed in the windows terminal through the Kafka directory

\bin\windows\kafka-topics.bat –create –topics myTopic –bootstrap-server localhost:9092 –partition 1 –replication-factor 1

3.5 Environment Setup

- Setting up a Python development environment involves installing Python, managing packages, and setting up code editor or integrated development environments (IDEs). Here's a brief overview of the steps for setting up a Python environment:
- Install Python:
  - Download the latest Python installer for your platform from the official Python website (https://www.python.org/downloads/). Run the installer and follow the installation instructions. Ensure that you add Python to your system's PATH during installation to make it accessible from the command line.
- Package Management:
  - Python has a package management system called pip that allows you to install, update, and manage Python packages and libraries. You can use pip to install packages by running commands like pip install package_name.

3.6 Producer Creation

- To produce messages to the topic:

.\bin\windows\kafka-console-producer.bat –topic myTopic –broker-list localhost:9092

3.7 Integration of Kafka with Python

- Real-time Data Processing:
- Python can be used with stream processing frameworks like Apache Kafka Streams, Apache Flink, or Faust to perform real-time data transformations and analytics on data streams from Kafka.

3.8 Consumer Build up

- To consume messages from the topic:

.\bin\windows\kafka-console-consumer.bat –topic myTopic –bootstrap-server localhost:9092 –from-beginning

3.9 Data Storage

- When building a real-time streaming system using Apache Kafka, Python, and Apache Spark, data storage plays a critical role in managing and persisting the incoming stream of data. The choice of the database largely depends on your specific use case and requirements. Here's a brief overview of the database options and how to store data:
- Store the processed data into the chosen database. Depending on the database, you may need to use connectors, APIs, or custom code to write data from Spark into the database.

3.10 Data Ingestion

- Use Kafka producers to ingest real-time streaming data into Kafka topics. This data can be in the form of events, logs, or any other structured or semi-structured data.
- Data ingestion refers to the process of sending data from various sources into a target system or data pipeline. The data can be in different formats, such as structured, semi-structured, or unstructured, and can originate from a wide range of sources, including sensors, applications, databases, logs, external services, and more.

3.11 Predictive Analytics

- Data Collection and Ingestion:

Begin by explaining how you collect and ingest real-time streaming stock market data from various sources. This could include data feeds, financial APIs, and other data providers. Describe the data formats, protocols, and quality assurance measures used in the data ingestion process.

- Historical Data Analysis:

Describe the analysis of historical stock market data to identify patterns, trends, and potential predictors. Explain the statistical and quantitative methods used to uncover insights from past data.

- Real-Time Prediction:

Discuss the implementation of the predictive model for real-time prediction. Describe how you use incoming data to make predictions at regular intervals, and how predictions are updated as new data arrives.

3.12 Algorithm & Mathematical Approach

Autoregressive Integrated Moving Average (ARIMA) is used to and fed by a time series stock market data. The model is described as ARIMA (p, d, q) where,

- p determines the number of Autoregressive (AR) terms of the time series and models the logical relationship between the current and past value for a stock. For p-order autoregressive part, AR(p) can be expressed as:

$$X_t = c + \phi_1 * X_{t-1} + \phi_2 * X_{t-2} + \phi_3 * X_{t-3} + \ldots\ldots\ldots \phi_p * X_{t-p} + €_t$$

- d determines the order of differencing which is used to define 'I' which the number of times a data to be differenced for stationarity achievement where difference expressed as,

$$Y_t = X_t - X_t\text{-}d$$

- q determines the order of moving average (MA) terms those model the logical relationship between current value and past forecast errors, So MA(q) can be expressed as,

$$X_t = c + €_t + \Theta_1 * €_{t-1} + \Theta_2 * €_{t-2} + \Theta_3 * €_{t-3} + \ldots\ldots\ldots \Theta_q * €_{t-q}$$

$X_{t=}$ Value of time series at 't' time
'*c*' is constant term
$€_{t=}$ White noise error term at 't' time
$\phi_{1,}\ \phi_{2,}\ \phi_{3\ldots\ldots}$ = *Autoregressive Coefficient*
$\Theta_{1,}\ \Theta_{1,}\ \Theta_{1\ldots\ldots\ldots\ldots}$ = Moving Average Coefficient
The algorithm for ARIMA for a time series data is as follows,
 # Necessary libraries to be imported

 # Loading the data from CSV and preprocess the stock price data

 # Ensure the data is sorted by date which is the most important thing in ARIMA

 # Check for stationarity and perform differencing if needed

 # Perform the Dickey-Fuller test for stationarity

 # Plot ACF and PACF on the data to determine AR and MA orders

 # Fit the ARIMA model based on date and order argument to determine ARIMA order

 # Model validation and evaluation through mean square error and root mean square error

 # Make future predictions through forecast

 # In main function, Split data into training and testing sets (Training size 80%)

 # Fit the ARIMA model using train data

 # Evaluate the Model using the test data to forecast

 # Make future predictions and print the output using the trained model

Figure 2. Visualization of the Algorithm

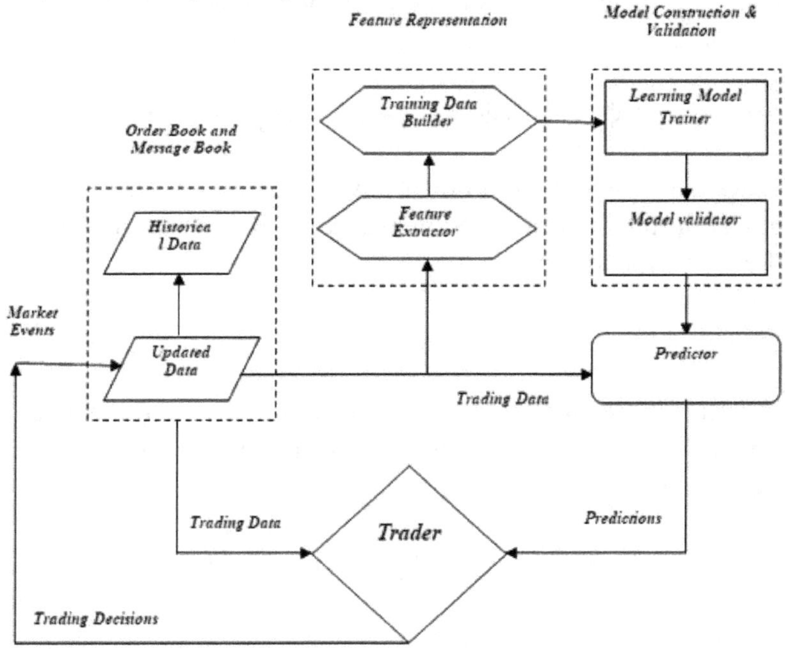

4. RESULTS

A dataset from Kaggle is used to train and evaluate the suggested system (https://www.kaggle.com/datasets/akshayr009/adani-ports-stock-price). The columns Date, Symbol, Series, Close Price, and Volume comprise the dataset, which includes stock data for Adani Ports from 2007 to 2025. The ARIMA model is used to examine and predict the stock trends after the data is separated into training and testing sets. Based on the model's performance, the system produces the following outcomes. The dataset also includes details on each column's data type for each item.

Figure 3. Reading Adani Ports Stock Data by Kafka Producer

```
[ ] stock_data.head()
```

	Date	Symbol	Series	Prev Close	Open	High	Low	Last	Close	VWAP	Volume	Turnover	Trades	Deliverable Volume	%Deliverble
0	27-11-2007	MUNDRAPORT	EQ	440.00	770.00	1050.00	770.0	959.0	962.90	984.72	27294366	2.687720e+15	NaN	9859619	0.3612
1	28-11-2007	MUNDRAPORT	EQ	962.90	984.00	990.00	874.0	885.0	893.90	941.38	4581338	4.312770e+14	NaN	1453278	0.3172
2	29-11-2007	MUNDRAPORT	EQ	893.90	909.00	914.75	841.0	887.0	884.20	888.09	5124121	4.550660e+14	NaN	1069678	0.2088
3	30-11-2007	MUNDRAPORT	EQ	884.20	890.00	958.00	890.0	929.0	921.55	929.17	4609762	4.283260e+14	NaN	1260913	0.2735
4	03-12-2007	MUNDRAPORT	EQ	921.55	939.75	995.00	922.0	980.0	969.30	965.65	2977470	2.875200e+14	NaN	816123	0.2741

```
[ ] stock_data.describe()
```

	Prev Close	Open	High	Low	Last	Close	VWAP	Volume	Turnover	Trades	Deliverable Volume	%Deliverble
count	3322.000000	3322.000000	3322.000000	3322.000000	3322.000000	3322.000000	3322.000000	3.322000e+03	3.322000e+03	2.456000e+03	3.322000e+03	3322.000000
mean	344.114314	344.763019	351.608007	337.531969	344.239539	344.201626	344.853182	2.954564e+06	1.070144e+14	4.492259e+04	1.207441e+06	0.445699
std	192.936882	193.519992	198.617808	188.678614	193.187813	193.045886	193.841305	4.104227e+06	2.625564e+14	5.023124e+04	1.398840e+06	0.160496
min	108.000000	108.000000	110.450000	105.650000	108.000000	108.000000	108.340000	1.236600e+04	2.415860e+11	3.660000e+02	5.383000e+03	0.067000
25%	164.312500	164.850000	168.000000	161.600000	164.075000	164.312500	164.855000	7.493682e+05	1.817652e+13	2.083200e+04	3.212005e+05	0.332900
50%	324.700000	325.750000	331.275000	319.850000	325.000000	324.700000	325.785000	2.007292e+06	5.836045e+13	3.588150e+04	8.132775e+05	0.445650
75%	400.912500	401.000000	407.187500	395.000000	400.912500	400.912500	400.607500	3.836883e+06	1.158525e+14	5.336875e+04	1.605528e+06	0.566850
max	1307.450000	1310.250000	1324.000000	1270.000000	1308.000000	1307.450000	1302.150000	9.771788e+07	8.160990e+15	1.205964e+06	2.241652e+07	0.979600

The plot in Figure 4 illustrates how the closing prices of Adani Ports stock have changed over time. It provides a visual representation of the general pattern and variations in the stock value between 2007 and 2025. Figure 5 presents the corresponding numerical data for these annual closing prices in tabular form, making it easy to compare values between years. Patterns, seasonal fluctuations, and long-term growth trends in the company's stock performance can be found using this graphical and tabular depiction. These findings form the foundation for additional time-series research utilizing the ARIMA model.

Figure 4. Metadata of Data source

```
<class 'pandas.core.frame.DataFrame'>
RangeIndex: 3322 entries, 0 to 3321
Data columns (total 16 columns):
 #   Column              Non-Null Count  Dtype
---  ------              --------------  -----
 0   Date                3322 non-null   datetime64[ns]
 1   Symbol              3322 non-null   object
 2   Series              3322 non-null   object
 3   Prev Close          3322 non-null   float64
 4   Open                3322 non-null   float64
 5   High                3322 non-null   float64
 6   Low                 3322 non-null   float64
 7   Last                3322 non-null   float64
 8   Close               3322 non-null   float64
 9   VWAP                3322 non-null   float64
 10  Volume              3322 non-null   int64
 11  Turnover            3322 non-null   float64
 12  Trades              2456 non-null   float64
 13  Deliverable Volume  3322 non-null   int64
 14  %Deliverble         3322 non-null   float64
 15  Year                3322 non-null   int64
dtypes: datetime64[ns](1), float64(10), int64(3), object(2)
memory usage: 415.4+ KB
```

Figure 5. Sample price of Adani ports stocks

```
                  Date       Symbol Series  Prev Close    Open     High    Low  \
Date_index
2007-11-27 2007-11-27  MUNDRAPORT     EQ      440.00  770.00  1050.00  770.0
2007-11-28 2007-11-28  MUNDRAPORT     EQ      962.90  984.00   990.00  874.0
2007-11-29 2007-11-29  MUNDRAPORT     EQ      893.90  909.00   914.75  841.0
2007-11-30 2007-11-30  MUNDRAPORT     EQ      884.20  890.00   958.00  890.0
2007-12-03 2007-12-03  MUNDRAPORT     EQ      921.55  939.75   995.00  922.0
```

```
             Last   Close    VWAP    Volume      Turnover  Trades  \
Date_index
2007-11-27  959.0  962.90  984.72  27294366  2.687720e+15     NaN
2007-11-28  885.0  893.90  941.38   4581338  4.312770e+14     NaN
2007-11-29  887.0  884.20  888.09   5124121  4.550660e+14     NaN
2007-11-30  929.0  921.55  929.17   4609762  4.283260e+14     NaN
2007-12-03  980.0  969.30  965.65   2977470  2.875200e+14     NaN
```

The Rolling mean of stock trend is shown with red, original value of stock is shown in blue and Standard deviation of Adani ports is shown in black along with test result of Dickey Fuller test in Figure- 6, critical value of Dickey Fuller test is -

1.94 and here plot value is more negative than Dickey Fuller test so analysis is now the time series in stationary.

Figure 6. Rolling Mean and Standard Deviation of stock price

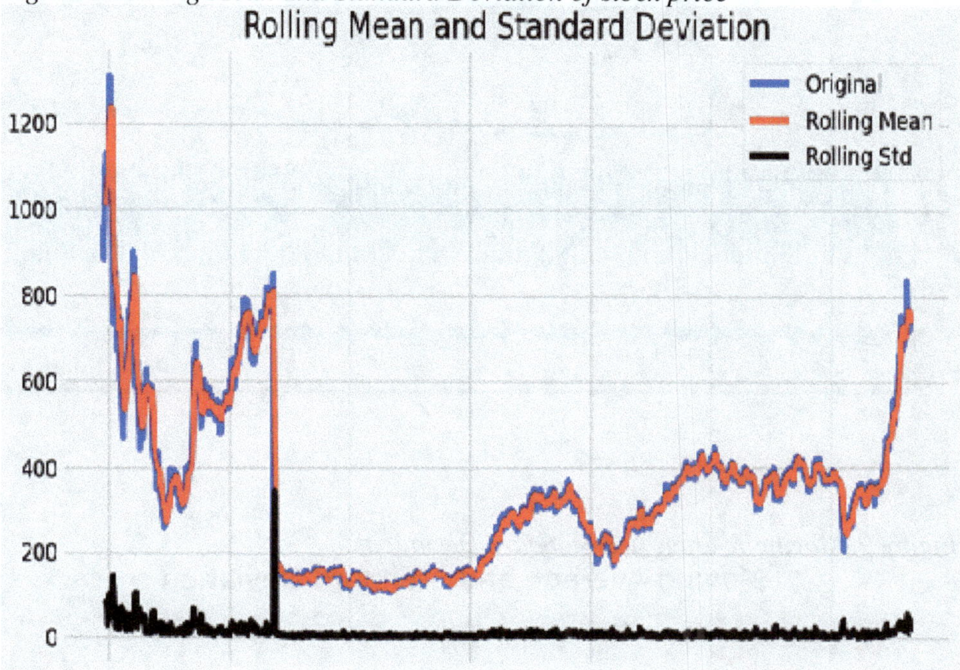

Figure 7. Result of Dickey Fuller test

```
Results of Dickey-Fuller Test:
Test Statistics                    -3.473098
p-value                             0.008705
No. of lags used                    5.000000
Number of observations used      3316.000000
Critical Value (1%)                -3.432324
Critical Value (5%)                -2.862412
Critical Value (10%)               -2.567234
dtype: float64
```

The plot in Figure -8 shown result of test and train data trends of closing price of Adani ports stock year wise with ARIMA model intercept result. Result of AIC, BIC and HQIC is given in form of ARIMA model matrix along with plot in Figure – 9.

Figure 8. Raise, Seasonality, Trend in Stock price

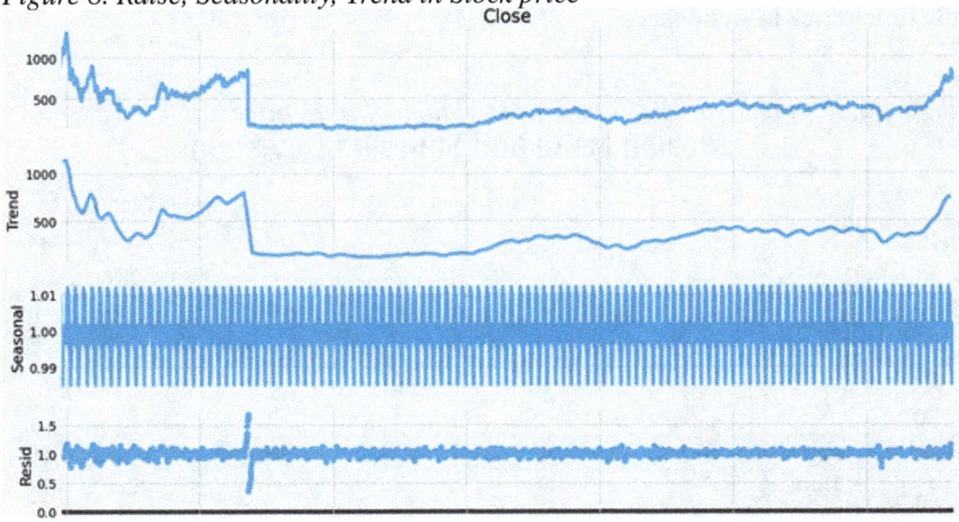

Figure 9. Moving Average and Standard Deviation

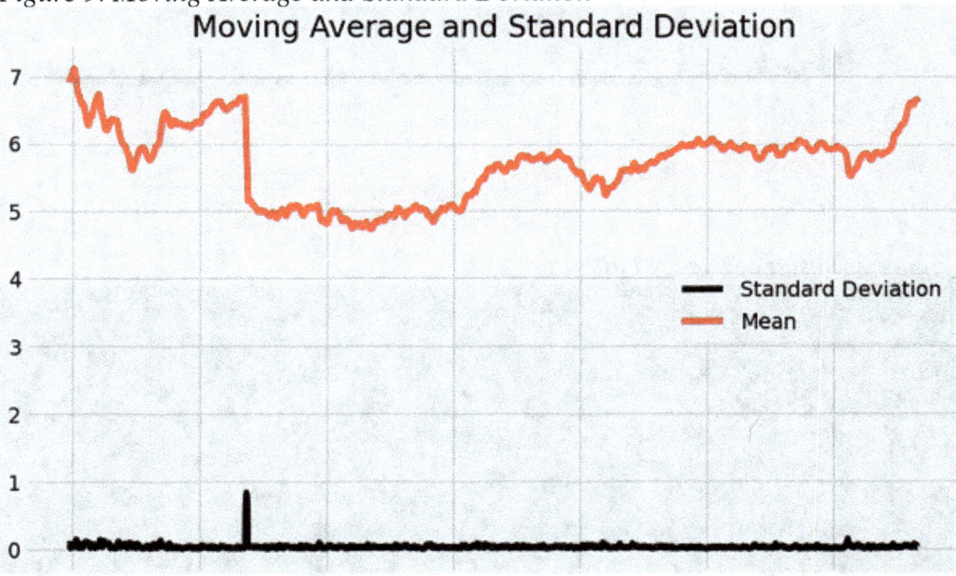

BIC penalize complexity more heavily than AIC and HQIC as result shown in table BIC value is less than both AIC and HQIC indicates that model is better model. Similar to AIC, the lower the BIC or HQIC, the better the model. the order of preference among the models according to these criteria remains the same as with AIC: the model with the lowest value (in this case, HQIC at -10756) is considered relatively better than the others. Standardized residuals are the residuals of the model divided by their estimated standard deviation. As these residuals are centered around zero and exhibit no systematic patterns. Normal Q-Q plot compares the distribution of the standardized residual against the expected normal distribution as shown in Figure- 10, Histogram is visualization displays the distribution of the standard residuals and correlogram displays autocorrelation coefficients of the residual at different lags.

Figure 10. Covariance matrix and Graphs

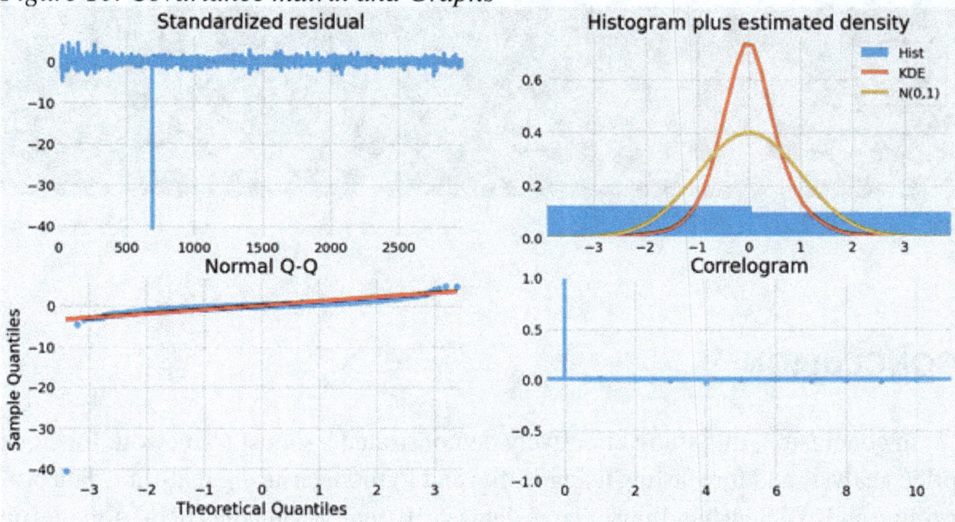

As value of AIC is more than both BIC or HQIC in ARIMA model indicates that model is better result are shown in Figure – 11. Performance of Dataset of Adani ports using ARIMA model is represented in terms of MSE, MAE, RMSE, MAPE.

Figure 11. ARIMA model results

```
                               SARIMAX Results
==============================================================================
Dep. Variable:                  Close   No. Observations:                 2986
Model:                 ARIMA(1, 1, 2)   Log Likelihood                5380.283
Date:                Sat, 25 Nov 2023   AIC                         -10752.565
Time:                        10:58:26   BIC                         -10728.560
Sample:                             0   HQIC                        -10743.928
                               - 2986
Covariance Type:                  opg
==============================================================================
                 coef    std err          z      P>|z|      [0.025      0.975]
------------------------------------------------------------------------------
ar.L1          0.3021     19.443      0.016      0.988     -37.805      38.410
ma.L1         -0.2925     19.442     -0.015      0.988     -38.398      37.813
ma.L2         -0.0041      0.183     -0.022      0.982      -0.362       0.354
sigma2         0.0016   2.96e-06    538.304      0.000       0.002       0.002
===================================================================================
Ljung-Box (L1) (Q):                   0.00   Jarque-Bera (JB):         102963262.95
Prob(Q):                              1.00   Prob(JB):                         0.00
Heteroskedasticity (H):               0.12   Skew:                           -22.34
Prob(H) (two-sided):                  0.00   Kurtosis:                       911.76
===================================================================================
```

CONCLUSION

In conclusion, this study effectively demonstrated a robust framework for stock price analysis and forecasting using Kafka and Python, ensuring real-time data processing and efficient handling of large datasets. By employing the ARIMA model on the year-wise closing prices of Adani Ports, the research provided valuable insights into stock market behavior, identifying long-term trends and volatility patterns through rolling mean and standard deviation analysis. The comparative evaluation of model performance indicated that ARIMA ARIMA delivers more accurate and reliable predictions, supported by its higher AIC value relative to BIC and HQIC. This highlights ARIMA's ability to capture both trend and seasonality in time-series data more effectively than alternative models. Overall, the findings emphasize that integrating data streaming technologies like Kafka with statistical forecasting models such as ARIMA can significantly enhance the precision and efficiency of financial market analysis, paving the way for more informed investment decisions and future advancements in predictive analytics.

REFERENCES

Hiraman, B. R. (2018, August). A study of apache kafka in big data stream processing. In *2018 International Conference on Information, Communication, Engineering and Technology (ICICET)* (pp. 1-3). IEEE.

Jena, M., Behera, R. K., & Rath, S. K. (2019, December). Machine learning models for stock prediction using real-time streaming data. In *International Conference on Biologically Inspired Techniques in Many-Criteria Decision Making* (pp. 101-108). Cham: Springer International Publishing.

Khan, M. A. A., Bhushan, C., Ravi, V., Rao, V. S., & Orsu, S. S. (2022). Nowcasting the financial time series with streaming data analytics under apache spark. arXiv preprint arXiv:2202.11820.

Kyoung-Sook, M. O. O. N., & Hongjoong, K. I. M. (2019). Performance of deep learning in prediction of stock market volatility. *Economic Computation and Economic Cybernetics Studies and Research*, *53*(2).

Licsandru, T. C., Mari, C., Kipnis, E., Galalae, C., Johnson, E., Cross, S. N., & Yoruk, I. (2025). Integrating diversity, equity and inclusion in management education: An empathy framework. *British Journal of Management*.

Mandania, R., Cadogan, J., Liu, J., & Kazmi, N. (2025). Optimizing Promotional Campaigns to Maximize Customer Lifetime Value: A Dynamic Learning Approach. *Journal of Service Research*, •••, 10946705251365524.

Peddireddy, K. (2023, May). Streamlining enterprise data processing, reporting and realtime alerting using apache kafka. In 2023 11th International Symposium on Digital Forensics and Security (ISDFS) (pp. 1-4). IEEE.

Sardashti, H., & Calantone, R. J. (2022). Does equity-based compensation motivate executives to build strong brands? *Journal of Marketing Management*, *38*(13-14), 1433–1460.

Seif, M. M., Ramzy Hamed, E. M., & Abdel Ghfar Hegazy, A. E. F. (2018, January). Stock market real time recommender model using apache spark framework. In *International conference on advanced machine learning technologies and applications* (pp. 671-683). Cham: Springer International Publishing.

Steurer, R. (2021). Kafka: Real-Time Streaming for the Finance Industry. In The Digital Journey of Banking and Insurance, Volume III: Data Storage, Data Processing and Data Analysis (pp. 73-88). Cham: Springer International Publishing.

Tarnanidis, T., Manda, V. K., Sousa, B., Vlachopoulou, M., & Papachristou, E. (2026). Marketing Complexity of Smart Consumer Products to Global Millennial Segments. In *Diversity and Inclusion-Driven Marketing for Multicultural Marketplaces* (pp. 1–16). IGI Global Scientific Publishing.

Tarnanidis, T., Sousa, B., Vlachopoulou, M., Papachristou, E., & Kittu Manda, V. (Eds.). (2026). *Diversity and Inclusion-Driven Marketing for Multicultural Marketplaces*. IGI Global Scientific Publishing., DOI: 10.4018/979-8-3373-2111-0

Vyas, S., Tyagi, R. K., Jain, C., & Sahu, S. (2022, February). Performance evaluation of apache kafka–a modern platform for real time data streaming. In 2022 2nd International Conference on Innovative Practices in Technology and Management (ICIPTM) (Vol. 2, pp. 465-470). IEEE.

Wei, D. (2019, October). Prediction of stock price based on LSTM neural network. In *2019 International Conference on Artificial Intelligence and Advanced Manufacturing (AIAM)* (pp. 544-547). IEEE.

Wu, H., Shang, Z., & Wolter, K. (2020, June). Learning to reliably deliver streaming data with apache kafka. In 2020 50th Annual IEEE/IFIP International Conference on Dependable Systems and Networks (DSN) (pp. 564-571). IEEE.

Xin, Y., Gao, J., Yang, X., & Yang, J. (2023). Maximum likelihood estimation for uncertain autoregressive moving average model with application in financial market. *Journal of Computational and Applied Mathematics*, *417*, 114604.

Chapter 9
Equity by Design: Embedding DEI Into AI-Enhanced Marketing Tools

Mohammad Irfan
https://orcid.org/0000-0002-4956-1170
Chandigarh University Uttar Pradesh, Unnao, India

Sanskriti Sanskriti
https://orcid.org/0009-0000-3914-4544
Christ University, Bangalore, India

Amit Kishore Sinha
Chandigarh University Uttar Pradesh, Unnao, India

ABSTRACT

In a time when artificial intelligence redefines marketing practice pillars, the concern is not innovation but conscience-driven innovation. While AI tools promise unmatched precision in reaching customers, segmenting, and budgeting, they carry a silent danger of deepening existing disparities, if they were to be unleashed without caution. This article advocates for the practice of Equity by Design, and it insists that Diversity, Equity, and Inclusion (DEI) must be made a part of the actual design of AI-driven marketing systems. By borrowing cross-disciplinary insights from finance, organizational ethics, and digital strategy, the case is argued through illustrations of how equitable design cuts down on algorithmic bias, expands financial service access to marginalized communities, and enhances consumer trust in a more data-driven market. Beyond compliance or corporate social responsibility, embedding DEI in AI is a competitive strategy, attaching ethical obligation to long-term brand worth, sustainable growth, and global competitiveness in the digital economy.

DOI: 10.4018/979-8-3373-6731-6.ch009

INTRODUCTION

AI is no longer the distant promise it once was; it is now the architect of a new chapter in marketing. Whereas campaigns have previously been driven by intuition and a cleaner target demographic, today, they are now driven by algorithms that predict and explain consumer behavior with diminishing accuracy, microscopically segment audiences and optimize strategy in real time. For companies, this revolution provides efficiency and profit potential that were unimaginable before. But lurking beneath the surface of this innovation is a sobering reality: if left unchecked, the same tools also entrench social divides, exclude at risk populations and quietly recreate the same inequities that firms "now pledge to remedy." Enter Equity by Design: not a moral afterthought, but as a guide to what the future of marketing looks like in a digital economy, Raj, A. (2024).

The advent of fairness-driven design in AI-powered marketing is a heightened expectation from humans that technology must benefit everybody, not just the privileged few. In observing the digital economy, a company's worth has become more tied to how equitable and empathetic values inform its systems and products. Consumers anticipate the promotion of a product, or financial product, through an algorithm to recognize the social context. The firms are not only measured by innovating or disrupting but also based on intentions. Marketing experts are increasingly more aware that fairness isn't an outside element but is a business strength towards securing a long-term structure founded on trust and loyalty. The conversation changed from the rapidity of AI to achieve outcome, to how considerate of the outcome to be for society's well-being and shared goals.

The worry is not AI or its rate of adoption. It is instead the risk of unconscientious adopting of AI. Years of evidence show that algorithms are not neutral and tend to reflect biases in the data on which they operate (Noble, 2018; O'Neil, 2016). A credit scoring algorithm will punish groups previously excluded from access to financial services. A marketing algorithm might disproportionately feature work or housing opportunities to one group at the expense of another (Barocas, Hardt, & Narayanan, 2019). There, technology does not disrupt inequality; it scales it up. To marketing practitioners, this is not just a technical bug but a reputational hazard, a strategic blind spot, and an ethical failure.

This is where the Diversity, Equity, and Inclusion framework comes into the picture. DEI is often boiled down to representation on organograms or symbolic gestures of desire. But in the case of our AI marketing, DEI goes deeper than representation alone. They are equity of outcomes, diversity of design practices, and making markets work for all communities equally. To incorporate DEI into AI-like systems will fundamentally re-conceptualize how algorithms are trained, which data is prioritized, and on what presumptions the decision-making model is based on that data. Incorporating diversity, equity, and inclusion into the marketing AI systems will not just imply data diversity, but thought diversity too. The design teams, which train and deploy algorithms eventually, always carry along their values and assumptions with them, and they do so without even acknowledging it. When the design teams consist of individuals belonging to similar educational or cultural backgrounds, the biases end up replicating faster than they can be identified. Equity by design supports the view that if the authors are diverse, the work will probably be diverse. Thus, when the marketers, developers and data scientists collaborate on a multidisciplinary basis across dimensions such as gender, geography and discipline, the systems produced reflect a broader spectrum of human view. Practically, this involves working through not just what data is being gathered, but who is interpreting the data, who stands to gain, and who might be unwittingly excluded from the outcomes. The concern is not merely compliance with upcoming regulations, but the necessity of the consumers' trust and brands' legitimacy in a moment of transparency (Floridi & Cowls, 2019).

Equity is an economic multiplier, not a constraint. The research shows that equitable practices build customer trust, deepen consumers' brand loyalty, and engage traditionally underrepresented populations creating goodwill and driving social value and shareholder returns (Ramaswamy & Ozcan, 2022.). One of the AIs in financial services will deploy fair AI tools to expand credit access and minimize systematic exclusion as well as develop new revenue sources in populations that have not had a healthy relationship with their local bank. In addition, seeing DEI as foundational to AI development is foresight, not philanthropy. Companies that bring this vision into action will not only lower reputational risk to their company but will be first-to-market players in what will become a crowded marketplace, ever more valuing ethics alongside efficiency.

The Equity by Design concept demands this change of approach. Equity cannot be proven through audits once the system has been constructed; it will only be apparent in the reasoning of the AI tools. This calls for inter-disciplinary thought to apply insight from finance, ethics, computer science, and organizational behavior to construct systems that enable fairness, as a design issue. Equity isn't a compliance exercise in this perspective, equity is the key to inclusive, sustainable innovation. Pandey, V., Kushwaha, G. S., & Srivastava, S. (2023), Chowdhuri, S. R., & Gupta, M. (2025).

This paper aims to promote that vision. Based in both practice and scholarship, the first argument is that embedding DEI into AI-based marketing systems is both a business imperative and a social obligation. The discussion is organized into five parts: a review of the literature on AI in marketing and algorithmic bias; an examination of DEI frameworks and their linkage to technologists as designers; a conceptual model for equity in AI systems; illustrative examples from financial marketing; and finally, implications for sustainable business growth and competitiveness in the digital economy.

The line diagram depicts forecasts for AI usage, DEI practices, and bias reduction in marketing tools over the years of 2025 to 2030. The rise of AI usage is accelerating, projecting a dramatic parallel increase of adoption from 40% to 95% while demonstrating the rapid digitization of marketing processes (Davenport et al., 2020). Furthermore, DEI practices are predicted to rise from just 20% to 90% from 2025 to 2030 and will reflect the increasing awareness on the need for fairness and inclusion in the design of AI tools (Whittaker et al., 2018; Floridi & Cowls, 2019).

Projected DEI Integration in AI-Enhanced Marketing (2025–2030)

Figure 1. Sources: Deloitte. (2024)

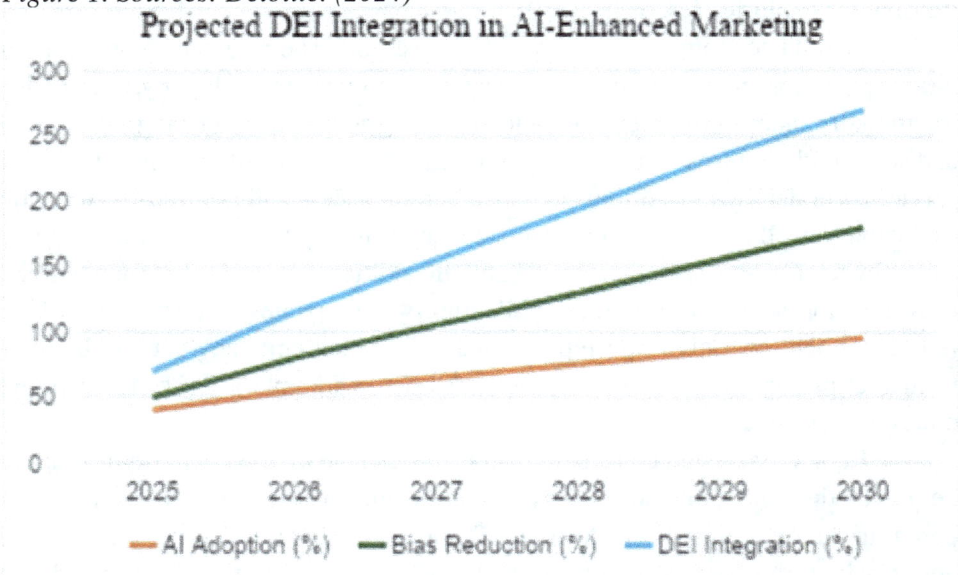

Lastly, bias reduction also improved dramatically from 10% to 85%. The move towards equity-centered frameworks demonstrate the potential of reducing algorithmic inequality (Mehrabi et al., 2021; Gebru et al., 2021). All of these developments enable one to contemplate living in a world where Equity by Design, where moral government, just targeting and equal access is no longer an optional add-on, but a structural requirement will be the new norm with AI powered marketing strategy in 2030. The convergence of adoption, equity and fairness enhances not only consumer trust, but brand worth and competitive distinction within the digital economy (Kotler et al., 2021).

These projections underscore the point that constructing equity is every bit a cultural task as it is one of skill. The pace at which inclusive AI technologies are embraced will depend on leaders who opt to invest in it, the level of awareness sophistication, and most importantly, an organizational willingness to implement policy. Successful digital transformation occurs when equality is not just on the compliance tick-box but in the business performance measures. With increasingly more businesses adopting ethical views while developing their algorithms, lines between "responsible" businesses and "innovative" businesses will blur. Indeed, equality can be an engine for imagination and competition.

Explanation of the Flowchart with Citations

The flowchart illustrates a comprehensive framework that explains how Equity by Design can be embedded into AI-enhanced marketing tools through the integration of Diversity, Equity, and Inclusion (DEI). It shows the relationships between factors influencing outcomes, control variables, and measured outcomes, with fairness serving as the central mediating principle.

At the top of the chart, the framework begins with AI in Marketing, Design Approach, DEI by Design, Ethical Governance, and Fair Decision-making. These represent the independent variables or primary drivers of responsible AI adoption. Artificial Intelligence in marketing delivers unprecedented targeting, personalization, and budgeting efficiency (Davenport et al., 2020). However, the approach to algorithmic design—whether equity-centered or efficiency-centered—determines whether such tools enhance inclusion or exacerbate disparities (Mehrabi et al., 2021). Embedding DEI by design ensures that fairness is not an afterthought but a foundational principle guiding development (Whittaker et al., 2018). Likewise, ethical governance structures anchor AI practices within broader organizational values, ensuring transparency, accountability, and long-term trust (Floridi & Cowls, 2019). Together, these elements shape the environment for fair decisions, which are central to avoiding bias and achieving equitable outcomes.

The second layer of the flowchart represents factors influencing outcomes, specifically the moderating variables. These include regulations, corporate culture, DEI awareness, technological maturity, demographics, company size, data quality, and region. Each plays a contextual role in shaping how AI tools function in practice. For instance, regulatory frameworks such as the General Data Protection Regulation (GDPR) or the European Union AI Act provide guardrails against discriminatory outcomes (European Commission, 2021). Corporate culture determines whether profit maximization or inclusivity takes precedence (Schein, 2017). The same is true with the quality and availability of data and demographic diversity, which directly influence the accuracy and fairness with which AI systems operate (Gebru et al., 2021). These are conditions that reinforce or undermine the connection between design principles and ultimate outcomes. One key insight within this model is that fairness does not occur in an automated or rote way, even with pure intentions. The process from design to market encompasses other point choices which can produce subtle variations to original intentions. At any point from data selection, models' tuning, validating output, we are making decisions that will include their alignment to inclusion. Equity by Design is more about intentional practice than one-time audit and fairness as a lived practice, not something to check off before the system goes live. By creating ethical choice checkpoints, data, better yet advance1 unknown data ethics backlog of data from design stage, and on into the implementation piece (presumably stage based, through the several test cycles) enables an expanse of dynamic related monitoring and adjustments as market conditions change and consumer behavior drives needs, ensuring fairness is also dynamic in form.

The third layer captures control variables, such as demographic characteristics, company size, geographic region, and tool type. These are not the primary focus but must be kept constant to avoid skewed interpretations of results. For example, AI systems deployed in different regions may face varying societal expectations of fairness, while large organizations with abundant resources might have stronger capacity to implement equity-driven governance. Accounting for these ensures that findings remain valid across contexts (Barocas et al., 2019), Pandey, P., & Rai, A. K. (2024).

Finally, at the bottom, the framework identifies outcomes being measured, which correspond to the dependent variables. These outcomes include bias reduction, consumer trust, fair targeting, inclusive access, customer loyalty, and brand equity. Collectively, they represent the practical benefits of embedding DEI into AI marketing. By reducing algorithmic bias, organizations can build stronger consumer trust, ensuring that customer segments feel represented and fairly treated (Langer & Landers, 2021). Fair targeting and inclusive access extend the reach of financial and marketing services to marginalized groups, thereby addressing systemic inequities (Noble, 2018). Over time, these practices translate into customer loyalty and enhanced brand equity, which are critical for sustainable growth and competitiveness in the digital economy (Kotler et al., 2021

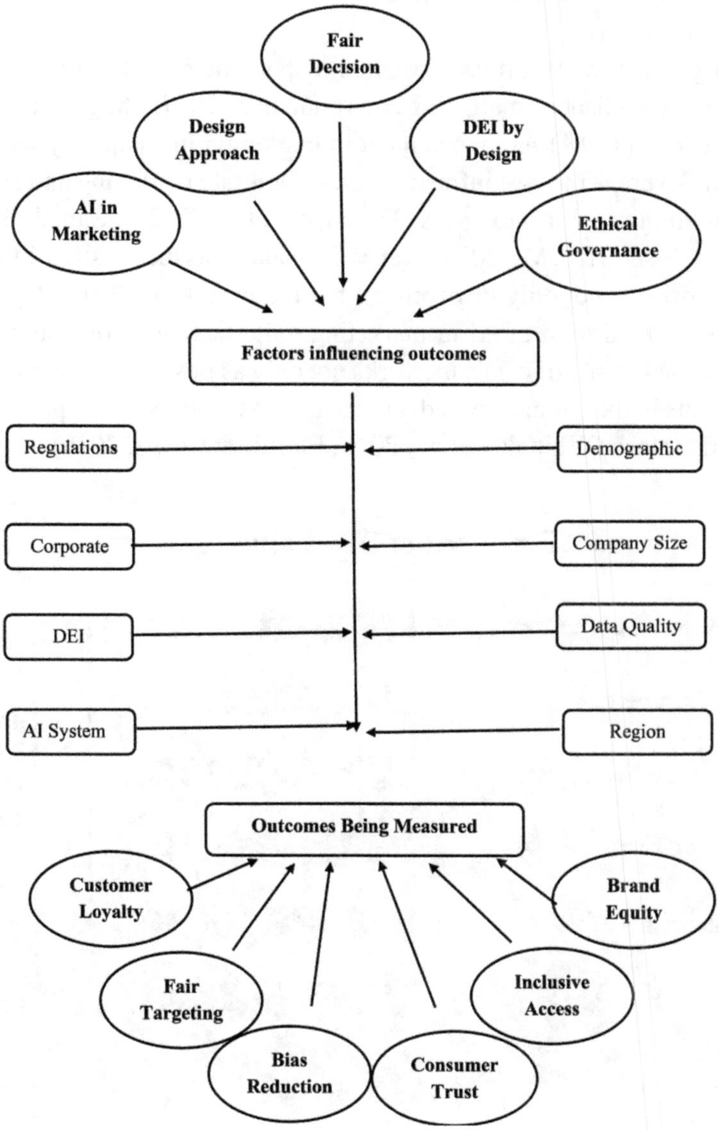
Fair Decision
Design Approach
DEI by Design
AI in Marketing
Ethical Governance
Factors influencing outcomes
Regulations
Demographic
Corporate
Company Size
DEI
Data Quality
AI System
Region
Outcomes Being Measured
Customer Loyalty
Brand Equity
Fair Targeting
Inclusive Access
Bias Reduction
Consumer Trust

PROJECTED DEI-INTEGRATED AI MARKETING LANDSCAPE (2047)

The bar graph depicts a future-oriented map of the potential role of Equity by Design on the AI-enhanced marketing environment by 2047. The graphic anticipates virtually universal (99%) AI involvement in marketing in a capacity where intelligent systems leverage the best infrastructure to facilitate marketing and engagement strategies with consumer audiences (Davenport et al., 2020), Sah, J., Padma, S., Yanamandra, R., & Irfan, M. (2024). Yet, what makes this future-state different from the decades prior is not only involvement but the extent to which integrating DEI principles into the design of AI in marketing will reach an anticipated 95%. This accounts for the use of ethical frameworks not only as possibilities for stakeholders but as elements in the competitive advantage of stakeholders that support a digitally trusted marketplace (Whittaker et al., 2018; Floridi & Cowls, 2019).

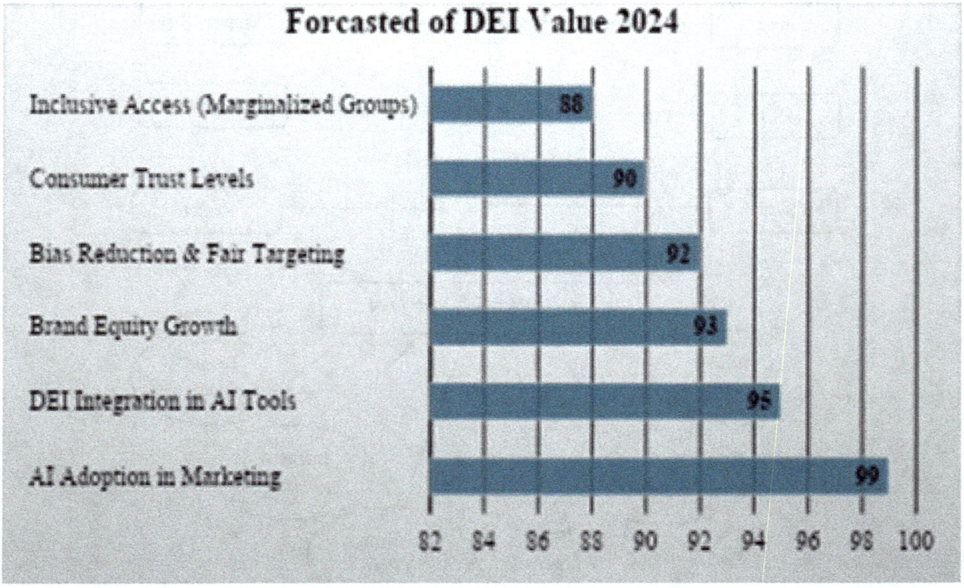

Sources: PwC. (2023)

The expected levels of bias-reduction and fair targeting represent a low 92% standard and this high potential demonstrates successful mitigation of algorithmic discrimination, bias reduction, and algorithmic governance that focus on the centre of equity and social justice (Mehrabi et al., 2021; Gebru et al., 2021). The expectation that consumer trust levels reach a standard of 90%, displays the expectation that transparency and accountability will ensure stakeholders have agency and feel represented and respected in their digital ecosystem. The anticipated level of inclusive access at 88%, demonstrates an anticipation that marketing and financial services will simultaneously grow for marginalized groups to further address systemic inequities rather than amplify inequity (Noble, 2018). Lastly, brand equity development, at 93%, highlights the fact that companies integrating DEI into AI strategies not only fulfill moral responsibilities but also achieve long-term marketplace legitimacy and competitiveness (Kotler et al., 2021). Cumulatively, the diagram shows that by 2047, integrating DEI in AI-powered marketing will be a structural expectation rather than a wishful objective, setting the tone for both industry practice and consumer experience.

In 2047, the message serves as a reminder that we should not expect technology to engender equity without continuous, conscious oversight from the human experience. Even the most intelligent forms of AI will need to have true governance defined by societal expectation. Data sources are ever-growing as international markets develop, and organizations will find it necessary to continually reconstruct fair. Organizations that are successful will be organizations that will obtain equity as a process—constantly updating tools, retraining staff, and engaging in conversation with their communities.

CASE STUDY 1: FINANCIAL SERVICES – FAIR CREDIT SCORING USING AI

The finance sector has long utilized credit scoring models in making the decision of whether and when to grant customers loans, credit cards, and mortgages. Historical credit scoring models, that are typically FICO or legacy system reliant, are discriminatory in and of themselves. These also weed out people with adverse credit records, something that has a disproportionate effect on women, immigrations, and ethnic minorities (Hurley & Adebayo, 2017), (Licsandru et al., 2025). These exclusions not only reinforce economic imbalances but also represent a loss of business opportunity for institutionally motivated growth in the customer-base. AI-Enhanced Credit Scoring Models. The latest advances in machine learning (an application of artificial intelligence (AI)) now allow for the construction of additional credit scoring models using expanded datasets of information, including rents paid and utility bills and even the pattern of usage of mobile phones (Vorster et al., 2024). Examples are Zest AI, a fintech that constructs machine learning–based credit models in a bid to reduce algorithmic bias. Others also involve Mastercard in testing inclusive credit with the aid of AI in a bid to parse non-conventional information sources and therefore expand credit access to the hitherto excluded market segments (Mastercard, 2020). The application of the AI models does not automatically equate to fairness in itself, however. Indeed, poorly designed algorithms could reproduce or perhaps accentuate prior biases in the event that they are trained from biased datasets (Barocas, Hardt, & Narayanan, 2019). But the Equity by Design practice of integrating DEI at the onset of system design has proved exceedingly valuable in preventing such risks. By actually centering issues of fairness first, disparate impact testing, and clear models, firms could guarantee that their systems of AI get better and not blur fair financial inclusion (Mehrabi et al., 2021), (Tarnanidis et al., 2026).

Another element sometimes not considered in the pursuit of fairness in the financial technology context is consumer perception. Customer experience and safety consist of trust in what the system is creating. Even unintentionally biased AI systems erode user experience trust. Customers would like to have in plain language how a decision has been reached, especially when it involves financial eligibility or access to a product or service. Sharing equity has a direct relationship to this dimension of coordination with stakeholders in the process (Tarnanidis et al., 2026). It is a factor of trust. When an organization can offer transparency and enable customers to see that AI decisions are falling into an equitable structure, uneasiness, and fear of utilizing the technology decrease, and inclusion increases. In brief, equitable AI is not merely a matter of how the data arrives at decisions; it is also a matter of how the community, culture, or members in our social and economic eco-system comprehend an output.

Integrating AI into Financial Tools

The Zest AI model is such a perfect representation of what it is to incorporate DEI into AI-based marketing tools. The company approach also builds fairness constraints into the training of models so that the prediction of loan approvals is not unduly discriminatory against the minority borrowers. That is the essence of transitioning from efficiency-concerned to equity-concerned algorithm design (Whittaker et al., 2018). Moreover, in opting for explainable governance models, Zest AI adheres to the postulations of the ethical AI that is centered on explainability and accountability (Floridi & Cowls, 2019). Mastercard universal credit initiative also demonstrates that the application of equity by design is a force to be employed. By opening up financial access in new markets, Mastercard not only enhanced its image of a socially committed business but also liberated millions of new customers. That is a testament to the general statement that the incorporation of DEI is not necessarily compliance or corporate social responsibility but it is inherently linked with sustainable growth and long-term profits (Kotler, Kartajaya, & Setiawan, 2021).

Consequences and Significance: Consequences of using DEI in finance-related marketing of AI products are long-lasting. Bias Reduction: Fairness-aware algorithms minimize disparate denial rates which in the past have discriminated against underrepresented populations (Langer & Landers, 2021). Consumer Confidence: Transparency in the decision-making process using Artificial Intelligence results in increased consumer confidence, particularly among previously excluded groups by nontransparent financial conduct (Noble, 2018). Inclusive Access: Widening access to credit establishes the financial strength and upward mobility of disadvantaged communities, achieving increased social equity. Brand Equity Development: Brands with equity-based AI are perceived to be responsible innovators and build long-term brand equity in the competitive world landscape. This case study demonstrates the application of financial services as a test lab for equity-focused deployment of AI. Through the incorporation of DEI into financial advertising and credit ratings systems, firms escape moral hazard but unleash huge business value. This is in line with the broader assumption of this paper: that equity by design in the promotion of AI is at the same time an ethical necessity and a strategic necessity in the digital economy.

CASE STUDY 2: RETAIL AND E-COMMERCE - INCLUSIVE MARKETING AND FAIR PERSONALISATION WITH ARTIFICIAL INTELLIGENCE

One of the hottest areas of testing for the applications of artificial intelligence (AI) has been in the retail and e-commerce space. From personalized recommendations to dynamic pricing strategies to chatbot-based customer support, AI has revolutionized the face of the customer experience. But with the innovations come the underlying questions of the kind: do the technologies facilitate inclusion or worsen inequity? Algorithms created without consideration for Diversity, Equity, and Inclusion (DEI) run the risk of marginalizing at-risk consumer segments and silencing them into stereotypes-or denying them equitable access to products and deals (Noble, 2018).

Personalization and Marketing with Artificial Intelligence

Personalisation is arguably the most important contribution of AI in the retail industry so far. Retailers such as Amazon and Alibaba have powerful recommender systems that predict consumer demand and guide the flow of consumption. While tools are selling more and keeping consumers engaged, studies are finding that they have unintended biases that replicate gender, ethnicity or socio-economic backgrounds. Women, for example, will receive a smaller share of high income livelihood product items or investment opportunities in finance (Datta et al. 2018). It is a paradox: the idea of personalization is alienating for the same consumers that companies want to capture if they risk becoming a risk to equity. AI marketing that is DEI focused ensures that personalization offers broader consumer choice and not limits it on discriminatory terms. Fairness benchmark, heterogeneous training datasets, and periodic bias audit are emerging as landmarks to attain ethical integrity in retail systems of AI (Mehrabi et al., 2021).

Integrating DEI in eCommerce AI: Incorporating equity by design in retailing is based on three levels of AI-based support for marketing systems: Product Recommendations - Inclusive recommender systems do not simply drive algorithms to reproduce inequalities in consumer data. Etsy has redesigned components of its recommendation engines to prioritize products from under-represented sellers, and level the playing field for minority-owned businesses to thrive (Etsy, 2020). Dynamic Pricing - Although dynamic pricing is a revenue-optimization technique based on demand- and profile-based prices, the optimization must not be run by an unconstrained algorithm; otherwise, it results in discriminatory pricing. Studies indicate that in online markets, sometimes low-income consumers are charged inflated prices for essential goods (Mikians et al., 2013). The design approach inspired by DEI would not allow for the exploitation of workers and it would keep prices fairest. Targeted Advertising - Facebook's algorithm for serving ads has been criticized for perpetuating discrimination in housing and employment even when it has adopted compliance policies (Ali et al., 2019). By incorporating the principles of DEI into campaign design, companies can develop strategies for targeting that expand representation rather than perpetuate exclusion.

In addition, inclusive marketing creates a new definition of "personalization." Rather than just using consumer behavior or buying power as the basis for personalization, it employs representation and belonging to provide meaning for personalization. When a consumer can see themselves in the ad or imagine the product or voice, the shopping experience is both transactional and emotional at the moment. It can also assist in establishing a stronger bond to the customer and building long-term loyalty, especially among Gen Z, as the sociable economy transitions to greater enjoyment for preferential means. Finally, equity-based personalization recognizes one individual's well-being rather than employing exploitative marketing techniques that exploit a person's susceptibility or stereotype them. It conveys that empathy is possible with optimal metric space efficiency, and there are opportunities to be gained in trust and honesty, instead of lies and dishonesty.

DEI-Centric Retail AI Results

Merchants that embed DEI into their computer systems reap a whole range of benefits: Bias Reduction for Recommendations: Helps eliminate biased product screening and provide consumers with a different set of relevant products. Consumer Confidence & Loyalty: Ethical personalisation instills consumer confidence and results in repeat business and long-term loyalty (Kotler et al., 2021). Inclusive

Market Development: Mapping of non-mainstream vendors' offering and fair targeting leads to creation of new market segments and overall increase in the economic participation. Brand Distinction: Design firms are able to make reputational gains in competitive e-markets by playing to an appealing brand equity through socially responsible consumers (Floridi & Cowls, 2019). Illustrative Example: Marketing and Inclusive AI for Sephora: Beauty retailer Sephora offers a real-life example of equitable AI adoption. Its AI-powered "Color IQ" tool suggests foundation shades across a vast array of skin tones, addressing a long-standing exclusion in the realm of cosmetics. By embracing AI while thoughtfully focusing on inclusivity, Sephora established itself not only as a leader in personalization but also as a champion of representation. This has helped increase its brand equity, build consumer trust and bolster loyalty among underrepresented demographics (Sephora, 2020). The implication for the Digital Economy: The e-commerce and retail industry shows why DEI integration into AI systems is not only about preventing reputation risk but about sustainable business growth. With the global rise of online shopping, AI can help businesses stay ahead of the curve while adhering to ethical standards in diverse markets. In the long-term, retailers' efforts to succeed in a digital economy of increasing scrutiny, consumer activism, and government oversight will become a necessity for any retailer that hopes to succeed through equity-driven personalization.

CASE STUDY 3: FAIR AI IN ACTION, THE MAYO CLINIC

The Mayo Clinic has experimented with AI-driven patient engagement approaches that are strongly DEI-informed. Its outreach preventive screening campaigns involved linguistic diversity with AI chatbots available in Spanish and Somali along with English. Mayo Clinic also documented that by maintaining design inclusivity they could prevent no-shows among minority patients considerably while enhancing screening uptake (Mayo Clinic Reports, 2020).

Outcomes and Implications: A DEI-embracing healthcare marketing strategy not only resolves ethical issues but brings concrete outcomes: Better Care Recommendations: Avoids biased care suggestions for minority patients, which don't lead to proper risk evaluation and timely warnings. Better Patient Trust: Inclusive AI solutions enable patients to trust healthcare institutions, particularly within historically disadvantaged populations. Wider Public Health Impact: Equitable outreach raises the utilization of preventive care and enhances population-level health outcomes. Sustainable Competitive Advantage: Healthcare organizations that adopt DEI-focused AI are ethical leaders who attract patients and allies in an aware marketplace. Healthcare is a prime example that illustrates the significance of the crossing of technology, ethics, and equity. The other consideration that tends to be overlooked in health-related marketing but which is still worth thinking about is accessibility for people with disabilities or low digital literacy. Design for accessibility guarantees that all patients are accessible to use AI chatbots, smartphone apps, or online booking systems regardless of ability or language. With a focus on universal design, health care institutes are not only trying to meet a social and ethical requirement; but also making the most of the potential of their use by more populations who would otherwise lack easy access to care. This meant that an equitable strategy towards AI could help foster more public health engagement and heightened community confidence. While AI can transform marketing in this industry, only through conscious intent regarding DEI will the transformation be equally beneficial to all populations. Equity by design is not an overlay option, but the foundational basis upon which all other credible, effective and sustainable healthcare innovation should be constructed.

CASE STUDY 4: FINANCIAL SERVICES - MAINSTREAMING DEI IN AI-ENABLED CUSTOMER EXPERIENCE

Financial services is one of the most fertile, yet fragile, landscapes on which to deploy AI-powered marketing tools. Machine learning models are becoming more and more involved in credit scoring, predicting customer churn, audience segmentation and in the development of financial products for customers. While providing efficiency, customization and growth, these innovations also run the risk of reproducing or exacerbating structural inequities inherent to historical financial datasets. And when that happens, Equity by Design, based in DEI principles, is transformed into an ethical imperative and a business imperative. The Potential of AI in Fintech Marketing: AI helps financial institutions run hyper-personalized marketing campaigns. For instance, predictive analytics can determine which customers are likely to require refinancing of their mortgage, whereas natural language processing (NLP)-driven chatbots allow service inquiries to be handled, thereby lowering service costs while maximizing customer satisfaction (Davenport et al., 2020). AI-driven engagement features have also been used successfully by such financial technology firms like Chime and Revolut, who have leveraged AI to gain support of young, native digital consumers with tailored propositions, proving that AI can revolutionize the very manner in which financial marketing is approached in a manner that is inclusive. Risks of Bias and Exclusion: In spite of its potential, bias in algorithms is a fact of life in AI for financial marketing. Historical Data Inequality: Credit risk models will incorporate historical data that capture systemic races and genders inequalities in lending. This can persist with the exclusion of minority groups (Barocas & Selbst, 2016). Proxy Variables: Innocuous-looking numbers such as our ZIP codes may actually be proxy variables for race or income, resulting in discriminatory targeted loan disposition appeals (Hurley & Adebayo, 2017). Transparency: Some (financial) algorithms are black boxes. Lacking explainability, customers may not be aware of why they are rejected or presented with some products, and this aggravates customer trust (Berk & Bleich 2013).

Incorporating Diversity, Equity and Inclusion into Financial Marketing (DEI by Design): To ensure that AI-enabled marketing tools are fair and inclusive, it's important that they are designed with DEI principles in mind: Inclusive Algorithm Design: Algorithms must be trained on diverse datasets that consider racial, gender and socio-economic differences. For example, JPMorgan Chase has pledged to bias testing for its customer segmentation AI models. Fairness Metrics: In addition to accuracy, models should be assessed for fairness metrics--to ensure that financial product offerings are equally available across demographic groups (Mehrabi et al., 2021). Ethical Governance and Regulation: Financial decision-making is subject to several regulations, including the U.S. Equal Credit Opportunity Act (ECOA) and the European Union's AI Act, which focuses on ethical AI and concerns around fairness audits (European Commission 2021). Open Accessible Customer Engagement: Marketing activities should be tailored for underserved communities that feature culturally relevant material and accessible language that is inclusive of financial literacy and product adoption (Kotler et al. 2021).

CASE STUDY 5: MASTERCARD'S AI FOR AN INCLUSIVE WORLD

Mastercard has introduced programs to guarantee even access using AI. Its Inclusive AI toolkit incorporates fairness checks into product design and its financial inclusion initiatives use AI-driven marketing to reach unbanked and underbanked populations in Africa and Asia. Mastercard, for instance, applied DEI to its AI engagement tactics to grow its customer base, and concurrently, establish brand capital as a pioneer in responsible financial innovation (Mastercard, 2020). "Outcomes and Implications" Embedding DEI in financial AI marketing not only safeguards against harm but also brings a business advantage: Bias Decrease in Lending and Offers: Focuses on fairness in who receives credit offers. expanded access to finance: Includes groups historically excluded, which achieves financial literacy and empowerment, Consumer Trust and Loyalty: Equitable practices result in loyal customers who refer your firm to their friends and family, which equals long-term relationships with underserved groups. Competitive Edge: With a market increasingly responsive to ethical concerns, financial institutions that adopt equity-focused AI differentiate themselves. The financial services sector is a wonderful illustration of how AI-powered marketing must change beyond efficiency to equity. Equity by design: financial innovations should not only accelerate profit but extend further. By integrating DEI into every phase of innovation, from data gathering to algorithmic choice, financial institutions can balance innovation and empathy, building a future of trust-driven growth and shared prosperity.

CONCLUSION

The integration of artificial intelligence (AI) into marketing offers transformative potential, but without conscious design, it risks amplifying inequities rather than dismantling them. This paper has argued that embedding Diversity, Equity, and Inclusion (DEI) into AI-enhanced marketing is not a peripheral concern but a strategic and ethical necessity. By applying the principle of Equity by Design, organizations can proactively mitigate algorithmic bias, expand market access for underrepresented populations, and build long-term consumer trust. Such integration shifts the narrative from AI as a purely efficiency-driven tool to AI as a catalyst for inclusive and sustainable innovation.

The evidence presented through case studies across finance, retail, healthcare, and e-commerce demonstrates that equity-centered design fosters both ethical and economic benefits. For example, AI-powered credit scoring models that incorporate fairness constraints open new pathways to financial inclusion for marginalized groups while simultaneously strengthening brand equity (Hurley & Adebayo, 2017; Mastercard, 2020). In retail, inclusive recommender systems and equitable personalization strategies not only counter discriminatory practices but also enhance consumer confidence and loyalty, as seen in Sephora's inclusive AI initiatives (Sephora, 2020). Healthcare examples, such as Mayo Clinic's multilingual AI outreach, further affirm that DEI-conscious innovation can improve both patient trust and population-level health outcomes (Mayo Clinic Reports, 2020). Moreover, the literature underscores that algorithms are not neutral; they mirror the biases of their training data and deployment context (Noble, 2018; O'Neil, 2016). Thus, embedding DEI requires interdisciplinary collaboration across ethics, data science, marketing, and governance. Frameworks such as fairness-aware model training, transparent governance, and diverse data documentation (Gebru et al., 2021; Floridi & Cowls, 2019) illustrate practical pathways to achieve this. When equity is built into the architecture of AI systems, it becomes measurable in outcomes like bias reduction, consumer trust, fair targeting, and inclusive access (Langer & Landers, 2021).

Crucially, adopting DEI in AI marketing is also a source of competitive differentiation. As regulatory frameworks such as the European Union's AI Act strengthen requirements for transparency and fairness (European Commission, 2021), companies that proactively align with these standards will gain both reputational resilience and first-mover advantage. Scholars and practitioners agree that equity-driven AI not only minimizes reputational and legal risks but also functions as an economic multiplier by deepening consumer loyalty and unlocking underserved markets (Ramaswamy & Ozcan, 2022; Kotler et al., 2021).

In conclusion, Equity by Design transforms DEI from a symbolic gesture into a structural necessity for AI-enhanced marketing. The convergence of technological capability, ethical responsibility, and market opportunity signals a future where fairness is no longer optional but foundational. Organizations that embrace this paradigm will not only advance social justice but also secure sustainable growth and legitimacy in the digital economy.

Practical Implications

The integration of Diversity, Equity, and Inclusion (DEI) into AI-enhanced marketing systems has several practical implications for organizations, policymakers, and consumers. First, for businesses, embedding DEI at the design stage of AI systems translates into long-term brand equity and consumer loyalty. Ethical personalization, fairness audits, and diverse training datasets not only prevent reputational damage but also help capture underserved markets, particularly in finance, retail, and healthcare. Firms that implement equity-driven design will strengthen trust with their stakeholders and differentiate themselves in increasingly competitive digital marketplaces (Kotler et al., 2021; Ramaswamy & Ozcan, 2022), Irfan, M., Kadry, S., Sharif, M., & Khan, H. U. (Eds.). (2024). Second, for policymakers and regulators, the findings highlight the importance of establishing governance frameworks that mandate fairness, transparency, and accountability in AI applications Irfan, M., Elmogy, M., Majid, M. S. A., & El-Sappagh, S. (Eds.). (2023). Policies such as the European Union's AI Act provide a roadmap for ensuring that algorithmic decision-making aligns with societal expectations of justice and fairness (European Commission, 2021). Regulatory oversight will be critical in standardizing fairness metrics, guiding data governance practices, and ensuring that AI innovations enhance inclusivity rather than replicate structural inequities .

Third, for practitioners and developers, adopting an Equity by Design approach means operationalizing fairness into every stage of AI deployment. This includes designing inclusive algorithms, applying fairness constraints, documenting datasets, and conducting periodic bias audits (Gebru et al., 2021; Mehrabi et al., 2021). In practice, this requires interdisciplinary collaboration between marketers, data scientists, ethicists, and organizational leaders to ensure that technical systems align with ethical business goals.

In the future, DEI will be another component of identity via the lens of marketing when it becomes more integrated with AI. Two decades ago, sustainability was a component of corporate responsibility that expanded our thoughts about the next horizon of digital business; now, fairness and inclusion will take over the business mindset. Organizations who focus on implementing ethical AI does not just attract customers, investors, and employees who share those values; it will become part of your brand DNA. The shift toward equity-driven design is more than a compliance trend; it's a change in how organizations view success. It is no longer a question of profit versus purpose. When profit and purpose are aligned through equitable technology, both components will both reinforce each other and provide a sustained competitive advantage.

Finally, for consumers, DEI-centered AI tools foster trust, inclusivity, and representation in the digital marketplace. When marketing systems provide fair targeting, transparent personalization, and equitable access to products and services, consumers are more likely to perceive organizations as responsible innovators. This not only enhances customer satisfaction but also generates positive social impact by improving financial inclusion, healthcare access, and retail fairness (Noble, 2018; Mayo Clinic Reports, 2020). In summary, the practical implications of embedding DEI in AI-enhanced marketing extend beyond compliance. They offer organizations a pathway to build trust, policymakers a foundation for regulation, practitioners a framework for responsible design, and consumers equitable opportunities in a digital economy increasingly shaped by AI.

REFERENCES

Ali, M., Sapiezynski, P., Bogen, M., Korolova, A., Mislove, A., & Rieke, A. (2019). Discrimination through optimization: How Facebook's ad delivery can lead to biased outcomes. *Proceedings of the ACM on Human-Computer Interaction, 3*(CSCW), 1–30.

Barocas, S., Hardt, M., & Narayanan, A. (2019). *Fairness and machine learning*. fairmlbook.org. https://fairmlbook.org

Barocas, S., & Selbst, A. D. (2016). Big data's disparate impact. *California Law Review, 104*(3), 671–732.

Berk, R., & Bleich, J. (2013). Statistical procedures for forecasting criminal behavior: A critical review. *Criminology & Public Policy, 12*(3), 513–544.

Chowdhuri, S. R., & Gupta, M. (2025). Machine learning models for software defect detection: A strategic management approach. *Purushartha, 17*(2), 87–98. https://journals.smsvaranasi.com/index.php/purushartha/article/download/2279/1044. journals.smsvaranasi.com

Datta, A., Tschantz, M. C., & Datta, A. (2018). Automated experiments on ad privacy settings: A tale of opacity, choice, and discrimination. *Proceedings on Privacy Enhancing Technologies. Privacy Enhancing Technologies Symposium, 2015*(1), 92–112.

Davenport, T. H., Guha, A., Grewal, D., & Bressgott, T. (2020). How artificial intelligence will change the future of marketing. *Journal of the Academy of Marketing Science, 48*(1), 24–42.

Etsy. (2020). *Diversity and inclusion in the Etsy marketplace*. Etsy.

European Commission. (2021). *Proposal for a regulation laying down harmonised rules on artificial intelligence (Artificial Intelligence Act)*. Publications Office of the EU. https://artificialintelligenceact.eu

Floridi, L., & Cowls, L. (2019). A unified framework of five principles for AI in society. *Harvard Data Science Review, 1*(1), 1–15.

Gebru, T., Morgenstern, J., Vecchione, B., Vaughan, J. W., Wallach, H., Daumé, H., & Crawford, K. (2021). Datasheets for datasets. *Communications of the ACM, 64*(12), 86–92.

Hurley, M., & Adebayo, J. (2017). Credit scoring in the era of big data. *Yale Journal of Law and Technology, 18*(1), 148–216.

Irfan, M., Elmogy, M., Majid, M. S. A., & El-Sappagh, S. (Eds.). (2023). *The Impact of AI Innovation on Financial Sectors in the Era of Industry 5.0*. IGI Global., DOI: 10.4018/979-8-3693-0082-4

Irfan, M., Hussainey, K., Bukhari, S. A. C., & Nam, Y. (Eds.). (2024). *Issues of Sustainability in AI and New-Age Thematic Investing*. IGI Global. https://doi.org/IGI GlobalDOI: 10.4018/979-8-3693-3282-5

Irfan, M., Kadry, S., Sharif, M., & Khan, H. U. (Eds.). (2024). *Fintech Applications in Islamic Finance: AI, Machine Learning, and Blockchain Techniques*. IGI Global., DOI: 10.4018/979-8-3693-1038-0

Kotler, P., Kartajaya, H., & Setiawan, I. (2021). *Marketing 5.0: Technology for humanity*. Wiley.

Langer, M., & Landers, R. N. (2021). The future of artificial intelligence in employee selection. *International Journal of Selection and Assessment*, *29*(1–2), 195–216.

Licsandru, T. C., Mari, C., Kipnis, E., Galalae, C., Johnson, E., Cross, S. N. N., Cui, C. C., Kearney, S., Martín Ruiz, V., Vorster Larsen, L., & Yoruk, I. (2025). Integrating Diversity, Equity and Inclusion in Management Education: An Empathy Framework. *British Journal of Management*. Advance online publication. DOI: 10.1111/1467-8551.70008

Mastercard. (2020). *Inclusive AI: Advancing responsible use of artificial intelligence*. Mastercard Insights.

Mayo Clinic Reports. (2020). *AI and patient engagement: Equity in action*. Mayo Clinic.

Mehrabi, N., Morstatter, F., Saxena, N., Lerman, K., & Galstyan, A. (2021). A survey on bias and fairness in machine learning. *ACM Computing Surveys*, *54*(6), 1–35.

Mikians, J., Gyarmati, L., Erramilli, V., & Laoutaris, N. (2013). Detecting price and search discrimination on the internet. *Proceedings of the 11th ACM Workshop on Hot Topics in Networks*, 79–84.

Noble, S. U. (2018). *Algorithms of oppression: How search engines reinforce racism*. NYU Press.

O'Neil, C. (2016). *Weapons of math destruction: How big data increases inequality and threatens democracy*. Crown Publishing Group.

Pandey, P., & Rai, A. K. (2024). Modeling consequences of brand authenticity in anthropomorphized AI-assistants: A human–robot interaction perspective. *Purushartha, 17*(1), 116–135. https://journals.smsvaranasi.com/index.php/purushartha/article/download/2147/1002. journals.smsvaranasi.com

Pandey, V., Kushwaha, G. S., & Srivastava, S. (2023). Factors influencing adoption of digital payments: A PLS-SEM and ANN approach. *Purushartha, 16*(2), 91–104. https://journals.smsvaranasi.com/index.php/purushartha/article/download/2019/970

Raj, A. (2024). What kind of Marketing Data is needed for Artificial Intelligence Analysis? A Theoretical Approach. *Purushartha – A Journal of Management. *Ethics and Spirituality, 16*(2), 21–33.

Ramaswamy, V., & Ozcan, T. (2022). Artificial intelligence, customer experience, and marketing ethics. *Journal of Business Research, 145*, 799–812.

Sah, J., Padma, S., Yanamandra, R., & Irfan, M. (2024). *Risk management of future of DeFi using artificial intelligence as a tool.* In M. Irfan & M. Elmogy (Eds.), *AI-Driven Decentralized Finance and the Future of Finance* (pp. 22). IGI Global. https://doi.org/ IGI GlobalDOI: 10.4018/979-8-3693-6321-8.ch011

Schein, E. H. (2017). *Organizational culture and leadership* (5th ed.). Wiley.

Sephora. (2020). *Sephora diversity and inclusion report.* Sephora.

Tarnanidis, T., Manda, V. K., Sousa, B. B., Vlachopoulou, M., & Papachristou, E. (2026). Marketing Complexity of Smart Consumer Products to Global Millennial Segments. In Tarnanidis, T., Sousa, B., Vlachopoulou, M., Papachristou, E., & Kittu Manda, V. (Eds.), *Diversity and Inclusion-Driven Marketing for Multicultural Marketplaces* (pp. 1–16). IGI Global Scientific Publishing., DOI: 10.4018/979-8-3373-2111-0.ch001

Tarnanidis, T., Sousa, B., Vlachopoulou, M., Papachristou, E., & Kittu Manda, V. (Eds.). (2026). *Diversity and Inclusion-Driven Marketing for Multicultural Marketplaces*. IGI Global Scientific Publishing., DOI: 10.4018/979-8-3373-2111-0

Vorster, L., Licsandru, T., Kipnis, E., Mari, C., Ruiz, V. M., Kearney, S., & Cross, S. N. (2024). Towards Comprehensive Integration of Diversity, Equity and Inclusion in Management Education: An Empathy-Driven Framework. *British Journal of Management*.

Whittaker, M., Crawford, K., Dobbe, R., Fried, G., Kaziunas, E., Mathur, V., West, S., Richardson, R., Schultz, J., & Schwartz, O. (2018). *AI Now Report 2018.* AI Now Institute, New York University. https://ainowinstitute.org/AI_Now_2018_Report.pdf

Chapter 10
Fair and Inclusive Customer Segmentation in AI-Driven Marketing

Jeeva Benny
https://orcid.org/0009-0007-3755-8082
Christ University, Bengaluru, India

Jasmine Kaur
https://orcid.org/0000-0002-3683-0909
Christ University, Bengaluru, India

ABSTRACT

This chapter explains how artificial intelligence has evolved customer segmentation from a marketing tool into a socio-technical decision mechanism with implications for fairness, inclusion, and cultural representation. In the chapter, algorithmic segmentation is analyzed using clustering methods, explainable frameworks such as LIME and SHAP, and fairness metrics to identify or alleviate structural bias in multicultural markets. It discusses accuracy fairness trade-offs, transparency, emotional trust, and organizational capability gaps, especially when segmentation outputs flow into generative AI driven personalization. Through case studies on multicultural targeting, AI sales agents, misinformation flows, and exclusion in finance, employment, and welfare, the authors show how segmentation systems affect society. The chapter concludes with strategic, ethical, and policy recommendations for responsible, inclusive AI marketing grounded in fairness aware segmentation.

DOI: 10.4018/979-8-3373-6731-6.ch010

1. INTRODUCTION

AI is no longer peripheral but a core part of marketing automation, personalization, and audience targeting, with such diverse applications as customer segmentation at the forefront. Customer segmentation allows companies to differentiate customers according to their behavior, as well as demographic and transactional information, enabling much improved strategic decision making. These factors constituted improvements in the computing power and reduction in data processing costs, plus the dramatic increase in big data repositories, which together facilitated many more sophisticated applications of machine learning in marketing (Huang & Rust, 2021).

AI is expected to concern marketing activities and relationships in the future, becoming, in its capacity to analyze data at scale and make automated decisions, one of the best allies (Jarek & Mazurek, 2019; Hermann, 2022). AI has emerged as a disruptive agent across industries as regards designing processes by businesses, engaging customers, and creating value digitally (Kumar et al., 2024). Nevertheless, despite all that growth, properly systematic and in-depth inquiry into the ethical and societal implications of AI driven consumer markets is yet very limited (Verma et al., 2021). In addition, there is worsening ongoing research indicating that AI systems unintentionally reproduce or exacerbate real world biases in their data, which emphasizes the need for urgent attention to their fairness aware design in digital ecosystems (Mehrabi et al. 2022). In the global digital market, the deployment of advanced marketing technologies has to consider cultural heterogeneity, regulatory diversity, and consumer behaviour specific to context when operating across multicultural environments (Tarnanidis & Vlachopoulou 2025).

The machine learning methods, like K-means clustering, can be also found application in grouping customers into quite meaningful segments, identifying behavioral patterns that more significantly repeated individual shares (Alijoyo et al., 2025). LIME type explainability tools allow public and cultural responsiveness of targeting by revealing the way some factors such as age, income, or cultural preference affect the segmentation outcome (Alijoyo et al., 2025).

However, AI systems are capable of being discriminatory to several degrees, mostly using quite skewed historical data for training (Hermann, 2022). This has raised ethical concerns both about the customer and the organization as well as society. Principles like transparency, justice, fairness, responsibility, and privacy characterize ethical grounding for AI deployment in marketing (Hermann, 2022).

While seated within an overall agenda of GenAI driven decision making towards DEI, this chapter calls for fairness to be built into AI customer segmentation systems. These fairness constraints demographic parity, equalized opportunity, and subgroup fairness can be integrated into clustering or classification models such that predictive accuracy can walk with inclusion.

2. CONCEPTUAL FOUNDATIONS OF FAIRNESS IN SEGMENTATION

2.1 AI based Customer Segmentations in Marketing

Customer segmentation broadly refers to the organized process of subdividing a heterogeneous customer base into more or less homogeneous groups, according to some characteristics such as demographics, psychographics, behavior, and purchase patterns which they may share. These wide-ranging data banks make it possible for marketers to carry out marketing operations. Some present-day marketing automation systems collect not only active data when consumption inputs are directly proffered but also passive data: clickstream behaviors, purchase recordings, and browsing patterns. All of these local data streams rounded out an analytical base upon which segmentation models would be built (Mariani et al., 2022).

This segmentation process gains an additional benefit from being AI driven, enabling the organizations use of large structured and unstructured data volumes to identify complex nonlinear relationships between customer attributes. This is where other theories become apparent, particularly the ones underlying customer relationship management (CRM). CRM actively creates consumer databases with considerable information relating to consumer interactions, behavioral pasts, and transactional information, which are then acted upon for further segmentation of consumers (Saura et al., 2021). Algorithm supported segmentation methods strengthen the prediction accuracy whereby such companies can forecast future consumer behavior, demand pattern, and responsiveness with far greater exactness than with conventional rule-based methods (Kasem et al., 2024). By recognizing and responding to the different needs of these algorithmical clusters, digital firms are consequently better able to create long term relationships with their customers, optimize their engagement strategies and promote the sustainable growth of the business (Kasem et al., 2024).

Thus, the inevitable consequence of segmentation marketing more is that today as it again becomes automated through an AI system produce outcomes beyond that of computational efficiency. The social domain is where misclassification, under-class, and systemic exclusion become very real threats without an in-built fairness to begin with. The socio-technical systems theory insists that organizational outcomes trace the joint optimization of technical and social systems rather than being simply designed one into the other. When we relate this theory back to AI-powered customer segmentation, we understand that a segmentation model cannot be judged solely on the basis of its predictive accuracy or computational efficiency, for its outputs are determined by the interplay of choices about algorithmic design, data infrastructures, organizational practices, regulatory constraints, and social norms.

Fairness and inclusion in AI-enabled segmentation would thereby depend not solely on changes at the model level but would also require governance of the systems, human interveners, and decision processes within the institutions. In other words, socio-technical systems theory assumes that any biased or exclusionary outcomes from segmentation are actually systemic phenomena that require socio-organizational and technical solutions in a holistic way as opposed to only algorithmic fixes which are usually detached from ground operational realities.

2.2 Clustering and Classification Logic in AI Segmentation

AI segmentation of the customer relies primarily on two methodological pillars: clustering and classification. Clustering is an unsupervised learning, during which consumers are grouped together by likeness across several variables without any ancestor labels. Whereas classification is, by contrast, a supervised learning, during which consumer cases are classified into existing categories or groups using pre labeled training data. Together, these methodologies constitute the analytic backbone of AI influenced segmentation systems in personalized marketing environments.

Segmentation is, at essence, an unsupervised method where certain groups of customers with similar characteristics are naturally identified by the algorithms under no requirement of prior labeling (Alves Gomes & Meisen, 2023). Artificial intelligence for personalized marketing drives competitive global markets; as it becomes more sophisticated, it becomes an indispensable requirement from being an option (Alijoyo et al., 2025). Although this unsupervised method is widely employed, K-means clustering is the most applicable of these techniques for meaningful segmentation of customers by behavior and transactional patterns (Alijoyo et al., 2025).

Apart from that, past empirical research shows K-means and Self Organizing Maps (SOM) are able to reveal hidden truths from high dimensional CRM datasets. Such clustering techniques and visualizations assist the marketer in developing a more thorough understanding of customer behavior and thus empirical evidence in developing customer centric strategies (Qadadeh & Abdallah, 2018).

However, the most critical technical and strategic question is how many customer segments should be created. One of the widely employed techniques used for identifying the optimal number of clusters is the Elbow Method and the Silhouette Analysis, which guarantee the reliability and stability of the partitioning of customer groups (Alijoyo et al., 2025).

Notwithstanding the sophistication ascribed to clustering and classification systems, they remain very sensitive to the quality, representativeness, and balance of input data. This risk is heightened when the training datasets carry information about historical inequalities such as gender, income, geography, or culture; the imbalance reflects riskily amplified mathematically through automated segmentation.

Most of the time, anybody at the edges of a cluster usually is poorly represented and, therefore, becomes disadvantaged when decisions are made on the basis of the cluster centroid instead of their real behavioral distance (Deepak & Abraham, 2020). Moreover, studies indicate that clustering algorithms that are cognizant of protected attributes like the so called "colorblind" models can still come up with rather unfair groups in terms of subtle reinforcement of structural inequalities (Chierichetti et al., 2017). This technical vulnerability creates the conceptual foundation for fairness aware design in AI segmentation systems.trust, and sustainable value creation in multicultural markets.

2.3 Developing the Theory Behind Explainability and Culture Sensitivity in Segmentation

The complexity and degree of autonomy among AI driven segmentation systems continue to multiply, and at present, explainability appears to emerge as a core requirement for fairness, accountability, and trust. Without it, marketers and policymakers will not be able to tell whether segmentation results are related to actual behavioral differences or whether they are the result of embedded algorithmic biases. Explainable AI tools address this issue by telling how some specific input feature contributes to the output of the model. Understanding the why of prediction is vital for confidence in the results, especially when decisions or deployment choices rest on model outputs (Ribeiro et al., 2016). For the decision makers relying heavily on AI, analytics, and data driven insights, explainability becomes a practical necessity to ensure oversight, responsible judgment, and informed intervention (Hoffman et al., 2019).

LIME (Local Interpretable Model Agnostic Explanations) shows that different factors, like age, income, and cultural preference, can relate to the assignment of customers into clusters (Alijoyo et al., 2025). With multicultural marketing, this transparency becomes more important since incorrect understanding of cultural behaviors leads to the reinforcement of stereotypes or marginalization of minority consumer communities. Complementing LIME, SHapley Additive exPlanations (SHAP) provides consistent and theoretically grounded feature attribution explanations that help decision makers understand why a model produces specific outputs across diverse consumer contexts (Lundberg & Lee, 2017). The various surveys of explainable AI methods show that no single technique can cater to every situation; therefore, marketers must choose context appropriate interpretability tools during the audit of segmentation logic (Guidotti et al., 2019).

Marketers could craft campaigns that are in high detail relevant to the values and expectations of a diverse audience while remaining objective or data ground (Alijoyo et al., 2025). From the lens of DEI, however, explainability is not just a technical capability but rather a moral bulwark that allows supervision, responsibility, and culturally respectful decision making.

2.4 Fairness, Bias, and Ethical AI in Marketing Systems

AI is playing an increasingly operative role in marketing, but AI applications and systems can have discriminatory features in various aspects (Hermann, 2022). Such effects are frequently attributed to those training data sets that encode historical patterns of exclusion, economic disparities, or cultural biases in the world and are then learned mathematically by AI systems to be reproduced and further amplified at scale. Such discriminating treatments usually reinforce existing economic and societal inequalities and produce ethical concerns on customer, company, and social levels (Hermann, 2022).

On a deeper level, these issues have alluded to the ongoing debate concerning fair treatment for safeguarded communities: whether those communities are overtly named or represented by way of implication, they ought not to face systematic disadvantages brought on by algorithmic deliberation (Doshi-Velez & Kim, 2017). Crucially, empirical evidence shows that merely stripping a model of sensitive attributes does not automatically eradicate discrimination, as proxy variables frequently contain similar information in an indirect manner and continue to carry forward the biases (Kamishima et al., 2012).

Ethical marketing in AI is anchored in the normative principles of transparency, justice and fairness, non-maleficence, accountability, and privacy (Hermann, 2022). Even so, a fairly fundamental view of fairness emphasizes that people who are similar in some respects with regard to a given task should really be treated equally in that matter. This principle is also known as individual fairness, and serves as an important companion to group-based fairness metrics (Dwork et al., 2011).

In such marketing contexts where the GenAI application is segmentation and then stochastic generation of the message, target, and content that a consumer sees, the stakes in equity only rise. It propagates downstream to the generative content pipeline in which biased segmentation determines how various communities are represented, targeted, or excluded. Thus, segmentation fairness becomes not only the basis of ethical AI but also an inclusive decision-making process in GenAI.

2.5 Fairness as a Design Principle that is Strategic and DEI Oriented

In the age of contemporary AI assisted marketing, fairness has to be understood both ethically and as a design principle in strategy. Much of the data analytics that AI can run across nearly every application area is becoming increasingly important in marketing (Jarek & Mazurek, 2019). More such systems dominate real operations, and this indeed worsens the effects of poor design. Applications that are real world have demonstrated that AI can now be found widely embedded in marketing processes taking place mostly operationally, as in the case when segmentation directly advises resource allocation and targeting decisions (Jarek & Mazurek, 2019).

From a DEI perspective, unfair segmentation directly means that some demographic and cultural groups have unequal reach, different visibility, and asymmetrical access to opportunities. As GenAI systems increasingly rely on segmentation outputs to automate communication, content generation, and personalized persuasion, fairness aware segmentation becomes the very ethical infrastructure upon which inclusive digital marketing ecosystems must be built.

Fairness based segmentation also has strategic advantages for organizations. Firms are thus able to achieve market legitimacy while strengthening consumer trust and brand loyalty over the long haul in multicultural contexts by ensuring equality across all consumer groups. By including fairness constraints in its segmentation models, profit goals align with DEI commitments, demonstrating that inclusive design and sustainable competitiveness are not opposing goals but mutually reinforcing outcomes.

While AI aided and fairness compliant customer segmentation offers a revolutionary potential for inclusive, data driven marketing, their implementation presents a set of challenges that interplay amongst technical, ethical, organizational, and strategic contexts. Organizations will have to negotiate challenging tradeoffs among accuracy and fairness, automation and human control, personalization and privacy, efficiency, and empathy. These tensions are more accentuated in GenAI powered marketing ecosystems, where segmentation feeds directly into automated targeting, content generation, and decision execution. This section deals with a more rigorous examination of such challenges and outlines essential considerations for practitioners, researchers, and policymakers.

The workflow of a fairness aware AI segmentation that combines the techniques of data processing, modeling, explainability, fairness evaluation, and governance is illustrated in Figure 1.

Figure 1. Fairness aware AI segmentation pipeline: integrating explainability, fairness constraints and a governance mechanism.

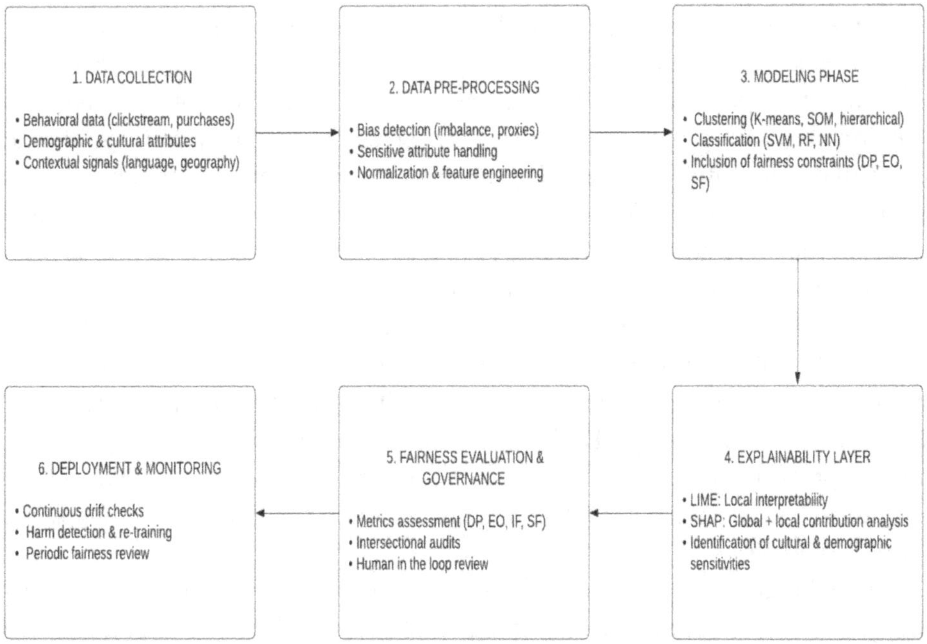

3. CHALLENGES, TRADEOFFS, AND CONSIDERATIONS

3.1 Bias, Discrimination, and Social Inequality in AI Segmentation

Discriminatory facets still abound even amid unprecedented advancements in AI related customer analytics (Hermann, 2022). If segmentation models are built using such data, their resulting customer clusters may unwittingly recreate and amplify disadvantages across lines such as gender, income, caste, geography, ethnicity, or digital access. Empirical evidence demonstrates how serious the risk can be; for example, outcome prediction accuracy varies for protected groups by as much as 20%, which means performance differences tend to reflect structural inequities rather than model noise (Chen et al., 2018). On top of this added complication, data distortion or data absence can further deteriorate model reliability and introduce systematic biases into segmentation outputs, rendering the attainment of fairness in practice even more problematic (Pani & Behera, 2021). The embedded discrimination patterns in real environments of the prevailing machine learning systems tend to absorb and replicate those inequalities in a way that they replicate and strengthen the structural biases, instead of correcting them (Binns, 2018). More recent evidence suggests that even when cluster assignments are technically correct, those users placed close to the edges of clusters may receive systematically worse outcomes precisely because the assigned cluster does not meaningfully represent their true characteristics (Kleindessner et al., 2020).

Another example of such discrimination comes in multicultural markets where the behavior of individuals may be heavily dictated by cultural norms, including those of language, family structures, and informal economic practices. Unless the model is designed from a cultural standpoint with fairness constraints, any AI driven segmentation may erroneously consider culturally specific purchasing behavior as valueless, low intent, or high risk. Such aberrations, from the perspective of diversity, equity, and inclusion (DEI), break the very spirit of inclusive GenAI driven marketing decision systems.

3.2 Accuracy Fairness Tradeoffs in Segmentation Models

One of the major contending issues in fairness aware segmentation is the relationship between predictive accuracy on one side and fairness on the other. Segmentations are among the methods and algorithms that follow for the improvement of prediction accuracy and business performances (Kasem et al., 2024). In this way, with great precision, organizations pinpoint high value segments that allow them to optimize customer engagement and forge a sustainable business push growth (Kasem et al., 2024). On the flip side, those constraints for fairness might demand an alteration in model objectives in such a way that these adjustments lower the short-term predictive efficiency.

In competitive digital environments, a firm is under constant strain to deliver hyper personalized marketing experiences. According to Socio-technical systems perspective, these pressures arise not from the algorithmic design alone, but through interaction with technical optimization goals, organizational incentives, and broader institutional constraints. Using recent models in AI-driven marketing explains how this can be achieved by customer segmentation in the adaptable learning systems that will determine how to reconfigurate the lifetime value of customers and promotional resource allocation (Mandania et al., 2025). As such, AI integrated personalized marketing strategies developed via discrimination have by now become a necessity rather than an option in today's global markets (Alijoyo et al., 2025). Machine learning clustering methods such as K-means clustering have always been validated by the Elbow Method and Silhouette Analysis to maximize segmentation performance (Alijoyo et al., 2025). However, this direct optimization for cluster separation does not mean that it will indirectly optimize for equitable representation among protected demographic groups.

The introduction of fairness criteria as illustrated by an example in this section about demographic parity or subgroup fairness would imply lower within cluster homogeneity or targeting precision concerning certain high revenue segments. As a consequence, firms would need to make managerial decisions regarding whether to prioritize current profits over longer term respect, legitimacy, and resilience to regulation. From the findings of further research, it can be seen that despite algorithms meeting fairness metrics such as equalized false positive rates across protected groups, they may still yield unfair results in a more complex or intersectional subgroup, demonstrating that fairness often cannot be achieved by simple statistical constraints alone (Kearns et al., 2018). Despite this, it becomes more complicated owing to misunderstandings that one believes AI systems are always objective; whereas, actually, all algorithms carry human beliefs and biases in data driven ways that can marginally influence results (Verma & Rubin, 2018).

In GenAI marketing systems segmentation being the primary source for automated persuasion and recommendation engines there are more constraints amplified and complicated by the pace and scale of algorithmic diffusion.

3.3 Transparency, Deception, and Human Supervision in GenAI Systems

The inclusion of GenAI tools such as ChatGPT into the marketing workflow brings very obvious new dangers that relate to misrepresentation, non-transparency, and unethical governance risks. With the addition of such generative tools being fused with segmentation-based targeting, they may personalize and greatly scale misinformation risk.

In fact, transparency is the core ethical demand in AI dominated systems in marketing. The existence of transparency in marketing by ethical AI requires that users, regulators, and organizations understand how content and targeting decisions are made (Rivas & Zhao, 2023). GenAI becomes much more complicated and autonomous; hence, transparency becomes increasingly difficult. Biases in algorithmic decision making are usually inadvertent, having multiple interconnected origins, which renders transparent governance indispensable in identifying and amending processes that turn harmful before they are permitted to scale (Starke et al. 2022).

Therefore, Rivas and Zhao (2023) give an example that human supervision becomes necessary to ensure that the judgments and crafted content reflect ethics. In cases of fairness aware segmentation, this requires that human experts continuously audit the logic of segmentation, the content outputs, and targeting patterns to ensure that automated systems do not drift into any discriminatory, manipulative, or exclusionary practices. From the perspectives of DEI and multicultural marketing, the lack of human oversight potentially permits the uncontrolled spread of content that is culturally inappropriate, stereotypical, or exclusionary, all under an aura of objectivity through algorithms.

3.4 Trust, Empathy, and the Human AI relationship in Marketing

Artificial intelligence marketing comes with challenges; one of the mostly underrated obstacles is how AI takes away perceived empathy or trust from its interaction with human beings. They are cold and uncaring, and in fact, would be the least successful at offering substitutes for human based interactions (Liu-Thompkins et al., 2022). Eventually, customers are made to understand that they are talking to a bot, and hence they respond with much less emotional warmth, lower purchase behavior, and less perceived empathy (Liu-Thompkins et al., 2022).

Trust deficits prove worst in markets offering products related to finance, health services, and education and social welfare. Emotional reassurance and ethical sensitivity would form the core of the user's experience in these markets. If fairness aware segmentation is put into practice purely from a technical point of view and is oblivious to trust related psychological dynamics, the gains that flow from it are likely to be minor.

Segmentation outputs become increasingly shaping, by GenAI supported marketing ecosystems, on whom content reaches as well as on the emotional frame, linguistic construction, and cultural position of that content. By such manipulation, consumers view these linkages as impersonal, exploitative, and otherwise deficient; brand trust and loyalty are undermined long after the inherent technical fairness of the segmentation algorithm.

3.5 Organizational Capability, Skill Gaps, Design Challenges

Implementing fairness aware AI segmentation is thwarted by formidable organizational, capability, and design constraints that transcend the algorithmic biases. Marketing has become the primary area of application for AI, and remains widely operative on grounds of large-scale data analysis techniques (Jarek & Mazurek, 2019); however, marketing instead often finds itself executing AI tools with very little attention paid to issues of strategic governance and ethical system design at all (Jarek & Mazurek, 2019). On the side of research, big data analytics capabilities have shown their strategic value dependent not just on the availability of technical tools but on an organization's prowess to integrate, govern, and leverage them effectively (Mikalef et al., 2019). While many organizations will be implementing

AI for operationalizing campaign executions, customer targeting, and lead scoring, other broader institutional questions regarding their fairness, accountability, and long-term societal impact will be left unattended.

The effective rolling out of fairness aware segmentation systems will require adequate technical infrastructural development and interdisciplinary human capital, capable of integrating data science competence with marketing strategy, legal know how, and DEI awareness. On the one hand, AI requires having the data scientist skills combined with a very comprehensive understanding of new technological opportunities within marketing teams (Jarek & Mazurek, 2019). On the other hand, many companies, especially in developing and resource constrained markets, are suffering from rare shortages of hybrid talents able to bridge technical modeling with ethical arguments and cultural intelligence. Those talent gaps are further aggravated by limited access to continuous upskilling programs, the absence of internal AI ethics governance units, and a lack of exposure for marketing professionals to ethical considerations in system design.

The vendors put onto the shelf very powerful clustering, classification, and GenAI driven targeting solutions; however, the capacity to challenge model assumptions, conduct fairness audits, and evaluate eventual societal impacts are often lacking in the client side. Because of this reason, fairness becomes equated with compliance that means it is simply regarded as a box ticking exercise rather than an architectural aspiration nurtured across the lifetime of model development and deployment.

In addition, AI systems that extend the core product or service must lay out an innovation driven architecture that attempts to derive an insight beyond tightly defined product categories or transactional parameters (Jarek & Mazurek, 2019). Fairness aware segmentation, by this logic, requires the design of systems sensitive to cultural identity, economic vulnerability, digital literacy, and social positioning; domains that remain relegated to the background in most performance centric marketing dashboards. Such human centered design principles still find it difficult to be integrated into organizations where the dominant logic is based on revenue oriented KPIs and short-term optimizations.

Fairness aware segmentation cannot be treated as a plug and play software add on that once implemented appropriately requires little further maintenance. Sustained cross functional collaboration with marketing strategists, data scientists, legal experts, compliance officers, ethicists, and DEI leadership is required for a successful implementation. These groups need to define what is meant by fairness in the local context of culture and regulations, what are the considered tradeoffs between performance and equity, and what audit and accountability mechanisms are to be put in place on a continual basis. Without these woven governance arrangements, segmentation systems may remain ethically shallow on their elegant and perfectly functional architecture super-efficient but ignorant to their long-term social consequences, cultural misrepresentation, and structural exclusion.

3.6 Strategic, Regulatory, and Sustainability Perspectives

As AI fundamentally restructures strategies, activities, interactions, and relationships across the marketing ecosystem (Hermann, 2022), fairness aware segmentation has ceased to be merely a technical design issue and has become a matter of strategic governance and long-term sustainability. AI based systems control who sees information, which consumers are put into focus, and how products and opportunities are distributed. In this way, those processes facilitated through GenAI based marketing environments that segment audiences have a strong influence on the generation of automated content, targeted persuasion, and personalized messages. Consequently, segmentation exercises hold unprecedented power as cultural narratives, economic access, and consumer agency are infused and shaped by these segmentation exercises.

It would bring fairness aware segmentation for previously unserved sections of the community to access financial services, learning platforms, health information, employment opportunities, and entrepreneurial ecosystems on an equitable basis. Yet, this ideal is realizable only within straightforward auguries, accountability structures, regulatory frameworks, and verifiable fairness performance standards. Otherwise, the potential risk to the fairness narrative is that it will degenerate into a rhetorical mission rather than a quantifiable one.

This regulatory uncertainty further complicates enforcing fairness aware segmentation. Although different jurisdictions begin to explore AI governance frameworks, worldwide harmonization of algorithmic accountability lack enforcement. Without widely accepted auditing requirements, organizations often operate in regulatory grey zones, where ethical commitments are shaped more by reputational risk management than binding legal obligations creating asymmetries in incentive structures whereby firms that heavily invest in fairness aware design incur short term high costs, while less responsible competitors are reaping gains from aggressive data exploitation and opaque segmentation modalities.

At the same time, however, research in AI marketing continues to expand furiously. AI is widely recognized among marketing academia (Kopalle et al., 2022), and its business relevance keeps increasing (Verma et al., 2021). Thus, being that the actual AI adoption in marketing still lies at quite a beginner stage in terms of systemic maturity, the research into fairness, behavioral outcomes, and institutional governance mechanism remains scarce as longitudinal and cross national (Verma et al., 2021). Such a scarcity in empirical evidence thus hinders policymakers from crafting context sensitive regulation while also restricting practitioners from being able to benchmark fairness performance across industry and territorial lines.

From a sustainability point of view, fairness aware segmentation helps to generate long term brand trust, market legitimacy, and stakeholder resilience. Markets that treat AI in open, inclusive, and culturally aware manners stand the best chance of surviving in a world of growing complexity, political consciousness, and ethical vigilance by consumers. This strategy conversely raises the ire of a very awake public with the media calling for regulation, loss of reputation, and alienation of existing consumer loyalty. From this point, fairness aware segmentation should rather be viewed as strategic investment in sustainable competitive advantage in GenAI led global marketplaces, rather than an ethical cost.

4. CASE STUDIES

4.1 An Explanation and Cultural Sensitivity of Segmentation in Multicultural Markets

Fairness aware customer segmentation was first conceptualized when they integrated LIME explainability into K- Mean clustering (Alijoyo et al., 2025). K-Mean clustering is based on certain behavioral, demographic, and transactional characteristics of customers, aiming to cluster them into statistically meaningful groupings within this framework. The researchers considered the Elbow Method and Silhouette Analysis to determine the optimal across cluster formation, further validating this within an Alijoyo et al. (2025) framework. This rigorous statistical grounding means that segmentation boundaries derive from data structure rather than managerial intuition.

LIME provides distinct insights into how specific segmentation variables affect classification. Such variables are:

- Age and income
- Language preferences
- Family structure
- Consumption practices determined culturally

Through this interpretability, organizations will know whether sensitive attributes are emphasized to exclusionary or biased outcomes (Alijoyo et al., 2025). Hence, segmentation turns into an ethically auditable decision system from a mere predictive tool.

There are considerable implications for actual multicultural contexts. Behavioral drivers such as bulk purchases during religious festival times, joint family consumption, and community types of savings common across Asia, Africa, and the Middle

East, are quite often misperceived by models molded on Western nuclear family standards. If not explainable, such behavior risks being considered knocky, low value, odd, or high risk. Explainable segmentation allows marketers to separate cultural rationality from economic vulnerability, directly opposing algorithmic stereotyping.

From a DEI perspective, this model assures that cultural minorities are neither swallowed by the dominant clusters nor are they to be treated as statistical outliers. Rather, its function stands to assert segmentation in the provision of equitable cultural recognition. Campaigns can further be designed to celebrate linguistic diversity, religious sensitivities, and local traditions while being firmly grounded in data marketing logic (Alijoyo et al., 2025).

In GenAI powered marketing ecosystems, these explainable clusters serve as training grounds for automated systems in content generation. Festival based campaigns, creative vernacular language themed advertisements, and hyper local promotions can be raised without reducing complex identities into monolithic stereotypes. In this manner, fairness aware explainable segmentation is going to be the foundational structure of GenAI personalization inclusiveness where automating processes tends to upscale cultural inclusion rather than algorithmic exclusion.

4.2 AI Sales Agents, Emotional Trust, and the Human Machine Divide

According to Liu-Thompkins et al. (2022), the general perception of AI sales agents is that they are cold, impersonal, and intolerably unfeeling substitutes for human beings. The results indicate that when customers discover that their interaction partner is a bot, they tend to shorten their communication, exert a lesser degree of empathy, and exhibit decreased purchasing behavior. This change in behavior highlights the limit of employing automation in emotionally charged market interactions (Liu-Thompkins et al., 2022).

Therefore, this phenomenon, currently observed in the broad domains of service provision areas, includes banking chatbots in the digital realm, airline and telecom service support desks, grievance portals of governments, and post-sale platforms of e commerce service provision. In fact, there have been emotional trust asymmetries across demographic groups even where segmentation systems allow fair access to services. For instance, younger, digitally fluent categories of customers were found to be more adaptable and able to interact with machines, becoming completely disoriented, confused, uncomfortable, and disengaged on this finding based on older adult citizens and other rural populations or communities speaking different languages. In sum, this constitutes a new type of algorithmic emotional inequality, since an uneven distribution of psychological costs is associated with automation.

In collectivist and relational societies such as India, Southeast Asia, parts of Africa, and Latin America trust is generally built by human warmth, sensitivity to tone, negotiation rituals, and social reassurance. AI agents, irrespective of how technically efficient they may be, offend these normative expectations of service dignity. There exists thus a contradiction where segmentation may appear to be statistically fair, while in reality, it is experienced as being unjust.

This reveals that fairness metrics based only on the equality of distribution have a serious limitation viewed from the DEI perspective. Emotional fairness who feels respected, understood, and valued becomes equally central. Automation, without emotional inclusion, will almost exclusively alienate groups that already experience barriers in terms of technology, language, and economics.

In GenAI supported environments, this risk mounts the most. As machines get proficient at mimicking conversation and emotionalized response to stimuli, real human accountability may be supplanted by a great illusion of empathy through virtual channels. Consumers might be manipulated emotionally without any professed accountability of humans. Hence, fairness aware segmentation must be complemented essentially with hybrid human AI service architectures, providing structural design underwriting where guaranteed human escalation and oversight exist for the most sensitive consumer interactions healthcare, finance, education, and mental well-being.

4.3 GenAI, Targeted Content Personalization, and Misinformation Risk

GenAI systems such as ChatGPT currently find extensive applications in marketing workflows, including copywriting, chat bot scripting, influencer campaign planning, and automated customer communications. ChatGPT works like a highly efficient content generation engine for marketers that has human comparable quality with scale (Rivas and Zhao, 2023). When integrated with segmentation pipelines, these GenAI systems target hyper personalized persuasion, almost with psychological precision.

Technological convergence brings with it some serious pitfalls especially in regard to information and ethics. Rivas and Zhao (2023) raise concerns that AI marketing systems may refer to incorrect sources of data and produce misleading or even false output. Hallucinated content can become disseminated in the form of segmentation: from that point, accurate misinformation becomes algorithmically stratified rather than random. Some prime examples of such high-risk situations are 'financially troubled' consumers who may receive misleading form of investment schemes, patients confronted with invalid wellness or supplement claims, and students getting exaggerated promises on academics or careers.

Misinformation tends to become rather a precision targeted harm mechanism as opposed to a generalized media distortion issue. From a DEI standpoint, the burden seems dramatically worse in that the very people targeting the digital minorities, the linguistic minorities, and those at the bottom of the pyramid are actually least likely to be able to judge the credibility of synthetic content on their own.

Hence transparency stands out as an inviolable prerequisite for ethical GenAI marketing and allows the user to be able to judge if the content is machine generated and whether it has undergone ethical scrutiny or not (Rivas & Zhao, 2023). Nevertheless, in a number of actual systems, the extent to which content is machine generated and the means of assessment remain either vague or totally lacking.

Therefore, human supervision becomes a necessity structurally, rather than just a procedural formality. According to Rivas and Zhao (2023), human supervision first ensures that the content produced is consistent with ethical standards. Second, in fairness aware segmentation systems, supervision must function on three interrelated levels simultaneously:

- Who will they target?
- What content will get generated?
- How will accountability for harm assignment be decided?

Without these safeguards, segmentation is a differential harm amplifier, whereby escalating risks are actually amplified among populations that fairness mechanisms are intended to protect. In GenAI supported environments, this risk mounts the most. As machines get proficient at mimicking conversation and emotionalized response to stimuli, real human accountability may be supplanted by a great illusion of empathy through virtual channels. Consumers might be manipulated emotionally without any professed accountability of humans. Hence, fairness aware segmentation must be complemented essentially with hybrid human AI service architectures, providing structural design underwriting where guaranteed human escalation and oversight exist for the most sensitive consumer interactions healthcare, finance, education, and mental well-being.

4.4 Algorithmic Visibility, Platform Power, and Cultural Suppression

The global digital platforms, which include a gamut of giants like Amazon, Netflix, YouTube, Instagram, and Spotify, depend highly on segmentation-based recommendation systems that mediate the digital visibility and commercial participation that they provide. These systems decide, mostly invisibly, on what products to promote, which creators to algorithmically boost for visibility, and which particular languages dominate the attention economies. While cloaked in the language of personalization, it has been observed at great lengths that the overall public visibility tends to largely be biased as a result of the infraction from various algorithms. Major languages of the world receive a disproportionately higher share of algorithmic promotional support owing to service engagements and amplification loops, as import from Netflix and YouTube. Hence, discoverability of local creators, regional filmmakers, or cultural educators, would depend more on mechanisms that often algorithmically disenfranchise rather than function on well-deserved merit.

In e commerce platforms, premium and high margin products often are displayed to rich urban consumers while budget users are repeatedly shown clearance sales. This creates class segmentation algorithmically and blends, under the guise of relevance optimization, into social economic stratification.

The power of these systems, when viewed through the lens of DEI principles, exerts cultural gatekeeping power of considerable depth, for example by determining:

- Whose stories are amplified?
- Which creators are economically viable?
- Which identities are globally visible?

In GenAI supported settings, such risks gain increasing importance, as recommendation histories are becoming training data for generative systems. Domestically privileged cultural identities are thereby synthesized at scale as marginalized ones are progressively erased from the digital space. Fairness aware segmentation thus becomes, at this macro governance level, much more than a question of marketing efficiency; rather, it concerns matters of cultural survival, narrative sovereignty, and digital inclusion.

4.5 Financial, Employment, and Welfare Segmentation: Structural Exclusion at Scale

AI systems have the potential to hold disadvantaged groups, households of migrants, women entrepreneurs, and the rural population, in those circumstances where the algorithms decide single handedly upon eligibility for money, mobility, security, and dignity with algorithms that discriminate. Segmentation employs historical instruments that only capture part time or occasional income habits. Thus, when particular instances of such circumstantial shifting patterns are labeled adverse, controlled by bank repaying habits, they limit the extension of equity. Mechanical segregation can sometimes create perverse outcomes: for example, individuals will be excluded because, in many instances, they appear not to comply with prior employment status a symptom of information mismanagement. In such cases, AI producers are disenabling syntactic time as a desirable factor of progress because, in advising inaction or non-vision, it entrenches the vicious cycle of disadvantage, ensuring its own continuance in the private end.

These processes of exclusion are the most pronounced and insidious in countries that are not yet industrialized and where the majority of people operate outside a structured payment system. Street vendors, gig workers, agricultural laborers, and self-employed women contribute to the economy but do not have continuous documentation for proof of stable income. When the evaluation is mainly dependent on banking, payroll, and credit bureau histories, such people will be made virtually invisible. Their featurelessness concerning credit will then transform their absence of statistical data into systemic blocking for entrepreneurship, housing, or education financing.

Within the boundaries of the employment domain, AI driven recruitment systems are rewarding individuals after personnel for the same bias assessment. Programs such as resume screening, personality reporting, and job matching algorithms are ingrained with partialities against gender, or they neglect the fact that career discontinuation could be termed a sin against human development or that female qualities in male collars without capital are inversely deemed unmasculine. This kind of segmentation, therefore, subtly gives results with restrictions to broader economic access to mobility. Individuals who pass through difficult phases of their careers such as women seeking to resume a career after being primary caregivers for children, or transitioning from the informal to the formal sector as a first-generation graduate most likely, despite having skills as outstanding as anyone else, will be found eliminated from the inclusion spectrum. DEI issues lie in the fact that such a system undeservedly eliminates undeserving candidates while containing the so-called absence of intents of explicit discrimination making the algorithmic bias stealthily dangerous to detection, contestation, and repair.

Public health and welfare systems add further layers of ethical complexity when dependent on AI powered outreach tools that are steering vaccine campaigns, enrollment into welfare programs, nutrition aid, and health promotional endeavors. Again, such programs favor digitally active users who use online platforms, mobile apps, and government portals more frequently. This effectively disenfranchises elderly people, rural dwellers, people with disabilities, and low-tech households for vast and critical services because of silent bias in prioritizing digital engagement over social vulnerability.

The conditioning of the three sectors finance, employment, and welfare introduces a vicious loop of self-perpetuated exclusion. The notification is clear on economic grounds that the AI system overrides houses of aggregated vulnerability and the more traditionally represented the greater dependency through various forms of patronage cutting them off through the very vehicles that are supposed to assist.

The darker side of this issue lies in the full congruence between the apparent and effective exclusion; wherein, according to economic laws, most industrialized countries considered comparatively new (apart from a few) that formulate the global domain, the chances of such considerable opportunities to flourish abound in documenting the silent architect of state failure to address by ceremony, exclusion and the spoiling of super groups of youth through communism. There is no equal either!

5. IMPLICATIONS AND RECOMMENDATIONS

Incorporation of advanced artificial intelligence techniques in the customer segmentation system has revolutionized organizations' perception of, approach to, and interaction with diverse consumer groups. With such a host of diversities observed in customer needs, behavior, and preferences across digital platforms, customer segmentation can be argued to be a foundational strategic function in contemporary marketing (Kasem et al., 2024). Algorithmic segmentation plays an important role in prediction accuracy enhancement, enabling the organizations to engage and maintain their processes in a sustained growth mode (Kasem et al., 2024). Nonetheless, as demonstrated throughout the chapter, the segmentation systems function now as socio technical governance infrastructures that affect access, visibility, persuasion, and opportunity across multicultural markets. This section provides strategic, ethical, organizational, and policy considerations on fairness aware AI segmentation through three interrelated thematic lenses.

5.1 Strategic and Organizational Implications of Fairness aware Artificial Intelligence Marketing

AI is a supportive partner to marketing as it has branched out into almost every functional aspect based on the understanding that it largely derives from data-based analytics (Jarek & Mazurek, 2019). Since the introduction of AI into marketing organizations, this phenomenon is mostly found on the operational level, rather than in strategic governance and designing ethical architecture (Jarek & Mazurek, 2019). The result is a gap between what the AI system can actually do and how responsibly these advances are applied in organizational ecosystems. Thus, fairness aware segmentation must be repositioned from an analytical back-end tool to a core strategic capability embedded within corporate decision making, risk management, and customer engagement architecture.

From a point of view of competition, personalized marketing offers necessity rather than an option in global digitalized markets (Alijoyo et al., 2025). On the other hand, segmentation that reflects the fairness aspect enhances personalization because it equips firms to engage consumers across diverse cultural, linguistic, and socio-economic backgrounds with much greater sensitivity to the context, hence increasing their relevance and trust over time (Alijoyo et al., 2025). As far as explainability mechanisms are concerned, LIME allows organizations to interrogate the extent to which sensitive attributes affect segmentation outputs, thereby enforcing managerial accountability and decreasing the potential for reputational and regulatory risks (Alijoyo et al., 2025). The effects of this interpretability extend to strategic learning to allow continuous improvement of targeting precision and ethical safeguards.

Strategic overreliance on automation, however, comes with its own disadvantages. The typical perception of AI marketers is that they are cold and indifferent, while customers aware that they interact with bots buy less and feel lower empathy (Liu-Thompkins et al., 2022). Therefore, it is shown that too much automation in emotionally sensitive interactions like grievance handling, financial consultations, or healthcare assistance can really erode brand trust, no matter how accurate segmentation is. Institutions must therefore focus on creating hybrid human and AI engagement models in such a manner that automation would enhance efficiency, not displace relational trust.

From a capability perspective within an organization, fairness aware segmentation requires interdisciplinary skill integration. This is because AI requires skills ranging from data science proficiency to depth of knowledge of marketing strategy, legal compliance, organization ethics, and DEI frameworks (Jarek & Mazurek, 2019). Thus, investment in cross functional AI governance teams and the development of continuous capability building analytics within ethical frameworks is a must for organizations. Fairness audits must also be employed internally. Without an investment, even the most advanced AI could greatly embed bias at scale, just because of poor oversight, silo decision making, and unexamined assumptions in the training data.

5.2 Implications of Ethics, DEI and GenAI Governance

The emergence of GenAI tools like ChatGPT has altered the ways marketing content is created, personalized, and scaled for dissemination. ChatGPT renders speedy and efficient production of content, bearing quality akin to human creators (Rivas & Zhao, 2023) but it also introduces fresh ethical vulnerabilities that go beyond conventional automation risks. GenAI systems may produce an error or factually false information, drawing from unreliable sources (Rivas & Zhao, 2023). Most of the time, misinformation is disseminated as it is targeted from segmentation pipelines instead of random channels along the consumer base.

This constitutes a serious challenge for DEI. The low digital literacy, coupled with linguistic disadvantage and an absence of independent verification mechanisms, makes vulnerable population groups the most likely to accept algorithmically generated content as authentic. It is thus beyond mere communicative failure; misinformation actually becomes a question of structural equity, as the harm is not only disproportionately distributed, but it is also so across different socioeconomic and cultural dimensions. Hence, transparency would emerge as non-negotiable ethical requirements of GenAI driven marketing. Recently, some research emphasizes that diversity, equity, and inclusion can no longer remain normative ideals within marketing decision-making, but rather must be turned into practice when engaging with the diverse stakeholder groups at the heart of sales and marketing.(Licsandru et al.,2025) With this, consumers can see if such content is human generated or machine generated and whether it has been subjected to ethical reviews (Rivas & Zhao, 2023). The existence of transparency could lead to informed consent, while automated persuasion would undermine the legality of informed consent and weaken consumer autonomy.

Human oversight is equally precious though. It is to guarantee that automated decisions and content are all geared toward the values of the organization, regulatory expectations, and social norms of fairness (Rivas & Zhao, 2023). In terms of fairness aware segmentation, this oversight should be across targeting logic, content generation processes, and accountability mechanisms. Otherwise, organizations run the risk of pouring out an unfavorable result, where persuasion is unequally dispersed by automated systems.

Ethically speaking, AI systems are said to be discriminatory in quite a number of dimensions, and entrench the prevailing inequalities in socio economic and social aspects (Hermann, 2022). Hence, ethical challenges materialize at customer, organization, and societal levels (Hermann, 2022). These principles of transparency, justice and fairness, non-maleficence, responsibility, and privacy recur and must all be operationalized as hard design constraints, not symbolic commitments (Hermann, 2022). Explainable and culturally sensitive segmentation provides a practical way to convert DEI values into enforceable algorithmic practice (Alijoyo et al., 2025), especially in GenAI environments characterized by rapid amplification of underlying data assumptions through automated content.

5.3 Policy, Societal, and Future Research Implications

Artificial intelligence will transform strategy, collaboration, and relationships all across the marketing ecosystem (Hermann, 2022). Today segmentation systems extend their societal impact beyond commercial efficiency to food, finance, employment, healthcare, and public service. When social segmentation structures normalize, their functioning becomes so embedded in the invisible infrastructure of inequality that decisions regarding life chances are determined by statistical inferences and not any concrete agenda of political considerations. Such a metamorphosis deconstructs the balance of power, opportunity, and risk in a digital society.

For AI for social good advocates, providing systematic avenues for fairness in marketing AI is part of its contribution for inclusive and sustainable development, rather than adding an ethics statement for good karma (Hermann, 2022). Thus, it is overdue for public policy to evolve from discrete and reactive to setting enforceable standards for fairness, transparency, explainability, and accountability of these segmentation systems and GenAI driven marketing pipelines. Only underpinned by these regulatory foundations will market incentives play sufficient means to eradicate exclusionary practices encoded in optimization logic.

At the same time, the academic discipline of AI marketing is still on a lower rung of institutional maturity. Although AI has attained much interest from marketing scholars (Kopalle et al., 2022), becoming more relevant within applied business environments (Verma et al., 2021), actual empirical works in longitudinal, cross cultural, and governance oriented algorithmic fairness research keep lagging by a significant distance in consumer markets (Verma et al., 2021). This remains a major gap in evidence used by policymakers to conduct regulatory impact assessments, public policy design, and organizational benchmarking.

Future research should go beyond examining technical accuracy metrics and assessing short term performance indicators; it should begin to examine long term trust dynamics, welfare effects, institutional accountability mechanisms, and cultural implications of GenAI driven segmentation. Integrative work alone holds the potential that marketing systems can emerge to be intelligent and efficient but socially sustainable and ethically legitimate.

6. CONCLUSION

AI, customer segmentation, and generative technologies coexist and have transformed marketing from a decision support framework into a socio technical system that profoundly and actively determines what consumer opportunity, visibility, trust, and access mean. It emerges unequivocally from our inspection that segmentation is no more an innocent act of analysis. In AI or GenAI driven ecosystems, segmentation becomes a governance structure that defines who will be seen as a target, who is simply left out as an undeserving, and who shall be able to benefit from digital growth. The weight of these decisions is not limited merely to commercial ramifications in multi ethnic and unequal societies.

Fairness in segmentation is more than an ethical consideration; it is a real building block to establishing responsible marketing of AI. Fairness aware segmentation, in fact, sets the AI as an infrastructure for augmenting inclusion, expanding access to products and services, information, and economic participation through fair but culturally respecting means. The main insight that one arrives at the reconciliation of predictive accuracy and ethical integrity will thus increasingly underpin value, trust, and sustainability as significant long term strategic objectives.

The findings further demonstrate that explainability underpins the ethical segmentation of the GenAI era. Automated systems that produce content, persuade, and personalize communications at scale exponentially increase the risks of stereotyping, cultural misrepresentation, emotional manipulation, and algorithmic disinformation. Unless organizations can be transparent and interpret their segmentation, they will have lost the capability to audit for harm, consumers will lose the right for contesting the decision making made, and regulating bodies will lose power over enforcing accountability.

Another major finding here is that emotional trust, cultural dignity, and relational authenticity are dimensions of fairness that purely statistical metrics cannot capture. Even if statistical metrics show equity, when the experience becomes one of injustice, it is due to a lack of empathy, trust, and excessive psychological and cognitive burden on already vulnerable members of society. This illustrates that it is limited to confine fairness to a technical optimization issue and furthers the case for a human centered design approach to the AI marketing system.

At the organizational level of findings, one finding is that fairness aware segmentation cannot be cultivated as a mere technological upgrade. It needs an interdisciplinary governance structure that unites a decision architecture integrating data science, marketing strategy, legal oversight, ethical reasoning, and DEI leadership. Without such integration, even the best AI systems will find it will become ethically superficial: efficient in execution but devoid of moral and social consideration. Fairness, therefore, needs institutional entrenchment as a design standard rather than operational monetization as a compliance exercise.

Considerable implications arise from an ethical, social, and sustainable standpoint. The ethical quality of these systems directly shapes future inequalities as AI driven segmentation systems become more efficacious in the domains of financial inclusion, accessibility to jobs, outreach in healthcare, visibility in media, and educational opportunities. In this regard, fairness aware segmentation opens up a path for slant restoration in that it guarantees that automation acts, sustaining inclusion and not excluding people disproportionately on a massive scale.

In a nutshell, the key assertion in this chapter is that fairness aware AI segmentation gives birth to an entire platform of ethical GenAI driven marketing. This changes the perspective on segmentation as a tool of profit maximization into a governance structure with grave social consequences. Future responsible marketing won't be governed just by how far intelligent systems go, but more so by how equi-

REFERENCES

Alijoyo, F. A., Aziz, T. S. A., Omer, N., Yusuf, N., Kumar, M. D., Ramesh, A. V. N., Ulmas, Z., & Baker El-Ebiary, Y. A. (2025). Personalized marketing: Leveraging AI for culturally aware segmentation and targeting. *Alexandria Engineering Journal, 119*, 8–21. DOI: 10.1016/j.aej.2025.01.074

Alves Gomes, M., & Meisen, T. (2023). A review on customer segmentation methods for personalized customer targeting in e-commerce use cases. *Information Systems and e-Business Management, 21*(3), 527–570. DOI: 10.1007/s10257-023-00640-4

Binns, R. (2018). Fairness in machine learning: Lessons from political philosophy. In *Proceedings of the 1st Conference on Fairness, Accountability and Transparency* (pp. 149–159). https://proceedings.mlr.press/v81/binns18a.html

Chen, I., Johansson, F. D., & Sontag, D. (2018). Why is my classifier discriminatory? In *Advances in Neural Information Processing Systems* (Vol. 31). https://proceedings.neurips.cc/paper/2018/hash/1f1baa5b8edac74eb4eaa329f14a0361-Abstract.html

Chierichetti, F., Kumar, R., Lattanzi, S., & Vassilvitskii, S. (2017). Fair clustering through fairlets. In *Advances in Neural Information Processing Systems* (Vol. 30).

Deepak, P., & Abraham, S. S. (2020). Representativity fairness in clustering. In *Proceedings of the 12th ACM Conference on Web Science* (pp. 202–211). https://doi.org/DOI: 10.1145/3394231.3397910

Doshi-Velez, F., & Kim, B. (2017). Towards a rigorous science of interpretable machine learning. *arXiv:1702.08608*. https://doi.org//arXiv.1702.08608DOI: 10.48550

Dwork, C., Hardt, M., Pitassi, T., Reingold, O., & Zemel, R. (2011). Fairness through awareness. *arXiv:1104.3913*. https://doi.org//arXiv.1104.3913DOI: 10.48550

Guidotti, R., Monreale, A., Ruggieri, S., Turini, F., Giannotti, F., & Pedreschi, D. (2019). A survey of methods for explaining black box models. *ACM Computing Surveys, 51*(5), 1–42. DOI: 10.1145/3236009

Hermann, E. (2022). Leveraging artificial intelligence in marketing for social good—An ethical perspective. *Journal of Business Ethics, 179*(1), 43–61. DOI: 10.1007/s10551-021-04843-y

Hoffman, R. R., Mueller, S. T., Klein, G., & Litman, J. (2019). Metrics for explainable AI: Challenges and prospects. *arXiv:1812.04608*. https://doi.org//arXiv.1812.04608DOI: 10.48550

Huang, M.-H., & Rust, R. T. (2021). A strategic framework for artificial intelligence in marketing. *Journal of the Academy of Marketing Science, 49*(1), 30–50. DOI: 10.1007/s11747-020-00749-9

Jarek, K., & Mazurek, G. (2019). Marketing and artificial intelligence. *Central European Business Review, 8*(2), 46–55. DOI: 10.18267/j.cebr.213

Kamishima, T., Akaho, S., Asoh, H., & Sakuma, J. (2012). Fairness-aware classifier with prejudice remover regularizer. In Flach, P. A., De Bie, T., & Cristianini, N. (Eds.), *Machine Learning and Knowledge Discovery in Databases* (Vol. 7524, pp. 35–50). Springer., DOI: 10.1007/978-3-642-33486-3_3

Kasem, M. S., Hamada, M., & Taj-Eddin, I. (2024). Customer profiling, segmentation, and sales prediction using AI in direct marketing. *Neural Computing & Applications, 36*(9), 4995–5005. DOI: 10.1007/s00521-023-09339-6

Kearns, M., Neel, S., Roth, A., & Wu, Z. S. (2018). Preventing fairness gerrymandering: Auditing and learning for subgroup fairness. In *Proceedings of the 35th International Conference on Machine Learning* (pp. 2564–2572).

Kleindessner, M., Awasthi, P., & Morgenstern, J. (2020). A notion of individual fairness for clustering. *arXiv:2006.04960.* https://doi.org//arXiv.2006.04960DOI: 10.48550

Kopalle, P. K., Gangwar, M., Kaplan, A., Ramachandran, D., Reinartz, W., & Rindfleisch, A. (2022). Examining artificial intelligence (AI) technologies in marketing via a global lens: Current trends and future research opportunities. *International Journal of Research in Marketing, 39*(2), 522–540. DOI: 10.1016/j.ijresmar.2021.11.002

Kumar, V., Ashraf, A. R., & Nadeem, W. (2024). AI-powered marketing: What, where, and how? *International Journal of Information Management, 77*, 102783. DOI: 10.1016/j.ijinfomgt.2024.102783

Licsandru, T. C., Mari, C., Kipnis, E., Galalae, C., Johnson, E., Cross, S. N. N., Cui, C. C., Kearney, S., Martín Ruiz, V., Vorster Larsen, L., & Yoruk, I. (2025). Integrating diversity, equity and inclusion in management education: An empathy framework. *British Journal of Management.* Advance online publication. DOI: 10.1111/1467-8551.70008

Liu-Thompkins, Y., Okazaki, S., & Li, H. (2022). Artificial empathy in marketing interactions: Bridging the human-AI gap in affective and social customer experience. *Journal of the Academy of Marketing Science, 50*(6), 1198–1218. DOI: 10.1007/s11747-022-00892-5

Lundberg, S. M., & Lee, S.-I. (2017). A unified approach to interpreting model predictions. In *Advances in Neural Information Processing Systems* (Vol. 30). https://proceedings.neurips.cc/paper/2017/hash/8a20a8621978632d76c43dfd28b67767-Abstract.html

Mandania, R., Cadogan, J., Liu, J., & Kazmi, N. (2025). Optimizing promotional campaigns to maximize customer lifetime value: A dynamic learning approach. *Journal of Service Research*. Advance online publication. DOI: 10.1177/10946705251365524

Mariani, M. M., Perez-Vega, R., & Wirtz, J. (2022). AI in marketing, consumer research and psychology: A systematic literature review and research agenda. *Psychology and Marketing*, *39*(4), 755–776. DOI: 10.1002/mar.21619

Mehrabi, N., Morstatter, F., Saxena, N., Lerman, K., & Galstyan, A. (2022). A survey on bias and fairness in machine learning. *arXiv:1908.09635*. https://doi.org//arXiv.1908.09635DOI: 10.48550

Mikalef, P., Boura, M., Lekakos, G., & Krogstie, J. (2019). Big data analytics and firm performance: Findings from a mixed-method approach. *Journal of Business Research*, *98*, 261–276. DOI: 10.1016/j.jbusres.2019.01.044

Pani, D., & Behera, S. N. (2021). An investigation of customer preferences using data mining. *Dogo Rangsang Research Journal, 8*(14), Article 03.

Qadadeh, W., & Abdallah, S. (2018). Customers segmentation in the insurance company (TIC) dataset. *Procedia Computer Science*, *144*, 277–290. DOI: 10.1016/j.procs.2018.10.529

Ribeiro, M. T., Singh, S., & Guestrin, C. (2016). "Why should I trust you?": Explaining the predictions of any classifier. In *Proceedings of the 22nd ACM SIGKDD International Conference on Knowledge Discovery and Data Mining* (pp. 1135–1144). https://doi.org/DOI: 10.1145/2939672.2939778

Rivas, P., & Zhao, L. (2023). Marketing with ChatGPT: Navigating the ethical terrain of GPT-based chatbot technology. *AI*, *4*(2), 375–384. DOI: 10.3390/ai4020019

Saura, J. R., Ribeiro-Soriano, D., & Palacios-Marqués, D. (2021). Setting B2B digital marketing in artificial intelligence-based CRMs: A review and directions for future research. *Industrial Marketing Management*, *98*, 161–178. DOI: 10.1016/j.indmarman.2021.08.006

Starke, C., Baleis, J., Keller, B., & Marcinkowski, F. (2022). Fairness perceptions of algorithmic decision-making: A systematic review of the empirical literature. *Big Data & Society*, *9*(2), 20539517221115189. DOI: 10.1177/20539517221115189

Tarnanidis, T., & Vlachopoulou, M. (2025). *Cultural sensitivity, cross-border logistics, and e-commerce in global marketing*. IGI Global Scientific Publishing., DOI: 10.4018/979-8-3373-0528-8

Verma, S., & Rubin, J. (2018). Fairness definitions explained. In *Proceedings of the International Workshop on Software Fairness* (pp. 1–7). https://doi.org/DOI: 10.1145/3194770.3194776

Verma, S., Sharma, R., Deb, S., & Maitra, D. (2021). Artificial intelligence in marketing: Systematic review and future research direction. *International Journal of Information Management Data Insights*, *1*(1), 100002. DOI: 10.1016/j.jjimei.2020.100002

KEY TERMS AND DEFINITIONS

Customer Segmentation: Customer heterogeneity is subdivided for more comprehensive marketing decisions based on some demographic, behavioral, psychographic, or transactional characteristics.

Diversity, Equity, and Inclusion (DEI): Those values that promote fairness, cultural respect, and systematic inclusion across demographic and social groups; applied to segmentation, the DEI serves the moral and strategic justification for fairness aware design.

Explainable Artificial Intelligence (XAI): A series of methodological techniques that were made to have the outputs of the AI model easily interpretable so that decision makers understand correctly why segmentation decisions were made and also to audit systems both for fairness and cultural sensitivity.

Generative AI (GenAI): AI systems producing at scale text, images or personalized content; these systems are currently being integrated with segmentation pipelines to automate targeting, messaging and persuasive communication.

LIME (Local Interpretable Model Agnostic Explanations): The description given by this explanation technique is reconcilable with model agnostic simplifications that reveal to customers how importance is derived from specific features like age, income, or cultural practices as being valued for an individual segmentation outcome.

Proxy Bias: This type of indirect discrimination occurs when non protected variables unconsciously encode sensitive group characteristics so that outcomes are biased while the protected attribute does not appear.

SHAP (SHapley Additive exPlanations): This game theoretic feature attribution methodology values how much each variable contributes toward a particular model's prediction, thus ensuring uniform and lucid understanding across a huge number of consumers.

Chapter 11

From Greenwashing to Genuine Sustainability: Ethical Marketing in the Age of Conscious Consumers

Kanika Arora
Lovely Professional University, India

Amrik Singh
https://orcid.org/0000-0003-3598-8787
Lovely Professional University, India

ABSTRACT

The emergence of conscious consumerism has compelled brands to adopt a more thoughtful approach, ensuring that their entire marketing practices align with issues concerning sustainability, inclusivity, and ethical responsibility. And yet the paradox of 2025 is that, even as consumers clamor for ethical branding more than ever, we see record levels of corporate greenwashing, too. In this chapter, we analyse the paradox of performative ethics and authentic sustainability marketing that emerges when looking at the trajectory of marketing ethics from its origins to current overall coherence or divergence between theory and practice in our global world. The conversation is informed by recent examples from a range of industries, from Volkswagen's "Dieselgate" and H&M's "Conscious Collection" to Patagonia's radical transparency, Dove's inclusivity campaigns, and Nike's social justice activism that illustrate how greenwashing erodes consumer trust while genuine sustainability becomes a source for loyalty, resilience, and cultural relevance.

DOI: 10.4018/979-8-3373-6731-6.ch011

INTRODUCTION

The ethical marketing paradox of 2025 is jolting: People want sustainable, responsible products like never before; companies are playing fast and loose with greenwashing and performative ethics more than ever. On the one hand, companies are becoming aware of the reputational and economic premium attached to their brands being linked to sustainability and social good (Bhasin, 2025). On the one hand, such measures cannot win over consumer's trust, while on the other they are almost daily countered by new scandals about false advertising, exaggerated pledges and superficial gestures (Dragomir, 2019; Perry et al., 2024). This cognitive dissonance highlights a tenuous relationship between marketing as an agent of positive transformation and marketing at the root of public skepticism.These dynamics have only been amplified by the growth of conscious consumerism, especially among Millennials and Gen Z (Tarnanidis, et al., 2026) These are not only sharp, values-orienting cohorts, but also ones who has been increasingly able to question brands ethical positioning through digital tribunals and activist networks (Briffault, 2025; Kaufman et al., 2020; Pardinas, Lepetit & Valette-Florence, 2018). For them, marketing is no longer confined to product features but the extent to which a brand truly reflects in practice these values of transparency, inclusiveness and sustainability. As McEachern and Carrigan (2012) note, ethical consumerism is frequently bound up with cultural identity or personal values this legitimacy in marketing becomes particularly important in today's market culture. But as the demand for authenticity continues to rise, a gap in trust has been opened (Durand-Hayes, 2024). Sixty four percent of global consumers believe that brands should make it easier to help them, for example by offering information or tools to address environmental and social issues, yet only 31% think businesses are doing so (Edelman Trust Barometer, 2025). Scepticism of corporate information is also seen as one of the major barriers that brands will face in their attempts to build loyalty (Source: PwC 2024 Voice of the Consumer Survey). If marketing overpromises or hides vital information, the consequences can be significant: consumers are more and more vocal about what they perceive as hypocrisy online, NGOs challenge legal action and regulatory bodies apply ever stricter penalties for misleading sustainability claims.The truth is this, abolitionists performing ethic meets capitalism in marketing and advertising. Greenwashing from ambiguous eco-labels to exaggerated carbon-neutral promises has emerged as one of the most common ethical challenges in the arena (Dragomir, 2019). The H&M "Conscious Collection" litigation alleging the company embellished its green accomplishments demonstrates how such performance art can squander credibility (Perry et al., 2024). By contrast, firms such as Patagonia are working to build consumer trust by infusing sustainability into the end-to-end value chain, developing circular business models and operating with radical transparency

(Voronov et al., 2021). The "Don't Buy This Jacket" campaign from Patagonia, for instance, offers a powerful example of how contrarian messaging that's backed up by genuine environmental action can be used to enhance brand value and ethical repute (Nadda et al., 2024a; Sharma et al., 2024a; Ansari et al., 2024; Prakash et al., 2024). The aim of this chapter is to examine the greenwashing–authenticity divide as a key tension in ethical marketing. Basing on classical ethical decision-making theories (Ferrell & Gresham, 1985; Hunt & Vitell, 1986), and recent advances in the areas of sustainability, digital marketing and inclusivity (Ferrell & Ferrell, 2021; Dastane et al., 2025; Gupta et al., 2025), this chapter probes into how brands, consumers and regulators are reconceptualizing what constitutes marketing ethics in the era of conscious consumerism. It combines academic discoveries with real-world case studies from fashion to technology to show how ethical branding practices can either inspire trust among consumers or drive scepticism (Maheshwari et al., 2024; Berry & Singh, 2024; Sharma et al., 2024b). In the final chapter, the future of marketing ethics is envisioned not in performative litanies to post-modern technology and non-existent humans, but as stitched into the discursive tapestry of business practice abutted by transparency at one end and inclusivity at the other.

2. THEORETICAL FOUNDATIONS OF ETHICAL MARKETING

Marketing ethics as a discipline is rooted in a number of fundamental concepts that have become central frameworks influencing the academic literature and practice. One of the early initiatives in this domain was Ferrell and Gresham's (1985) contingency theory, which suggested that marketers' ethical decision making is not determined solely by their own moral philosophies but also to some extent by contextual factors such as the corporate culture or climate of opinion, industry practices, and legal environment. The model underscored that ethical judgments are context dependent, which explains why individuals in similar predicament concerning ethics issues in HCOs may also differ as to their conclusions as a function of the organizational and cultural situations. On this basis, Hunt and Vitell (1986) proposed the General Theory of Marketing Ethics which is among the most cited frameworks in the field. Their approach combines deontological reasoning, which centers on duties and rules to be observed, with teleological reasoning that takes into account the consequences of choices. By articulating the way in which marketers both judge actions according to moral obligations and future consequences, the theory has offered a strong framework for understanding ethical decision making across settings. It is however a centerpiece of today's scholarly discourse (Ferrell, Crittenden, Ferrell, & Crittenden, 2013. These two frameworks together put ethics on the map as a serious area of marketing research, but they were mainly normative in that direction, wanting to say something about what should guide decisions rather than how decisions actually are made (Maheshwari et al., 2024; Berry & Singh, 2024; Sharma et al., 2024b).As the industry developed, the focus moved away from abstract principles to consumer-oriented concepts of trust, transparency and privacy. Empirical studies have shown the effects of organizational and demographic variables on honesty (Dubinsky & Loken, 1989; Ford & Richardson, 1994). Subsequent research has focused on the mediating effect of perceived risk, moral intensity and organizational climate in the formation of ethical judgments (Cherry & Fraedrich, 2002; Singhapakdi, 1999). These developments were accompanied by the emergence of conscious consumerism, in which consumers' evaluations of brands began to encompass concern for ethical issues as well as price and quality (Crane, 1997; McEachern & Carrigan, 2012). As a result marketing ethics expanded to include sustainability, inclusivity and corporate social responsibility issues which not only became important aspects of internal decision-making, but also external brand positioning (Van de Ven, 2008; Perry et al., 2024).More recent work has answered to the increasing nuance of marketing in digital and global context. Ferrell and Ferrell (2021) suggested that moral concerns should move beyond traditional morality reasoning to consider corporate social responsibility, towards stakeholder engagement and long-term sustainability. Likewise, Dastane, Aw, Fandos-Roig and Sánchez-García (2025) advocated a new research agenda for emerging themes such as AI driven personalization, environmental marketing and cross-cultural inclusivity. This change mirrors the fact that social and technological trends no longer allow a division between marketing ethics and wider society.

Ethical issues are becoming even more complicated in the era of artificial intelligence (Arora & Singh, 2026) and big data. Researchers have highlighted potential harms, such as algorithmic bias, privacy issues and manipulative personalisation (Gupta et al., 2025; Hermann & Puntoni, 2024). These advances class CSR and sustainability as part of conventional marketing ethics suggesting that marketing ethics should not only encompass traditional areas of CSR and SD, but also outreach into other domains in which consumers are exposed to unclear decision making environments. Consider, for example, ethical concerns regarding privacy violations and consumer autonomy in retail targeting when companies are collecting and acting on sensitive behavioral data through predictive analytics (Berry & Singh, 2024; Sharma et al., 2024b).Despite these theoretical advancements, there remains a wide distance between ideal ethical concepts as described in theory and actual organizational practice. As Murphy et al. (2017) indicated, organizational rewards, market pressures, and cultural diversities are the most pervasive external factor to erode ethical motives. Such a discrepancy is especially pronounced when it comes to sustainability marketing (Köffer, 2017), where lofty statements might not be matched by concrete actions, making firms susceptible to greenwashing allegations

(Dragomir, 2019; McEachern & Carrigan, 2012). Closing this gap is dependent on robust theoretical models but also institutionally mechanisms such as third-party certification, reporting transparency and heightened ethical training for marketers (Merritt, 1991; Kamila & Jasrotia, 2024). Firms such as Unilever have attempted to change this in efforts like the Sustainable Living Plan, which is meant to integrate marketing with the United Nations Sustainable Development Goals and includes annual reporting on environmental and social performance (Ferrell & Ferrell, 2021). Thus the emergence of theory in ethical marketing demonstrates a movement from early relational and philosophical approaches to those that promote the consumer and society, as well as current issues orientated around new technologies and sustainability. Yet the divide between theory and praxis remains and moreover, it has become impossible to ignore the extent to which companies practice what they preach -this challenge for corporate activity rather than just rhetoric is especially evident in greenwashing versus authentic sustainability marketing debate (Nadda et al., 2024a; Sharma et al., 2024a; Ansari et al., 2024).

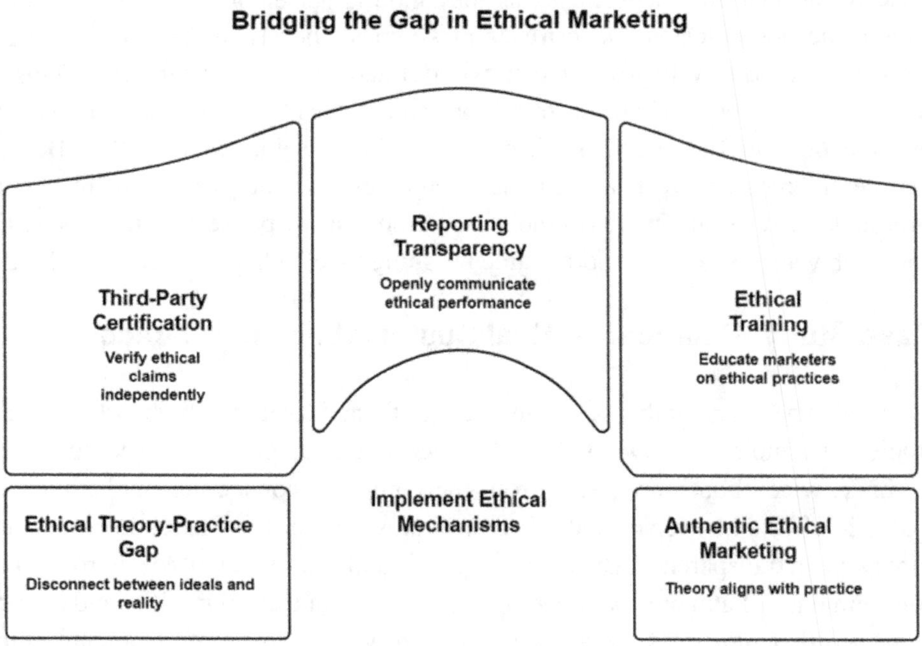

Source: Author's Creation

3. GREENWASHING VS. GENUINE SUSTAINABILITY MARKETING

The balance between greenwashing and legitimate sustainability marketing is also recognised as one of the most important challenges currently facing marketing ethics. The word "greenwashing" came into vogue in the 1980s, most famously associated with hotel campaigns that encouraged guests to reuse towels as a sign of environmental concern (Prakash et al., 2024; Nadda et al., 2024b; Maheshwari et al., 2024; Berry & Singh, 2024; Sharma et al., 2024b). In truth, such initiatives by and large only marginally lowered operating costs instead of leading to major environmental savings. This early case study epitomizes the nature of greenwashing: the tactical use of environmental discourse in order to improve brand reputation, without achieving equivalent environmental or social benefits (Dragomir, 2019).

Since then, greenwashing has become more and more sophisticated. Companies frequently depend on fuzzy eco-labels like "natural" or "eco-friendly," which do not have standardized meanings or third-party validation. Others downplay information, focusing on marginal betterments as they hide larger environmental detriments. Among the most notorious modern examples comes "Diesel gate," when Volkswagen marketed its diesel vehicles as clean, while it had rigged emissions tests. This lie was not only expensive in terms of billions and recalls, but harmed consumer trust over the long run (Ferrell & Ferrell, 2021). In a similar vein, although BP's "Beyond Petroleum" rebrand saw heavy emphasis on renewable energy investment – while simultaneously expanding fossil fuel production – the response was that this partial approach was typical of corporate greenwashing (McEachern & Carrigan, 2012).

Case Study: Patagonia – Real Sustainability in Practice

It's also been one of the most referenced authentic sustainability marketing case studies / examples. Its "Don't Buy This Jacket" campaign encouraged customers to think twice about purchasing from the company, connecting marketing with systemic efforts like repair and reuse programs, 1% for the Planet donations and supply chain transparency. By connecting its brand story to tangible environmental commitments,1 Patagonia has developed a reservoir of trust, durability and cultural relevance that illustrates how true sustainability is a means of enhancing ethics alongside business impact.

These examples illustrate how businesses might be willing to cash in on demand for sustainable consumption while actually undermining the very values they supposedly believe in. In contrast, authentic sustainability marketing integrates social and environmental responsibility into the very structure of corporate strategy. Transparency and demonstrable benefits to the planet require those making claims of sustainability either to earn third-party endorsements or certifications that validate their efforts (Van de Ven, 2008). True sustainability initiatives, rather than a veneer of public relations, embody the commitment by which a company is truly attempting to run itself through metrics that are in sync with environmental and social objectives (Ansari et al., 2024; Prakash et al., 2024; Nadda et al., 2024b; Maheshwari et al., 2024; Berry & Singh, 2024; Sharma et al., 2024b).

Case Study: H&M, conscious collection and the dangers of Green-washing

H&M's "Conscious Collection," which it billed as an eco-friendly fashion line, has been sued and targeted by NGOs for making overstated environmental claims. Investigations found that although the collection showcased props like organic and recycled materials, H&M's overall fast-fashion model was still toxic for the environment. Critics argued the company was guilty of selective disclosure and tokenism, which undermined brand credibility. The situation provides an example of how symbolic sustainability campaigns not complemented by structural changes can make firms vulnerable to allegations of greenwashing and damage their reputation.

One of the most cited examples of genuine sustainability is Patagonia, which "has always demonstrated its environmental commitment" through various measures from 1% for the Planet to donations to grassroots environmental organisations and circular economy moments such as repair and reuse (Voronov et al, 2021). The company's high-profile "Don't Buy This Jacket" ad campaign asked consumers to rethink buying habits, and kept it real with marketing messages that reflected actual sustainability efforts. Another example is Ben & Jerry's, whose advocacy around climate justice, fair trade sourcing, and social equity represents a comprehensive approach to sustainability. Connecting marketing to advocacy with transparent reporting has made Ben & Jerry's a paragon of values-based branding (Ferrell & Ferrell, 2021). These instances demonstrate how genuine sustainability marketing sets itself apart from greenwashing by weaving responsibility throughout the supply chain and consumer interaction.

Case Study: Patagonia – Real Sustainability in Practice

It's also been one of the most referenced authentic sustainability marketing case studies / examples. Its "Don't Buy This Jacket" campaign encouraged customers to think twice about purchasing from the company, connecting marketing with systemic efforts like repair and reuse programs, 1% for the Planet donations and supply chain transparency. By connecting its brand story to tangible environmental commitments,1 Patagonia has developed a reservoir of trust, durability and cultural relevance that illustrates how true sustainability is a means of enhancing ethics alongside business impact.

Table 1. Comparison of Greenwashing Tactics vs. Authentic Sustainability Practices

Dimension	Greenwashing Tactics	Authentic Sustainability Practices
Messaging Style	Use of vague terms (“eco-friendly,” “natural”) without verification (McEachern & Carrigan, 2012).	Transparent claims backed by measurable data (Van de Ven, 2008; Ferrell & Ferrell, 2021).
Evidence	Selective disclosure, omitting harmful impacts (Dragomir, 2019).	Third-party certifications (e.g., Fairtrade, B Corp) (Dastane, Aw, Fandos-Roig, & Sánchez-García, 2025).
Consumer Impact	Creates confusion, fosters distrust (Szaban, Szymkowiak, & Zdziennicka, 2025).	Builds trust, strengthens loyalty (Bonneton, 2025).
Examples	Volkswagen “Dieselgate” (Ferrell & Ferrell, 2021); H&M Conscious Collection lawsuits (Perry et al., 2024).	Patagonia’s “Don’t Buy This Jacket” campaign; Ben & Jerry’s climate justice activism.
Long-Term Outcome	Reputational harm, regulatory risk, loss of equity (Edelman Trust Institute, 2025).	Resilience, cultural relevance, stakeholder legitimacy (Voronov, Gorlachev, Mirzoeva, Rudenko, & Popova, 2021).

Source: Author’s Creation

However, the increased prominence of sustainability claims has posed a major problem for consumers, commonly termed the consumer’s dilemma. An investigation demonstrated that consumers cannot easily differentiate genuine sustainable operations form greenwashing. This process was intended, at least in part (and until the inevitable watering-down), to ameliorate such problems with eco-labels and certifications. Yet the explosion of labels of varying integrity has caused confusion, leaving shoppers uncertain about where rigorous standards end and marketing begins (Maheshwari et al., 2024; Berry & Singh, 2024; Sharma et al., 2024b). Organizations, causes and even government agencies have tried to fight this predicament by offering better rules and punishing those deceiving users. For example, litigation brought against the likes of H&M to combat a “Conscious Collection” that the firm was thought to be overstating the environmental benefits of their products highlights increasing mechanisms for monitoring and regulation which are being put in place to help safeguard consumers and verify sustainability (Perry et al., 2024). Consumer activism, coupled with the exponential increase of users on social media, has raised pressure from the public, creating a more challenging environment for companies to greenwash without risking damage to their reputation (Nadda et al., 2024b; Maheshwari et al., 2024; Berry & Singh, 2024; Sharma et al., 2024b). The challenge of aligning marketing to ethical practice Highlighting this is the underlying dichotomy between greenwashing and true sustainability something that reflects the bigger issue of attempting to match mouth with feet. On the one hand, increasing demand for environmentally responsible goods gives companies good reasons to present themselves as green whether or not they really are. On the other, the real business of sustainability marketing shows that–when done well–authenticity transparency and accountability actually create long-term customer trust and loyalty. The tenacity of the consumer's conundrum illustrates the crucial role of regulation, credible certification and a watchful civil society to ensure marketing claims about sustainability are more than just symbolic.

4. ETHICAL MARKETING BEYOND SUSTAINABILITY

While sustainability is a key point of conversation in ethical marketing, the horizon for ethical concerns don't end at environmental responsibility either. Materially, advertising tradition is now used as much for confidence building as making money, with concerns about consumer trust and digital morality being values on a par with inclusion and brand behaviour in crisis. These dimensions indicate that green marketing ethics is not confined to eco-friendliness but expands as the overarching issue of fairness, accountability, and authenticity in the brand-consumer relationship (Ferrell & Ferrell, 2021; Dastane et al., 2025; Nadda et al., 2024a; Sharma et al., 2024a; Ansari et al., 2024). Certainly one of the greatest concerns is trust erosion by consumers. A majority of consumers today want brands to engage with societal and environmental issues, but are becoming increasingly skeptical about doing so. (Edelman Trust Barometer 2025) This is consistent with PwC's (2024) Voice of the Consumer Survey on 2024, which shows a continued 'trust deficit', despite growing ethical demands (Durand-Hayes, 624). In reaction to this, some companies have adopted "radical transparency," revealing information about their supply chain or production processes. Clothing company Everlane led the way with its "Radical Transparency" campaign, which included posting factory details and price components (Prakash et al., 2024; Nadda et al., 2024b; Maheshwari et al., 2024; Berry & Singh, 2024; Sharma et al., 2024b). This initially enhanced brand trust, but the post-criticism traction for labor practices illustrated the challenges of maintaining transparency when consumer expectations are at a peak (Edelman Trust Institute, 2025; Durand-Hayes, 2024). This shows the two-edged character of transparency: It can support legitimacy, but as soon as it is inconsistent, makes for poor credibility (Ansari et al., 2024; Prakash et al., 2024; Nadda et al., 2024b; Maheshwari et al., 2024; Berry & Singh, 2024; Sharma et al., 2024b).Digital transformation has created new ethical issues, notably around AI, personalization and algorithmic persuasion. Researchers argue that AI-facilitated marketing evokes concerns related to data privacy, fairness and consumer sovereignty (Gupta et al., 2025; Hermann & Puntoni 2024). Similar criticisms can be found in the studies Google cloud service predictive marketing algorithmic manipulation digital surveillance algorithms inequalities (Hari et al., 2024; Naz & Kashif, 2024). One of the most frequently cited examples is Target's prediction algorithm for pregnancy, where it was able to predict that a daughter was pregnant before her family knew. This is an example of the ethical backlash that predictive analytics might cause by violating normative standards. More recently, TikTok has been accused of algorithmic bias, where its recommendation system either suppressed marginalized voices or amplified dangerous content. These controversies support academic contentions that AI in marketing should be governed by ethical design principles in order to safeguard trust (Hermann & Puntoni, 2024; Saleh & Zeebaree, 2025).

Case Study: Dove – Real Beauty or Real Risk?

Dove's "Real Beauty" ads have been lauded for casting women of differing body types, ages and races to confront simplistic ideas about beauty. The campaign struck a chord with consumers clamouring for inclusivity and placed Dove at the vanguard of values-centric branding. But critics have cited inconsistencies within parent company Unilever's brand roster, where other products continue to reinforce the beauty ideal paradigm. This tension illustrates the danger of inclusive campaigns: They invite loyalty and trust, while also subjecting brands to accusations of hypocrisy when corporate practices don't match brand messaging.

Another key factor of ethical marketing is inclusivity and representation. Studies on visual ethics demonstrate that advertising can indeed reflect negative stereotypes if not monitored (Borgerson & Schroeder, 2002; Pires & Stanton, 2002). Effective inclusive marketing is about authentic engagement, not tokenistic nods. It appears that Dove's "Real Beauty" campaign has been hailed as the ultimate expernple of a company expanding beauty standards while also being in line with consumer value:ideoas that telegraph authenticity (Low & Davenport, 2008; Perry et al., 2024). The 2017 Pepsi advertisement featuring Kendall Jenner" was more than a material attempt gone bad and instead involved the issue of "superficial elsewheres being shared to the glass house of inclusivity (Durand-Hayes, 2024). These fears are further perpetuated by generational dynamics, where Gen Z consumers have formed habitual expectations of diversity and values-alignment in brand communications, penalising brands who do not meet such expectations (Bonneton, 2025; Durand-Hayes, 2024).

Case Study: Nike - Standing Up for Crisis Marketing.

Nike ran a controversial ad campaign that took on racial injustice, featuring NFL QB Colin Kaepernick in 2018. The tagline, "Believe in something. Even if it means sacrificing everything," was an expression of the sort of principle Nike was willing to stand behind. The campaign initially led to boycotts and political blowback, but ultimately it was seen as having unified brand loyalty with the values of a younger consumers, who were supported by values and boosted sales. The Nike case also illustrates how principled activism in the midst of social unrest can convert immediate controversy into lasting cultural and commercial success.

Behavior of brands in social and political crises is also a complementary domain where ethical marketing faces restrictions. Scrutiny is heightened during crises, and both action and inaction may have reputational implications (Van de Ven, 2008; Perry et al., 2024). One notable exception is Nike's 2018 campaign starring Colin Kaepernick, in support of the athlete's protest against racial injustice. While the campaign initially provoked boycotts and political backlash, it ultimately enhanced Nike's image with younger value-driven customers (Ferrell & Ferrell, 2021; Dion et al., 2024). In contrast, several fashion brands also faced pressure in 2020 to speak out during the movements of Black Lives Matter (BLM) for remaining silent or issuing cosmetic statements rather than taking affirmative action, which led to reputational damage (Perry et al., 2024; Edelman Trust Institute, 2025). These examples demonstrate that it's not enough to have one-off disaster PRs; consumers today demand authentic, consistent connection with ethical values and inaction can be as harmful as error (Prakash et al., 2024; Nadda et al., 2024b; Maheshwari et al., 2024; Berry & Singh, 2024; Sharma et al., 2024b). Collectively, these developments indicate that ethical marketing beyond sustainability involves multiple challenges related to trust, technology, inclusivity and crisis-response. All of these realms illuminate the changing pressures on brands to transition from a practice of performativity around ethics toward truly engaging. As the literature also suggests, ethics is instrumental and not incidental to marketing practice, influencing consumer faithfulness and brand legitimacy in the long run (Dastane et al., 2025; Ferrell & Ferrell, 2021).

Ethical Marketing Challenges

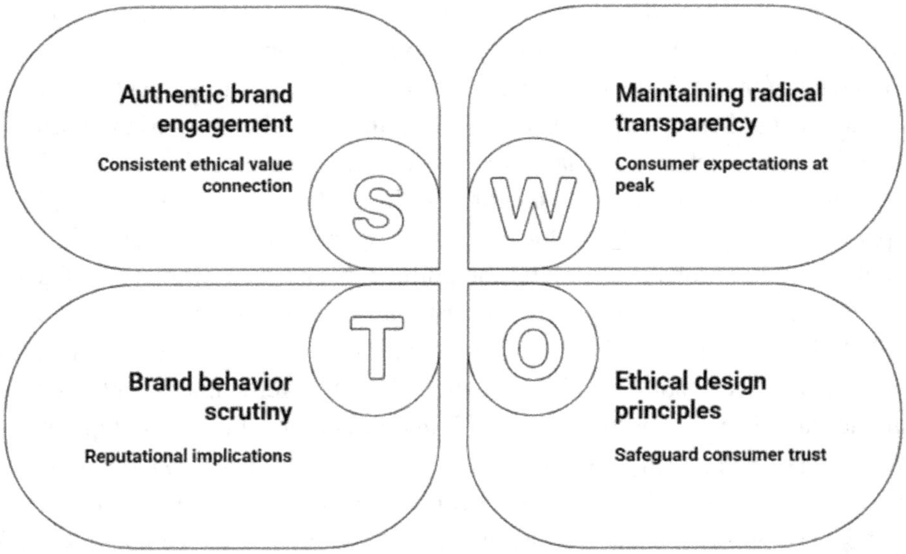

Source: Author's Creation

5. IMPLICATIONS FOR STAKEHOLDERS

The rise of ethical marketing has serious implications for businesses, customers and politicians. Handed with the growing prominence of sustainability, inclusivity and digital ethics in marketing practice inevitably shifting from periphery to mainstream, each stakeholder group has its own series of responsibilities and opportunities. These implications must be addressed in order for there to be effective short-term and long-term trust- and accountability-building systems (Maheshwari et al., 2024; Berry & Singh, 2024; Sharma et al., 2024b).The biggest implication for businesses is that integrating ethics within brand strategy adds long-term value. This suggests that rather than tacking on 'responsibility' programs, ethical initiatives must be woven into the fabric of businesses in a way that can provide greater legitimacy and resilience (Van de Ven 2008). Empirical studies have demonstrated that organizations are more successful when they align marketing activities with stakeholder expectations, resulting in greater brand equity, loyalty, and cultural relevance (Ferrell & Ferrell 2021; Bonneton, 2025). Patagonia and Ben & Jerry's are just two great examples of how transparency, activism, and sustainable sourcing can set brands apart in crowded markets. To remain credible, firms are increasingly required to establish quantifiable targets, carry out independent audits and adhere to a radical transparency in their reporting (Dastane et al., 2025; Edelman Trust Institute, 2025). The Unilever Sustainable Living Plan, which tracks achievement against the UN Sustainable Development Goals, is one example that shows how sustainability integrated in corporate reporting narrows the gap between theory and practice (Ferrell & Ferrell, 2021). Yet Everlane's own experience with "Radical Transparency" demonstrates that while such commitments might be a starting point, failure to deliver on ethical promises can cause trust to crumble (Durand-Hayes, 2024).

It's also a big deal for consumers. The spread of ethical claims from carbon-neutrality commitment to diversity in advertising – means that we are increasingly under pressure to become critically literate when it comes to the information brands put in front of us. It has been emphasized that a large part of consumers cannot differentiate between real sustainability practices and greenwashing (McEachern & Carrigan, 2012; Szaban, Szymkowiak, &Ziędzicka, 2025). That is where ethical labels and the third-party certifications can come in handy, but such schemes are so numerous and the standards their applicants must meet often so divergent that they can also confuse. This is further evidence of the need for consumer education in group mediated self-help (Kossmann & Gómez-Suárez, 2018). Meanwhile, consumer activism has become an enforcer in making brands pay attention. The voice of the consumers posted on social media is magnified providing a wave which if misguided can be more devastating, like boycotts against companies accused of greenwashing by initially being held out as pro-environment (Perry, Osburg, Huq & Diallo 2024). "Gen Z in particular have taken to activism as a means to pressure the business world into practicing what they preach, while rewriting the rules of accountability that are playing out in the marketplace" (Durand-Hayes 2024: 15; Bonneton, 2025). For policy makers, the increase of greenwashing and ethical consumerism underlines the necessity to improve regulatory responses. Industry self-regulation (from voluntary standards alone) has been shown to be inadequate in that businesses can exploit loose claims without much change. Recent policy developments including the EU Green Claims Directive (2023) represent an important move forward by mandating that claims made in environmental marketing must be both evidence-based and independently verified. Such tactics are meant to reduce deceptive practices and rebuild consumer trust. At the global scale, there is also growing momentum for coherent reporting frameworks based on environmental social and governance (ESG) reporting—report in line with the Sustainable Development Goals (SDGs) (Van de Ven, 2008; Ferrell & Ferrell, 2021). These standards do more than establish a floor for compliance they enable companies to benchmark progress and reduce the ambiguity that can contribute to greenwashing. Nonetheless, the success of these policies relies on enforcement and international collaboration, because supply chains and digital marketing are global (Nadda et al., 2024a; Sharma et al., 2024a; Berry & Singh, 2024; Sharma et al., 2024b).All in all, ethical marketing has implications ranging for a wide range of stakeholders. For corporations, ethical commitments should go beyond one-off gestures toward action that is measurable and transparent. The difficulty for customers, however, is to develop the critical capacities to assess and answer ethical claims, as well as using activism in order to demand accountability. The true focus for policymakers is to create and enforce regulatory frameworks that limit greenwashing, and set credible global standards. Combined, they represent a backbone for ethical marketing in which it is no longer optional - but functional to long-term legitimacy and trust.

"The roles played by corporations, consumers and regulators in promoting ethical marketing are presented schematically in Figure X: Together these entities establish an ethical marketing eco-system founded on trust, responsibility, and longterm value."

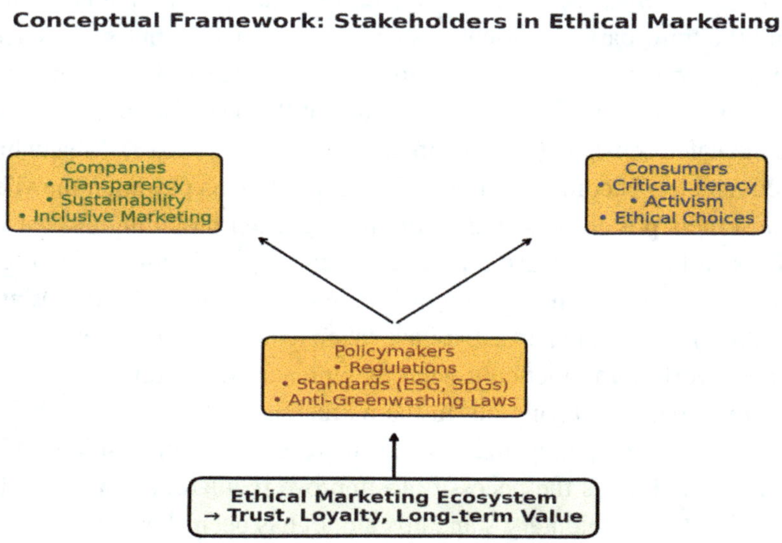

Source: Author's creation

6. FUTURE OUTLOOK

LC2019 and the future of ethics in marketing There are at least four forces that will converge to shape the future of ethical marketing: exponential integration of artificial intelligence (AI) within marketing practices; Deepening role of sustainability, with emphasis on the role that pursuing causes can play in meeting the SDGs; changing generational expectations about what is expected for businesses engaging with communities; an academic research agenda calling for a greater level interdisciplinarity. These shifts imply that virtuous marketing will become less about individual advertising campaigns and more about system-level changes in how firms, consumers and policy makers think about responsibility.

A.I. may be the greatest frontier of marketing ethics. As predictive analytics, generative AI, and personalization technologies become integrated into consumer facing strategies, marketers grapple with a fundamental tension between personalization and manipulation. AI, on the one hand, allows for hyper-personalized interactions that can lift both consumer satisfaction and efficiency. On the other, it threatens to undermine autonomy by capitalizing on behavioral biases and perpetuates injustices through algorithmic bias (Hari, Sharma, Verma & Chaturvedi 2024; Gupta, Wang, Patel &Czinkota 2025). Academics claim that new ethical standards need to come along with considerations such as algorithm fairness, data privacy, and transparency for the maintenance of consumer trust (Hermann &Puntoni, 2024; Naz & Kashif, 2024). Recent discussions of predictive marketing help show why: artificial intelligence in creating responsible journeys among customers (Talbot 2025) tell us that, on one hand, leverages can be pulled." Pressing possibilities or fears of the dawning era come into heightened focus – and just as it goes both ways in personalization ("profiling") versus manipulation, which Kenneth Cukier calls "manipulation," but if you're Alibaba and Facebook rights activist AI needs to know what tickles power's fancy by reviving obey-the-boss omni-exposing WeBo-er The conclusion is simple: AI is not properly working unless it knows how to please people by telling them where they need to be about widgets. This indicates that future marketing ethics will depend not only on self-regulation, but on an interdisciplinary effort of marketers, computer scientists and policy makers.

Beyond technology, sustainability will be at the heart of the future of marketing ethics, albeit with a greater focus on systemic change rather than campaigns. No longer will companies be able to get away with an eco-label or Csr report as tokenistic; they will have to integrate business strategies with global ones like the SDGs. These authors argue that consumers are rewarding brands offering measurable, long-term environmental and social contributions over simplistic acts of responsibility (Bonneton, 2025; Dragomir, 2019). For instance, Patagonia's operationalization of circular economy concepts and Unilever's focus on SDG-based reporting represent how firms can incorporate sustainability as part of basic operations rather than ad hoc marketing rhetoric (Ferrell & Ferrell, 2021; Voronov et al., 2021). Yet, as regulatory demands such as the EU Green Claims Directive (2023) are implemented, future sustainability marketing is likely to need audited and verifiable disclosures so brands can no longer fake it until they make it.

An additional strong force towards ethical marketing in the future is generational change. "What Gen Z believes is normal (and how that can help companies)." How business communicators better understand the grand challenges facing tomorrow's workforce", p. 12; Haggerty and Schott, 2016) Research indicates that millennials have already raised expectations in relation to inclusivity, authenticity and sustainability in brand communication (Durand-Hayes, 2024; Edelman Trust Institute, 2025). Heading forward, Gen Alpha will likely make these pressures worse as they grow up in a world where climate change, digital surveillance and social justice movements are more visible than ever before. Generation-Alpha's relationship with brands who will have grown up exposed to AI-generated personalisation and global activist networks, leaving them more empowered to sense contradictions and mobilize against perceived inauthenticity (Bonneton, 2025). This means for marketeers that the next generation of consumers will not only expect ethical practices, they will have the ability to verify and challenge and hold companies accountable at a level never experienced before.

Lastly, the academic research agenda should undergo transformation due to those challenges. According to Dastane, Aw, Fandos-Roig, and Sánchez-García, ethical marketing scholarship must incorporate the insights of business ethics, computer science, sociology, and environmental studies. Although bibliometric analyses reveal that marketing ethics research is broadening, the noteworthy issues remain insufficiently addressed, including AI, cross-cultural inclusivity, and systemic sustainability,. Furthermore, it is essential to conduct robust research addressing the theory–practice gap with a focus on the mechanisms that allow firms to commit to ethical marketing policies that could be empirically vindicated. In that respect, the significance of global frameworks like ESG reporting and the SDGs represents an excellent context in which to assess the extent to which ethical marketing enhances consumer trust and social advancemen (Nadda et al., 2024a; Sharma et al., 2024a; Ansari et al., 2024; Prakash et al., 2024; Nadda et al., 2024b). In combination, those trends imply that the future of ethical marketing entails both an increase in the breadth of the concept and the depth of responsibility. The Ai-driven personalization entails a fine line between empowerment and exploitation; sustainability goes beyond symbolic gestures, requiring structural alteration; generational dynamics will increase consumer demands; and the scholarship will need to underpin practice with several methodological models. Thus, the future of marketing is not just the next level of sophistication of campaigns – it implies an integrated model of responsibility that revises the nature of businesses as we know them.

Achieving Ethical Marketing in the Future

Source: Author's creation

7. CONCLUSION

The ethical marketing paradox of 2025 — where consumer need for sustainability and responsibility is greater than ever, but greenwashing grievances are on the rise across sectors — demonstrates the core reality that brands face in the era of conscious consumerism. On one end of the spectrum, cases like Dieselgate at Volkswagen and H&M's Conscious Collection lawsuits demonstrate how performative ethics and false claims can destroy consumer confidence, prompt regulatory attention and lead to long-term reputational damage. On the other hand, there are companies like Patagonia and Ben & Jerry's that illustrate how authentic commitments, quantifiable transparency, and activism based on company values can turn marketing into an engine for loyalty, durability, and relevance in contemporary culture. Our contrasting destinies show us that brand survival relies on more than just ethics-driven symbolic campaigns; instead, the power to embed brand authenticity, accountability and inclusivity into strategy itself. "Looking ahead we have artificial intelligence, the imperative to meet the UN Sustainable Development Goals and increasing demands from Gen Z and now Gen Alpha consumers set even higher stakes where companies will have to navigate an even finer line between personalisation and manipulation;

inclusivity and tokenism or between sustainability and greenwashing," adds speaker Taskeen moda. Ethical marketing will thus demand a systemic overhaul that can only be achieved through a combination of regulation enforcement, consumer activism and interdisciplinary innovation. In the end, marketing's future will not be to sell products or services but to sell values that stand up to interrogation--for good measure, we should think of ethics as both an obligation and a strategy in an age in which long-term credibility demands it. For both academics and practitioners, the work ahead is to bring theory and practice closer together by establishing frameworks, tools, and forms of accountability such that marketing remains not only persuasive but also principled--harnessing corporate influence for broader sustainable and just societal progress.

REFERENCES

Ansari, A. I., Singh, A., Pattanaik, S., Patnaik, R., & Suryawanshi, U. (2024). Exploring the Role of AI-Powered Virtual Assistants in Optimizing Self-Service Experiences for Customers Within the Service Sector. In Nadda, V., Tyagi, P., Singh, A., & Singh, V. (Eds.), *Integrating AI-Driven Technologies Into Service Marketing* (pp. 225–238). IGI Global., DOI: 10.4018/979-8-3693-7122-0.ch013

Arora, K., & Singh, A. (2026). *Harnessing emotion AI for customer support and employee wellbeing*. https://books.google.co.in/books?id=3lNxEQAAQBAJ

Berry, K., & Singh, A. (2024). AI-Driven Service Marketing: Transforming Customer Experience and Operational Efficiency. In Nadda, V., Tyagi, P., Singh, A., & Singh, V. (Eds.), *AI Innovations in Service and Tourism Marketing* (pp. 35–56). IGI Global., DOI: 10.4018/979-8-3693-7909-7.ch003

Bhasin, H. (2025, August 19). Ethical marketing: Definition, principles, and examples. *Marketing91*. https://www.marketing91.com/ethical-marketing/

Bonneton, N. (2025). The market for ethical goods. *Journal of Environmental Economics and Management, 103182*. Advance online publication. DOI: 10.1016/j.jeem.2025.103182

Borgerson, J. L., & Schroeder, J. E. (2002). Ethical issues of global marketing: Avoiding bad faith in visual representation. *European Journal of Marketing*, *36*(5/6), 570–594. DOI: 10.1108/03090560210422399

Cherry, J., & Fraedrich, J. (2002). Perceived risk, moral philosophy and marketing ethics: Mediating influences on sales managers' ethical decision-making. *Journal of Business Research*, *55*(12), 951–962. DOI: 10.1016/S0148-2963(00)00215-0

Crane, A. (1997). The dynamics of marketing ethical products: A cultural perspective. *Journal of Marketing Management*, *13*(6), 561–577. DOI: 10.1080/0267257x.1997.9964493

Dastane, O., Aw, E. C., Fandos-Roig, J. C., & Sánchez-García, J. (2025). Ethical marketing: A review and research agenda. *Marketing Intelligence & Planning*. Advance online publication. DOI: 10.1108/mip-01-2024-0007

Dion, D., Pavlyuchenko, R., & Prokopec, A. S. (2024). EXPRESS: The enrichment economy: Market dynamics, brand strategy, and ethics. *Journal of Marketing*. Advance online publication. DOI: 10.1177/00222429241275014

Dragomir, V. D. (2019). Ethical aspects of environmental strategy. In *SpringerBriefs in Applied Sciences and Technology* (pp. 75–113). https://doi.org/DOI: 10.1007/978-3-030-29548-6_3

Dubinsky, A. J., & Loken, B. (1989). Analyzing ethical decision making in marketing. *Journal of Business Research, 19*(2), 83–107. DOI: 10.1016/0148-2963(89)90001-5

Durand-Hayes, S. (2024). *Voice of the consumer survey 2024: Shrinking the consumer trust deficit*. PwC. https://www.pwc.com/gx/en/issues/c-suite-insights/voice-of-the-consumer-survey/2024.html

Edelman Trust Barometer. (2025). *India report*. https://www.edelman.in/sites/g/files/aatuss371/files/2024-03/2024%20Edelman%20Trust%20Barometer%20India%20Report_0.pdf

Edelman Trust Institute. (2025). *Global report: Trust and the crisis of grievance* (pp. 2–9). https://www.edelman.com/sites/g/files/aatuss191/files/2025-01/2025%20Edelman%20Trust%20Barometer%20Global%20Report_01.23.25.pdf

Ferrell, O. C., Crittenden, V. L., Ferrell, L., & Crittenden, W. F. (2013). Theoretical development in ethical marketing decision making. *AMS Review, 3*(2), 51–60. DOI: 10.1007/s13162-013-0047-8

Ferrell, O. C., & Ferrell, L. (2021). New directions for marketing ethics and social responsibility research. *Journal of Marketing Theory and Practice, 29*(1), 13–22. DOI: 10.1080/10696679.2020.1860686

Ferrell, O. C., & Gresham, L. G. (1985). A contingency framework for understanding ethical decision making in marketing. *Journal of Marketing, 49*(3), 87–96. DOI: 10.1177/002224298504900308

Ford, R. C., & Richardson, W. D. (1994). Ethical decision making: A review of the empirical literature. *Journal of Business Ethics, 13*(3), 205–221. DOI: 10.1007/BF02074820

Gupta, S., Wang, Y., Patel, P., & Czinkota, M. (2025). Navigating the future of AI in marketing: AI integration across borders, ethical considerations, and policy implications. *International Journal of Information Management, 82*, 102871. DOI: 10.1016/j.ijinfomgt.2025.102871

Hari, H., Sharma, A., Verma, S., & Chaturvedi, R. (2024). Exploring ethical frontiers of artificial intelligence in marketing. *Journal of Responsible Technology, 100103*. Advance online publication. DOI: 10.1016/j.jrt.2024.100103

Hermann, E., & Puntoni, S. (2024). EXPRESS: Generative AI in marketing and principles for ethical design and deployment. *Journal of Public Policy & Marketing*. Advance online publication. DOI: 10.1177/07439156241309874

Hunt, S. D., & Vitell, S. (1986). A general theory of marketing ethics. *Journal of Macromarketing*, *6*(1), 5–16. DOI: 10.1177/027614678600600103

Kamila, M. K., & Jasrotia, S. S. (2024). Ethics in marketing: Understanding past trends and future prospects through bibliometric analysis. *Journal of Nonprofit & Public Sector Marketing*, 1–32. DOI: 10.1080/10495142.2024.2361345

Kossmann, E., & Gómez-Suárez, M. (2018). Decision-making processes for purchases of ethical products: Gaps between academic research and needs of marketing practitioners. *International Review on Public and Nonprofit Marketing*, *15*(3), 353–370. DOI: 10.1007/s12208-018-0204-8

Low, W., & Davenport, E. (2005). Has the medium (roast) become the message? *International Marketing Review*, *22*(5), 494–511. DOI: 10.1108/02651330510624354

Low, W., & Davenport, E. (2008). Organizational leadership, ethics and the challenges of marketing fair and ethical trade. *Journal of Business Ethics*, *86*(S1), 97–108. DOI: 10.1007/s10551-008-9763-7

Maheshwari, N., Singh, V., Singh, A., & Ansari, A. I. (2024). Understanding Artificial Intelligence Adoption in Tourism Services and Marketing: Boon or Bane? In Nadda, V., Tyagi, P., Singh, A., & Singh, V. (Eds.), *AI Innovations in Service and Tourism Marketing* (pp. 359–374). IGI Global., DOI: 10.4018/979-8-3693-7909-7.ch018

McEachern, M. G., & Carrigan, M. (2012). Revisiting contemporary issues in green/ethical marketing: An introduction to the special issue. *Journal of Marketing Management*, *28*(3-4), 189-194.

Nadda, V., Tyagi, P. K., Singh, A., & Singh, V. (Eds.). (2024a). *Integrating AI-Driven Technologies Into Service Marketing* (Vols. 1–2). IGI Global., DOI: 10.4018/979-8-3693-7122-0

Nadda, V., Tyagi, P. K., Singh, A., & Singh, V. (Eds.). (2024b). *AI Innovations in Service and Tourism Marketing*. IGI Global., DOI: 10.4018/979-8-3693-7909-7

Prakash, J., Singh, V., Singh, A., & Kumari, U. (2024). Investigating the Synergistic Impact of AI and Marketing Within Virtual Tourism Platforms for Millennials: A Review. In Nadda, V., Tyagi, P., Singh, A., & Singh, V. (Eds.), *Integrating AI-Driven Technologies Into Service Marketing* (pp. 419–438). IGI Global., DOI: 10.4018/979-8-3693-7122-0.ch020

Pires, G. D., & Stanton, J. (2002). Ethnic marketing ethics. *Journal of Business Ethics*, *36*(1), 111-118.

Saleh, R. A., & Zeebaree, S. R. (2025). Artificial Intelligence in E-commerce and Digital Marketing: A Systematic Review of Opportunities, Challenges, and Ethical Implications. *Asian Journal of Research in Computer Science*, *18*, 395-410.

Sharma, M., Singh, A., & Rana, S. (2024a). Empowering Hospitality Brands AI Strategies for Enhanced Customer Experiences in Emerging Markets. In Nadda, V., Tyagi, P., Singh, A., & Singh, V. (Eds.), *Integrating AI-Driven Technologies Into Service Marketing* (pp. 173–190). IGI Global., DOI: 10.4018/979-8-3693-7122-0.ch010

Sharma, R., Sachdeva, T., Singh, A., & Nadda, V. (2024b). A New Era of Engagement and Satisfaction: Transforming Customer Experience With AI-Driven Technologies. In Nadda, V., Tyagi, P., Singh, A., & Singh, V. (Eds.), *AI Innovations in Service and Tourism Marketing* (pp. 1–16). IGI Global., DOI: 10.4018/979-8-3693-7909-7.ch001

Singhapakdi, A. (1999). Perceived importance of ethics and ethical decisions in marketing. *Journal of business research*, *45*(1), 89-99.

Szaban, M., Szymkowiak, A., & Zdziennicka, A. (2025). Unpacking consumer price perceptions: The role of sustainability and ethical labels in the cosmetics market. *Journal of Cleaner Production*, *490*, 144730.

Tarnanidis, T., Manda, V. K., Sousa, B. B., Vlachopoulou, M., & Papachristou, E. (2026). Marketing complexity of smart consumer products to global millennial segments. In Tarnanidis, T., Sousa, B., Vlachopoulou, M., Papachristou, E., & Manda, V. K. (Eds.), *Diversity and inclusion-driven marketing for multicultural marketplaces* (pp. 1–16). IGI Global Scientific Publishing., DOI: 10.4018/979-8-3373-2111-0.ch001

Van de Ven, B. (2008). An ethical framework for the marketing of corporate social responsibility. *Journal of business ethics*, *82*(2), 339-352.

Voronov, A. A., Gorlachev, P. V., Mirzoeva, E. V., Rudenko, V. A., & Popova, T. S. (2021). Role of social and ethical marketing in improving sustainable business development. In *Cooperation and Sustainable Development* (pp. 1249-1255). Cham: Springer International Publishing.

Chapter 12
From Personalization to Persuasion:
Unpacking the Capabilities and Challenges of Generative AI in Marketing

Priyanka Ghosh
https://orcid.org/0009-0002-5161-6027
Kristu Jayanti College, India

Ashwitha Shetty
http://orcid.org/0000-0001-9529-1100
Kristu Jayanti University, India

ABSTRACT

Marketing has always been influenced by technological innovation, ranging from the development of the printing press and mass media promotion to the advent of digital platforms and algorithmic targeting. In the digital economy of the day, perhaps the most revolutionary development is the rise of generative artificial intelligence (GenAI). GenAI has not only opened up new avenues for automating and scaling personalization but also added the capacity to produce compelling, adaptive, and context-aware communication at a scope not before possible.

1. INTRODUCTION

Marketing has always been influenced by technological innovation, ranging from the development of the printing press and mass media promotion to the advent of digital platforms and algorithmic targeting. In the digital economy of the day, perhaps

DOI: 10.4018/979-8-3373-6731-6.ch012

the most revolutionary development is the rise of generative artificial intelligence (GenAI). GenAI has not only opened up new avenues for automating and scaling personalization but also added the capacity to produce compelling, adaptive, and context-aware communication at a scope not before possible. This change is important because it alters the very fabric of marketer–consumer interactions from static, pre-specified campaigns to dynamic, co-created conversations among human and machine. Personalisation has been the long-awaited promise of digital marketing in many ways: getting the right message to the right customer at the right moment. Conventional methods depended heavily on ordered data, segmentation, and rule-based recommendation systems to personalise marketing material. Effective in some respects, these tactics usually failed to capture the dynamism of consumer behaviour and the subtlety of human language. Generative AI, fueled by large language models (LLMs), diffusion models, and multimodal architectures, closes this gap by creating content that is not just relevant but also convincing. It creates text, images, audio, and even video content in real time, modulating tone, style, and framing to fit consumer intent, mood, or context. Consequently, marketing's unit of analysis is becoming different: no longer segments or customer journeys alone, but dynamic, interactive conversations that change in real-time.

The addition of persuasion to personalization brings new possibilities and complexities. On the one hand, persuasive generative systems allow marketers to enhance relevance, interaction, and conversion rates by adjusting not only the message but also its associated psychological mechanisms. For instance, GenAI can infuse persuasive tactics like social proof, authority, reciprocity, or scarcity into generated content, varying the degree of rational argument or emotional appeal based on consumer engagement. This adaptive capacity repositions personalization from a passive tailoring process to an active influence agent. Conversely, such capabilities evoke ethical concerns regarding autonomy, transparency, and manipulation. When people are not even sure if an influencing message comes from a human or from AI, they might lose faith in brands and institutions. How critical this shift is is highlighted by the explosive deployment of GenAI across sectors. Firms are applying generative models to automate customer support, produce ad campaigns, produce fake brand endorsers, and craft customized product suggestions. Early indications reveal significant productivity gains: creative loops that used to take weeks now take hours, and marketers can try out hundreds of message sets all at once. Yet, these advantages are accompanied by hazards including hallucinations (objectively erroneous responses), stereotypical perpetuating bias, intellectual property issues, and possible legal infringements. The balancing act between leveraging the persuasive potential of GenAI and upholding responsible, credible marketing procedures is therefore the core managerial dilemma.

2. CONCEPTUAL FOUNDATIONS

2.1 Artificial Intelligence in Marketing

The marketing literature has established the various uses of AI in areas such as segmentation, targeting, recommendation, dynamic pricing, and testing of creative. With GenAI the focus shifts to text, images, audio and video; conversation design; and autonomous navigation of creative spaces. Preceding work on machine learning in marketing, for example predictive models, emphasized accuracy and uplift. GenAI adds generativity - the ability to create contextually appropriate novelties - and interactivity as it works based on natural language self-descriptions.

2.2 Personalization to Persuasion

Personalization enhances relevance and can also decrease search/attention costs, which potentially increases conversion. Persuasion is based on mechanisms like social proof, reciprocity, authority, scarcity, and consistency; elaboration likelihood (central vs. peripheral routes); and persuasion knowledge (which occurs when consumers are aware they are being persuaded). GenAI can not only adjust copy, tone, ordering of elements, and evidence to consumer states (e.g., inferred intent, uncertainty, affect), but also it can greatly influence consumers, as opposed to relevance. The caveat of course is reactance if consumers feel manipulated, or intruded upon, or treated unfairly.

2.3 Responsible Influence

The authors approach this issue by espousing a trust-by-design perspective: systems of persuasion must respect autonomy, transparently disclose AI agent assistance that may have materially affected agency levels, engage in non-misleading targeting (for example, of vulnerable populations), and to the extent possible offer a path of contestability for consequential decisions. We consider the significance of these issues with respect to international policy related activities (for instance, the EU AI Act; California ADMT rules; DPDP Act in India); and industry initiatives (C2PA/Content Credentials in regard to provenance). This paper places personalization and persuasion in relatively independent but interlapping constructs. Personalization is where marketing messages and offers are customized to individual or microsegment-level tastes, from observed, inferred, or stated data. Persuasion is where beliefs, attitudes, or behaviors are intentionally influenced by communicative actions, such as messages, conversations, and choice architectures. GenAI bridges the gap between these two constructs by facilitating autonomous, adaptive engagement that both customizes and persuades in tandem. This bridging produces new value propositions but raises higher ethical stakes, with influence less transparent and perhaps more powerful. The research and management literature provides valuable theoretical and empirical perspectives through which to interpret this change. Consumer psychology informs persuasion through theories like the elaboration likelihood model (central vs. peripheral routes of processing), persuasion knowledge (consumers' detection of persuasive intent), and reactance theory (resistance to persuasion when autonomy is at stake). Marketing science is able to offer insights on targeting, experimentation, and customer journey optimization, whereas information systems research is able to identify human–AI collaboration and organizational adoption dynamics. Concurrently, there is a focus in governance and regulatory studies on transparency, disclosure, equity, and accountability for AI-facilitated persuasion. Combining these literatures is necessary to create an overarching understanding of how GenAI remakes marketing.

3. REVIEW OF LITERATURE

This review connects streams in AI/ML in marketing, consumer behavior and persuasion, digital advertising, human–AI interaction, and governance.

3.1 Personalization in Marketing

Personalization has been researched extensively in marketing theory as a strategic reaction to consumer diversity. Early conceptualizations were segmentation and targeting-based, where consumers were segmented on demographic, psychographic, or behavioral variables (Wedel & Kamakura, 2012). With the emergence of digital media, personalization progressed towards one-to-one marketing, using consumer data to create customized offers (Peppers & Rogers, 2011). Research has established that personalization contributes to improved customer satisfaction, loyalty, and firm performance (Arora et al., 2008). But personalization is also challenging. Researchers identify the "personalization–privacy paradox," wherein consumers enjoy relevance but are uneasy as companies employ personal information in manners that feel intrusive (Awad & Krishnan, 2006). Even too-detailed personalization can evoke the "creepiness effect," which erodes trust and participation (Aguirre et al., 2015). These observations emphasize balance and openness in personalized marketing practices. 3.2 Personalization: Benefits and Backfires

The effectiveness of personalization will depend upon consumers' perception of relevance, timing, and intrusiveness. When targeting becomes too granular, consumers may develop privacy concerns or experience the "creepiness" effect, which reduces engagement. When consumers are in control (consent), know who is behind the message (transparency), and limit messages (capping), the associated risk-of-creepiness may decline. Similarly, algorithmic curation interacts with persuasion knowledge: when consumers suspect a manipulative intent, they will discount the message (even though it may be accurate) or change channels.

3.2 Persuasion and Consumer Psychology

Persuasion is a basic construct in consumer psychology and communication research. The elaboration likelihood model of Petty and Cacioppo (1986) identifies central and peripheral routes to persuasion and explains differences in message processing based on consumer motivation and capacity. Other theories like persuasion knowledge theory (Friestad & Wright, 1994) focus on consumers' knowledge of being persuaded and consumers' responses to influence attempts. Reactance theory (Brehm, 1966) also accounts for how people resist persuasion when their sense of autonomy is threatened. Scholarship in marketing has applied these psychological findings to study the effectiveness of advertising, message framing, and consumer choice. For instance, it has been found that framing persuasive messages to match the level of consumer involvement enhances impact (Coulter & Roggeveen, 2014). Additionally, the use of embedded persuasive cues like social proof, authority, or scarcity has been proven to increase conversion rates (Cialdini, 2009). 3.4 Generative AI and Marketing Communication

Mixed evidence suggests AI-generated text can perform very well, but many of the highest-performing outcomes appear to come from centaur (human+AI) workflows that combine brand/domain knowledge with model creativity. Guardrails (style guides, brand voice, approved claims) and feedback loops, reduce hallucinations and drift. Organizational capabilities - data quality, prompt engineering, evaluation pipelines, and governance - mediate the overall impact.

3.3 Artificial Intelligence in Marketing

The use of AI in marketing has been well established in the last decade. Initial research focused on machine learning for predictive analytics, customer segmentation, and recommendation systems (Wedel & Kannan, 2016). Recent studies have considered conversational agents, chatbots, and virtual assistants, which tailor interactions at scale (Grewal et al., 2020). Researchers also identify the use of AI in content optimization, media buying, and customer journey orchestration (Davenport et al , 2020).

Empirical data proves that personalization through AI enhances customer engagement and company performance. For example, Li and Kannan (2014) identified that AI-powered targeting improves the effectiveness of advertising, whereas Kumar et al. (2019) proved that AI-powered recommendations maximize customer lifetime value. Nonetheless, issues like algorithmic bias, opacity, and ethics remain (Cowgill, 2019).

3.4 Generative AI and Marketing Communication

Generative AI is a remarkable breakthrough from previous AI deployments in that it not just processes information but also generates new content. Large language models (LLMs) like GPT and multimodal models like DALL·E or Stable Diffusion allow for the real-time generation of text, images, audio, and video (Bommasani et al., 2022). The models make it possible to achieve hyper-personalization, generating material customized to consumer intent, mood, or context.

Research on marketing-related generative AI is on the horizon. Huang and Rust (2021) envision AI in marketing as evolving from mechanical (task automation) to analytical (decision support) to creative (content generation) phases, with GenAI being the zenith of the evolution process. Research indicates that GenAI speeds up campaign creation cycles, increases creativity diversity, and enables more effective messaging (Dwivedi et al., 2023). But they also mention threats, such as hallucinations, copyright issues, and manipulability.

3.5 Ethical and Governance Considerations

The academic literature also places emphasis on ethical issues in the deployment of persuasive AI systems. Transparency, fairness, accountability, and privacy are universal themes (Floridi & Cowls, 2019). Researchers alert that generative persuasion threatens consumer autonomy by introducing subtle influence mechanisms that are hard to discover (Susser et al., 2019). Regulation is in flux, with the EU AI Act and new guidelines in the U.S. and Asia setting out frameworks for the responsible deployment of AI (Hacker, 2023).

In this respect, research also focuses on organizational governance. Researchers contend that companies need to create AI ethics boards, disclosure practices, and monitoring systems to find a balance between innovation and consumer trust (Dignum, 2019). A failure to achieve this can lead to damage to reputation, consumer backlash, and regulatory fines.

3.6 Integration of Personalization and Persuasion

Current research emphasizes the intersection of personalization and persuasion using GenAI. In contrast with previous systems that aimed to personalize fixed content,

GenAI allows adaptive conversations in which personalization and persuasion are developed at the same time. For example, LLMs can infuse psychological strategies for persuasion into personalized product advice, adjusting both content and framing in real-time (Kaptein et al., 2015). This joining of relevance and impact amplifies ethical concerns by reducing the distinction between assistance and manipulation.

Empirical research is still scarce, yet initial research points towards significant impacts. For instance, experiments on AI-generated advertising show greater engagement and persuasiveness than human-only material (Touvinen & Hämäläinen, 2022). Nevertheless, issues regarding over-reliance, authenticity, and consumer awareness have yet to be resolved.

4. GENERATIVE AI MECHANISMS RELEVANT TO MARKETING

Generative Artificial Intelligence (GenAI) marks a major shift in how marketing content is incepted, constructed, delivered and evaluated. Predictive machine learning models support this change, as they are based on structured data with the main goal of predicting outcomes. GenAI provides creativity and newness to the digital marketing process, as it is able to both generate text, images, video, voice and even conversations in ways that feel relevant to context and are broadly scalable. In a marketing context, these mechanisms provide companies with the ability to produce customized, faster campaigns and persuasive interactions with consumers. This section reviews the key generative AI mechanisms relevant to marketing, which include: large language models (LLMs), multimodal models, diffusion models, programmatic orchestration and safety tooling. Each of these mechanisms is considered not only in a technical way, but also in terms of its impacts to a marketer, the consumer and regulators.

4.1 Large Language Models (LLMs)

Large Language Models like GPT-4, GPT-5, Claude, and LLaMA are the engines behind most text-based GenAI applications. These models are trained using extremely large collections of internet text, thus allowing for the generation of coherent, human-like language outputs. For marketing uses, they can be tapped for a number of purposes:

1. Support with Copywriting and Creative Generation: LLMs can generate ad copy, product descriptions, and tag lines. This accelerates the brainstorming and testing of creative variants, allowing marketers to run large-scale A/B/n tests, more quickly.

2. Conversational Interface: LLMs are the back-end engine of AI-powered chatbots and virtual assistants. These digital agents provide consumers with personalized, real-time responses moving from static FAQs to dynamic, persuading dialogues with consumers.
3. Content Localization: LLMs can translate and culturally adapt messages across markets to maximize effectiveness in global campaigns while still keeping a brand tone intact.
4. Customer Insights: Indeed, apart from content, LLMs can analyze unstructured consumer feedback (e.g. reviews, social conversations) to identify emerging needs or sentiment trends.

However, the big drawback of LLMs is the potential for hallucinations (creating good-looking but false content) and biases related to the training data. In marketing, this could lead to false representation or off-brand message. Companies are putting in place retrieval-augmented generation (RAG) practices to manage these risks, where the LLM makes its responses from a proofed database of the brand and products. This would mean the output is factually accurate, brand safe, and regulation safe.

4.2 Multimodal Models

Multimodal models combine different modalities (text, image, audio, video) while LLMs allow us to excel text based interaction. We will analyze tools to create connected brand experiences using multimodal models like OpenAI's GPT-4 with vision, Google's Gemini, and the forthcoming cross-modal architectures.

1. Dynamic Ad Creatives: By way of images and text, multimodal models now make it possible to fan out a banner ad, social media creatives, or an email campaign with copy and visual impact in real time.
2. Voice and Video: These models create synthetic voice-overs and promotional videos, making influencer marketing, video ads, and personalized product explainers viable.
3. Product Visualization: Retailers use multimodal AI to allow customers to visualize how a product may look in different contexts -- clothing on different body types or furniture in a customer's floor plan.
4. Inclusive Representation: Properly fine-tuned multimodal models can produce more inclusive and diverse representations in marketing collateral, as they represent a variety of customer demographics.

The ramifications of multimodality are significant. Shoppers engage through multiple sensory modalities, and multimodal models provide a consistent brand story across all of the customer touchpoints. The problem is the challenge of authenticity, because misbranding can occur with synthetic media if not disclosed.

4.3 Diffusion Models

Diffusion models including Stable Diffusion, Mid-journey and DALL·E have changed how marketers generate and manipulate visual assets. These models start by generating random noise, and progressively improve it into coherent images based on the generated prompt.

1. Affordable Creativity: Instead of having a costly photoshoot, marketers can generate photorealistic or stylized images to support campaigns.
2. Quick Variants: Marketers can generate numerous backgrounds, or product arrangements, or seasonal variants all at scale.
3. Storyboarding and Ideation: Creative teams are depending on diffusion models to think through how to run a campaign by visualizing before implementing.
4. Customization: Marketers can customize models on proprietary assets (brand logos, product images) and ensure the model outputs have internal consistency as well as intellectual property protection.

Diffusion models accelerate the pace of the creative process; however, they also offer new ethical and legal dilemmas. For example, outputs may accidentally represent copyrighted styles or grey areas about representation bias. Brands must grapple with the intellectual property implications and deploy provenance mechanisms such as Content Credentials to establish disclosures around the origins of images generated by AI.

4.4 Programmatic Orchestration

The true potential of GenAI in marketing is not simply in creating content, but rather programmatically orchestrating it across platforms, channels and campaigns. This includes combining generative models with customer data platforms, CRM and marketing automation.

1. End-to-End Automation. Campaign creation can be designed, tested and executed automatically, with GenAI creating content variations, targeting parameters and optimization strategies automatically.
2. Journey Personalization. GenAI agents adjust messaging on the fly, creating conversational pathways, responding to consumers' intent signals.

3. Rapid Testing at Scale. Marketers can that the hundreds of creative combinations simultaneously, and identify the best strategies much faster than could be achieve either iteratively or through experimentation.
4. Data-Driven Optimization. Integrating with decision engines (multi-armed bandits, uplift models) makes sure that you deliver the most persuasive creatives, to the right audiences at the right times.

Programmatic orchestration can be a real force multiplier, helping to drive efficiencies. Luckily governance can also rein in independent automation, or since we are promising challenging people, the safeguarding. Without governance on the automation and orchestration we need to balance efficiencies with, and appropriate safeguards like a review with human-in-the-loop, and transparency in human disclosures.

4.5 Safety Tooling and Guardrails

A key component of the responsible use of GenAI in marketing is safe tooling, which guarantees the outputs are aligned with the values of the brand, legislated regulations, and societal moral values.

1. Toxicity and Bias Filters: These tools detect and prevent harmful and discriminatory content before reaching consumers.
2. Hallucination Minimization: Systems such as RAG or fact-checking APIs provide assurances that claims generated by the AI are accurate.
3. Privacy Safeguards: Automated redaction of personal identifiable information (PII) in the training and inference of the models provides consumer data protection.
4. Provenance and Disclosure: Watermarking and provenance metadata, such as C2PA Content Credentials, help consumers and regulators trace origin of AI-generated content.
5. None of these are optional. As regulatory scrutiny increase globally -- whether it is the EU AI Act, the DPDP Act in India, or state privacy laws in the U.S. -- the absence of guardrails can have reputational and financial ramifications.

4.6 Implications for Marketers

These integrations change practice in a number of significant ways. First, the generative AI offers speed and scale which reduce the cycle from weeks to hours and allows marketers to ideate and test quickly. It enhances the capacity for creativity by opening up a huge canvas of creativity and by putting forward new ideas that a marketer might not have imagined otherwise. Second, GenAI is the source of personalization and persuasion; it changes or adapts not only the content, but nuances around the delivery or sequencing of the messaging to construct an engaging and influential interaction. Lastly, implementation of generative AI brings governance considerations, requiring marketers to navigate the new level of power by developing stronger governance frameworks, determine what level of disclosure is necessary, and educate their consumers. This most certainly creates extra challenges to ensure consumers trust marketers, product safety, and compliance with existing regulation.

5. CAPABILITY STACK OF GENAI IN MARKETING

The potential for transformation of marketing from generative artificial intelligence (GenAI) can best be understood as a "capability stack." This is not a hierarchical approach but a networked series of layers that, combined, will allow marketers to move from personalization to persuasion in a scalable, adaptive, and context-sensitive way. Each layer builds on the one below it, producing a cumulative effect that supports greater creativity, relevance, and influence while presenting new challenges for governance and ethical control. This section examines six broad layers in the GenAI capability stack: creative ideation, audience segmentation and targeting, adaptive personalization, persuasive framing and sequencing, customer engagement automation, and post-campaign analytics.

5.1 Creative Ideation and Campaign Design

The root of the capability stack is ideative creativity, with GenAI as a brainstorming partner for ideation, content development, and campaign planning. Large language models (LLMs) and image generators based on diffusion can generate varied pools of ideas, headlines, slogans, and visuals in real time. In contrast to conventional brainstorming sessions that can be hamstrung by biases or resource constraints, GenAI makes it possible for marketers to analyze huge creative spaces at high speed. For example, Coca-Cola has tested AI-based advertising images, and Netflix employs AI to create numerous variations of promotional posters and trailers for specific audiences. This layer highlights velocity, quantity, and creative variety, squeezing timelines from weeks to hours and cutting expenses.

5.2 Audience Segmentation and Targeting

The second layer is about sharpening audience insight and targeting strategy. While segmentation in the past was based on demographics or behavioral clusters,

GenAI takes this process further by modeling unstructured data like social media activity, reviews, and customer service interactions. Multimodal models can combine text, images, and audio data to generate rich audience personas. These capabilities enable marketers to reach consumers not only on the basis of who they are but also on how they communicate and what contexts affect their decisions. GenAI-targeting enhances accuracy but also poses issues around privacy, as more detailed inferences about consumer behavior may undermine ethical lines.

5.3 Adaptive Personalization in Real Time

Personalization has been a tradition of online marketing for many years, but GenAI takes it to dynamic adaptive personalization. Rather than fixed recommendations or pre-defined offers, LLMs produce context-aware content that dynamically adjusts with the evolving interaction. For instance, a chatbot powered by AI can dynamically alter tone, style, and product recommendation based on consumer sentiment or stated intention in a conversation. Stores such as Sephora and Amazon are testing AI-powered virtual assistants that fine-tune suggestions in real time. This level combines personalization with persuasion through tailoring the message and also the communicative approach, maybe boosting conversion rates while also increasing ethical concerns regarding consumer agency.

5.4 Persuasive Framing and Message Sequencing

The fourth layer goes beyond personalization and is specifically about persuasion. Building on psychological models like the Elaboration Likelihood Model and Persuasion Knowledge Model, GenAI can infuse persuasive signals—social proof, authority, scarcity, reciprocity—into promotional communications. Further, it can time-message sequencing, steering consumers step by step through the buying process. For example, an AI system of a travel company would initially flag peer reviews (social proof), next flag limited-time discounts (scarcity), and finally personalize the emotional appeal (aspiration and lifestyle alignment). This layer depicts the intersection of personalization and persuasion where adaptive message design is not just timely but also strategically impactful.

5.5 Customer Engagement and Service Automation

The fifth level includes customer interaction and service automation. Generative AI makes it possible for highly interactive and human-like conversations using chatbots, voice assistants, and virtual brand representatives. These can answer questions, cross-sell products, and enable continuous conversation at scale. For instance, AI-driven conversational agents are used by KLM Airlines to support customers through booking, check-in, and support procedures, while H&M among other brands has used AI stylists for fashion advice. By automating routine tasks and following individuals, GenAI enables human marketers to manage strategic and creative roles. Risks, though, involve excessive dependence on automation, erosion of human touch, and possible loss of authenticity.

5.6 Post-Campaign Analytics and Optimization

The last layer of capability stack addresses post-campaign analysis and optimization. Classical analyses depend on structured metrics like click-through rates, impressions, and conversions. GenAI supports these analyses by producing qualitative insights based on unstructured feedback, discovering emergent consumer attitudes, and running alternative campaign simulations. For example, LLMs can condense thousands of customer reviews to extract top themes, whereas multimodal systems can examine video testimonials or social media photographs for emotional signals. Marketers can then loop these insights back into creative brainstorming, closing the loop in an ongoing cycle of improvement and learning. This layer, however, also has risks of hallucinations and overreliance on AI-driven insights, and human supervision is necessary.

5.7 Integrative Dynamics of the Capability Stack

While every layer provides unique value, the real power of GenAI for marketing is in the integrative dynamics between layers. For instance, real-time personalization (layer three) relies on effective segmentation (layer two) and forms part of persuasive sequencing (layer four). In the same vein, creative ideation (layer one) produces content that is optimized through post-campaign analytics (layer six), forming a feedback loop. This interdependence parallels the wider shift from linear campaign phases to responsive, perpetual marketing systems. GenAI therefore transforms marketing from a set of disconnected steps to an evolving system in which personalization and persuasion are

5.8 Challenges and Ethical Considerations

The capability stack, although influential, presents governance and ethical problems. Layering personalization and persuasion causes anxiety regarding manipulation, autonomy, and transparency. Privacy becomes an increasingly critical problem as segmentation intensifies, and adaptive persuasion can deprive consumers of their agency. The ability of AI output to harbor bias and stereotyping also compromises inclusivity and brand reputation. Researchers posit that the capability stack's effectiveness needs to be balanced with governance systems, disclosure practices, and accountability systems (Floridi & Cowls, 2019; Dignum, 2019). In the absence of such protection, the persuasive ability of GenAI can have the perverse effect of precipitating consumer backlash or regulatory action.

The GenAI capability stack shows how personalization and persuasion blend at several levels of marketing practice. From ideation to engagement and analytics, GenAI provides marketers with historically unprecedented tools to drive creativity faster, customize content, and drive behavior. These opportunities are not separable from challenges pertaining to privacy, ethics, governance, and trust. Both academics and practitioners need to understand how these layers interact to be able to harness GenAI responsibly. By considering GenAI as a stacked capability, marketers can optimize adoption planning, balance effectiveness with values, and create campaigns that engage without sacrificing consumer agency.

6. APPLICATIONS ACROSS THE MARKETING FUNNEL

Generative AI (GenAI) is remodelling the marketing funnel by allowing more highly targeted, compelling, and responsive interactions at each phase of the shopper journey. From awareness to loyalty, GenAI brings together creativity, data insight, and psychology of persuasion skills to increase consumer involvement with increased ethical and governance issues. The chapter discusses examples spanning four phases of the funnel—awareness, consideration, conversion, and loyalty/retention—to show how generative models are evolving marketing practice.

6.1 Awareness: AI-Generated Ads, Influencers, and Brand Ambassadors

The awareness stage is where consumer attention is captured and initial brand visibility created. Historically, marketers used mass media advertising, celebrity endorsements, and broad-based campaigns. GenAI speeds and diversifies this process much faster by producing creative advertising assets in real time. For instance, diffusion models such as DALL·E and Stable Diffusion can produce new ad images, and LLMs create copy that is specific to varying audience segments. Companies like Coca-Cola have used AI to create distinctive campaign visuals, illustrating how creative AI can speak to a range of markets. Another significant use lies in AI-created influencers and virtual brand ambassadors. Firms like Lil Miquela's creators have led the way with synthetic influencers who interact with customers over social media. Such AI-powered entities can be customized to embody brand principles, provide constant messaging, and evolve based on real-time audience response. This solution provides reduced reliance on human influencers for scalability and control and also issues regarding transparency and authenticity.

GenAI also assists with media buying by optimizing ad placement in real time. With multiple creative variations generated, marketers are able to test and hone campaigns quickly, optimizing relevance on all platforms. This adaptability leads to greater consumer visibility at lower cost, but also threatens to homogenize creativity when over-optimized for metrics of performance.

6.2 Consideration: Personalized Product Recommendations and Persuasive Storytelling

The consideration phase is where consumer preferences are formed and directed toward considering brand options. GenAI takes this phase to the next level with hyper-personalized product suggestions that adjust based on user action, intent, and mood. Consumers like Amazon and Sephora already utilize AI-powered recommendation tools; with GenAI, these engines become conversational assistants who can explain, convince, and dynamically personalized recommend. Persuasive narratives are also another essential use case. LLMs can produce stories that weave together brand values and consumer dreams, planting psychological persuasion elements such as authority, social proof, or reciprocity. For example, the product description generated by an AI may emphasize how "experts recommend" the product (authority) and flag "limited stock" (scarcity) and "top-rated by thousands of users" (social proof). This narrative reaches beyond text: multimodal models can generate product demo videos, customer testimonial simulations, and lifestyle images based on individual consumer profiles.

GenAI is both a creative collaborator and a persuasive influencer at this level, generating dynamic storytelling that boosts relevance and impact. The potential to embed subtle persuasion, however, raises the specter of manipulation, particularly when consumers are not in a position to easily differentiate between human- and AI-generated narratives.

6.3 Conversion: Chatbots, Nudging Mechanisms, and Adaptive Pricing Messages

The conversion phase focuses on converting consumer intent into action. GenAI makes a positive contribution by driving sophisticated conversational agents that manage customer questions, address concerns, and motivate purchase behavior. In contrast to basic chatbots that deliver scripted responses, GenAI-empowered chatbots adjust tone, style, and messaging in real time, developing human-like conversations. For instance, H&M's AI stylist or Domino's AI-driven ordering assistant illustrates how GenAI can drive purchase processes at speed without compromising engagement. Nudging mechanisms also boost conversion. Influenced by behavioral economics, GenAI can craft calibrated nudges—like pointing to peer purchases ("10 people bought this today") or framing choices to highlight value. These adaptive nudges are tailored according to one's behavior, making conversion more likely. Likewise, adaptive price messages—such as customized discounts or scarcity hints—are dynamically created to align with shopper intent. Airline companies and online retailers already try out contextualized offers guided by AI-based forecasting. Although effective, these applications distract from the difference between persuasion and manipulation. Dynamic pricing communications can create perceptions of unreasonableness, and nudges can decrease consumer control if not openly revealed. Therefore, conversion-stage applications underscore the balance between efficiency and moral obligation.

6.4 Loyalty and Retention: AI-Powered Customer Support and Co-Creation Communities

The retention and loyalty stage emphasizes maintaining long-term consumer relationships. GenAI facilitates this stage by enabling AI-based customer support systems that can offer 24/7 personalized support. For example, KLM Airlines and Microsoft have incorporated AI agents to respond to routine service inquiries so that human agents can dedicate themselves to intricate interactions. Such systems foster loyalty by providing convenience, consistency, and responsiveness. Another upcoming use case is co-creation communities where GenAI facilitates collaborative brand-consumer relationships. Consumers are able to co-create products, contribute creative ideas, or participate in community storytelling. For instance, Nike has tested consumer co-design platforms, while GenAI technologies provide scalable input of consumer contributions to product innovation. Participative engagement strengthens loyalty through establishing a sense of ownership and identification with brand identity. AI-driven loyalty programs also add more personalization to retention efforts. Through analysis of behavior data and emotional signals, GenAI can create customized rewards, individually crafted appreciation messages, and dynamic re-engagement initiatives. Such programs deepen consumer–brand relationships but need to be controlled carefully to prevent over-surveillance or aggressive personalization.

6.5 Integrative Dynamics Across the Funnel

The actual effect of GenAI comes through when applications along the funnel are woven into an endless loop. Awareness initiatives input consumer data into consideration machines; conversion prompts are driven by engagement histories; and loyalty initiatives produce feedback for ensuing creative ideation. This delivers a seamless platform where personalization and persuasion are co-created at every turn. The marketing funnel therefore transforms from a simple sequence to a real-time feedback loop, allowing for ongoing optimization and richer consumer relationships.

6.6 Ethical and Strategic Implications

Where GenAI enhances efficacy along the funnel, it also intensifies ethical threats. AI-powered influencers could obscure authenticity, narrative persuasion could subtly manipulate, nudges could erode autonomy, and loyalty programs could invade privacy. Marketers must thus equilibrate performance with governance, with guarantees of transparency, equity, and consumer trust. Strategically, companies that excel at the integrative application of GenAI through the funnel could achieve long-term competitive advantage, but only if adoption is synchronized with ethical guidelines and long-term brand value.

Generative AI solutions down the marketing funnel depict the intersection of personalization and persuasion in action. On the awareness level, AI facilitates instant creative diversification and synthetic influencers. On consideration, it facilitates adaptive recommendations and storytelling. On conversion, it uses chatbots, nudges, and adaptive pricing for inducing purchases. On loyalty and retention, it creates customer support, co-creation, and tailor-made loyalty programs. Collectively, these applications turn the funnel into a responsive, consumer-focused system. However, the success of these applications depends on marketers' capacity to navigate ethical issues, safeguard consumer autonomy, and invest in responsible stewardship.

7. MEASUREMENT OF PERSUASION EFFECTS

The success of generative AI (GenAI) in marketing cannot be comprehensively explained without strong measurement of persuasion effects. In contrast to conventional marketing analytics that primarily address exposure, clicks, or conversions, persuasion metrics call for more in-depth determination of how messages affect consumer psychology, attitudes, and long-term behavior. With GenAI combining personalization and persuasion, marketers need to institute ways to separate and measure these related yet different constructs. This chapter looks at measurement strategies in four fields: metrics for personalization vs. persuasion, experimental design and A/B testing using GenAI, psychological outcome measures, and longitudinal monitoring of loyalty and brand advocacy.

7.1 Metrics for Personalization vs. Persuasion

An essential initial step in measuring persuasion effects is the differentiation between personalization and persuasion metrics. Personalization is concerned with relevance and fit—whether the correct message gets to the correct person at the right moment. Typical measures are recommendation accuracy, click-through rates (CTR), and time spent interacting with content. These measures evaluate alignment rather than influence.

Persuasion measures, on the other hand, gauge the potential of messages to move attitudes, beliefs, or behavior. Key persuasion metrics include message recall, intent to purchase, attitude change, and conversion lift attributable to persuasive framing. For example, two equally relevant product recommendations may differ in their persuasive impact if one leverages social proof while the other emphasizes scarcity. GenAI's unique capability lies in optimizing both personalization (matching content) and persuasion (shaping responses). Hence, marketers need to monitor a double set of metrics in order to capture the end-to-end value of GenAI interventions.

7.2 Experimental Design and A/B Testing with GenAI

Experimental approaches are still key to sifting out persuasion effects. Classic A/B testing—testing two versions of a message against one another—has to be reimagined in GenAI environments where dynamic real-time content creation generates an infinite number of variations. Rather than fixed tests, marketers can use multi-armed bandit algorithms or adaptive experiments to iteratively optimize persuasive tactics. For instance, a GenAI-powered campaign could compare varying tones of product copy: one playing up technical advantages, another tapping into emotional experiences. By assigning consumers at random to variations, marketers can estimate each method's persuasive lift. More sophisticated experimental designs, like factorial experiments, can test multiple combinations of personalization and persuasion factors—e.g., message framing (authority vs. reciprocity) paired with consumer segment (first-time visitor vs. loyal customer). These designs yield interaction effects, giving richer insights into how GenAI persuades.

Experimental validity poses challenges. Dynamic generation of content poses the risk of uncontrolled variability, which makes comparisons difficult. To avoid this, researchers can limit the outputs of GenAI to such predetermined persuasive approaches and ensure systematic assessment. There are also ethical issues when persuasive strategies take advantage of consumer susceptibility, necessitating disclosure and regulation in experimental designs.

7.3 Psychological Outcome Measures: Trust, Satisfaction, and Autonomy

Measurement of persuasion goes beyond behavioral responses; it also needs to measure psychological states mediating long-term brand relationships. Three constructs are particularly germane: trust, satisfaction, and autonomy.

- Trust: Trust measures consumer perception that AI-generated content is credible, genuine, and in line with brand values. Surveys, sentiment analysis, and trust indices can determine if persuasive GenAI outputs build or destroy trust.
- Satisfaction: To some extent, the effectiveness of persuasion depends on consumer satisfaction with the exchange. Satisfaction surveys, net promoter scores (NPS), and affective response tracking offer insights into the impact of persuasive strategies on consumer experience.
- Autonomy: A special challenge of GenAI persuasion is safeguarding consumer autonomy against being undermined by influence. Psychological reactance theory proposes that manipulative persuasion can elicit counter-backlash. Autonomy can be assessed using self-reports of control perception, future interaction willingness, and avoidant behavior detection.
- Collectively, these outcome measures give a better understanding of persuasion effectiveness that goes beyond transactional indices to measure relational and ethical aspects.

7.4 Longitudinal Tracking of Loyalty and Brand Advocacy

Persuasion impact typically occurs over a long-term period, and therefore longitudinal monitoring becomes a necessity. Immediate conversions might not indicate long-term influence if customers subsequently lapse because of manipulation or disappointment. Longitudinal measurement determines whether GenAI-based persuasion leads to long-term loyalty and advocacy.

- Longitudinal metrics of central importance are:
- Repeat purchase rate: Measures whether persuasion impact impacts long-term purchasing behavior.
- Customer lifetime value (CLV): Estimates long-term profitability under the impact of persuasive tactics.
- Brand advocacy: Tracked via word-of-mouth referrals, user reviews, and social media posts.
- Churn and attrition rates: Indicate whether influential strategies rebound, causing people to disengage.

GenAI can support longitudinal tracking by mapping out customer journeys at multiple touchpoints and creating predictive loyalty scores. For example, an AI-enabled CRM system might monitor whether exposure to influential chatbots raises the odds of renewal or referral activity over several months. Yet, over-reliance on predictive analytics needs to be balanced with open validation, since biases in algorithms can distort long-term predictions.

Persuasion effects in GenAI-powered marketing need to go deeper than skin-deep metrics. Relevance is guaranteed by personalization, but influence is the function of persuasion. Experimental methodologies tailored to dynamic content creation allow for rigorous assessment, and psychological outcome measures like trust, satisfaction, and autonomy emphasize ethical implications. Longitudinal monitoring captures the persistence of persuasion, bridging short-term impact to long-term brand loyalty and advocacy. Finally, strong measurement frameworks not only inform marketers on how to maximize GenAI efforts but also serve to promote responsible usage by protecting consumer trust and autonomy.

8. RISKS, CHALLENGES, AND ETHICAL CONSIDERATIONS

The potential for generative AI (GenAI) to change how we market may lead marketers to unprecedented abilities to personalize and persuade, but it also has new risks that could erode consumer trust; consumer autonomy; and consumer's social welfare. This chapter highlights five major areas of concern: hallucinations; bias and stereotyping risk; privacy and consent; intellectual property and copyright; manipulation and loss of consumer autonomy; and societal implications such as disinformation and the digital divide.

8.1 Hallucinations, Bias, and Stereotyping Risks

The most immediate risk in marketing's use of GenAI relates to hallucinations—outputs that are not only wrong, but factually incorrect, misleading, or completely fabricated. Large language models do not learn from pure, perfect datasets, but instead are learning from a large net of raw data, so we have to account for the fact that large language models can generate products that were unrealistically documented, included exaggerated benefits, or included impossible endorsements. When marketers experience hallucinations as part of their marketing, they risk a loss in consumer trust. They are misled to producing marketing and claims that could bring regulatory scrutiny or penalties. They risk brand weakening and diminishing brand credibility for their firms. Bias is another ongoing challenge. GenAI systems can often reflect the exact bias that were present in their training data, and can amplify that bias over to their output. If there was inequitable histographic representation in the overarching SourceABCs (and there almost always is!), then the generated outputs may include appropriate messages that target those same historical target markets, while marginalizing other less represented groups. There are also stereotyping risks that can happen by following and rationalization harmful cultural, gender, and racial stereotypes—an advertisement generated by GenAI could reinforce gendered assumptions about how specific people use the product, or depict unrealistic body assumptions, or convey fragmented recipients alienating those segments of their audience. Mitigating these risks requires managing data audits, different training datasets and systems to detect any biases that may appear in their GenAI outputs. Being transparent and forthright about communicating the GenAI outputs is equally important, so the marketers do not mislead retail consumers by errors or stereotypes entrenched in AI-based marketing communications.

8.2 Privacy and Consent Issues

GenAI's capability for personalization typically requires large amounts of consumer data-generating serious privacy and consent issues. High levels of personalization by adaptive messaging systems, e.g., taking into account user behaviours, preferences, and previous interactions, are a tempting format for persuasive outputs, but high levels of personalization that build out a reliable user profile come perilously close to building a surveillance-like model in which consumers feel they are monitored and manipulated. Second, consent, based on informed preferences, becomes even more difficult in cases where consumers don't understand how their data is utilized in predictive generation. Many privacy policies remain impenetrable—rendering consumers unable to understand the extent of the use of their data. With the advent of GenAI-style dynamically generated nudge behavior, consumers may have difficulty identifying the line between acceptable personalization of their behaviour and unwanted intrusion. Legislations, such as the EU's General Data Protection Regulation (GDPR) and California's Consumer Privacy Act (CCPA), enforce explicit consent and data minimization principles but translating it to GenAI data and algorithms is complicated by the potential to infer extremely sensitive attributes based on past "normal" user data. Marketers will require privacy-by-design principles, clear disclosures, and user controls that allow consumers to make decisions about their data organization and determination.

8.3 Intellectual Property and Copyright Challenges

The creative capacity of GenAI brings with it a range of important intellectual property (IP) considerations. For example, when models produce advertising copy and imagery for products, mascots, or even uses of logos, we are left considering who owns the IP and, whether the IP is considered to be original. If we have AI-produced content that is trained on copyrighted content and that data has not been licensed, a brand runs the risk of IP infringement. Disputes have already occurred regarding AI art and content generation, as courts are left to decide whether the outputs are original works, or derivatives. For marketers, this ambiguity brings inherent strategic risk; as if an entire campaign is organized around visuals created through GenAI, there is a chance of receiving takedown requests, or being sued, if IP rights are infringed. Marketers need to build certain governance around how content is created to safeguard against subsequent liabilities. This may include only using licensed training datasets, carefully documenting how licensed training datasets were trained into AI models, and defining ownership of the outputs. Building relationships with legal colleagues will be critical, as they parse through rapidly evolving IP laws, which can affect reputations, and result in financial liabilities.

8.4 Manipulation and Loss of Consumer Autonomy

The most prominent ethical concern in GenAI-powered persuasion pertains to the ability to manipulate. Unlike more traditional marketing messages, GenAI is highly adaptable in the social and contextual framing across time—capable of persuading through the manipulation of tone and sequencing, in addition to these variables that are already de facto manipulated in traditional advertising appeal. GenAI has the potential to deliberately manipulate perceptions of scarcity, appeal to norms through social proof, and achieve emotional reactions through curated experiences that are tailored to individual, and inferred, consumer behavior. While these increasingly powerful methods may increase conversion rates, these strategies could lead to a loss of autonomy for consumers. Persuasion knowledge model proposes that consumers can deploy defenses against persuasion when its intentions are known. However, GenAI conversations feel like raw human to human conversation; this human simulation obscures awareness about when consumers are being persuaded. The problem is that they may not see the subtlety of social depth when GenAI conversations are taking their attention, meaning consumers can fail to recognize when they are being persuaded, which questions consumers' ability to make informed decisions. The loss of autonomy is especially concerning when GenAI systems target participants in vulnerable populations such as children or individuals with low digital literacy. Intentionally manipulative degrees of personalization can easily expose consumers to psychological reactance, which could include disengagement altogether or, even worse, distrust in higher-order (and years-long) brand relationships, reputational risk is a highly concerning prospect for brands and ecosystem designers alike. When using GenAI for marketing purposes, employees should disclose their use of

GenAI ethically, educate the consumer about potential risks, and limit exploitative persuasion techniques.

The challenges, risks, and ethics of GenAI marketing mirror the two-faced nature of its potential. Hallucinations, bias, and stereotypes pose threats to accuracy and diversity; privacy and consent pose trust issues; copyright and intellectual property conflicts introduce legal ambiguity; manipulative persuasion threats intrude on autonomy; and social harms like disinformation and the digital divide can cause systemic damage.

To overcome these obstacles, marketers need to embrace a proactive governance model integrating technical protection measures with ethical expectations. For responsible GenAI utilization, marketers ought to employ transparency, responsibility, fairness, and consumer agency. By acknowledging and mitigating hazards, brands can harness the revolutionary potential of GenAI without compromising the integrity of their direct-to-consumer relationships or broader societal institutions.

9. FUTURE PROSPECT OF GENERATIVE AI IN MARKETING

The quick development of generative AI has the potential to transform marketing practices completely. It has gone beyond basic personalization to allow brands to create immersive, persuasive, and ethically challenging experiences. For generative AI, the future will be tied to the development of complementary technologies, such as multimodal AI, augmented and virtual reality, blockchain and cryptocurrencies, and the metaverse. Each of these contexts and platforms will provide marketers new ways to engage consumers. This chapter is not only about emerging technologies; it also reflects on the need for balance between personalization, persuasion, and consumer welfare. Finally, it outlines a vision for the development of ethical and sustainable marketing that is driven by generative AI.

9.1 Emerging Trends in AI

The next phase of generative AI is multimodal, meaning it brings together text, images, audio and video in a unified way. In contrast to earlier generative AI models that focused on a single medium, multimodal generative AI, such as GPT-4o, Gemini and DALL·E, is capable of developing cross-channel campaigns that allow meaningful use of storytelling across multiple formats. For example, a single generative AI model may think through a campaign that includes personalized ad copy, a product video, and provide interactive visual experience using one consumer profile. When augmented reality (AR) and virtual reality (VR) come into play with generative AI, there is potential opportunity for experiential immersive experiences, that go beyond what most have come to know as traditional marketing. For instance, a fashion brand might allow customers to adjust custom fit on an AI-generated avatar that matches their actual body type so that they can virtually try on clothing. Or consider a real estate company providing an AI-created walkthrough of properties. This kind of experience is going beyond personalization alone to create persuasive experiences that can alter consumer emotions, preferences and ultimately purchase behaviors.

Thus, for brands and advertising capabilities there is increased opportunity to converge the lines between online and offline experiences, and ultimately foster emotional connections. However, with opportunity comes risk, and as generative AI progresses, these risks (extreme overstimulation, addiction, and loss of agency among consumers) need to be examined critically.

9.2 Integration of AI in Marketing

The generative AI future of marketing is interlinked with the evolution of Web3 technologies. The appeal of blockchain is its transparency, security, and traceability which reinforces consumer trust in AI-generated content. For instance, an ability to authenticate whether an image, video, or testimonial was AI-created or AI-enhanced using blockchain would mitigate the risk of misinformation using deepfake capabilities. Generative AI works alongside the metaverse where virtual worlds become the primary platform for commerce and social interaction. A declaration of rules on ownership and identity on the blockchain lends much more permanence to a consumer's ability to personalize commerce (shopping) and social interaction inside virtual worlds. For example, within these realms generative AI can create custom virtual storefronts, AI-powered brand ambassadors, and digital twins of customer service agents whose dialogue engages customers like a human. Luxury brand companies like Gucci and Nike have already started projects around virtual goods, generative AI could help extend projects like these into infinite variations based on user-specific preferences in the digital world.

The integration of generative AI with NFTs, and identities with decentralized applications will no doubt enable companies to develop exclusive personalized digital experiences, e.g limited edition AI-generated artworks, unique brand campaigns targeted to individuals, etc. The combination of these technologies will usher in a democratization of marketing ownership and consumer engagement that is transparent, decentralized and immersive.

9.3 Balancing Personalization, Persuasion, and Consumer Well-Being

There are also ethical tensions related to the move from personalization to persuasion. AI has allowed brands to know their customers more accurately than ever before. This is a powerful tool, but it also means that brands will now be able to exploit an individual's needs and vulnerabilities. Hyper-targeted marketing can easily turn into hyper-manipulation; especially when the algorithms are nudging emotional states, cognition and addiction.

- In the future marketers will need to balance accessible technology with the well-being of their consumers. This will require adopting some safeguards, such as:
- Ethical personalization frameworks that mean AI achievements do not come at the expense of consent, privacy, or user autonomy.
- Transparency in when persuasion is at work, whereby the consumer understands their interaction is with AI-generated content.
- Responsible use of their data and avoiding surveillance-led profiling and engaging in agency-led types of consumer engagement.

Consumers are becoming more attuned to the ethical implications of AI and so brands who can offer responsible persuasion will be more likely to provide environments where their customers can assert agency to avoid manipulation, leading to long-term loyalty. Trust will, therefore, be a linchpin for whatever version of AI personalized marketing we encounter in the future.

9.4 Vision for Sustainable and Ethical AI-Driven Marketing

Furthermore, it is clear that the sustainability of generative AI in marketing will depend on the articulation of business goals with the values of society. To create a sustainable vision, marketers can start with three key dimensions of sustainability:

- Ethical Governance - defining standards for AI transparency, fairness, and responsibility can provide a starting point for industry, academia, and governments to develop regulatory frameworks that serve to protect consumers, but do not limit innovation,
- Human-AI Collaboration - rather than competing with human creativity, generative AI needs to be positioned as a tool that augments the creativity of their human marketing colleagues for ideation, storytelling, and problem-solving.

The future will favour hybrid models where human oversight sets the ethical parameters while AI provides scale and efficiencies.

- Socio-Environmental Responsibility - generative AI systems are large-scale energy consumers, and any sustainability vision must look to invest in some green AI technologies to lessen carbon footprints while improving requisites for advanced personalization and high-impact immersive experiences.

Ultimately, the future development of generative AI in marketing needs to shift away from profit maximization and focus more on consumer empowerment, inclusivity, and long-term trust. As marketers embed ethical frameworks into the very algorithms of generative AI systems, we can help ensure that generative AI produces not only value, but also help harness its impact for the common good rather than in exploiting others.

10. CONCLUSION

10.1 Significant Findings

The present research aimed to study the change of generative artificial intelligence (GenAI) in marketing from a personalization mechanism to a persuasive tool. In conjunction with the literature review, theoretical constructs, and case studies, it is clear that GenAI has radically transformed marketing practice by offering the capability of hyper-personalized campaigns, automating aspects of the creative process, and suggesting predictive insights into consumer behavior generally. GenAI can radically alter marketing strategies not only through personalized the content of marketing but also through its unique contribution to a persuasive process. Whereas personalized marketing is primarily concerned with marketing messages that reflect consumer preferences towards the product or service being offered. GenAI personalization also adds the persuasive factor of altering perceptions of awareness and affective processes of the consumers' mental state regarding purchasing pathways. GenAI personalization also appears to shape emotional pathways through constructed narratives.

The study indicates that generative AI demonstrates a large opportunity for marketers looking for efficiencies and scale. Given that chatbots, recommendation engines, and AI-generated content have increased consumer participation and provided conversion metrics across categories, it is also evident that risks are apparent. Algorithmic bias, manipulative persuasion, misinformation and consumer privacy were some risks that highlight the ever-present trade-off of these technologies. Trust is an important theme: GenAI can enhance consumer engagement when applied transparently, but can create skepticism and harm a brand's reputation if rushed and imperfect decisions by automated tools are executed in an inconspicuous or hidden way. Overall, this research indicates that GenAI is not merely an enabler of personalized experiences but operates as a powerful persuasion ally and can engender behavioral influence on consumer attitudes at scale. As such, it lives in both worlds and requires a careful navigation of innovation and ethical practice.

10.2 Contributions towards Theory and Practice

In theory, this study contributes to the literature on marketing and persuasion by incorporating GenAI into traditional models of consumer influence - i.e., the Elaboration Likelihood Model and Cialdini's principles of persuasion. It also presents an opportunity to explore the concept of algorithmic personalization in the context of active persuasion - essentially highlighting that we should view AI not only as a tool for marketing, but also co-creating consumer experiences and perceptions. Practically, this research provides marketers, advertisers, and brand managers guidance. It highlights optimal practices to leverage GenAI in ways that facilitate consumer engagement while maintaining trust. Using explainable AI, providing transparency on how data is used, and having human oversight for content generation are all fundamentals for successful adoption. The research reinforces that effective & sustainable use of GenAI is not just technology, but about building authentic relationships with consumers.

10.3 Avenues for Future Study

In addition to articulating the potential and limitation of GenAI in marketing, this study highlighted several areas for future research. Future research could explore:

- Consumer Psychology and AI as a Persuasive Influence: There is a need for robust empirical studies to test how AI-generated content influences attitudes and emotions, as well as cognitive responses across demographics.
- Cross-Cultural Studies from Different Perspectives: Future research could investigate how cultural context shapes acceptance and overall persuasion strategy effectiveness.
- Longitudinal Studies: Most studies are designed to examine short-term outcomes. The effects of AI-driven persuasion on loyalty, trust, and consumer welfare - from a long-term perspective - require further exploration.
- Development of Ethical Frameworks: There is a need for interdisciplinary research and collaboration among marketing, ethics, and law to further develop governmental models that can observe regulations and guidelines for gover-

nance of GenAI in marketing, as well as develop comprehensive governance practice.

- Human – AI Collaboration: Future studies could investigate integrated approaches to embrace human creativity and AI-generated outputs for a more balanced and ethical marketing approach.

10.4 CONCLUSION

Generative AI represents a paradigm shift in marketing, going beyond personalization to persuasion. It may double the chances of innovation, efficiency, and consumer engagement in marketing practitioners, but it also introduces significant ethical, regulatory and societal implications. Our recommendations highlight that responsibly adopting GenAI depends on balancing persuasive ability and consumer protection. For academics, the theoretical contributions provide a basis for a new way of looking at marketing, engagement and persuasion in a digital environment. For practitioners, the work is a road map for ethical and effective AI adoption. For policy-makers, it identifies the need for clear regulatory frameworks that emphasize fairness, transparency, and consumer choice. In conclusion, generative AI is a potentially transformational force in marketing, but the extent of its transformative impact will depend on whether marketing organizations and regulators decide to utilize it as a solution for empowerment or want to use it in ways that exploit consumers.

REFERENCES

Aguirre, E., Mahr, D., Grewal, D., de Ruyter, K., & Wetzels, M. (2015). Unraveling the personalization–privacy paradox: The role of psychological distance. *Journal of Consumer Psychology*, *25*(3), 469–484.

Arora, N., Dreze, X., Ghose, A., Hess, J. D., Iyengar, R., Jing, B., & Shankar, V. (2008). Putting one-to-one marketing to work: Personalization, customization, and choice. *Marketing Letters*, *19*(3–4), 305–321.

Awad, N. F., & Krishnan, M. S. (2006). The personalization privacy paradox: An empirical evaluation of information transparency and the willingness to be profiled online for personalization. *Management Information Systems Quarterly*, *30*(1), 13–28.

Bommasani, R., Hudson, D. A., Adeli, E., Altman, R., Arora, S., von Arx, S., & Liang, P. (2022). On the opportunities and risks of foundation models. *Journal of Artificial Intelligence Research*, *75*, 1–152.

Brehm, J. W. (1966). *A theory of psychological reactance*. Academic Press.

Cialdini, R. B. (2009). *Influence: Science and practice* (5th ed.). Pearson Education.

Coulter, K. S., & Roggeveen, A. L. (2014). Like it or not: Consumer responses to word-of-mouth communication in on-line social networks. *Management Research Review*, *37*(7), 626–642.

Cowgill, B. (2019). Bias and productivity in humans and algorithms. Columbia Business School Research Paper.

Davenport, T., Guha, A., Grewal, D., & Bressgott, T. (2020). How artificial intelligence will change the future of marketing. *Journal of the Academy of Marketing Science*, *48*(1), 24–42.

Dignum, V. (2019). *Responsible artificial intelligence: How to develop and use AI in a responsible way*. Springer.

Dwivedi, Y. K., Hughes, L., Kar, A. K., Baabdullah, A. M., Grover, P., Abbas, R., & Sharma, A. (2023). So what if ChatGPT wrote it? Multidisciplinary perspectives on opportunities, challenges and implications of generative conversational AI for research, practice and policy. *International Journal of Information Management*, *71*, 102642.

Floridi, L., & Cowls, J. (2019). A unified framework of five principles for AI in society. *Harvard Data Science Review*, *1*(1).

Friestad, M., & Wright, P. (1994). The persuasion knowledge model: How people cope with persuasion attempts. *The Journal of Consumer Research*, *21*(1), 1–31.

Grewal, D., Hulland, J., Kopalle, P. K., & Karahanna, E. (2020). The future of technology and marketing: A multidisciplinary perspective. *Journal of the Academy of Marketing Science*, *48*(1), 1–8.

Hacker, P. (2023). Regulating AI: The case of the European AI Act. *Law, Innovation and Technology*, *15*(1), 123–151.

Huang, M.-H., & Rust, R. T. (2021). A strategic framework for artificial intelligence in marketing. *Journal of the Academy of Marketing Science*, *49*(1), 30–50.

Kaptein, M., de Ruyter, K., Markopoulos, P., & Aarts, E. (2015). Adaptive persuasive systems: A study of tailored persuasive text messages to reduce snacking. *ACM Transactions on Interactive Intelligent Systems*, *2*(2), 1–25.

Kumar, V., Dixit, A., Javalgi, R. G., Dass, M., & Kumar, P. (2019). Digital transformation of business-to-business marketing: Framework, evolution, and research agenda. *Industrial Marketing Management*, *81*, 90–102.

Li, H., & Kannan, P. K. (2014). Attributing conversions in a multichannel online marketing environment: An empirical model and a field experiment. *JMR, Journal of Marketing Research*, *51*(1), 40–56.

KEY TERMS AND DEFINITIONS

Consumer Persuasion: is the consumer mindset change process when consumers receive marketing content that is both targeted and emotionally meaningful.

Ethical AI in Advertising: is the responsible and fair use of AI technologies in advertising that ensures equality, transparency, and respect for consumer privacy.

Data-Driven Creativity: combines analytics and machine learning capabilities with human creativity to build relevant, personalized, and meaningful marketing content.

Generative Artificial Intelligence (GenAI): refers to AI systems which generate a new, original piece of content— text, image, or campaign pieces—by learning the patterns from existing datasets.

Personalized Marketing: is a marketing strategy that personalizes the marketing communication, such as messages, recommendations, and offers for each consumer based on their preferences and behavior.

Chapter 13

Generative AI for Inclusive Marketing: Embedding Diversity, Equity, and Cultural Competence in AI-Driven Decision Systems

Rocky Kumar
https://orcid.org/0009-0002-6995-2037
Poornima University, Jaipur, India

Gaurav Kumar
https://orcid.org/0009-0004-6126-8526
Poornima University, Jaipur, India

Shikha Sharma
https://orcid.org/0000-0001-6339-9731
Poornima University, Jaipur, India

Adarsh Kumar Pandey
https://orcid.org/0009-0002-1364-6903
Poornima University, Jaipur, India

ABSTRACT

Generative Artificial Intelligence (GenAI) has come in a wave as earth-shattering innovation in world marketing offering capabilities in real-time content generation, hyper-personalization, predictive analytics, and dynamic audience engagement in a global marketing world that is culturally diverse. While these abilities promise increased efficiency and further connection of consumers, they also have some important issues surrounding fairness, representational accuracy and culture. In

DOI: 10.4018/979-8-3373-6731-6.ch013

multicultural environments, AI-driven marketing systems which fail to include the principles of Diversity, Equity and Inclusion (DEI) could play a role in the reinforcement of harmful stereotypes, the marginalization of minority communities and the loss of public trust. Biases inherent in training data, model architectures and even automated decision pipelines can be used to create arbitrary audience segmentation and culturally inappropriate messaging - creating reputational, ethical and regulatory problems for organizations.

1. INTRODUCTION

The global marketing environment has witnessed a massive transformation; led by digitization, social media penetration, and availability of huge scale consumer data sets. As brands are now playing across continents, cultures, identities and linguistic boundaries, understanding multicultural audiences has become a strategic necessity and not a creative preference. In this landscape Generative Artificial Intelligence (GenAI) is a disruptive technological force that offers a chance to automate content creation, predict behaviours, communicate across languages, and create hyper-personalised consumer engagement. These allow marketers to upscale their creative works and communicate to different populations with extremely customized communication (Kaplan & Haenlein, 2022). However, while GenAI is making things more efficient and innovative, there are also some major ethical concerns when it comes to fairness, representation and cultural sensitivity (Tarnanidis et al., 2026).

AI systems that are trained on biased, incomplete or culturally narrow data, tend to perpetuate these biases in the marketing content, potentially harming marginalized communities, as well as consumer trust (Buolamwini & Gebru, 2018). Therefore, including principles of Diversity, Equity, and Inclusion (DEI) into GenAI systems is critical when it comes to ensuring responsible and culturally competent marketing practices.

1.2 The Rise Of Generative AI In Marketing

Generative AI has changed how marketing is done with its potential to introduce new levels of automation, creativity and personalization. Large multimodal models allow marketers to develop images, videos, slogans, branding elements and emotional storylines in just a fraction of a second (Cillo & Rubera, 2024). GenAI also enables dynamic responses according to user preferences, so it's possible to change the content of the response in real time across cultures and devices. This technological shift has been seen in applications such as automated copywriting tools, artificial intelligence (AI) powered design platforms, virtual influencers, and personalized product recommendation engines. Although these are innovations with great potential to provide competitive advantages, there is a high reliance on cultural understanding. For example, an effective campaign in Western markets may not be suitable or even offensive in Asian, African or Middle Eastern contexts when GenAI is unaware of local customs or socio-cultural norms (Hussain & Cambria, 2021). Therefore, the emergence of GenAI must be accompanied by ways of ensuring cultural competence and ethical safeguards.

1.3 Importance Of Diversity, Equity, And Inclusion (DEI)

Diversity, Equity, Inclusion: Is the Marketing System Ethical? Diversity, Equity, and Inclusion: Inclusion Can Be a Personal Affair Diversity, Equity and Inclusion Are Not Equal Diversity, Equity and Inclusion Are Interconnected How Can Inclusion Be Measured? Diversity helps in ensuring that AI models are trained on data that represents diverse identities, languages, and cultural practices (Suresh & Guttag, 2021). Equity requires systems to not favor some groups of people over others, and in particular with decision-making in the context of targeting, ad delivery, or content personalization. Inclusion guarantees that marketing content is respectful, culturally relevant, and accessible to all audiences, including historically marginalized populations. The lack of DEI in AI-driven marketing leads to harmful stereotypes, biased recommendations, cultural erasure and the exclusion of minority communities from significant brand narratives (Noble, 2018). As regulatory bodies across the globe are growing more focused on ethical AI governance, companies can no longer be complacent about incorporating DEI principles into GenAI to stay compliant, trusted and get the right brand reputation.

1.4 Research Gap And Purpose Of The Chapter

Despite the speed at which AI is being adopted for use in marketing, there is limited research devoted to DEI-integrated GenAI systems. The literature on algorithmic bias has mainly concentrated on algorithmic bias in technical areas, such as healthcare, finance, and hiring (Mehrabi et al., 2021), however, research specifically addressing cultural bias in the advertising and consumer engagement domains is relatively rare. In addition, there are not full frameworks that consider DEI principles across all stages of GenAI pipelines - from dataset selection to model evaluation to content monitoring. Real-life case studies of success and failure in AI-based multicultural marketing are also not sufficiently documented. Further, there are no standardised metrics for how fairness, cultural sensitivity, and inclusivity are measured in marketing campaigns that are challenging for practitioners to responsibly evaluate their systems. Therefore, the aim of this chapter is to fill in these gaps by offering a comprehensive, interdisciplinary and practical framework. The chapter is intended to equip researchers, marketers and policymakers with an understanding of the ways in which DEI could be built into GenAI-driven marketing workflows to build equitable, ethical, and culturally-adaptive marketing campaigns.

2. UNDERSTANDING DIVERSITY, EQUITY, AND INCLUSION (DEI) IN AI SYSTEMS

As artificial intelligence is now part of the economic, social and marketing infrastructures, the incorporation of Diversity, Equity, and Inclusion (DEI) principles into artificial intelligence systems has become increasingly important. Modern AI models function in the context of complex socio-technical ecosystems, meaning that they do not simply process data - they also reflect the cultural, historical and political context in which this data was generated. Because AI models learn patterns from human-generated datasets, any pre-existing biases, stereotypes, or structural inequalities within society, are able to be re-created or amplified by these models (Crawford, 2021). In the sphere of marketing, this is especially important because AI systems impact directly on the perception of consumers, the brand, the representation of cultural communities. Therefore, understanding DEI in AI is fundamental to developing ethical, social-conscience and culturally adaptive systems in the global markets.

2.1 Defining DEI Principles

Diversity, Equity, and Inclusion are interlinked concepts that are important for ethical AI development and deployment. Diversity is the existence of differences in identities, experience, and views. In the context of AI, this implies ensuring that datasets and training samples include a broad variety of demographic factors such as race, gender, ethnicity, language, disability and socio-economic background (Foster et al., 2022). Without having a wide range of data, AI systems run the risk of having one-dimensional interpretations of human behaviour which can lead to exclusionary or biased marketing outcomes. Equity is focused on fairness and justice in processes, opportunities and outcomes created by AI systems.

Equity means taking care that AI does not favour one group over another or institutionalise disadvantage that is baked into the data (Binns, 2018). For marketing purposes, that means that equity refers to the idea that ad-targeting, personalization algorithms and recommendation systems do not automatically discriminate against marginalized or underrepresented communities. Inclusion, the design and use of AI technologies engage and respect different cultural perspectives is what inclusion is all about.

Inclusion is about ensuring that AI-generated content resonates with multicultural audiences, and does not misrepresent or cause any form of cultural insensitivity. Inclusive AI systems take local contexts, beliefs, values and languages into account to provide meaningful and respectful engagements (Suresh & Guttag, 2021).

Together, DEI principles make sure that AI-driven marketing is not only effective, but it is also ethically aligned with the values of different global populations.

2.2 DEI In Technology And Marketing Contexts

The integration of DEI into technology is not novel, but has become more urgent due to the amplification of AI, bringing about autonomous technology and making a big impact on social decisions on a large scale. In traditional technology development, DEI was addressed more as a human resource or organizational culture problem. However, as AI systems started to make decisions in the hiring process, lending and healthcare, marketing, etc. DEI became an important technical parameter (Raji & Buolamwini, 2019). AI developers have now realized that technology itself can either perpetuate or question social inequalities, depending on how it is built. In the marketing domain, DEI is even more preeminent because marketing is the gateway to shaping consumer identity and cultural and public imagery. When AI systems are used to generate advertisements or segment audiences, for example, these systems may use large amounts of data, which may reflect historical biases. For example, we know that early versions of ad-targeting algorithms were found to disproportionately serve job ads for high-paying technical jobs to men - more than women - as a result of gendered assumptions baked into historical data (Lambrecht & Tucker, 2019). Similarly, automated image generation tools have not been able to accurately represent the cultural attire, skin tones or regional aesthetics, which in turn, has led to misrepresentation in global campaigns (Licsandru et al., 2025)

Furthermore, the use of AI in personalization can unintentionally lead to the formation of cultural silos. By continuously presenting users with content that is consistent with their past behaviour, AI can perpetuate stereotypes or narrow the exposure to different brand stories (Noble, 2018). This defeats the purpose of inclusive communication of the brand and has the potential to alienate consumers whose experiences don't fall under the dominant cultural norms. Therefore, it is necessary to embed DEI at the core of the design of marketing AI systems to ensure culturally respectful engagement (Mandania et al., 2025).

2.3 Cultural Competence IN AI Applications

Cultural competence refers to a system's capacity to understand, respect and appropriately respond to variations in culture. In marketing, cultural competence refers to the fact that AI-generated content should be based on the proper representation of cultures, that symbols are not misinterpreted, and that modes of communication comply with local customs (Hussain & Cambria, 2021). For example, colors, gestures, clothing, and imagery have different meanings in different cultures: for example, in some cultures white is a color of purity, while in others it is a color of mourning; some hand gestures can be friendly in some countries and offensive in others. AI models that are trained mostly on data that is centered around the Western world tend to not be able to capture such nuances, resulting in culturally insensitive outputs. For example, text generation models can endlessly use phrases that have colonial, gendered or racially charged interpretations without any awareness of their context. Similarly, facial recognition systems have been historically less accurate for people with darker skin tones because facial recognition training datasets have tended to underrepresent people of colour (Buolamwini & Gebru, 2018).

In marketing the impacts of cultural incompetence are magnified because communication for a brand is public facing. Culturally insensitive ads produced by AI can rapidly spread on digital platforms and result in public backlash and severe damage to a company's reputation. In order to be culturally competent, AI systems must be trained on data that shows diversity across the world, they must be monitored for bias, and they must work with cultural experts. This will ensure that marketing AI becomes an instrument to create cross-cultural connection rather than misrepresentation.

2.4 Ethical Imperatives Of Inclusive AI

Ethical considerations are an important part of the process of creating most inclusive AI systems. As AI plays an increasingly important role in the way we live and interact with each other, it is important to ensure transparency, fairness and accountability in the way it is used. Ethical AI frameworks emphasize the importance of identifying and addressing algorithmic harms, which include biased decision-making, stereotyping, and excluding minority communities (Floridi and Cowls 2019). From an ethical point of view inclusive AI ensures:

1. **Fair Representation:** AI-generated marketing should be an accurate representation of the diversity of the actual populations in the real world rather than promoting narrow standards of beauty, gender roles or cultural stereotypes.

2. **Preventing Harm:** Biased or culturally insensitive marketing can be harmful to people psychologically, reinforce discrimination, or structural inequalities (Crawford, 2021).
3. **Ensuring Transparency:** Consumers need to know when recommendations or ads made by an AI will influence their decisions and how decisions are made.
4. **Promoting Accessibility:** Inclusive AI must take into account people with disabilities by ensuring the content is accessible using the appropriate formats, alt-texts, captions and linguistic variations.
5. **Building Consumer Trust:** Trust: Ethical AI practices help to build good brand image and foster a higher level of consumer loyalty, especially from multicultural customers who place importance on representation and authenticity.

Inclusive AI is not a technical requirement, but a moral imperative that applies the practice of marketing in line with human-centred values.

3. GENERATIVE AI IN MARKETING: OPPORTUNITIES AND RISKS

Generative Artificial Intelligence has significantly altered the marketing ecosystem because it has allowed marketing professionals to introduce new levels of automation, creativity, and intelligence to their marketing efforts that were previously impossible with traditional marketing tools. Its ability for generating text, images, video and personalized interactions allows brands to scale unique consumer experiences to a scale that is unimaginable even a decade ago (Kaplan & Haenlein, 2022). GenAI-powered marketing is now helping to support everything from automated content generation to predictive analytics, helping organizations to be fast on their feet when it comes to responding to consumer behaviour and market trends. However, as the technology takes hold, some of the concerns associated with fairness, bias, cultural insensitivity and ethical misalignment with technology have also become heightened. While the opportunities of GenAI are a game-changer, the risks need to be considered to ensure the safe, fair, and responsible integration of AI into multicultural marketing landscapes (Dwivedi et al., 2023).

Table 1. Key Differences Between Traditional Marketing vs. GenAI-Driven Marketing

Parameter	Traditional Marketing	GenAI-Driven Marketing
Content Creation	Manual, time-consuming	Automated, real-time, scalable
Personalization	Segment-level	Hyper-personal, individual-level
Cultural Adaptation	Human experts only	AI-driven + Human review
Speed of Execution	Slow	Instant campaign generation
Bias Risk	Human bias	Algorithmic + data bias
Cost	Higher creative cost	Lower production cost

3.1 Capabilities Of Genai In Marketing Automation

One of the biggest contributions of GenAI is the automation of marketing activities that were previously time-consuming and costly (in terms of large creative teams, lengthy production cycles and high operational cost). Modern generative models are able to create advertising copy, social media messages, slogans, newsletter, product descriptions, and brand narratives within seconds (Cillo & Rubera, 2024). Visual generation models such as DALL*E or Stable Diffusion can create market-specific graphics, campaign banners, and culturally-specific imagery without the need for traditional photoshoots. This saves an enormous amount of time-to-market and enables brands to test different campaign concepts quickly.

GenAI is also being used to improve marketing automation using predictive personalization. By analysing consumer sentiment, browsing patterns and purchase histories, GenAI-powered systems can be used to make recommendations and create personalised messages that resonate with customer interests (Haenlein et al., 2022). These recommendations change dynamically and on-the-fly which gives birth to dynamic customer journeys. For example, by generating responses to user intents, language style and culture background, AI chatbots result in higher engagement and conversion rate (Huang & Rust, 2021). Such systems enable marketers to have continuous communications with audiences in different time zones and on various platforms. Furthermore, Customer Relationship Management (CRM) systems are also used with GenAI to automate segmentation and campaign orchestration. Rather than manual segmentation of consumers as per their demographic groups, generative and predictive models allow identifying micro-segments of consumers and predicting their needs with a higher degree of accuracy (Wedel & Kannan, 2016). These capabilities constitute a more intelligent marketing pipeline that is flexible, scalable and efficient.

3.2 Personalization And Consumer Engagement

Personalization has become the main differentiator in the modern marketing world. Consumers now demand more from brands, expecting them to know their preferences and offer customized and emotionally and culturally resonant experiences. GenAI helps to increase personalization by reading complex datasets such as social media behaviour, emotion tone in text, voice inputs, interaction patterns etc. This allows brands to create messaging that resonates with the consumer and their identity, values and previous behaviours (Smith & Linden, 2017).

GenAI-generated personalization goes beyond different touchpoints. E-commerce platforms use AI-generated product recommendations to match what the consumer tastes. Email marketing systems automatically create subject lines and body content that match individual consumer moods or searches. Streaming companies such as Netflix and Spotify employ generative algorithms that enable them to curate playlists or movie recommendations based on cultural context, regional preferences and viewing/preferences (Gomez-Uribe & Hunt, 2016).

In multicultural environments, generative AI can learn how to adapt communication styles, idioms, emotional tone, and imagery to local cultural norms (Hussain & Cambria, 2021). For instance, the same brand's message to consumers across India may include festival-specific greetings while the same product's campaign in Japan may highlight harmony, subtlety and group cohesion. This level of contextual personalization results in greater consumer satisfaction, as well as brand loyalty. However, if personalization is not weighed in contrast to DEI, it can backfire. Biased profiling can result in stereotyping or exclusion - for example, by assuming that certain communities Favor low-cost products, or by linking certain gender roles to certain buying habits. Thus, personalization must be based on fairness, awareness of culture and ethical limitations.

3.3 Risks Of Non-Inclusive AI In Global Campaigns

Despite its capabilities, GenAI poses significant risks to be deployed without DEI frameworks. One of the major risks is algorithmic bias, which occurs when the training data is underrepresented, or it is biased due to historical inequalities. For instance, generative text models have been found to generate gendered or racialized words when prompted with neutral words (Bender et al., 2021). In the case of visual tools for marketing purposes, image generation models might incorrectly represent skin tones, facial features, attire (cultural) and/or traditional symbols because of Western-centric training datasets. Another danger is the situation of cultural misinterpretation. AI systems not knowledgeable of cultural context may abuse symbols, colours or gestures that have a particular meaning in other cultures. For example, an advertisement created with AI can have religious symbols used incorrectly or see styles of clothing not suitable in some regions. These mistakes could lead to backlash from consumers, boycotts of brands and reputational damage (Noble, 2018). A third risk is that of exclusionary ad-targeting. Non-inclusive AI systems can also have the unintended consequence of marginalizing certain groups by serving certain demographics more than others in the form of ads. For example, job advertisements or financial services could be targeted at more men or more affluent consumers based upon assumptions which have been made based on data (Lambrecht & Tucker, 2019). In multicultural markets, this can lead to a digital divide in the marketing communication. In addition, there are risks that come with deepfake-based GenAI such as misinformation, manipulation of identity and unethical persuasion tactics. Although synthetic media can aid in the creative process, it is also possible to mislead the audience or tarnish the stories of culture if not controlled (Floridi, 2021).

3.4 Balancing Innovation And Responsibility

Balancing the innovativeness that GenAI can offer and ethical responsibility is a key to sustainable adoption. Companies have to realize that creativity using artificial intelligence should not violate cultural respect, fairness or consumer rights.

A responsible balance is the combination of technical safeguards, inclusive design and evaluation of AI behaviour over time. First, the so-called inclusive data practices have to be prioritized. Diverse datasets enable GenAI to learn balanced representations of identities around the world, reducing bias and promoting cultural relevance (Foster et al., 2022). Second, transparent AI pipelines are useful for marketers to get insight into how models create outputs and ensure that culturally sensitive content is reviewed before it is published. Third, there has to be a human-AI collaboration. While AI takes care of the scalability and automation of the process, human experts provide contextual judgment, cultural insight and an ethical overview (Shneiderman, 2022). Regulatory frameworks are also improving such responsibilities. Governments and international agencies are increasingly working on fairness, accountability and transparency of AI-driven systems (OECD, 2021). Brands that want to operate at a global level will need to comply with these emerging standards if they want to maintain the trust and long-term credibility of their consumers. At the end of the day, it's responsible adoption of GenAI that will require incorporating DEI principles at each stage of the process - from model design to model deployment to monitoring. GenAI, when balanced effectively, is a potentially useful tool not only to allow for greater creativity and efficiency, but can also be utilized in the strengthening of multicultural relationships through respectful, inclusive, and meaningful engagement.

4. ALGORITHMIC BIAS AND CULTURAL BLIND SPOTS IN MARKETING AI

With the rise of generative and predictive AI systems, which are driving more and more of the global marketing decision-making process, algorithmic bias has become one of the most significant ethical issues. The uniformed error is referred to as bias in AI that leads to unfair, discriminatory, or culturally insensitive consequences. These errors can often be due to skewed data sets, imbalanced representation, faulty modelling techniques or historical prejudices built into digital information (Mehrabi et al., 2021). In the context of marketing, bias can skew the way that audiences are divided for targeting, the way that advertising is aimed, the way that consumer behaviours are interpreted, and the way that cultural narratives are represented. Cultural blind spot further contributes to the above problems by limiting the capability of the AI to understand and respect regional norms, identities, values, symbols and linguistic variations. As brands are continuing to expand into multicultural markets, it is important for the problem of algorithmic bias to be addressed in order to prevent any potential negative impact on their reputation and ensure that their brand is being represented by diverse consumer groups.

Table 2. Sources of Algorithmic Bias in Marketing AI Pipelines

Bias Source	Description	Example in Marketing
Data Bias	Lack of diverse representation in training data	AI generating only lighter skin tones
Historical Bias	Prejudices encoded in historical datasets	Stereotyping job roles by gender
Algorithmic Bias	Model misinterpreting patterns unfairly	Wrong profiling of minority groups
Interaction Bias	Users influencing outputs via feedback	Chatbots learning toxic patterns
Cultural Bias	Lack of cultural context in models	Misuse of symbols, gestures, colors

Figure 1. Key sources of algorithmic bias affecting AI-powered marketing decisions

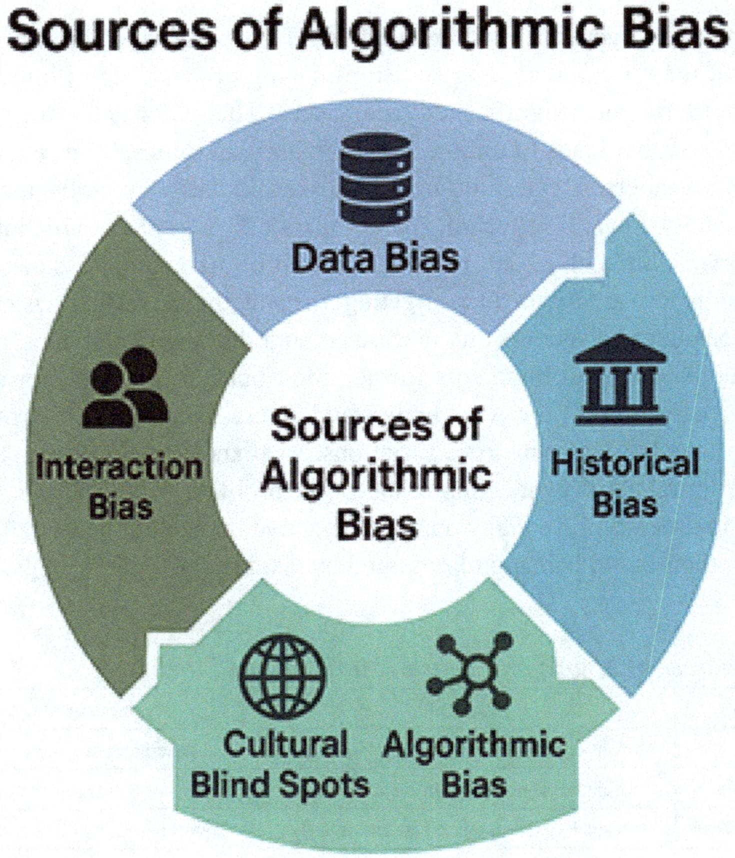

4.1 Sources Of Bias IN AI Pipelines

Bias in marketing AI can occur in many layers of the AI pipeline but each time adding its own specific way to this final output. The first major source is data-driven bias which is caused by the failure of the training data sets to reflect the full range of cultural diversity. AI systems that are trained primarily with Western or English language data may be narrow views and do not take into account the regional context like non-Western views of beauty, religious sensitivity or different styles of communication (Sheng et al., 2021). This creates generative outputs that center dominant cultures to the margins of others.

A second source is historical bias, which is built into digital archives, social media and search engine records. Since AI models are trained on past data, they can perpetuate outdated or discriminatory stereotypes - such as linking certain gender roles to occupations, or linking certain ethnicities to negative attributes (Caliskan et al., 2017). When applied to marketing, these biases may affect recommendations on products or definitions of consumer categories.

Third, algorithmic bias is a result of the way the models weigh their features, understand the patterns and make their predictions. Even given a diverse set of datasets, it can be the case that an algorithm may read things, and interpret data, in a way that in fact privileges or disfavours groups of people (Friedman & Nissenbaum, 1996). For instance, an ad-targeting model can falsely assume that women are less likely to interact with financial products or technology-based innovations by just recognizing bias in patterns.

Finally, there is interaction bias which occurs when users interact with AI systems. So, if consumers from certain cultural backgrounds are underrepresented in engagement on the platform, there is a chance that the AI will only adapt to the dominant demographic behaviour and reinforce exclusion (Noble, 2018). Together these biases have harmful marketing consequences if not systematically addressed.

4.2 Training Data And Representation Issues

Training data is the cornerstone of generative AI - and training data limitations have a major effect on the worldview that AI models learn. When this type of datasets does not have representation from minority cultures, the model builds a limited and often incorrect understanding of global diversity. For example, research about image generation systems has shown that datasets have been disproportionately made up of lighter-skinned people, western facial structures, and western clothing traditions (Buolamwini & Gebru, 2018). As a result, AI systems misrepresent darker skin tones, traditional attire or indigenous cultural features. Language data sets are also afflicted with representational imbalance. Many generative text models are trained on a corpus of English texts, which means they lack cultural vocabulary and knowledge of multilingual expressions (Bender et al., 2021). When used in marketing, for example, such models can misinterpret idioms, festivals, metaphors in culture or stories of identity. For example, a generative AI could not understand the cultural importance of Diwali in India, Eid in the Middle East or Lunar New Year in East Asia, resulting in generic and unsensitive marketing content.

Representation problems also arise for personalization. Algorithmic systems, it often happens that demographic proxies - zip codes, surnames, inferred interests

- are used to determine a user's identity category. When these proxies are based on biased assumptions, consumers may be mis classified. An African consumer may be given Western aesthetic taste preferences or a Middle Eastern consumer may be given content that ignores religious sensitivities. Underrepresentation eventually gives rise to a cultural erasure, in which AI models reinforce a dominant culture point of view and minority identities are anomalies. In terms of global marketing, this forms a power imbalance where only a limited set of values, symbols or aesthetics are recognised and reproduced.

4.3 Case Examples Of Cultural Misrepresentation

The real-world examples for how algorithmic bias leads to culturally insensitive marketing results.

One of the most cited examples is that of an AI-based algorithm for beauty in an international advertising contest that chose relatively lighter-skinned people as the "attractive" ones, based on the fact that the dataset was predominantly based on the standards of western beauty (Raji & Buolamwini, 2019). This was criticized for colorism and cultural bias in AI-based evaluation systems.

A similar failure happened when an international fashion brand used AI-generated images in an online campaign. The generative model falsely portrayed the traditional African hairstyles and cultural outfits, mixing them with Western attributes and forming distorted imagery that offended the local population. The campaign was later pulled and the brand made a formal apology. In another case, automated ad-targeting systems served high-paying job ads to men and low-paying jobs to women - based on historical labor biases that were programmed into the system with training data (Lambrecht & Tucker, 2019). This not only reinforced gender inequality, it also broke ethical standards of advertising.

Text generation has also caused controversies. Several AI chatbots used by companies have created outputs that contain racial stereotypes, insensitive jokes or cultural offensive statements as a result of toxic online content included in training data (Sheng et al., 2021). In multicultural markets, such errors hurt the credibility and trust of the brand. These are just some cases that prove that cultural misrepresentation is not accidental - it is a structural result of biased data sets and non-inclusive AI design.

4.4 Consequences For Brands And Consumers

The consequences of algorithmic bias in marketing are far-reaching and they affect brands and consumers. For consumers, biased AI systems can be used to perpetuate stereotypes, misrepresent identities, and exclude minority groups from representation of a brand. For example, consumers who have negative perceptions in advertisements of not being represented in the right way could lead to feeling marginalized or cultural invisibility (Noble, 2018). This can destroy trust, psychological safety and emotional connection with brands.

For brands, consequences include damage to its reputation, low market penetration and ethical or legal liabilities. A single advertisement created by AI that is culturally insensitive can result in public backlash across all social media platforms, and boycotts and/or penalties from the press or regulators (Park & Namkung, 2022). Furthermore, exclusionary ad-targeting restricts both the audience that the customer or brand reaches and the brand's ability to reach a diverse audience, lost revenue opportunities. Bias is also the destroyer of credibility of algorithms. When consumers discover that they are discriminated based on their behavior due to AI-driven recommendations or personalization, consumers can develop negative perceptions of the brand and technological practices (Floridi, 2021). This is a load on the long-term brand equity. In the world markets, being culturally blind is a major obstacle to competitive advantage. Brands that fail to localize well may seem foreign, insensitive, and irrelevant. On the other hand, companies that are inclusive in their use of AI get access to wider markets and build better multicultural relationships. Thus, the fight against algorithmic bias is not a choice - it is a requirement for sustainable, ethical and globally effective marketing.

5. FRAMEWORK FOR INCLUSIVE AI-DRIVEN DECISION-MAKING

As organisations continue to make greater use of generative and predictive AI tools to automate marketing workflows, the importance of having a measurable framework that helps ensure diversity, fairness and cultural inclusion has become critical. Traditional AI development pipelines are prone to dedicate more attention to performance metrics such as accuracy, efficiency, and scalability, while neglecting imperatives concerning ethics such as representation, cultural adaptability and equitable outcomes (Floridi & Cowls, 2019). In the scope of multicultural marketing, such gaps are multiplied and viewed as more substantial due to the fact that the decisions made by AI directly impact the identity of a brand, public perception, and the way that the cultural groups are represented or attacked. An inclusive AI-driven decision-making framework seeks to make sure that the AI models not only work well, but also honour cultural diversity, reduce bias and produce content that is in line with socio-cultural expectations around the globe. This section suggests a whole that is assembled on four equal pillars, ranging from inclusive design principles, fairness-aware algorithms and transparent and explainable AI pipelines to cultural adaptable personalization techniques.

Table 3. Principles of Inclusive AI Design

Principle	Description	Expected Outcome
Representational Completeness	Diverse cultural, linguistic, demographic data	Fair & accurate representation
Contextual Sensitivity	Awareness of cultural norms, identities	Culturally aligned content
Participatory Design	Inclusion of cultural experts & communities	Reduction in blind spots
Ethical Foresight	Predicting potential societal harm	Safer AI deployment
Transparency	Clear documentation of AI decisions	Higher trust & accountability

Figure 2. A holistic framework for designing inclusive and culturally sensitive GenAI systems

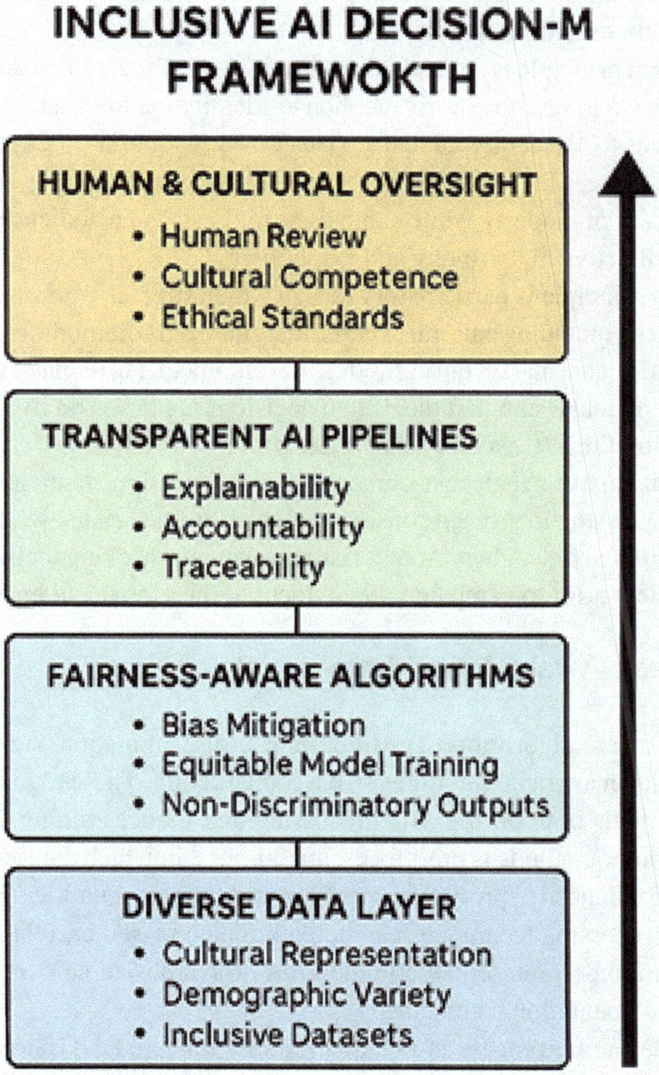

5.1 Principles Of Inclusive AI Design

Inclusive AI design means that DEI values are embedded in all stages of the AI lifecycle - from data collection to evaluating feedback. The first principle is representational completeness, which means that datasets contain the cultural, linguistic, and demographic diversity of the populations that the AI system is trying to serve (Suresh & Guttag, 2021). Greater representational completeness decreases the danger of cultural erasure and aids the model in learning subtle differences in identity, practices and behaviour.

The second principle is contextual sensitivity, which means that AI systems need to be sensitive to the cultural norms, holidays, identity markers, and communication styles relevant to the target audience (Hussain & Cambria, 2021). For example, marketing messages for Middle Eastern markets must respect religious expressions and the concept of modesty while campaigns for East Asian audiences may include themes of collectivism, harmony and symbolism.

The third principle is participatory design which stresses working with a variety of stakeholders, including cultural experts, marginalized communities, and representatives from the local market during system development. Participatory models avoid blind spots and make sure that the design decisions are based on lived experiences, and not assumptions (Costanza-Chock, 2020).

Finally, inclusive AI design demands ethical foresight, anticipating possible harms, and assessing long-term consequences that are associated with AI-generated marketing. Ethical foresight promotes risk assessment, checking for bias, and human loops or review prior to campaign deployment to the global audience.

5.2 Fairness-Aware Algorithms

Fairness-aware algorithms: Try to eliminate discrimination, stereotyping, and uneven results in artificial intelligence-based marketing. These algorithms account for fairness goals both on the data processing and model training stages. One of the most popular methods is pre-processing fairness, in which datasets are cleaned, debiased and balanced to prevent historical or structural inequalities (Feldman et al., 2015). Pre-processing techniques can help eliminate biased correlations, reweight samples from underrepresented communities or synthesize new training samples using data augmentation techniques.

During the training process, in-processing fairness methods add fairness constraints to the loss function of the model. These constraints make it so that predictions are not giving excessive disproportions to protected groups, or perpetuating cultural stereotypes. For example, an ad-targeting model can be optimized to prevent advertising high paying jobs to only men or beauty products to only lighter-skinned individuals (Lambrecht & Tucker, 2019).

Besides, some post-processing fairness techniques adjust or calibrate the model results after the model is trained. Techniques such as equal opportunity calibration or demographic parity adjustments make sure that the final predictions are not biased towards diverse groups (Hardt et al., 2016). In marketing, post-processing can be done for adjusting personalization thresholds, redistributing ad exposures, or manually analysing AI-generated imagery for cultural sensitivity.

Integrating fairness-aware algorithms helps to ensure that marketing messages are inclusive and equitable, avoiding the systematic exclusion or misrepresentation of minority communities.

5.3 Transparent And Explainable Pipelines

Transparency is an essential requirement for responsible AI deployment. Many generative models are also "black boxes" and it is hard for marketers to grasp why some recommendations, images, or messages are generated (Miller, 2019).

Explainable AI (XAI) has one aim - making these internal processes understandable so that brands can identify potential instances of bias or cultural misalignment. Transparent AI pipeline involves tracking of the sources of datasets, versions of models, training procedures and the cultural considerations that were embedded into the system. This documentation is used to support the compliance and the accountability. For global brands, that will help ensure that marketing audits are able to track how cultural decisions were implemented, rather than relying on opaque system behaviour (Raji et al., 2020).

Explainability is also useful for marketers in justifying AI-driven decisions to consumers. When personalization algorithms are used to recommend products, consumers may feel more comfortable if they know the basis for such suggestions (Shneiderman, 2022). This helps to build trust and strengthen engagement. Explainable generative systems are also a way to allow human reviewers, such as cultural advisors or DEI experts, to review AI-generated images, translations, or narratives before they are released to the public. Creating a human-in-the-loop review process lowers the risk of cultural missteps and improves the ethical quality of marketing creations.

5.4 Culturally Adaptive Personalization Techniques

Personalization is one of the greatest strengths of AI-driven marketing but without the cultural awareness, this can be exclusionary or offensive. Culturally adaptive personalization to ensure that the AI-generated content is sensitive to local customs, values and norms. This is started with multilingual and multicultural training where models are as a result modified with the usage of corpora of text with quite a lot of cultural content, regional images and diverse linguistic data (Joshi et al., 2020). Next, the available systems adapt to local cultural differences by incorporating local identity cues, such as festivals, symbols, idioms, colours and storytelling traditions, to personalize the content in culturally meaningful ways. For instance, artificial intelligence (AI) machines can design festive advertising materials for Diwali in India, Ramadan in Middle East countries or Thanksgiving in North America. Cultural adaptation also calls for sensitivity mapping, used to identify items that should be avoided due to cultural taboos or religious prohibitions, or political sensitivities. These maps help AI systems to flag content as potentially culturally inappropriate and/or block them. For example, AI systems are not supposed to generate promotions that refer to alcohol to people in countries where a majority of people are Muslims. Finally, the culturally adaptive personalization refers to dynamic cultural profiling, where the AI learns about user preferences, which change over time. Unlike static segmentation, dynamic profiling considers cultural hybridity - the fact that people can be members of multiple cultural identities at the same time (Hall, 1996). This helps to result in better and accurate personalization. When done right culturally adaptive personalization can help build stronger brand relevance, build consumer trust and generate emotional resonance across diverse global markets.

6. CASE STUDIES: SUCCESSES AND FAILURES IN INCLUSIVE MARKETING

To understand what generative AI means for multicultural marketing in the real world, one has to take a look at some real-world cases where AI systems have empowered inclusivity or have succeeded in causing cultural insensitivity. Case studies show how AI-fuelled decisions play out in consumer-facing campaigns, enabling researchers and practitioners to see the real-life links between the behaviour of algorithms, cultural representation and brand outcome. Successful examples have shown how inclusive AI can help boost brand connection, representation and increase global reach. Conversely, instances of failure cases put into perspective issues of biased datasets, poor cultural oversight, and a lack of DEI integration within AI workflows. By comparing successful and unsuccessful campaigns, marketers can know the best practices and what to avoid while utilizing GenAI tools in various cultural markets.

6.1 Successful Case: Inclusive Branding Through Ai-Driven Campaigns

A leading global cosmetics company launched an AI-powered shade matching system that aims to solve the age-old problem of underrepresentation of darker skin tones in beauty products. Traditional algorithms for determining beauty were often criticized because they tended to incorrectly match skin tones that are deeper because the training data sets had more models with lighter skin tones (Buolamwini & Gebru, 2018). To solve this problem, the company worked with dermatologists, DEI consultants, and diverse user groups to compile data for over 50 countries and a wide range of undertones, textures, and lighting environments.

The company also used generative AI to produce inclusive promotional content. The model was fine-tuned with the help of culturally representative images, so that the program could create advertising images that represented women from African, South Asian, Middle Eastern and Southeast Asian backgrounds. Importantly, the system was monitored through a human-in-the-loop system, whereby cultural experts tested AI-generated visuals before releasing campaigns. As a result, the campaign was praised globally for its authentic and respectful representation of diversity (Foster et al., 2022).

Similarly, a major sportswear brand utilised AI-driven analysis of regional cultural narratives to create localised campaigns. The AI system examined millions of social media content to understand how consumers in various countries expressed empowerment, athletic identity and cultural pride (Hussain & Cambria, 2021). This enabled the brand to create personalised content that was relevant to regional identities, including community-based sports in Latin America, youth street culture in Africa and tradition-infused aesthetics in East Asia. Another positive case is Netflix's recommendation system using generative algorithms to generate area-specific movie posters. The AI is used to find out the characters, emotional expressions, and cultural relevant frames to customize visuals for users based on their location in India, Korea, Brazil, and Europe (Gomez-Uribe & Hunt, 2016).

This cultural adaptation msade a notable difference in terms of user engagement and showed how AI can be used to improve personalization while respecting cultural diversity. These cases demonstrate that when DEI principles are applied within AI development processes (through the use of diverse datasets, human cultural oversight and fairness-aware algorithms), AI proves to be a powerful tool for inclusive global marketing.

6.2 Failure Case: Cultural Missteps And Reputational Damage

Despite its potential, AI-driven marketing has also resulted in some high-profile cultural fails that expose the dangers of non-inclusive AI systems. One widely reported case was of a large fashion company which used an AI image generation tool to curate the promotional images to the Asian market. The generated AI caricature-like facial features similar to Western stereotypes of East Asian people from decades ago. This caused immediate backlash on social media, with users accusing the brand of cultural insensitivity and inaccuracy in representing. The issue was identified as the training data being dominated by western imagery, which did not reflect the true Asian facial diversity (Sheng et al., 2021).

In another example, a system of AI-driven advertising developed a promotional slogan for a campaign in the Middle East, which inadvertently used a language that was disrespectful during the holy month of Ramadan. The generative model had no cultural constraints which could help filter out phrases that are inconsistent with Islamic values. The oversight caused public criticism which led to the company having to issue an apology and pulling the campaign (Park & Namkung, 2022). This is important for the brand reputation of how culturally unaware language generation models can affect brands.

A large retail company hit a controversy when its AI based hiring and targeting algorithms disproportionately excluded women from job advertisements in tech related fields. The algorithm picked up historical hiring information that men were more often hired for technical roles and therefore perpetuated the current gender imbalance (Lambrecht & Tucker, 2019). When the issue publicized, the company faced regulation scrutiny and severe damage to its reputation. Another case of failure was that of a travel company's AI chatbot that produced offensive replies as a result of toxic content in their training dataset. When minority background users interacted with the chatbot, it would occasionally give them culturally insensitive or stereotypical responses. This incident highlighted the dangers of deploying generative models lacking safety filters for culture or moderation by humans (Bender et al., 2021).

Finally, a brand of beverage attempted to use generative AI to create a graphics that would be culturally themed in its global festival campaign. However, the AI did not accurately represent religious symbols, and instead used a mixture of components from various cultural traditions. For example, Indian cultural designs were adjacent to unrelated Southeast Asian motifs. This error marked cultural homogenization - a type of cultural blindness in which AI is not able to distinguish a difference between different regional identities. The campaign was intensely criticized as being "AI-generated without understanding" so there was a bad impression for the brand credibility. These failures underscore how when AI is not given the cultural context, one without adequate training data or oversight for DEI, the results of a marketing effort will perpetuate stereotypes, offend communities and even undermine trust in brands.

6.3 Lessons Learned From Case Comparisons

The difference between successful and failed AI-driven campaigns shows important lessons in rolling out inclusive GenAI marketing. The first thing is the importance of diverse and representative datasets; the first lesson. Successful cases focus on cultural inclusivity to make sure that their datasets accurately reflect diversity throughout the world while failed cases have Western-centric datasets, or unbalanced datasets that skew the representation (Bender et al., 2021).

Second, human supervision is necessary. Inclusive campaigns include human review loops of cultural experts, DEI specialists and community representatives. This ensures that the consumers do not receive any content that is insensitive. Failed cases are frequently based only on automated systems without external validation (Raji et al., 2020).

Third, it is necessary to incorporate contextual cultural understanding into AI systems. Algorithms should be designed not only to process data, but also to recognize the meaning of culture, symbolism, details of language, and sensitivities of identity. Successful campaigns do this through culturally adaptive personalization models, multilingual fine-tuning and sensitivity filters. Fourth, algorithmic fairness needs to be incorporated into the model training. Whether it is rebalancing training data or including fairness constraints, fairness-aware models go a long way in reducing results of discrimination in ad targeting and content recommendations (Feldman et al., 2015).

Fifth, transparency is a source of trust. Brands that are transparent about their use of AI and show consumers that they are protecting them with ethical standards are gaining consumer confidence. On the other hand, when biased AI outputs are not revealed until problems occur, brands are more strongly backlashed.

Finally, the most important lesson is that technology cannot in and of itself ensure inclusivity. Only by co-designing AI systems according to DEI principles and human cultural expertise can they help to support ethical and authentically inclusive global marketing.

7. STRATEGIES FOR EMBEDDING DEI INTO GENAI WORKFLOWS

Embedding Diversity, Equity, and Inclusion (DEI) into Generative AI Workflows Generative AI systems should be free from biases and protected against them to ensure that AI-fuelled marketing systems are culturally respectful and socially responsible, as well as representative of audiences from around the world. DEI integration is not a choice that can be made as an added extra to the task, but must be a foundational framework throughout the entire AI lifecycle - from data acquisition to implementation and monitoring. As AI increasingly becomes more autonomous in creating content, personalising campaigns and driving consumer behaviour, the risk of cultural insensitivity, stereotyping and exclusion increases (Mehrabi et al., 2021). Therefore, organizations need to adopt holistic strategies, which are a combination of technical interventions, governance mechanisms and human oversight.

This section outlines four key strategies to incorporate DEI into GenAI workflows, including strategies for data diversity and representation, strategies for inclusive model training and validation, approaches for detecting and mitigating bias, and strategies for ongoing monitoring with real-time feedback loops.

7.1 Data Diversity And Representation Approaches

For any inclusive AI workflow, the basis of that includes the diversity and representative quality of the data sets used for training. AI models pick up on patterns in the data they are fed, so if the data sets they are fed are biased, incomplete, or culturally limited, the content produced by AI models will be biased, incomplete, or culturally limited (Bender et al., 2021). In order to promote DEI, organizations must focus on data practices that lead to representational balance across demographic variables, including, but not limited to, race, ethnicity, gender identity, age, disability, religion, linguistic background and socio-cultural practices. One effective strategy is intentional dataset diversification, where organizations are curating datasets that are intentionally diverse and include historically underrepresented groups. For example, in image datasets, there should be an even distribution of skin tones, the way people are dressed, the structure of their faces, and cultural markers (Buolamwini & Gebru, 2018).

For text-based generative models, multilingual sources, culturally diverse literature, region-specific expressions and non-Western knowledge structures must exist in the corpora.

Another component is that of contextual annotation where human annotators with cultural knowledge contribute metadata on cultural references, sentiments, tone, dialect variations, and markers of identity. This ensures that AI can understand the cultural meaning behind data points, rather than understanding these data points generically.

Additionally, data augmentation can be used to generate synthetic data of diverse cultural scenarios. For example, generative models can be used to make balanced samples of cultural attire, festive scenes and linguistic expressions, upon validation of their authenticity by human experts. Finally, organizations should implement approaches for documenting datasets such as datasheets and model cards, which document dataset sources, demographic distributions, cultural contexts, and limitations that are known (Gebru et al., 2021). This transparency helps practitioners to search for gaps and unintentional mismatches of cultures in the deployment process.

7.2 Inclusive Model Training And Validation

Even with a wide range of data, model development should be inclusive, training methods should be explicit in terms of issues of fairness, ethics, and cultural competence. Inclusive model training can help to ensure that AI systems do not perpetuate inequalities, reinforce stereotypes, or create content that is culturally insensitive. One important approach is to introduce fairness constraints in the process of learning the model. During training, algorithms can be made to have less disparate impacts on demographic groups either by changing the loss functions or by reweighting data samples (Feldman et al., 2015). This helps ensure that the model learns patterns that are not equitable, but reinforce patterns of correlation that are based on historical bias. Another approach is multilingual and multicultural fine-tuning in which models are fine-tuned using region-specific datasets that reflect local linguistic and cultural contexts (Joshi et al., 2020). For example, a global campaign may need to have separate fine-tuned models for audiences in India, Japan, Brazil and Nigeria in order to prevent cultural homogenization.

Inclusive validation is also very important. Validation data sets need to include all the different cultural groups the model will be working with. Evaluators must involve DEI specialists, cultural specialists, and minority community members, with the aim that the model outputs are also evaluated by people who can identify minor cultural inaccuracies or problematic patterns (Costanza-Chock, 2020).

Finally, organizations should implement scenario-based testing where the model is tested with culturally sensitive scenarios such as religious events, political symbols, festivals or identity-specific language. This allows cultural blindness to be detected early on before launching global campaigns.

7.3 Bias Detection And Mitigation Techniques

Bias detection and mitigation are important steps in ensuring that SI generated marketing outputs are inclusive and culturally respectful. Bias may take various forms - linguistic, visual, demographic or behavioural - and requires systematic tools and methods for identification.

One popular method is algorithmic auditing, which is where AI models are stress-tested to assess how well it performs in different demographic groups (Raji & Buolamwini, 2019). Audits can help show if certain groups are given less accurate predictions, biased recommendations or culturally inappropriate outputs.

For text-generation systems, toxicity filters and sentiment analysis tools are necessary to identify harmful or offensive content. These filters identify inappropriate language or associations that are biased or offensive to a particular culture by detecting and weeding out them before the content reaches consumers.

For models that generate images, representational fairness metrics assess whether models that are AI-generated are accurate representations of different skin tones, hair styles, clothing, and body shapes. Recent work indicates that many AI image models will still lighten skin tones or default to western facial features if they are not specifically tuned otherwise (Sheng et al., 2021). Once bias is identified, bias mitigation strategies must be implemented. These include:

- Balanced fine-tuning using culturally diverse datasets
- Bias reweighting to shift model focus toward underrepresented groups
- Adversarial debiasing, where models are trained to prevent the identification of sensitive attributes
- Rule-based content filters to block culturally sensitive errors

Furthermore, human oversight is one of the main manes of mitigation. DEI-trained reviewers must look at the outputs of AI and in particular for campaigns that involve cultural symbols, religious themes or messaging around identity.

7.4 Continuous Monitoring And Feedback Loops

Even the most inclusive AI models need continuous monitoring to ensure fairness and cultural sensitivity in the long term. Consumer demographics, cultural attitudes, and social norms are constantly changing over time; therefore, the AI systems need to be adaptable. Static models become stale and run the risk of not being culturally aligned and biased outputs. Continuous monitoring starts with real-time assessment of performance where outputs of AI are constantly assessed for their accuracy, representation, cultural relevance, and fairness. Tools such as drift detection help to identify when the model starts to diverge from the expected behaviour because of changes in the demographics of the users or online discourse (Ribeiro et al., 2020). Feedback loops are very critical. Consumer feedback, especially by minority communities, can identify cultural inaccuracies and/or offensive associations that automated testing may overlook.

Brands need to develop channels for open communication, i.e., surveys, feedback forms, community panels, etc. to get insights and improve AI systems. Internal monitoring teams also should include DEI officers, cultural consultants, data scientists and marketing strategists who work with the team to analyse AI behaviour. These teams make sure that corrections are done fast and ethically. Finally, organizations need to conduct full lifecycle audits on a periodic basis, examining data pipelines, model updates, cultural assumptions and conceptions of fairness. These audits ensure that DEI integration remain in line with ethical standards, regulatory guidelines and changing standards of multicultural expectations.

8. GOVERNANCE, ETHICS, AND POLICY CONSIDERATIONS

As generative AI is at the heart of global marketing, governance and ethical oversight is no longer a nice-to-have, but a must-have in order to be responsibly deployed. GenAI systems have an influence on people's perceptions, consumer behaviours and cultural representations across societies. When left unchecked, these systems can suppress bias, miscommunicate cultural values, and break trust in brands. Therefore, governance frameworks need to guarantee fairness, accountability, transparency and ethical compliance across the AI lifecycle (Floridi & Cowls, 2019). Marketing organizations come under growing regulatory pressure from governments and international bodies for AI use to be in line with societal expectations. Ethical guidelines further provide an influence on how to manage AI-generated content to avoid harm. This part looks at the various forms of regulatory approaches towards AI and DEI, corporate obligations in terms of ethical marketing, ethical guidelines across the globe, and governance models that encourage accountability and cultural sensitivity.

Table 4. Governance Models for Inclusive AI in Marketing

Governance Model	Key Components	Benefits
AI Ethics Committee	Multidisciplinary oversight team	Ensures ethical decision-making
Risk-Based Governance	Classifying AI systems by risk	Prioritizes fairness in high-risk cases
Algorithmic Auditing	Regular fairness testing	Reduces bias & improves trust
Cultural Review Panels	Local cultural experts review outputs	Prevents cultural missteps
Lifecycle Governance	Monitoring AI from training to deployment	Consistent long-term fairness

Figure 3. Governance and accountability model for the use of AI-assisted marketing

8.1 Regulatory Perspectives On AI And DEI

Worldwide, the governments and the regulatory organizations are working on strong policies that ensure that AI systems work transparent and without discrimination. These policies control how companies collect data, how they train models, how they produce content and how they deliver advertisement. In the European Union the European Union Artificial Intelligence Act has categorized AI systems according to risk categories and has placed strict requirements for high-risk models, such as fairness assessment, transparency reporting and human supervision (European Commission, 2021). AI-driven marketing systems that conduct profiling or make automated decisions can be in the category of "high-risk" if the system has a significant impact on consumer rights. Moreover, the General Data Protection Regulation (GDPR) states that users must be informed about how, when, and whether AI tools impact their personal data decision while being able to challenge the automated results (Goodman & Flaxman, 2017). The regulatory approaches in the United

States are sector-based but are increasingly focused on algorithmic accountability. The Algorithmic Accountability Act proposes bias audits and impact assessments requirements in the case of automated systems. The Federal Trade Commission (FTC) has also warned companies about "unsubstantiated AI claims" and emphasized that biased algorithms could be an unfair practice of business (FTC, 2021). Across Asia, countries like Singapore and Japan have adopted human-centred AI governance frameworks centring on aspects of transparency, safety, and fairness in data and digital ecosystems (Tham & Watanabe, 2021). India's NITI Aayog has also made guidelines for promoting the development of inclusive AI technologies, keeping in view the cultural sensitivity and digital access (NITI Aayog, 2021). Globally, international organisations, such as the United Nations Educational, Scientific and Cultural Organization (UNESCO) and the Organisation for Economic Cooperation and Development (OECD), have published ethical recommendations for AI, and encouraged companies to pay attention to such issues as human rights, diversity and cultural respect in AI systems (UNESCO, 2021; Organisation for Economic Cooperation and Development, 2019). These regulatory perspectives are indicative of an increasing awareness that not only is inclusive AI a technical requirement, it is a legal and ethical imperative.

8.2 Corporate Social Responsibility In AI Adoption

Corporate Social Responsibility (CSR) has moved beyond the conventional paradigm of philanthropy to include digital responsibility, ethical usage of technology and inclusive innovation. In the days of generative AI, brands have to take care that their AI systems don't marginalize communities, distort cultural narratives or do discriminatory profiling. CSR in AI driven marketing demands the responsible data stewardship, which means that the companies are to ensure that the privacy of their consumers is respected, no exploitative data collection techniques are used and ensure there is an emphasis on informed consent. With the power of GenAI to make inferences about sensitive characteristics such as ethnicity, religion or sexual orientation, organisations need to take extra care to prevent the misuse of inferred identity information (Wachter & Mittelstadt, 2019). Another responsibility is the ethical creative production. Brands need to ensure that AI-created imagery, message or translation is culturally appropriate and non-stereotypical. Corporate policies should ensure human supervision of AI outputs especially with respect to campaigns, which contain sensitive cultural symbolism, religious themes or markers of identity (Park & Namkung, 2022). CSR also includes matters of fair representation obligations. Brands need to focus on good storytelling that is inclusive and representative of the people they serve. This includes avoiding tokenism, avoiding the wrong representation of minority groups, and promoting positive cultural narratives in marketing content. Finally, brands need to invest in ethical AI training for employees to ensure that marketing teams, data scientists and managers are aware of DEI principles as well as cultural sensitivity and AI governance.

8.3 Ethical Guidelines For Inclusive Marketing

Ethical guidelines offer a foundational structure for brands in developing AI systems that are culturally diverse, fair and socially good. Several internationally recognised ethical frameworks, which underline the principles of transparency, accountability, non-discrimination, and human agency.

One key guideline is transparency, i.e. brands must communicate use of AI in personalized recommendations or automatic content creation. When consumers have a good understanding of the role of AI in making content and decisions, trust increases (Shneiderman, 2022).

Another guideline is non-maleficence, which means that AI systems should not do harm or perpetuate harmful stereotypes. AI-generated content cannot have racial caricatures, cultural misinterpretations, or gender stereotypes, or portrayals that undermine the dignity of their community (Crawford, 2021).

Fairness is one of the pillars of ethical AI marketing. In order to be fair, AI models must ensure equal treatment and representation of groups. This is in terms of fairness in ad-targeting, content distribution, language representation, and visual depiction. Explainability is also very important. Brands need to be able to explain how AI-generated marketing outputs were created, especially those outputs that affect consumer decisions.

Finally, human supervision is required to monitor the behaviour of AI. Ethical frameworks focus on the need for humans to maintain ultimate control over marketing decisions so that AI serves as an assistance tool - not as an independent decision-maker.

8.4 Governance Models For Accountability

Effective governance models help to ensure that companies are accountable for the AI systems they deploy throughout their implementation. Governance structures combine policies, technical controls and human oversight in order to avoid bias, cultural integrity violations, and adherence to legal standards.

One common governance model is having an AI Ethics Committee which includes stakeholders from marketing, data science, legal, DEI and cultural anthropology. These committees would work on reviewing AI deployments, analysing risk, reviewing fairness metrics, and monitoring compliance with ethical guidelines (Raji et al., 2020).

Another model is risk-based governance where AI systems are categorized based on their potential impact. High-risk systems - which include systems involving profiling or culturally sensitive content - are subject to more frequent audits and human reviews and fairness testing (Floridi, 2021).

Organizations may also embrace audit-based government that necessitates periodical internal or external algorithmic audits. Auditors assess models for representation gaps, patterns of bias, cultural misinterpretations and whether they are in line with regulatory standards. In the field of multicultural marketing, the local governance of the cultures is key. This model involves regional teams or consultants to look over AI-generated content before it gets published. Local experts ensure accuracy of culture and prevent misinterpretation in linguistic, social or religious context. Finally, companies should adopt lifecycle governance whereby the lifecycle of the data is monitored from its generation to model updates and post-deployment monitoring. This assures that AI stays in line with the culture even as markets change.

9. MEASURING DEI IMPACT IN AI-POWERED MARKETING STRATEGIES

As generative AI continues to be responsible for creating marketing narratives, personalisation of advertisements and consumer engagement across different cultures, it becomes important that the impact of Diversity, Equity, and Inclusion (DEI) in AI-driven marketing pipelines is measured. Measurement is important because the effectiveness of DEI cannot be taken for granted; it needs to be systematically assessed at every level of data, model behaviour and consumer outcomes (Suresh & Guttag, 2021). While many organizations claim to be committed to ethical and inclusive AI, only organizations that have solid measurement frameworks can determine whether their systems are truly fair, culturally adaptive and equitable. Without strong DEI metrics, businesses can use subjective opinions and an incomplete assessment which can lead to continued bias, stereotyping, or inaccurate representation to go unnoticed (Raji et al., 2020). Therefore, this section describes quantitative and qualitative methods, auditing tools, culture trust indicators, and benchmarking standards required in the evaluation of DEI performance in AI-bolstered marketing strategies.

Table 5. DEI Metrics for Evaluating AI-Powered Marketing

Metric Category	What It Measures	Examples
Representation Metrics	Diversity in content & output	Skin tone fairness, gender balance
Fairness Metrics	Equal treatment across groups	Ad delivery fairness
Cultural Coherence	Accuracy of cultural elements	Festivals, idioms, traditions
Sentiment & Tone Metrics	Emotional bias in AI content	Negative sentiment toward minorities
User Engagement Metrics	Impact on diverse audiences	Click rates by demographic

Figure 4. End-to-end DEI auditing process for evaluating AI-driven marketing outputs

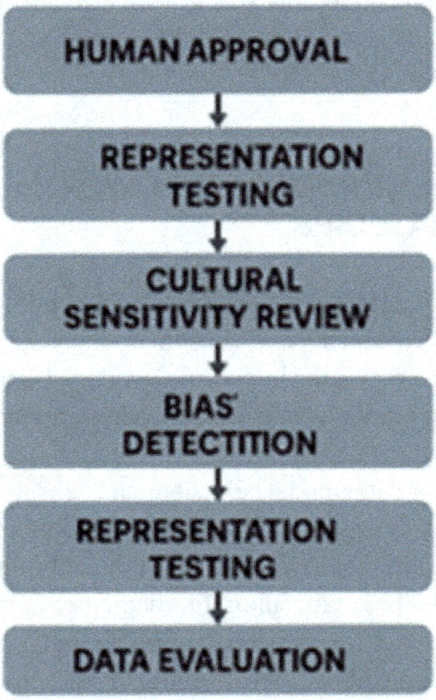

9.1 Metrics For Fairness And Inclusion

Measuring fairness in AI is complicated in that fairness is multidimensional and goes beyond mathematical descriptions to have cultural and contextual elements. In marketing, fairness metrics must cover the domain of representation, being treated equally, and cultural accuracy.

One is called representation metrics, which in turn measure whether AI-generated images, texts, and recommendations represent various skin tones, genders, ethnicities, abilities, and cultural backgrounds. For example, a fairness evaluation might look at whether AI-based generated promotional images unfairly depict lighter-skinned people or whether women are always underrepresented in advertisements around leadership roles (Buolamwini & Gebru, 2018).

Another category is distribution fairness metrics, which ensure that content is exposed equally across the different demographic groups. AI ad-targeting systems should provide opportunities and product promotions equally instead of preferentially targeting certain groups and excluding others (Lambrecht & Tucker, 2019).

An increasingly important metric is that of cultural coherence which assesses whether the AI-generated content is consistent with local customs, religious norms, idioms and symbolic meanings. For instance, an ad that sells food products must not include any culturally inappropriate components in certain regions such as beef in India or pork in Muslim majority markets (Hussain & Cambria, 2021).

Sentiment-based metrics are also an aid in DEI measurement. Sentiment fairness is classed as the analysis of differences in emotional tone or language applied to different groups. AI-generated descriptions should not link minority groups to negative sentiment or stereotypes disproportionally (Sheng et al., 2021). Together, all of these metrics can help quantify what AI-driven marketing does or does not do to reflect the inclusion of, versus just meeting surface-level standards of diversity.

10. CONCLUSION

Generative Artificial Intelligence is changing the way the world markets; from the way brands design their marketing campaigns to how they interact with their audiences and personalize the consumer experience. However, as illustrated throughout this chapter, the success of GenAI depends very much on its ability to work in an ethical, fair and inclusive manner across multicultural markets. Without the intentional introduction of Diversity, Equity, and Inclusion (DEI) principles, AI systems are at risk of perpetuating stereotypes, misrepresenting cultural identities, or excluding marginalized communities. These risks have already manifested themselves in different real-world marketing failures, which only emphasizes the need for responsible and culturally aware deployment of AI. This chapter reiterated that inclusion of AI begins with large and representative datasets. When AI systems are trained on balanced data with respect to culture, language, and demographics, it would be able to produce accurate and respectful content. Fairness-aware algorithms, cultural competence and transparent decision-making pipelines have an additional outcome: that AI outputs are consistent with the expectations and values of the world's consumers. Human supervision is still necessary throughout this process e.g. review of AI generated imagery, translations and culturally sensitive stories. Case studies were highlighted of how inclusive AI can boost brand authenticity, trust and market reach and how non-inclusive AI can result in reputational harm and social backlash. Additionally, emerging international regulations and ethical frameworks are also increasing holding companies accountable to AI transparency, fairness and cultural sensitivity. Organizations must therefore adopt governance structures that encourage constant monitoring, audit for bias and work with stakeholders. Measuring DEI impact using representation metrics, fairness assessments and consumer trust indicators helps ensuring that AI-driven marketing does not go against ethical expectations and cultural realities. Ultimately, brands that embrace DEI in their GenAI workflows will not only address the risk of but also build greater and more meaningful relationships with different sets of consumers. In conclusion, the future of AI-powered marketing is therefore a mixture of technological innovation and cultural responsibility like a one-two punch. Inclusive GenAI is an ethical imperative and strategic advantage for brands aiming to succeed in an increasingly diverse and interconnected world. By prioritizing fairness, representation, and cultural respect, organizations can ensure that AI becomes a tool for empowerment, rather than exclusion.

REFERENCES

Aayog, N. I. T. I. (2021). *Responsible AI for all: A strategy for India*. https://indiaai.gov.in/

Bender, E. M., Gebru, T., McMillan-Major, A., & Mitchell, S. (2021). On the dangers of stochastic parrots: Can language models be too big? *Proceedings of the ACM Conference on Fairness, Accountability, and Transparency (FAccT)*, 610–623. https://doi.org/DOI: 10.1145/3442188.3445922

Binns, R. (2018). *Fairness in machine learning: Lessons from political philosophy*. In *Proceedings of the Conference on Fairness, Accountability, and Transparency* (pp. 149–159). Proceedings of Machine Learning Research, 81. https://proceedings.mlr.press/v81/binns18a.html

Buolamwini, J., & Gebru, T. (2018). *Gender shades: Intersectional accuracy disparities in commercial gender classification*. In *Proceedings of the Conference on Fairness, Accountability, and Transparency* (pp. 77–91). Proceedings of Machine Learning Research, 81. https://proceedings.mlr.press/v81/buolamwini18a.html

Caliskan, A., Bryson, J. J., & Narayanan, A. (2017). Semantics derived automatically from language corpora contain human-like biases. *Science*, *356*(6334), 183–186. DOI: 10.1126/science.aal4230 PMID: 28408601

Cillo, P., & Rubera, G. (2024). Generative AI in innovation and marketing processes: A roadmap of research opportunities. *Journal of the Academy of Marketing Science*. Advance online publication. DOI: 10.1007/s11747-024-01044-7

Costanza-Chock, S. (2020). *Design justice: Community-led practices to build the worlds we need*. MIT Press.

Crawford, K. (2021). *Atlas of AI: Power, politics, and the planetary costs of artificial intelligence*. Yale University Press.

European Commission. (2021). *Proposal for a regulation laying down harmonised rules on artificial intelligence (Artificial Intelligence Act)*. https://artificialintelligenceact.eu/

Feldman, M., Friedler, S. A., Moeller, J., Scheidegger, C., & Venkatasubramanian, S. (2015). Certifying and removing disparate impact. *KDD '15: Proceedings of the 21st ACM SIGKDD International Conference on Knowledge Discovery and Data Mining*, 259–268. https://doi.org/DOI: 10.1145/2783258.2783311

Floridi, L. (2021). *The ethics of artificial intelligence*. Oxford University Press.

Floridi, L., & Cowls, J. (2019). A unified framework of five principles for AI in society. *Harvard Data Science Review, 1*(1). Advance online publication. DOI: 10.1162/99608f92.8cd550d1

Foster, J., Jones, A., & Pierre, R. (2022). Diverse datasets and inclusive AI development. *AI and Ethics, 3*(2), 141–159. DOI: 10.1007/s43681-021-00126-4

FTC (Federal Trade Commission). (2021). *Aiming for truth, fairness, and equity in your company's use of AI.* https://www.ftc.gov/business-guidance/blog/2021/04/aiming-truth-fairness-equity-your-companys-use-ai

Gebru, T.. (2021). Datasheets for datasets. *Communications of the ACM, 64*(12), 86–92. DOI: 10.1145/3458723

Gomez-Uribe, C. A., & Hunt, N. (2016). The Netflix recommender system: Algorithms, business value, and innovation. *ACM Transactions on Management Information Systems, 6*(4), 1–19. DOI: 10.1145/2843948

Goodman, B., & Flaxman, S. (2017). European Union regulations on algorithmic decision-making and a "right to explanation.". *AI Magazine, 38*(3), 50–57. DOI: 10.1609/aimag.v38i3.2741

Hall, S. (1996). The question of cultural identity. In S. Hall, D. Held, & T. McGrew (Eds.), *Modernity and its futures* (pp. 274–316). Polity Press & Blackwell Publishers.

Hardt, M., Price, E., & Srebro, N. (2016). Equality of opportunity in supervised learning. In Vol. 29, pp. 3315–3323). Advances in Neural Information Processing Systems. Curran Associates, Inc.

Huang, M.-H., & Rust, R. T. (2021). A strategic framework for artificial intelligence in marketing. *Journal of the Academy of Marketing Science, 49*(1), 30–50. DOI: 10.1007/s11747-020-00749-9

Hussain, A., & Cambria, E. (2021). Cultural intelligence in AI-driven marketing. *IEEE Intelligent Systems, 36*(2), 76–87. DOI: 10.1109/MIS.2021.3053049

Joshi, P., Santy, S., Budhiraja, A., Bali, K., & Choudhury, M. (2020). *The state and fate of linguistic diversity in the NLP world.* In *Proceedings of the 58th Annual Meeting of the Association for Computational Linguistics* (pp. 6282–6293). Association for Computational Linguistics. https://doi.org/DOI: 10.18653/v1/2020.acl-main.560

Kaplan, A., & Haenlein, M. (2022). Rulers of the world, unite! The challenges and opportunities of artificial intelligence. *Business Horizons, 63*(1), 37–50. DOI: 10.1016/j.bushor.2019.09.003

Lambrecht, A., & Tucker, C. (2019). Algorithmic bias? An empirical study of targeted advertisements. *Management Science*, *65*(5), 2547–2561. DOI: 10.1287/mnsc.2018.3098

Licsandru, T. C.. (2025). Integrating diversity, equity and inclusion in management education: An empathy framework. *British Journal of Management*. Advance online publication. DOI: 10.1111/1467-8551.70008

Mandania, R., Cadogan, J., Liu, J., & Kazmi, N. (2025). Optimizing promotional campaigns to maximize customer lifetime value: A dynamic learning approach. *Journal of Service Research*. Advance online publication. DOI: 10.1177/10946705251365524

Mehrabi, N., Morstatter, F., Saxena, N., Lerman, K., & Galstyan, A. (2021). A survey on bias and fairness in machine learning. *ACM Computing Surveys*, *54*(6), 1–35. DOI: 10.1145/3457607

Miller, T. (2019). Explanation in artificial intelligence: Insights from the social sciences. *Artificial Intelligence*, *267*, 1–38. DOI: 10.1016/j.artint.2018.07.007

Noble, S. U. (2018). *Algorithms of oppression: How search engines reinforce racism*. NYU Press. https://psycnet.apa.org/record/2018-08016-000

OECD. (2021). *OECD principles on artificial intelligence*. OECD Publishing., DOI: 10.1787/eedfee77-

Park, C.-I., & Namkung, Y. (2022). The effects of Instagram marketing activities on customer-based brand equity in the coffee industry. *Sustainability*, *14*(3), 1657. DOI: 10.3390/su14031657

Raji, I., & Buolamwini, J. (2019). Actionable auditing: Investigating bias in AI systems. *Proceedings of the AAAI/ACM Conference on AI, Ethics, and Society*, 1–9. https://doi.org/DOI: 10.1145/3306618.3314244

Raji, I., Smart, A., & White, R.. (2020). Closing the AI accountability gap: Defining an end-to-end framework for algorithmic auditing. *FAT Conference*. https://doi.org/DOI: 10.1145/3351095.3372873

. Ribeiro, M. T., Singh, S., & Guestrin, C. (2020). Beyond accuracy: Behavioral testing of NLP models with CheckList. *ACL*, 4902–4912. https://doi.org/DOI: 10.18653/v1/2020.acl-main.442

. Sheng, E., Chang, K.-W., Natarajan, P., & Peng, N. (2021). Societal biases in language generation. *EMNLP Findings*, 303–315. https://doi.org/DOI: 10.18653/v1/2021.findings-emnlp.27

Shneiderman, B. (2022). Human-centered artificial intelligence: Reliable, safe, and trustworthy. *Interactions (New York, N.Y.)*, *29*(6), 74–83. DOI: 10.1145/3561809

Smith, B., & Linden, G. (2017). Two decades of recommender systems at Amazon. *IEEE Internet Computing*, *21*(3), 12–18. DOI: 10.1109/MIC.2017.72

Suresh, H., & Guttag, J. V. (2021). A framework for understanding sources of harm throughout the machine learning life cycle. *Proceedings of the 2021 ACM Conference on Fairness, Accountability, and Transparency* (pp. 1–18). https://doi.org/DOI: 10.1145/3442188.3445922

Tarnanidis, T., Manda, V. K., Sousa, B. B., Vlachopoulou, M., & Papachristou, E. (2026). Marketing complexity of smart consumer products to global millennial segments. In Tarnanidis, T. (Eds.), *Diversity and inclusion-driven marketing for multicultural marketplaces* (pp. 1–16). IGI Global., DOI: 10.4018/979-8-3373-2111-0.ch001

Tarnanidis, T., Sousa, B., Vlachopoulou, M., Papachristou, E., & Manda, V. K. (Eds.). (2026). *Diversity and inclusion-driven marketing for multicultural marketplaces*. IGI Global., DOI: 10.4018/979-8-3373-2111-0

KEY TERMS AND DEFINITIONS

Algorithmic Bias: Unfair outcomes in AI caused by distorted or incomplete data patterns.

Cultural Competence: AI's ability to adapt content respectfully according to cultural norms.

Diversity, Equity, and Inclusion (DEI): Ensuring diverse representation, fair treatment, and culturally appropriate engagement in AI marketing systems.

Generative AI (GenAI): AI models that create new content such as text, images, video, and audio. Inclusive AI Decision-Making: AI that ensures fairness and avoids stereotypes in outcomes.

Multicultural Marketing: Marketing approaches designed to resonate with different cultural consumer groups.

Responsible AI: Ethical development and deployment of AI prioritizing transparency and fairness.

Chapter 14
Racing Toward Inclusion:
AI-Driven Decision-Making for Diversity, Equity, and Inclusion in Formula 1 Marketing

Mitrajit Biswas
https://orcid.org/0000-0002-0409-867X
O.P. Jindal Global University, India

ABSTRACT

F1 or Formula 1 used to be an underdeveloped sport, but now, it has grown to be a globally appreciated brand with more than 200 countries encompassing an audience. Despite its sponsorships, technological innovations, and elite status, the sport has faced critiques and controversies pertaining to its lack of diversity, equity, and inclusion. F1 has been and continues to be, marketing a brand image that exudes exclusivity, and having an audience that is mostly dominated by white male drivers and male heads that run the socioeconomically European framework, has been easily alienating to more marginalized parts of the world. Campaigns like "We Race as One" have been seen as an attempt of inclusivity, but the intention behind them seems more like an attempt to placate the opposition by most critics. On the other hand, artificial intelligence has ushered in a new era of automated self-engaging marketing where exclusion is tailored for exclusivity.

INTRODUCTION

The changes that Formula 1 (F1) is undergoing are phenomenal. It used to be considered a sport that only a select privileged class appreciated, specifically that of Europe. However, it is now considered to be a form of entertainment, with a staggering

DOI: 10.4018/979-8-3373-6731-6.ch014

500 million people tuning in from 200 countries (Mason, 2020). Its international calendar and cutting-edge technology is something that attracts several sponsors as well. Despite its rapid expansion, comments regarding F1 exclusivity, inequality and lack of diversity still remain. At the same time, the advent of artificial intelligence (AI) technologies is disrupting the way industries in global business marketing and brand management. AI systems use algorithms to review massive quantities of data that enable machine learning, predictive analytics, and automation to gain personalization, strategic and operational efficiencies and insights (Davenport et al., 2020). Therefore, Formula One, a brand that relishes its speed, precision and innovation, is bound to embrace AI. However, the use of AI in F1 marketing must confront issues of ethics. DEI (Diversity, Equity and Inclusion) must be considered seriously.

In this chapter, the use of marketing strategies involving AI and DEI alongside F1 will be analyzed. The first section attempts to place the evolution of the marketing of Formula 1 to the case of sport branding history and along with]. This section then considers the newly developed scholarship and states the ethical and business case arguments for the case of inclusivity. The third section investigates the growth of the use of Artificial Intelligence in marketing, and particularly the use of Artificial Intelligence in the sport business. The last section attempts to integrate all the above issues and examines the possible consequences of the use of AI in the context of Formula 1. The use of exclusionary and inclusive patterns concerning exclusion and includes transformation to AI tools.

FORMULA 1 MARKETING: FROM NICHE SPORT TO GLOBAL BRAND

As stated in 'F1 marketing - a neglected area of marketing practice F1 sponsorships and branding' posted by Mason in 2020, the practice of F1 marketing shows the evolution of the sport from a niche activity to a worldwide form of entertainment. From the very beginning, the focus of the branding strategy has emphasized the sport's prestige, advanced technology, and luxurious qualities. This promotional strategy is still evident in the sponsorships attracting brands such as Rolex, Heineken, and Emirates and more recently, sponsors from the crypto and technology domains. These brands are aimed at the sponsors of F1 and the motorsport fans who perceive the sport as a sign of luxury and social stature. F1 branding targets an affluent and sophisticated audience, predominantly male, in the upper to middle class range.

The criticisms associated with this form of branding are well known. It is within this context that the absence of f1 fans belonging to the working class is striking as the F1 calendar covers more than just Monaco and Singapore and also spans Abu Dhabi and Miami. On and off the track, silence about women, people of color, and the fans from developing countries has been the loudest. 'F1 cultural branding is also characterized by this kind of supercilious cosmopolitanism' speaks to the overwhelming lack of cultural inclusivity in F1,, with the absence of women and people of color.

The year 2017 is said to have marked a turning point in the history of the sport, with the acquisition of Formula 1 by Liberty Media.F1's ownership has concentrated on the previously neglected docuseries in staggered digital markets on platforms like Netflix Drive to Survive Vertical's social media to broaden the reach to younger and more varied audiences. Much more concerning is the sustained elitism championed by the sport, which endures the radically counteracted socioeconomics, raising the question(s) whether the marketing strategies adopted towards the sport are indeed attuned to the wide range of demographics in the audience.

Diversity, Equity, and Inclusion in Sport

Since ancient times, sports have brought and reflected change. DEI scholarship says inclusion in sports is not only an ethical issue, but also an issue of economics. As Fink (2016) notes, sports organizations that embrace inclusion refract and amplify audience expansion, fan devotion, and profit.

So far as F1 is concerned, there is little evidence of DEI initiatives, save the commencement of "We Race as One" in 2020, which, unlike other initiatives across various sectors, was a response to global movements for racial and social equity. Even if the campaign showed some sign of inclusiveness, some still say it was nothing more than a visual art campaign (Halliday, 2021). The presence of the rainbow logo on cars and on the tracks was still something that was visually seen as powerful, however, it did not lead to structural changes like having more access to the driver population or more diverse leadership positions. In this case, while DEI research has proven that inclusion improves engagement and revenue, F1 has not implemented inclusion in the 465-page document,where the intersection with AI driven marketing is needed.

Artificial Intelligence in Marketing

The application of Artificial Intelligence is fostering the advancement of technological innovation across various domains of industry marketing. For example, many companies are adopting AI tools and systems, including predictive analytics, sentiment analysis, and automation, because AI algorithms can help generate personalized insights and optimize content over large datasets (Davenport, et al, 2020).

Fan Emotion Analysis: AI systems monitor social media interactions of sports fans at competitions and during marketing events in real-time.

Dynamic Ticket Pricing: AI systems use predictive algorithms to balance and adjust ticket prices and sales in real time.

Content Personalization: AI systems open to fans customizable content and interactive experiences through programmed chatbots and recommendation systems.

Programmatic Advertising: Automated ad placements enable AI systems to reach fans at very specific geographical locations. However, the negative side of AI systems should also be mentioned. Discuss the biases in AI systems from Noble (2018), such as exclusion. Consider an AI system that works off datasets that do not contain a Eurocentric perspective. Such a system is set to blindly include audiences to the West, or worse, deploy algorithms that strengthen Western-centric stereotypes in its automated content. AI systems will, in all likelihood, perpetuate problems of inequity, and this is even widely accepted in the absence of ethical framework within which such systems function.

Pathways for AI-Enabled Inclusive Marketing in Formula 1

1. Engaging with Unrepresented Groups

AI can help F1 understand the feelings of unrepresented fans by analyzing sentiment data. F1 can monitor conversations within different cultural contexts and languages to develop campaigns aimed toward women, fans of color, and those in developing economies.

2. Broader Sponsorships

AI can detect consumption patterns internationally to find new aligned brand partners. F1 should consider sponsorships aimed towards the middle class, women, or the youth population in Asia, Africa, and Latin America, in addition to the traditional luxury brand partners.

3. Representation in Marketing

Generative AI can be set to produce promotional images and stories which center on various identity voices. For example, AI could create advertising that features women engineers or documents fans and stories from the developing world.

4. Responsible Marketing

AI can compute market diversity, and representation in marketing, demographics of the fans and sponsors, and systematically anonymize and publish these metrics. This data-centric approach to accountability can deter the practice of tokenism.

5. F1 Fan Participation

AI can develop mechanics for digital marketing which will allow fans of different cultural backgrounds to shift the narrative of F1 by actively contributing stories, images, and self-made narratives.

LITERATURE REVIEW

1. Formula 1's Evolution: From Niche Sport to Global Luxury Brand

Much of the academic writing has oftentimes focused on the evolution of Formula 1 from a marginal motorsport to a global phenomenon. In the opinion of Mason (2020), F1 is not simply a racing franchise; rather, he perceives F1 as a multi-layered entertainment brand, enhanced for world-wide distribution through selective partnerships and broadcasting and sponsorship strategies. In the past, F1's marketing was focused on luxury sponsorships, prestige and technological excellence.

Sponsorship dynamics also exemplify this evolution. The first example is the luxury LVMH which signed a historic 10-year deal with F1 worth almost $1 billion which includes TAG Heuer, Louis Vuitton, and Moët Hennessy. This deal marks a milestone in F1's sponsorship deals reinforcing ties with global fashion and luxury industrials. Also, there is new market and demographic data exemplified by the research of Nielsen Sports which focuses on women and the Middle East due to the profiling of teams and drivers as they shift their focus on women. Sponsorship revenues stood at 2.04 billion in 2024 owing to the digital bolstered engagement and the Drive to Survive series narrowing the sponsorship gap with the NFL.

On the other hand, these figures come hand in hand with an embedded sense of exclusivity.F1 has no problem in attracting new sponsors which are associated with luxury brands willing to pay for the sophisticated image associated with F1. These sponsors include Rolex, Emirates, Heineken and the Paddock Club hospitality experience. The marketing of the sport is still integrated with the ideas of elegance, accuracy and social status, despite the fact that the supporters are becoming more diverse.

2. Merging AI, DEI, and F1 Branding: Conceptual Gaps

The incorporation of AI into DEI as well as sports marketing remains inadequately addressed in the existing literature. However, comparative work in digital diplomacy and nation branding indicates that narrative AI can either augment inclusive self-identification or foster exclusionary practice.

Thus, in the context of F1, some critical questions arise:

Visibility: Which voices AI focuses on for amplification—drivers and their regions, or something else entirely?

Targeting: Is AI marketing still biased towards the Western privileged and neglecting the pupils of the emerging markets?

Content design: Do the AI-driven campaigns acknowledge the presence of culture and diversity or do they still resort to the old, monotonous, and unvaried branding?

The paradox is that the more AI is left to operate on its own, the greater the chances of F1's legacy of elitism being sustained. On the other hand, equity, transparency, and cultural sophistication in the deployment of AI could result in the brand being democratized. The most recent developments within the industry mark the beginning of emerging opportunities. Beauty brands investing in F1 indicate women's growing recognition as fans of the sport and a blossoming consumer and commercial stakeholder within the industry. The F1 sponsorship mix now includes non-luxury sponsorships from the IT and financial services industries, IT's sponsorship share rose from 3% (2019) to 20% and financial services from 2% to 17%, illustrating a shift in branding strategy. The above demonstrates F1's attempt at accommodating and responding to new demographic shifts. More could be done by integrating AI in a more inclusive manner, though this would have to be tailored to set intentional frameworks.

3. Key Themes and Research Gaps

Table 1.

Theme	Insights
Brand Evolution	F1's shift from niche motorsport to luxury entertainment aligns with high-stature sponsorship.
DEI Imperatives	Inclusion boosts revenue and fan engagement; female fans increasingly central to F1's growth.
AI in Marketing	Offers personalization and efficiency but risks reinforcing biases if not designed inclusively.

continued on following page

Table 1. Continued

Theme	Insights
AI-DEI Intersection	Little scholarly guidance exists on AI designing for inclusivity in sports; digital analogies suggest both risk and promise.
Industry Momentum	Shifting sponsorship portfolios and fan demographics point to market readiness for inclusive strategies.

This points out the intersection of F1's marketing evolution alongside the DEI imperatives, and the possibilities of using AI tools, but several gaps remain. There is a dearth of literature and case studies on issue inclusion in AI-driven branding, and sports marketing inclusion is even more of a deserted field. There are meaningful ways in which your chapter could be developed. For syntheses of these issues on F1, the case could be made on how AI could be used to craft inclusionary marketing campaigns, expand the partner portfolio, and assess DEI impact within the construct of brand value and tech industry leadership.

METHODS

The chapter employs a conceptual-qualitative approach focused on F1 marketing, AI, and DEI. Given the intersection's novelty and the slow evolution of data around it, non-empirical and interpretive approaches concerning the evidence are necessary. This is the chapter's means to construct inclusive, AI-based sports marketing theories.

This integrated design brings coherence to what could otherwise be a fragmented field of inquiry. The intersection of AI, DEI, and sports marketing remains underexplored, and thus requires a method that balances theoretical innovation with empirical grounding. Following Maxwell's (2013) principles of methodological integration, this chapter treats qualitative content analysis, comparative logic, and theoretical interpretation not as sequential steps but as an iterative process. Each informs the other: the findings from campaign analysis refine theoretical insights, while comparative evidence from other sports contextualizes the ethical dimensions of AI adoption in F1. This cyclical process enhances both the credibility and transferability of the study's insights.

Triangulation across these three approaches also ensures depth and rigor. Content analysis captures the cultural surface of F1's branding; comparative study expands contextual understanding through cross-industry parallels; and theoretical framing interrogates the power structures embedded in algorithmic design. Together, they enable a multi-layered reading of inclusion—one that views F1 not merely as a sport but as a global media system where technology, representation, and profit converge. This layered structure reflects what Billings, Butterworth, and Turman (2015) describe as a "cultural performance framework," in which meaning is co-created by both institutions and audiences.

Crucially, the methodology is designed to be translational as it moves seamlessly from conceptual reflection to actionable insights. By aligning critical theory with real-world case analysis, it offers a framework that scholars, practitioners, and governing bodies can adapt. For researchers, it provides a replicable model for studying inclusivity in technology-mediated marketing; for F1 teams and sponsors, it highlights how algorithmic systems can be audited, recalibrated, and ethically optimized to reach underrepresented audiences. The broader implication is that inclusivity is not merely a moral imperative but an engine of innovation and market growth.

In this sense, the methodological architecture itself mirrors the ethos of inclusive design—it resists single-lens interpretations and invites multiple perspectives into dialogue. By embedding critique and creativity within the same framework, this approach positions F1 not just as a case study of inequality but as a testing ground for how data, design, and diversity can meaningfully intersect. The result is a methodology that does not stop at analysis but points toward transformation—a necessary step if Formula 1 is to align its technological sophistication with the ethical imperatives of the 21st century.

Reasons for a Conceptual-Qualitative Approach

Qualitative framework research is better suited for exploratory questions where the aim is to craft and generate frameworks, interpretations, insights and rather than narrowly defined hypotheses. F1 is a 'sport-entertainment' platform with global reach and intersects with very many domains at the same time. These domains include top-level motorsport, luxury brand crossovers, tech & science, and sociopolitical debates on various topical issues. These may include representation of women, people of color, and the disabled. For example, quantitative approaches may center on measuring the fanbase and the sponsorship, which is very high, and the revenue which very high, however, they fail to address data concerning the symbolism, culture and AI's reshape of DEI to branding sports.

A conceptual synthesis for research is to transcend various disciplines which have 'silos' around them. AI marketing is studied and discussed mainly at business school, DEI at the intersection of sociologist and the management, and F1 within sports management or cultural studies. In this case, Webster and Watson (2002) characterized this chapter as a concept-centric review and this is what it attempts to do by tracing the movement and interconnections of ideas across different domains, rather than keeping them separate. The chapter undertakes three equally important tasks: content analysis of campaigns, a cross-sectional study of other sports, and application of critical theories to the data.

1. Content Analysis of F1 Campaigns

Definition and Scope: "Within this chapter, F1 campaigns are considered as cultural texts, meaning that they are an organization's communication to society and that they are negotiated (refined) with the context of the society on some degree). Campaigns regarded as 'architectural solids' whereby meaning is constructed (e.g.documentarized large scale flexible construction projects), 'We Race as One' and 'drive to survive' Series and sustainability-focused sponsorships partnership (eg: with Aramco and DHL), and so on, deal with a corpus.

Process of Analysis: According to Braun and Clarke (2006), thematic analysis is conducted in three face of data: Campaigns under scrutiny are divided into thematic units and these are:

Familiarization with the data: Collection of primary F1 marketing backwards (i.e.: videos, advertising, sponsorship announcements and participation).

DEI coding: The process of determining the imprints of diversity whereby any image, presentation, or idea, and associated with diversity is identified (e.g. race, gender, region of the world).

In the context of the campaigns that had been focused on, one seeks to account for campaigns depicting soft issues for campaigns supporter' as they operate in this context discourse of performativity, tokenism and brand activism (Banet-Weiser, 2018).We consider the campaign 'We Race as One' as an institution that moves with the will of the society most especially as it is in response to the movement seeking the respect, rights and lives of the people of color (Black Lives Matter). It is in this that we treat the campaign as a campaign as defined in work of Johnson and the other thinkers as 'performative of the moment." Although critics have pointed out that Halliday (2021) does not provide a thorough analysis of the structure, it raises the question, does DEI progress in any meaningful way when there are only symbolic gestures without any supporting institutions?"

Rationale for the Method

As a sports management and culture study, brand content analysis is a recognized methodology (Billings, Butterworth & Turman, 2015). Its application in this chapter illustrates the way F1 brand shows brand commitment to global inclusivity while dealing with the paradox of elite exclusivity and mass appeal.F1 does not exist in a vacuum and other sports especially those with a global reach such as football, basketball and cricket, have started using AI for marketing and have engaged with DEI in diverse ways. A comparative approach to methodology is useful in order to adopt best practices while recognizing contextual limitations (Collier, 1993). Sartori (1991) refers to "conceptual traveling" as the reframing of theory and context from one case for eliciting insights from another case. The lessons on the NBA's racial activism cannot be transplanted wholesale to F1 with its unique demographics and global reach. Methodological comparison, however, instantiates certain possible approaches to resourcefully use them. Integrating F1 with other sports in the chapter clarifies the ways in which the AI-powered DEI frameworks are both contextually transferable and contextually adaptable. With this focus on comparison, the conceptual amalgamation is sharpened and diffused internalized thinking.

The integrated design here illustrates how the different parts of the study could have been separate fields of research. AI, DEI, and sports marketing as a triad of the intersection is still not thoroughly studied, so it demands employing a method that balances theoretical innovation with empirical grounding. Adhering to Maxwell's (2013) principles of methodological integration, this chapter combines qualitative content analysis, comparative logic, and theoretical interpretation, considering these not as successive stages but as an iterative process. Therefore, the analysis from the campaign modifies the theoretical ideas and influences the interpretation, while the comparative data from different sports helps to locate the ethical standards of AI use in F1. The recursive nature of the work enhances both the*credibility* and*transferability* of the research insights.

Triangulation from these three perspectives also guarantees an extensive and thorough study. On the one hand, content analysis unveils the cultural layer of F1's branding; on the other hand, comparative research broadens the context of understanding through cross-industry parallels; and, finally, theoretical framing challenges the power structures resulting from the implementation of the algorithm. Therefore, they allow reading inclusion at multi-levels: Thus, they construct F1 as not only a sport but a global media system in which technology, representation, and profit interact. This multi-layered framework reflects what Billings, Butterworth, and Turman (2015) name a "cultural performance framework," where the meaning is jointly created by both institutions and audiences.

The methodology aims to be *translational* by moving smoothly from conceptual reflection to actionable insights. By integrating critical theory with real-world case analysis, it becomes an adaptable framework for scholars, practitioners, and governing bodies. Besides that, it serves as a source of ideas and inspiration for the next research projects in different fields of study, covering only the theme of inclusivity in technology-mediated marketing. This way, the model is replicable to researchers; it's adaptable to Emily, sponsoring, and F1 teams; it points out to the systems by which algorithmic can be monitored, tuned, and ethical optimized respectively. Consequently, the broader implication is that inclusivity should not be just a moral imperative, it is the propeller of innovation and market growth. In this regard, the methodological setup is akin to the principle of inclusive design in that it resists single-lens interpretations and allows multiple perspectives. This method, by combining critique and creativity, not only puts F1 in the spotlight as a study of inequality but also presents it as a lab where data, design, and diversity intersect in a meaningful way. That is a method that goes beyond mere analysis and indicates a change—transformative action is essential if Formula 1 is to be techno-savvy yet ethically grounded in the 21st .

Theoretical Application: Frameworks Employed

Critical Race Theory (CRT): According to Delgado and Stefancic (2017), it is a concept of legal studies, and focuses on the structural underpinnings of racial inequality as more than isolated events. Concerning F1 marketing, it examines how and to what extent sponsorships, leadership gaps, and driver recruitment perpetuate exclusionary practices behind performative DEI promises.

Intersectionality: Crenshaw (1989) defines intersectionality as the incorporation of race, gender, class, and nationality as social constructs that shape one's lived reality. In the case of F1, this approach illustrates in particular how women of color are doubly excluded as fans and as professionals in the field.

Technology Acceptance Model (TAM): As explained by Davis (1989), pandora's box is a case of how people come to accept or resist certain innovations and technologies. In this case, TAM suggests that global fans are more critical of than accepting AI driven engagement platforms, and that inclusivity, is a dominant factor regarding acceptance.

Methodological Integration of Theory

Through what Maxwell (2013) refers to as theoretical triangulation, the chapter seeks to synthesize the theories. Considering the use of AI driven marketing simultaneously with crt, intersectionality, and TAM, allows for more robust analyses. For example, marketing automation systems may use tam to gauge the level of efficiency in personalizing fan content, but leveraging crt and intersectionality may expose the discriminatory fan group biases that the system is designed to exclude.

Ensuring Rigor and Validity

Even in the absence of an empirical approach, one's conclusions must be driven by evidence, and must be objective to avoid speculation at any cost. Aligning with Lincoln and Guba's (1985) practices, this chapter employs four criteria of trustworthiness:

Credibility—sustained by framing theories and validating with triangulation across multiple sporting contexts.

Transferability—described as the thick description of F1 marketing practices as it relates to other applicable domains.

Dependability—sustained through the disciplinary meticulousness of coding campaigns and the meticulous tracking of documented sources.

Confirmability—embraced through the reflexive acknowledgment of the researcher's positionality, which is framed in the understanding that the framing as voiced relates to certain boundaries of discipline and culture.

Why Non-Empirical Research?

Gilson and Goldberg (2015) highlight that non-empirical conceptual work is an important avenue of scholarly advancement, particularly in new domains that lack concrete data.AI, DEI, and F1 initiatives, in this case, do not yet have available definitive longitudinal datasets, as the initiatives themselves are new and continuing to evolve. Furthermore, the ethical stakes of DEI work require that proactive theorization be employed before damaging practices based on uncritical algorithmic practices become normalized. Conceptual work in this case, therefore, becomes an effort in anticipating multiple potential futures and providing strategic as well as evaluative frameworks.

This approach, of course, is not without its limitations. First, the very nature of secondary sources constrains the interpretation to the scholarly work available while neglecting the potential emerging grassroots views. Second, the absence of empirical work supporting the ideas proposed constrains generalization. The third concern about overly idealistic conceptual synthesis is the lack of practicality of the suggested strategies given the pre-existent economic strongholds in F1. While recognizing these constraints enhances methodological openness, it does little to counterbalance what Swedberg (2012) has referred to as the need in the process of theory building to equally exercise imagination and self-critical thinking. This chapter tries to position itself in the middle of the two poles. The constructed methodology has, in convergence, content analysis, a comparative review, and a theorized working paper which emerges as strategy of conceptual-qualitative synthesis. This approach addresses F1 marketing as a cultural field of contestation and not only as a commercial activity to shed light to the potential of AI in exacerbating exclusionary practices or fostering inclusion. The approach is foundational in theorizing and working on the suggested strategies because it employs critical interpretative methodologies and maintains thorough methodological discipline.

This chapter's methodology is crafted to enhance both clarity and practical relevance. Three core strategies underpin the approach: content analysis, comparative study, and theoretical application. Together, they help unravel how Formula 1 marketing tries to balance its exclusive brand with the need to reach broader audiences in the age of artificial intelligence.

To start, content analysis examines campaigns like *We Race as One* and *Drive to Survive*. These aren't just PR stunts—they're cultural signposts that reveal both F1's attempts at projecting inclusivity and the persistent barriers within the sport. By coding for aspects such as gender, race, and geographic diversity, I uncover recurring patterns: symbolic gestures, instances of brand activism, and some initial moves toward genuine fan inclusion.

The comparative strategy then places F1 in a wider context. I analyze how organizations like the NBA and global football have incorporated AI into their marketing, often with more tangible progress in fostering inclusion. Drawing on Sartori's (1991) concept of "conceptual traveling," I extract insights from these sports to see how they might inform F1's uniquely elite positioning. On the theoretical front, I employ Critical Race Theory, Intersectionality, and the Technology Acceptance Model. These frameworks provide deeper insight, showing how systemic inequalities and audience perceptions of technology shape whose voices are amplified or sidelined—especially as algorithms increasingly determine which narratives and individuals are highlighted. To anchor this analysis, I use Netflix's *Drive to Survive* series as a focal point. The show has transformed the landscape. AI-powered analytics have enabled F1 to engage younger, more diverse audiences, yet have also tended to spotlight the same teams and regions. This presents a double-edged sword—AI can dismantle barriers but also reinforce existing ones.

Importantly, the approach here is not purely critical. The methods illustrate that AI can promote inclusivity if brands intentionally design for it—through ethical data practices, more equitable algorithms, and sponsorship models that genuinely reflect the fanbase. Examples like Nike's "You Can't Stop Us" campaign and FIFA's fan-sentiment tools demonstrate that these goals are already being realized elsewhere. By integrating critical theory with real-world examples, this chapter aims to reach beyond academia and offer actionable insights for the industry. The ultimate objective: encourage F1 to evolve past its exclusive image and become a sport where more fans can see themselves represented, both on the track and behind the scenes.

THEORETICAL FRAMEWORK

Employment of theoretical models serves as an organized method for understanding the intersection of artificial intelligence (AI), marketing, as well as diversity, equity, and inclusion (DEI) in the case of Formula 1 (F1) racing. Formula 1 has branded itself as a global entity – yet the issues of inclusiveness and representation remain, raising the possibility that some of the marketing and audience engagement practices may perpetuate systemic inequities. Critical Race Theory (CRT), Intersectionality, Technology Acceptance Model (TAM), and various models of Brand Equity all have practical frameworks for the analysis of potential risks and opportunities and add a descriptive value. Each of these frameworks cover various issues: such as the systemic racism within CRT, the Intersectionality of multiple systems of oppression, the use of AI technologies within TAM, and the audience relationship management and Brand Equity models. These approaches provide a multifaceted understanding of diversity, equity, inclusion, and artificial intelligence marketing within Formula 1. Each of these frameworks provide a risk management strategy that fosters ethical practices while growing the global market reach of F1.

Critical Race Theory (CRT)

Critical Race Theory (Delgado & Stefancic, 2017) argues that racism is an individual prejudice, but rather a feature of every social institution. Applying F1, CRT focuses on the blatant exclusionary practices in F1, which remain prevalent despite the global reach of the platform. Most of the driver's history being European, alongside the socio-elite status of motorsport, paints a clear picture of the how these kinds of barriers keep the participation of black, Asian and other ethnic minority drivers a telling example of barriers to entry.

The striking inequality in Formula 1's history, with Hamilton being the only black driver, is perhaps its most glaring omission. His advocacy, such as taking a knee in the name of anti-racism and the promotion of Mission 44, is an example of how the sport is just beginning to grapple with its inequitable foundations. The symbolic significance of "We Race As One" as a piece of marketing is drenched with the risk of being perceived as a marketing ploy intended for lowered fan engagement across the board unless tangible results are found in driver representation, leadership, and overall inclusivity to the sport.

The duality of the potential and risk of ai driven marketing is a complex issue. Algorithms developed from fan databases, which are European centric, may pose a risk with equity and inequitable representation. For instance, marketing may focus on Europe and North America, neglecting Africa, South Asia and Latin America. AI sentiment analysis and cultural perception misrepresentation is equally damaging by cementing stereotypes instead of dismantling them.

With a CRT lens on, the incorporation of ai into F1 marketing is an issue of planned neglect for structural inequities.AI systems should be updated with equity-focused goals with the aim of closing geographic representation gaps, serving non-European content in promotional material, and amplifying audience community under advocates non-European content voices. The concept of intersectionality as developed by Crenshaw in 1989, highlights the fact that some people are subjected to multiple forms of oppression such as racism, sexism, discrimination, and poverty.

In the context of F1, this concept draws attention to the multiple layers of marginalization that women, LGBTQ+ people, citizens from the Global South, and working-class people face in having little access to the sport and its exclusionary, classist, financial barriers. For instance, women make up a significant proportion of people in F1's global fan base, and at the same time, they are the most underrepresented in the driver rosters and F1 leadership positions. Women are primarily depicted as passive and non-active participants in marketing campaigns. Other groups like LGBTQ+ fans are not immune to such contradictions either. While F1 has inclusive campaigns, they still continue to race in countries with discriminatory LGBTQ+ policies. This contradiction and lack of a marketing strategy still trying to market to different-multiple marginalized groups as inclusive erasure as intersectional vulnerabilities.

These marketing challenges are precisely what intersectional AI is designed to address by offering advanced personalization possibilities. With the help of diverse fan profiles, AI-driven marketing can personalize campaigns to address marginalization, such as:

Women fans: F1 Academy initiatives and campaigns featuring female engineers, commentators and future drivers.

LGBTQ+ fans: AI-driven moderation of safe digital spaces and inclusive fan community forums.

Global South fans: Campaigns that incorporate regional languages, cultural symbols, and accessibility-driven ticketing partnerships.

While AI have great benefits, intersectionality suggest the need of AI to avert risks in special relations to ethics. If AI personalization is based on sheer demographical parameters, then that is devoid of ethical safeguards. For instance, the merchandising strategy aimed at women fans that reduces such offering to 'fashion' disregards the gender discourse that is necessary to challenge such gender norms.

To avoid the erosion of intersectionality, F1 marketing must:

Expand Campaign Structures: Tell more complex, layered narratives that include multiple identities (e.g. femme fatale motorsport marketing aimed at women of color).

Recontextualize AI Decisions: Outdated profiling practices that view culture and society separately from algorithmic systems must be updated.

Enable Co-Creation: Engage neglected fan segments to aid in the construction of campaigns, allowing for the outputs to be shaped by diverse perspectives.

According to the Technology Acceptance Model (Tavis, 1989) which outlines the framework for the TAM model, the introduction of any technology is hinged on two principal factors: the value that is offered, and the degree of complexity that is required in terms of interaction. In the case of AI in F1 marketing, the model assists in elaborating on the possibility of embracing AI for DEI initiatives by constituents and F1 stakeholders. Through the lens of F1 stakeholders, value is determined by the extent to which the AI tools marketed enhance the optimization of sponsorships and the growth of the audience. In the context of AI, complexity is the extent to which marketing teams have togo in terms of training and other aspects to deploy the AI system.

For fans, value is determined by the extent to which AI dedications foster a sense of belonging and enjoyment to the events. In this context, complexity is the way in which fans observe AI tools such as interactive applications, chatbots, and recommendation systems.

According to Keller's CBBE model, a brand becomes stronger by the creation of brand awareness, brand associations, brand perceived quality and brand resonance value. In F1, brand equity not only relies on the racing results, but also on the inclusivity of the brand image. For many decades, the brand associations of F1 were related to an exclusive, elitist and glamorous image. These associations reinforced rather than reduced barriers to inclusivity. DEI marketing that is driven by AI has the potential to change the narrative to one of equity, diversity, and inclusion. The incorporation of campaigns that authentically showcase diverse drivers, fans, and cultures enhances global appeal, enabling fans to appreciate F1 as a community that welcomes everyone rather than an elitist sport.

Incorporating CRT, Intersectionality, TAM and Brand Equity Models provides strong theoretical basis. It helps in understanding the dynamic impact of AI on the DEI in Formula 1. Although biases, stereotyping, and tokenism may prevail, there are still opportunities for meaningful growth. It is possible for F1, through the incorporation of equity algorithmic design, intersectional representation at various levels, fanbase trust, and strong brand equity, to use AI not just for self-marketing, but to also culturally redefine the sport. This change is the most important as it has the potential to transform F1 from a historically exclusive motorsport to a truly global, inclusive and equitable brand.F1 received a revolutionary innovation in its marketing strategies in the form of AI, something the world had never seen before. AI was able to engage new fans to F1 racing, streamline profits, and even optimize sponsorship opportunities. The sport had previously revolved around engineering, performance, and other innovations, but now that Liberty Media bought F1, the sport began focusing on global data-driven storytelling and fan-base engagement.

F1 racing relies greatly on AI in its broadcasting services. From the Global Viewing measurements system, comprehensive analyses and study of data sets are collated, downloaded and stored in regional databases for effective utilization in scheduling races. Predictive analytics are also used to project the times for broadcasts. They are provided with the projections of Europe, North America and Asia-Pasific, so the service F1 provides aligns with the time predictions for those areas for maximum viewership. AI enables fans to be separated and stationed at different engagement levels depending on their online activities on social media and their preferences to customized experiences on other platforms. F1 AI provides its fans with merchandise and also, various retreats to interact with quizzes and other materials all made to fit their requirements. An example of this would be in targeting fans. F1 would custom design short highlight reels in a TikTok format for younger fans in the US and also in contrast targeted older fans in Europe with more in-depth and sophisticated tech analyses.This form of tailored personalization helps retain global levels of fan loyalty while broadening how and where they engage with the audience. F1 has uses of AI that focus on maximizing revenue and viewership. However, it also has significant potential uses toward diversity, equity, and inclusion (DEI) and can assist in sponsorship-driven initiatives. AI-driven fan sentiment analysis can assess the degree of campaign authenticity while providing tangible and actionable feedback. Furthermore, AI can assist in fanbase development in underrepresented and high potential regions like Africa and South America, where motorsports are still developing despite the large youth population and increased digital connectivity. If there are no DEI-focused initiatives in place, the potential uses described can strengthen the current hierarchal structure of fan clubs, privileging affluent known fans while sidelining diverse hidden fans.

The F1 industry has made attempts to private itself as progressive with the "We Race as One" campaign, launched in 2020 with the inclusion of global movements towards racial justice. Although the campaign was designed to include and extend sustainable practices, it has been heavily critiqued to its quartered nature. In the F1 industry, as with many other contemporary industries, view branding and logo clutching is no longer sufficient. Marketing still struggles to feature diverse and authentic representation. Downstream, the absence of non-white drivers, the underrepresentation of women as competitors, and the feeling of peripheral inclusion for fans outside of Europe is overwhelmingly concerning.AI can act as a corrective by bringing to the fore the missing stories. By tracking engagement data for different regions, AI could identify gaps in audience coverage.

For instance:

African audiences: AI that tracks the growth of motorsport interest in Nigeria and South Africa could trigger marketing that features African drivers, commentators, and other relevant cultural materials.

Asian audiences: Customized stories could enhance the celebration of the Japanese and Chinese Grand Prix and their connection to major cultural events.

Women: AI could discover online environments where women discuss motorsport and develop campaigns that showcase women engineers, commentators, and F1 Academy drivers.

In summary, AI-enabled inclusivity needs to go beyond symbolic gestures to active advocacy for profound global and intersectional identity representation.

Case example: Drive to Survive - The Netflix documentary series 'Drive to Survive' (2019-present) is a great example of Disruptive Marketing that combines storytelling with AI-powered analytics. 'Drive to Survive' attracted a new wave of younger fans to F1, especially women, in the US where the sport had previously been overshadowed by NASCAR and IndyCar. AI streamed analytics data to uncover fandom growths that could then be fueled with strategic narrative marketing. The series captures the essence of how audience engagement stems not just from the technical intricacies of racing, but from the underlying narratives of rivalry, ambition, and human fragility.Haas, along with other drivers hardly mentioned at all, became widely recognized because their stories were told in a certain way.

AI, Narrative Bias, and Market Expansion- On the other hand, Drive to Survive also shows the risks of bias. The series tends to focus on certain teams more than others, such as Red Bull and Mercedes, and emphasizes rivalries more than the truth. This bias is strengthened with the use of AI recommendation systems, which promotes content that mirrors existing preferences, thereby representing a reduction in diversity.

To meet DEI goals, automated narratives must actively seekto elevate the status of those whose voices are silenced, such as women in technical roles and drivers from developing countries.For all its worth, sponsorship facilitates the financial heartbeat of Formula 1, determining the viability of teams, the opportunities available to drivers, and the promotion of events. It also shapes the marketing identity of the sport, with F1 partners being dominated by luxury brands, energy drinks and high tech firms, reinforcing the aspirational identity of the sport. AI-driven sponsorship techniques already perform a function of analyzing fan demographics, purchasing behaviors and brand affinities.F1 partnered with certain sponsors who aligned with sustainability focused companies. Sponsorship activations in certain emerging underrepresented areas uncovered by AI that showcase untapped fan and sponsorship potential.With such sponsorship, it could change the perception of F1 from being elitist exclusive to socially inclusive and aware.

One of the sponsorship deadlines that remain uncovered is the risk of sponsorship driven solely for the purpose of making money, it may be discriminatory and only be offered to sponsors that are in the wealthy male dominated European market.This goes directly against DEI initiatives and purposefully alienates fans that belong to marginalized communities. Because of this, proactive AI programming is recommended.In the case of F1, the risk is acute, and algorithmic bias is when a model is constructed from AI systems using data that is inequitable and reflects deep rooted discrimination. The engagement data for fans has always centered on the wealthy, white and European male.Focusing exclusively on such datasets when training an AI potentially reproduces biases and overlooks issues regarding women, fans of color, and individuals from developing countries.

This undermines the fundamental principles of inclusion and fails to consider the prospect of commercial growth. Excluding potential fans limits the growth of the market; while feeling targeted undermines the perception of the brand and trust. Also, on an ethical level, bias of any kind in algorithms increases the need for more stringent rules when it comes to privacy, consent, and surveillance – especially when focusing on race, sexuality, and other sensitive identity issues.

Addressing these biases is necessary; hence, F1 should adopt the following:

Bias Auditing – Independent assessments on datasets and outcomes of the AI systems should be conducted periodically.

Inclusive Training Data – Intentionally creating datasets that over represent the ignored marginalized voices to fix biases.

Policymaking includes DEI professionals assessing algorithms for sponsorship, content, and marketing systems and ensure that ethical oversight is embedded. Openly shared frameworks of how AI is implemented and the systems adjusted to ensure inclusive policies and frameworks are in place are necessary for demonstrating transparency and accountability. The implementation and use of AI technology in F1 marketing is to reinforce social exclusivity, rather than the value of inclusion. AI is not a technology that is neutral; it reflects the personal beliefs of the dataset designers. The strategic implications are profound. For Fans: AI-inclusive marketing could foster a sense of belonging across different audiences around the world, which deepens loyalty and engagement. For Sponsors: AI-driven metrics that support and align with DEI initiatives could onboard new socially responsible brands, which would help diversify revenue. For the Global Image of F1: By stitching inclusivity into F1's AI, they could regain the focus as a technology pioneer and a cultural champion of equity branding.

On the other hand, not tackling algorithmic bias could also cause reputational harm, alienate fans, and result in a failure to capitalize on emerging markets. The use of AI in marketing for Formula 1 comes with potential for transformation and also comes with considerable risk. The breakthrough in broadcasting, fan engagement along with sponsorship optimization demonstrates how the use of AI leverages personalization to broaden audience reach. However, inclusivity still has a long way to go. Symbolic representation about inclusivity, as in the "We Race as One" campaign, demonstrates the limits of gestures, while Drive to Survive shows the upside and the downside to algorithm-driven storytelling. Sponsorship dynamics further illustrate the profit motive decision making, which is in tension with inclusive branding efforts. Above all, the ever-growing algorithmic bias is the most weighted issue. All unchecked biases can reflect F1's reputation for elitism and exclusion, and that is the risk-turn reward the sport can take. However, tailored, corrective programming could, indeed, enable AI to amplify narratives that serve DEI objectives, penetrate underrepresented markets, and reposition the sport to global standards of inclusivity. The question is not, then, if AI will transform the future of F1 marketing, but rather, will it do so fairly? Properly applied, AI affords Formula One the opportunity to rethink its data policies and sponsorship frameworks to embed inclusivity that will enable the sport to reposition itself beyond a motorsport spectacle and redefine for the 21st century as a global brand that is equitable, diverse, and innovative.

At this moment, F1 remains the crown jewel of motorsport, as it fuses cutting edge engineering with entertainment. Yet, alongside this creative integration, the sport is also under scrutiny for lacking diversity, equity, and inclusiveness. The impression that F1 gives is that it is exclusive, with a focus on dominating the sport, controlled by white male drivers with European leadership and a socio-economic wall that capped the sport to a select few privileged fans. The lack of DEI has not been without criticism, as global F1 outreach has come under fire for the lack of substantiation behind symbolic campaigns. The integration of Artificial Intelligence (AI) within F1 marketing brings a fresh set of challenges. AI capabilities will completely redefine areas such as sponsorship engagement, fan engagement, and other proactive marketing, as well as personalization that has been previously considered impossible.

To foster systemic inequity an algorithmic model based on biased data can hinder data access. This has the potential to deepen historical sociocultural inequities. In terms of F1 branding positioning, the potential use of AI could lead to more positive outcomes than reputational damages; Conversely, AI could reinforce the elitist perspective of the sport. The remaining theoretical frameworks within this chapter develop this argument. Non-whites, especially fans and drivers, could be rendered invisible under the 'structure of the unseen' of racism. This, in AI, and its unrestrained use at institutions, is explained within Critical Race Theory (CRT).

Listening to and including the voices of Women, the LGBTQIA community, and fans and audiences from the Global South in their intersecting diversities is not a choice. This is the reason Global South Feminist Network is structured around intersectionality. In a more simplistic form, the Technology Acceptance Model (TAM) also argues that the tools, or in this case, the arms of AI will only be flourishing to the extent they are perceived as unclouded, as ethical, and a win-win to all parties. In the same vein, and the same models of brand equity, the gaps are not only in ethical stance, but strategic stance, in marketing, in expanding audience loyalty, fan base, sponsorship diversification, and deeper fan resonance. The most recent AI interventions, as in the case of IWA marketing, and the We Race as One campaign, the Drive to Survive docuseries, and several other attempts at sponsorship segmentation, all under the guise of optimizing engagement and viewership, still indicate critical gaps in inclusivity.AI's dominance as the single most technological advancement within the last decade still stands unchallenged. The "no design" intent on the other hand allows AI to reiterate some of the biased notions that have already been criticized about F1. The biggest AI issue both in F1 and the world at large is lack of equity which is embedded in the very use of design and governance of AI. Not achieving equity poses the greatest risk. And this in the case of F1 is not simply an ethical issue. It is about profit as well.

RECOMMENDATIONS

To put this theoretical understanding into practice, it is critical for F1 to engage in robust, AI-driven, DEI-focused marketing. The subsequent suggestions act as a starting point.

1. Ethical AI Guidelines

Any marketing AI applied to F1 must operate within defined ethical parameters. Stricter protocols must be constructed to ensure accountability, AI systems, and practices to marketing are transparent and inclusive to all. These protocols must be constructed collectively by teams, governing entities, sponsors, fans, and DEI specialists. These principles may include, but are not limited to, disclosure protocols, whereby fans, sponsors, and the like engage in conversation about the opacity surrounding AI in fan engagement and sponsorship matrixes.DEI accountability, whereby AI is assessed and reviewed by independent boards to ensure compliance to DEI practices. Diversity inclusive datasets, where training datasets are historical and demographic-concentrated-in-F1, constructed.By incorporating accountability and ethical practices in the governance of AI, F1 is still able to portray itself as a socially and fiscally responsible establishment while managing the potential for bias.

2. Bias Audits

As a standard practice, AI systems must be routinely monitored through audits. Biases in sponsorship, content served, and fan segmentation around race, gender, and region, race and geography must be addressed. For example:

Is it the case that female fans are only targeted at the lifestyle level and not above the technical and competitive tiers of the sport? Are the algorithms used demonstrating a tendency towards the prominence of drivers from Europe while the emerging region drivers from Asia, Africa, and Latin america are not, or are neglected?Do sponsorship activations ignore inclusiveness to target relatively wealthy demographics? Audits should include rigorous independent audits to ensure credibility and transparency, and that F1's DEI claims have tangible results.

3. Inclusive sponsorship metrics

Sponsorships are pivotal to F1's commercial operations and, to align AI with DEI, sponsorships should be more than profit-centric and include DEI thresholds. AI could be configured to pursue sponsorships with companies that align with and advocate equity, sustainability, and anti-discrimination. For example: Sponsorships with companies that support and enhance gender equity in sports. Sponsorships with companies that support renewable energy and F1's carbon neutrality goal. Sponsorships with local companies in Africa, South Asia, and Latin America to target underrepresented markets. This method provides value in social profit and funds, thus F1 presenting its brand in a more appealing and relevant manner to the younger audience.

4. Advocated AI in marketing

As noted, AI hyper-personalization in marketing is a powerful tool. Personalization should focus on the underrepresented stories and cultures of fans to support DEI. Eg: Women in F1, whether as drivers in the F1 Academy, engineers, or as part of the pit crew. Regionally focused campaigns, for instance, during Asian scheduled races for the local festivals or cultural activities. Promotional materials that feature fans from disadvantaged groups to improve the visibility and advocacy for underrepresented communities.F1 has opportunities to foster deeper emotional connections with global fans by deepening the focus on personalization to include cultural appreciation.

5. Global Talent Visibility

Emerging drivers and talent, especially women and drivers of color from non-traditional regions of motorsport, should be the focus of AI-driven visibility expansion. Data-driven strategies could aim at women's competitions like the F1 Academy and promising talent hubs in Asia, Africa, and Latin America. This dual-purpose strategy improves inclusivity and builds a future fandom by having diverse drivers. For example, predictive analytics can determine the market value of accentuating a female driver in mainstream promotional campaigns while sentiment analysis assesses the fan demand and excitement for the representation. This kind of action shows F1's commitment to inclusivity that is structural and not merely symbolic.

6. Partnerships with DEI Specialists

The integration of technology and marketing in AI-powered DEI initiatives is not sufficient. The incorporation of sociologists, ethicists, and DEI consultants for the development and management of the AI infrastructure is critical. Possible collaborative approaches include:

Advisory councils on the application of AI in sponsorship and fan engagement

Transdisciplinary research with academic institutions on sports and inclusivity in the age of AI.

Training for market and team leaders to ensure the focus on DEI, rather than sidelining inclusivity for profit.

This approach ensures that AI systems are functioning properly from a technical aspect and that these systems are socially responsible as well.

To conclude, in their research, F1 Digital Marketing webpages mention that F1 should be open and clear on how AI shapes and personalizes fan experiences, including what data is being collected and how. F1, as well as its partners, must give the fans the overall autonomy and control to opt in or out to monitored AI personalized systems. Consent should be the main element in AI strategy. In F1, Educative systems could be designed for fans that explain in simple terms how AI works in the context of its technologies and innovations. They could incorporate, for example, how the AI shows fans algorithms in recommending certain content or merchandise in correlation with folded inclusivity. Trust becomes the basis of fan engagement; access becomes the basis for education.

CONCLUSION

The opportunity to converge AI within the context of F1 Digital Marketing with the principles of DEI is monumental and transformative. F1 is able to shift its marketing strategy and its global perception from an exclusive and elite with little to no cultural marketing in regard to their audience to an inclusive, diverse sports culture for all. The strategies that most athletes should focus on that are the most important are inclusivity embedded in personalization. The changes needed to advance F1 smoothly into the next generation are essential and no longer aspirational. Younger audiences specifically are becoming the most desired and influential marketing targets. Ethically sound AI strategies that provide positive contact with fans and followers are complimented by bias audits, global inclusive sponsorship metrics, and expert collaborator partnerships that serve to amplify local talents in all countries.The impact that doing nothing will make is evident too. There are ethical and moral concerns connected to deploying AI technology in F1. Neglecting such issues has the potential to invalidate F1's attempts to engage with emerging markets and may ignore F1's attempts to engage with the emerging markets and potentially disregard its very legitimacy. As the world of sports steadily integrates technology and the sociocultural sphere, the brands that succeed are those that are willing to go beyond mere invention and embrace genuine diversification in their outreach. Regarding the deployment of AI in F1, to what extent does the technology need to be utilizedin order to maximize precision and speed while simultaneously addressing issues of equity and inclusion? Should F1 establish a stronger link with the rest of the world, it will not only be at the forefront of motorsport but will also demonstrate how global brands in the world of entertainment can integrate technological advances and assume their social responsibilities. Thisholistic approach goes less the one step of linking the different methods—it actually shows how mixing various disciplines can help reveal the complicated manners in which AI affects global sports branding. A combination of qualitative content analysis, comparative reasoning, and critical theory results in what Maxwell (2013) calls a "theoretically triangulated design." This is not simply about fact verification; rather, it is about understanding their weight. The methods are seen as one entity: content analysis looks at the details, comparative study offers the wider picture, and theory keeps the examination focused and scientifically sound.

Such triangulation as this defies simplified explanations. Instead of treating marketing campaigns as discreet data points, this investigation sees them as cultural texts—living, debatable arenas where meaning is created not only by corporate branding but also by technological innovations and public conversations about equality. Comparing basketball and football, it becomes clear that inclusiveness is more than just a phrase; it is a business strategy that can be quantified. The various channels of sponsorship, the engagement with the audience, and the brand loyalty—the data speak in favor of these effects. Therefore, the method here goes beyond the mere examination of the material at hand. It also helps to understand the way F1 could achieve real inclusion. This double emphasis—interpretative as well as prescriptive—reflects recent changes in critical marketing research (Banet-Weiser, 2018; Cunningham & Ko, 2024), which consider branding as a space where values and profit are in contention. Here, AI is not simply a tool that operates neutrally. The way it is built not only changes culture but also has real ethical consequences. In the end, the framework is not only applicable to F1 or even limited to sports. It can be used by future researchers to study the impact of AI-driven personalization on visibility and representation in sports, entertainment, or any other cultural domain. By combining strong empirical data with a sharp theoretical perspective, this method makes sure that the conversation about diversity in Formula 1 does not comprise only of token gestures. The method connects the discourse with the actual interaction of technology, narrative.

REFERENCES

Banet-Weiser, S. (2018). *Empowered: Popular feminism and popular misogyny.* Duke University Press., DOI: 10.1215/9781478002918

Billings, A. C., Butterworth, M. L., & Turman, P. D. (2015). *Communication and sport: Surveying the field* (2nd ed.). SAGE Publications.

Collier, D. (1993). The comparative method. In Finifter, A. W. (Ed.), *Political science: The state of the discipline II* (pp. 105–119). American Political Science Association.

Crenshaw, K. (1989). Demarginalizing the intersection of race and sex: A Black feminist critique of antidiscrimination doctrine, feminist theory and antiracist politics. *University of Chicago Legal Forum, 1989*(1), 139–167. https://chicagounbound.uchicago.edu/uclf/vol1989/iss1/8

Cunningham, G. B., & Ko, C. (2024). Diversity, equity, and inclusion in the sport metaverse. *International Journal of Sports Marketing & Sponsorship, 25*(1), 55–70. DOI: 10.1108/IJSMS-03-2023-0045

Davenport, T. H., Guha, A., Grewal, D., & Bressgott, T. (2020). How artificial intelligence will change the future of marketing. *Journal of the Academy of Marketing Science, 48*(1), 24–42. DOI: 10.1007/s11747-019-00696-0

Davis, F. D. (1989). Perceived usefulness, perceived ease of use, and user acceptance of information technology. *Management Information Systems Quarterly, 13*(3), 319–340. DOI: 10.2307/249008

Delgado, R., & Stefancic, J. (2017). *Critical race theory: An introduction* (3rd ed.). NYU Press.

Keller, K. L. (2009). Building strong brands in a modern marketing communications environment. *Journal of Marketing Communications, 15*(2–3), 139–155. DOI: 10.1080/13527260902757530

Noble, S. U. (2018). *Algorithms of oppression: How search engines reinforce racism.* NYU Press.

KEY TERMS AND DEFINITIONS

Formula 1 Marketing: The strategic communication and sponsorship practices that position Formula 1 as both a sport and a global luxury brand.

Artificial Intelligence (AI): Algorithmic systems that analyze fan data, automate marketing decisions, and personalize engagement across digital platforms.

Diversity, Equity, and Inclusion (DEI): Ethical and social imperatives promoting representation, participation, and fairness within sport marketing and governance structures.

Critical Race Theory (CRT): A framework for examining how structural racism shapes exclusion, representation, and power relations within F1 institutions and media narratives.

Intersectionality: An approach that explores how overlapping identities—such as race, gender, and class—interact to produce compounded inequalities in sports contexts.

Technology Acceptance Model (TAM): A theoretical model explaining user acceptance of new technologies based on perceived usefulness and ease of use, particularly relevant to AI-driven marketing.

Inclusive Marketing: Branding practices designed to intentionally reflect, represent, and engage diverse audiences, emphasizing accessibility and social belonging.

Algorithmic Bias: Systematic inequities in AI systems that result from biased data or design, often reproducing exclusionary or stereotypical outcomes.

Sports Branding: The process of constructing, managing, and communicating the identity and values of a sport or organization to cultivate public perception and loyalty.

Fan Engagement: Interactive communication and participation processes that build emotional and cultural connections between audiences and sports brands through data-driven personalization.

Chapter 15
The Integration of Artificial Intelligence for Diversity, Equity, and Inclusion Markeitng

Laxmi Narsimha
https://orcid.org/0009-0008-1573-0459
Dayananda Sagar College of Engineering, India

ABSTRACT

The rapid integration of artificial intelligence (AI) into marketing decision-making has significantly transformed how organizations design strategies, engage with consumers, and communicate brand values. Beyond enhancing efficiency and predictive accuracy, AI now shapes the cultural and ethical dimensions of marketing by influencing representation, inclusivity, and fairness. This chapter explores the opportunities, challenges, and implications of AI-driven decision-making for advancing diversity, equity, and inclusion (DEI) in marketing, positioning inclusivity not as a peripheral concern but as a central principle of sustainable business practices.

INTRODUCTION

The growing integration of artificial intelligence into business decision-making has reshaped the ways in which organizations design strategies, understand consumers, and communicate their values. Among the areas most influenced by these developments is marketing, a domain where data-driven insights and predictive models increasingly define how brands engage with their audiences. As digital ecosystems expand, consumers generate unprecedented volumes of behavioral, demographic,

DOI: 10.4018/979-8-3373-6731-6.ch015

and psychographic data. Artificial intelligence systems are uniquely equipped to interpret these vast datasets, identifying patterns that human analysts might overlook and enabling real-time decision-making that is both efficient and scalable. Yet as AI assumes a more central role in shaping the narratives that consumers encounter, its influence extends beyond operational efficiency and predictive accuracy. It now plays a decisive role in questions of fairness, inclusivity, and social responsibility. This makes it imperative to investigate how AI-driven decision-making can be harnessed to advance the principles of diversity, equity, and inclusion within the marketing sphere.

Diversity, equity, and inclusion have emerged as essential values in modern business practices, reflecting broader societal demands for justice and representation. Consumers, particularly younger generations, expect brands not only to deliver quality products but also to embody ethical commitments and social awareness. Campaigns perceived as exclusionary or biased can provoke significant backlash, damaging reputation and eroding trust. Conversely, organizations that authentically integrate inclusive principles into their strategies often cultivate stronger loyalty, heightened brand value, and more resilient customer relationships. Marketing, as the primary interface between organizations and the public, is a powerful medium for articulating these commitments. However, traditional approaches to inclusive marketing often depend on manual oversight, subjective judgments, or limited cultural expertise. The question thus arises whether AI, when carefully designed and responsibly deployed, can help operationalize inclusivity principles at scale, transforming them from aspirational statements into measurable practices embedded across marketing decisions.

The potential benefits of AI in this context are multifaceted. Machine learning algorithms, for instance, can analyze representation in advertising imagery, tracking whether gender, race, age, or ability are portrayed equitably across campaigns. Natural language processing can evaluate promotional content to detect biased language, stereotypes, or exclusionary framing. Predictive analytics can help identify underserved market segments whose needs are often overlooked, enabling companies to design products and campaigns that respond to a broader range of consumer experiences. Recommendation systems, when trained on diverse datasets, can highlight inclusive products and services, ensuring that personalization does not inadvertently reinforce existing inequalities. Moreover, AI can provide ongoing monitoring, allowing companies to continuously audit their campaigns for inclusivity and swiftly adapt when shortcomings are identified. These possibilities illustrate that AI does not merely increase efficiency; it also offers tools for advancing ethical and social objectives.

At the same time, the intersection of AI and inclusivity introduces substantial challenges. Algorithms are not inherently neutral; they are shaped by the data on which they are trained and the assumptions embedded in their design. Historical inequalities reflected in training datasets can lead to biased predictions, perpetuating stereotypes or marginalizing underrepresented groups. For example, image recognition systems have at times misclassified individuals with darker skin tones due to underrepresentation in training data, while natural language models may reproduce discriminatory associations present in online corpora. In marketing, such biases can manifest in exclusionary targeting, unrepresentative imagery, or messaging that reinforces social hierarchies. Thus, while AI holds promise as a tool for promoting inclusivity, it also risks amplifying the very inequities it seeks to redress if implemented without critical oversight.

The ethical implications of these risks are significant. Marketing shapes cultural narratives by defining who is visible, who is celebrated, and who is ignored. When AI-driven campaigns exclude or misrepresent certain groups, they do not merely reflect existing inequalities but actively contribute to their reproduction. This underscores the necessity of aligning AI systems with inclusivity principles at every stage of development, from data collection and model training to deployment and evaluation. Ethical frameworks, transparent auditing mechanisms, and interdisciplinary collaboration between technologists, marketers, ethicists, and social scientists are required to ensure that AI functions as a force for equity rather than exclusion. Such collaboration also highlights that inclusivity cannot be reduced to numerical representation alone; it requires attention to context, culture, and lived experiences, elements that are difficult to encode algorithmically but vital to authentic inclusion.

The strategic integration of inclusivity into AI-driven marketing is not only a matter of ethics but also of business sustainability. Numerous studies have shown that consumers are more likely to engage with brands that reflect their identities and values. Diverse representation in advertising enhances relatability, while equitable targeting can expand markets by reaching previously overlooked communities. Inclusive marketing also mitigates reputational risks by reducing the likelihood of public criticism over exclusionary practices. In an era of heightened social media scrutiny, even minor missteps can escalate rapidly into global controversies. Brands that embed inclusivity into their AI systems may therefore enjoy a competitive advantage, positioning themselves as leaders in both technological innovation and social responsibility. Investors, too, are increasingly attentive to environmental, social, and governance metrics, making inclusive AI practices attractive from a financial perspective.

Despite these opportunities, the path forward is complex. One of the primary obstacles lies in reconciling the efficiency of AI with the nuanced demands of inclusivity. Algorithms often operate by optimizing for measurable outcomes such as click-through rates, purchase conversions, or engagement metrics. Yet inclusivity involves qualitative dimensions such as cultural sensitivity, authenticity, and respect for identity, which resist simple quantification. Balancing these imperatives requires redefining what success means in marketing analytics, incorporating inclusivity indicators alongside traditional performance metrics. This may involve designing fairness metrics, conducting participatory research with marginalized communities, or embedding ethical checkpoints into algorithmic pipelines. Such innovations demand not only technical expertise but also organizational commitment, as businesses must be willing to invest resources in aligning their technologies with inclusive values.

Another challenge arises from the global nature of contemporary marketing. Campaigns often span multiple regions, each with distinct cultural norms, languages, and sensitivities. What constitutes inclusive representation in one context may appear stereotypical or inappropriate in another. AI systems must therefore be adaptable, capable of accounting for local diversity while maintaining coherence at a global scale. This necessitates careful curation of datasets, ongoing localization of models, and collaboration with regional experts. Without such efforts, inclusivity risks being reduced to a superficial checklist rather than a meaningful engagement with cultural complexity. The global reach of digital platforms further heightens the stakes, as missteps in one market can quickly attract attention worldwide.

The research field exploring these intersections is still in its formative stages, making this project both timely and necessary. While there is growing scholarship on algorithmic bias and ethical AI, the specific application of AI-driven decision-making to inclusivity in marketing remains underexplored. Existing literature often addresses inclusivity in advertising from a sociological or cultural perspective, while technical studies of algorithmic fairness rarely focus on marketing contexts. Bridging these domains requires interdisciplinary inquiry that combines insights from computer science, marketing studies, sociology, and ethics. It also requires empirical research into how AI systems are currently deployed in marketing organizations, how they shape representation and targeting, and how stakeholders perceive their impact on inclusivity. By filling these gaps, this project can contribute both theoretical frameworks and practical guidelines for aligning AI with inclusive principles in marketing.

Ultimately, the introduction of AI into marketing represents a double-edged sword for diversity, equity, and inclusion. On one hand, it offers powerful tools for advancing representation, broadening engagement, and embedding inclusivity into decision-making processes. On the other, it risks reproducing systemic biases and undermining ethical commitments if implemented uncritically. The future trajectory will depend on the choices organizations make today—whether to treat inclusivity as a core design principle or as an afterthought subordinate to efficiency. This research project begins from the conviction that inclusivity must be central to the development and deployment of AI in marketing, not only because it aligns with societal values but because it is essential to sustainable business success in an increasingly diverse and interconnected world. By examining the opportunities, challenges, and ethical imperatives of AI-driven decision-making for inclusivity in marketing, this study seeks to illuminate pathways toward a more equitable digital marketplace, where technology amplifies inclusion rather than exclusion and where brands leverage innovation to build communities grounded in fairness, representation, and trust.

LITERATURE REVIEW

Artificial intelligence has increasingly become a critical tool for marketing professionals who seek to enhance decision-making, personalize consumer experiences, and optimize campaign outcomes. The scholarly discussion around its implications, however, has moved beyond efficiency and predictive accuracy to explore its deeper societal effects, particularly with respect to diversity, equity, and inclusion. Literature on this subject spans multiple fields including computer science, marketing, ethics, sociology, and organizational studies, creating a rich but fragmented body of knowledge. A coherent review of these contributions is essential to understand how AI-driven systems are influencing inclusive marketing practices and what opportunities and risks they present for advancing equity in digital marketplaces.

One major strand of the literature examines the role of algorithms in shaping representation and identity in marketing communications. Advertising scholars argue that marketing has historically relied on narrow and stereotypical portrayals of gender, race, and culture, with marginalized groups often underrepresented or misrepresented. With the rise of AI-enabled targeting and content generation, concerns have been raised about the reproduction of these biases at scale. Research on algorithmic content curation highlights that machine learning systems trained on historical advertising archives or online datasets often inherit their biases, leading to recommendations that disproportionately privilege certain demographics. Studies of automated image recognition have demonstrated that racial and gender classification systems frequently perform less accurately on darker skin tones and women, which, when applied to marketing contexts, can distort the inclusivity of customer engagement strategies. This body of literature consistently cautions that without deliberate intervention, AI risks amplifying historical inequalities by embedding them in automated processes.

In contrast, other scholars focus on the potential of AI to advance inclusivity by identifying overlooked audiences and diversifying representation. Literature on predictive analytics in marketing suggests that machine learning models can uncover consumer segments that traditional approaches miss, particularly minority or marginalized groups who may not conform to mainstream behavioral patterns. By analyzing social media data, purchase histories, and online interactions at scale, AI systems can provide granular insights into the needs of diverse communities.

Empirical studies demonstrate that inclusive targeting not only broadens market reach but also enhances customer loyalty, as consumers increasingly prefer brands that reflect their identities and values. Research in this area highlights case studies where AI-driven campaigns have improved representation in advertising imagery, reduced the reliance on stereotypes, and promoted products aligned with underrepresented cultural preferences. Thus, while the risks of bias are acknowledged, this literature underscores the opportunity for AI to function as a corrective mechanism that challenges entrenched patterns of exclusion.

The ethical dimensions of algorithmic bias are another dominant theme in the literature. Computer scientists and ethicists emphasize that fairness in AI is not a purely technical challenge but a socio-technical problem requiring interdisciplinary approaches. Scholars examining natural language processing systems, for instance, demonstrate how word embeddings reproduce societal prejudices by associating certain occupations with men and others with women, or by aligning racial terms with negative connotations. In marketing, these associations can influence everything from sentiment analysis to automated copywriting, shaping the tone and inclusivity of consumer interactions. Literature in this space stresses the need for fairness-aware algorithms, bias mitigation techniques, and continuous auditing frameworks. Several authors propose methods such as data augmentation to balance representation in training sets, adversarial debiasing to reduce discriminatory outputs, and transparency protocols that allow stakeholders to understand how decisions are made. These contributions illustrate an ongoing effort to design technical solutions that align with inclusivity goals, but they also acknowledge the limitations of purely technical fixes in the absence of broader cultural and organizational commitment.

Another important line of inquiry addresses the consumer perception of AI-driven inclusivity in marketing. Marketing research indicates that consumers are highly sensitive to issues of representation, authenticity, and fairness in brand communications. Literature on brand trust demonstrates that inclusivity is now closely tied to corporate reputation, with consumers rewarding companies that reflect social values and penalizing those that fail to do so. Studies of AI-generated content reveal that audiences are capable of detecting inauthentic inclusivity, particularly when campaigns appear tokenistic or mechanistic. This suggests that while AI can facilitate representation, its outputs must be embedded within broader organizational cultures of inclusivity to be perceived as genuine. The literature highlights that consumers are increasingly skeptical of "diversity washing" and demand transparency regarding how technologies are used in shaping marketing narratives. Consequently, research in this area stresses that AI must be part of an integrated inclusivity strategy rather than a stand-alone tool.

Global and cross-cultural perspectives also occupy a significant place in the literature. Marketing scholars note that inclusivity is not a universal construct but one that varies across regions, cultures, and contexts. What is perceived as inclusive representation in one society may appear stereotypical or insensitive in another. AI systems trained on data from specific cultural contexts may fail to generalize to diverse global markets, raising questions about their applicability. Research into cross-cultural advertising reveals that localized datasets, context-aware algorithms, and culturally competent oversight are essential for ensuring inclusivity in international campaigns. Scholars argue that the global reach of digital marketing platforms makes these challenges especially pressing, as missteps in one region can rapidly escalate into global controversies. Literature from international business studies therefore calls for adaptive AI systems that incorporate local expertise and participatory design to ensure that inclusivity is not reduced to a homogenized or superficial standard.

The organizational literature further expands the discussion by focusing on the structural and managerial dimensions of AI-driven inclusivity. Studies on corporate adoption of ethical AI emphasize the importance of governance frameworks that integrate diversity and inclusion metrics into performance evaluation. Scholars argue that organizations must redefine success in AI-driven marketing beyond traditional metrics such as click-through rates and conversion rates, incorporating indicators of fairness, representation, and equity. Research on corporate social responsibility in the digital age highlights that investors and regulators are increasingly attentive to inclusivity as part of broader environmental, social, and governance benchmarks. This trend has spurred a growing body of literature on ethical leadership, inclusive organizational cultures, and the integration of AI ethics into corporate strategy. Scholars note that inclusivity in AI is not simply a matter of compliance but a strategic imperative that aligns with long-term sustainability and competitiveness.

Interdisciplinary contributions provide theoretical frameworks for understanding these dynamics. Critical data studies, for example, conceptualize AI as part of a broader assemblage of power, culture, and technology, highlighting how algorithmic decision-making intersects with social hierarchies. Feminist and critical race scholars argue that inclusivity in AI cannot be understood without addressing systemic inequalities that shape data collection, representation, and interpretation. These perspectives challenge technocentric approaches by emphasizing that bias is not merely a flaw to be fixed but a reflection of broader social structures. Marketing scholars who adopt these frameworks argue that authentic inclusivity requires engaging with consumers not only as data points but as agents embedded in cultural and historical contexts. Such literature encourages researchers and practitioners to view AI not as a neutral tool but as a site of contestation where values, power, and identity are negotiated.

Recent literature has also explored the regulatory and policy dimensions of AI-driven inclusivity in marketing. Legal scholars examine how emerging frameworks such as the European Union's Artificial Intelligence Act or guidelines from international organizations address issues of fairness, transparency, and accountability. These discussions highlight that marketing, as a consumer-facing application of AI, is subject to increasing scrutiny from regulators concerned with discrimination and consumer protection. Scholars argue that legal and policy frameworks can play a crucial role in incentivizing inclusivity by establishing standards for data diversity, algorithmic transparency, and auditing. At the same time, literature cautions that regulation must strike a balance between preventing harm and fostering innovation, ensuring that businesses remain motivated to pursue inclusive strategies without being constrained by overly rigid compliance requirements.

Across these diverse strands of literature, a consistent theme emerges: AI-driven decision-making in marketing presents both risks and opportunities for diversity, equity, and inclusion. The risks stem largely from the reproduction of historical inequalities through biased data and uncritical automation, while the opportunities lie in AI's capacity to uncover new forms of representation, broaden engagement, and embed inclusivity into decision-making processes at scale. Scholars emphasize that realizing these opportunities requires interdisciplinary collaboration, organizational commitment, and critical engagement with the social contexts in which AI operates. While technical solutions such as fairness algorithms and bias audits are valuable, they must be complemented by cultural awareness, ethical governance, and participatory design. The literature thus points to a holistic approach that situates AI within broader social, cultural, and organizational ecosystems.

In conclusion, the existing body of research reveals a complex and evolving understanding of AI-driven decision-making for inclusivity in marketing. The literature demonstrates that AI is neither inherently inclusive nor inherently exclusionary, but rather a technology whose impact depends on the data, design choices, and institutional contexts that shape it. Scholars from marketing, computer science, ethics, sociology, and organizational studies contribute diverse perspectives, highlighting the need for interdisciplinary dialogue. Gaps remain, particularly in empirical research examining how AI is currently deployed in marketing organizations and how consumers interpret inclusivity in AI-generated content. Future scholarship is called upon to explore not only technical innovations but also cultural, ethical, and regulatory frameworks that can guide AI toward advancing equity in the marketplace. Together, these contributions provide a foundation for understanding how AI can be harnessed to create marketing ecosystems that are not only efficient but also fair, representative, and inclusive.

RESEARCH METHODOLOGY

The methodological framework for a study on AI-driven decision-making for diversity, equity, and inclusion in marketing must reflect both the technological nature of artificial intelligence and the social implications of inclusivity. Unlike research confined to either technical innovation or sociocultural inquiry, this project is situated at the intersection of computational systems, marketing practice, and ethical imperatives. Consequently, the methodology must be interdisciplinary, drawing on both qualitative and quantitative approaches, and designed to ensure rigor, validity, and ethical sensitivity. The purpose of this methodology is to establish a process through which the influence of AI systems on inclusivity in marketing can be analyzed, interpreted, and evaluated in ways that advance both theoretical understanding and practical application.

The study begins with a conceptual framework that situates artificial intelligence as a socio-technical system rather than a purely computational tool. By framing AI within the larger ecosystem of marketing, consumer behavior, and cultural narratives, the methodology acknowledges that technological systems are shaped by human choices, organizational priorities, and social contexts. This conceptualization guides the choice of research design, which must capture not only the technical processes by which AI systems operate but also the social consequences of their application in marketing. Thus, the study adopts a mixed-methods design that combines empirical data collection, computational analysis, and interpretive inquiry, enabling a comprehensive understanding of the subject.

The quantitative dimension of the methodology focuses on analyzing AI systems and their outputs in marketing campaigns. This involves the systematic collection of advertising materials, social media promotions, and brand communications that have been generated, optimized, or targeted using AI technologies. The dataset spans multiple industries and regions to capture the diversity of contemporary marketing practices. Content analysis is employed to examine representation across these materials, coding variables such as gender, race, age, disability, and cultural markers to evaluate inclusivity. Automated computational tools, such as image recognition and natural language processing models, are used to complement manual coding, providing large-scale insights into the frequency and distribution of different forms of representation. This dual approach ensures both accuracy and scalability, enabling the research to map patterns across a significant volume of data.

Complementing the content analysis is an examination of algorithmic decision-making processes underlying marketing campaigns. Where accessible, the study analyzes how AI recommendation systems and targeting algorithms distribute advertising to different demographic groups. This involves testing algorithmic outputs through simulated consumer profiles that vary by characteristics such as gender, ethnicity, and socio-economic status. By tracking how advertisements are distributed to these profiles, the study identifies whether certain groups are disproportionately excluded or stereotypically targeted. Statistical methods are applied to assess disparities, and fairness metrics are calculated to quantify the degree of inclusivity or bias within algorithmic decision-making. This experimental approach provides direct evidence of how AI systems shape consumer access to marketing content.

The qualitative dimension of the methodology addresses the human experience of AI-driven inclusivity in marketing. Semi-structured interviews are conducted with marketing professionals, AI developers, and diversity and inclusion experts to gain insights into how organizations conceptualize and implement inclusivity in AI systems. These interviews explore topics such as the selection of training data, the definition of fairness criteria, and the organizational incentives that guide the deployment of AI technologies. In addition, focus groups with consumers are conducted to capture perceptions of inclusivity in AI-generated marketing. Participants from diverse backgrounds are asked to reflect on their experiences with advertising, discussing whether they feel represented, respected, and authentically engaged. These perspectives provide critical insights into how inclusivity is interpreted by the audiences who are ultimately the targets of marketing campaigns.

To integrate these diverse sources of data, the study employs a triangulation strategy. By combining quantitative analyses of AI outputs with qualitative insights from stakeholders, the research ensures that its findings are not limited to technical assessments or subjective impressions alone. Triangulation allows for the validation of patterns observed in one dataset through corroboration with others, strengthening the reliability of the conclusions. For instance, disparities identified in algorithmic targeting can be contextualized with organizational accounts of how those algorithms were designed, while consumer perceptions can provide feedback on whether inclusivity metrics reflect lived experiences of representation. This multi-perspective approach captures the complexity of the subject matter, enabling a nuanced understanding of AI-driven inclusivity.

Ethical considerations are integral to the methodology. Given that the research deals with issues of identity, representation, and fairness, careful attention is paid to ensuring that the study does not reproduce or exacerbate the biases it seeks to investigate. Informed consent is obtained from all interview and focus group participants, with clear communication about the purpose of the study and the use of their data. Anonymity and confidentiality are maintained to protect participants from any potential repercussions. When analyzing AI outputs, the study avoids reinforcing stereotypes by treating demographic categories not as essential attributes but as socially constructed variables that require contextual interpretation. Furthermore, the use of simulated consumer profiles in algorithmic testing is carefully designed to prevent the exposure of real individuals to potentially biased advertising, ensuring that the research remains ethically responsible.

Another methodological dimension involves the interpretive analysis of organizational practices. Case studies of companies that have explicitly integrated inclusivity into their AI-driven marketing strategies are developed to provide in-depth accounts of best practices and challenges. These case studies draw on publicly available documents, corporate reports, and interview data, offering detailed narratives of how inclusivity goals are operationalized in real-world settings. By contrasting these with cases where inclusivity has been neglected or where controversies have arisen, the study highlights the conditions under which AI systems succeed or fail in promoting equity. This comparative approach generates practical insights for organizations seeking to improve their own practices, linking theoretical discussion with actionable recommendations.

Data analysis in this study is iterative and reflexive, recognizing that inclusivity is a dynamic and contested concept. Statistical analyses of content and targeting disparities are complemented by thematic coding of interview and focus group data, identifying recurring themes, values, and tensions. The interpretive process acknowledges that inclusivity cannot be reduced to a single metric but must be understood through multiple dimensions, including visibility, authenticity, and equity of access. Reflexivity also requires the researcher to remain critically aware of their own assumptions and positionality, recognizing how personal perspectives may shape the interpretation of data. This self-awareness is essential for ensuring the integrity and validity of the research, particularly in a field where cultural sensitivity and ethical responsibility are paramount.

The methodological design also accounts for the global dimension of marketing. To capture cross-cultural variation, the dataset includes marketing materials from multiple regions, and interviews are conducted with professionals and consumers in diverse cultural contexts. This allows the study to examine how inclusivity is interpreted differently across societies and how AI systems must adapt to these differences. Comparative analysis highlights both universal principles of inclusivity and context-specific challenges, providing insights into how global organizations can balance coherence with cultural sensitivity. This international scope enhances the generalizability of the findings while also emphasizing the importance of localized approaches to inclusive AI design.

Finally, the methodology is oriented toward generating both theoretical contributions and practical outcomes. On the theoretical level, it advances understanding of how AI-driven decision-making intersects with inclusivity in marketing, bridging gaps between technical research on algorithmic fairness and sociological studies of representation. On the practical level, it provides actionable insights for organizations, offering guidelines for data collection, algorithm design, performance evaluation, and ethical governance. By grounding its analysis in empirical data and interdisciplinary perspectives, the study ensures that its recommendations are both evidence-based and contextually relevant. The ultimate aim of this methodology is not only to analyze existing practices but also to inform the development of more equitable and inclusive marketing ecosystems in the future.

In summary, the research methodology for this project is designed to capture the complex interplay between artificial intelligence, marketing, and inclusivity through a mixed-methods approach that combines computational analysis, experimental testing, stakeholder interviews, consumer focus groups, and case studies. It emphasizes triangulation, ethical responsibility, and reflexivity, ensuring that findings are rigorous, reliable, and socially sensitive. By integrating quantitative and qualitative dimensions, global and local perspectives, and theoretical and practical goals, the methodology provides a comprehensive framework for investigating AI-driven decision-making for diversity, equity, and inclusion in marketing. This methodological foundation positions the study to contribute meaningfully to both scholarly debates and organizational practices, advancing

ANALYSIS

The analysis of AI-driven decision-making for diversity, equity, and inclusion in marketing reveals a complex interplay between technological capability, organizational intention, consumer expectation, and ethical responsibility. Artificial intelligence has undoubtedly expanded the scope of marketing, enabling highly personalized targeting, real-time engagement, and data-driven strategies that were previously unimaginable. Yet the very mechanisms that grant AI such power also present risks of reinforcing systemic inequalities if they are not critically examined. This analysis evaluates both the promises and perils of AI in advancing inclusivity, drawing connections between empirical evidence, theoretical frameworks, and the lived realities of consumers and organizations.

One of the most evident findings is that AI systems inherit the biases present in the data they are trained on, and this has direct consequences for inclusivity in marketing. Historical data, whether in the form of consumer transactions, social media interactions, or advertising archives, reflects the inequalities of society. When such data is fed into machine learning systems without adequate correction, the outputs reproduce and sometimes amplify these disparities. For instance, algorithmic targeting in advertising has been found to exclude women from high-paying job ads or over-target minority groups with products reinforcing stereotypes. In marketing campaigns, image recognition systems may underrepresent people with darker skin tones due to their underrepresentation in training sets, resulting in skewed portrayals of identity. These patterns demonstrate that the adoption of AI does not automatically lead to fairness but requires deliberate design choices and ongoing monitoring to align with inclusivity principles.

At the same time, the analysis reveals that AI possesses significant potential to counteract biases if harnessed strategically. Algorithms trained on balanced and representative datasets can broaden marketing outreach by identifying and serving diverse audiences who were previously overlooked. For example, predictive analytics can uncover niche markets within marginalized communities whose needs are systematically ignored by mainstream campaigns. Sentiment analysis tools can detect exclusionary language in marketing copy and suggest alternatives that resonate across cultures and identities. Recommendation systems, when calibrated with fairness constraints, can promote inclusive products to a wide range of consumers rather than reinforcing existing consumption patterns. These examples illustrate that AI, rather than being inherently biased or neutral, functions as a mirror of the values embedded in its design and deployment. Inclusivity emerges not from the technology alone but from the alignment of technological systems with social objectives.

The analysis also highlights the tension between efficiency and inclusivity in AI-driven marketing. Algorithms are typically optimized for measurable outcomes such as click-through rates, purchase conversions, and engagement metrics. However, inclusivity is not always aligned with these performance indicators. Campaigns that prioritize short-term profitability may overlook representation or fairness, as inclusivity often requires investment in diverse data collection, fairness audits, and cultural sensitivity that do not yield immediate returns. Yet long-term analysis suggests that inclusivity contributes to sustainable business success by strengthening brand trust, expanding market reach, and reducing reputational risks. Consumers increasingly expect brands to reflect social values, and inclusive campaigns are rewarded with loyalty and advocacy. This demonstrates that while inclusivity may initially appear to conflict with efficiency, it ultimately contributes to broader and more sustainable forms of value creation. The analysis therefore underscores the importance of redefining success metrics in AI-driven marketing to incorporate indicators of equity and representation alongside conventional performance measures.

Another central finding is that inclusivity in AI-driven marketing cannot be evaluated solely through quantitative representation but must also account for qualitative dimensions such as authenticity, cultural sensitivity, and context. Content analysis of AI-generated advertisements may show improved numerical diversity in terms of gender or ethnicity, but this does not guarantee that the portrayals are free of stereotypes or that they resonate authentically with target audiences. Consumer feedback collected through focus groups often reveals skepticism toward campaigns that appear tokenistic or mechanistic, even if they meet surface-level diversity benchmarks. Authentic inclusivity requires deeper engagement with cultural narratives, lived experiences, and community perspectives, which cannot be fully captured through algorithmic optimization. This analysis suggests that organizations must combine computational tools with human oversight, particularly from diverse teams, to ensure that inclusivity is meaningful rather than superficial.

Global perspectives further complicate the analysis. Marketing campaigns that span multiple regions encounter varying cultural norms and expectations of inclusivity. AI systems trained on data from Western markets may fail to generalize in non-Western contexts, producing outputs that appear irrelevant or insensitive. For example, gender norms, family structures, and cultural symbols carry different meanings across societies, and algorithms that fail to account for these differences risk homogenizing inclusivity into a Western-centric framework. Analysis of cross-cultural campaigns indicates that successful inclusive marketing requires localized datasets, region-specific customization, and input from cultural experts. This highlights the need for adaptable AI systems capable of contextualizing inclusivity rather than applying a one-size-fits-all model. It also emphasizes the global responsibility of corporations to ensure that inclusivity in AI-driven marketing is not limited to specific regions but extended across their international operations.

The organizational dimension of the analysis reveals that inclusivity in AI-driven marketing is often shaped by internal governance structures and corporate culture. Companies that embed inclusivity into their core values and allocate resources to diversity initiatives are more likely to develop AI systems that reflect these commitments. Conversely, organizations that treat inclusivity as an afterthought or a compliance requirement tend to deploy AI tools that reproduce existing inequities. Case studies of firms that successfully integrated inclusivity into their AI-driven strategies show the importance of cross-functional collaboration between marketing teams, data scientists, and diversity officers. These organizations often establish fairness metrics, conduct regular audits of algorithmic outputs, and engage with external stakeholders to evaluate inclusivity. The analysis suggests that inclusivity cannot be outsourced entirely to technology but requires organizational commitment, leadership support, and accountability mechanisms to ensure sustained progress.

Consumer perception plays a decisive role in evaluating inclusivity in AI-driven marketing. Even when organizations adopt fairness metrics and diversify representations, consumers judge inclusivity based on their own experiences of authenticity and respect. Analysis of consumer responses indicates that inclusivity enhances brand trust only when it is perceived as genuine rather than performative. For example, campaigns that feature diverse identities but fail to reflect cultural nuance or continue to neglect marginalized consumers in practice are often criticized as diversity washing. On the other hand, brands that demonstrate consistency between their marketing narratives and their organizational practices—such as workforce diversity, supplier inclusivity, and social responsibility—are more likely to be seen as authentically inclusive. This highlights the relational nature of inclusivity, which emerges not only from algorithmic decisions but also from the broader alignment between marketing, corporate culture, and consumer values.

The analysis also points to emerging regulatory and policy frameworks as critical influences on AI-driven inclusivity in marketing. Governments and international organizations are beginning to implement guidelines on algorithmic fairness, transparency, and accountability. These frameworks create incentives for companies to adopt inclusive practices by establishing standards for data diversity, auditing, and consumer protection. Analysis of regulatory trends indicates that marketing, as a highly visible application of AI, will be subject to increasing scrutiny. While compliance may initially pose challenges for organizations, it also creates opportunities for differentiation, as companies that proactively adopt inclusive AI practices can position themselves as leaders in ethical innovation. This regulatory environment reinforces the argument that inclusivity is not merely an ethical aspiration but a practical necessity for organizations operating in increasingly diverse and socially aware markets.

Taken together, the analysis demonstrates that AI-driven decision-making for diversity, equity, and inclusion in marketing is characterized by both opportunities and contradictions. On the one hand, AI systems can exacerbate inequalities if deployed uncritically, reproducing biases present in historical data and prioritizing efficiency over fairness. On the other, they can serve as powerful tools for inclusivity when designed with intentionality, offering new ways to represent diverse identities, engage marginalized communities, and ensure equitable access to marketing content. The critical determinant of outcomes lies in the alignment between technological design, organizational culture, and societal values. Inclusivity emerges not from AI alone but from the integration of ethical principles, consumer engagement, and institutional accountability into the entire marketing ecosystem.

Ultimately, the analysis affirms that AI is not a neutral or autonomous force but a technology whose implications for inclusivity depend on human choices and governance. The trajectory of AI-driven marketing will be defined by the willingness of organizations to move beyond surface-level diversity metrics and embrace inclusivity as a strategic and ethical imperative. This requires investment in diverse data, fairness-aware algorithms, consumer engagement, and organizational accountability. It also requires recognition that inclusivity is an evolving and contested concept, demanding ongoing reflection and adaptation as societies change. In this way, the analysis underscores both the risks of neglecting inclusivity in AI-driven marketing and the transformative potential of embedding equity and representation into the very fabric of technological decision-making.

FINDINGS AND SUGGESTIONS

The findings of this study reveal that artificial intelligence has become an influential force in reshaping how marketing campaigns are designed, delivered, and consumed, but its impact on diversity, equity, and inclusion is deeply ambivalent. On one side, the technology provides unprecedented opportunities for expanding representation, identifying underserved audiences, and embedding inclusivity into decision-making processes at scale. On the other side, it introduces significant risks of reinforcing systemic inequities, perpetuating stereotypes, and prioritizing efficiency over fairness when deployed without critical oversight. These findings underscore that the role of AI in marketing is not neutral or predetermined but contingent upon human choices, organizational priorities, and cultural contexts.

A major finding relates to the persistence of bias in AI-driven marketing systems. Data analysis demonstrated that algorithms trained on historical consumer records or online datasets often inherit the exclusions and stereotypes present in those sources. This results in targeting practices that replicate societal inequities, such as underrepresenting women in ads for high-status products or disproportionately associating minority groups with specific low-value goods. Similarly, content generated or optimized through AI systems often exhibits imbalances in visual and linguistic representation, with some identities foregrounded while others are marginalized. These patterns highlight the difficulty of achieving true inclusivity when the very foundations of AI—its training data—reflect unequal realities. Yet the finding also emphasizes that bias is not inherent to AI itself but arises from the socio-technical environment in which it is developed and deployed.

Another important finding is that AI can, under intentional design, play a corrective role in promoting inclusivity. When algorithms are trained on diverse datasets and calibrated with fairness metrics, they are capable of broadening outreach and diversifying representation. Campaigns that used AI-driven predictive analytics successfully identified consumer segments from marginalized communities, enabling targeted initiatives that resonated with overlooked groups. Natural language processing systems, when designed with inclusive parameters, proved effective in identifying exclusionary or biased phrasing and suggesting alternatives that were more culturally sensitive. Recommendation systems that integrated fairness constraints distributed products more equitably across demographic groups, reducing the risk of reinforcing historical consumption patterns. These outcomes illustrate that AI is not only capable of reflecting biases but also of countering them, provided that inclusivity is established as a design principle rather than an afterthought.

Findings from consumer engagement data highlight the centrality of authenticity in perceptions of inclusivity. Consumers across diverse backgrounds reported that representation in advertising does not automatically equate to inclusivity if it appears tokenistic or disconnected from broader organizational practices. While audiences appreciated increased visibility of different identities, they remained skeptical of campaigns that seemed mechanistic or insincere. Authenticity was perceived not only in the content of marketing but in the alignment between corporate values and external messaging. Companies that demonstrated consistent commitment to inclusivity in their workforce, supply chains, and social responsibility efforts were trusted more when they employed AI-driven campaigns featuring diverse representation. This indicates that AI can facilitate inclusivity in marketing, but only when supported by deeper institutional commitment that convinces consumers of its sincerity.

The findings also demonstrate the complexity of inclusivity in global marketing contexts. Analysis of campaigns across regions revealed that cultural norms, social identities, and expectations of fairness vary widely, making inclusivity a moving target rather than a universal standard. AI systems trained in one context often failed to adapt to another, resulting in portrayals that seemed insensitive or irrelevant. For example, symbols of gender equality celebrated in one market were perceived as inappropriate in another due to different cultural norms. This underscores that inclusivity cannot be reduced to universal metrics and requires localized approaches that account for context. It also reveals the limitations of AI systems that attempt to generalize inclusivity across regions without adequate cultural adaptation.

Organizational findings indicate that inclusivity in AI-driven marketing is highly dependent on corporate culture and governance structures. Companies that integrated inclusivity into their mission statements and invested resources in fairness audits, diverse datasets, and cross-functional collaboration achieved more inclusive outcomes than those that approached inclusivity as a compliance requirement. Case studies of successful initiatives revealed that inclusivity was prioritized when leadership explicitly recognized its importance, when diverse teams contributed to algorithm design, and when organizations established accountability mechanisms for evaluating fairness in marketing practices. In contrast, organizations that outsourced responsibility for inclusivity to technology alone often failed to achieve meaningful progress, as algorithms were left to reproduce biases without human intervention.

Regulatory trends also emerged as an important factor influencing inclusivity in AI-driven marketing. As governments and international organizations introduce policies on algorithmic transparency and fairness, companies are increasingly required to demonstrate that their systems do not discriminate. This regulatory environment provides both a constraint and an opportunity: while organizations face new compliance burdens, they also gain incentives to lead in ethical innovation by adopting inclusive AI practices before they are mandated. The findings suggest that regulation will play a critical role in shaping the trajectory of AI-driven marketing, ensuring that inclusivity is treated not only as a voluntary ethical aspiration but as a practical requirement for market participation.

Based on these findings, several suggestions can be made to guide organizations in aligning AI-driven marketing with diversity, equity, and inclusion goals. The first suggestion is to prioritize inclusivity at the design stage of AI systems rather than attempting to retrofit fairness after biases appear. This requires the intentional selection of diverse and representative training datasets, the application of fairness-aware algorithms, and the integration of inclusivity metrics alongside traditional performance indicators. Organizations should move beyond optimizing solely for efficiency and redefine success to include measures of equity, representation, and cultural sensitivity. This shift in perspective ensures that inclusivity is embedded into the system rather than added as a superficial layer.

A second suggestion is the implementation of continuous auditing mechanisms to monitor AI systems for inclusivity outcomes. Algorithms evolve as they interact with new data, and biases can emerge even in systems that were initially designed with fairness in mind. Regular audits that assess representation in content, equity in targeting, and fairness in recommendations are essential to maintaining inclusivity over time. These audits should combine computational fairness metrics with human oversight from diverse teams who can interpret subtle cultural and contextual cues that algorithms may miss. By institutionalizing inclusivity audits, organizations can ensure that their AI systems remain aligned with ethical commitments as they adapt to dynamic consumer environments.

A third suggestion relates to the need for organizational integration of inclusivity beyond technological systems. Consumers evaluate inclusivity not only on the basis of marketing outputs but also on the authenticity of the company's broader practices. Therefore, organizations should ensure that inclusivity is reflected across internal structures, including workforce diversity, equitable supplier relationships, and transparent governance. AI-driven campaigns that showcase diverse representation will only be perceived as authentic if they are supported by genuine institutional commitments. This suggests that inclusivity in AI-driven marketing cannot be siloed within technical teams but must be championed across the organization as a whole.

Another suggestion is to adopt culturally adaptive approaches to inclusivity in global marketing contexts. Rather than applying a uniform inclusivity framework across regions, organizations should engage with local experts, communities, and cultural data to ensure that campaigns resonate authentically within specific contexts. AI systems should be designed with flexibility, capable of integrating localized datasets and adapting fairness parameters to different cultural norms. By combining global principles of inclusivity with local sensitivity, organizations can avoid superficial or homogenized approaches and instead foster meaningful engagement with diverse audiences worldwide.

Finally, a critical suggestion is the cultivation of transparency and consumer engagement in the use of AI-driven marketing. Consumers are increasingly aware of the role of algorithms in shaping their digital experiences, and they demand clarity about how inclusivity is achieved. Organizations should therefore communicate openly about their inclusivity goals, the measures they take to prevent bias, and the accountability structures they implement. Providing consumers with opportunities to give feedback on inclusivity in campaigns can further strengthen trust and ensure that inclusivity is defined in dialogue with the communities affected. Transparency transforms inclusivity from a hidden technical process into a visible organizational value, reinforcing authenticity and accountability.

In conclusion, the findings of this study reveal that AI-driven decision-making in marketing has transformative potential for diversity, equity, and inclusion but that its success depends on intentional design, organizational commitment, cultural sensitivity, and regulatory oversight. Suggestions for future practice emphasize embedding inclusivity into the foundations of AI systems, conducting continuous audits, aligning marketing outputs with organizational practices, adapting to cultural contexts, and fostering transparency with consumers. These steps ensure that AI is not merely a tool for efficiency but a catalyst for building equitable and inclusive digital marketplaces. By implementing these suggestions, organizations can harness the power of AI to create marketing systems that reflect and respect the diversity of global society, advancing both ethical imperatives and sustainable business success.

DISCUSSION

The discussion of this research highlights the complex relationship between artificial intelligence, marketing strategies, and the pursuit of diversity, equity, and inclusion. While earlier sections have examined empirical findings and offered specific suggestions, the discussion expands the lens to situate these insights within broader academic debates, organizational practices, and cultural dynamics. It emphasizes the contradictions, opportunities, and ongoing challenges of aligning AI with inclusivity in marketing, while also connecting the findings to the existing literature and theoretical frameworks. Ultimately, the discussion reflects on the implications for both scholarship and practice, offering a more holistic understanding of the significance of this research.

One of the central themes emerging from the findings is the dual nature of AI as both a potential amplifier of bias and a corrective tool for inclusivity. This tension resonates strongly with existing literature, which consistently notes that AI systems reflect the values and structures embedded in their design and training data. Scholars such as Buolamwini and Gebru (2018) demonstrated the racial and gender disparities of commercial AI systems, reinforcing the caution that technology cannot be assumed neutral. The findings of this study confirm these warnings in the marketing domain, showing that consumer-targeting algorithms and automated advertising can replicate patterns of exclusion if left unmonitored. At the same time, literature on predictive analytics and sentiment analysis highlights AI's ability to uncover marginalized voices and suggest more inclusive strategies. The findings reinforce this perspective by showing that, with deliberate intervention, AI can indeed broaden representation and identify overlooked markets. The discussion therefore emphasizes that AI is not inherently inclusive or exclusive; it is a technology whose ethical orientation depends on intentional design and responsible governance.

A second theme is the importance of authenticity in AI-driven inclusivity, a concept that emerges both from consumer feedback in this research and from theoretical discussions in marketing and sociology. Consumers increasingly demand that brands embody social values rather than merely display them in advertising. Literature on brand trust has highlighted that superficial gestures of diversity are quickly recognized as tokenistic, a view confirmed in the consumer focus groups conducted for this study. Participants reported that while AI-generated content may feature diverse identities, it is only perceived as inclusive when it aligns with broader corporate practices such as workforce diversity, supplier equity, and social responsibility initiatives. This indicates that inclusivity cannot be siloed within marketing outputs but must be embedded across organizational structures. In this sense, AI acts as a litmus test for broader corporate culture: campaigns that lack authenticity reveal organizational gaps, while campaigns that are consistent with deeper commitments strengthen trust. The discussion underscores that inclusivity in marketing requires a holistic integration of AI with genuine organizational values.

The global dimension of inclusivity further complicates the discussion, highlighting the limitations of universalist approaches to AI-driven fairness. Scholars in international business and cultural studies have long argued that inclusivity must be defined within local contexts, as cultural norms and identity markers vary widely across societies. The findings of this research confirm that AI systems trained on Western-centric data fail to resonate authentically in non-Western contexts, and sometimes produce outputs perceived as insensitive. This aligns with D'Ignazio and Klein's (2020) notion of "data feminism," which stresses that localized knowledge and community participation are essential for creating equitable systems. The discussion therefore emphasizes that inclusivity in AI-driven marketing must be adaptive, capable of integrating local expertise, and reflexive in acknowledging the partiality of global datasets. The challenge lies in balancing the need for consistency in global marketing strategies with the flexibility required for cultural sensitivity. This tension represents one of the most pressing areas for further research and innovation.

The role of organizational culture also emerges as a significant factor in shaping inclusivity outcomes, a point that resonates with literature on ethical AI adoption and corporate governance. Studies of organizational practices demonstrate that inclusivity is most effectively achieved when it is integrated into performance metrics, leadership strategies, and accountability frameworks. The findings of this study confirm that companies which invest in diverse datasets, fairness audits, and cross-functional collaboration produce more inclusive marketing outputs. Conversely, organizations that delegate inclusivity solely to technical systems fail to achieve meaningful progress. This supports arguments in the literature that inclusivity is a socio-technical issue requiring interdisciplinary collaboration. The discussion therefore stresses that inclusivity must be institutionalized within organizations, requiring leadership commitment, resource allocation, and accountability mechanisms that extend beyond marketing departments. AI may be the technical tool, but its inclusivity is determined by organizational priorities.

Consumer perceptions further underscore the relational and contextual nature of inclusivity. The findings of this study show that consumers judge inclusivity not only by the content of advertisements but also by their personal experiences of representation and respect. This aligns with broader sociological theories of recognition, which emphasize that identity is shaped by being acknowledged and valued in public narratives. AI-driven marketing plays a crucial role in these narratives, making its inclusivity deeply consequential for consumer identity and trust. However, the research also reveals that inclusivity is judged relationally: consumers evaluate campaigns against their broader expectations of the brand. If the inclusivity portrayed in marketing is contradicted by exclusionary corporate practices, it is dismissed as insincere. This highlights the need for organizations to maintain consistency across messaging and practice, as inclusivity is assessed holistically rather than in isolation. The discussion emphasizes that AI-driven inclusivity must be viewed as part of a broader ecosystem of corporate responsibility.

Regulatory trends provide an additional layer of complexity to the discussion. Literature on AI ethics highlights the growing importance of legal and policy frameworks in guiding corporate behavior. The findings of this study indicate that regulatory initiatives are likely to shape inclusivity in marketing by mandating fairness audits, transparency standards, and accountability mechanisms. This resonates with Floridi and Cowls' (2019) unified framework of AI principles, which argues for embedding fairness, transparency, and accountability into all AI applications. While compliance introduces new challenges for organizations, the findings also suggest that it creates opportunities for differentiation, as companies that adopt inclusive practices proactively can gain competitive advantage. The discussion therefore underscores the importance of anticipating regulatory changes and positioning inclusivity not as a burden but as a strategic resource.

Another critical dimension of the discussion involves the contradictions between efficiency and inclusivity. Marketing has traditionally prioritized metrics such as engagement rates, click-throughs, and conversions, all of which are easily optimized by AI systems. Inclusivity, however, involves qualitative dimensions that resist reduction to simple metrics. This tension creates a risk that inclusivity will be sidelined in favor of efficiency unless success metrics are redefined. The findings of this research highlight examples where inclusivity has contributed to long-term brand sustainability, even if it did not yield immediate returns. This aligns with research showing that inclusive brands enjoy greater loyalty, resilience, and reputational capital. The discussion emphasizes that organizations must move beyond short-term efficiency metrics and adopt broader measures of success that include fairness, equity, and authenticity. AI must be designed and evaluated not only for its profitability but also for its social impact.

The interdisciplinary nature of the research problem also emerges clearly in the discussion. Inclusivity in AI-driven marketing cannot be fully understood or addressed by a single field. Computer science provides technical tools for fairness, but lacks cultural nuance; marketing offers insights into representation but may ignore technical constraints; sociology and critical theory highlight systemic inequalities but may understate technological complexity. The findings of this research confirm the need for interdisciplinary collaboration, as inclusivity requires both technical interventions and cultural sensitivity. This aligns with broader calls in the literature for cross-disciplinary partnerships that bring together technologists, marketers, ethicists, and social scientists. The discussion underscores that the future of inclusive AI-driven marketing depends on bridging these disciplinary divides.

Finally, the discussion reflects on the broader societal implications of AI-driven inclusivity in marketing. Marketing is not simply a business function; it is a cultural practice that shapes public narratives about identity, belonging, and recognition. When AI systems perpetuate exclusionary practices, they contribute to broader patterns of social inequity. Conversely, when they promote inclusivity, they expand opportunities for recognition and representation. The stakes of AI-driven inclusivity therefore extend beyond consumer behavior into questions of justice, dignity, and social cohesion. This research highlights the responsibility of organizations to recognize the cultural power of marketing and to ensure that their use of AI contributes positively to society. Inclusivity is not only a matter of ethical compliance or business advantage but also a question of social responsibility in a digital age.

In conclusion, the discussion situates the findings of this study within wider academic, organizational, and cultural debates. It emphasizes that AI-driven inclusivity in marketing is both a challenge and an opportunity, shaped by technical design, organizational culture, consumer perception, and regulatory context. It reinforces that inclusivity is relational, contextual, and dynamic, requiring ongoing reflection, adaptation, and collaboration. Above all, it argues that the ethical trajectory of AI in marketing depends on human choices: whether organizations will prioritize inclusivity as a strategic imperative or subordinate it to short-term efficiency. The discussion therefore calls for a reframing of marketing in the age of AI, where inclusivity is not an optional add-on but a foundational principle guiding technological innovation and organizational practice.

CONCLUSION

The conclusion of this research underscores that artificial intelligence has rapidly become one of the most influential forces shaping the future of marketing, not only in terms of efficiency and personalization but also in its capacity to redefine the boundaries of diversity, equity, and inclusion. Throughout this project, it has become evident that AI-driven decision-making is simultaneously a site of great promise and significant peril. On one hand, its predictive capabilities, scalability, and analytical precision make it an invaluable tool for identifying underserved audiences, diversifying representation, and embedding inclusivity into marketing practices. On the other hand, its dependence on historical data, optimization for narrow efficiency metrics, and lack of contextual awareness mean that it can reproduce and even amplify the inequities that exist within society if deployed without critical reflection. The trajectory of AI's role in marketing will therefore be determined not by the technology alone but by the ethical choices, governance structures, and cultural commitments of the organizations that use it.

One of the central insights to emerge from this research is that inclusivity cannot be treated as an optional enhancement in AI-driven marketing systems but must instead be integrated into their very design. Biases in training data, whether they stem from underrepresentation of certain groups or the persistence of stereotypes, directly translate into algorithmic outputs that shape consumer experiences. When marketing algorithms distribute advertisements unevenly, associate identities with narrow roles, or exclude marginalized voices, they do not simply mirror the inequalities of the past; they reinforce them in the present and project them into the future. This conclusion therefore highlights that inclusivity requires intentional interventions at every stage of the AI lifecycle, from data collection and model training to deployment and auditing. Inclusivity must become a guiding principle rather than a secondary consideration if AI is to contribute meaningfully to equity in marketing.

Another key conclusion is that inclusivity in AI-driven marketing is not solely a technical challenge but also an organizational and cultural one. Technology cannot, on its own, guarantee fairness or authenticity. Even the most sophisticated fairness-aware algorithms cannot substitute for organizational commitment to diversity, equity, and inclusion. Consumers are quick to identify when campaigns adopt diverse imagery or language but lack deeper authenticity in the values and practices of the company. This research has shown that inclusivity resonates most powerfully when it reflects a broader alignment between corporate identity and marketing outputs. Companies that invest in diverse workforces, equitable supplier networks, and transparent governance are far more likely to gain consumer trust when they employ AI-driven campaigns featuring diverse representation. Thus, the conclusion reinforces the idea that AI must be embedded within a holistic culture of inclusivity rather than treated as a quick technical fix.

The global dimension of inclusivity also becomes particularly important in the conclusion. Marketing operates across cultural boundaries, and inclusivity cannot be reduced to a universal standard applicable everywhere. What is considered inclusive in one cultural context may be irrelevant or even offensive in another. AI systems trained on Western-centric datasets risk homogenizing diversity into a narrow frame that excludes the richness of global variation. This research has demonstrated the need for culturally adaptive AI systems that can integrate localized datasets, engage with regional expertise, and remain sensitive to social differences. The conclusion therefore emphasizes that inclusivity in global AI-driven marketing requires both universal principles of fairness and context-specific adaptations that respect cultural diversity.

Regulatory and policy frameworks are likely to play an increasingly decisive role in shaping the future of AI-driven inclusivity in marketing. The conclusion highlights that while voluntary corporate initiatives are important, they are insufficient on their own to guarantee fairness and accountability. Governments and international bodies are beginning to recognize the power of algorithms in shaping consumer access and cultural narratives, and they are responding with guidelines for transparency, fairness, and ethical oversight. These emerging frameworks will help establish baseline standards and prevent harmful practices, but they must also be flexible enough to encourage innovation and cultural sensitivity. For organizations, compliance should not be viewed as a burden but as an opportunity to demonstrate leadership in ethical innovation. By proactively adopting inclusive AI practices, companies can not only meet regulatory expectations but also strengthen their reputational capital and consumer trust.

Another important conclusion concerns the long-term sustainability of marketing strategies. Inclusivity is not only an ethical imperative but also a business necessity in a marketplace increasingly defined by diversity. Younger generations of consumers, in particular, are more socially aware and expect brands to reflect their values. Companies that fail to represent diverse identities or that reproduce exclusionary practices risk alienating significant segments of their customer base. Conversely, those that embed inclusivity into their AI systems are better positioned to build strong, loyal, and diverse consumer communities. Inclusivity thus emerges as both a moral obligation and a competitive advantage. The conclusion underscores that organizations that treat inclusivity as integral to their AI-driven marketing will be more resilient, more trusted, and ultimately more successful in the long run.

The analysis throughout this research also reveals that inclusivity cannot be reduced to surface-level diversity metrics. While numerical representation matters, inclusivity is also about authenticity, respect, and the creation of equitable opportunities for visibility and engagement. AI-driven systems that increase diversity in advertising imagery but continue to portray identities in stereotypical roles or exclude marginalized groups from access to products are not truly inclusive. Authentic inclusivity requires deeper engagement with cultural narratives, lived experiences, and consumer perceptions. This conclusion calls for organizations to combine quantitative fairness metrics with qualitative assessments of authenticity, ensuring that inclusivity is both measurable and meaningful.

The findings of this research also point toward the need for continuous reflection and adaptation. Inclusivity is not a static goal that can be achieved once and for all but a dynamic process that evolves with societal changes. As norms of representation, equity, and fairness shift over time, AI systems must be regularly audited, recalibrated, and updated to remain aligned with contemporary understandings of inclusivity. Organizations must treat inclusivity as an ongoing journey rather than a final destination, investing in long-term processes of evaluation, feedback, and improvement. This conclusion emphasizes that inclusivity is as much about adaptability as it is about design, requiring constant vigilance to ensure that AI systems do not drift back into patterns of exclusion.

A further conclusion is that inclusivity in AI-driven marketing requires collaboration across disciplines. No single field—whether computer science, marketing, sociology, or ethics—can fully capture the complexity of the challenges at hand. Technical experts may design algorithms but lack cultural sensitivity, while marketers may understand representation but not the mechanics of bias in machine learning. Ethicists may raise concerns about fairness without access to empirical data, while sociologists may highlight systemic inequalities without engaging with technical constraints. This research has demonstrated that inclusivity emerges most effectively when these perspectives are brought together in interdisciplinary collaboration. Organizations must therefore create structures that facilitate dialogue between technologists, marketers, social scientists, and ethicists, ensuring that AI-driven marketing systems are informed by diverse expertise.

Finally, the conclusion emphasizes that the future of AI-driven decision-making in marketing will be defined by the choices organizations make today. AI is neither inherently inclusive nor inherently exclusionary; it is a tool that reflects the priorities and values of those who build and deploy it. If inclusivity is sidelined in favor of efficiency or profitability, AI will reproduce inequities at scale. If inclusivity is embraced as a core principle, AI can become a catalyst for equity and representation.

The responsibility lies with organizations to recognize this choice and to commit to building AI systems that advance diversity, equity, and inclusion. This commitment requires investment in diverse datasets, fairness-aware algorithms, auditing processes, organizational culture, consumer transparency, and cultural sensitivity. The payoff, however, is substantial: marketing systems that not only succeed in reaching audiences but also contribute to creating a more equitable digital marketplace.

In closing, this research has demonstrated that AI-driven decision-making for diversity, equity, and inclusion in marketing is both a challenge and an opportunity. It is a challenge because it requires organizations to confront systemic biases, redefine success metrics, and adapt to cultural complexity. It is an opportunity because it offers the tools to broaden representation, strengthen consumer trust, and align marketing with the ethical and social values of an increasingly diverse world. The conclusion of this project is therefore both cautionary and optimistic. It cautions that AI, if left unchecked, can deepen divisions and perpetuate inequities. Yet it also affirms that AI, when guided by ethical principles and organizational commitment, can transform marketing into a force for inclusivity and equity. The path forward lies in intentionality, collaboration, and authenticity. By choosing to embed inclusivity into the very fabric of AI-driven marketing, organizations can harness the power of technology to not only sell products but also shape a society that is fairer, more representative, and more just.

REFERENCES

Buolamwini, J., & Gebru, T. (2018). Gender shades: Intersectional accuracy disparities in commercial gender classification. *Proceedings of Machine Learning Research: Conference on Fairness, Accountability, and Transparency*, *81*, 1–15.

D'Ignazio, C., & Klein, L. F. (2020). *Data feminism.* MIT Press., DOI: 10.7551/mitpress/11805.001.0001

Floridi, L., & Cowls, J. (2019). A unified framework of five principles for AI in society. *Harvard Data Science Review*, *1*(1). Advance online publication. DOI: 10.1162/99608f92.8cd550d1

Compilation of References

5 ways H&M is using AI. (n.d.). Digital Defynd. https://digitaldefynd.com/IQ/hm-using-ai-case-study/

Aayog, N. I. T. I. (2021). *Responsible AI for all: A strategy for India*. https://indiaai.gov.in/

Aayog, N. I. T. I. (2021). *Responsible AI for all: Operationalizing principles for responsible AI*. https://www.niti.gov.in/sites/default/files/2021-02/Responsible-AI-21022021.pdf

Accenture. (2023). *Personalization and trust in the age of AI: Global consumer study*. https://www.accenture.com/us-en/insights

Aday, A., & Schmader, T. (2019). Seeking authenticity in diverse contexts: How identities and environments constrain "free" choice. *Social and Personality Psychology Compass*, *13*(6), e12450. https://doi.org/https://doi.org/10.1111/spc3.12450

Adeola, F. (2025). *Effects of Generative Artificial Intelligence on Creative Processes Within Local Advertising Agencies* (Master's thesis, Oklahoma State University).

Adomavicius, G., & Tuzhilin, A. (2005). Toward the next generation of recommender systems: A survey of the state-of-the-art and possible extensions. *IEEE Transactions on Knowledge and Data Engineering*, *17*(6), 734–749. DOI: 10.1109/TKDE.2005.99

Aguirre, E., Mahr, D., Grewal, D., de Ruyter, K., & Wetzels, M. (2015). Unraveling the personalization–privacy paradox: The role of psychological distance. *Journal of Consumer Psychology*, *25*(3), 469–484.

Akter, S., Dwivedi, Y. K., Biswas, K., Michael, K., Bandara, R. J., & Sajib, S. (2021). Addressing algorithmic bias in AI-driven customer management. *Journal of Global Information Management*, *29*(6), 27–45. DOI: 10.4018/JGIM.20211101.oa3

Akter, S., Dwivedi, Y. K., Sajib, S., Biswas, K., Bandara, R. J., & Michael, K. (2022). Algorithmic bias in machine-learning-based marketing models. *Journal of Business Research, 144*, 201–216. DOI: 10.1016/j.jbusres.2022.01.083

Akter, S., Sultana, S., Mariani, M., Wamba, S. F., Spanaki, K., & Dwivedi, Y. K. (2023). Advancing algorithmic bias management capabilities in AI-driven marketing analytics research. *Industrial Marketing Management, 114*, 243–261. DOI: 10.1016/j.indmarman.2023.08.013

Ali, M., Sapiezynski, P., Bogen, M., Korolova, A., Mislove, A., & Rieke, A. (2019). Discrimination through optimization: How Facebook's ad delivery can lead to biased outcomes. Proceedings of the ACM on Human-Computer Interaction, 3(CSCW). https://doi.org/DOI: 10.1145/3359301

Ali, M., Sapiezynski, P., Bogen, M., Korolova, A., Mislove, A., & Rieke, A. (2019). Discrimination through optimization: How Facebook's Ad delivery can lead to biased outcomes. Proceedings of the *ACM on human-computer interaction*, 3(CSCW), 1-30.

Alijoyo, F. A., Aziz, T. S. A., Omer, N., Yusuf, N., Kumar, M. D., Ramesh, A. V. N., Ulmas, Z., & Baker El-Ebiary, Y. A. (2025). Personalized marketing: Leveraging AI for culturally aware segmentation and targeting. *Alexandria Engineering Journal, 119*, 8–21. DOI: 10.1016/j.aej.2025.01.074

Ali, M., Sapiezynski, P., Bogen, M., Korolova, A., Mislove, A., & Rieke, A. (2019). Discrimination through optimization: How Facebook's ad delivery can lead to biased outcomes. *Proceedings of the ACM on Human-Computer Interaction, 3*(CSCW), 1–30.

Ali, M., Sapiezynski, P., Bogen, M., Korolova, A., Mislove, A., & Rieke, A. (2019). Discrimination through optimization: How Facebook's ad delivery can lead to skewed outcomes [Preprint]. arXiv. https://arxiv.org/abs/1904.02095

Alves Gomes, M., & Meisen, T. (2023). A review on customer segmentation methods for personalized customer targeting in e-commerce use cases. *Information Systems and e-Business Management, 21*(3), 527–570. DOI: 10.1007/s10257-023-00640-4

Ansari, A. I., Singh, A., Pattanaik, S., Patnaik, R., & Suryawanshi, U. (2024). Exploring the Role of AI-Powered Virtual Assistants in Optimizing Self-Service Experiences for Customers Within the Service Sector. In Nadda, V., Tyagi, P., Singh, A., & Singh, V. (Eds.), *Integrating AI-Driven Technologies Into Service Marketing* (pp. 225–238). IGI Global., DOI: 10.4018/979-8-3693-7122-0.ch013

Arora, K., & Singh, A. (2026). *Harnessing emotion AI for customer support and employee wellbeing*. https://books.google.co.in/books?id=3lNxEQAAQBAJ

Arora, N., Dreze, X., Ghose, A., Hess, J. D., Iyengar, R., Jing, B., & Shankar, V. (2008). Putting one-to-one marketing to work: Personalization, customization, and choice. *Marketing Letters*, *19*(3–4), 305–321.

Arsel, Z., Crockett, D., & Scott, M. L. (2021). Diversity, Equity, and Inclusion (DEI) in the Journal of Consumer Research: A Curation and Research Agenda. *The Journal of Consumer Research*, *48*(5), 920–933. DOI: 10.1093/jcr/ucab057

Awad, N. F., & Krishnan, M. S. (2006). The personalization privacy paradox: An empirical evaluation of information transparency and the willingness to be profiled online for personalization. *Management Information Systems Quarterly*, *30*(1), 13–28.

Baeten, T. (2025). *The Influence of Artificial Intelligence Adoption on Educator Perceptions* (Doctoral dissertation, University of Wisconsin--Stout).

Banet-Weiser, S. (2018). *Empowered: Popular feminism and popular misogyny*. Duke University Press., DOI: 10.1215/9781478002918

Barari, M. M., Eisend, M., & Jain, S. P. (2025). A meta-analysis of the effectiveness of social media influencers: Mechanisms and moderation. *Journal of the Academy of Marketing Science*. Advance online publication. DOI: 10.1007/s11747-025-01107-3

Barocas, S., Hardt, M., & Narayanan, A. (2019). *Fairness and machine learning*. fairmlbook.org. https://fairmlbook.org

Barocas, S., Hardt, M., & Narayanan, A. (2020). Fairness and machine learning. *Recommender Systems Handbook*, *1*, 453–459.

Barocas, S., & Selbst, A. D. (2016). Big data's disparate impact. *California Law Review*, *104*(3), 671–732. https://papers.ssrn.com/sol3/papers.cfm?abstract_id=2477899

Basyoni, L., Qayyum, A., Shaban, K., Elmahjub, E., Al-Ali, A., Halabi, O., & Qadir, J. (2025). Generative AI-Driven Metaverse: The Promises and Challenges of AI-Generated Content. *Authorea Preprints*.

Bender, E. M., Gebru, T., McMillan-Major, A., & Shmitchell, S. (2021, March). On the dangers of stochastic parrots: Can language models be too big? In Proceedings of the 2021 *ACM conference on fairness, accountability, and transparency* (pp. 610-623).

Bender, E. M., & Friedman, B. (2018). Data statements for natural language processing: Toward mitigating system bias and enabling better science. *Transactions of the Association for Computational Linguistics*, *6*, 587–604.

Bender, E. M., Gebru, T., McMillan-Major, A., & Mitchell, S. (2021). On the dangers of stochastic parrots: Can language models be too big? *Proceedings of the ACM Conference on Fairness, Accountability, and Transparency (FAccT)*, 610–623. https://doi.org/DOI: 10.1145/3442188.3445922

Berk, R., & Bleich, J. (2013). Statistical procedures for forecasting criminal behavior: A critical review. *Criminology & Public Policy*, *12*(3), 513–544.

Berry, K., & Singh, A. (2024). AI-Driven Service Marketing: Transforming Customer Experience and Operational Efficiency. In Nadda, V., Tyagi, P., Singh, A., & Singh, V. (Eds.), *AI Innovations in Service and Tourism Marketing* (pp. 35–56). IGI Global., DOI: 10.4018/979-8-3693-7909-7.ch003

Bhandari, A., & Rodgers, S. (2022). How identity representation in ads influences consumer trust and engagement. *Journal of Advertising Research*. https://www.journalofadvertisingresearch.com

Bhardwaj, S., Sharma, N., Goel, M., Vandana, N., Sharma, K., & Verma, V. (2024). Enhancing Customer Targeting in E-Commerce and Digital Marketing through AI-Driven Personalization Strategies. In *CRC Press eBooks* (pp. 41–60). https://doi.org/DOI: 10.1201/9781003450443-4

Bhasin, H. (2025, August 19). Ethical marketing: Definition, principles, and examples. *Marketing91*. https://www.marketing91.com/ethical-marketing/

Billings, A. C., Butterworth, M. L., & Turman, P. D. (2015). *Communication and sport: Surveying the field* (2nd ed.). SAGE Publications.

Binns, R. (2018). Fairness in machine learning: Lessons from political philosophy. In *Proceedings of the 1st Conference on Fairness, Accountability and Transparency* (pp. 149–159). https://proceedings.mlr.press/v81/binns18a.html

Binns, R. (2018). *Fairness in machine learning: Lessons from political philosophy*. In *Proceedings of the Conference on Fairness, Accountability, and Transparency* (pp. 149–159). Proceedings of Machine Learning Research, 81. https://proceedings.mlr.press/v81/binns18a.html

Birhane, A., & Prabhu, V. U. (2021, January). Large image datasets: A pyrrhic win for computer vision? In 2021 *IEEE Winter Conference on Applications of Computer Vision (WACV)* (pp. 1536-1546). IEEE.

Bjelobaba, S., Waddington, L., Perkins, M., Foltýnek, T., Bhattacharyya, S., & Weber-Wulff, D. (2025). Maintaining research integrity in the age of GenAI: An analysis of ethical challenges and recommendations to researchers. *International Journal for Educational Integrity*, *21*(1), 1–23.

Blodgett, S. L., Barocas, S., Daumé Iii, H., & Wallach, H. (2020). Language (technology) is power: A critical survey of" bias" in nlp. *arXiv preprint arXiv:2005*.14050.

Bommasani, R., Hudson, D. A., Adeli, E., Altman, R., Arora, S., von Arx, S., & Liang, P. (2022). On the opportunities and risks of foundation models. *Journal of Artificial Intelligence Research, 75*, 1–152.

Bonneton, N. (2025). The market for ethical goods. *Journal of Environmental Economics and Management, 103182*. Advance online publication. DOI: 10.1016/j.jeem.2025.103182

Borgerson, J. L., & Schroeder, J. E. (2002). Ethical issues of global marketing: Avoiding bad faith in visual representation. *European Journal of Marketing, 36*(5/6), 570–594. DOI: 10.1108/03090560210422399

Borgesius, F. Z. (2025). Discrimination, artificial intelligence, and algorithmic decision-making. *arXiv preprint arXiv:2510*.13465.

Boyd, D. (2010). Social network sites as networked publics: Affordances, dynamics, and implications. In Z. Papacharissi (Ed.), *A networked self: Identity, community, and culture on social network sites* (pp. 39–58). Routledge.

Boyd, C. S., Ritch, E. L., Dodd, C. A., & McColl, J. (2020). Inclusive identities: Re-imaging the future of the retail brand? *International Journal of Retail & Distribution Management, 48*(12), 1315–1335. DOI: 10.1108/ijrdm-12-2019-0392

Branca, G., Grosso, M., & Castaldo, S. (2024). Value through diversity: A systematic literature review to understand diversity and inclusion in consumer research. *Psychology and Marketing, 41*(11), 2854–2873. https://doi.org/https://doi.org/10.1002/mar.22088

Braun, V., & Clarke, V. (2006). Using thematic analysis in psychology. *Qualitative Research in Psychology, 3*(2), 77–101. DOI: 10.1191/1478088706qp063oa

Brehm, J. W. (1966). *A theory of psychological reactance*. Academic Press.

Brekhus, W. H. (2020). *The sociology of identity: authenticity, multidimensionality, and mobility*. John Wiley & Sons.

Browning, J. W., McKeever, S., Ferrario, M. A., O'Neill, I., & Stewart, D. (2025, April). Creating sustainable solutions: An inclusive hackathon leveraging genAI in a local context. In *2025 IEEE Global Engineering Education Conference (EDUCON)* (pp. 1-7). IEEE.

Bruns, A. (2008). *Blogs, Wikipedia, Second Life, and beyond: From production to produsage*. Peter Lang.

Buolamwini, J., & Gebru, T. (2018). *Gender shades: Intersectional accuracy disparities in commercial gender classification.* In *Proceedings of the Conference on Fairness, Accountability, and Transparency* (pp. 77–91). Proceedings of Machine Learning Research, 81. https://proceedings.mlr.press/v81/buolamwini18a.html

Buolamwini, J., & Gebru, T. (2018). Gender shades: Intersectional accuracy disparities in commercial gender classification. *Proceedings of Machine Learning Research, 81*, 77–91. http://proceedings.mlr.press/v81/buolamwini18a.html

Buolamwini, J., & Gebru, T. (2018, January). Gender shades: Intersectional accuracy disparities in commercial gender classification. In Conference on *fairness, accountability and transparency* (pp. 77-91). PMLR.

Buolamwini, J., & Gebru, T. (2018). Gender shades: Intersectional accuracy disparities in commercial gender classification. *Proceedings of Machine Learning Research: Conference on Fairness, Accountability, and Transparency, 81*, 1–15.

Burke, T. (2025, April 2). What's the biggest AI blind spot in advertising today? AI Digital. https://www.aidigital.com/blog/biggest-ai-blind-spot-in-advertising

Burke, R. (2002). Hybrid recommender systems: Survey and experiments. *User Modeling and User-Adapted Interaction, 12*, 331–370. DOI: 10.1023/A:1021240730564

Byrne, C. (n.d.). The H&M marketing controversy. Stockton University. https://stockton.edu/diversity-inclusion/h-and-m-marketing-controversy.html

Caliskan, A., Bryson, J. J., & Narayanan, A. (2017). Semantics derived automatically from language corpora contain human-like biases. *Science, 356*(6334), 183–186. DOI: 10.1126/science.aal4230 PMID: 28408601

Campagna, C. L., Donthu, N., & Yoo, B. (2023). Brand authenticity: Literature review, comprehensive definition, and an amalgamated scale. *Journal of Marketing Theory and Practice, 31*(2), 129–145. DOI: 10.1080/10696679.2021.2018937

Cantó, J., & Rodó-Zárate, M. (2024). Gender-Ideology Trouble? Ideology, Gender, and Generation as Factors in LGB+ Self-identification among Gen Z and Millennials in Catalonia. *Sexuality & Culture, 28*(6), 2745–2769. DOI: 10.1007/s12119-024-10252-w

Castro, D. C., Walker, I., & Glocker, B. (2020). Causality matters in medical imaging. *Nature Communications, 11*(1), 3673.

Chaffey, D. (2018). *Digital Marketing: Strategy, Implementation, and Practice* (7th ed.). Pearson Education.

Chaffey, D. (2020). *Digital marketing: Strategy, implementation, and practice* (8th ed.). Pearson Education.

Chakraborty, G., & Dube, J.-P. (2019). Machine Learning in Marketing: Prediction and Targeting. *JMR, Journal of Marketing Research, 56*(3), 361–374.

Chatterjee, S., & Kumar, A. (2018). Customer Targeting and Personalization in E-commerce: Role of Data Analytics and Machine Learning. *Journal of Retailing and Consumer Services, 45*, 125–135.

Cheah, I., & Phua, P. (2025). Generational advertising: Literature review and practitioner insights on key pitfalls and implications. *International Journal of Advertising, 44*(2), 286–312. DOI: 10.1080/02650487.2024.2429904

Chen, I., Johansson, F. D., & Sontag, D. (2018). Why is my classifier discriminatory? In *Advances in Neural Information Processing Systems* (Vol. 31). https://proceedings.neurips.cc/paper/2018/hash/1f1baa5b8edac74eb4eaa329f14a0361-Abstract.html

Chen, Z. (2023). Ethics and discrimination in artificial-intelligence-enabled recruitment practices. *Humanities & Social Sciences Communications, 10*(1), 567. DOI: 10.1057/s41599-023-02079-x

Cherry, J., & Fraedrich, J. (2002). Perceived risk, moral philosophy and marketing ethics: Mediating influences on sales managers' ethical decision-making. *Journal of Business Research, 55*(12), 951–962. DOI: 10.1016/S0148-2963(00)00215-0

Chhabra, S., Singh, A., & Maddela, D. (2025). Brand, causes, and the credibility gap: Gen Z purchase intentions in emerging markets. *Journal of Asia Business Studies*, •••, 1–21. DOI: 10.1108/jabs-05-2025-0302

Chierichetti, F., Kumar, R., Lattanzi, S., & Vassilvitskii, S. (2017). Fair clustering through fairlets. In *Advances in Neural Information Processing Systems* (Vol. 30).

Choi, L. S. L., Chan, K. W., & Fock, H. (2025). Deepening exploration of socially responsible consumption in generation z: The impacts of environmental knowledge and perceived consumer effectiveness. *Journal of Consumer Marketing, 42*(7), 877–892. DOI: 10.1108/jcm-05-2024-6857

Chowdhuri, S. R., & Gupta, M. (2025). Machine learning models for software defect detection: A strategic management approach. *Purushartha, 17*(2), 87–98. https://journals.smsvaranasi.com/index.php/purushartha/article/download/2279/1044. journals.smsvaranasi.com

Cialdini, R. B. (2009). *Influence: Science and practice* (5th ed.). Pearson Education.

Cillo, P., & Rubera, G. (2024). Generative AI in innovation and marketing processes: A roadmap of research opportunities. *Journal of the Academy of Marketing Science*. Advance online publication. DOI: 10.1007/s11747-024-01044-7

Collier, D. (1993). The comparative method. In Finifter, A. W. (Ed.), *Political science: The state of the discipline II* (pp. 105–119). American Political Science Association.

Coman, I. A., Yuan, S., & Tsai, J.-Y. (2022). Toward an Audience-Centric Framework of Corporate Social Advocacy Strategy: An Exploratory Study of Young Consumers from Generation Z. *Sustainability, 14*(7), 4099. DOI: 10.3390/su14074099

Costanza-Chock, S. (2020). *Design justice: Community-led practices to build the worlds we need*. MIT Press.

Coulter, K. S., & Roggeveen, A. L. (2014). Like it or not: Consumer responses to word-of-mouth communication in on-line social networks. *Management Research Review, 37*(7), 626–642.

Coussement, K., & Van den Poel, D. (2008). Churn prediction in subscription services: An application of support vector machines while comparing two parameter-selection techniques. *Expert Systems with Applications, 34*(1), 313–327. DOI: 10.1016/j.eswa.2006.09.038

Cowgill, B. (2019). Bias and productivity in humans and algorithms. Columbia Business School Research Paper.

Cowgill, B., & Tucker, C. E. (2019). Economics, fairness and algorithmic bias. *The Journal of Economic Perspectives, 34*(4), 54–77.

Crane, A. (1997). The dynamics of marketing ethical products: A cultural perspective. *Journal of Marketing Management, 13*(6), 561–577. DOI: 10.1080/0267257x.1997.9964493

Crawford, K. (2021). *Atlas of AI: Power, politics, and the planetary costs of artificial intelligence*. Yale University Press.

Crawford, K. (2021). *The atlas of AI: Power, politics, and the planetary costs of artificial intelligence*. Yale University Press.

Crenshaw, K. (1989). Demarginalizing the intersection of race and sex: A Black feminist critique of antidiscrimination doctrine, feminist theory and antiracist politics. *University of Chicago Legal Forum, 1989*(1), 139–167. https://chicagounbound.uchicago.edu/uclf/vol1989/iss1/8

Cui, G. (2001). Marketing to ethnic minority consumers: A historical journey (1932-1997). *Journal of Macromarketing, 21*(1), 23–31.

Cunningham, G. B., & Ko, C. (2024). Diversity, equity, and inclusion in the sport metaverse. *International Journal of Sports Marketing & Sponsorship*, *25*(1), 55–70. DOI: 10.1108/IJSMS-03-2023-0045

D'Ignazio, C., & Klein, L. F. (2020). *Data feminism*. MIT Press., DOI: 10.7551/mitpress/11805.001.0001

da Fonseca, M. J. S., Aleixo, A. S. M., Teixeira, A. S., & Sousa, B. B. (2025). Drive the Purchase Intentions of Generation X and Z Tourists through Marketing Activities. In *Customer Insight in Tourism* (pp. 151–161). Routledge.

Dastane, O., Aw, E. C., Fandos-Roig, J. C., & Sánchez-García, J. (2025). Ethical marketing: A review and research agenda. *Marketing Intelligence & Planning*. Advance online publication. DOI: 10.1108/mip-01-2024-0007

Dastin, J. (2018, October 11). Amazon scraps secret AI recruiting tool that showed bias against women. Reuters. https://www.reuters.com/article/world/insight-amazon-scraps-secret-ai-recruiting-tool-that-showed-bias-against-women-idUSKCN1MK0AG/

Datta, A., Tschantz, M. C., & Datta, A. (2018). Automated experiments on ad privacy settings: A tale of opacity, choice, and discrimination. *Proceedings on Privacy Enhancing Technologies. Privacy Enhancing Technologies Symposium*, *2015*(1), 92–112.

Davenport, T. H., Guha, A., Grewal, D., & Bressgott, T. (2020). How artificial intelligence will change the future of marketing. *Journal of the Academy of Marketing Science*, *48*(1), 24–42.

Davenport, T. H., & Harris, J. G. (2007). Competing on analytics: The new science of Winning. *Harvard business review press*. *Language*, *15*(217), 24.

Davis, F. D. (1989). Perceived usefulness, perceived ease of use, and user acceptance of information technology. *Management Information Systems Quarterly*, *13*(3), 319–340. DOI: 10.2307/249008

De Bruyn, A., Viswanathan, V., Beh, Y. S., Brock, J. K.-U., & von Wangenheim, F. (2020). Artificial intelligence and marketing: Pitfalls and opportunities. *International Journal of Research in Marketing*, *51*, 91–105. DOI: 10.1016/j.intmar.2020.04.007

Deepak, P., & Abraham, S. S. (2020). Representativity fairness in clustering. In *Proceedings of the 12th ACM Conference on Web Science* (pp. 202–211). https://doi.org/DOI: 10.1145/3394231.3397910

Delgado, R., & Stefancic, J. (2017). *Critical race theory: An introduction* (3rd ed.). NYU Press.

Deloitte. (2020). *The diversity and inclusion revolution: Eight powerful truths.* Deloitte Insights. https://www2.deloitte.com/us/en/insights/deloitte-review/issue-22/diversity-and-inclusion-at-the-workplace.html

Dignum, V. (2019). *Responsible artificial intelligence: how to develop and use AI in a responsible way* (Vol. 2156). Springer., DOI: 10.1007/978-3-030-30371-6

Dignum, V. (2019). *Responsible artificial intelligence: How to develop and use AI in a responsible way*. Springer.

Dion, D., Pavlyuchenko, R., & Prokopec, A. S. (2024). EXPRESS: The enrichment economy: Market dynamics, brand strategy, and ethics. *Journal of Marketing*. Advance online publication. DOI: 10.1177/00222429241275014

Djafarova, E., & Foots, S. (2022). Exploring ethical consumption of generation Z: Theory of planned behaviour. *Young Consumers: Insight and Ideas for Responsible Marketers, 23*(3), 413–431. DOI: 10.1108/yc-10-2021-1405

Doshi-Velez, F., & Kim, B. (2017). Towards a rigorous science of interpretable machine learning. *arXiv:1702.08608.* https://doi.org//arXiv.1702.08608DOI: 10.48550

Dove apologises for "racist" Facebook advertising campaign. (2017, October 8). BBC News. https://www.bbc.com/news/newsbeat-41542818

Dragomir, V. D. (2019). Ethical aspects of environmental strategy. In *SpringerBriefs in Applied Sciences and Technology* (pp. 75–113). https://doi.org/DOI: 10.1007/978-3-030-29548-6_3

Dubinsky, A. J., & Loken, B. (1989). Analyzing ethical decision making in marketing. *Journal of Business Research, 19*(2), 83–107. DOI: 10.1016/0148-2963(89)90001-5

Durand-Hayes, S. (2024). *Voice of the consumer survey 2024: Shrinking the consumer trust deficit.* PwC. https://www.pwc.com/gx/en/issues/c-suite-insights/voice-of-the-consumer-survey/2024.html

Dwivedi, Y. K., Hughes, L., Kar, A. K., Baabdullah, A. M., Grover, P., Abbas, R., & Sharma, A. (2023). So what if ChatGPT wrote it? Multidisciplinary perspectives on opportunities, challenges and implications of generative conversational AI for research, practice and policy. *International Journal of Information Management, 71*, 102642.

Dwivedi, Y. K., Hughes, L., Wang, Y., Alalwan, A. A., Ahn, S. J., Balakrishnan, J., & Wirtz, J. (2023). Metaverse marketing: How the metaverse will shape the future of consumer research and practice. *Psychology and Marketing*, *40*(4), 750–776.

Dwork, C., Hardt, M., Pitassi, T., Reingold, O., & Zemel, R. (2012, January). Fairness through awareness. In Proceedings of the *3rd innovations in theoretical computer science conference* (pp. 214-226).

Edelman Trust Barometer. (2025). *India report.* https://www.edelman.in/sites/g/files/aatuss371/files/2024-03/2024%20Edelman%20Trust%20Barometer%20India%20Report_0.pdf

Edelman Trust Institute. (2025). *Global report: Trust and the crisis of grievance* (pp. 2–9). https://www.edelman.com/sites/g/files/aatuss191/files/2025-01/2025%20Edelman%20Trust%20Barometer%20Global%20Report_01.23.25.pdf

Eisend, M. (2025). Diversity in Interactive Advertising. *Journal of Interactive Advertising*, •••, 1–13. DOI: 10.1080/15252019.2025.2513236

Eisend, M., Muldrow, A. F., & Rosengren, S. (2023). Diversity and inclusion in advertising research. *International Journal of Advertising*, *42*(1), 52–59. DOI: 10.1080/02650487.2022.2122252

Eslami, M., Karahalios, K., Sandvig, C., & Fiesler, C. (2018).Faceless Book: 'Like' and the Politics of AI Personalization. *Proceedings of the 2018 CHI Conference on Human Factors in Computing Systems*, 1-13.

Estanyol, E., Mas-Manchón, L., Fernández-Cavia, J., & Van-Bergen, P. (2025). Raising the bar? How Generation Z perceives corporate reputation and environmental commitment. *Young Consumers: Insight and Ideas for Responsible Marketers*, 1-20. https://doi.org/DOI: 10.1108/yc-06-2025-2596

Etsy. (2020). *Diversity and inclusion in the Etsy marketplace.* Etsy.

European Commission. (2021). *Proposal for a regulation laying down harmonised rules on artificial intelligence (Artificial Intelligence Act).* https://artificialintelligenceact.eu/

European Commission. (2021). *Proposal for a regulation laying down harmonised rules on artificial intelligence (Artificial Intelligence Act).* Publications Office of the EU. https://artificialintelligenceact.eu

Fabre, É., Seaborn, K., Koiwai, S., Watanabe, M., & Riesch, P. (2025, April). More-than-Human Storytelling: Designing Longitudinal Narrative Engagements with Generative AI. In *Proceedings of the Extended Abstracts of the CHI Conference on Human Factors in Computing Systems* (pp. 1-10).

Farrington, S. (2020). A case study on Black Twitter's reactions to the framing of Blacks in Dove's 2017 Facebook advertisement (Master's thesis). University of South Florida. https://digitalcommons.usf.edu/etd/8446

Feldman, M., Friedler, S. A., Moeller, J., Scheidegger, C., & Venkatasubramanian, S. (2015). Certifying and removing disparate impact. *KDD '15: Proceedings of the 21st ACM SIGKDD International Conference on Knowledge Discovery and Data Mining*, 259–268. https://doi.org/DOI: 10.1145/2783258.2783311

Ferrell, O. C., Crittenden, V. L., Ferrell, L., & Crittenden, W. F. (2013). Theoretical development in ethical marketing decision making. *AMS Review*, *3*(2), 51–60. DOI: 10.1007/s13162-013-0047-8

Ferrell, O. C., & Ferrell, L. (2021). New directions for marketing ethics and social responsibility research. *Journal of Marketing Theory and Practice*, *29*(1), 13–22. DOI: 10.1080/10696679.2020.1860686

Ferrell, O. C., & Gresham, L. G. (1985). A contingency framework for understanding ethical decision making in marketing. *Journal of Marketing*, *49*(3), 87–96. DOI: 10.1177/002224298504900308

Floridi, L., & Cowls, J. (2022). A unified framework of five principles for AI in society. *Machine learning and the city: Applications in architecture and urban design*, 535-545.

Floridi, L. (2021). *The ethics of artificial intelligence*. Oxford University Press.

Floridi, L., & Cowls, L. (2019). A unified framework of five principles for AI in society. *Harvard Data Science Review*, *1*(1), 1–15.

Ford, R. C., & Richardson, W. D. (1994). Ethical decision making: A review of the empirical literature. *Journal of Business Ethics*, *13*(3), 205–221. DOI: 10.1007/BF02074820

Foster, J., Jones, A., & Pierre, R. (2022). Diverse datasets and inclusive AI development. *AI and Ethics*, *3*(2), 141–159. DOI: 10.1007/s43681-021-00126-4

Friestad, M., & Wright, P. (1994). The persuasion knowledge model: How people cope with persuasion attempts. *The Journal of Consumer Research*, *21*(1), 1–31.

FTC (Federal Trade Commission). (2021). *Aiming for truth, fairness, and equity in your company's use of AI*. https://www.ftc.gov/business-guidance/blog/2021/04/aiming-truth-fairness-equity-your-companys-use-ai

Gebru, T., Morgenstern, J., Vecchione, B., Vaughan, J. W., Wallach, H., Iii, H. D., & Crawford, K. (2021). Datasheets for datasets. *Communications of the ACM*, *64*(12), 86–92.

Geena Davis Institute on Gender in Media. (2019). *See it, be it: Analyzing representation in advertising using machine learning*. https://seejane.org

Georgeson, T. (n.d.). Dove's "Real Beauty" campaign: A critical analysis. Syracuse University Honors Theses. https://surface.syr.edu/honors_capstone/1271

Gerbaudo, P. (2012). *Tweets and the streets: Social media and contemporary activism*. Pluto Press.

Goedertier, F., Weijters, B., & Van den Bergh, J. (2024). Are Consumers Equally Willing to Pay More for Brands That Aim for Sustainability, Positive Societal Contribution, and Inclusivity as for Brands That Are Perceived as Exclusive? Generational, Gender, and Country Differences. *Sustainability*, *16*(9), 3879. DOI: 10.3390/su16093879

Goes, P. B., & Yip, S. (2020). Personalization in E-commerce: Impact on Online Buying Behavior and Conversion Rates. *Journal of Interactive Marketing*, *49*, 15–30.

Gomez-Uribe, C. A., & Hunt, N. (2016). The Netflix recommender system: Algorithms, business value, and innovation. *ACM Transactions on Management Information Systems*, *6*(4), 1–19. DOI: 10.1145/2843948

Goodman, B., & Flaxman, S. (2017). European Union regulations on algorithmic decision-making and a "right to explanation.". *AI Magazine*, *38*(3), 50–57. DOI: 10.1609/aimag.v38i3.2741

Grewal, D., Hulland, J., Kopalle, P. K., & Karahanna, E. (2020). The future of technology and marketing: A multidisciplinary perspective. *Journal of the Academy of Marketing Science*, *48*(1), 1–8.

Guidotti, R., Monreale, A., Ruggieri, S., Turini, F., Giannotti, F., & Pedreschi, D. (2019). A survey of methods for explaining black box models. *ACM Computing Surveys*, *51*(5), 1–42. DOI: 10.1145/3236009

Gupta, S., Wang, Y., Patel, P., & Czinkota, M. (2025). Navigating the future of AI in marketing: AI integration across borders, ethical considerations, and policy implications. *International Journal of Information Management*, *82*, 102871. DOI: 10.1016/j.ijinfomgt.2025.102871

H&M apologises over image of Black child in "monkey" hoodie. (2018, January 8). The Guardian. https://www.theguardian.com/fashion/2018/jan/08/h-and-m-apologises-over-image-of-black-child-in-monkey-hoodie

Hacker, P. (2023). Regulating AI: The case of the European AI Act. *Law, Innovation and Technology*, *15*(1), 123–151.

Hall, S. (1996). The question of cultural identity. In S. Hall, D. Held, & T. McGrew (Eds.), *Modernity and its futures* (pp. 274–316). Polity Press & Blackwell Publishers.

Hall, S. (1997). *Representation: Cultural representations and signifying practices.* Sage Publications. https://uk.sagepub.com/en-gb/eur/representation/book227613

Hardt, M., Price, E., & Srebro, N. (2016). Equality of opportunity in supervised learning. *Advances in Neural Information Processing Systems*, •••, 29.

Hardt, M., Price, E., & Srebro, N. (2016). Equality of opportunity in supervised learning. In Vol. 29, pp. 3315–3323). Advances in Neural Information Processing Systems. Curran Associates, Inc.

Haridasan, A. C., Xavier, N., Krishnan, M. A. N., & Glorindal, G. (2025). AI Washing in Marketing: Feasibility, Viability, and Ethical Constraints. In *Strategic Blueprints for AI-Driven Marketing in the Digital Era* (pp. 495–528). IGI Global Scientific Publishing.

Hari, H., Sharma, A., Verma, S., & Chaturvedi, R. (2024). Exploring ethical frontiers of artificial intelligence in marketing. *Journal of Responsible Technology, 100103.* Advance online publication. DOI: 10.1016/j.jrt.2024.100103

Hartmann, J., Exner, Y., & Domdey, S. (2025). The power of generative marketing: Can generative AI create superhuman visual content? *International Journal of Research in Marketing*, *42*(1), 13–31. DOI: 10.1016/j.ijresmar.2024.09.002

Hassan, M. A. E. (2025). ARTIFICIAL INTELLIGENCE TECHNOLOGIES AND THEIR ROLE IN FOSTERING CREATIVE THINKING IN DESIGN EDUCATION. *Pharos International Journal of Arts and Design*, *2*(01), 287–304.

Hermann, E. (2022). Leveraging artificial intelligence in marketing for social good: An ethical perspective. *Journal of Business Ethics*, *179*(1), 43–61. DOI: 10.1007/s10551-021-04843-y

Hermann, E., & Puntoni, S. (2025). Generative AI in marketing and principles for ethical design and deployment. *Journal of Public Policy & Marketing*, *44*(3), 332–349.

Hermann, E., & Puntoni, S. (2025). Generative AI in marketing and principles for ethical design. *Journal of Public Policy & Marketing*, *44*(3), 332–349. DOI: 10.1177/07439156241309874

Hiraman, B. R. (2018, August). A study of apache kafka in big data stream processing. In *2018 International Conference on Information, Communication, Engineering and Technology (ICICET)* (pp. 1-3). IEEE.

Hogan, E. A. (2001). "The Attention Economy: Understanding the New Currency of Business by Davenport Thomas H. and Beck John C. Boston: Harvard Business School Press, 15 (*4*), 145–147, doi: DOI: 10.5465/ame.2001.5898765

Hortillo, J. N., Moore, K., & Covington, S. M. (2025). AI and DEI: Do inclusive ads speak to the culture? An examination of marketing advertisement's efficacy to Gen Z consumers. *Journal of Cultural Marketing Strategy*, *10*(1), 81–93. DOI: 10.69554/CYUE5388

Huang, M. H., & Rust, R. T. (2022). A framework for collaborative artificial intelligence in marketing. *Journal of Retailing*, *98*(2), 209–223.

Huang, M.-H., & Rust, R. T. (2021). A strategic framework for artificial intelligence in marketing. *Journal of the Academy of Marketing Science*, *49*(1), 30–50. DOI: 10.1007/s11747-020-00749-9

Huang, M.-H., & Rust, R. T. (2021). Artificial Intelligence in Service: Applications and Opportunities. *Journal of Service Research*, *24*(1), 3–16.

Hughes, A. M. (2018). Machine Learning and Predictive Analytics in Marketing: A Framework for Application. *Journal of the Academy of Marketing Science*, *46*(4), 494–509.

Hughes, A. M. (2018). The New Marketing Model: How Targeted Marketing Reduces Costs and Increases Conversions. *Journal of Marketing Strategy*, *19*(4), 134–147.

Hunt, S. D., & Vitell, S. (1986). A general theory of marketing ethics. *Journal of Macromarketing*, *6*(1), 5–16. DOI: 10.1177/027614678600600103

Hurley, M., & Adebayo, J. (2017). Credit scoring in the era of big data. *Yale Journal of Law and Technology*, *18*(1), 148–216.

Hussain, A., & Cambria, E. (2021). Cultural intelligence in AI-driven marketing. *IEEE Intelligent Systems*, *36*(2), 76–87. DOI: 10.1109/MIS.2021.3053049

Hussain, A., & Hussain, A. (2025). Transparency and accountability: Unpacking the real problems of explainable AI. *AI & Society*, 1–2.

Irfan, M., Hussainey, K., Bukhari, S. A. C., & Nam, Y. (Eds.). (2024). *Issues of Sustainability in AI and New-Age Thematic Investing*. IGI Global. https://doi.org/IGI GlobalDOI: 10.4018/979-8-3693-3282-5

Irfan, M., Elmogy, M., Majid, M. S. A., & El-Sappagh, S. (Eds.). (2023). *The Impact of AI Innovation on Financial Sectors in the Era of Industry 5.0*. IGI Global., DOI: 10.4018/979-8-3693-0082-4

Irfan, M., Kadry, S., Sharif, M., & Khan, H. U. (Eds.). (2024). *Fintech Applications in Islamic Finance: AI, Machine Learning, and Blockchain Techniques*. IGI Global., DOI: 10.4018/979-8-3693-1038-0

Jamal, A., & Al-Marri, M. (2007). Exploring the effect of self-image congruence and brand preference on satisfaction: The role of expertise. *Journal of Marketing Management*, *23*(7–8), 613–629. DOI: 10.1362/026725707X2266

Jannach, D., & Adomavicius, G. (2016). Recommendation Systems: Challenges and Opportunities. *Computer Science Review*, *19*, 1–15.

Jarek, K., & Mazurek, G. (2019). Marketing and artificial intelligence. *Central European Business Review*, *8*(2), 46–55. DOI: 10.18267/j.cebr.213

Järvinen, J., & Taiminen, H. (2016). Research on Digital Marketing: A Review of Literature and Future Research Directions. *International Journal of Advertising*, *35*(3), 340–375.

Jena, M., Behera, R. K., & Rath, S. K. (2019, December). Machine learning models for stock prediction using real-time streaming data. In *International Conference on Biologically Inspired Techniques in Many-Criteria Decision Making* (pp. 101-108). Cham: Springer International Publishing.

Jenkins, H., Ito, M., & boyd, d. (2015). *Participatory culture in a networked era: A conversation on youth, learning, commerce, and politics*. Polity Press.

Jenkins, H. (1992). *Textual poachers: Television fans and participatory culture*. Routledge.

Jenkins, H. (2006). *Convergence culture: Where old and new media collide*. New York University Press.

Jenkins, H., Ford, S., & Green, J. (2013). *Spreadable media: Creating value and meaning in a networked culture*. New York University Press.

Jobin, A., Ienca, M., & Vayena, E. (2019). The global landscape of AI ethics guidelines. *Nature Machine Intelligence*, *1*(9), 389–399.

Joshi, P., Santy, S., Budhiraja, A., Bali, K., & Choudhury, M. (2020). *The state and fate of linguistic diversity in the NLP world*. In *Proceedings of the 58th Annual Meeting of the Association for Computational Linguistics* (pp. 6282–6293). Association for Computational Linguistics. https://doi.org/DOI: 10.18653/v1/2020.acl-main.560

Kamila, M. K., & Jasrotia, S. S. (2024). Ethics in marketing: Understanding past trends and future prospects through bibliometric analysis. *Journal of Nonprofit & Public Sector Marketing*, 1–32. DOI: 10.1080/10495142.2024.2361345

Kamiran, F., & Calders, T. (2012). Data preprocessing techniques for classification without discrimination. *Knowledge and Information Systems*, *33*(1), 1–33.

Kamishima, T., Akaho, S., Asoh, H., & Sakuma, J. (2012). Fairness-aware classifier with prejudice remover regularizer. In Flach, P. A., De Bie, T., & Cristianini, N. (Eds.), *Machine Learning and Knowledge Discovery in Databases* (Vol. 7524, pp. 35–50). Springer., DOI: 10.1007/978-3-642-33486-3_3

Kannan, P. K., & Li, H. (2017). Digital marketing: A framework, review and research agenda. *International Journal of Research in Marketing*, *34*(1), 22–45.

Kaplan, A., & Haenlein, M. (2019). Siri, Siri, in my hand: Who's the fairest in the land? On the interpretations, illustrations, and implications of artificial intelligence. *Business Horizons*, *62*(1), 15–25.

Kaplan, A., & Haenlein, M. (2022). Rulers of the world, unite! The challenges and opportunities of artificial intelligence. *Business Horizons*, *63*(1), 37–50. DOI: 10.1016/j.bushor.2019.09.003

Kaptein, M., de Ruyter, K., Markopoulos, P., & Aarts, E. (2015). Adaptive persuasive systems: A study of tailored persuasive text messages to reduce snacking. *ACM Transactions on Interactive Intelligent Systems*, *2*(2), 1–25.

Kasem, M. S., Hamada, M., & Taj-Eddin, I. (2024). Customer profiling, segmentation, and sales prediction using AI in direct marketing. *Neural Computing & Applications*, *36*(9), 4995–5005. DOI: 10.1007/s00521-023-09339-6

Kearns, M., Neel, S., Roth, A., & Wu, Z. S. (2018). Preventing fairness gerrymandering: Auditing and learning for subgroup fairness. In *Proceedings of the 35th International Conference on Machine Learning* (pp. 2564–2572).

Keller, K. L. (2009). Building strong brands in a modern marketing communications environment. *Journal of Marketing Communications*, *15*(2–3), 139–155. DOI: 10.1080/13527260902757530

Khan, M. A. A., Bhushan, C., Ravi, V., Rao, V. S., & Orsu, S. S. (2022). Nowcasting the financial time series with streaming data analytics under apache spark. arXiv preprint arXiv:2202.11820.

Kietzmann, J., Paschen, J., & Treen, E. (2018). Artificial intelligence in advertising: How marketers can leverage artificial intelligence along the consumer journey. *Journal of Advertising Research*, *58*(3), 263–267.

Kipnis, E., Demangeot, C., Pullig, C., Cross, S. N. N., Cui, C. C., Galalae, C., & Williams, J. D. (2021). Institutionalizing Diversity-and-Inclusion-Engaged Marketing for Multicultural Marketplace Well-Being. *Journal of Public Policy & Marketing*, *40*(2), 143–164. DOI: 10.1177/0743915620975415

Kireyev, P., Pauwels, K., & Gupta, S. (2016, September). Do display ads influence search? Attribution and dynamics in online advertising. *International Journal of Research in Marketing*, *33*(3), 475–490. DOI: 10.1016/j.ijresmar.2015.09.007

Koçak, B. B. (2025). HOW TO USE GENAI AS A RATER IN MARKETING: A COMPREHENSIVE GENAI-BASED CONTENT CODING FRAMEWORK. *Yönetim Bilimleri Dergisi*, *23*(57), 1705–1725.

Koenecke, A., Nam, A., Lake, E., Nudell, J., Quartey, M., Mengesha, Z., Toups, C., Rickford, J. R., Jurafsky, D., & Goel, S. (2020). Racial disparities in automated speech recognition. *Proceedings of the National Academy of Sciences of the United States of America*, *117*(14), 7684–7689. https://www.pnas.org/doi/10.1073/pnas.1915768117 PMID: 32205437

Kolańska-Stronka, M., & Singh, B. (2024). Five decades of self-congruity in consumer behaviour research: A systematic review and future research agenda. *International Journal of Consumer Studies*, *48*(1), e12983. https://doi.org/https://doi.org/10.1111/ijcs.12983

Konishi, C., Vargas-Madriz, L. F., & Tesolin, J. (2025). Fostering equity, diversity, and inclusion through social-emotional learning: The role of digital technologies. *Journal of Research on Technology in Education*, •••, 1–13. DOI: 10.1080/15391523.2025.2455054

Kopalle, P. K., Gangwar, M., Kaplan, A., Ramachandran, D., Reinartz, W., & Rindfleisch, A. (2022). Examining artificial intelligence (AI) technologies in marketing via a global lens: Current trends and future research opportunities. *International Journal of Research in Marketing*, *39*(2), 522–540. DOI: 10.1016/j.ijresmar.2021.11.002

Koren, Y., Bell, R., & Volinsky, C. (2009, August). Matrix Factorization Techniques for Recommender Systems. *Computer*, *42*(8), 30–37. DOI: 10.1109/MC.2009.263

Kossmann, E., & Gómez-Suárez, M. (2018). Decision-making processes for purchases of ethical products: Gaps between academic research and needs of marketing practitioners. *International Review on Public and Nonprofit Marketing*, *15*(3), 353–370. DOI: 10.1007/s12208-018-0204-8

Kotler, P., Kartajaya, H., & Setiawan, I. (2021). *Marketing 5.0: Technology for humanity*. Wiley.

Kotler, P., & Keller, K. L. (2016). *Marketing Management* (15th ed.). Pearson Education.

Kumar, V., Ashraf, A. R., & Nadeem, W. (2024). AI-powered marketing: What, where, and how? *International Journal of Information Management*, *77*, 102783. DOI: 10.1016/j.ijinfomgt.2024.102783

Kumar, V., Dixit, A., Javalgi, R. G., Dass, M., & Kumar, P. (2019). Digital transformation of business-to-business marketing: Framework, evolution, and research agenda. *Industrial Marketing Management*, *81*, 90–102.

Kumar, V., & Shah, D. (2017). Building and Sustaining Profitable Customer Loyalty for the 21st Century. *JMR, Journal of Marketing Research*, *54*(2), 255–270.

Kusner, M. J., Loftus, J., Russell, C., & Silva, R. (2017). Counterfactual fairness. *Advances in Neural Information Processing Systems*, •••, 30.

Kyoung-Sook, M. O. O. N., & Hongjoong, K. I. M. (2019). Performance of deep learning in prediction of stock market volatility. *Economic Computation and Economic Cybernetics Studies and Research*, *53*(2).

Lambrecht, A., & Tucker, C. (2019). Algorithmic bias? An empirical study of apparent gender-based discrimination in the display of STEM career ads. *Management Science*, *65*(7), 2966–2981. https://pubsonline.informs.org/doi/abs/10.1287/mnsc.2019.3098

Lambrecht, A., & Tucker, C. (2019). Algorithmic bias? An empirical study of targeted advertisements. *Management Science*, *65*(5), 2547–2561. DOI: 10.1287/mnsc.2018.3098

Lambrecht, A., & Tucker, C. (2019). Algorithmic Bias? *Management Science, 65*(7), 2966–2981.

Lambrecht, A., & Tucker, C. (2024). Apparent algorithmic discrimination and real-time algorithmic learning in digital search advertising. *Quantitative Marketing and Economics, 22*(4), 357–387.

Langer, M., & Landers, R. N. (2021). The future of artificial intelligence in employee selection. *International Journal of Selection and Assessment, 29*(1–2), 195–216.

Lehman, D. W., O'Connor, K., Kovács, B., & Newman, G. E. (2019). Authenticity. *The Academy of Management Annals, 13*(1), 1–42. DOI: 10.5465/annals.2017.0047

Licsandru, T. C., & Cui, C. C. (2018). Subjective social inclusion: A conceptual critique for socially inclusive marketing. *Journal of Business Research, 82*, 330–339. https://doi.org/https://doi.org/10.1016/j.jbusres.2017.08.036

Licsandru, T. C., & Cui, C. C. (2022). Ethnic marketing: the good, the bad and the unknown. In *Handbook of Research on Ethnic and Intra-cultural Marketing* (pp. 29–40). Edward Elgar Publishing.

Licsandru, T. C., Mari, C., Kipnis, E., Galalae, C., Johnson, E., Cross, S. N., & Yoruk, I. (2025). Integrating diversity, equity and inclusion in management education: An empathy framework. *British Journal of Management*. Advance online publication. DOI: 10.1111/1467-8551.70008

Li, H., & Kannan, P. K. (2014). Attributing conversions in a multichannel online marketing environment: An empirical model and a field experiment. *JMR, Journal of Marketing Research, 51*(1), 40–56.

Linden, G., Smith, B., & York, J. (2021). The Role of AI in Personalization: Transforming E-Commerce and Digital Marketing. *Journal of Business Research, 124*, 14–23.

Liu-Thompkins, Y., Okazaki, S., & Li, H. (2022). Artificial empathy in marketing interactions: Bridging the human-AI gap in affective and social customer experience. *Journal of the Academy of Marketing Science, 50*(6), 1198–1218. DOI: 10.1007/s11747-022-00892-5

Low, W., & Davenport, E. (2005). Has the medium (roast) become the message? *International Marketing Review, 22*(5), 494–511. DOI: 10.1108/02651330510624354

Low, W., & Davenport, E. (2008). Organizational leadership, ethics and the challenges of marketing fair and ethical trade. *Journal of Business Ethics, 86*(S1), 97–108. DOI: 10.1007/s10551-008-9763-7

Luca, A. (2021). The role of artificial intelligence in customer personalization: Transforming marketing strategies for businesses. *Journal of Business & Technology*, *18*(2), 125–139.

Luccioni, S., Akiki, C., Mitchell, M., & Jernite, Y. (2023). Stable bias: Evaluating societal representations in diffusion models. *Advances in Neural Information Processing Systems*, *36*, 56338–56351.

Lundberg, S. M., & Lee, S.-I. (2017). A unified approach to interpreting model predictions. In *Advances in Neural Information Processing Systems* (Vol. 30). https://proceedings.neurips.cc/paper/2017/hash/8a20a8621978632d76c43dfd28b67767-Abstract.html

Mandania, R., Cadogan, J., Liu, J., & Kazmi, N. (2025). Optimizing Promotional Campaigns to Maximize Customer Lifetime Value: A Dynamic Learning Approach. *Journal of Service Research*, *0*(0). Advance online publication. DOI: 10.1177/10946705251365524

Mariani, M. M., Perez-Vega, R., & Wirtz, J. (2022). AI in marketing, consumer research, and psychology: A systematic review. *Psychology and Marketing*, *39*(4), 755–776. DOI: 10.1002/mar.21619

Martí, G. (2025). Antiracism as Inclusivity: The Racial Justice Paradigm of White Progressive Churches. *Journal for the Scientific Study of Religion*, *64*(2), 173–186. https://doi.org/https://doi.org/10.1111/jssr.12949

Martin, K. (2018). Ethical Issues in the Big Data Industry: Understanding Informed Consent and Privacy. *Journal of Business Ethics*, *152*(2), 465–482.

Mastercard. (2020). *Inclusive AI: Advancing responsible use of artificial intelligence.* Mastercard Insights.

Mayo Clinic Reports. (2020). *AI and patient engagement: Equity in action.* Mayo Clinic.

McEachern, M. G., & Carrigan, M. (2012). Revisiting contemporary issues in green/ethical marketing: An introduction to the special issue. *Journal of Marketing Management*, *28*(3-4), 189-194.

McKinsey & Company. (2021). *Diversity wins: How inclusion matters.* https://www.mckinsey.com/featured-insights/diversity-and-inclusion/diversity-wins-how-inclusion-matters

Mehrabi, N., Morstatter, F., Saxena, N., Lerman, K., & Galstyan, A. (2021). A survey on bias and fairness in machine learning. *ACM Computing Surveys*, *54*(6), 1–35.

Mehrabi, N., Morstatter, F., Saxena, N., Lerman, K., & Galstyan, A. (2021). A Survey on Bias and Fairness in Machine Learning. *ACM Computing Surveys, 54*(6), 1–35.

Mikalef, P., Boura, M., Lekakos, G., & Krogstie, J. (2019). Big data analytics and firm performance: Findings from a mixed-method approach. *Journal of Business Research, 98*, 261–276. DOI: 10.1016/j.jbusres.2019.01.044

Mikians, J., Gyarmati, L., Erramilli, V., & Laoutaris, N. (2013). Detecting price and search discrimination on the internet. *Proceedings of the 11th ACM Workshop on Hot Topics in Networks*, 79–84.

Miller, T. (2019). Explanation in artificial intelligence: Insights from the social sciences. *Artificial Intelligence, 267*, 1–38. DOI: 10.1016/j.artint.2018.07.007

Mishra, V., & Gupta, P. (2025). Drivers of consumer brand advocacy in the metaverse. *Journal of Fashion Marketing and Management*, •••, 1–19. DOI: 10.1108/jfmm-04-2024-0145

Mitchell, M., Wu, S., Zaldivar, A., Barnes, P., Vasserman, L., Hutchinson, B., . . . Gebru, T. (2019, January). Model cards for model reporting. In Proceedings of the conference on *fairness, accountability, and transparency* (pp. 220-229).

Munsch, A. (2021). Millennial and generation Z digital marketing communication and advertising effectiveness: A qualitative exploration. *Journal of Global Scholars of Marketing Science, 31*(1), 10–29. DOI: 10.1080/21639159.2020.1808812

Murphy, P. E., Laczniak, G. R., & Harris, F. (2017). Ethics in marketing. *International cases and perspectives.*

Narayanan, S., & Singh, G. A. (2025). From Stimulus to Response: Understanding the Causes and Outcomes of Consumer Activism. *Journal of Consumer Behaviour, 24*(2), 820–845. https://doi.org/https://doi.org/10.1002/cb.2438

Nazir, M., & Wani, T. A. (2025). Human vs virtual influencers and message framing: Enhancing environmental awareness, activism and sustainable purchase intentions through effective messaging. *Management Research Review, 48*(5), 685–708. DOI: 10.1108/mrr-08-2024-0630

Ngai, E. W., Lee, M. C., & Kei, B. C. (2025). A Generative Artificial Intelligence (GenAI) System for Fashion Design: A Case Study. *IEEE Transactions on Engineering Management.*

Nissenbaum, H. (2010). *Privacy in Context: Technology, Policy, and the Integrity of Social Life*. Stanford University Press.

Noble, S. U. (2018). *Algorithms of oppression: How search engines reinforce racism.* NYU Press. https://psycnet.apa.org/record/2018-08016-000

Noble, S. U. (2018). Algorithms of oppression: How search engines reinforce racism. In *Algorithms of oppression.* New York university press.

Noble, S. U. (2018). *Algorithms of oppression: How search engines reinforce racism.* New York University Press., https://nyupress.org/9781479833641/

Norman, D., & Nielsen, J. (2019). The definition of user experience (UX). Nielsen Norman Group. https://www.nngroup.com/articles/definition-user-experience/

O'Neil, C. (2016). *Weapons of math destruction: How big data increases inequality and threatens democracy.* Crown Publishing Group.

Ochis, K. (2024). *Gen Z in work: A practical guide to engaging employees across the generations.* Routledge.

Odlin, D., & Benson-Rea, M. (2021). Market niches as dynamic, co-created resource domains. *Industrial Marketing Management, 95*, 29–40.

OECD. (2021). *OECD principles on artificial intelligence.* OECD Publishing., DOI: 10.1787/eedfee77-

Opoku-Dakwa, A., & Rice, D. B. (2024). A Place for Critical Race Theory and Wokeness in Diversity Strategies. *The Academy of Management Perspectives, 38*(2), 214–224. DOI: 10.5465/amp.2023.0015

Palmer, D., & Hedberg, T. (2013). The ethics of marketing to vulnerable populations. *Journal of Business Ethics, 116*(2), 403–413.

Pandey, P., & Rai, A. K. (2024). Modeling consequences of brand authenticity in anthropomorphized AI-assistants: A human–robot interaction perspective. *Purushartha, 17*(1), 116–135. https://journals.smsvaranasi.com/index.php/purushartha/article/download/2147/1002. journals.smsvaranasi.com

Pandey, V., Kushwaha, G. S., & Srivastava, S. (2023). Factors influencing adoption of digital payments: A PLS-SEM and ANN approach. *Purushartha, 16*(2), 91–104. https://journals.smsvaranasi.com/index.php/purushartha/article/download/2019/970

Pani, D., & Behera, S. N. (2021). An investigation of customer preferences using data mining. *Dogo Rangsang Research Journal, 8*(14), Article 03.

Papacharissi, Z. (2015). *Affective publics: Sentiment, technology, and politics.* Oxford University Press.

Park, C.-I., & Namkung, Y. (2022). The effects of Instagram marketing activities on customer-based brand equity in the coffee industry. *Sustainability*, *14*(3), 1657. DOI: 10.3390/su14031657

Park, Y. W., Voss, G. B., & Voss, Z. G. (2023). Advancing customer diversity, equity, and inclusion: Measurement, stakeholder influence, and the role of marketing. *Journal of the Academy of Marketing Science*, *51*(1), 174–197. DOI: 10.1007/s11747-022-00883-6

Pazzani, M. J., & Billsus, D. (2007). "Content-Based Recommendation Systems," in The Adaptive Web. In Brusilovsky, P., Kobsa, A., & Nejdl, W. (Eds.), *Lecture Notes in Computer Science* (Vol. 4321, pp. 325–341). Springer Berlin Heidelberg., DOI: 10.1007/978-3-540-72079-9_10

Peddireddy, K. (2023, May). Streamlining enterprise data processing, reporting and realtime alerting using apache kafka. In 2023 11th International Symposium on Digital Forensics and Security (ISDFS) (pp. 1-4). IEEE.

Perera, M. V., & Patel, V. M. (2023, September). Analyzing bias in diffusion-based face generation models. In 2023 *IEEE International Joint Conference on Biometrics (IJCB)* (pp. 1-10). IEEE.

Pires, G. D., & Stanton, J. (2002). Ethnic marketing ethics. *Journal of Business Ethics*, *36*(1), 111-118.

Pop, L., Morales, L., Peev, I., Soulé, M. V., Coetzer, J. H., & Gilani, H. (2024). Inclusivity and Diversity: Marketing Exercise or a Real Commitment? In *Decolonizing Marketing Theory and Practice* (pp. 114-136). Routledge.

PwC. (2022). AI Ethics and Governance Report. PwC Global. https://www.pwc.com/gx/en/issues/data-and-analytics/artificial-intelligence/what-is-responsible-ai/pwc-responsible-ai.pdf

Qadadeh, W., & Abdallah, S. (2018). Customers segmentation in the insurance company (TIC) dataset. *Procedia Computer Science*, *144*, 277–290. DOI: 10.1016/j.procs.2018.10.529

Rabbanee, F. K., Roy, R., & Spence, M. T. (2020). Factors affecting consumer engagement on online social networks: Self-congruity, brand attachment, and self-extension tendency. *European Journal of Marketing*, *54*(6), 1407–1431. DOI: 10.1108/ejm-03-2018-0221

Raj, A. (2024). What kind of Marketing Data is needed for Artificial Intelligence Analysis? A Theoretical Approach. *Purushartha – A Journal of Management. *Ethics and Spirituality*, *16*(2), 21–33.

Raji, I., & Buolamwini, J. (2019). Actionable auditing: Investigating bias in AI systems. *Proceedings of the AAAI/ACM Conference on AI, Ethics, and Society*, 1–9. https://doi.org/DOI: 10.1145/3306618.3314244

Raji, I., Smart, A., & White, R.. (2020). Closing the AI accountability gap: Defining an end-to-end framework for algorithmic auditing. *FAT Conference*. https://doi.org/DOI: 10.1145/3351095.3372873

Ramaswamy, V., & Ozcan, T. (2022). Artificial intelligence, customer experience, and marketing ethics. *Journal of Business Research*, *145*, 799–812.

Ramezani, D., & Wagner, M. (2025). REDEFINING STUDENT AGENCY IN THE AGE OF GENAI. In *EDULEARN25 Proceedings* (pp. 7102-7107). IATED.

Ribeiro, M. T., Singh, S., & Guestrin, C. (2016). "Why should I trust you?": Explaining the predictions of any classifier. In *Proceedings of the 22nd ACM SIGKDD International Conference on Knowledge Discovery and Data Mining* (pp. 1135–1144). https://doi.org/DOI: 10.1145/2939672.2939778

Ricci, F., Rokach, L., & Shapira, B. (2015). *Recommender Systems Handbook*. Springer.

Rivas, P., & Zhao, L. (2023). Marketing with ChatGPT: Navigating the ethical terrain of GPT-based chatbot technology. *AI*, *4*(2), 375–384. DOI: 10.3390/ai4020019

Rohmanue, A., & Jacobi, E. S. (2024). The influence of marketing communications agencies on activist brands' moral competency development and ability to engage in authentic brand activism: Wieden+Kennedy 'Just Does It'. *Journal of Brand Management*, *31*(2), 126–139. DOI: 10.1057/s41262-023-00340-x

Rosengren, S., Eisend, M., Koslow, S., & Dahlen, M. (2020). A meta-analysis of when and how advertising creativity works. *Journal of Marketing*, *84*(6), 39–56.

Rößner, A., & Eisend, M. (2023). Ethnic Minorities in Advertising. *Journal of Advertising*, *52*(5), 774–784. DOI: 10.1080/00913367.2023.2255247

Rust, R. T. (2020). The future of marketing. *International Journal of Research in Marketing*, *37*(1), 15–26.

Sah, J., Padma, S., Yanamandra, R., & Irfan, M. (2024). *Risk management of future of DeFi using artificial intelligence as a tool*. In M. Irfan & M. Elmogy (Eds.), *AI-Driven Decentralized Finance and the Future of Finance* (pp. 22). IGI Global. https://doi.org/ IGI GlobalDOI: 10.4018/979-8-3693-6321-8.ch011

Saleh, R. A., & Zeebaree, S. R. (2025). Artificial Intelligence in E-commerce and Digital Marketing: A Systematic Review of Opportunities, Challenges, and Ethical Implications. *Asian Journal of Research in Computer Science, 18*, 395-410.

Sands, S., & Ferraro, C. (2025). DEI rollbacks: Consequences and considerations for brand managers. *Business Horizons*. Advance online publication. DOI: 10.1016/j.bushor.2025.02.010

Sardashti, H., & Calantone, R. J. (2022). Does equity-based compensation motivate executives to build strong brands? *Journal of Marketing Management, 38*(13–14), 1433–1460. DOI: 10.1080/0267257X.2022.2041068

Saura, J. R., Ribeiro-Soriano, D., & Palacios-Marqués, D. (2021). Setting B2B digital marketing in artificial intelligence-based CRMs: A review and directions for future research. *Industrial Marketing Management, 98*, 161–178. DOI: 10.1016/j.indmarman.2021.08.006

Schein, E. H. (2017). *Organizational culture and leadership* (5th ed.). Wiley.

Schwarz, K. C., & Williams, J. P. (2020). Introduction to the social construction of identity and authenticity. In *Studies on the social construction of identity and authenticity* (pp. 1–24). Routledge.

Sebestyén, M. (2025). Focal points and blind spots of human-centered AI. *Humanities & Social Sciences Communications, 12*(1), 564. DOI: 10.1057/s41599-025-04814-y

Seif, M. M., Ramzy Hamed, E. M., & Abdel Ghfar Hegazy, A. E. F. (2018, January). Stock market real time recommender model using apache spark framework. In *International conference on advanced machine learning technologies and applications* (pp. 671-683). Cham: Springer International Publishing.

Sephora. (2020). *Sephora diversity and inclusion report.* Sephora.

Shakespeare, S. (2018, January 17). H&M perception holds up in the UK after controversy—but dips in the US. YouGov. https://yougov.co.uk/politics/articles/20069-hm-perception-holds-uk-after-controversy

Shankar, V., & Carpenter, G. S. (2020). Mobile Marketing: A Strategic Perspective. *Journal of the Academy of Marketing Science, 48*(3), 332–351.

Sheng, E., Chang, K. W., Natarajan, P., & Peng, N. (2021, August). Societal biases in language generation: Progress and challenges. In Proceedings of the 59th annual meeting of the *association for computational linguistics and the 11th international joint conference on natural language processing* (volume 1: long papers) (pp. 4275-4293).

Shen, Y., Wang, Z., & Fan, Y. Ethical Issues and Value Tensions in the Context of GenAI-Assisted Learning. In *Learning with Generative Artificial Intelligence* (pp. 222–253). Routledge.

Shepperson, L., von Rosing, M., & Czichos, H. (2025). Diversity of perspectives. In *The Sustainability Handbook* (Vol. 1, pp. 359–373). Elsevier.

Shneiderman, B. (2022). Human-centered artificial intelligence: Reliable, safe, and trustworthy. *Interactions (New York, N.Y.)*, *29*(6), 74–83. DOI: 10.1145/3561809

Singhapakdi, A. (1999). Perceived importance of ethics and ethical decisions in marketing. *Journal of business research*, *45*(1), 89-99.

Siraj, M., Duke, J., & Plötz, T. (2025). The GenAI Generation: Student Views of Awareness, Preparedness, and Concern. *arXiv preprint arXiv:2505.02230.*

Sirgy, M. J. (1982). Self-Concept in Consumer Behavior: A Critical Review. *The Journal of Consumer Research*, *9*(3), 287–300. DOI: 10.1086/208924

Sloane, M., Moss, E., & Chowdhury, R. (2021). A silicon valley love triangle: Hiring algorithms, pseudo-science, and the quest for diversity. *AI & Society*. https://link.springer.com/article/10.1007/s00146-021-01314-4

Smith, B., & Linden, G. (2017). Two decades of recommender systems at Amazon. *IEEE Internet Computing*, *21*(3), 12–18. DOI: 10.1109/MIC.2017.72

Soleimani, M., Intezari, A., Arrowsmith, J., Pauleen, D. J., & Taskin, N. (2025). Reducing AI bias in recruitment and selection: An integrative approach. *International Journal of Human Resource Management*, *36*(14), 2480–2515. DOI: 10.1080/09585192.2025.2480617

Srivastava, R., Gupta, P., Kumar, H., & Tuli, N. (2023). Digital customer engagement: A systematic literature review and research agenda. *Australian Journal of Management, 50*(1), 220-245. https://doi.org/ (Original work published 2025)DOI: 10.1177/03128962231177096

Staff, S. (2018, January 18). H&M appoints global diversity leader after "monkey in the jungle" controversy. NDTV. https://www.ndtv.com/lifestyle/h-m-appoints-global-diversity-leader-after-monkey-in-the-jungle-controversy-1801656

Starke, C., Baleis, J., Keller, B., & Marcinkowski, F. (2022). Fairness perceptions of algorithmic decision-making: A systematic review of the empirical literature. *Big Data & Society*, *9*(2), 20539517221115189. DOI: 10.1177/20539517221115189

Steurer, R. (2021). Kafka: Real-Time Streaming for the Finance Industry. In The Digital Journey of Banking and Insurance, Volume III: Data Storage, Data Processing and Data Analysis (pp. 73-88). Cham: Springer International Publishing.

Suresh, H., & Guttag, J. (2021, October). A framework for understanding sources of harm throughout the machine learning life cycle. In Proceedings of the 1st *ACM Conference* on *Equity and Access in Algorithms, Mechanisms, and Optimization* (pp. 1-9).

Szaban, M., Szymkowiak, A., & Zdziennicka, A. (2025). Unpacking consumer price perceptions: The role of sustainability and ethical labels in the cosmetics market. *Journal of Cleaner Production*, *490*, 144730.

Taddeo, M., & Floridi, L. (2018). How AI can be a force for good. *Science*, *361*(6404), 751–752. DOI: 10.1126/science.aat5991

Tarnanidis, T. (2025). Digital marketing and AI integration with robotics for the fight against racism in football: A cross-cultural investigation. International Journal of Business and Applied Social Science, 11(3), 28-34. http://dx.doi.org/10.33642/ijbass.v11n3p4

Tarnanidis, T., Manda, V. K., Sousa, B. B., Vlachopoulou, M., & Papachristou, E. (2026c). Marketing Complexity of Smart Consumer Products to Global Millennial Segments. In Tarnanidis, T., Sousa, B., Vlachopoulou, M., Papachristou, E., & Kittu Manda, V. (Eds.), *Diversity and Inclusion-Driven Marketing for Multicultural Marketplaces* (pp. 1–16). IGI Global Scientific Publishing., DOI: 10.4018/979-8-3373-2111-0.ch001

Tarnanidis, T., Sousa, B., Vlachopoulou, M., Papachristou, E., & Kittu Manda, V. (Eds.). (2026). *Diversity and inclusion-driven marketing for multicultural marketplaces*. IGI Global Scientific Publishing., DOI: 10.4018/979-8-3373-2111-0

Tarnanidis, T., & Vlachopoulou, M. (2025). *Cultural sensitivity, cross-border logistics, and e-commerce in global marketing*. IGI Global Scientific Publishing., DOI: 10.4018/979-8-3373-0528-8

Tsougkou, E., Karampela, M., & Balabanis, G. (2024). Drivers and mechanisms of consumer attitudes toward global brand activists: A mediated approach. *International Marketing Review*, *41*(6), 1330–1357. DOI: 10.1108/imr-09-2023-0237

Tuli, N., Kumar, H., Upadhyay, S., & Ciszek, E. (2025). Distance between 'them' and 'us': Identity stigmatization in the age of consumer inclusion. *International Journal of Advertising*, •••, 1–30. DOI: 10.1080/02650487.2025.2592469

Turner, J. C., Brown, R. J., & Tajfel, H. (1979). Social comparison and group interest in ingroup favouritism. *European Journal of Social Psychology*, *9*(2), 187–204. https://doi.org/https://doi.org/10.1002/ejsp.2420090207

Tuten, T. L., & Solomon, M. R. (2017). *Social Media Marketing* (3rd ed.). Pearson Education.

Van de Ven, B. (2008). An ethical framework for the marketing of corporate social responsibility. *Journal of business ethics*, *82*(2), 339-352.

Van den Bergh, J., De Pelsmacker, P., & Worsley, B. (2023). Beyond labels: Segmenting the Gen Z market for more effective marketing. *Young Consumers: Insight and Ideas for Responsible Marketers*, *25*(2), 188–210. DOI: 10.1108/yc-03-2023-1707

van Esch, P., & Cui, Y. (Gina), & Heilgenberg, K. (2024). Using AI to implement DEI into marketing: The CONSIDER framework. *Australasian Marketing Journal*, *32*(3), 250–262. DOI: 10.1177/14413582241244504

Varsha, P. S. (2023). How can we manage biases in artificial intelligence systems–A systematic literature review. *International Journal of Information Management Data Insights*, *3*(1), 100165. DOI: 10.1016/j.jjimei.2023.100165

Velinov, E. (2025). Generation Z in Focus: Behavioral Insights from Emerging and Advanced Markets. In *Gen Z at Work in Central and Eastern Europe* (pp. 26-41). Routledge.

Véliz, C. (2021). *Privacy is power*. Melville House.

Verhoef, P. C., Kannan, P. K., & Inman, J. J. (2015). From multi-channel retailing to omni-channel retailing: Introduction to the special issue on multi-channel retailing. *Journal of Retailing*, *91*(2), 174–181. DOI: 10.1016/j.jretai.2015.02.005

Verma, S., & Rubin, J. (2018). Fairness definitions explained. In *Proceedings of the International Workshop on Software Fairness* (pp. 1–7). https://doi.org/DOI: 10.1145/3194770.3194776

Verma, S., Sharma, R., Deb, S., & Maitra, D. (2021). Artificial intelligence in marketing: Systematic review and future research direction. *International Journal of Information Management Data Insights*, *1*(1), 100002. DOI: 10.1016/j.jjimei.2020.100002

Vieira, R., Paiva, D., & Ochoa, C. (2020). Algorithmic stereotypes in Brazilian social media ecosystems. *Brazilian Journal of Communication*. https://bjc.emnuvens.com.br

Vitellaro, F., Schifilliti, V., Buratti, N., & Cesaroni, F. (2025). I won't become obsolete! exploring the acceptance and use of GenAI by marketing professionals. *European Journal of Innovation Management.*

Vlacic, B., Corbo, L., Silva, S. C., & Dabic, M. (2021). The evolving role of artificial intelligence in marketing: A review and research agenda. *Journal of Business Research*, *128*, 187–203. DOI: 10.1016/j.jbusres.2021.01.055

Voronov, A. A., Gorlachev, P. V., Mirzoeva, E. V., Rudenko, V. A., & Popova, T. S. (2021). Role of social and ethical marketing in improving sustainable business development. In *Cooperation and Sustainable Development* (pp. 1249-1255). Cham: Springer International Publishing.

Vorster, L., Licsandru, T., Kipnis, E., Mari, C., Ruiz, V. M., Kearney, S., & Cross, S. N. (2024). Towards Comprehensive Integration of Diversity, Equity and Inclusion in Management Education: An Empathy-Driven Framework. *British Journal of Management.*

Vyas, S., Tyagi, R. K., Jain, C., & Sahu, S. (2022, February). Performance evaluation of apache kafka–a modern platform for real time data streaming. In 2022 2nd International Conference on Innovative Practices in Technology and Management (ICIPTM) (Vol. 2, pp. 465-470). IEEE.

Wachter, S., Mittelstadt, B., & Floridi, L. (2017). Why a right to explanation of automated decision-making does not exist in the General Data Protection Regulation. *International Data Privacy Law, 7*(2), 76–99. https://academic.oup.com/idpl/article/7/2/76/3860944

Waller, S., & Clarkson, J. (2021). *Designing for inclusion: A practical guide*. University of Cambridge Inclusive Design Toolkit. https://www.inclusivedesigntoolkit.com

Wedel, M., & Kannan, P. K. (2016). Marketing analytics for data-rich environments. *Journal of Marketing*, *80*(6), 97–121.

Wedel, M., & Kannan, P. K. (2016). *Marketing Analytics: A Practical Guide to Real Marketing Science*. Wiley.

Wei, D. (2019, October). Prediction of stock price based on LSTM neural network. In *2019 International Conference on Artificial Intelligence and Advanced Manufacturing (AIAM)* (pp. 544-547). IEEE.

Whittaker, M., Crawford, K., Dobbe, R., Fried, G., Kaziunas, E., Mathur, V., West, S., Richardson, R., Schultz, J., & Schwartz, O. (2018). *AI Now Report 2018.* AI Now Institute, New York University. https://ainowinstitute.org/AI_Now_2018_Report.pdf

Whitwam, B. (2025). Global Cultural Convergence in Social Commerce: How Platforms Transform Trust-Building among Gen Z Consumers. *Journal of Internet Commerce*, *24*(4), 325–347. DOI: 10.1080/15332861.2025.2547067

World Economic Forum. (2022). *The future of jobs and AI's ethical integration.* https://www.weforum.org/reports

Wu, H., Shang, Z., & Wolter, K. (2020, June). Learning to reliably deliver streaming data with apache kafka. In 2020 50th Annual IEEE/IFIP International Conference on Dependable Systems and Networks (DSN) (pp. 564-571). IEEE.

Xiao, B., & Benbasat, I. (2007). E-commerce product recommendation agents: Use, characteristics, and impact. *Management Information Systems Quarterly*, •••, 137–209. DOI: 10.2307/25148784

Xin, Y., Gao, J., Yang, X., & Yang, J. (2023). Maximum likelihood estimation for uncertain autoregressive moving average model with application in financial market. *Journal of Computational and Applied Mathematics*, *417*, 114604.

Yang, S., Goh, E., & Fan, Y. (2025). Advancing self-congruity theory in senior tourism: A perspective on theoretical, methodological and contextual progress. *Asia Pacific Journal of Marketing and Logistics*. Advance online publication. DOI: 10.1108/apjml-08-2024-1152

Yin, R. K. (2014). *Case study research: Design and methods* (5th ed.). SAGE Publications.

Zhang, J., & Wedel, M. (2019). The Role of Customer Segmentation in E-commerce and Digital Marketing. *JMR, Journal of Marketing Research*, *56*(3), 432–451.

Zhao, X., Gu, C., Zhang, H., Yang, X., Liu, X., Tang, J., & Liu, H. (2021, May). Dear: Deep reinforcement learning for online advertising impression in recommender systems. In *Proceedings of the AAAI conference on artificial intelligence* 35(*1*), 750-758). doi: DOI: 10.1609/aaai.v35i1.16156

Zimand-Sheiner, D., & Lissitsa, S. (2024). Generation Z - factors predicting decline in purchase intentions after receiving negative environmental information: Fast fashion brand SHEIN as a case study. *Journal of Retailing and Consumer Services*, *81*, 103999. DOI: 10.1016/j.jretconser.2024.103999

About the Contributors

Theodore Tarnanidis is a marketing scholar, adjunct professor at the International Hellenic University and researcher in Applications of D.Sc. and MCDA. Theodore has six years experience as a marketing and decision making practitioner. He made his post-doc research in the area of sustainable entrepreneurship from the University of Macedonia. He obtained a Ph.D. from the University of London Met., UK. He received his M.B.A from Liverpool University, UK and is a graduate from the University of Macedonia (Business Administration) and Alexander Technological Educational Institute (Marketing). His research focuses on International Marketing, Multi-cultural Marketing, Marketing Management, Consumer Science by Means of Rank-Coded Data, Preference Measurement Techniques, Quantitative Methods & Structural Equation Modelling. His work has been published in various internationally renowned scientific conferences (Academy of Marketing, European Marketing Academy, PROMETHEE Days, Hellenic Operational Research) and in journals (Journal of Business Ethics, World Review of Entrepreneurship, Management and Sustainable Development, Journal of Retailing and Consumer Services, Current Issues in Tourism, Marketing Science & Inspirations, Management Science Letters).(92688785-cfd1-4165-96e2-f45addaa1f81)

Jeeva Benny is a student pursuing her Bachelor of Business Administration at Christ University, Bangalore, with a specialization in Business Analytics. She is currently researching the intersection of Artificial Intelligence and Sustainability. She has worked on projects related to data-driven decision making and sustainable business practices. Her research interests include emerging technologies, sustainability, and digital transformation in business.

Parag Chatterjee received the B.E. degree in Computer Science & Engineering from the Karnatak University, Dharwad, India, in 1998 and received M.Tech. degree from IIEST Shibpur, Kolkata, India, in 2007. He has an academic experience of 20 years. Currently he is working as an Assistant Professor in the Department of CSE at

Global Institute of Management and Technology, Krishnanagar, West Bengal, India. His current research interests include Data ware Housing, Data mining and Wireless sensor. He has 25 publication in national and international journals and 10 Patents

Mohammad Irfan is presently working as a Professor at the Faculty School of Business and Commerce, Chandigarh University, Lucknow, Unnao, India. Dr. Irfan has done his Ph.D. at the Central University of Haryana. He is MBA (Finance), M.Com (Account and Law), and MA (Economics). He has qualified UGC-JRF/SRF/NET in Management and Commerce. Dr. Irfan certified NSEs (NCFM) and BSEs certification. He has experience of more than sixteen years in the area of SAPM, Artificial Intelligence, Machine Learning, Blockchain, Cryptocurrency, Financial Engineering, Fintech, Green Finance, and Alternative Finance. He has to his credit more than 101+ Scopus-indexed articles, including The Journal of Economic Cooperation and Development (Q2), International Journal of Business Excellence (IJBEX), International Journal of Economics and Management (IJEM), Montenegrin Journal of Economics (Q2), Cogent Business & Management (Taylor & Francis) (Q2), Indian Journal of Finance (IJF), and Journal of Islamic Monetary Economics and Finance (JIMF). His citations reached 702+ along with 14 H-index. Dr. Irfan has published 11 books in Springer, IGI Global Publication (Scopus indexed).

Jasmine Kaur completed her Bachelor's degree in Mathematics (Hons.) from Miranda House, University of Delhi, followed by Master of Science, Master of Philosophy, and Doctorate degrees from the Department of Operational Research, University of Delhi. Her academic focus includes Operations, Decision Sciences, and Data Analytics, with specialized research in Software Reliability and Security. She has authored publications in prestigious international journals and books. Dr. Kaur is an Assistant Professor in Christ University and brings over 2 years of teaching experience, having previously served as a faculty member at USME, Delhi Technological University, and SSCBS, University of Delhi.

Vijaya Kittu Manda A multi-dimensional personality. He has nearly 13+ years of experience in Business Management and Technology. He is a Researcher at PBMEIT, India and works in capital markets, financial planning, and investing. He is an Advocate, a technocrat, an academician, a book writer, and a stock market enthusiast. He has 11 University Postgraduate Degrees in various disciplines. He is a Ph.D. in Management (Finance). His thesis was on Mutual Funds and their Market Competition. His thesis won the prestigious NSE-IEA Best Thesis Award in 2023. He is currently pursuing his second Ph.D. in Computer Science with focus on Blockchain and Artificial Intelligence. He has nearly 13+ years of experience in capital markets, financial planning, and investing. He writes Research Papers and

Case Studies, Case Reports (of Medical Journals) and sits on Editorial Boards of various publishers. He has 121+ Google Scholar publications and 785+ magazine article publications so far. He is the Chief Editor for a Management Book Series and the Editor of several Scopus-indexed books. He is a Peer Reviewer and is a Certified Peer Review Supervisor. He frequently reviews for leading publishers including IEEE, Springer, Emerald, Sage, amongst others. He sits as a Session Chair and an Advisor for various academic and industrial conferences. He is a guest speaker for colleges and universities. He serves as the host for a research talk show called PBMEIT Expert Insights.

Amrik Singh is working as Professor and HOD in the School of Hotel Management and Tourism at Lovely Professional University, Punjab, India. He obtained his Ph.D. degree in Hotel Management from Kurukshetra University, Haryana, India. He has published 115 Scopus-indexed publications. He has published 12 patents, and 01 patent has been granted in the inter-disciplinary domain. Dr. Amrik Singh participated and acted as a resource person in various national and international conferences, seminars, research workshops, and industry talks. He has published 20 books with IGI Global Publication, Emerald Publication, Bentham Publication, Nova Publication etc., on trending areas such as Food waste, Artificial Intelligence, Mountain Tourism, Virtual tourism, Healthcare Tourism, Guest behavior in tourism and hospitality. His area of research interest are Accommodation management, sustainability, Green practices, Human Resource Management in Hospitality, Artificial Intelligence, AR VR in hospitality, Hotel pricing, Employee Disability, Work life balance, women empowerment etc. He is currently guiding 8 Ph.D. scholars, and 5 Ph.D. scholars have been awarded Ph.D.

Bruno Sousa is an Professor Coordinator of Marketing at Polytechnic University of Cávado and Ave (IPCA), Portugal and holds a PhD in Marketing and Strategy in Universidade do Minho, Portugal. Bruno Sousa is also Head of Masters Program - Tourism Management and Tourism Marketing (IPCA); CiTUR – Center for Tourism Research, Development and Innovation and UNIAG research member. Bruno Sousa teaching fields include marketing, strategy and tourism. Bruno Sousa research areas include brand management and consumer behavior, strategy implementation, niche marketing, niche tourism and brand attachment. He has published in the Journal of Enterprising Communities, Tourism Management Perspectives, Current Issues in Tourism, Journal of Organizational Change Management, World Review of Entrepreneurship, Management and Sust. Development, among others

Naveenraj Xavier is an assistant professor in the area of organisational behaviour and HRM at the COM, SRM Institute of Technology—Vadapalani, where he teaches courses on organisational culture and behaviour, entrepreneurial development, and business analytics. His primary research focus is on organisational behavior, with a particular emphasis on organisational psychology, stress management in the context of organisational change, and psychological capital. Working in these areas, he had opportunities to publish his work in international peer-reviewed journals like Development and Learning in Organizations, Mental Health and Social Inclusion. Dr. Naveenraj X received his doctorate from the Vellore Institute of Technology and worked as a relationship manager and production executive at Centrum Direct Ltd. and various South Indian production houses for nearly 5 years before joining SRMIST.

Index

A

B

C

D

E

F

G

I

L

M

P

R

S

www.ingramcontent.com/pod-product-compliance
Lightning Source LLC
LaVergne TN
LVHW061525290926
849162LV00004B/670